"Composed in the style of the great medieval *catenae*, this new anthology of patristic commentary on Holy Scripture, conveniently arranged by chapter and verse, will be a valuable resource for prayer, study and proclamation. By calling attention to the rich Christian heritage preceding the separations between East and West and between Protestant and Catholic, this series will perform a major service to the cause of ecumenism."

**AVERY CARDINAL DULLES, S.J.**
*Laurence J. McGinley Professor of Religion and Society*
*Fordham University*

---

"The initial cry of the Reformation was *ad fontes*—back to the sources! The Ancient Christian Commentary on Scripture is a marvelous tool for the recovery of biblical wisdom in today's church. Not just another scholarly project, the ACCS is a major resource for the renewal of preaching, theology and Christian devotion."

**TIMOTHY GEORGE**
*Dean, Beeson Divinity School, Samford University*

---

"Modern church members often do not realize that they are participants in the vast company of the communion of saints that reaches far back into the past and that will continue into the future, until the kingdom comes. This Commentary should help them begin to see themselves as participants in that redeemed community."

**ELIZABETH ACHTEMEIER**
*Union Professor Emerita of Bible and Homiletics*
*Union Theological Seminary in Virginia*

---

"Contemporary pastors do not stand alone. We are not the first generation of preachers to wrestle with the challenges of communicating the gospel. The Ancient Christian Commentary on Scripture puts us in conversation with our colleagues from the past, that great cloud of witnesses who preceded us in this vocation. This Commentary enables us to receive their deep spiritual insights, their encouragement and guidance for present-day interpretation and preaching of the Word. What a wonderful addition to any pastor's library!"

**WILLIAM H. WILLIMON**
*Dean of the Chapel and Professor of Christian Ministry*
*Duke University*

---

"Here is a nonpareil series which reclaims the Bible as the book of the church by making accessible to earnest readers of the twenty-first century the classrooms of Clement of Alexandria and Didymus the Blind, the study and lecture hall of Origen, the cathedrae of Chrysostom and Augustine, the scriptorium of Jerome in his Bethlehem monastery."

**GEORGE LAWLESS**
*Augustinian Patristic Institute and Gregorian University, Rome*

"We are pleased to witness publication of the
Ancient Christian Commentary on Scripture. It is most beneficial for us to learn
how the ancient Christians, especially the saints of the church
who proved through their lives their devotion to God and his Word, interpreted
Scripture. Let us heed the witness of those who have gone before us in the faith."

**METROPOLITAN THEODOSIUS**
*Primate, Orthodox Church in America*

---

"Across Christendom there has emerged a widespread interest
in early Christianity, both at the popular and scholarly level. . . .
Christians of all traditions stand to benefit from this project, especially clergy
and those who study the Bible. Moreover, it will allow us to see how our traditions are
both rooted in the scriptural interpretations of the church fathers while at
the same time seeing how we have developed new perspectives."

**ALBERTO FERREIRO**
*Professor of History, Seattle Pacific University*

---

"The Ancient Christian Commentary on Scripture fills a long overdue need for scholars and
students of the church fathers. . . . Such information will be of immeasurable
worth to those of us who have felt inundated by contemporary interpreters and novel theories
of the biblical text. We welcome some 'new' insight from the
ancient authors in the early centuries of the church."

**H. WAYNE HOUSE**
*Professor of Theology and Law*
*Trinity University School of Law*

---

"Chronological snobbery—the assumption that our ancestors working without benefit of
computers have nothing to teach us—is exposed as nonsense by this magnificent
new series. Surfeited with knowledge but starved of wisdom, many of us are
more than ready to sit at table with our ancestors and listen to their holy
conversations on Scripture. I know I am."

**EUGENE H. PETERSON**
*Professor Emeritus of Spiritual Theology*
*Regent College*

"Few publishing projects have encouraged me as much as the recently announced Ancient Christian Commentary on Scripture with Dr. Thomas Oden serving as general editor. . . . How is it that so many of us who are dedicated to serve the Lord received seminary educations which omitted familiarity with such incredible students of the Scriptures as St. John Chrysostom, St. Athanasius the Great and St. John of Damascus? I am greatly anticipating the publication of this Commentary."

### Fr. Peter E. Gillquist
*Director, Department of Missions and Evangelism*
*Antiochian Orthodox Christian Archdiocese of North America*

---

"The Scriptures have been read with love and attention for nearly two thousand years, and listening to the voice of believers from previous centuries opens us to unexpected insight and deepened faith. Those who studied Scripture in the centuries closest to its writing, the centuries during and following persecution and martyrdom, speak with particular authority. The Ancient Christian Commentary on Scripture will bring to life the truth that we are invisibly surrounded by a 'great cloud of witnesses.'"

### Frederica Mathewes-Green
*Commentator, National Public Radio*

---

"For those who think that church history began around 1941 when their pastor was born, this Commentary will be a great surprise. Christians throughout the centuries have read the biblical text, nursed their spirits with it and then applied it to their lives. These commentaries reflect that the witness of the Holy Spirit was present in his church throughout the centuries. As a result, we can profit by allowing the ancient Christians to speak to us today."

### Haddon Robinson
*Harold John Ockenga Distinguished Professor of Preaching*
*Gordon-Conwell Theological Seminary*

---

"All who are interested in the interpretation of the Bible will welcome the forthcoming multivolume series Ancient Christian Commentary on Scripture. Here the insights of scores of early church fathers will be assembled and made readily available for significant passages throughout the Bible and the Apocrypha. It is hard to think of a more worthy ecumenical project to be undertaken by the publisher."

### Bruce M. Metzger
*Professor of New Testament, Emeritus*
*Princeton Theological Seminary*

ANCIENT CHRISTIAN
COMMENTARY ON SCRIPTURE

NEW TESTAMENT
XII

# REVELATION

EDITED BY

## WILLIAM C. WEINRICH

GENERAL EDITOR
THOMAS C. ODEN

InterVarsity Press
Downers Grove, Illinois

InterVarsity Press
P.O. Box 1400, Downers Grove, IL 60515-1426
World Wide Web: www.ivpress.com
E-mail: mail@ivpress.com

InterVarsity Press* is the book-publishing division of InterVarsity Christian Fellowship/USA*, a student movement active on campus at hundreds of universities, colleges and schools of nursing in the United States of America, and a member movement of the International Fellowship of Evangelical Students. For information about local and regional activities, write Public Relations Dept., InterVarsity Christian Fellowship/USA, 6400 Schroeder Rd., P.O. Box 7895, Madison, WI 53707-7895, or visit the IVCF website at <www.intervarsity.org>.

Scripture quotations, unless otherwise noted, are from the Revised Standard Version of the Bible, copyright 1946, 1952, 1971 by the Division of Christian Education of the National Council of the Churches of Christ in the U.S.A., and are used by permission.

Selected excerpts from Fathers of the Church: A New Translation, ©1947-. Used by permission of The Catholic University of America Press, Washington, D.C. Full bibliographic information on volumes of Fathers of the Church may be found in the Bibliography of Works in English Translation.

Selected excerpts from Bede the Venerable, Homilies on the Gospels, translated by Lawrence Martin and David Hurst, Cistercian Studies Series 110 and 111, ©1991. Used by permission of Cistercian Publications, Kalamazoo, Michigan.

Selected excerpts from Bede the Venerable, On the Tabernacle, translated by Arthur Holder, Translated Texts for Historians 18, ©1994. Used by permission of Liverpool University Press, Liverpool, United Kingdom.

Selected excerpts from Rufinus, A Commentary on the Apostles' Creed, translated by J. N. D. Kelly, Ancient Christian Writers 20, ©1954; St. Methodius, The Symposium: A Treatise on Chastity, translated by Herbert Musurillo, Ancient Christian Writers 27, ©1958; Tertullian, Treatises on Penance: On Penitence and On Purity, translated by William P. Le Saint, Ancient Christian Writers 28, ©1959; St. Maximus of Turin, Sermons, translated and annotated by Boniface Ramsey, Ancient Christian Writers 50, ©1989; Cassiodorus, Explanation of the Psalms, translated by P. G. Walsh, Ancient Christian Writers 52 and 53, ©1990-1991. Used by permission of Paulist Press, Mahwah, New Jersey, <www.paulistpress.com>.

Selected excerpts from Augustine: Earlier Writings, translated by John Burleigh, The Library of Christian Classics 6, ©1953. Used by permission of Westminster John Knox Press, Louisville, Kentucky.

Selected excerpts from The Works of Saint Augustine: A Translation for the 21st Century, ©1990-. Used by permission of the Augustinian Heritage Institute, Ardmore, Pennsylvania.

Selected excerpts from The Panarion of Epiphanius of Salamis, translated by Frank Williams, Nag Hammadi Manichean Studies 36, ©1994. Used by permission of E. J. Brill, Leiden, The Netherlands.

Cover photograph: Scala/Art Resource, New York. View of the apse. S. Vitale, Ravenna, Italy.

Spine photograph: Byzantine Collection, Dumbarton Oaks, Washington D.C. Pendant cross (gold and enamel). Constantinople, late sixth century.

ISBN-10 0-8308-1497-3
ISBN-13 978-0-8308-1497-8

Printed in the United States of America ∞

**Library of Congress Cataloging-in-Publication Data**

Revelation/edited by William C. Weinrich.

     p. cm.—(Ancient Christian commentary on Scripture. New

Testament; 12)

    Includes bibliographical references and index.

    ISBN 0-8308-1497-3 (hardcover: alk. paper)

    1. Bible. N.T. Revelation—Commentaries.  I. Weinrich, William

C.  II. Series.

    BS2825.53.R48 2005

    228'.077'09—dc22                                             2005018544

| P | 25 | 24 | 23 | 22 | 21 | 20 | 19 | 18 | 17 | 16 | 15 | 14 | 13 | 12 | 11 | 10 | 9 | 8 | 7 | 6 | 5 | 4 | 3 | 2 |
|---|----|----|----|----|----|----|----|----|----|----|----|----|----|----|----|----|---|---|---|---|---|---|---|---|
| Y | 27 | 26 | 25 | 24 | 23 | 22 | 21 | 20 | 19 | 18 | 17 | 16 | 15 | 14 | 13 | 12 | 11 | 10 | 09 | 08 | 07 | 06 | | |

# CONTENTS

# GENERAL INTRODUCTION

The Ancient Christian Commentary on Scripture has as its goal the revitalization of Christian teaching based on classical Christian exegesis, the intensified study of Scripture by lay persons who wish to think with the early church about the canonical text, and the stimulation of Christian historical, biblical, theological and pastoral scholars toward further inquiry into scriptural interpretation by ancient Christian writers.

The time frame of these documents spans seven centuries of exegesis, from Clement of Rome to John of Damascus, from the end of the New Testament era to A.D. 750, including the Venerable Bede.

Lay readers are asking how they might study sacred texts under the instruction of the great minds of the ancient church. This commentary has been intentionally prepared for a general lay audience of nonprofessionals who study the Bible regularly and who earnestly wish to have classic Christian observation on the text readily available to them. The series is targeted to anyone who wants to reflect and meditate with the early church about the plain sense, theological wisdom and moral meaning of particular Scripture texts.

A commentary dedicated to allowing ancient Christian exegetes to speak for themselves will refrain from the temptation to fixate endlessly upon contemporary criticism. Rather, it will stand ready to provide textual resources from a distinguished history of exegesis that has remained massively inaccessible and shockingly disregarded during the last century. We seek to make available to our present-day audiences the multicultural, multilingual, transgenerational resources of the early ecumenical Christian tradition.

Preaching at the end of the first millennium focused primarily on the text of Scripture as understood by the earlier esteemed tradition of comment, largely converging on those writers that best reflected classic Christian consensual thinking. Preaching at the end of the second millennium has reversed that pattern. It has so forgotten most of these classic comments that they are vexing to find anywhere, and even when located they are often available only in archaic editions and inadequate translations. The preached word in our time has remained largely bereft of previously influential patristic inspiration. Recent scholarship has so focused attention upon post-Enlightenment historical and literary methods that it has left this longing largely unattended and unserviced.

This series provides the pastor, exegete, student and lay reader with convenient means to see what Athanasius or John Chrysostom or the desert fathers and mothers had to say about a particular text for preaching, for study and for meditation. There is an emerging awareness among Catholic, Protestant and Orthodox laity that vital biblical preaching and spiritual formation need deeper grounding beyond the scope of the historical-critical orientations that have governed biblical studies in our day.

Hence this work is directed toward a much broader audience than the highly technical and specialized scholarly field of patristic studies. The audience is not limited to the university scholar concentrating on the study of the history of the transmission of the text or to those with highly focused philological interests in textual morphology or historical-critical issues. Though these are crucial concerns for specialists, they are not the paramount interests of this series.

This work is a Christian Talmud. The Talmud is a Jewish collection of rabbinic arguments and comments on the Mishnah, which epitomized the laws of the Torah. The Talmud originated in approximately the same period that the patristic writers were commenting on texts of the Christian tradition. Christians from the late patristic age through the medieval period had documents analogous to the Jewish Talmud and Midrash (Jewish commentaries) available to them in the *glossa ordinaria* and catena traditions, two forms of compiling extracts of patristic exegesis. In Talmudic fashion the sacred text of Christian Scripture was thus clarified and interpreted by the classic commentators.

The Ancient Christian Commentary on Scripture has venerable antecedents in medieval exegesis of both eastern and western traditions, as well as in the Reformation tradition. It offers for the first time in this century the earliest Christian comments and reflections on the Old and New Testaments to a modern audience. Intrinsically an ecumenical project, this series is designed to serve Protestant, Catholic and Orthodox lay, pastoral and scholarly audiences.

In cases where Greek, Latin, Syriac and Coptic texts have remained untranslated into English, we provide new translations. Wherever current English translations are already well rendered, they will be utilized, but if necessary their language will be brought up to date. We seek to present fresh dynamic equivalency translations of long-neglected texts which historically have been regarded as authoritative models of biblical interpretation.

These foundational sources are finding their way into many public libraries and into the core book collections of many pastors and lay persons. It is our intent and the publisher's commitment to keep the whole series in print for many years to come.

Thomas C. Oden
General Editor

# A Guide to Using This Commentary

Several features have been incorporated into the design of this commentary. The following comments are intended to assist readers in making full use of this volume.

## Pericopes of Scripture

The scriptural text has been divided into pericopes, or passages, usually several verses in length. Each of these pericopes is given a heading, which appears at the beginning of the pericope. For example, the first pericope in the commentary on Revelation is "1:1-9 The Revelation of Jesus Christ." This heading is followed by the Scripture passage quoted in the Revised Standard Version (RSV) across the full width of the page. The Scripture passage is provided for the convenience of readers, but it is also in keeping with medieval patristic commentaries, in which the citations of the Fathers were arranged around the text of Scripture.

## Overviews

Following each pericope of text is an overview of the patristic comments on that pericope. The format of this overview varies within the volumes of this series, depending on the requirements of the specific book of Scripture. The function of the overview is to provide a brief summary of all the comments to follow. It tracks a reasonably cohesive thread of argument among patristic comments, even though they are derived from diverse sources and generations. Thus the summaries do not proceed chronologically or by verse sequence. Rather they seek to rehearse the overall course of the patristic comment on that pericope.

We do not assume that the commentators themselves anticipated or expressed a formally received cohesive argument but rather that the various arguments tend to flow in a plausible, recognizable pattern. Modern readers can thus glimpse aspects of continuity in the flow of diverse exegetical traditions representing various generations and geographical locations.

## Topical Headings

An abundance of varied patristic comment is available for each pericope of these letters. For this reason we have broken the pericopes into two levels. First is the verse with its topical heading. The patristic comments are then focused on aspects of each verse, with topical headings summarizing the essence of the patristic comment by evoking a key phrase, metaphor or idea. This feature provides a bridge by which modern readers can enter into the heart of the patristic comment.

**Identifying the Patristic Texts**

Following the topical heading of each section of comment, the name of the patristic commentator is given. An English translation of the patristic comment is then provided. This is immediately followed by the title of the patristic work and the textual reference—either by book, section and subsection or by book-and-verse references.

**The Footnotes**

Readers who wish to pursue a deeper investigation of the patristic works cited in this commentary will find the footnotes especially valuable. A footnote number directs the reader to the notes at the bottom of the right-hand column, where in addition to other notations (clarifications or biblical cross references) one will find information on English translations (where available) and standard original-language editions of the work cited. An abbreviated citation (normally citing the book, volume and page number) of the work is provided. A key to the abbreviations is provided on page xv. Where there is any serious ambiguity or textual problem in the selection, we have tried to reflect the best available textual tradition.

Where original language texts have remained untranslated into English, we provide new translations. Wherever current English translations are already well rendered, they are utilized, but where necessary they are stylistically updated. A single asterisk (*) indicates that a previous English translation has been updated to modern English or amended for easier reading. The double asterisk (**) indicates either that a new translation has been provided or that some extant translation has been significantly amended. We have standardized spellings and made grammatical variables uniform so that our English references will not reflect the odd spelling variables of the older English translations. For ease of reading we have in some cases edited out superfluous conjunctions.

For the convenience of computer database users the digital database references are provided to either the Thesaurus Linguae Graecae (Greek texts) or to the Cetedoc (Latin texts) in the appendix found on pages 410-17.

# Abbreviations

| | |
|---|---|
| *ABC* | P. G. Walsh, ed. and trans. *Augustine: De bono coniugali, De sancta virginitate*. Oxford: Clarendon Press, 2001. |
| ACM | Herbert Musurillo, trans. *The Acts of the Christian Martyrs*. Oxford Early Christian Texts. Oxford: Clarendon Press, 1972. |
| ACW | Ancient Christian Writers: The Works of the Fathers in Translation. Mahwah, N.J.: Paulist Press, 1946-. |
| ANCL | Alexander Roberts and James Donaldson, eds. The Ante-Nicene Christian Library: Translations of the Writings of the Fathers Down to A.D. 325. Edinburgh: T & T Clark, 1867-1897. |
| ANF | Alexander Roberts and James Donaldson, eds. Ante-Nicene Fathers. 10 vols. Buffalo, N.Y.: Christian Literature, 1885-1896. Reprint, Grand Rapids, Mich.: Eerdmans, 1951-1956; Reprint, Peabody, Mass.: Hendrickson, 1994. |
| CCL | Corpus Christianorum. Series Latina. Turnhout, Belgium: Brepols, 1953-. |
| CS | Cistercian Studies. Kalamazoo, Mich.: Cistercian Publications, 1973-. |
| CSEL | Corpus Scriptorum Ecclesiasticorum Latinorum. Vienna, 1866-. |
| FC | Fathers of the Church: A New Translation. Washington, D.C.: Catholic University of America Press, 1947-. |
| GCS | Die griechischen christlichen Schriftsteller der ersten Jahrhunderte. Berlin: Akademie-Verlag, 1897-. |
| LCC | J. Baillie et al., eds. The Library of Christian Classics. 26 vols. Philadelphia: Westminster, 1953-1966. |
| MTS | Franz Zaver Seppelt, Joseph Pascher and Klaus Mörsdorf, eds. Münchener Theologische Studien, Historische Abteilung. Munich: Karl Zink, 1950-. |
| *NKZ* | *Neue kirchliche Zeitschrift*. Leipzig: A. Deichertsche Verlagsbuchhandlung, 1890-1933. |
| NHMS | J. M. Robinson and H. J. Klimkeit, eds. Nag Hammadi and Manichaean Studies. Leiden: E. J. Brill, 1993-. |
| NPNF | P. Schaff et al., eds. A Select Library of the Nicene and Post-Nicene Fathers of the Christian Church. 2 series (14 vols. each). Buffalo, N.Y.: Christian Literature, 1887-1894; Reprint, Grand Rapids, Mich.: Eerdmans, 1952-1956; Reprint, Peabody, Mass.: Hendrickson, 1994. |
| *OFP* | Origen. *On First Principles*. Translated by G. W. Butterworth. London: SPCK, 1936; Reprint, Gloucester, Mass.: Peter Smith, 1973. |
| PG | J.-P. Migne, ed. Patrologia cursus completus. Series Graeca. 166 vols. Paris: Migne, 1857-1886. |
| PL | J.-P. Migne, ed. Patrologia cursus completus. Series Latina. 221 vols. Paris: Migne, 1844-1864. |
| PTS | Patristische Texte und Studien. New York: de Gruyter, 1964-. |
| SC | H. de Lubac, J. Daniélou et al., eds. Sources Chrétiennes. Paris: Éditions du Cerf, 1941-. |
| SEHL | Scriptores ecclesiastici Hispano-Latini veteris et medii aevi. Madrid: typis Augustinianis Monasterii Escurialensis, 1940-. |
| *TAM* | Ernest Evans, ed. and trans. *Tertullian: Adversus Marcionem*. 2 vols. Oxford Early Christian Tests. Oxford: Clarendon Press, 1972. |
| TEG | Traditio Exegetica Graeca. Louvain: Peeters, 1991-. |

TS        Texts and Studies. 3 Series. Cambridge: Cambridge University Press, 1891-.

TTH       G. Clark, M. Gibson and M. Whitby, eds. Translated Texts for Historians. Liverpool: Liverpool University Press, 1985-.

*WSA*      J. E. Rotelle, ed. *Works of St. Augustine: A Translation for the Twenty-First Century.* Hyde Park, N.Y.: New City Press, 1995.

WUNT     Wissenschaftliche Untersuchungen zum Neuen Testament. Tübingen, Mohr, 1950-.

# Introduction to the Revelation to John

The New Testament is replete with the conviction that Jesus of Nazareth is the fulfillment of the Old Testament expectations. The apostle Paul gives classic expression to the view that with the coming of Jesus and the rise of the Christian community the consummation of all things is coming to pass: "[events of the Old Testament] were written down for our instruction, upon whom the end of the ages [τὰ τέλη τῶν αἰώνων] has come" (1 Cor 10:11). In view of such a conviction concerning the significance of Jesus and the church, Christian thinking and interpretation could not escape the importance of the eschaton for Christian faith and life. Christian reality continued to be lived within situations characterized by temptation, sin and persecution, although, in some manner, the final good of God's ultimate intentions had been fulfilled in the death, resurrection and ascension of Jesus. It is not surprising, therefore, that the Revelation of John, of all the New Testament writings the most explicitly and pervasively eschatological, was from a very early time one of the most systematically read and used books of the New Testament.

## Authorship and Canonicity of the Revelation

Isbon Beckwith has noted that "so much external testimony to the personality of the author, traceable back to almost contemporaneous sources, is found in the case of almost no other book of the New Testament."[1] Indeed, at its beginning and at its end the book of Revelation claims to be the prophecy of "John" (Rev 1:1, 4, 9; 22:8). Although nowhere in the Revelation is this John identified with the apostle and evangelist John, this identification was virtually universal in the early church. In the middle of the second century, Justin Martyr (d. c. 165) writes of "John, one of the apostles of Christ, who prophesied by a revelation that was made to him."[2] Irenaeus (c. 180) makes extensive use of the Revelation and likewise ascribes it to "John, the Lord's disciple."[3] Tertullian (c. 220) is similarly explicit in his belief that the apostle John was author of the Revelation,[4] as was Hippolytus (c. 235), who writes of "the blessed John, apostle and disciple of the Lord."[5] In view of the history of the reception of the Revelation in the East, it is especially noteworthy that Origen (d. c. 254) frequently and without any hint of doubt attributes the Revelation to John the apostle. In his *Commentary on John*, Origen writes that "the apostle and evangelist—but now also a prophet in addition through the Apocalypse—says

---

[1]Isbon Beckwith, *The Apocalypse of John* (New York: Macmillan, 1919; reprint ed., Grand Rapids, Mich.: Baker, 1979), 351. For general studies of the reception of the Revelation in the early church, see Ned B. Stonehouse, *The Apocalypse in the Ancient Church: A Study in the History of the New Testament Canon* (Goes: Oosterbaan & Le Cointre, 1929); Gerhard Maier, *Die Johannesoffenbarung und die Kirche* (WUNT 25; Tübingen: J. C. B. Mohr, 1981).

[2]Justin Martyr *Dialogue with Trypho* 81 (ANF 1:178).

[3]Irenaeus *Against Heresies* 4.20.11 (ANF 1:491).

[4]Tertullian *Against Marcion* 3.24 (TAM 1: 247).

[5]Hippolytus *On the Antichrist* 36 (ANF 5:211).

correctly ... that he saw the Word of God riding on a white horse in the opened heaven."[6]

Despite this testimony, there were some few who rejected attribution of the Revelation to the apostle. Two instances are worthy of mention. Irenaeus mentions certain persons who rejected the Gospel of John because the Paraclete is promised in it.[7] These persons are most probably, but not certainly, the group called the Alogoi by Epiphanius of Salamis in his *Panarion*. Epiphanius writes of a group who, apparently for anti-Montanist reasons, rejected the Gospel of John and the Revelation saying that "these are not of John but of Cerinthus and that these are not worthy to exist in the church."[8] Later, Epiphanius informs us that this same group rejected the Revelation because its symbolism was vulgar and unedifying and because it contained errors, such as including a letter to the church at Thyatira when no church existed at Thyatira.[9] Eusebius of Caesarea informs us of a certain Roman presbyter by the name of Gaius who was active against the Montanists during the episcopacy of Zephyrinus (c. 198-c. 217). Whether Gaius was a member of the Alogoi or not is uncertain. However, he also attributed the Revelation to the Gnostic Cerinthus. Eusebius quotes Gaius:

> Yes, Cerinthus also, by means of revelations purported to be written by a great apostle, fraudulently foists marvelous tales upon us, on the ground that they were shown to him by angels. He says that after the resurrection the kingdom of Christ will be on earth, and that the flesh, dwelling at Jerusalem, will once more serve lusts and pleasures.[10]

We know from a twelfth-century commentary on the Revelation by Dionysius Bar Salibi that Hippolytus polemicized against Gaius in a work entitled "Heads Against Gaius."

More important for the history of interpretation was the argument of Dionysius of Alexandria (247-265) against the authenticity of the Revelation. Eusebius provides lengthy sections of Dionysius's book, *On the Promises*, which he wrote against a certain Egyptian bishop named Nepos who had defended the view that the kingdom of Christ would be on the earth. However, on the basis of his comparison between the Revelation and the Gospel and epistles of John, Dionysius concluded that while the Gospel and the epistles are by the same person, namely, the apostle John, the Revelation is "utterly different from, and foreign to, these writings; it has no connection, no affinity, in any way with them; it scarcely, so to speak, has even a syllable in common with them."[11] Dionysius rejects the view of Gaius that the Revelation was written by Cerinthus, and noting that the name John was common, rejects also the idea that the John of the Revelation could be the John Mark mentioned in the Acts. Rather, Dionysius surmises that the Revelation was written by a second John who lived at Ephesus, even as the apostle John lived at Ephesus.[12]

It is likely that the spiritualizing exegesis of Origen and the antimillennialist position of Dionysius served to foster the general reserve of the Eastern church toward the Revelation. Be that as it may, the

---

[6]Origen *Commentary on the Gospel of John* 2.45 (FC 80:106). The reference of Origen is to Rev 19:13. See also *Commentary on the Gospel of John* 1.84; 2.42; 5.3. For Origen's attitude toward the Revelation, see D. Strathmann, "Origenes und die Johannesoffenbarung," *NKZ* 34 (1923): 228-36.

[7]Irenaeus *Against Heresies* 3.11.9 (ANF 1:429).

[8]Epiphanius *Panarion* 51.3 (GCS 31:251).

[9]Epiphanius *Panarion* 51.32, 33 (GCS 31:305, 306).

[10]Eusebius *Ecclesiastical History* 3.28.2. From Eusebius we know that Dionysius of Alexandria had read the "Dialogue" of Gaius against the Montanist Proclus (*Ecclesiastical History* 3.28.3-5). On Gaius see also Jerome *Lives of Illustrious Men* 59 (NPNF, 2nd series, 3:374-75).

[11]Eusebius *Ecclesiastical History* 7.25.1-27, here para. 22.

[12]On Dionysius, see Wolfgang A. Bienert, *Dionysius von Alexandrien: Zur Frage des Origenismus im dritten Jahrhundert* (PTS 21; Berlin and New York: Walter de Gruyter, 1978), 193-200; Stonehouse, *The Apocalypse*, 123-28.

view that the Revelation was from John the apostle became the universal opinion of the broad catholic tradition. This is, for example, the common conviction of the various commentaries that are featured in this volume. They all agree with Apringius of Beja that the Revelation was given "to John, the most blessed of the apostles."[13]

As we learn from the Revelation itself, it was from the beginning sent to seven churches. This, no doubt, contributed to its early and widespread dissemination. Nothing with certainty can be found of the Revelation in the Apostolic Fathers. However, Irenaeus writes of certain "most approved and ancient copies" of the Revelation.[14] This is testimony to the early circulation of the book. As we might expect, evidence of its early use in Asia Minor is rather abundant. The evidence that Eusebius gives about Papias of Hierapolis (c. 120) mentions nothing explicit of the Revelation, but the chiliasm of Papias makes it likely that he knew of it.[15] Indeed, in the prologue to his *Commentary on the Apocalypse*, Andrew of Caesarea mentions Papias along with Irenaeus, Methodius and Hippolytus as early exponents of the Revelation.[16] The first explicit mention of the Revelation is in Justin Martyr's *Dialogue with Trypho*, in which Justin refers to the Revelation in conjunction with Isaiah 65:17-25 to justify his millennialist understanding of the new Jerusalem.[17] It is probable that Justin came to know the Revelation while in Asia Minor. As I have noted, Irenaeus makes frequent and substantive use of the Revelation, especially in book 5 of *Against Heresies*, where he extensively discourses upon the thousand-year reign of Christ upon the earth.[18] Since one of the seven letters was sent to the church at Sardis, it is highly plausible that Melito of Sardis (c. 170) knew of the Revelation. Eusebius comments that Melito wrote "On the Devil and the Apocalypse of John."[19] H. B. Swete suggests that this was "probably a treatise on the Devil in which certain passages in the Apocalypse came under discussion," not a commentary.[20] Given its connections with Asia Minor we should note here also the *Letter of the Lyons Martyrs* (177), which cites the Revelation five times, once as Scripture.[21] Finally, for use of the Revelation in Asia Minor we should note the anti-Montanist writer, Apollonius, who, according to Eusebius "makes use of testimonies drawn from the Apocalypse of John."[22]

Swete suggests that from the beginning texts of the Revelation went west rather than east, for "few copies seem to have penetrated to Antioch, and fewer or none to Edessa and Nisibis."[23] In any case, the Revelation was early and steadfastly recognized and used by Western Christian writers. In Africa, Tertullian (c. 220) makes significant use of Revelation, as does Cyprian (d. 258). In Rome, the *Shepherd* of Hermas (c. 140) makes use of the Revelation, and Hippolytus (c. 230) quotes extensively from the Rev-

---

[13]Apringius *Tractate on the Apocalypse* 1.1 (CCL 107:33).

[14]Irenaeus *Against Heresies* 5.30.1 (ANF 1:558).

[15]Eusebius *Ecclesiastical History* 3.39.1-17.

[16]Andrew of Caesarea *Commentary on the Apocalypse* prologue (MTS 1 Sup 1:10).

[17]For an informative summary of eschatological beliefs in the early fathers, see Brian E. Daley, *The Hope of the Early Church: A Handbook of Patristic Eschatology* (Cambridge: Cambridge University Press, 1991; Peabody, Mass.: Hendrickson, 2003); for Justin, 20-22.

[18]Daley, *Hope of the Early Church*, 28-32.

[19]Eusebius *Ecclesiastical History* 3.26.2.

[20]H. B. Swete, *Commentary on Revelation* (London: Macmillan, 1911; reprint ed., Grand Rapids, Mich.: Kregel, 1977), cxcvii-cxcviii.

[21]Eusebius *Ecclesiastical History* 5.1.3-5.2.7 (Revelation as Scripture, 5.1.58).

[22]Eusebius *Ecclesiastical History* 5.18.1-14, esp. 14.

[23]Swete, *Commentary on Revelation*, cxvii.

elation and perhaps even wrote a commentary on the book. The Revelation is listed in the Muratorian Canon, which may reflect the Scriptures in use in Rome in the early third century.[24] To be sure, the canonicity of the Revelation was never really in doubt within Western Christianity. Not surprisingly, therefore, the Revelation of John is among the books listed as canonical Scripture by the third Council of Carthage in 397.[25] The Revelation also received its most continuous comment in the West, from the commentary of Victorinus of Petovium through those of Tyconius, Primasius, Apringius, Caesarius of Arles, the Venerable Bede, Ambrosius Autpertus, Beatus of Liebana, Alcuin and Haimo of Auxerre.[26]

Although the Revelation received its greatest support in the West, testimony to it is by no means lacking in the East. According to Eusebius, Theophilus, bishop of Antioch (c. 180), wrote a treatise against the Gnostic Hermogenes "in which he has made use of testimonies drawn from the Apocalypse of John."[27] Clement of Alexandria and Origen, despite their allegorizing interpretations, make frequent use of the terminology and images of the Revelation. However, during the fourth century especially the Revelation receives only an inconsistent reception. Cyril of Jerusalem (c. 360) omits the Revelation from his canonical listing in the *Catechetical Lectures*. It is also missing from the catalogues of Gregory of Nazianzus, the *Apostolic Canons* and the Syriac Peshitta. In addition, it appears that Theodore of Mopsuestia, John Chrysostom[28] and Theodoret never quoted the Revelation. Its disputed character is clear from the comments of Eusebius of Caesarea and Amphilochius of Iconium.[29] However, the Revelation is listed in the catalogues of Epiphanius and of Athanasius,[30] who make use of the Revelation in their writings, as do Basil of Caesarea and Cyril of Alexandria. Although the Revelation appears to have been approved by the Quinisext Council of 692, the continuing peripheral use of the Revelation in the East is seen in the fact that no Greek commentary of the Revelation appears before the sixth century (Oecumenius and Andrew of Caesarea), and that after the commentary of Arethas (c. 900), who largely works over the commentary of Andrew of Caesarea, no additional commentary of significance arises from the Eastern church. To this day the Revelation is not used for liturgical reading in the Eastern church.

## Commentaries and Interpretation of the Revelation

Although the earliest extant commentary on the Revelation is that of Victorinus of Petovium (d. 304),

---

[24]See B. F. Westcott, *A General Survey of the History of the Canon of the New Testament*, 6th ed. (London: Macmillan, 1889; reprint ed., Grand Rapids, Mich.: Baker, 1980), 211-20, 521-38. See, however, Geoffrey Mark Hahneman, *The Muratorian Fragment and the Development of the Canon* (Oxford: Clarendon Press, 1992), who with some cogency argues that "the Muratorian Fragment is not a Western late second-century document, but is instead a late fourth-century Eastern catalogue, probably deriving from Western Syria or Palestine" (217).

[25]Westcott, *History of the Canon*, 439-41, 541-42.

[26]For a helpful summary, see E. Ann Matter, "The Apocalypse in Early Medieval Exegesis," in *The Apocalypse in the Middle Ages*, ed. Richard K. Emmerson and Bernard McGinn (Ithaca, N.Y.: Cornell University Press, 1992), 38-50.

[27]Eusebius *Ecclesiastical History* 4.24.1.

[28]The tenth-century lexicographer, Suidas, claims that Chrysostom "received both the three letters [of John] and the Apocalypse" (Westcott, *The History of the Canon*, 442 n. 3).

[29]Westcott, *The History of the Canon*, 445-46.

[30]See esp. Hahneman, *The Muratorian Fragment*, 132-182, esp. 134-35. On the disputed canon of the Synod of Laodicea (c. 360), which does not list the Revelation, see Hahneman, 157; Westcott, *The History of the Canon*, 431-39.

[31]For surveys of early commentaries, see Swete, *Commentary on Revelation*, cxcvii-cciv; Charles Kannengiesser, *Handbook of Patristic Exegesis: The Bible in Ancient Christianity*, 2 vols. (Leiden: E. J. Brill, 2004), 1:368-73; esp. the thorough listing by Francis X. Gumerlock, "Ancient Commentaries on the Book of Revelation: A Bibliographical Guide," a paper delivered at the Southwest Regional Meeting of the Evangelical Theological Society, March 2003, available online at http://www.tren.com. I thank Dr. Gumerlock for permission to use material from his paper.

there is evidence that commentaries existed in the third century and perhaps even in the second.[31] Jerome writes that Justin and Irenaeus "interpreted" the Revelation.[32] However, this may only mean, as Swete observed, that in their writings they commented on certain passages rather than claiming that they dedicated a whole work to the book. Perhaps the work of Melito of Sardis *On the Devil and the Apocalypse of John*, mentioned by Eusebius,[33] was something closer to a commentary, but the work is lost. We are on more solid footing with Hippolytus (c. 230). Jerome writes that Hippolytus wrote "some commentaries on the Scriptures" among which he mentions *On the Apocalypse*.[34] Most likely this refers to the *Apology for the Apocalypse and Gospel of John*, fragments of which have been preserved in the sixth-century commentary of Andrew of Caesarea, a thirteenth-century Arabic commentary and the twelfth-century Syriac commentary of Dionysius Bar Salibi.[35] In the commentary of Bar Salibi, fragments of another work of Hippolytus, *Heads Against Gaius*, a defense of the authenticity and authority of the Revelation, are contained.[36] Importantly, Origen appears to have intended a commentary on the Revelation, a project that seems, however, never to have been effected.[37] Nonetheless, certain scholia of Origen on the Revelation have been preserved,[38] and it is possible that the Revelation was the subject matter of a number of homilies delivered by Origen.[39] Finally, from the Alexandrian context we may note that in his commentary on Zechariah, Didymus the Blind mentions that he had written a commentary on Revelation.[40]

Although the Revelation clearly received some attention in the first three centuries, the first commentary on the Revelation that we possess is that of Victorinus, bishop of Petovium (in Upper Pannonia) and martyr in the "great persecution" of Diocletian (d. c. 304). Jerome writes that Victorinus wrote commentaries on the Old Testament but also a commentary on the Apocalypse.[41] Although in Jerome's judgment Victorinus was "deficient in learning" but "not deficient in the wish to use the learning he has,"[42] he was nonetheless personally acquainted with the writings of Victorinus and mentions him with some frequency. Indeed, it is possible that Victorinus was rather well known in Rome during the fourth century, for Helvidius appealed to Victorinus for support of his view that after Jesus the Virgin Mary had children by natural childbirth.[43] Jerome further tells us that Victorinus was an imitator of Origen and rendered Origen's interpretations "not in exact versions but in independent paraphrases."[44] The

---

[32]Jerome *Lives of Illustrious Men* 9 (NPNF 2 3:364).

[33]Eusebius *Ecclesiastical History* 4.26.2.

[34]Jerome *Lives of Illustrious Men* 61 (NPNF, 2 3:375).

[35]The fragments of this commentary are in French translation in Pierre Prigent, "Hippolyte, commentateur de l'Apocalypse," *Theologische Zeitschrift* 28 (1972): 391-412; and in Pierre Prigent and R. Stehly, "Les fragments du De Apocalypsi d'Hippolyte," *Theologische Zeitschrift* 29 (1973): 313-33.

[36]An English translation of these fragments is in John Gwynn, "Hippolytus and His 'Heads Against Gaius,'" *Hermathena* 14 (Dublin: 1888), 397-418; a French translation in Prigent, "Hippolyte," 407-12.

[37]Origen expresses this intent in his *Commentary on the Gospel of Matthew* 49 (PG 13:1673-74).

[38]For discussion and texts, see A. de Boysson, "Avons-nous un commentaire d'Origene sur l'Apocalypse," *Revue Biblique* 10 (1913): 555-67; C. H. Turner, "Document. Origen Scholia in Apocalypsin," *Journal of Theological Studies* 25 (1923): 1-16. For discussion of the eschatology of Origen, including his use of material and ideas from the Revelation, see Daley, *Hope of the Early Church*, 47-64, and Charles E. Hill, *Regnum Caelorum: Patterns of Millennial Thought in Early Christianity*, 2nd ed. (Grand Rapids, Mich.: Eerdmans, 2001), 176-89, esp. 181-87.

[39]See Joseph F. T. Kelly, "Early Medieval Evidence for Twelve Homilies by Origen on the Apocalypse," *Vigiliae Christianae* 39 (1985): 273-79.

[40]SC 83:123; 84:654-65.

[41]Jerome *Lives of Illustrious Men* 74 (NPNF, 2nd series, 3:377).

[42]Jerome *Letter* 70.5 (NPNF 2 6:151).

[43]Jerome *Against Helvidius* 19 (NPNF 2 6:343). Apparently Helvidius based his ideas on a commentary on Matthew by Victorinus, now lost. According to Jerome, Helvidius had misinterpreted Victorinus.

[44]Jerome *Letter* 61.2; 84.7 (NPNF 2 6:132, 179).

commentary on the Apocalypse by Victorinus, perhaps written as early as the reign of Gallienus (c. 258-260),[45] is not easily characterized. It is certainly true that he had used Irenaeus and Hippolytus and that he interpreted the Revelation in broadly millennialist terms. This is especially clear in his remarks concerning the thousand years and the new Jerusalem where traditional chiliastic interpretations, already to be found in Irenaeus, appear. Moreover, Victorinus is the first to use the legend of *Nero redivivus*[46] to interpret the antichrist figure. Yet, while much of the Revelation was interpreted as referring to the last days of the earth and the earthly kingdom of Christ, much was also interpreted in a modest allegorical manner, most likely reflecting the influence of Origen. So, for example, the letters to the seven churches are understood to address and to represent seven classes of saints. Perhaps the most important contribution of Victorinus to the interpretation of the Revelation is the idea of recapitulation, whereby the visions of the book do not depict a sequential series of future occurrences but rather depict the same realities that repeatedly occur throughout salvation history and are rendered through differing images and symbols. Thus the antichrist can be perceived both in the Roman emperors as well as in the end-time imitator of the Christ, the antichrist. The idea of recapitulation as a principle for the interpretation of the Revelation would be adopted by Tyconius into his *Rules* and through him would enter into the Middle Ages as a common method of interpreting Revelation.

Indeed, in the Western, Latin exegetical tradition on the Revelation the interpretative method of Tyconius (c. 370-390) transformed and to a great extent determined commentary on the Revelation for the following eight centuries. Little is known of Tyconius, and what we know is largely derived from Gennadius of Marseilles (c. 490).[47] Tyconius was a Donatist who in addition to two works in defense of the Donatist cause wrote the *Book of Rules* for the study and understanding of the meaning of Scripture and a "comprehensive" exposition of the Revelation of John. The *Book of Rules* is the sole remaining work of Tyconius, and through it we can infer the exegetical approach of Tyconius to the Scriptures which had such a profound influence upon the Latin exegetical tradition.[48] In the prologue to the *Rules* Tyconius writes that he intends "to fashion keys and lamps, as it were, to the secrets of the law" [i.e., the whole Bible]. These rules are seven in number: the Lord and his body; the Lord's bipartite body; the promises and the law; the particular and the general; times; recapitulation; and the devil and his body. The seven rules, says Tyconius, are "mystic," that is, they "obtain in the inner recesses of the entire law and keep the rich treasures of the truth hidden from some people." By "mystic" Tyconius seems to mean that these rules are the compositional principles of the scriptural text that the Holy Spirit used to structure and form the very wording of the text itself.[49] Apart from these rules the truth of the text remains "hidden" from some people. One must, as it were, understand how the mind of the

---

[45]So M. Dulaey, *Victorin de Poetovio: Sur L'Apocalypse* (SC 423; Paris: Les Editions du Cerf, 1997), 15. For a complete discussion of Victorinus, see Martine Dulaey, *Victorin de Poetovio, Premier Exegete Latin*, 2 vols. (Collection des Etudes Augustiniennes 139, 140; Paris: Institut d'Etudes Augustiniennes, 1993).

[46]A popular belief that Nero would return, based on Rev 13:11-18 where a beast numbered 666 is described. Each letter of the Greek and Hebrew alphabets has a numerical value; Nero's name in Hebrew totals 666.

[47]Gennadius *Lives of Illustrious Men* 18 (NPNF 2 3:389).

[48]For text and translation of the *Book of Rules*, see William S. Babcock, trans., *Tyconius: The Book of Rules*, Society of Biblical Literature Texts and Translations 31 (Atlanta: Scholars Press, 1989); for a thorough study of the Tyconian *Rules*, see Pamela Bright, *The Book of Rules of Tyconius: Its Purpose and Inner Logic*, Christianity and Judaism in Antiquity 2 (Notre Dame, Ind.: University of Notre Dame Press, 1988).

[49]See esp. Charles Kannengiesser, "Augustine and Tyconius: A Conflict of Christian Hermeneutics in Roman Africa," in *Augustine and the Bible*, ed. Pamela Bright (Notre Dame, Ind.: University of Notre Dame Press, 1999), 149-77, esp. 155-62.

Spirit works in order to understand the speech of the Spirit. Given the Donatist conviction that there were two churches, the true, spiritual church of the Donatists and the false church of the Catholic *traditores*,[50] perhaps Tyconius understood his rules to be the spiritual basis for interpreting the Bible in such a way as to justify the Donatist church as the one, holy community of the Spirit. As it happened, the *Rules* of Tyconius in fact worked against the separatist ecclesiology of the Donatist schism. In them Tyconius argued that in this world a separation between the good and the evil was impossible; the church militant was itself a "mixed church" in which the holy and the unholy lived. Similarly, Tyconius erodes the distinction of "new" and "old" dispensation as a distinction of times. Throughout time, according to Tyconius, the divine activity of grace and judgment has been at work in all nations and peoples and individuals. The effect of this understanding was to undercut millennialist assumptions about the last days as a temporal period of time. Determinative for the last days was the birth, death and resurrection of Christ. The thousand years of Christ's reign with his saints was, therefore, the time from Christ to the time of his second coming, and the "first resurrection" was the coming to faith in baptism.

It is evident that these "mystic rules" guided Tyconius in his commentary on the Revelation.[51] According to Gennadius, Tyconius understood nothing in the Revelation "in a carnal sense, but all in a spiritual sense." Moreover, Gennadius rather exactly describes Tyconius's interpretation of the Revelation as a revelation, not of the (temporal) last times, but of the time of the church: "He doubts that there will be a reign of the righteous on earth for a thousand years after the resurrection, or that there will be two resurrections of the dead in the flesh, one of the righteous and the other of the unrighteous, but maintains that there will be one simultaneous resurrection of all mankind." The "first resurrection" of the Revelation concerns only "the growth of the church" wherein the just "are raised from the dead bodies of their sins through baptism to eternal life." The "second resurrection" of the Revelation is, then, "the general resurrection of all men in the flesh."[52] A couple of examples will illustrate the use of the rules in Tyconius's commentary on the Revelation. Rule two of Tyconius teaches of the Lord's "bipartite Body," that is, that the church in this world is a mixed community including pious and impious. In his *Rules* Tyconius quotes the Song of Songs 1:5, "I [the church] am black and beautiful," and sees this fact also in the Revelation where "the Lord now calls the seven angels [i.e., the septiform church] holy and keepers of his precepts and now shows the same angels to be guilty of many crimes and in need of repentance."[53] The idea of an *ecclesia mixta* (mixed church) is frequent also in the commentary of Tyconius. For example, writing of Revelation 8:12 that a third part of the sun, moon and stars were struck down and darkened, Tyconius interprets the heavenly bodies to be the church, for "there are two peoples within the church, that part of God which is compared to the light, and that part of the devil which is surrounded by the darkness of shadows. . . . This part was struck so that it might become apparent who is of God and who of the devil."[54] Rule seven of Tyconius speaks of "The Devil and His Body." Just as the church is the body of Christ, so that in

---

[50]The "betrayers," i.e., North African clergy who handed over the Scriptures to be burned during the Great Persecution of A.D. 303-305 under Diocletian.

[51]See Kannengiesser, "Augustine and Tyconius," 157-65. Kannengiesser notes in Tyconius's commentary the "massive and constant use" of technical terms elaborated in the Rules and claims that "Tyconius' interpretation of the famous seven letters addressed to the churches in the Johannine Apocalypse conforms closely to the logic and the sequence of the Tyconian seven rules" (162).

[52]Gennadius *Lives of Illustrious Men* 18 (NPNF 2 3:389).

[53]Babock, *Tyconius*, 19.

[54]TS 2 7:96-97 §§172-73.

Christ the church is also noted and Christ in the church, so also the devil has his body, so that when the devil is seen, his body is also to be noted. Commenting on the dragon who wishes to devour the child of the woman (Rev 12:4), Tyconius thinks of Herod, who wished to kill the baby Jesus, and writes that "the devil in heaven [i.e., the church] is always seeking to devour that person who is being born through heavenly things and who is born to God and is caught up to his throne.... For, in the person of Herod the whole company of persecutors is revealed."[55]

Tyconius's conversion of millennialist calculations to commentary on the universal and unitary time of the church became common to Western interpretation of the Revelation primarily through the massive influence of Augustine of Hippo (d. 430). It is certain that Augustine knew the seven rules of Tyconius, for he explicitly enumerates and comments upon them in *On Christian Doctrine*. Although the Donatism of Tyconius occasioned a certain reserve toward him in Augustine, the influence of Tyconius on Augustine is evident in Augustine's commentary on Revelation 20:1-6 in book 20 of *City of God*.[56] Although he had once held chiliastic beliefs, in *City of God* Augustine provides a sustained and developed understanding of the last times as the time of the church militant. This time had begun with the death and resurrection of Christ, and these events were the fulfillment of Old Testament prophecy; no events after these allowed for a further, more calculated determination of the end of the world.[57] After Christ, in the world there is "nothing solid, nothing stable"; all of history is homogenous.[58] Therefore, the thousand years of Revelation 20 symbolize all the years of the Christian era during which the church is always beset by the devil within through heresy and hypocrisy and without through persecution. The abyss in which Satan is chained is the hearts of the wicked, so that when Satan is "loosed" and gathers Gog and Magog for battle, these are not to be regarded as specific nations. Rather, the anger of the devil arises whenever the church is persecuted and attacked by his body of the impious. The "first resurrection" and the "second resurrection" represent two kinds of life, that of the soul and that of the body. The first resurrection, then, is the coming to life of the soul in baptism, and the second resurrection is the coming to life of the body in the final and general resurrection. Finally, the thrones upon which the saints sit and judge are the positions of authority in the church.[59]

In addition to Augustine, the other major influence for mediating the Tyconian interpretation of the Revelation to the Middle Ages was Jerome (d. 420). Sometime shortly before 400 a certain Anatolius sent a copy of Victorinus's commentary on the Apocalypse to Jerome and asked him to evaluate its contents. Respectful of the fact that Victorinus had been a bishop and a martyr, Jerome reveals a certain hesitation to do this, for like Papias of Hierapolis and Nepos of Egypt before him, Victorinus had believed in an earthly kingdom of one thousand years. Nonetheless, the response of Jerome to Anatolius was a revision of the commentary of Victorinus. In the prologue to his commentary, Jerome indicates that he had corrected the millennialist errors of

---

[55]TS 2 7:184-85 §§463-64.

[56]For the relation between Tyconius and Augustine, see Paula Fredriksen, "Tyconius and Augustine on the Apocalypse," in *The Apocalypse in the Middle Ages*, ed. Richard K. Emmerson and Bernard McGinn (Ithaca, N.Y.: Cornell University Press, 1992), 20-37; Martine Dulaey, "L'Apocalypse: Augustine et Tyconius," in *Saint Augustine et la Bible*, ed. Anne-Marie la Bonnardiere (Paris: Beauchesne, 1986), 369-86; Pamela Bright, "'The Preponderating Influence of Augustine': A Study of the Epitomes of the *Book of Rules* of the Donatist Tyconius," in *Augustine and the Bible*, ed. Pamela Bright (Notre Dame, Ind.: University of Notre Dame Press, 1999), 109-28.

[57]For Augustine's fight against ongoing chiliastic belief, see esp. his letters to Hesychius of Salone (*Letters* 197, 198, 199).

[58]For discussion of Augustine's change of view in eschatological matters, see R. A. Markus, *Saeculum: History and Society in the Theology of St Augustine* (Cambridge: Cambridge University Press, 1970), 1-71.

[59]For a good summary of Augustine's eschatological views, see Daley, *Hope of the Early Church*, 131-50.

Victorinus and had added his own comments.[60] Jerome's interpretation of the thousand years is thoroughly amillennial and is governed by his interests in monastic virtue and the church's struggle with heresy. He does not think that the kingdom of a thousand years will be an earthly one. Rather, the number ten represents the Decalogue and the number one hundred represents "the crown of virginity," so that one who preserves intact his virginity, who faithfully fulfills the precepts of the Decalogue and binds impure habits and thoughts within the inner chamber of his heart is one who has fulfilled the number thousand and reigns with Christ as a true priest of Christ.[61]

The Tyconian tradition through Jerome and Augustine and the Victorine tradition through Jerome governed commentary on the Revelation well into the Middle Ages.[62] We might notice first a work that bears perhaps the least of this influence. Cassiodorus (d. c. 590), born into a patrician family, was statesman under Theodoric the Ostrogoth but retired to found the famous monastery at Vivarium in southern Italy. There he oversaw the writing and copying of numerous manuscripts, including his own considerable output. Among these were his *Complexiones* on apostolic letters, the Acts of the Apostles and the Revelation, written toward the end of his life. In the *Complexiones* Cassiodorus provided brief abstracts of biblical books in which he combined several verses together in order to paraphrase them. Of the four explicit mentions of Tyconius in the writings of Cassiodorus, three of them are in the *Complexiones* and two of these in the *complexiones* on Revelation. Any influence on him by Tyconius's commentary, however, is impossible to ascertain.[63]

Caesarius of Arles (d. 543), however, reveals a considerable influence of Augustine, Tyconius and Victorinus. Caesarius was widely read in Augustine and the Fathers and at an early age committed himself to the monastery at Lerins. However, in 503 he was elevated to the episcopal see at Arles, where he became a leader in monastic and theological affairs. Caesarius was a prolific preacher whose sermons reflect his struggles to free his people from pagan superstition and the heresies of Arianism and semi-Pelagianism.[64] In his *Expositiones* on the Revelation of Saint John, Caesarius presents brief comments on the Revelation that are rather artificially divided as homilies. According to Kenneth B. Steinhauser, the *Expositiones* of Caesarius demonstrate that he possessed the unrevised commentary of Victorinus and two copies of Tyconius's commentary on the Apocalypse.[65] In any case, these homilies reveal a thorough ecclesial interpretation of the Revelation typical of Tyconius and Augustine. For example, Caesarius interprets the "heaven" of Revelation 4:1 to be the church, as he does the twenty-four elders, who represent both the leaders and the people of the church. From the throne proceeds thunder and voices (Rev 4:5), that is, "heretics come forth from the church" even as does the preaching of the church.[66]

The most important commentary for mediating the Tyconian-Augustinian interpretation of Revelation to

---

[60]CSEL 49:14-15.

[61]CSEL 49:145-47. For discussion of Jerome's revision of Victorinus, see Kenneth B. Steinhauser, *The Apocalypse Commentary of Tyconius: A History of Its Reception and Influence* (European University Studies 301; Frankfurt and New York: Peter Lang, 1987), 35-44.

[62]See the helpful chart of text influences by E. Ann Matter, "Apocalypse in Early Medieval Exegesis," 42. For a persuasive study of the influence of Tyconius's commentary and its reconstruction through later commentaries, see Steinhauser, *The Apocalypse Commentary of Tyconius*.

[63]For a critical edition of the *Complexiones in Apocalypsin*, see CCL 107:99-129 (also PL 70:1405-18). For discussion, see Steinhauser, *The Apocalypse Commentary of Tyconius*, 89-98. For the life and work of Cassiodorus, see James J. O'Donnell, *Cassiodorus* (Berkeley: University of California Press, 1979).

[64]For an English translation, see FC 31 (sermons 1-80), FC 47 (sermons 81-186), FC 66 (sermons 187-238).

[65]Steinhauser, *The Apocalypse Commentary of Tyconius*, 52-68.

[66]Homily 3 (PL 35:2422).

the Middle Ages was that of Primasius of Hadrumetum (d. after 553). We know virtually nothing of the life of Primasius.[67] Only one event of his life is clearly in view. He was deeply involved in the so-called Three Chapters controversy of the sixth century. To gain Monophysite support, Justinian I determined to condemn writings of three significant Antiochene theologians, Theodore of Mopsuestia, Theodoret of Cyr and Ibas of Edessa. This action was widely decried in the Latin West, and at first Vigilius, bishop of Rome, also opposed. However, ordered by Justinian to Constantinople (551), Vigilius eventually gave his assent to Justinian's actions as well as the formal condemnation of the Three Chapters by the Fifth Ecumenical Council (553). In this entire episode Primasius proved a loyal and faithful follower of Vigilius. He too was summoned to Constantinople in 551 and returned to Africa after agreeing to the condemnations of the council in 553. Sometime upon his return he was consecrated bishop of Hadrumetum, principal city of the province of Byzancena.

Primasius's commentary on the Apocalypse is the only work of his that survives. Its date of composition is unknown, but since it is mentioned by Cassiodorus in his *Institutes*, it was written before the outbreak of the Three Chapters controversy, perhaps around 540. In the prologue, Primasius explicitly makes clear his indebtedness to Augustine and to Tyconius.[68] Nowhere is the influence of Augustine more evident than in the wholesale incorporation of Augustine's comments on Revelation 20:1-6 from *City of God* 20.7-17 into his commentary. Although Primasius is defensive about his use of Tyconius, indicating that one can acquire jewels from a dunghill, and mentions Tyconius only twice, it is evident that throughout his commentary Primasius borrows extensively from Tyconius.[69] Primasius interprets the Revelation as a text of the earthly church, and at times the theological issues of his day are evident. He interprets Revelation 12:1 as the church that has put on Christ and now sojourns amid many heretics, among whom is Timothy Aelurus, Monophysite patriarch of Alexandria.[70] The ongoing vigor of Arianism in North Africa is evidenced by his comments on the Alpha and Omega of Revelation 22:13. The letters alpha and omega have the same value as does the Greek word for "dove," indicating the equality of natures between the Father, Son and Holy Spirit. The importance of Primasius's *Commentary on the Apocalypse* is clear from the fact that it was itself a major source for all important eighth-century commentaries, those of Bede, Ambrosius Autpertus and Beatus of Liebana.

The continuing influence of Jerome's edition of Victorinus's commentary is evident in the commentary of Apringius, Bishop of Beja (Portugal). Apringius wrote his commentary during the reign of the Arian Visigothic king, Theudis (531-548). His commentary also shows opposition to Arian denial of Christ's deity. The commentary exists in one copy only, which contains original material by Apringius on Revelation 1:1—5:7 and Revelation 18:6—22:21. The remaining commentary consists of whole sections of Jerome's corrected version of Victorinus. Interesting is the interpretation of the seven seals, which Apringius understands christologically as the incarnation, birth, passion, death, resurrection, glory and kingdom. In his humanity these together complete all that was sealed in the Old Testament.[71] It has been suggested that Apringius's text may originally have been homilies preached between Easter and Pentecost, when portions of the Revelation were read in the

[67]See Johannes Haussleiter, *Die lateinische Apokalypse der alten afrikanischen Kirche,* in Forschungen zur Geschichte des neutestamentlichen Kanons und der altkirchlichen Literatur, part 4 (Erlangen and Leipzig: Andr. Deichert'sche Verlagsbuchhandlung, 1891), 1-8.
[68]CCL 92:1-2.
[69]Steinhauser, *The Apocalypse Commentary of Tyconius,* 81-88: "Tyconius may rightly be considered his chief source."
[70]CCL 92:179-80.
[71]CCL 107:65-66.

Visigothic church. In any case, the influence of Apringius's commentary seems to have been confined to the Iberian Peninsula, since Beatus of Liebana is the only later author to make reference to it.[72] It does not appear that Apringius knew the commentary on Revelation by Tyconius.

The commentary of Bede the Venerable (d. 735) makes extensive use of Jerome's edition of Victorinus, of Tyconius and of Primasius. Often quoted are Augustine and Gregory the Great as well. Born about 673, at seven years Bede was given into the care of the monks of Jarrow, where he lived the rest of his life. His *Explanation of the Apocalypse* is dedicated to Hwaetberct, named Eusebius because of his piety, who succeeded as abbot of Wearmouth and Jarrow in 716. The commentary was written some time before that date. In his dedicatory letter to Eusebius, Bede, using Augustine's *On Christian Doctrine*, explicitly mentions the seven rules of Tyconius and openly admits to his significant use of them. Bede divides the Revelation into seven sections that correspond to seven ages of the world through which the church moves. It is likely that this schema was inspired by the seven rules of Tyconius, even if he were not the origin of it.[73] Along with the other eighth-century commentaries of Autpertus (d. 781) and Beatus (d. 798),[74] that of Bede marks a transition in the history of Western interpretation of the Revelation. Especially the commentaries of Bede and Autpertus fully incorporate Augustine, Tyconius and Primasius and become the principal means by which those traditions come to Carolingian interpreters such as Alcuin and Haimo.

The first full Greek commentary on the Revelation comes from Oecumenius (early sixth century), who seems to have been a layman of high rank. Various manuscripts call him "philosophos," "rhetor" and "scholasticus," which would indicate broad learning. Moreover, he was the recipient of correspondence from Severus of Antioch, the most important Monophysite theologian of the sixth century. This would suggest a date of writing toward the early part of the sixth century, perhaps about 510.[75] The commentary of Oecumenius is characterized by broad reading, knowledge of contemporary events and the mild allegory of the Alexandrian exegetical tradition. It also evinces considerable independence and originality, for Oecumenius shows no knowledge of any earlier commentary. At the beginning of his commentary Oecumenius explicitly mentions Athanasius, Basil, Gregory of Nazianzus, Methodius, Cyril of Alexandria and Hippolytus.[76] However, his familiarity with earlier patristic literature is considerable, for he cites in addition Justin Martyr, Irenaeus, Eusebius, Clement of Alexandria, and others.[77]

For the most part Oecumenius interprets the visions of the Revelation to refer to events surrounding the future parousia of Christ. However, from time to time a distinct christological interest is evident. At the beginning of his comments on the Revelation, Oecumenius lays out what he believes is "the pattern of pure theol-

---

[72]Matter, "The Apocalypse in Early Medieval Exegesis," 45-46.

[73]Steinhauser, *The Apocalypse Commentary of Tyconius*, 117-22. See also Gerald Bonner, *Saint Bede in the Tradition of Western Apocalyptic Commentary* (Newcastle upon Tyne: J. & P. Bealls, 1966).

[74]For the critical text of Autpertus, see CCL 27A *(continuatio mediaevalis)*; for Beatus, Henry A. Sanders, *Beati in Apocalipsin Libri Duodecim*, Papers and Monographs of the American Academy in Rome, vol. 7 (Rome: American Academy in Rome, 1930).

[75]John C. Lamoreux, "The Provenance of Ecumenius' Commentary on the Apocalypse," *Vigiliae Christianae* 52 (1998): 88-108, who argues for a date between 508 and 518.

[76]TEG 8:65.

[77]For a full listing of references, see TEG 8:326-36. For discussion of Oecumenius, see Fr. Diekamp, "Mittheilungen ueber den neuaufgefundenen Commentar des Oekumenius zur Apokalypse," *Sitzungsberichte der Koeniglichen Preussischen Akademie der Wissenschaften* 43 (1901): 1046-56; Clifford H. DuRousseau, "The Commentary of Oecumenius on the Apocalypse of John: A Lost Chapter in the History of Interpretation," *Biblical Research* 29 (1984): 21-34; Daley, *Hope of the Early Church*, 179-83.

ogy," namely, that "God the Word [consubstantial with the Father and the Spirit] was begotten from God the Father before all ages" and that "in the last days for us and our salvation he became man, not by any loss of divinity, but by the assumption of human flesh together with a rational soul, so that he who is Emmanuel may be recognized as united from two natures, from divinity and humanity, the natures subsisting perfectly according to their own integrity and distinction which arises from their natural qualities and peculiarities, neither being mixed nor changed by coming together into unity, nor being separated after the ineffable and real union." Nestorius and Eutyches are explicitly rejected.[78] A similar statement occurs toward the end of the commentary, this time containing a variation of the famous four adverbs of Chalcedon and the interesting claim that after the union there are "one person, one hypostasis, and one energy."[79] Such statements show clearly that while Oecumenius may not have been opposed to the Council of Chalcedon, he interpreted it in a manner congenial to the Monophysite interests of Severus of Antioch.

Interest in the incarnate life of Christ is manifest especially in two contexts. Like Apringius, Oecumenius interprets the seven seals as symbols for events in the life of Jesus. The first seal symbolizes the incarnation, the second his baptism, the third his miracles, the fourth his trial before Pilate, the fifth his crucifixion, the sixth his burial, and the seventh his descent into hades. Unique to Oecumenius is also his interpretation of the thousand years, which he understands to refer to the "day" of salvation, namely, to the time of the incarnation of Christ. The short time during which the devil is loose is the time between Christ and his second coming.[80] Oecumenius's knowledge of natural philosophy is employed in his discussion of the four beasts around God's throne, which he believes to represent the four elements. The lion is fire; the ox is earth; the man is air; and the eagle is water.[81]

Another sixth-century Greek commentator on the Revelation was Andrew of Caesarea (early sixth century). Since Andrew seems at times to refer to the attacks of the Huns, Franz Diekamp dates Andrew's commentary about 515.[82] Although Andrew adduces with some frequency the writings of earlier writers such as Papias, Irenaeus, Hippolytus, Methodius, Eusebius, Epiphanius, Gregory of Nazianzus and Cyril of Alexandria, he never refers to any earlier commentary. However, it is clear that Andrew knew the commentary of Oecumenius and often summarizes the views of Oecumenius only to offer an alternative opinion. More than Oecumenius, Andrew is concerned with the moral life of the Christian. In the epilogue to his commentary, Andrew reminds readers that "through the seven churches we are taught steadfastness in temptations, zeal in the doing of good, and other forms of virtue."[83] Andrew rarely speculates, offering rather a careful biblical narrative and one anchored in traditional interpretation. The thousand years represents "the time from the incarnation of the Lord until the arrival of the antichrist," the number thousand signifying perfection and completion, and only God knows how long the completion of the church will take.[84] Andrew reveals opposition to the positions of Origen, indicating that he is not unaware of the issues of the Origenistic controversies

---

[78]TEG 8:66-67.
[79]TEG 8:287.
[80]TEG 8:248-50.
[81]TEG 8:109-10.
[82]Franz Diekamp, "Das Zeitalter des Erzbischofs Andreas von Caesarea," *Historisches Jahrbuch* 18 (Munich: Kommissions-Verlag von Herder, 1897): 1-36.
[83]MTS 1 Sup 1:263.
[84]MTS 1 Sup 1:216.

of the sixth century. He speaks against the "restoration of all things" and in another work, *Therapeutike*, opposes the view that resurrection bodies will be spherical.[85] The commentary of Andrew provided the basis for the commentary of Arethas (c. 900), a successor of Andrew as bishop of Cappadocian Caesarea. After Arethas no significant commentary on the Revelation has been written. Indeed, that of Andrew of Caesarea became the standard commentary on the book for the later Byzantine tradition.

## Criteria and Selection of Commentaries

The Revelation of John was read and used by Christian writers from the second century onwards. Sometimes this use was more thematic, such as the use of the last chapters of Revelation by Irenaeus to substantiate his millennialism. Others, such as Tertullian and Cyprian, used the Revelation for specific moral exhortations. Others, such as Jerome and Augustine, use the Revelation to advance the practice of virginity. Still others, such as Athanasius, might cite the Revelation for theological and doctrinal reasons. Selections from such writers have been chosen to illustrate such use. Many of these selections possess their own intrinsic interest and significance, and they provide a certain enrichment to the more formal commentaries selected.

However, the great share of the selected texts are from the commentaries and homilies surveyed in the previous section. The use of commentaries not only gives a sense of the exegetical and theological tradition of Revelation interpretation but also to some extent provides a sequential and homogeneous interpretation of the text of the Revelation. The commentaries selected for regular citation are eight in number.

1. Victorinus of Petovium. The commentary of Victorinus is not only the earliest commentary of the Revelation that we possess, it is also the only one that comes from the pre-Nicaean period and does not reflect later doctrinal and disciplinary issues. Moreover, Victorinus is deeply influenced by early Christian interpretations and expectations, and for that reason alone its inclusion seemed to be necessary. To be sure, the text of Victorinus may not be perfectly secure. The critical edition of Johannes Haussleiter used in this volume was established from fifteenth- and sixteenth-century manuscripts. Nonetheless, before Haussleiter's work Victorinus was known only through the various recensions of Jerome's version. For the translation of Victorinus here I have used Haussleiter's critical edition, *Commentarii in Apocalypsin Editio Victorini* (CSEL 49; Leipzig: G. Freytag, 1916).[86] Mention should be made also of the Latin text with French translation of Martine Dulaey, *Victorin de Poetovio. Sur l'Apocalypse* (SC 423; Paris: Éditions du Cerf, 1997). Her notes are helpful and at times used in the footnotes of this volume.

2. Tyconius. The (lost) commentary of Tyconius presents special problems. Given the wide influence of Tyconius on later exegetical tradition, he could not be overlooked. However, the commentary of Tyconius exists only in quotation and through its use by others often embarrassed by Tyconius's Donatist origins. Fragments of the commentary, extant in a manuscript from the Italian monastery at Bobbio, have been edited by Francesco Lo Bue, *The Turin Fragments of Tyconius' Commentary on Revelation* (Texts and Studies, n.s. 7; Cambridge: Cambridge University Press, 1963). It is generally known that some aspects of these fragments cannot have come from Tyconius, and Lo Bue suggested that the Tyconian text had probably early received "a redac-

---

[85]Diekamp, "Das Zeitalter des Andreas von Caesarea," 29 n. 2.

[86]On facing pages Haussleiter gives the Latin of a *Recensio hieronymiuna cum posteriorum additamentis*, a rendering of Jerome's edition.

tion for Catholic use."[87] With this reservation in mind, the Turin fragments also possess Tyconian affinities, and in the absence of any English translation of the fragments in the Lo Bue edition, I have used the Turin fragments as from Tyconius.

Tyconius's commentary survived through its use in early medieval Latin commentaries. Nowhere is this more the case than in the eighth-century commentary of Beatus of Liebana.[88] However, Beatus was slightly outside the chronological scope of the ACCS series, and I decided rather to incorporate as much as possible of another, earlier commentary that also contained significant Tyconian material. For this purpose, the sixth-century commentary of Primasius was selected. To identify material from Tyconius in Primasius, "The Tyconian Synopsis" of Kenneth Steinhauser was used as guide.[89] Therefore, some selections of Tyconius are noted as from the critical edition of Primasius's commentary (CCL 92). By using Primasius as a source for Tyconius, more of the important commentary of Primasius could be translated for the first time.

3. Primasius. In the judgment of E. Ann Matter, the commentary of Primasius exerted "extraordinary influence on the [Latin exegetical] tradition." "All later commentaries," she writes, "were influenced by this one, either directly or indirectly."[90] Primasius incorporates Augustine, Tyconius and Victorinus/Jerome and influences all later interpretations. This in itself justifies the extensive use of Primasius in this volume. For the translation here I have used A. W. Adams's critical edition of *Commentarius in Apocalypsin* (CCL 92).

4. Caesarius of Arles. The series of homilies known as the *Expositio in Apocalypsim* circulated for a long time under the name of Augustine and sometimes are referred to as the Pseudo-Augustine homilies. Some have attributed these sermons, or perhaps they are sermon notes, to Gennadius of Marseilles. However, Germain Morin has demonstrated that they come from Caesarius of Arles.[91] In addition, Morin has published a critical edition of the *Expositio* in *Sancti Caesarii Episcopi Arelatensis Opera Omnia*, vol. 2 (Maretioli, 1942). Under the name of Augustine the Latin text also exists in J.-P. Migne's *Patrologiae cursus completus, Series Latinae*, vol. 35 (Paris, 1845). For the translation here I have used the text in PL 35:2417-52, since it is more accessible than is the edition of Morin.

5. Apringius of Beja. The *Tractatus in Apocalypsin* of Apringius stands outside the tradition of Tyconius and possesses interpretation not to be found in other early medieval Latin commentaries. His commentary survives only in one twelfth-century manuscript, and its influence seems to have been limited to the Iberian peninsula. The single manuscript combines comment by Apringius (Rev 1:1—5:7; 18:6—22:20) with that of Jerome's version of Victorinus. The commentary was first edited by Marius Férotin in *Apringius e Béja: Son Commentaire de l'Apocalypse écrit sous Theudis, roi des Wisigoths (531-548)* (Paris: Alphanse Picard, 1900). A Latin edition was later published in P. A. C. Vega, *Apringii Pacensis Episcopi Tractatus in Apocalypsin*, Scriptores Ecclesiastici Hispano-Latini Veteris et Medii Aevi, fasc. 10-11 (Madrid: Typis Augustianis Monasterii Escurialensis, 1940). A much superior critical edition is that of Roger Gryson, *Apringi Pacensis Episcopi Tractatus in Apocalypsin*

---

[87]Lo Bue, *The Turin Fragments*, 32-38; see also the careful analysis by Steinhauser, *The Apocalypse Commentary of Tyconius*, 198-211, who concludes that the fragments "cannot be considered the best representative of the Tyconian archetype."

[88]For a listing of passages from Tyconius in the commentary of Beatus, see Traugott Hahn, *Tyconius-Studien: Ein Beitrag zur Kirchen- und Dogmengeschichte d. 4. Jahrhunderts* (Leipzig: Dieterich, 1900; reprint ed., Aalen: Scienta Verlag, 1971), 11-12; also "The Tyconian Synopsis" in Steinhauser, *The Apocalypse Commentary of Tyconius*, 265-316.

[89]Steinhauser, *The Apocalypse Commentary of Tyconius*, 265-316.

[90]Matter, *The Apocalypse in Early Medieval Exegesis*, 43.

[91]Germain Morin, "Le commentaire homiletique de S. Cesaire sur l'Apocalypse," *Revue Benedictine* 45 (1933): 43-61.

*Fragmenta quae Supersunt* (CCL 107). While a Latin text with Spanish translation exists in Alberto del Campo Hernandez, *Comentario al Apocalipsis de Apringio de Beja: Introduccion, Texto Latino y Traduccion* (Estella: Editorio Verbo Divino, 1991), this volume offers an English translation of Apringius for the first time. For the translation the edition of Gryson was utilized (CCL 107).

6. Bede the Venerable. For the purpose of this volume, Bede the Venerable represents the outcome of patristic comment characteristic of the eighth-century commentaries, especially that of Autpertus. At the same time he was much used by the Carolingian commentators Alcuin and Haimo. An English translation by Edward Marshall exists in *The Explanation of the Apocalypse by Venerable Bede* (Oxford/London: James Parker & Co., 1878). I was not able to see that translation. My translation is based upon the critical edition of Roger Gryson, *Bedae Presbyteri: Expositio Apocalypseos* (CCL 121A).

7. Oecumenius. Oecumenius takes pride of place as the first Greek commentary of the Revelation. A Greek edition was published by H. C. Hoskier, *The Complete Commentary of Oecumenius on the Apocalypse* (Ann Arbor, Mich.: University of Michigan Press, 1928). This edition has been superseded by that of Marc de Groote, *Oecumenii Commentarius in Apocalypsin*, Traditio Exegetica Graeca 8 (Louvain: Peeters, 1999). A rough English translation of Oecumenius's commentary was kindly provided to me by Clifford H. DuRousseau. The translation of Oecumenius in this volume is based upon the critical edition of de Groote (TEG 8).

8. Andrew of Caesarea. Andrew's *Commentary on the Apocalypse* is the standard commentary of the Byzantine tradition. Its interest lies not only in its historical importance but also in the fact that he often engages the interpretations of Oecumenius. The commentary of Oecumenius is divided into twelve discourses, but there is no apparent attempt by Oecumenius to divide the Revelation into meaningful sections. It is Andrew of Caesarea who seems to have the distinction of being the first to divide the Revelation according to a conceived pattern. In the prologue to his commentary Andrew indicates that he has divided the Revelation into twenty-four books (λόγοι) corresponding to the twenty-four elders. Each of these books is further divided into three chapters (κεφάλαια) corresponding to the three-fold nature of man, body, soul and spirit.[92] There are, therefore, seventy-two chapters in all. In keeping with the spirit of the ACCS series, this volume divides the Revelation according to the pattern of Andrew of Caesarea. The critical edition of Andrew's commentary is that of Josef Schmid, *Studien zur Geschichte des Griechischen Apokalypse-Textes*, 1, Teil: *Der Apokalypse-Kommentar des Andreas von Kaisareia*, Muenchener Theologische Studien (Munich: K. Zink, 1955). My translation is based upon this edition by Schmid (MTS 1 Sup 1). English quotations from Andrew are also available in Averky Taushev, *The Apocalypse: In the Teachings of Ancient Christianity*, translated by Father Seraphim Rose (Platina, Calif.: St. Herman of Alaska Brotherhood, 1985, 1995).

It is my hope that the selections in this volume will give an adequate idea of the broad use of the Revelation by the patristic writers as they attempted to guide and to encourage their readers on their way to the new Jerusalem. As space has permitted, I have attempted to give adequate context so that the creative use of Scripture, the theological interest and the pastoral intent can be discerned. It is an honor and privilege to participate in a project that invites laypeople and clergy to hear the voice of the Fathers and to recognize in them the faith that unites all Christians. Especially do I thank Thomas Oden for the opportunity to participate is this wonderful

---

[92]MTS 1 Sup 1:10.

series. I thank also the editorial team of ACCS at Drew University, led by Joel Elowsky, for their effort in providing me the first gathering of texts for use in this volume and for their editing and encouragement along the way. The Reverend Robert Smith of Walther Theological Library, Concordia Theological Seminary, Fort Wayne, Indiana, was also most helpful in structuring and formatting the text.

William C. Weinrich

# THE REVELATION TO JOHN

## 1:1-9 THE REVELATION OF JESUS CHRIST

[1]The revelation of Jesus Christ, which God gave him to show to his servants what must soon take place; and he made it known by sending his angel to his servant John, [2]who bore witness to the word of God and to the testimony of Jesus Christ, even to all that he saw. [3]Blessed is he who reads aloud the words of the prophecy, and blessed are those who hear, and who keep what is written therein; for the time is near.

[4]John to the seven churches that are in Asia:
Grace to you and peace from him who is and who was and who is to come, and from the seven spirits who are before his throne, [5]and from Jesus Christ the faithful witness, the first-born of the dead, and the ruler of kings on earth.
To him who loves us and has freed us from our sins by his blood [6]and made us a kingdom, priests to his God and Father, to him be glory and dominion for ever and ever. Amen. [7]Behold, he is coming with the clouds, and every eye will see him, every one who pierced him; and all tribes of the earth will wail on account of him. Even so. Amen.
[8]"I am the Alpha and the Omega," says the Lord God, who is and who was and who is to come, the Almighty.
[9]I John, your brother, who share with you in Jesus the tribulation and the kingdom and the patient endurance, was on the island called Patmos on account of the word of God and the testimony of Jesus.

**OVERVIEW:** As the Word and Son of God, Christ reveals to the saints what he is given from his Father. By calling the saints "servants," Christ shows that he is their Creator (OECUMENIUS). The revelation from Christ unveils heavenly secrets inaccessible to human senses (APRINGIUS). In the Revelation, Christ discloses the course of the life of the church to her perfection at the end (BEDE). Writing to seven churches, John is in fact writing to all churches and to all ages, for the number seven represents the present life (APRINGIUS, ANDREW OF CAESAREA). Through these churches the grace of God comes by the Holy Spirit to a prideful human race (CAESARIUS OF ARLES). John addresses the churches in the name of the Trinity who "was" and "is" and "is to come" (ANDREW OF CAESAREA). The seven spirits are seven angels who are ministers of Christ (OECUMENIUS), or they represent the one Holy Spirit in his sevenfold grace (APRINGIUS).

John also addresses the churches in the name of Jesus Christ, for in his humanity Christ was the faithful witness of his deity and cleansed us from sin by his blood (APRINGIUS). Christian martyrs are witnesses of this faithful witness (EUSEBIUS). As the firstborn of the dead, Christ abolished death and became the source and pattern of our salvation (IRENAEUS, ATHANASIUS). As the firstborn, Christ gave the adoption of sonship even to those who lived before the incarnation (BEDE), and he initiated the general resurrection (OECUMENIUS). Christ will come again in that same flesh in which he ascended into heaven (FULGENTIUS OF RUSPE), and his angels, who are called "clouds," will accompany him (OECUMENIUS). Christ calls himself the "Alpha and Omega" because he is both Creator and Redeemer (AUGUSTINE), and in him all things at the end return as they were at the beginning (TERTULLIAN). Christ calls himself "the Almighty," indicating that he shares one Godhead with the Father (ATHANASIUS). John received this revelation during the reign of Caesar Claudius (APRINGIUS), or in another opinion, at the time of Domitian (BEDE).

## 1:1 The Revelation of Jesus Christ

**REVELATION MAKES KNOWN WHAT WE CANNOT KNOW.** APRINGIUS OF BEJA: From this we learn that this [book] is called an Apocalypse, that is, "revelation," which manifests those secrets which are hidden and unknown to the senses, and that unless [Christ] himself reveals them, he who perceives [the revelation] will not have the strength to understand what he sees. TRACTATE ON THE APOCALYPSE 1.1.[1]

**"SOON" INDICATES A RELATION TO ETERNITY.** OECUMENIUS: When it is said to him, "The Revelation of Jesus Christ, which God gave to him," it is as though he said, "This revelation is given from the Father to the Son, and then from the Son to us," his servants. By calling the saints the "servants" of Christ, he safeguards what is proper to his deity. For, to whom would men belong, unless to him who is the Maker and Creator of

humankind? And who is the Creator of humankind and of all creation? No one other than the only begotten Word and Son of God! For, the present author says in the Gospel, "All things were made through him."[2] And why does he wish to add "what must soon take place," although those events which will take place have not yet occurred, even though a considerable span of time has passed, more than five hundred years, since these words were spoken? Because to the eyes of the eternal and endless God all ages are regarded as nothing, for, as the prophet says, "A thousand years in your sight, O Lord, are as yesterday when it is past, or as a watch in the night."[3] For this reason, therefore, he added "soon," not to indicate a measure of time which must pass before the fulfillment of what must happen, but to indicate the power and eternality of God. For to him who is, any passage of time, even should it be great and considerable, is something small when compared with that which is unending. COMMENTARY ON THE APOCALYPSE 1.1-2.[4]

**THE REVELATION REVEALS THE HISTORY OF THE CHURCH.** BEDE: When the church had been established by the apostles, it was proper that it be revealed by what course [the church] was to be extended and was to be perfected at the end, so that the preachers of the faith might be strengthened against the adversaries of the world. As was his custom, John refers the glory of the Son to the Father and testifies that Jesus Christ received the revelation of this mystery from God. EXPLANATION OF THE APOCALYPSE 1.1.[5]

## 1:3 Blessed Are Those Who Read and Hear

**PERFECTION IS TO DO WHAT YOU READ AND HEAR.** APRINGIUS OF BEJA: He wishes to make clear that the reading does not accomplish the obedience of the commandments, nor does the hearing display the completion of an accom-

---

[1]CCL 107:33. [2]Jn 1:3. [3]Ps 90:4 (89:4 LXX). [4]TEG 8:67-68. [5]CCL 121A:235.

plished deed. Rather, that alone is perfection, when you perform with understanding what you read and what you hear. "The time is short." For those who accomplish these things, he does not prolong the time of recompense, but he says that the giving of the divine reward is near. TRACTATE ON THE APOCALYPSE 1.3.[6]

## 1:4 To the Seven Churches

PERTAINING TO ALL THE CHURCHES. APRINGIUS OF BEJA: What is the importance of the people of Asia that they alone deserve to receive the apostolic revelation? However, there is a mystery in the number and a sacrament in the name of the province. First, let us discuss the meaning of the number, because both the number six and the number seven are always used in the law with a mystical meaning: "For God made heaven and earth in six days,"[7] and "on the seventh day he rested from his works"[8] and "on it," it says, "they shall enter again into my rest."[9] The number seven, therefore, signifies the period of the present life, so that the apostle is not merely writing to seven churches and to that world in which he was then present, but it is understood that he is giving these writings to all future ages, even to the consummation of the world. Therefore, he mentions the number in a most holy manner, and he names "Asia," which means "elevated" or "walking," indicating that celestial fatherland which we call the "catholic church." For exalted by the Lord and always moving toward the things which are above, it is the church which advances by spiritual exercises and is always desirous of the things of heaven. TRACTATE ON THE APOCALYPSE 1.4.[10]

THROUGH THE SPIRIT THE APOSTLES BRING GRACE. CAESARIUS OF ARLES: Asia means "elevated," by which the human race is indicated. These seven churches and the lampstands are to be seriously considered because it is the sevenfold grace which is given by God through Jesus Christ, our Lord, to us of the human race who

have believed. For he himself promised to send to us the Spirit Paraclete from heaven, whom he also sent to the apostles who were seen to be in Asia, that is, in the prideful world, where he also gave the sevenfold grace to the seven churches, that is to us, through his servant John. EXPOSITION ON THE APOCALYPSE 1.4, HOMILY 1.[11]

GREETINGS FROM THE TRINITY. ANDREW OF CAESAREA: Although there are many churches in every place, he wrote to seven only. For through the number seven he indicates the mystery of the church which exists everywhere and that which corresponds to the present life in which there is a sevenfold period of days. And therefore he makes mention of seven angels and seven churches to which he says, "Grace to you and peace from the tri-hypostatic[12] deity." Through the phrase "who is" the Father is indicated, who spoke to Moses: "I am Who I am."[13] Through the phrase "who was" the Word is indicated, who was in the beginning with God. And through the phrase "who is to come" the Paraclete is indicated, who always visits the children of the church in holy baptism but will come more perfectly and more clearly in the age to come. It is possible to recognize in the seven spirits the seven angels who have received the governance of the churches. These are not numbered with the most divine and royal Trinity but are mentioned together with it as servants, even as the divine apostle says: "I testify to you before God and the elect angels."[14] These phrases may be understood also in another manner. The phrase "who is and who was and who is to come" may signify the Father, who encompasses in himself the beginning, the middle and the end of all things. COMMENTARY ON THE APOCALYPSE 1.4.[15]

THE SEVEN SPIRITS CORRESPOND WITH THE SEVENFOLD GIFTS OF THE HOLY SPIRIT. APRINGIUS OF BEJA: Here is that mystery of the

---

[6]CCL 107:34. [7]Gen 2:2. [8]Ex 20:11. [9]Heb 4:4-5. [10]CCL 107:34-35. [11]PL 35:2417. [12]One God in three persons. [13]Ex 3:14. [14]1 Tim 5:21. [15]MTS 1 Sup 1:13-14.

number seven which is everywhere indicated. Here the seven spirits are introduced, which are one and the same Spirit, that is, the Holy Spirit, who is one in name, sevenfold in power, invisible and incorporeal, and whose form is impossible to comprehend. The great Isaiah revealed the number of its sevenfold powers when he wrote: "the Spirit of wisdom and understanding"—that through understanding and wisdom he might teach that he is the creator of all things—"the Spirit of counsel and might"—who conceived these things that he might create them—"the Spirit of knowledge and piety"—who governs the creation with piety by the exercise of his knowledge and whose purposes are always according to mercy—"the Spirit of the fear of the Lord"—by whose gift the fear of the Lord is manifested to rational creatures.[16] This is itself the sacred character of the Spirit who is to be worshiped. It includes rather the ineffable praise, and does not indicate any form of nature. TRACTATE ON THE APOCALYPSE 1.4.[17]

### THE SEVEN SPIRITS ARE SEVEN ANGELS.

OECUMENIUS: The seven spirits are seven angels. However, they are not to be regarded as of equal honor or co-eternal with the Holy Trinity, by no means, but as true assistants and faithful servants. For the prophet says to God, "All things are your servants,"[18] and among "all things" are included also the angels. And in another place he says concerning them, "Bless the Lord, all his hosts, his ministers that do his will."[19] And the apostle uses this manner of speaking in his first letter to Timothy: "I urge you before God and Jesus Christ and the elect angels."[20] And so when he says, "which are before his throne," he is giving added witness to their order as servants and ministers, but in no way to any equality in honor. COMMENTARY ON THE APOCALYPSE 1.4B.[21]

## 1:5 Jesus Christ the Faithful Witness

### THE WORD MADE FLESH IS WITNESS.

APRINGIUS OF BEJA: Since earlier he had recalled

that Word who, before the assumption of the flesh, was with the Father in glory, he of necessity adds the humanity of the assumed flesh when he says, "And from Jesus Christ, the faithful witness." For through the humanity which he had assumed, he gave a faithful testimony to his divinity, and by his passion and blood he interceded for our sins and cleansed us from all unrighteousness. And so, for the sake of our frailty and weakness he brought a faithful witness to God the Father "with whom there is no variation or shadow due to change."[22] TRACTATE ON THE APOCALYPSE 1.5.[23]

### THE MARTYR IS WITNESS OF HIM WHO IS TRUE WITNESS.

EUSEBIUS OF CAESAREA[24]: They did not proclaim themselves witnesses, nor did they allow us to address them by this name. If any one of us, in letter or conversation, spoke of them as witnesses, they rebuked him sharply. For they conceded cheerfully the appellation of "Witness" to Christ "the faithful and true Witness,"[25] "firstborn of the dead," and prince of the life of God. They reminded us of the witnesses who had already departed, and said, "They are already witnesses whom Christ has deemed worthy to be taken up in their confession, having sealed their testimony by their departure. But we are lowly and humble confessors." ECCLESIASTICAL HISTORY 5.2.2-3.[26]

### AS FIRSTBORN OF THE DEAD, CHRIST IS SOURCE OF LIFE.

IRENAEUS: Great, then, was the mercy of God the Father. He sent the creative Word, who, when he came to save us, put himself in our position, and in the same situation in which we lost life. He loosed the prison bonds, and his light appeared and dispelled the darkness in the prison, and he sanctified our birth and abolished death, loosing those same bonds by

---

[16]Is 11:2-3. Victorinus of Petovium also quotes this passage to interpret the seven spirits as the one Holy Spirit.  [17]CCL 107:35-36.  [18]Ps 119:91 (118:91 LXX).  [19]Ps 103:21 (102:21 LXX).  [20]1 Tim 5:21.  [21]TEG 8:70.  [22]Jas 1:17.  [23]CCL 107:36.  [24]Eusebius is quoting the *Letter of the Lyons Martyrs*.  [25]Rev 3:14.  [26]NPNF 2 1:217-18*.

which we were held. He showed forth the resurrection, becoming himself the firstborn from the dead, and raised in himself prostrate man, being lifted up to the heights of heaven, at the right hand of the glory of the Father. Just as God had promised through the prophet, saying, "I will raise up the tabernacle of David."[27] This means that which is fallen, the body sprung from David. This was in truth accomplished by our Lord Jesus Christ, in the triumph of our redemption, that he raise us in truth, setting us free to the Father. . . . as the firstborn of the dead, head and source also of the life unto God. PROOF OF THE APOSTOLIC PREACHING 38-39.[28]

**As Firstborn from the Dead, Christ Is the Pattern of Our Salvation.** ATHANASIUS: Although it was after us that he was made man for us and became our brother by likeness of body, still he is called and is the firstborn of us. Since all people were lost through the transgression of Adam, Christ's flesh was saved first of all and was liberated, because it was the Word's body. Henceforth also we, having become joined together with his body, are saved through it. For in his body the Lord becomes our guide to the kingdom of heaven and to his own Father, saying, "I am the way"[29] and "the door," and "through me all must enter."[30] Wherefore he is also said to be "firstborn from the dead," not because he died before us, since we died first, but because he suffered death for us and abolished it, and therefore, as man, was the first to rise, raising his own body for our sakes. Therefore, since he has risen, we too shall rise from the dead from him and through him. DISCOURSES AGAINST THE ARIANS 2.61.[31]

**In Christ the General Resurrection Is Begun.** OECUMENIUS: Paul also ascribes to him this phrase, saying, "Who is the firstfruits, the firstborn from the dead."[32] They call him the "firstborn from the dead" since he initiated the general resurrection and "has renewed for us a new and living way (namely, the resurrection of the dead) through the veil, that is, through his flesh," as it is written.[33] For all of those who rose again from the dead before the coming of the Lord were again handed over to death, for that was not the true resurrection but merely a reprieve from the time of death. Therefore, none of them is named the "firstborn from the dead," but the Lord is indeed called this, since he is become the source and cause of the true resurrection and, as it were, has become a certain firstfruits of the resurrection of men, becoming such as they were and going forth as from a certain bridal chamber out of death unto life. COMMENTARY ON THE APOCALYPSE 1.5.[34]

**Christ Is the Firstborn Even of Those Who Preceded His Birth.** BEDE: It can be understood that, for a special reason, the Lord was said to be firstborn, according to what John says in the Apocalypse about him. . . . And the apostle Paul says, "Now those whom he has foreknown he has also predestined to become conformed to the image of his Son, that he himself should be the firstborn among many brothers."[35] He is the firstborn among many brothers because "to as many as received him he gave the power to become sons of God,"[36] of whom he is rightly named the firstborn because in dignity he came before all the sons of adoption, even those who in their birth preceded the time of his incarnation. Therefore, they can with the greatest truth bear witness with John, "He who comes after us was before us."[37] That is, "He was born in the world after us, but by the merit of his virtue and kingdom he is rightfully called the firstborn of us all." HOMILIES ON THE GOSPELS 1.5.[38]

### 1:6 A Kingdom and Priests

**We Are Priests in Christ, the Eternal Priest.** BEDE: Since the King of kings and the

---

[27]Amos 9:11. [28]ACW 16:71-73*. [29]Jn 14:6. [30]Jn 10:9. [31]NPNF 2 4:381**. [32]Col 1:18. [33]Heb 10:20. [34]TEG 8:70-71. [35]Rom 8:29. [36]Jn 1:12. [37]Jn 1:15. [38]CS 110:48-49.

celestial Priest united us to his own body by offering himself up for us, there is no one of the saints who is spiritually deprived of the office of the priesthood, since everyone is a member of the eternal Priest. EXPLANATION OF THE APOCALYPSE 1.6.[39]

## 1:7 All Shall See His Coming

CHRIST WILL RETURN IN THE FLESH. FULGENTIUS OF RUSPE: Hold most firmly and never doubt that the Word made flesh always has the same truly human flesh with which God the Word was born of the Virgin, with which he was crucified and died, with which he rose and ascended to heaven and sits at the right hand of God, with which he will come again to judge the living and the dead. For this reason, the apostles heard from the angels, "He . . . will return in the same way as you have seen him going into heaven,"[40] and the blessed John says, "Behold, he will come amid the clouds, and every eye will see him, even those who pierced him; and all the tribes of the earth will see him." LETTER TO PETER ON THE FAITH 20.63.[41]

THE HOLY ANGELS WILL ACCOMPANY CHRIST WHEN HE RETURNS VISIBLY. OECUMENIUS: I think that the divine Scripture figuratively calls the holy angels "clouds" because of their lightness and sublimity and movement in the air, as though it were saying, "The Lord will come, being carried and attended by his holy angels." And the prophet speaks of him in this way: "And he rode upon a cherub and he flew; he flew upon the wings of the wind."[42] And he writes, "every eye will see him, every one who pierced him." At his second and glorious coming, he will not come as though he were hiding in a corner. Nor will he come secretly as he did in his previous coming, when he visited the world in the flesh. The prophet showed that this coming would be hidden, when he said, "He will come down as rain upon a fleece and as rain drops which fall upon the earth." He will rather come

openly and visibly, so that he will be seen by every eye, even by those who are especially sinful and impious. And of these, those who maltreated or pierced him must be regarded as a class of their own. "And all tribes of the earth will wail on account of him," namely, those peoples who have remained in unbelief and have not come to bend their neck to his saving yoke. COMMENTARY ON THE APOCALYPSE 1.7.[43]

## 1:8 The Alpha and the Omega

IN CHRIST THE END RETURNS TO THE BEGINNING. TERTULLIAN: In the same way the Lord applied to himself two Greek letters, the first and the last, as figures of the beginning and the end which are united in himself. For just as Alpha continues on until it reaches Omega and Omega completes the cycle back again to Alpha, so he meant to show us that in him is found the course of all things from the beginning to the end and from the end back to the beginning. Every divine dispensation should end in him through whom it first began, that is, in the Word made flesh.[44] Accordingly, it should also end in the same way in which it first began. So truly in Christ are all things recalled to their beginning. So the faith has turned away from circumcision back to the integrity of the flesh, as it was in the beginning. So, too, there is liberty now to eat any kind of food, with abstention from blood alone, as it was in the beginning.[45] There is a unity of marriage, as it was in the beginning. There is a prohibition of divorce, which was not in the beginning.[46] Finally, the whole man is called once more to paradise, where he was in the beginning. ON MONOGAMY 5.[47]

CHRIST IS ALPHA AND OMEGA, CREATOR AND REDEEMER. AUGUSTINE: The martyrdom of the blessed apostles has consecrated this day for us. It

---

[39]CCL 121A: 239. [40]Acts 1:11. [41]FC 95:97-98. [42]Ps 18:10 (17:11 LXX). [43]TEG 8:73. [44]Jn 1:14. [45]Cf. Gen 9:3-4; Acts 15:29. [46]Mt 19:8. [47]ACW 13:78-79. Jerome makes the same argument (*Against Jovinian* 1.18, NPNF 2 6:360).

was by despising the world that they earned this renown throughout the whole world. Peter was the first of the apostles and Paul the last of the apostles. The first and the last were brought to one and the same day for martyrdom by the First and the Last, by Christ. In order to grasp what I've said, turn your minds to the Alpha and the Omega. The Lord himself said plainly in the Apocalypse, "I am the Alpha and the Omega, the first"—before whom is nobody—"the last"—after whom is nobody;[48] he precedes all things and sets a term to all things. Do you want to gaze upon him as the first? "All things were made through him."[49] Do you seek him as the last? "For Christ is the end of the law, that every one who has faith may be justified."[50] In order for you to live at some time or other, you had him as your creator. In order for you to live always, you have him as your redeemer. SERMON 299B.1, ON THE BIRTHDAY OF THE HOLY APOSTLES PETER AND PAUL.[51]

**AS THE ALMIGHTY, CHRIST IS ONE GOD WITH THE FATHER.** ATHANASIUS: The Godhead of the Son is the Father's. It is indivisible. Thus there is one God and none other but he. So, since they are one, and the Godhead itself one, the same things are said of the Son, which are said of the Father, except his being said to be Father. For instance, it is said that he is God: "And the Word was God."[52] It is said that he is Almighty, "Thus says he who was and is and is to come, the Almighty."[53] It is said that he is Lord, "one Lord Jesus Christ."[54] It is said that he is Light, "I am the Light,"[55] that he wipes out sins, "that you may know," he says, "that the Son of man has power upon earth to forgive sins,"[56] and so with other attributes. For "all things," says the Son himself, "whatsoever the Father has, are mine"; and again,

"And mine are yours."[57] DISCOURSES AGAINST THE ARIANS 3.4.[58]

### 1:9 John on the Island of Patmos

**JOHN ON PATMOS DURING THE REIGN OF CLAUDIUS.** APRINGIUS OF BEJA: The ecclesiastical writers have taught that at the time of Claudius Caesar, when that famine which the prophet Agabus had announced in the Acts of the Apostles[59] would come in ten years time was at its height, that during that difficulty this same Caesar, impelled by his usual vanity, had instituted a persecution of the churches. It was during this time that he ordered John, the apostle of our Lord, Jesus Christ, to be transported into exile, and he was taken to the island of Patmos, and while there confirmed this writing. That he might present the trials of suffering which he was bearing at that time, he recalls that he was a participant in suffering, and then he adds the kingdom to the suffering of tribulation, and because of the kingdom to be received he further adds the patient endurance which he bore for the sake of Jesus. TRACTATE ON THE APOCALYPSE 1.9.[60]

**JOHN ON PATMOS DURING THE REIGN OF DOMITIAN.** BEDE: History notes that John had been banished to this island by the emperor Domitian on account of the gospel, and that then he was, appropriately, allowed to penetrate the secrets of heaven while [at the same time] prohibited from leaving a small space of the earth. EXPLANATION OF THE APOCALYPSE 1.9.[61]

---

[48]Rev 1:8, 17. [49]Jn 1:3. [50]Rom 10:4. [51]*WSA* 3 8:244*. [52]Jn 1:1. [53]This passage is often quoted to affirm the deity of Christ (also Gregory of Nazianzus *Oration* 29.17; NPNF 2 7:307). [54]1 Cor 8:6. [55]Jn 8:12. [56]Mk 2:10; Mt 9:6. [57]Jn 16:15; 17:10. [58]NPNF 2 4:395*. [59]Acts 11:28. [60]CCL 107:39. [61]CCL 121A:241.

## 1:10-20 JOHN SEES THE VOICE SPEAKING TO HIM

$^{10}$*I was in the Spirit on the Lord's day, and I heard behind me a loud voice like a trumpet* $^{11}$*saying, "Write what you see in a book and send it to the seven churches, to Ephesus and to Smyrna and to Pergamum and to Thyatira and to Sardis and to Philadelphia and to La-odicea."*

$^{12}$*Then I turned to see the voice that was speaking to me, and on turning I saw seven golden lampstands,* $^{13}$*and in the midst of the lampstands one like a son of man, clothed with a long robe and with a golden girdle round his breast;* $^{14}$*his head and his hair were white as white wool, white as snow; his eyes were like a flame of fire,* $^{15}$*his feet were like burnished bronze, refined as in a furnace, and his voice was like the sound of many waters;* $^{16}$*in his right hand he held seven stars, from his mouth issued a sharp two-edged sword, and his face was like the sun shining in full strength.*

$^{17}$*When I saw him, I fell at his feet as though dead. But he laid his right hand upon me, saying, "Fear not, I am the first and the last,* $^{18}$*and the living one; I died, and behold I am alive for evermore, and I have the keys of Death and Hades.* $^{19}$*Now write what you see, what is and what is to take place hereafter.* $^{20}$*As for the mystery of the seven stars which you saw in my right hand, and the seven golden lampstands, the seven stars are the angels of the seven churches and the seven lampstands are the seven churches.*

**OVERVIEW:** Despite the weakness of his human nature, John was raised up to see the secrets of God (APRINGIUS). In the Spirit he wrote to seven churches which represent the one catholic church and whose names mystically indicate the struggle between truth and error in the church to the end of time (VICTORINUS, APRINGIUS). The vision of Christ who speaks to John reveals the invisible glory of the Father (IRENAEUS). Christ walks in the midst of seven lampstands, for he is the Light upon which the light of the churches rests (APRINGIUS). The churches are therefore called lampstands, not lights (OECUMENIUS).

Christ is "like" a son of man, for he is now ascended and united to the Spirit (VICTORINUS). Moreover, his two natures are indicated (OECUMENIUS), as well as the unity of Christ with the church (PRIMASIUS). Christ is dressed in the robe of his flesh (VICTORINUS) and wears a girdle about his breasts, which are the two Testaments (APRINGIUS) or the two Testaments that nourish Christians unto eternal life (CAESARIUS OF ARLES). The girdle is about the breasts, not the loins, for the gospel deepens the commandments of the law (JEROME) and restrains the wrath of God by the benevolence of our High Priest (ANDREW OF CAESAREA).

The white head of Christ indicates that God is his head (VICTORINUS), that he is pure and merciful (APRINGIUS) and that the mystery of the gospel is ancient (OECUMENIUS). The white hairs indicate also the newly baptized who are the sheep of Christ and the new Jerusalem, which comes down from heaven as does the snow (CAESARIUS OF ARLES). The feet of Christ are the apostles who bring the good news (VICTORINUS) or the human nature of Christ, which is refined by the divine nature (APRINGIUS, ANDREW OF CAESAREA). Refined by fire, the feet refer also to the church of the endtime, which will be tested by afflictions (BEDE). The voice of Christ is like many waters, for God works in many ways and his preaching goes throughout the world (IRENAEUS, OECUMENIUS). The sword of his mouth is variously viewed as the law and the gospel (VIC-TORINUS), the Holy Spirit (FULGENTIUS OF RUSPE), the letter and the spirit of the divine teaching (JEROME) or the judgment (OECUMENIUS). The face of Christ is compared with the sun, for he died and rose again (VICTORINUS). Moreover, united to Christ, the church also will shine like the sun (BEDE).

At the vision of Christ, John fell down out of fear and humility (APRINGIUS), but Christ raised him up, for he died that we might live (OECUMENIUS). The seven stars are the church to the end of time (APRINGIUS), and the lampstands are the church, which bears the light of Christ to the world through the unity of its faith and preaching (IRENAEUS).

## 1:10 A Voice Like a Trumpet

**JOHN SAW THE SECRET THINGS OF GOD.**
APRINGIUS OF BEJA: He says that he was taken up in the spirit, that is, that he was raised up to the secret things of God, in order that he might see those things which he was to speak. Moreover, he says that he did not enter into the heights of heaven in a bodily manner, but that he entered in the spirit, recalling this word, "No one has ascended into heaven except he who has descended, namely the Son of man, who is in heaven."[1] The holy apostle Paul also says that he was taken up, but in what way? He says, "Whether in the body or out of the body, I do not know, God knows."[2] He writes that he had been taken up into ecstasy, in the spirit. But since the day of the Lord is mentioned in this passage, when he says that he had been taken up in the spirit, he is indicating that he had been cleansed of any work of a profane kind. For, on the Lord's day the apostle could only devote himself to divine things and holy duties. . . . Concerning the preachers of the gospel, it is written, "Cry aloud, do not cease, lift up your voice as a trumpet."[3] And concerning the words "behind me," the prophet said, "And they shall hear a voice from behind of one teaching."[4] Let all humanity be

exalted to whatever degree of sanctity, in comparison to the holy acts of God and to the divine words, it can by no means ever stand as an equal before his presence and face. But our flesh, weighed down by a certain weakness, is instructed, as it were, from behind by the words of God. Therefore, in saying "behind me" he indicates the weakness of his human nature. TRACTATE ON THE APOCALYPSE 1.10.[5]

## 1:11 Write to the Seven Churches

**THE SEVEN CHURCHES REPRESENT THE ONE CATHOLIC CHURCH.** VICTORINUS OF PETOVIUM: He mentions seven churches by the explicit use of their own names to which he has sent letters. He does this not because they are the only churches, or even the most important of the churches, but because what he says to one, he says to all. For it makes no difference whether one speaks to a cohort, in number only a few soldiers, or whether one speaks through it to the entire army. Whether in Asia or in the whole world, Paul taught that all of the seven churches which are named are one catholic [church].[6] And therefore, that he might preserve this understanding, he did not exceed the number of seven churches, but wrote to the Romans, to the Corinthians, to the Ephesians, to the Thessalonians, to the Galatians, to the Philippians and to the Colossians. Later he wrote only to individual persons, lest he exceed the number of seven churches. . . . We read that this type was announced by the Holy Spirit through Isaiah [who spoke] of seven women who seized one man.[7] However, this one man is Christ, who was not born of seed. And the seven women are churches who received their own bread and wear their own clothes but who ask that their reproach be taken away and that his name be invoked over them. The "bread" is the

[1]Jn 3:13. [2]2 Cor 12:2. [3]Is 58:1. [4]Is 30:21. [5]CCL 107:39-40. [6]That in writing to seven churches John and Paul were speaking to all churches of the one catholic church is a common idea (Apringius; Primasius; Bede; already in the Muratorian Canon, c. 200). [7]Is 4:1.

Holy Spirit, who nourishes to eternal life. It is "their own" because it has been promised to them through faith, and "their own clothes" refers to the promises which have been made to them and by which they wish to be covered, as Paul says: "It is necessary that this corruptible be clothed with incorruption and that this mortal be clothed with immortality."[8] And the words "that their reproach be taken away" refer to that first sin which is taken away in baptism when each person begins to be called a "Christian," which is the meaning of the words "your name will be invoked over us." In these seven churches, therefore, we are to think of the one church. COMMENTARY ON THE APOCALYPSE 1.7.[9]

**THE NAMES OF THE CHURCHES CONTAIN MYSTERIES.** APRINGIUS OF BEJA: We have already said that he addressed one church which exists during the time of the whole world, that is, from that time when he spoke to the consummation of the world. Since he now mentions the names of these churches specifically, let us see what meanings they have.... There is a mighty mystery in the names which we will examine and discuss to the extent that God allows. Ephesus means "my will" or "my plan." He wills that we know that the whole reality of our faith and the dignity of the catholic church is not to be ascribed to human merit, but they are the will of God and the disposition of the divine purpose. Smyrna means "their song." And what else is the song of the perfect if not the celestial doctrine and the preaching of the gospel and the advance of the Christian religion, or the melodious confession of the catholic church? Pergamum means "to him who divides their horns." This refers either to the insolence of the powers of the air, or to the arrogance of the heretics. And he teaches that the pride of the powers is always to be separated and divided from the congregation of the church, for the horns are either power or arrogance. He writes to Thyatira, that is "enlightened." This signifies that, after the expulsion of heretical pride and after the defeat of temptations

from the powers of the air, the holy church is deserving of the light of righteousness. Sardis means the "beginning of beauty." The church is seized by the sun of righteousness and is illumined by the light of truth, so that she might have the beginning of beauty, the Lord Jesus Christ, and might always shine in perpetual light. Philadelphia means "preserving devotion to the Lord." After possessing the sun of righteousness, after the illumination of holiness, after the comeliness of holy beauty, the church rightly is devoted to the Lord and preserves herself by an inviolable observation of devotion. Laodicea means either "a tribe beloved of the Lord," or, as some would have it, "a birth is expected." Both are meaningful, for she who has merited the beauty of faith and the sun of righteousness and knows that through faith the Lord cleaves to her, might also be a tribe whom the Lord loves, who is both loved by the Lord and preserved by the Lord. Furthermore, the church might well await her own birth, either the regeneration of baptism or the glory of the resurrection, whenever she preserves herself by humility and patience. TRACTATE ON THE APOCALYPSE 1.11.[10]

## 1:12a *The Voice Speaking to John*

**CHRIST REVEALS THE GLORY OF THE INVISIBLE FATHER.** IRENAEUS: Neither Moses nor Elijah nor Ezekiel, who all had many celestial visions, saw God. Rather, what they did see were likenesses of the splendor of the Lord and prophecies of things to come. It is evident that the Father is indeed invisible, of whom also the Lord said, "No man has seen God at any time."[11] But his Word, as he himself willed it, and for the benefit of those who beheld, did show the Father's brightness and explained his purposes, as also the Lord said, "The only begotten God, which is in the bosom of the Father, he has declared [him]."[12] ... John also, the Lord's disciple, when seeing the

---

[8]1 Cor 15:53. [9]CSEL 49:26-30. [10]CCL 107:41-42. Primasius gives the same spiritual meanings to the cities. [11]Jn 1:18. [12]Jn 1:18.

priestly and glorious advent of his kingdom, says in the Apocalypse: "I turned to see the voice that spoke with me. And, being turned, I saw seven golden candlesticks, and in their midst One like the Son of man, clothed with a garment reaching to the feet, and wrapped around the chest with a golden girdle. His head and his hair were white, as white as wool, and as snow. His eyes were like a flame of fire. His feet were like fine brass, as if they were forged in a furnace. His voice [was] like the sound of waters. He had in his right hand seven stars. Out of his mouth came a sharp two-edged sword. He looked like the sun shining at full strength." For in these words he sets forth something of the glory [which he has received] from his Father, as the head. He sets forth something of the priestly office, as in the case of the long garment reaching to the feet. And this was the reason why Moses vested the high priest after this fashion. Something also alludes to the end [of all things], as [where he speaks of] the fine brass being forged in the fire, which denotes the power of faith, and constant prayer, because of the consuming fire which is to come at the end of time. AGAINST HERESIES 4.20.11.[13]

**THE VOICE WAS NOT SENSORY.** ANDREW OF CAESAREA: He shows that the voice was not sensory when he says, "I turned," not to hear but "to see the voice." For spiritual hearing and spiritual seeing are the same thing. COMMENTARY ON THE APOCALYPSE 1.12.[14]

## 1:12b Seven Golden Lampstands

**THE LIGHT OF THE CHURCH RESTS ON CHRIST.** APRINGIUS OF BEJA: Resting on three arms, a lampstand raises the body of a single shaft, and upon this shaft there is placed a lamp of light. "For no other foundation can any one lay than that which is laid, which is Jesus Christ,"[15] says the apostle, "from which the whole body, joined and knit together by every joint with which it is supplied, makes bodily growth and upbuilds itself in love, according to the work and ability of each

member."[16] This is that branch of which it is said: "There shall come forth a branch from the stump of Jesse."[17] Upon this branch a light is placed, that is, the light of the catholic church is made ready, so that seized by the truth of his light, she might herself bring forth perpetual light, and marked by the manifestation of one faith, she might be exalted by the light of the divine majesty. TRACTATE ON THE APOCALYPSE 1.12.[18]

**THE CHURCHES ARE LAMPSTANDS, NOT LIGHTS.** OECUMENIUS: As he himself will explain a little later, the seven lampstands are the seven churches to which he is commanded to write. He calls them "lampstands" since they carry in themselves the "illumination of the glory of Christ."[19] He did not call them "lamps" but "lampstands," for a lampstand itself does not possess the capacity to shine, but it bears that which is capable of illumination. Likewise, Christ mentally illuminates his churches. For just as the holy apostle exhorts those who have received the Faith, "be as lights in the world, holding fast the word of life"[20]—for indeed the lamp does not in itself possess light, but it is receptive of that light which comes to it—so also here the Evangelist saw the churches as lampstands and not as lights. For it is said concerning Christ, "You shine forth marvelously from the everlasting mountains,"[21] probably meaning the angelic powers; and again he says to the Father, "Send out your light and your truth"[22]; and again, "the light of your countenance, O Lord."[23] And so, those who partake of the divine light are described on the one hand as lights and on the other hand as lampstands. He says that the lampstands are "golden" on account of the value and excellence of those made worthy to receive the divine light. COMMENTARY ON THE APOCALYPSE 1.12-16.[24]

---

[13]ANF 1:491. No one sees God and lives (Ex 33:20). Upon seeing this vision, John "fell at his feet as dead" (Rev 1:17). According to Irenaeus, this fulfilled the OT passage. [14]MTS 1 Sup 1:20. [15]1 Cor 3:11. [16]Eph 4:16. [17]Is 11:1. [18]CCL 107:43. [19]2 Cor 4:4. [20]Phil. 2:15-16. [21]See Ps 76:4 (75:5 LXX). [22]Ps 43:3 (42:3 LXX). [23]Ps 44:3 (43:4 LXX). [24]TEG 8:76.

## 1:13a *One Like a Son of Man*

**THE ASCENDED CHRIST IS MORE THAN SON OF MAN.** VICTORINUS OF PETOVIUM: It says that "in the midst of the golden lampstands there was one walking similar to a son of man." It says "similar," because death had been destroyed. For when he had ascended into heaven, and when his body was united to the Spirit of glory which he received from the Father, henceforth he could be called as though Son of God and no longer as though son of man. COMMENTARY ON THE APOCALYPSE 1.2.[25]

**CHRIST AND THE CHURCH ARE ONE.** PRIMASIUS: "And I saw seven golden lampstands, and in the midst of the lampstands was one like a son of man." He saw Christ who rather often desires to be called by this name. He who is the enclothed Christ is the seven lampstands themselves. Whether the seven lampstands or the seven stars, both refer to the church. . . . On account of the exalted nature of the divine discourse, on occasion the genus cannot be described clearly, because it is more easily seen than expressed. . . . So also in this passage, among the seven lampstands he is describing the church in the Son of man. "For," the apostle says, "the two shall become one flesh, and I am saying that it refers to Christ and the church."[26] As I said above, the genus is clarified through various species.[27] COMMENTARY ON THE APOCALYPSE 1.12.[28]

**"LIKE A SON OF MAN" INDICATES THE TWO NATURES.** OECUMENIUS: He calls him "son of man" who for our sakes humbled himself to the form of a servant, namely, Christ, who became "fruit of the womb,"[29] as the holy psalmist says, that is, the womb of the unwedded and ever-virgin Mary. For since Mary is a human being and our sister, it is appropriate that God the Word, conceived virginally according to the flesh, is also called "son of man." And he has spoken with precision, for he did not say "son of man" but "like a son of man," since he is also God and Lord of all,

the Emmanuel. COMMENTARY ON THE APOCALYPSE 1.12-16.[30]

## 1:13b *Clothed with a Long Robe*

**THE ROBE IS THE FLESH OF CHRIST.** VICTORINUS OF PETOVIUM: The words "in priestly garment" most clearly indicate the flesh, which was not corrupted by death and which possesses through his death an eternal priesthood. "A golden girdle was tied to his breast." These words suggest that a vibrant knowledge and a pure spiritual understanding have been given to the churches. COMMENTARY ON THE APOCALYPSE 1.4.[31]

**THE GOSPEL DEEPENS THE LAW.** JEROME: In the law, John had a leather girdle because the Jews thought that to sin in act was the only sin. . . . In the Apocalypse of John, our Lord Jesus, who is seen in the middle of the seven lampstands, also wore a girdle, a golden girdle, not about his loins but about the breasts. The law is girdled about the loins, but Christ, that is, the gospel and the fortitude of the monks, binds not only wanton passion but also mind and heart. In the gospel, one is not even supposed to think anything evil; in the law, the fornicator is accused for judgment. . . . "It is written," he says, "in the law, 'You shall not commit adultery.'"[32] This is the leather girdle clinging about the loins. "I say to you, anyone who even looks with lust at a woman has already committed adultery with her in his heart." This is the golden girdle that is wrapped around the mind and heart. HOMILIES ON MARK 75 (1).[33]

---

[25]CSEL 49:18-20. Victorinus seems to say that upon his ascension Christ assumed his divine sonship and so the title *Son of man* was no longer adequate. Now he is "similar" to a son of man. [26]Eph 5:31-32. [27]Primasius understands the flesh of Christ to be the church. Therefore, in the "Son of man", the enclothed or enfleshed Christ, he perceives also the church. Ephesians 5:31-32 is often quoted for this idea. He argues that the complex idea that the same is Christ and the church is more easily described through a variety of images, here a son of man and seven lampstands, than through words. [28]CCL 92:15-16. [29]Ps 127:3 (126:3 LXX). [30]TEG 8:77. [31]CSEL 49:22. [32]See Mt 5:27. [33]FC 57:125-26.*

**LAW AND GOSPEL ARE GIRD BY THE PASSION.**
APRINGIUS OF BEJA: The breasts of the Lord are
the holy teaching of the law and the gospel. This
girding is a sign of the passion, concerning
which the Lord himself spoke to Peter: "When
you are old, another will gird you and lead you
where you do not wish"[34] The "golden girdle" is
his everlasting power, washed in the blood of
the Lord's passion. There is a variety of this girdle in the diversity of powers, yet there is one
power behind the multitude of wonders.
Another interpretation: The golden girdle is the
chorus of the saints, tested as gold through fire.
Another: The golden girdle around the chest is
the fervent conscience and the pure spiritual
understanding refined as though by fire, and so
it was given to the churches. TRACTATE ON THE
APOCALYPSE 1.13.[35]

**THE TWO TESTAMENTS NOURISH CHRIS-
TIANS TO ETERNAL LIFE.** CAESARIUS OF ARLES:
He who is girded signifies Christ the Lord. By
the two breasts understand the two Testaments
which receive from the breast of our Lord and
Savior as though from a perennial fountain and
from which they nourish the Christian people
unto eternal life. The golden girdle is a chorus or
the multitude of saints. For just as the breast is
bound by a girdle, so the multitude of the saints is
bound to Christ, so that as the two Testaments
encompass the two breasts they are nourished by
them as by holy paps. EXPOSITION ON THE APOC-
ALYPSE 1.13, HOMILY 1.[36]

**CHRIST IS OUR BENEVOLENT HIGH PRIEST.**
ANDREW OF CAESAREA: He was clothed with a
long robe, as a high priest of those things above
"according to the order of Melchizedek."[37] Moreover, he was girded with a golden girdle, not
around the loins, as other men are to check
desires (for the divine flesh is not accessible to
these), but at the chest, around the breasts, so
that the boundlessness of the divine wrath might
be restrained by benevolence and that the truth
might be revealed girding about the two Testa-

ments which are the dominical breasts through
which the faithful are nourished. It is a golden
girdle to indicate its excellence and purity and
genuineness. COMMENTARY ON THE APOCALYPSE
1.12-13.[38]

## 1:14a His Head and Hair Were White

**CHRIST IS ANCIENT AND IMMORTAL.** VICTORI-
NUS OF PETOVIUM: By the "whiteness on the
head" is shown his antiquity and immortality,
and the source of his majesty, for "the head of
Christ is God."[39] COMMENTARY ON THE APOCA-
LYPSE 1.2.[40]

**CHRIST POSSESSES THE PURITY OF GOD AND
IS TENDER TOWARD SINNERS.** APRINGIUS OF
BEJA: The head of Christ is God,[41] and he himself
is white on account of the brightness of the purity
of the Unbegotten and on account of the unmixed
light of the Only Begotten and on account of the
pure radiance of the Holy Spirit and the immaculate glory of his righteousness. And not without
reason is he called white, because he is compared
to white wool and to snow on account of his ten-
derness which he gives without ceasing to the sinners. As it is written: "Though your sins are like
scarlet, they shall be as white as snow; and
though they are red as crimson, they shall
become as wool."[42] TRACTATE ON THE APOCA-
LYPSE 1.14.[43]

**THE MYSTERY OF CHRIST IS ANCIENT.** OECU-
MENIUS: "His head," it says, "and his hairs were
like white wool, like snow," for the mystery in
Christ was new at its appearance, although to be
sure eternal according to good pleasure. The
holy apostle has written concerning this: "the
mystery which was hidden from the ages and
generations, which has now been revealed to his
saints, to those whom he willed."[44] Therefore,

---

[34]Jn 21:18. [35]CCL 107:43-44. [36]PL 35:2417. [37]Ps 110:4 (109:4 LXX);
Heb 5:6, 10; 6:20; 7:17. [38]MTS 1 Sup 1:20. [39]1 Cor 11:3. [40]CSEL
49:20. [41]1 Cor 11:3. [42]Is 1:18. [43]CCL 107:44. [44]Col 1:26-27,

the whiteness of his head, which is compared with wool and with snow, represents the antiquity of the mystery, such as relates to the good pleasure of God. COMMENTARY ON THE APOCALYPSE 1.12-16.[45]

**THE BAPTIZED ARE THE SHEEP OF CHRIST AND THE NEW JERUSALEM.** CAESARIUS OF ARLES: The white hair is the multitude of those made white, that is, he is speaking of the neophytes who come forth from baptism. He speaks of wool because they are the sheep of Christ. He speaks of snow because just as snow falls freely from heaven, so also the grace of baptism comes apart from any preceding merits. For those who are baptized are Jerusalem, which each day comes down as though snow from heaven. That is, the church is said to descend from heaven because that grace is from heaven through which she is both freed from sins and joined to Christ, who is her eternal head and heavenly spouse. . . . The beast from the abyss is said to ascend, that is, an evil people is born from an evil people. For just as by descending humbly Jerusalem is exalted, so the beast, that is, that prideful people which arrogantly ascends, is cast down. EXPOSITION ON THE APOCALYPSE 1.14, HOMILY 1.[46]

## 1:14b *His Eyes Were Like Fire*

**CHRIST IS LIGHT AND JUDGE.** OECUMENIUS: "And his eyes," it says, "were as a flame of fire." The flame indicates either his radiance, since Christ is indeed a light and calls himself this, saying, "I am the light and the truth,"[47] or it represents his fearsomeness and the threat made against the seven churches to which the visions of the Revelations are being sent, since they are not perfectly following his laws. COMMENTARY ON THE APOCALYPSE 1.12-16.[48]

## 1:15a *His Feet Were Like Bronze*

**HIS FEET ARE THE APOSTLES.** VICTORINUS OF PETOVIUM: "His feet were like burnished bronze refined in a furnace." He is speaking of the apostles, because refined through suffering they preached his word. For those through whom the proclamation is extended are properly called feet. And the prophet understood this beforehand in saying, "Let us worship where his feet have stood,"[49] because where they as the first stood and established the church, namely, in Judea, there all the saints will come together and worship their God.[50] COMMENTARY ON THE APOCALYPSE 1.5.[51]

**THE FEET ARE THE TWO NATURES AND THE HARMONY OF PREACHING.** ANDREW OF CAESAREA: And the feet are also the foundations of the church. And they are "like bronze incense," which, the medical people say, possesses a good smell when burned, and which is called by them masculine incense. There is another interpretation: since the bronze refers to the human nature and the incense refers to the divine nature, through these is indicated the sweet odor of the faith and the unconfusedness of the unity. Or another interpretation: the bronze shows the euphony of the proclamation, while the incense shows the conversion of the nations, from which the Bride is commanded to come. COMMENTARY ON THE APOCALYPSE 1.15.[52]

**THE FEET ARE THE HUMAN NATURE OF CHRIST.** APRINGIUS OF BEJA: The feet are the human nature which he possessed in himself which he assumed out of mercy for our salvation. For just as when copper ore is refined in a furnace there is no accretion or rusty buildup on the outside, so the most pure and perfect flesh of the assumed man, taken up by deity and remaining in deity, continues without any defect of human nature, without any guilt of the parent. TRACTATE ON THE APOCALYPSE 1.15.[53]

---

[45]TEG 8:77-78. [46]PL 35:2417. [47]Jn 8:12; 14:6. [48]TEG 8:78. [49]Ps 131:7 LXX. [50]Apringius also gives this interpretation. [51]CSEL 49:26. [52]MTS 1 Sup 1:21. Andrew gives the human nature and the apostles as two other possible interpretations. [53]CCL 107:44.

## THE FEET ARE THE CHURCH OF THE END

**TIME.** BEDE: The phrase "feet refined by fire" refers to the church of the end time, which will be examined and tested by terrible afflictions. For indeed orichalcum is bronze, which is brought to a golden color by a very hot fire and added elements. Another translation, which renders with "like burnished bronze of Lebanon," signifies that the church in Judea, in which Lebanon is a mountain, will be persecuted, especially at the end time. For even the temple is often referred to as "Lebanon," for it is said to it, "Open, O Lebanon, your gates, and let fire consume your cedars."[54] EXPLANATION OF THE APOCALYPSE 1.15.[55]

### 1:15b *His Voice Was Like Many Waters*

**GOD WORKS IN MANY WAYS TO FULFILL HIS PURPOSES.** IRENAEUS: Thus, in a variety of ways, he adjusted the human race to an agreement with salvation. On this account also does John declare in the Apocalypse that his voice is "as the sound of many waters." For the Spirit [of God] is truly [like] many waters, since the Father is both rich and great. And the Word, passing through all those [men], did liberally confer benefits upon his subjects, by drawing up in writing a law adapted and applicable to every class [among them]. AGAINST HERESIES 4.14.2.[56]

**HIS VOICE REACHES INTO ALL THE EARTH.** OECUMENIUS: "And his voice was as the sound of many waters." This is an appropriate way of speaking. For how would his voice reach into all the earth and the proclamation concerning him into the corners of the world, unless it were audible, and not merely by virtue of the perceptible voice but by the power of the proclamation? COMMENTARY ON THE APOCALYPSE 1.12-16.[57]

### 1:16a *In His Right Hand Were Seven Stars*

**THE STARS ARE SEVEN ANGELS.** OECUMENIUS: I think that he calls the holy angels "stars" because of the abundant brightness of Christ

which they have in themselves. They are in his right hand, for they were found worthy of this most exalted status before God and, as it were, they rest upon the hand of God. COMMENTARY ON THE APOCALYPSE 1.12-16.[58]

### 1:16b *From His Mouth Issued a Sharp Sword*

**THE TWO-EDGED SWORD IS THE LAW AND THE GOSPEL.** VICTORINUS OF PETOVIUM: The phrase "a sharp two-edged sword issued from his mouth" shows that it is he himself who earlier gave to the whole world knowledge of the law through Moses but now gives the blessings of the gospel. And since by the same word every human race will be judged, whether of the Old or of the New Testament, he is called a "sword." For a sword arms a soldier, a sword kills the enemy, and a sword punishes the deserter. And that he might show the apostles that he was announcing judgment, he said, "I have not come to send peace, but a sword."[59] And when he had fulfilled all the parables, he said to them, "'Have you understood all this?' And they said, 'Yes.' And he said, 'Therefore, every scribe who has been trained for the kingdom of heaven is like a householder who brings of his treasury what is new and what is old,'"[60] by the *new things* meaning the words of the gospel, and by the *old things* meaning the law and the prophets. That these had come from his own mouth he told to Peter: "Go to the sea and cast a hook, and take the first fish that comes up, and when you open its mouth you will find a shekel—that is two denarii. Give that for me and for you."[61] And David spoke in a similar way through the Spirit: "Once has God spoken, twice have I heard this,"[62] meaning that the Lord once decreed from the beginning what was going to be unto the end. Therefore these things are the two Testaments which, according to an understanding of

---

[54]Zech 11:1. [55]CCL 121A:245-47. [56]ANF 1:479. [57]TEG 8:79. [58]TEG 8:79. [59]Mt 10:34. [60]Mt 13:51-52. [61]Mt 17:27. [62]Ps 62:11 (61:12 LXX).

time, are called either two denarii, or new things and old things, or a sharp two-edged sword. And finally, since he himself is made judge by the Father, he wishes to show that people will be judged by the word of [his] preaching, and so he said, "Do you think that I will judge you on the last day? The word which I have spoken to you, that will judge you on the last day."[63] And Paul wrote to the Thessalonians in view of the antichrist: "Whom the Lord will kill by the breath of his mouth."[64] This is, therefore, the two-edged sword which issues from his mouth. COMMENTARY ON THE APOCALYPSE 1.4.[65]

**THE SAINTS HAVE THE TWO-EDGED SWORD OF THE LETTER AND THE SPIRIT.** JEROME: "Let two-edged swords be in their hands." They who sing for joy upon their couches—this means the saints surely, perfect men—what else do they have? "Let two-edged swords be in their hands." "Two-edged swords"—the swords of the saints are two-edged. We read in the Apocalypse of John—which, by the way, is read in the churches and is accepted, for it is not held among the Apocrypha but is included in the canonical writings—as I was saying, it is written there of the Lord Savior: "Out of his mouth came forth a sharp two-edged sword." Mark well that these saints receive from the mouth of God the two-edged swords that they hold in their hands. The Lord, therefore, gives the sword from his mouth to his disciples. It is a two-edged sword, namely, the word of his teachings. It is a two-edged sword, historically and allegorically, the letter and the spirit. It is a two-edged sword that slays adversaries and at the same time defends his faithful. "A two-edged sword"—the sword has two heads. It speaks of the present and future world. Here below, it strikes down adversaries; above, it opens the kingdom of heaven. HOMILIES ON THE PSALMS 59 (Ps 149).[66]

**THE SWORD IS THE HOLY SPIRIT.** FULGENTIUS OF RUSPE: Hold most firmly and never doubt that the same Holy Spirit, who is the one Spirit of the Father and the Son, proceeds from the Father and the Son. For the Son says, "When the Spirit of Truth comes, who has proceeded from the Father,"[67] where he taught that the Spirit is his, because he is the Truth. That the Holy Spirit proceeds from the Son, the prophetic and apostolic teaching shows us. So Isaiah says concerning the Son: "He shall strike the earth with the rod of his mouth, and with the breath of his lips he shall kill the wicked."[68] Concerning him the apostle also says, "Whom the Lord Jesus will kill with the breath of his mouth."[69] The one Son of God himself, showing who the Spirit of his mouth is, after his resurrection, breathing on his disciples, says, "receive the Holy Spirit."[70] "From the mouth," indeed, of the Lord Jesus himself, says John in the Apocalypse, "a sharp two-edged word came forth." The very Spirit of his mouth is the sword itself which comes forth from his mouth. LETTER TO PETER ON THE FAITH 11.54.[71]

**THE SWORD IS AN IMAGE OF JUDGMENT.** OECUMENIUS: "And from his mouth issued a sharp, two-edged sword." Therefore, the holy David said to the Lord: "Gird your sword upon your thigh, O mighty One."[72] For he did not yet at that time command to us the evangelical precepts, the transgression of which was destruction. Therefore, the place where the sword was put suggests the delay of punishment, for it was not prepared for slaughter. But now the sword comes forth from the mouth, the image showing that those who are disobedient to the evangelical commandments will have a threat to their souls to be cut into two by the sword, which the Lord indeed mentions in the Gospels. COMMENTARY ON THE APOCALYPSE 1.12-16.[73]

### 1:16b *His Face Was Like the Sun*

**THE SON DIED AND ROSE AGAIN.** VICTORINUS OF PETOVIUM: "The brightness of the sun was in

---

[63]Jn 12:48. [64]2 Thess 2:8. [65]CSEL 49:22-24. [66]FC 48:426-27*. [67]Jn 15:26. [68]Is 11:4. [69]2 Thess 2:8. [70]Jn 20:22. [71]FC 95:93-94. [72]Ps 45:3 (44:4 LXX). [73]TEG 8:79-80.

his face." His face was his appearance by which he conversed with man face to face. For, although the glory of the sun is less than the glory of the Lord, yet because of the rising and setting [of the sun] and its rising again, the Scripture says that his face was like the glory of the sun, because he was born and suffered and rose again. COMMENTARY ON THE APOCALYPSE 1.3.[74]

**THE CHURCH WILL SHINE AS THE SUN.** BEDE: As he appeared to his disciples on the mountain, so will the Lord appear after the judgment to all the saints. For at the judgment the impious will see him whom they pierced. And this circumstance concerning the Son of man is true also of the church, with whom Christ himself was made one nature, since he gives to her the priestly honor and the power to judge that she also might shine as the sun in the kingdom of his Father. EXPLANATION OF THE APOCALYPSE 1.16.[75]

## 1:17 John Fell as Though Dead

**THE LORD STRENGTHENS THE FAITHFUL AND HUMBLE.** APRINGIUS OF BEJA: Thoroughly terrified by fear of his weakness, insignificance and inferiority, he fell down, not falling only to some degree, but wholly giving himself over to the Lord in humility and faith. And, therefore, the Lord also felt compassion in view of this most pious devotion. "He laid his right hand on me, saying, 'Fear not.'" Here he both rewards faith and strengthens the faithful, who is terrified not by unbelief but by an awe-filled wonder, and he urges John not to fear. TRACTATE ON THE APOCALYPSE 1.17.[76]

## 1:18 The First and the Last

**JESUS, THE WELLSPRING OF LIFE.** OECUMENIUS: The holy John would not have been strong enough to survive his astonishment had the saving right hand of the Son of God not touched him, which by the mere touch had accomplished so many wonderful things. And he said to me, "I am the first and the last," which is as though he had said, "I am he who for the salvation of you all sojourned among you in the flesh at the end of times, even though I am the First and the firstborn of all creation. How is it possible that anything evil transpire from my appearance? For if I who am living and am the wellspring of life became dead for you, and trampled death underfoot and lived again, how is it possible that you who are living become dead on account of me and my appearance? And if 'I have the keys of death and of hades,' so that I make dead and make alive those whom I wish, and that I will bring down to hades and bring up again, as it is written concerning me, and that, as the prophet says, escape from death belongs to me,[77] I would not have sent my own worshipers and disciples to an untimely death." COMMENTARY ON THE APOCALYPSE 1.17-19.[78]

## 1:20 Seven Stars, Seven Lampstands

**THE STARS ARE THE ENTIRE CONGREGATION OF THE BLESSED.** APRINGIUS OF BEJA: The stars placed in the right hand of God are the souls of the saints, or, what is the same thing, the entire congregation of the blessed who have been and who will be until the consummation of the world. In a similar way, we have said that the seven lampstands are the one true church that has been established during the seven-day period of this world, which is founded by faith in the Trinity and which is made strong by the sacrament of the heavenly mystery. TRACTATE ON THE APOCALYPSE 1.20.[79]

**THE WHOLE CHURCH BEARS THE LIGHT OF CHRIST.** IRENAEUS: But the path of those belonging to the church surrounds the whole world. It possesses the sure tradition from the apostles and

---

[74]CSEL 49:20. Also Apringius, Primasius. The incarnation is the supreme moment when Christ shows himself to humankind face to face. [75]CCL 121A:247-49. [76]CCL 107:46. [77]Ps 68:20 (67:21 LXX). [78]TEG 8:81. [79]CCL 107:47.

allows us to see that the faith of all is one and the same, since all receive one and the same God the Father. All believe in the same dispensation regarding the incarnation of the Son of God. All are cognizant of the same gift of the Spirit. All are conversant with the same commandments. All preserve the same form of ecclesiastical constitution. And all expect the same advent of the Lord and await the same salvation of the complete man, that is, of the soul and body. Undoubtedly the preaching of the church is true and steadfast, in which one and the same way of salva-tion is shown throughout the whole world. For to her is entrusted the light of God. Therefore the "wisdom" of God, by means of which she saves all people, "is declared in [its] going forth; it speaks faithfully in the streets, is preached on the tops of the walls, and speaks continually in the gates of the city."[80] For the church preaches the truth everywhere, and she is the seven-branched candlestick that bears the light of Christ. AGAINST HERESIES 5.20.1.[81]

---

[80]Prov 1:20-21. [81]ANF 1:548.

---

# 2:1-7 TO THE ANGEL OF THE CHURCH IN EPHESUS

[1]"To the angel of the church in Ephesus write: 'The words of him who holds the seven stars in his right hand, who walks among the seven golden lampstands.

[2]"'I know your works, your toil and your patient endurance, and how you cannot bear evil men but have tested those who call themselves apostles but are not, and found them to be false; [3]I know you are enduring patiently and bearing up for my name's sake, and you have not grown weary. [4]But I have this against you, that you have abandoned the love you had at first. [5]Remember then from what you have fallen, repent and do the works you did at first. If not, I will come to you and remove your lampstand from its place, unless you repent. [6]Yet this you have, you hate the works of the Nicolaitans, which I also hate. [7]He who has an ear, let him hear what the Spirit says to the churches. To him who conquers I will grant to eat of the tree of life, which is in the paradise of God.'"

---

**OVERVIEW:** In writing to the churches, John addresses angels (ORIGEN). Or, in writing to the angel of the church, John is addressing each church directly (OECUMENIUS). The Evangelist finds each church worthy of praise and of blame, for each church is representative of the whole church (BEDE). In every church there will be false teachers and there will be the failure of sin. Therefore, John reminds this church that teachers must be tested for truth (OECUMENIUS), and he reminds this church that God has promised to pardon sinners (TERTULLIAN, CYPRIAN). However, good works, especially that of love, must follow repentence (VICTORINUS, APRINGIUS); otherwise God will move from patience to punishment (OECUMENIUS). Christ threatens also to come and judge those who are evil in the church even as he blesses the good (CAESARIUS OF ARLES).

Excessive desire and the slough of vice are the results of the perverse heresy of the Nicolaitans.

---

18

Such heresy makes the church weak (APRINGIUS). The obedient must hear the Spirit, or Christ (OECUMENIUS), who promises rewards to those who conquer, either to the martyr (TERTULLIAN) or to the repentant (APRINGIUS). The fruit of the tree of life is the new life of knowledge and love that comes through the gospel (METHODIUS). To eat of this tree refers to the eternal life given to those who resisted the evil demons (ANDREW OF CAESAREA). The church is itelf the spiritual paradise in which the celestial bread is given from the tree of life, Jesus Christ, who hung on the cross (TYCONIUS).

## 2:1 Write to the Angel of the Church in Ephesus

**PATIENCE, STEADFAST LOVE AND HATRED OF FALSEHOOD.** VICTORINUS OF PETOVIUM: In the first letter, [John] says, "I know your work and toil and your patient suffering"—I know that you work and toil, and I see that you are patient; lest you think that I will remain a long time away from you—"and that you are not able to bear evil persons and those who call themselves apostles you have found to be liars, and you have suffered patiently for the sake of my name." All of these things are in view of praise, and no ordinary praise. And yet it is good that such persons and such a class of people and such elect persons be admonished in every way, lest they be robbed of those blessings which are their due. But he said that he had a few things against them. "You have forsaken your first love," he said. "Remember from where you have fallen." When someone falls, he falls from a height, and therefore he says "from where," since even to the very end works of love must be practised, for this is the principal commandment. And, therefore, unless this be done, he threatened to "move the lampstand from its place," that is, to scatter the people. However, they hate the works of the Nicolaitans, which he also hates, and this is deserving of praise. "Works of the Nicolaitans" refer to the fact that before that time there were factious and troublesome

men who as ministers made for themselves a heresy in the name of Nicolaus, so that what had been offered to idols could be exorcised and eaten, and that anyone who had committed fornication might receive the peace on the eighth day. And, therefore, he praised those to whom he wrote and promised to such great people the tree of life, which is in the paradise of their God. COMMENTARY ON THE APOCALYPSE 2.1.[1]

**THE SPIRITUAL PERSON MAY ADDRESS EVEN ANGELS.** ORIGEN: In many places, and especially in the Psalms, you will find speech addressed to the angels. Power has been given to man—at least to him who has the Holy Spirit—to speak even to the angels. I shall give one example from these instances, so that we might realize that angels too can be taught by human voices. It has been written in the Apocalypse of John, "Write to the angel of the church of the Ephesians, 'I have something against you.'" And again, "Write to the angel of the church of Pergamum, 'I have something against you.'"[2] Clearly it is a man who writes to angels and enjoins something. HOMILIES ON THE GOSPEL OF LUKE 23.7.[3]

**THE ANGEL IS THE CHURCH.** OECUMENIUS: He speaks periphrastically of the church in Ephesus as an "angel of the church in Ephesus." For the guardian angel of the church has not sinned, so that it requires the admonition to repent. He is rather most holy and for this reason exists at the right hand of the Lord, giving as proof of this the purity of his nature and flashes as of light. Moreover, what need would there be for him who is conversing with the Evangelist to say, "write to him [the angel]," since the holy angel was present and was listening to the conversation (being on the right hand of the one speaking)? And, finally, the saint himself interprets the vision seen by

---

[1]CSEL 49:32-34. Victorinus is the sole witness to give us these details about the Nicolaitans, that they exorcised meat of the demons to whom it had been consecrated and that they were lax in issues of penance. [2]Rev 2:12, 14. [3]FC 94:100-101.

him and says, "He who has ears, let him hear what the Spirit is saying to the churches." He did not say "to the angels of the churches" but "to the churches." And so, also in the remaining interpretations you will find the words "write the following to the angel of the church," not that he is speaking about the angel but about the church. COMMENTARY ON THE APOCALYPSE 2.1-7.[4]

**EVERY CHURCH IS WORTHY OF PRAISE AND BLAME.** BEDE: He blames part of this church, and he praises part of this church, according to the quality of its name. For *Ephesus* may be interpreted as either "great fall" or "my will in it." ... He shows that what he writes to the individual churches, he is saying to all the churches. For, it was not the church of the Ephesians alone, which, should it not repent, was to be moved from its place, nor was Pergamum only the seat of Satan, and not everywhere. Likewise, the remaining things of the individual churches are common to every church. ... The "tree of life" is Christ, by the vision of whom holy souls are nourished in the celestial paradise and in the present body of the church. EXPLANATION OF THE APOCALYPSE 2.1, 7.[5]

### 2:2 Testing Those Who Call Themselves Apostles

**IT IS NECESSARY TO TEST THOSE WHO PREACH.** OECUMENIUS: And he says, "You are not able to bear evil men," for you have acquired the habit of hating evil, and "you have tested those who have called themselves apostles but are not, and you have found them to be false." Those in Ephesus fulfilled the divine command that they should not believe every spirit but test the spirits to see whether they are from God. Therefore, they tested those who preached the gospel among them, and through this testing they found some to be false apostles who were proclaiming counterfeit doctrines. He speaks of those who were disciples of Cerinthus, who were contemporary with the Evangelist and were proclaiming

profane teachings. COMMENTARY ON THE APOCALYPSE 2.1-7.[6]

### 2:4 I Have This Against You

**GOD WILLS TO PARDON THE PENITENT.** TERTULLIAN: You have sinned, yet you still can be reconciled. You have someone to whom you can make satisfaction, yes, and one who wills it. If you doubt that this is true, consider what the Spirit says to the churches. He charges the Ephesians with "having abandoned charity." He reproaches the Thyatirenes with fornication and "eating food sacrificed to idols."[7] He accuses the Sardians of "works that are not complete."[8] He censures the people of Pergamos for teaching false doctrines.[9] He upbraids the Laodiceans for "placing their trust in riches."[10] And yet he warns them all to repent—even adding threats. But he would not threaten the impenitent if he failed to pardon the penitent. ON PENITENCE 7-8.[11]

### 2:5a Repent and Do the Works You Did at First

**THE CALL TO REPENTANCE IS A PROMISE OF FORGIVENESS TO THE PENITENT.** CYPRIAN: But I wonder that some are so obstinate as to think that penance ought not to be allowed to the lapsed or as to consider that pardon ought to be denied to the penitent when it is written, "Remember whence you have fallen and repent and do the former works." This is certainly said to him who, it is ascertained, has fallen and whom the Lord exhorts to rise again through works since is it written, "Alms deliver ... from death."[12] Certainly not from that death which once the blood of Christ extinguished and from which the water of beneficial baptism and the grace of our Redeemer freed us, but from that which afterward creeps in through sins. In another place, also, time is given for repentance, and the Lord

---

[4]TEG 8:84. [5]CCL 121A: 249-53. [6]TEG 8:84-85. [7]Rev 2:20. [8]Rev 3:1. [9]Rev 2:14. [10]Rev 3:17. [11]ACW 28:29-30. [12]Tob 4:11.

threatens the one who does not do penance. "I have," he says, "many things against you: that you permit your wife Jezebel, who calls herself a prophetess, to teach, and to seduce my servants, to commit fornication and to eat of things sacrificed to idols. And I gave her time that she might repent, and she does not want to repent of her fornication. Behold, I will cast her upon a bed, and those who commit fornication with her are in the greatest tribulation, unless they repent of their deeds."[13] The Lord certainly would not exhort to repentance if it were not because he promises pardon to the penitent. LETTER 55.22, TO ANTONIAN.[14]

### REPENTANCE IS TO BE FOLLOWED BY ACTIONS THAT EXPRESS REPENTANCE.

APRINGIUS OF BEJA: For although he wishes that we remember those instances in which we have badly fallen, he exhorts that we might not fall again. And that our faults which we have committed might be cleansed, he shows a way by which one might come to pardon when he says, "Repent." That is, wash away your sins with tears, just as "that sinful woman," as a type of the church, "washed the feet of Jesus with her tears and wiped them with her hair."[15] And he exhorts and commands what one should do after repentance: "Do your first works," either by an extraordinary goodness or do those works which you had done in the earnestness of your first conversion. TRACTATE ON THE APOCALYPSE 2.5.[16]

### 2:5 I Will Come and Remove Your Lampstand

### GOD MOVES FROM PATIENCE TO PUNISHMENT.

OECUMENIUS: By the words "I will come to you," he does not suggest any movement that involves a change of position, since God fills all things. Rather, he indicates, as it were, a change from his longsuffering to punishment. He speaks of the removal of the lampstands, that is, of the churches as his own abandonment [of them], which, when it comes against the sinners, brings

them into every kind of distress and trouble, so that they might also say, "My eye was troubled with anger," and "My heart was troubled within me."[17] COMMENTARY ON THE APOCALYPSE 2.1-7.[18]

### THE LAMPSTAND MOVED BUT NOT TAKEN AWAY.

CAESARIUS OF ARLES: Note that he did not say that he "takes away" [the lampstand] but that he "moves." For the lampstand signifies the one Christian people. Therefore, he says that this lampstand is to be moved, not taken away, so that we might understand that in the very same church the evil are moved and the good confirmed. Moreover, he means that by the hidden but nonetheless just judgment of God, that which is taken from the evil is given as increase to the good. This fulfills that which is written, "He who has, it will be added to him; but to him who has not, even that which he has shall be taken from him."[19] EXPOSITION OF THE APOCALYPSE 2.5, HOMILY 2.[20]

### 2:6 The Works of the Nicolaitans

### NICOLAITAN INDULGENCE NOT TRUE TO THE APOSTOLIC NICOLAUS.

CLEMENT OF ALEXANDRIA: Similar, too, are those who claim to be followers of Nicolaus. They keep one of the man's sayings, forcing its meaning: "One must misuse the flesh." But this admirable man showed that we ought to curtail pleasures and desires and to use this discipline to weaken the impulses and onset of the flesh. Those who wallow in pleasure like goats are (you might say) violating the body and are plunged in the delights of passion. They do not realize that the body, whose nature is fleeting, falls into rags, while the soul is buried in a slough of vice, when they follow the instructions of pleasure rather than a man of apostolic faith. STROMATEIS 2.118.3-5.[21]

---

[13]See Rev 2:20-22. [14]FC 51:147*. [15]Lk 7:44. [16]CCL 107:48-49. [17]Ps 55:4 (54:5 LXX). [18]TEG 8:85. [19]Mt 25:29. [20]PL 35:2421. [21]FC 85:234-35. Bede agrees with Clement's interpretation. However, others did accuse the deacon Nicolaus as source of this heresy (Irenaeus *Against Heresies* 1.26.3).

**HERESY MAKES THE CHURCH WEAK.** APRING-IUS OF BEJA: Of the Nicolaitans, it is interpreted as "a pouring out" or "the folly of a fainting church." And this is rightly said of heretics who have been poured out from the container of the truth and have tumbled headlong into the mud of deceit. And, concerning this pouring out, it is said in the Law: "You are poured out as water; you will not rise up."[22] Clearly, the foolishness of a fainting church is the perverse teaching of the heretics, for they do not bring healing to the wound of the people, but they afflict upon the people the greatest of weaknesses, thinking foolish thoughts about God and being themselves fully taken over by ridiculous ideas. Concerning such persons it is said: "They have restored the sorrow of my people to dishonor, saying, 'Peace, peace,' when there is no peace."[23] TRACTATE ON THE APOCALYPSE 2.6.[24]

## 2:7a Hear What the Spirit Says

**LET THE OBEDIENT HEAR.** OECUMENIUS: "He who has an ear," that is, who is obedient by obeying the divine precepts, "let him hear what the Spirit says to the churches." He says "the Spirit," either because the visions of the Revelation are effected by the Spirit, or he calls Christ "spirit," in that he is and is known to be God. Just as he does not fail to be called "Son of man" in that he is and is known to be man. For the Godhead is said to be all together "spirit," as the Lord himself says in speaking to the Samaritan woman: "God is a spirit, and it is necessary that those who worship him, worship in spirit and in truth."[25] COMMENTARY ON THE APOCALYPSE 2.1-7.[26]

## 2:7b Who Conquers Will Eat of the Tree of Life

**GOD DETERMINES THE PRIZE FOR THE MARTYR.** TERTULLIAN: In still another sense, a persecution can be considered as a contest. Who sets the terms of any contest if not the one who provides the crown and the prizes? You will find the terms of this contest decreed in the Apocalypse, where he proclaims the rewards of victory, especially for those who really come through persecution victorious, [27] and in their victorious struggle have fought not merely against flesh and blood but against the spirits of wickedness.[28] Obviously, then, the superintendent of the games and the one who sets the prize is the one who decides who is the winner of the contest. The essence, then, of a persecution is the glory of God, whether he approves or condemns, raises up or casts down. ON FLIGHT IN TIME OF PERSECUTION 1.5.[29]

**THE FRUIT OF THE TREE OF LIFE COMES THROUGH THE GOSPEL.** METHODIUS: The tree of life which paradise once bore, now again the church has produced for all, even the ripe and comely fruit of faith. It is necessary that we bring such fruit when we come to the judgment seat of Christ, on the first day of the feast. For if we are without it we shall not be able to feast with God nor to have part, according to John,[30] in the first resurrection. For the tree of life is wisdom first begotten of all. "She is a tree of life to them that lay hold upon her," says the prophet, "and happy is every one that retains her."[31] "A tree planted by the waterside, that will bring forth its fruit in due season."[32] That is, learning and charity and discretion are imparted in due time to those who come to the waters of redemption. One who has not believed in Christ nor understood that he is the first principle and the tree of life, since he cannot show to God his tabernacle adorned with the best of fruits, how shall [this person] celebrate the feast? How shall he rejoice? Do you desire to know good fruit of the tree? Consider the words of our Lord Jesus Christ, how pleasant they are beyond mere human words. Good fruit came by Moses, that is the law, but not as good as the gospel. For the law is a kind of figure and shadow of

---

[22]See Gen 49:4. [23]Jer 8:11. [24]CCL 107:49-50. [25]Jn 4:24. [26]TEG 8:86. [27]Rev 2:7, 10, 11, 17, 26-28; 3:5, 12, 21. [28]Eph 6:12. [29]FC 40:276-77*. [30]Rev 20:6. [31]Prov 3:18. [32]Ps 1:3.

things to come, but the gospel is truth and the grace of life. The fruit of the prophets was pleasant, but not so pleasant as the fruit of immortality which is plucked from the gospel. BANQUET OF THE TEN VIRGINS 9.3.[33]

**WE FEED ON CHRIST IN THE CHURCH.** TYCONIUS: "Who conquers, I will grant to eat from the tree of life," that is, from the fruit of the cross, "which is in the paradise of my God." The church is to be regarded as paradise, for "all things were done in figure," and Adam was "the shadow of the one to come," as the apostle teaches.[34] Indeed, the tree of life is the wisdom of God, the Lord Jesus Christ, who hung on the cross. In the church and in the spiritual paradise, he gives to the faithful food of life and the sacrament of the celestial bread, of which you read, "Wisdom is the tree of life to those who embrace her."[35] COMMENTARY ON THE APOCALYPSE 2.7.[36]

**REWARDS ARE PROMISED TO THOSE WHO REPENT.** APRINGIUS OF BEJA: He has spoken of the toil of the church. He has described the perversity of the heretics. Now to those still in their failures, he exhorts to repentance, and [he] promises rewards after this toil to those who are victorious, so that, entering into paradise, they might freely eat from the tree of life, for which Adam was expelled from paradise, lest he eat anything from it. And so he says, "which is in the paradise of my God," where, namely, the wind breathes life, where the mysteries give virtue, and he furnishes the fruit of the tree of life, that is, an eternity which does not fade away. TRACTATE ON THE APOCALYPSE 2.7.[37]

**CHRIST IS WISDOM AND ETERNAL LIFE.** ANDREW OF CAESAREA: Every person has a physical ear, but only the spiritual person has a spiritual ear, such as was granted to Isaiah.[38] And to such as conquer in the struggle against the demons, he promised to give "to eat from the tree of life," that is, to grant them to share in the blessings of the future age, for eternal life is figuratively depicted through the tree. And Christ is said to be both, as is clear from what Solomon says and what our apostle writes in another passage. For, concerning wisdom, Solomon says, "She is the tree of life,"[39] while John writes about Christ, "This is God and eternal life."[40] If, therefore, we are allowed to attain to these things, let us accomplish the victory over our sufferings. For, most certainly proper recompense will follow our trials, by the grace and beneficence of our Lord, Jesus Christ, with whom be glory to the Father together with the Holy Spirit for ever and ever. Amen. COMMENTARY ON THE APOCALYPSE 2.7.[41]

---

[33]ANCL 14:96-97*. [34]Rom 5:14. [35]Prov 3:18. [36]CCL 92:25-26. [37]CCL 107:50. [38]Is 50:5. [39]Prov 3:18. [40]1 Jn 5:20. [41]MTS 1 Sup 1:26-27.

---

## 2:8-11 TO THE ANGEL OF THE CHURCH IN SMYRNA

[8]*"And to the angel of the church in Smyrna write: 'The words of the first and the last, who died and came to life.*

[9]*"'I know your tribulation and your poverty (but you are rich) and the slander of those who say that they are Jews and are not, but are a synagogue of Satan.* [10]*Do not fear what you are about to*

*suffer. Behold, the devil is about to throw some of you into prison, that you may be tested, and for ten days you will have tribulation. Be faithful unto death, and I will give you the crown of life.* [11]*He who has an ear, let him hear what the Spirit says to the churches. He who conquers shall not be hurt by the second death.'"*

**OVERVIEW:** Jesus, who is true God and true man, addresses the church at Smyrna (OECUMENIUS). He speaks to every church that is poor in spirit and despises the wealth of the present age (APRINGIUS, ANDREW OF CAESAREA, PRIMASIUS). Nonetheless, Christians are rich, for they have a wealthy patron in Christ who for us became poor (OECUMENIUS). Therefore, Christians are wealthy in the things of the Spirit (ANDREW OF CAESAREA) and possess the riches of faith and blessing (APRINGIUS).

Meanwhile, the church does suffer under those who have failed to confess Christ (OECUMENIUS) and who will be instruments of the antichrist (VICTORINUS). Moreover, the church suffers much because of false Christians who are Jews within the church since they are pious only on the outside (TYCONIUS). Yet, the church will suffer until the end of time, for the devil will always persecute the church through the impious, the heretics and finally the antichrist (APRINGIUS, PRIMASIUS). The devil will also attack the church throughout the present age by bringing her into temptation, just as he did against Adam, who fell, and against Christ, who withstood the threefold temptation (PRIMASIUS). The sufferings of the present age, however, will not compare with the perpetuity of future blessedness (APRINGIUS), and so Christians should remain faithful to the end in faith, love, and holiness (PRIMASIUS), as did the martyrs and the confessors who received a crown of life (CYPRIAN). Through such faithfulness the justification of forgiveness and conversion will issue into the glorification of eternity (FULGENTIUS OF RUSPE) and into freedom from the results of sin (OECUMENIUS). For through the tree of the cross Christ has conquered death, which was the gift which Adam gave to posterity by eating of the forbidden tree (PRIMASIUS).

### 2:8a *Write to the Angel of the Church in Smyrna*

**CHRIST EXHORTS TO ENDURANCE IN PERSECUTION.** BEDE: He speaks to this church concerning the endurance of persecution, and to this the name also corresponds. For "Smyrna" may be rendered "myrrh," which designates the mortification of the flesh. EXPLANATION OF THE APOCALYPSE 2.8.[1]

### 2:8b *The First and the Last*

**BY DEATH HE PUT DEATH TO DEATH.** OECUMENIUS: The Lord calls himself "first" because of the essence of his deity but calls himself "last" because of the incarnation and the economy of the flesh. "Who was dead," he says, "and came to life." He who came into the trial of death, he says, by death put death to death. COMMENTARY ON THE APOCALYPSE 2.8-11.[2]

### 2:9 *I Know Your Suffering and Poverty*

**YOU PERSEVERE THROUGH SLANDER.** VICTORINUS OF PETOVIUM: The next letter shows the following manner of life and habit of another group. And so he says, "I know you that you are poor and labor, but you are rich." For he knows that for such persons there are hidden riches with him. [And he knows] the slander of the Jews, whom he denies that they are Jews, but rather a synagogue of Satan, for they are gathered together by the antichrist. That they might persevere even to death, he says to them: "Whoever will persevere, will not be harmed

---

[1]CCL 121A:253. [2]TEG 8:87.

by the second death," that is, he will not be punished in hell. COMMENTARY OF THE APOCA-LYPSE 2.2.[3]

RICH IN FAITH AND BLESSINGS. APRINGIUS OF BEJA: He praises the works of his church, for through many tribulations she contends for the kingdom. He indicates expressly the grace of poverty, because [the church] despises very much the things of the present time, so that she might acquire future things. "But you are rich." You are rich in faith and are filled with an abundance of blessings. "And you are slandered by those who say that they are Jews and are not, but are a synagogue of Satan." For the church often sustains much insult from those who claim that they confess God, but do not confess him. Rather, their congregation is bound to the devil as its source. For that reason, he exhorts his church not to fear those who kill the body, but afterward have nothing which they can do.[4] TRACTATE ON THE APOC-ALYPSE 2.9.[5]

SOME SAY THEY ARE JEWS BUT ARE NOT. OECUMENIUS: "I know your tribulation and your poverty"—indeed, you do not speak, as do the wicked Jews, who say, "Why have we fasted, and you did not notice it? Why have we humbled ourselves, and you paid no heed?"[6] But "you are rich," he says, since you have Christ as a wealthy patron, although indeed for us he became poor, "taking the form of a slave."[7] "and the blasphemy" of those falsely called "Jews." *Judah* means "confession," and *Israel* means "those who spiritually see God." Therefore, those who are true Jews and the spiritual Israel would be those who confess Christ. "For he is not a Jew who is one outwardly, nor is the circumcision which is outward and physical" pleasing to God, as Paul says, "rather, he is a Jew who is one inwardly, and the circumcision is a matter of the heart," not of the flesh.[8] For that reason, those who have remained Jews in unbelief are a blasphemous synagogue, under the leadership of Satan. COMMENTARY ON THE APOC-ALYPSE 2.8-11.[9]

RICH IN THE THINGS OF THE SPIRIT. ANDREW OF CAESAREA: In the things of the flesh you have tribulation and poverty, which you endure for my sake, being beaten by unbelievers and being deprived of present goods. But in the things of the Spirit you are rich, for you have the "hidden treasure in the field"[10] of your heart. COMMEN-TARY ON THE APOCALYPSE 2.9.[11]

FALSE CHRISTIANS ALSO INHABIT THE CHURCH: TYCONIUS: He speaks to every church that is poor in spirit yet possesses all things, as the apostle says, "as having nothing, and yet possessing everything."[12] "And you are slandered by those who say that they are Jews and are not, but are a synagogue of Satan." Here certainly it is shown that he was not speaking only to a special church, for it was not only at Smyrna where there were or are Jews who slander. However, it is possible that there is a double meaning of "Jews" here, either those who are openly Jews outside or those who are Jews within [the church], that is, false Christians. For religiosity is characteristic of the Jews, as the apostle says, "He is a Jew who is one inwardly, and real circumcision is a matter of the heart, spiritual and not literal."[13] And again he says, "We are the circumcision who worship God in spirit, and put no confidence in the flesh."[14] Nor ought we ourselves to abandon those [in the church] when they are even called a synagogue of Satan. For we know that the Lord has presented us with an example of longsuffering by tolerating Judas even unto the end. COMMENTARY ON THE APOCALYPSE 2.9.[15]

### 2:10a Do Not Fear What You Will Suffer

DO NOT FEAR THE TORTURES OF PERSECU-TORS. APRINGIUS OF BEJA: He speaks of those future trials and evils which will come upon them from the impious, and he comforts his faithful,

---

[3]CSEL 49:34-36. Victorinus believed that in the last days the Jews will collude with the antichrist. [4]See Lk 12:4. [5]CCL 107:50-51. [6]Is 58:3. [7]Phil 2:7. [8]Rom 2:28-29. [9]TEG 8:87. [10]Mt 13:44. [11]MTS 1 Sup 1:27. [12]2 Cor 6:10. [13]Rom 2:29. [14]Phil 3:3. [15]CCL 92:26.

that they not be fearful of the tortures of the persecutors. And he indicates what they would be strong enough to suffer and what the enemy would be able to do. . . . For, just as in the early period of the catholic church, after the banishment of the apostle, whose sayings these are, the sufferings continued and many tribulations were inflicted upon the church, so we know that also in the future more [sufferings] will be inflicted when the antichrist arrives, although even now the church often sustains many sufferings in various places and regions from heretics and from native populations. TRACTATE ON THE APOCALYPSE 2.10[16]

## 2:10b *You Will Have Tribulation for Ten Days*

**PRESENT SUFFERING, FUTURE BLISS.** APRINGIUS OF BEJA: But he says, "You will have tribulation for ten days." This is to say, should you consider the present evils which you suffer in comparison to the perpetuity of the future blessedness, you will regard these without doubt as small and as quickly transient as though of ten days duration. And therefore, the apostle said: "I consider that the sufferings of this present time are not worth comparing with the glory that is to be revealed to us."[17] TRACTATE ON THE APOCALYPSE 2.10.[18]

**TEN REPRESENTS THE COURSE OF THE PRESENT LIFE.** PRIMASIUS: "Behold, the devil is about to throw some of you into prison, that you may be tested, and for ten days you will have tribulation." These words are fitting for the universal church, against whom the devil is always waging war with unavoidable hostilities. And for this reason the course of the present life is signified by the ten days, since in the Decalogue there exists in brief form a summary of the law. For here are the required divine commandments where there is need for continence. For this reason also the Lord said, "Agree with your accuser," that is, the law, "while you are with him in the way of this age."[19] In this way he indicates the entire time when, with the law instructing you, there is con-

flict against the manifold allurements of desire, so that when the five physical senses are subdued through the grace of God, victory is achieved. And when duplicated on account of the twofold sexes, the five senses become ten.

I also think that the ten days may be interpreted as the total course of this life in which there will never fail to be a threefold temptation for the faithful. For "the life of man upon the earth is a trial,"[20] and this is so as the seven days pass by and continue to pass by until the whole time of the present life is unfolded. The devil was permitted to bring this temptation even upon our Lord Jesus Christ as the head of the church. This spiritual battle of the church of Christ is further indicated in the figure of a woman who is in struggle. For the Lord said to the serpent, "I will put enmity between you and the woman. She will watch[21] your head, and you will lie in wait for her heel."[22] It is, therefore, clearly recognized that in this age, which is completed in the course of seven days, the church of Christ is subjected to various trials. These receive their most powerful and principal expression in the three sins, in the passion of fleshly desire and the unrestrained gluttony of forbidden excesses.[23]

---

[16]CCL 107:51. [17]Rom 8:18 [18]CCL 107:51. [19]See Mt 5:25. [20]See Job 7:1. [21]Latin *observabit*. [22]Gen 3:15 *Vetus Latina*. [23]A familiar pattern of rabbinic exegesis is here employed by the commentator. Accordingly, every word, indeed every letter of the Torah had meaning, some hidden, some multiple. Wherever a number appears in a sacred text, whether Old or New Testament, it is closely investigated by the rabbinic or patristic commentator. Revelation 2:10 makes better sense to one who is aware of certain standard and familiar numerical equivalents. Primasius had doubtless already preached on the fall, man and woman, the law, the temptation narrative and the sabbath. This reference to ten days gives him the opportunity to bring together a wide range of biblical allusions with which his audience was already familiar. There are two sexes, each with five senses. Hence in the struggle of men and women there are symbolically ten days of temptation and trial. Ten days means the present life, lived under the law, constrained by the Decalogue. The five sensual desires, complicated by sexuality, conflict with the law in these ten days. The three forms of temptation are encompassed and symbolized in the temptation of Jesus by the devil. At the end of seven days a final struggle is occurring in which there is a new birthing of man and woman coming into being. The pain of giving birth begins with the fall of Adam and Eve and looks toward a new Adam and Eve.

The enemy attempted to deceive the Lord by way of bread, as though he were a second Adam, since he had given the first Adam a draught of death when he persuaded him to taste what was forbidden to humankind. And so by rendering the first Adam a captive to the belly, he intended to bind him in addiction also to other desires of the flesh. And the enemy was also allowed to attack the Lord with the temptation to vainglory when he exhorted him to throw himself headlong from the pinnacle of the temple, adding the witness of the psalm which says, "He has given his angels charge over you" and the following.[24] And just as the enemy had deceived the first man with the suggestion, "You shall be like gods knowing good and evil,"[25] so he exhorted the Lord to throw himself down incautiously out of the desire to display the deity which he had laid aside. And the enemy tempts also a third time through which it is indicated that greed for the glory of earthly kingdoms and the pomp of worldly wealth must be condemned.[26] When this threefold temptation is added to the times of this life, which are indicated by the seven days, the number ten is fulfilled, and for this reason it is said, "for ten days you will have tribulation." COMMENTARY ON THE APOCALYPSE 2.10.[27]

## 2:10c Be Faithful unto Death

**CONFESSORS ARE TO BE HONORED EVEN AS MARTYRS ARE.** CYPRIAN: Let very willing vigilance and care be bestowed, moreover, upon the bodies of all who, although they have not been tortured, yet depart from the prison by the glorious exit of death. Neither their valor nor their honor is less that they themselves should not be among the blessed martyrs. They have endured, as far as it is in their power, whatever they were prepared and ready to endure. In the eyes of God, the one who offered himself to torments and to death suffered whatever he was willing to suffer. For he himself did not fail the torments, but the torments failed him. "He who has acknowledged me before men, I also will acknowledge him

before my Father,"[28] says the Lord. They have acknowledged him. "He who has persevered even to the end, he will be saved,"[29] says the Lord. They have their virtues incorrupt and immaculate. And again it is written: "Be faithful unto death, and I will give you the crown of life." They endured even unto death, faithful and steadfast and invincible. When to our wish and to our confession in prison and in chains is added also the end of dying, the glory of martyrdom is consummated. LETTER 12.1, TO PRIESTS AND DEACONS.[30]

**THE CHURCH MUST ALWAYS BE FAITHFUL.** PRIMASIUS: These words pertain to the entire church. For also the apostle teaches this when he speaks of Adam and says, "Adam was not deceived, but the woman was deceived and became a transgressor."[31] And thereupon he indicated the church by moving to figurative speech, saying, "She will be saved through the bearing of sons, if she continues in faith and love and holiness with modesty."[32] No one believes that this is spoken of a woman who is dead, and not rather of the church of Christ. COMMENTARY ON THE APOCALYPSE 2.10.[33]

## 2:11 One Who Conquers Is Not Hurt by the Second Death

**THE GRACE OF JUSTIFICATION IS COMPLETED IN THE PERFECT GLORIFICATION.** FULGENTIUS OF RUSPE: This then is done in them through grace so that the change brought about by divine gift may begin in them here. The change begins first through justification, in which there is a spiritual resurrection, and afterwards, in the resurrection of the body, in which the change of the justified is brought to completion; the perfected glorification, remaining for eternity, is not changed. To this end, first the grace of justifica-

[24]Ps 91:11 (90:11 LXX). [25]Gen 3:5. [26]Lk 4:1-13. [27]CCL 92:27-28. Bede, who follows the interpretation of Primasius, adds that some interpret the ten days to refer "to the ten persecutions of the nations from Caesar Nero unto Diocletian." [28]Mt 10:32. [29]Mt 10:22. [30]FC 51:35. [31]Tim 2:14. [32]Tim 2:15. [33]CCL 92:28.

tion, then the grace of glorification changes them so that the glorification itself remains, unchangeable and eternal in them. For here they are changed through the first resurrection by which they are enlightened that they may be converted. That is, they change from death to life by this, from iniquity to justice, from infidelity to faith, and from evil acts to a holy way of life. Therefore, the second death has no power over them. Concerning such people, it is said in the Apocalypse: "Blessed is the one who shares in the first resurrection. The second death has no power over them."[34] Again it is said in the same book: "The victor shall not be harmed by the second death." Therefore, just as the first resurrection is found in conversion of the heart, so the second death is found in eternal punishment. Let every person who does not wish to be condemned by eternal punishment of the second death hasten here to become a participant of the first resurrection. ON THE FORGIVENESS OF SINS 2.12.3-4.[35]

**THOSE WHO OVERCOME TEMPTATION.** OECUMENIUS: "He who has an ear, let him hear what the Spirit says to the churches. He who conquers will not be hurt by the second death." This is a very apt statement. For, while all, the just and the sinner alike, are subject to the first death, which is the separation of the soul from the body, so that the divine judgment might be enforced: "You are earth and to earth you will return,"[36] those who have overcome temptations should not be harmed by the second death, which is the result of sin, and which the Lord specified when he said, "Let the dead bury their own dead."[37] COMMENTARY ON THE APOCALYPSE 2.8-11.[38]

**THE DEATH FROM ADAM IS OVERCOME IN THE VICTORY OF CHRIST.** PRIMASIUS: "He who conquers shall not be hurt by the second death." Having eaten of the forbidden tree, [Adam] procured this [death] for posterity. However, watering the tree of the cross by the water and blood which flowed from the holy place of his side, Christ caused the firstfruits of salvation to sprout up where he knew the original evil had arisen, saying, "Rejoice, I have overcome the world."[39] Thus, if anyone conquers, he will conquer in him. COMMENTARY ON THE APOCALYPSE 2.11.[40]

---

[34]Rev 20:6. [35]FC 95:166-67*. [36]Gen 3:19. [37]Mt 8:22. [38]TEG 8:88. [39]Jn 16:33. [40]CCL 92:28.

---

## 2:12-17 TO THE ANGEL OF THE CHURCH IN PERGAMUM

[12]"And to the angel of the church in Pergamum write: 'The words of him who has the sharp two-edged sword.

[13]" 'I know where you dwell, where Satan's throne is; you hold fast my name and you did not deny my faith even in the days of Antipas my witness, my faithful one, who was killed among you, where Satan dwells. [14]But I have a few things against you: you have some there who hold the teaching of Balaam, who taught Balak to put a stumbling block before the sons of Israel, that they might eat food sacrificed to idols and practice immorality. [15]So you also have some who hold the teaching of the Nicolaitans. [16]Repent then. If not, I will come to you soon and war against them with the sword of my mouth. [17]He who has an ear, let him hear what the Spirit says to the churches. To him

*who conquers I will give some of the hidden manna, and I will give him a white stone, with a new name written on the stone which no one knows except him who receives it.'"*

**Overview:** "Pergamum" refers to the divine judgment by the "two-edged sword" which distinguishes between the faithful and the unfaithful (Andrew of Caesarea, Bede). Here Christ speaks to every church, for the devil everywhere works temptation and wickedness (Tyconius). Christ praises this church for its steadfastness, exemplified in the martyrdom of Antipas (Andrew of Caesarea). But Christ is everywhere killed by sin and unbelief (Tyconius). Yet, he also blames this church, for she has within her some who follow the teachings of Balaam. Through this heresy the devil induces some to be devoured by pleasure and causes the church to be destroyed and scattered (Apringius, Andrew of Caesarea). Through the teachings of Balaam the Nicolaitans promote a spiritual fornication and pagan ideas (Tyconius, Bede). Nonetheless, the Lord encourages these heretics to repent, lest they be judged by the divine law (Primasius). To be restored to the church, however, they do not require another baptism (Jerome). Those who conquer the devil will receive immortality (Victorinus), which comes through the incarnate Bread from heaven (Tyconius), who now offers himself to us in the Eucharist (Andrew of Caesarea, Tyconius). They will also receive the adoption of sonship and the name of Christian (Victorinus) and the knowledge of the Son of man (Caesarius of Arles).

### 2:12a Write to the Angel of the Church in Pergamum

**Christians Strong in Faith Retain the Gifts of Baptism.** Victorinus of Petovium: The third class of saints are persons who are strong in the faith and are not frightened by persecution. But since there are even among them some who are inclined toward illicit indulgences, he says, "I will fight with them by the sword of my mouth," that is, "I will say what I will com-

mand, and I will tell you what you are to do." For there are some "who have taught the doctrine of Balaam and have placed a stone of stumbling before the eyes of the sons of Israel, to eat what is sacrificed to idols and to commit fornication." And this was known a long time ago. For he gave this advice to the king of the Moabites that in this way he had scandalized the people.[1] "So," he says, "you have some among you who hold to this teaching," and under the pretext of mercy you corrupt others. "Whoever conquers," he says, "I will give to him from the hidden manna." The "hidden manna" is immortality. The "white stone" is the adoption as a son of God. The "new name" is that of Christian. Commentary on the Apocalypse 2.3.[2]

**God Distinguishes Between the Just and the Sinner.** Bede: "Pergamum" may be rendered "dividing their horns," for by his judgment he distinguishes between the virtue of the faithful and the deceit of the Nicolaitans, so that the horns of the sinners may be broken and the horns of the just one may be exalted. Explanation of the Apocalypse 2.12.[3]

### 2:12b The Two-Edged Sword

**The Sword Separates Faithful and Unfaithful.** Andrew of Caesarea: The city to which this is said was given to idolatry, but he is expressing approval of those in it who remained faithful through the endurance of trials. The "two-edged sword" is either the word of the gospel, which cuts the heart and separates the faithful from the unfaithful, or it is the relentless judgment against the impious. Commentary on the Apocalypse 2.12-13.[4]

---

[1]Num 25:1-2. [2]CSEL 49:36-38. [3]CCL 121A:255. [4]MTS 1 Sup 1:29.

## 2:13a *Satan's Throne*

**SATAN RULES WHEREVER THERE IS EVIL.**
TYCONIUS: "I know where you dwell, where
Satan's throne is." This he says to every church,
since the tempter is everywhere, and to him it is
said, "She shall watch your head, and you shall
watch for her heel."[5] "For the world is placed in
evil."[6] Those persons are the throne of Satan
whom he owns in wickedness.[7] The Evangelist
reverts to the species, for although the entire sevenfold church is symbolized by these seven
locales, nonetheless certain things have occurred
in them specifically which he either praises or
rebukes. COMMENTARY ON THE APOCALYPSE
2.13.[8]

## 2:13b *You Did Not Deny*

**THE MARTYR RECALLS THE ENDURANCE OF
FAITH.** ANDREW OF CAESAREA: Antipas was a
most courageous martyr in Pergamum, whose
martyrdom I have read.[9] Here the Evangelist
recalls his memory as a demonstration of their
endurance, as well as of the cruelty of those who
were deceived. COMMENTARY ON THE APOCA-
LYPSE 2.13.[10]

**CHRIST IS MARTYRED BY UNBELIEF AND SIN.**
TYCONIUS: "You hold my name and you did not
deny my faith, even in the days of Antipas my
witness, my faithful one, who was killed among
you." Indeed, Christ is killed among many, who
either do not believe that he rose again, or who
deny him among themselves through condem-
nable faults, and this is "where Satan dwells."
COMMENTARY ON THE APOCALYPSE 2.13.[11]

## 2:14 *The Teaching of Balaam*

**HERESY DESTROYS A PEOPLE.** APRINGIUS OF
BEJA: Nevertheless, the Lord has something
against this church because there are some who
"hold the teaching of Balaam," which is interpreted "without people" or "without property."

For Balaam is a type of the adversary who does
not gather a people for salvation, nor does he
rejoice in the number of the multitude that is
being saved. Rather, as long as he destroys all and
remains without a people and without any property, then he rejoices. It is he himself who "taught
Balak to put a stumbling block before the sons of
Israel." For Balak is interpreted to mean "throwing down" or "devouring." He has thrown Israel
down so that it might be consecrated to the idol,
Phogor[12], and he has devoured them by the eating
of pleasure and luxury. TRACTATE ON THE APOC-
ALYPSE 2.14.[13]

**THE DEVIL SOWS HERESY THROUGH PLEA-
SURE.** ANDREW OF CAESAREA: It seems that this
city had two evils. There were a good number of
Greeks, and among those regarded as faithful the
shameful Nicolaitans were sown as evil weeds
among the wheat.[14] And therefore he reminds
them of Balaam, saying, "who through Balaam
taught Balak." Through these words it is clear
that he refers to the mental Balaam, that is, the
devil, who through the sensual Balaam taught
Balak to throw a stone of stumbling before the
Israelites, namely, to sacrifice to idols and to commit fornication. Through the pleasure of this heresy, they fell so low that they offered sacrifices to
Beelphegor[15]. COMMENTARY ON THE APOCALYPSE
2.14-15.[16]

**IDOLATRY IS A FORNICATION OF THE SPIRIT.**
TYCONIUS: "But I have a few things against you."
To be sure, he speaks against some members who
must be blamed, but not against those to whom
he says, "But you did not deny my faith. You have
there some who hold the teaching of Balaam, who
taught Balak to put a stumbling block before the

---

[5]Gen 3:15 *Vetus Latina.*  [6]1 Jn 5:19.  [7]Caesarius of Arles explains that
"Satan lives everywhere in his body, which is arrogant and evil men."
[8]CCL 92:29.  [9]This account, which Andrew had read, is no longer
extant.  [10]MTS 1 Sup 1:29.  [11]CCL 92:29.  [12]A god of Moab, as designated by LXX and Vg. Its English equivalent is Peor.  [13]CCL 107:52.
[14]Mt 13:24-30.  [15]The name given to the god Baal on Mt. Phegor in
Moab.  [16]MTS 1 Sup 1:30.

sons of Israel, to eat food sacrificed to idols and to practice immorality." To eat and to commit fornication are the two principle forms [of sin] that the hypocrites struggle to enjoy, as the Lord says, "Inside you are full of plunder and incontinence and every iniquity."[17] Idolatry is spiritual fornication. "You have lost," it says, "all who go whoring from you."[18] COMMENTARY ON THE APOCALYPSE 2.14.[19]

## 2:15 The Teaching of the Nicolaitans

**THE NICOLAITANS WERE PROMISCUOUS AND HAD PAGAN IDEAS.** BEDE: The Nicolaitans receive their name from the deacon, Nicolaus, of whom Clement[20] reports that, when he was reproached for jealousy of his very beautiful wife, he responded that whoever wanted might take her as wife. On account of this, the faithless taught that the apostles had permitted to everyone a promiscuous and communal intercourse with women. In addition, the Nicolaitans are said to have proclaimed certain fabulous and virtually pagan ideas concerning the beginning of the world and not to have kept their foods separate from those which had been offered to idols. EXPLANATION OF THE APOCALYPSE 2.16.[21]

## 2:16 Repent!

**HERETICS NEED ONLY TO REPENT.** JEROME: Let us show from the Apocalypse that repentance unaccompanied by baptism ought to be allowed valid in the case of heretics. It is imputed to the angel of Ephesus that he has forsaken his first love. In the angel of the church of Pergamum the eating of idol sacrifices is censured, and the doctrine of the Nicolaitans. Likewise the angel of Thyatira is rebuked on account of Jezebel the prophetess, and the idol meats, and fornication. And yet the Lord encourages all these to repent and adds a threat, moreover, of future punishment if they do not turn. Now he would not urge them to repent unless he intended to grant pardon to the penitents. Is there any indication of his

having said, Let them be rebaptized who have been baptized in the faith of the Nicolaitans? Or let hands be laid upon those of the people of Pergamum who at that time believed, having held the doctrine of Balaam? No, rather, "Repent therefore," he says, "or else I come to you quickly, and I will make war against them with the sword of my mouth." DIALOGUE AGAINST THE LUCIFERIANS 24.[22]

**THE COMMANDMENTS WILL JUDGE THE CONTEMPTUOUS.** PRIMASIUS: "You also have some who hold the teaching of the Nicolaitans. Repent then. If not, I will come to you soon and war against you with the sword[23] of my mouth." He speaks of a sword.[24] . . . The sword is the commandments of both Testaments by which the contemptuous are spiritually overcome. "For those who have sinned under the law will be judged by the law."[25] COMMENTARY ON THE APOCALYPSE 2.16.[26]

## 2:17 Hidden Manna and a White Stone

**THE GLORY OF VICTORY CANNOT NOW BE DESCRIBED.** OECUMENIUS: "And I will give to him a white stone," that is, a stone indicating victory and bright with glory, "and upon the stone a new name which no one knows except him who receives it." For it is said, "What eye has not seen, nor ear heard, nor has come into the heart of man, that has God prepared for those who love him."[27] COMMENTARY ON THE APOCALYPSE 2.12-17.[28]

**THE BREAD FROM HEAVEN.** TYCONIUS: "To him who conquers I will give some of the hidden manna." This manna is the invisible Bread which

---

[17]See Mt 23:25.  [18]See Ps 73:27 (72:27 LXX).  [19]CCL 92:29.
[20]Clement of Alexandria. See *Stromateis* 3.4 (ANF 2:385), although the ANF editors chose to leave the text in Latin.  [21]CCL 121A:257.
[22]NPNF 2 6:332-33*. Jerome argues against the opinion of Cyprian, who recognized as valid only those baptisms administered in the orthodox church.  [23]Latin *rumphea*.  [24]Latin *gladius*.  [25]Rom 2:12.
[26]CCL 92:29-30.  [27]1 Cor 2:9.  [28]TEG 8:90.

came down from heaven, which indeed was made man, so that "man might eat the bread of angels."[29] And the figure of this was indicated beforehand in the manna given in the desert. Whoever ate of that bread were said by the Lord to have died, because remaining faithless, they did not eat of this hidden and uniquely spiritual manna by which [Christ] offers immortality to the faithful. For he said, "Unless you eat the flesh of the Son of man and drink his blood, you will not have eternal life in you."[30] For, indeed, whoever at that time was able to eat spiritually, they were worthy to obtain the same immortality, as were Moses and others. As the apostle teaches, "They ate the same spiritual food."[31] For the visible manna was in no way detrimental to those who used the bodily food in a spiritual manner. So also now, the spiritual manna of the Lord's body does not profit persons in the present if they receive it unworthily, for "they eat and drink judgment upon themselves."[32] COMMENTARY ON THE APOCALYPSE 2.17.[33]

**THE NAME CHRISTIAN MARKS BAPTISM AND MARTYRDOM.** PRIMASIUS: "And I will give him a white stone," that is, the adoption of the sons of God. This stone is a precious gem and may be understood as similar to that pearl that the merchant found and valued as equal to all his possessions which he sold.[34] Another translation renders this as "pearl."[35] "And upon the stone is a new name," that is, the name of *Christian*, for which reason we read, "And you shall be called by a new name which the mouth of the Lord will give."[36] And besides baptism I mention also martyrdom, "which no one knows except him who

receives it." Although hypocrites seem to bear the name superficially, they are unable to enter the power of its meaning, "having the form of religion but denying the power of it."[37] Therefore, the same John says, "He who says that he knows him but disobeys his commandments is a liar, and the truth is not in him."[38] COMMENTARY ON THE APOCALYPSE 2.17.[39]

**REVELATION ONLY GIVES KNOWLEDGE OF THE SON OF MAN.** CAESARIUS OF ARLES: "And I shall give to him a white stone," that is, the body made white by baptism. "And on the stone is written a new name," that is, the knowledge of the Son of man. "Which no one knows except him who receives it." That is, no one knows it except through revelation, and for that reason it is said of the Jews, "For had they known," they would not have crucified the Lord of glory."[40] EXPOSITION ON THE APOCALYPSE 2.17, HOMILY 2.[41]

**THE BLESSINGS OF VICTORY.** ANDREW OF CAESAREA: The "hidden manna" is "the Bread of Life" which came down from heaven for us and became edible. Figuratively, those good things are also called "manna" which are in the future going to come down from heaven, from where comes also the "new Jerusalem." Those who conquer the devil shall obtain these things. COMMENTARY ON THE APOCALYPSE 2.17.[42]

---

[29]Ps 78:25 (77:25 LXX). [30]Jn 6:53. [31]1 Cor 10:3. [32]1 Cor 11:29. [33]CCL 92:30. [34]See Mt 13:45-46. [35]See *Vetus Latina* on this verse. [36]Is 62:2. [37]2 Tim 3:5. [38]1 Jn 2:4. [39]CCL 92:30-31. [40]1 Cor 2:8. [41]PL 35:2421. [42]MTS 1 Sup 1:31.

# 2:18-29 TO THE ANGEL OF THE CHURCH
## IN THYATIRA

[18]"And to the angel of the church in Thyatira write: 'The words of the Son of God, who has eyes like a flame of fire, and whose feet are like burnished bronze.

[19]"'I know your works, your love and faith and service and patient endurance, and that your latter works exceed the first. [20]But I have this against you, that you tolerate the woman Jezebel, who calls herself a prophetess and is teaching and beguiling my servants to practice immorality and to eat food sacrificed to idols. [21]I gave her time to repent, but she refuses to repent of her immorality. [22]Behold, I will throw her on a sickbed, and those who commit adultery with her I will throw into great tribulation, unless they repent of her doings; [23]and I will strike her children dead. And all the churches shall know that I am he who searches mind and heart, and I will give to each of you as your works deserve. [24]But to the rest of you in Thyatira, who do not hold this teaching, who have not learned what some call the deep things of Satan, to you I say, I do not lay upon you any other burden; [25]only hold fast what you have, until I come. [26]He who conquers and who keeps my works until the end, I will give him power over the nations, [27]and he shall rule them with a rod of iron, as when earthen pots are broken in pieces, even as I myself have received power from my Father; [28]and I will give him the morning star. [29]He who has an ear, let him hear what the Spirit says to the churches.'"

**OVERVIEW**: Thyatira means "for sacrifice," for the life of the saints is one of living sacrifice (BEDE). Yet, among the noble faithful there are some who endanger the simple by an unwarranted leniency and by allowing new, false prophecies (VICTORINUS, CAESARIUS OF ARLES). Therefore Christ addresses both those who are faithful and those who are unsteady and faithless. He who is true God and true man discerns all things and is a threat to sinners (APRINGIUS, OECUMENIUS, ANDREW OF CAESAREA), even as he is the object of immutable faith and a spiritual fragrance and ointment to those who are being saved (OECUMENIUS, ANDREW OF CAESAREA). Christ recognizes that many are devoted and do works of love toward the needy, that they increase in obedience to his commandments and that they will even suffer martyrdom (APRINGIUS, OECUMENIUS).

However, some allow a heresy to exist that tempts the simple of mind to sin and idolatry (OECUMENIUS, ANDREW OF CAESAREA). For this spiritual harlotry Christ threatens a future condemnation, unless they repent (APRINGIUS, ANDREW OF CAESAREA). For that reason he has given them a time for repentance, for Christ desires the conversion and life of the sinner (OECUMENIUS). Some, however, do not repent, for they have been given over by God to a false security that comes from the absence of temporal punishment (PRIMASIUS). By faith the church knows that such persons will receive the hidden judgment of spiritual death (TYCONIUS), since God sees not only works and words but also thoughts and intentions and inner pleasures (CYPRIAN, BEDE).

Christ exhorts those who have not turned from the truth of the church to persevere in the apostolic teaching so that God might acknowledge them (TYCONIUS, ANDREW OF CAESAREA). To those who do remain faithful, Christ promises that the church will be given the power of Christ to judge (TYCONIUS), and therefore the saints will judge the apostate angels (APRINGIUS) and the faithless who allowed themselves to be deceived (ANDREW OF CAESAREA). For like a morning star that has fallen from heaven, Satan will be trampled by the saints (OECUMENIUS). However, Christ, the true Morning Star, is himself light and is always in light (APRINGIUS). Therefore, with his coming is heralded the new day of the first resurrection in which the darkness of error and the gloom of the present life are dispelled (TYCONIUS, APRINGIUS, ANDREW OF CAESAREA).

## 2:18a *Write to the Angel of the Church in Thyatira*

**CHRISTIANS OUGHT NOT GIVE WAY TO A FALSE MERCY.** VICTORINUS OF PETOVIUM: The fourth class indicates the nobility of the faithful who do good works every day and who do greater works. But even among these the Lord shows that there are persons who too easily grant an unlawful peace and pay attention to new prophecies, and he urges and admonishes the others, to whom this is not pleasing, who know the iniquity of the adversary. And for these evils and deceptions he seeks to bring dangers upon the head of the faithful. And therefore he says, "I do not place upon you any further burden"—that is, "I have not given to you the observations and duties of the law," which is another burden—"but hold fast to that which you have, until I come. And to him who conquers, I will give power over the nations"—that is "he will be established as judge among the rest of the saints"—and "I will give to him the morning star," that is, Christ promises the first resurrection. For the morning star drives the night away and announces the light, that is, the beginning of the day. COMMENTARY ON THE APOCALYPSE 2.4.[1]

**CHRISTIAN LIFE IS A LIVING SACRIFICE.** BEDE: *Thyatira* may be translated "for sacrifice." For the saints present their bodies as a living sacrifice. EXPLANATION ON THE APOCALYPSE 2.18.[2]

## 2:18b *Who Has Eyes Like Flames and Feet Like Bronze*

**CHRIST IS RESPLENDENT IN HIS SINLESSNESS.** APRINGIUS OF BEJA: [His eyes like flames signify] his gaze which discerns all things, and [his feet like burnished bronze signify] his unstained flesh which glows, just like bronze in a fire is bright with clarity. TRACTATE ON THE APOCALYPSE 2.18.[3]

**CHRIST IS A THREAT TO SINNERS.** OECUMENIUS: "The words of the Son of God, who has eyes like flames of fire" indicates the terrifying threat against sinners, and "whose feet are as burnished bronze," denotes either the steadfast immutability of faith in him or the spiritual fragrance of the evangelical teachings. COMMENTARY ON THE APOCALYPSE 2.18-29.[4]

**CHRIST IS THE SPIRITUAL OINTMENT OF THOSE BEING SAVED.** ANDREW OF CAESAREA: The text speaks of the fiery likeness of the eyes, which signifies the illumination of the righteous and the punishment of the sinners. The feet and the burnished bronze symbolize the fragrance of Christ, the spiritual ointment, among those who are being saved.[5] They symbolize as well the undivided and unmixed unity of the divinity and humanity. For this unity, as though hardened in fire by the Holy Spirit, is incomprehensible to human reasoning. COMMENTARY ON THE APOCALYPSE 2.18.[6]

## 2:19 *I Know Your Works*

**MANY SAINTS WILL BE MARTYRED.** APRINGIUS OF BEJA: He says that he knows the work, the love, the faith, the service and the patience of his church. "And that your latter works exceed the first." He indicates that at the end of time there

---

[1]CSEL 49:38. The "new prophecies" most likely refer to Montanism. [2]CCL 121A:259. [3]CCL 107:53. [4]TEG 8:91. [5]See 2 Cor 2:15. [6]MTS 1 Sup 1:32.

will be a great number of saints, when, with the coming of the man of sin, the son of perdition, innumerable thousands of saints will be consecrated with their own blood. TRACTATE ON THE APOCALYPSE 2.19.[7]

**ONE MAY INCREASE IN OBEDIENCE.** OECUMENIUS: "I know your works and your love and your faith and your service." This is as though he said, "I praise you for your total devotion." He says, "I know," rather than "I praise," since he had said to Moses, "I know you beyond all men,"[8] and "the Lord knows the path of the righteous."[9] By "service" he means the succor which one gives to those in need. "And your latter works are more than the first." This shows that as they progressed, they improved in their obedience to the commandments. COMMENTARY ON THE APOCALYPSE 2.18-29.[10]

## 2:20-21 The Woman Jezebel

**CHRIST OPPOSES BISHOPS WHO FAIL TO DISCIPLINE SINNERS.** CAESARIUS OF ARLES: He is speaking to the leaders of the churches who fail to impose the severity of ecclesiastical discipline upon the extravagant and the fornicator and those who do whatever other kind of evil. It is possible that this also refers to heretics. "Who calls herself a prophetess," that is, a Christian, for many heresies flatter themselves with this name. EXPOSITION OF THE APOCALYPSE 2.20, HOMILY 2.[11]

**THE LORD DOES NOT WISH THE DEATH OF SINNERS.** OECUMENIUS: To show that God alone possesses perfect sinlessness, he says, "I have this against you." And what do I have [against you]? "That you have the woman, Jezebel, who calls herself a prophetess," and you do not throw her out. For in the person of Jezebel, the wife of Ahab, he sees a paradigm for the wickedness of that woman who lived at that time. And she, he says, "who calls herself a prophetess, teaches and deceives" many to commit fornication and to eat food sacrificed to idols.

He refers either to physical fornication or to that apostasy from God of which it is said, "And they committed fornication in their works,"[12] and again, "They committed adultery with wood."[13] But the Lord does not wish the death of a sinner but rather his conversion and life, and so he says that he gave to her an opportunity for repentance. But if she does not wish to repent, he says, I will do such and such to her and to those who commit adultery with her, so that all might know that it is I who am God—for it is the prerogative of God to search minds and the hearts. For it is said, "It is God who searches the heart and mind." But, indeed, to those who have nothing in common with that adulterous woman, that is, those who are more simple and do not know the deceitful crafts of the evil one—for this is what you say—upon you I will place no greater burden, for your simplicity suffices. Only hold fast the teaching which has been handed over to you until my second coming. COMMENTARY ON THE APOCALYPSE 2.18-29.[14]

**HERESY CANNOT BE ALLOWED TO DECEIVE THE SIMPLE.** ANDREW OF CAESAREA: Although on account of [your] faithfulness and your service for those in need I acknowledge your piety and your endurance, nonetheless I rightly blame you, because you allow the heresy of the Nicolaitans to exist openly. This heresy is figuratively called "Jezebel" because of its impiety and licentiousness. Because of this [heresy] my servants, through their simplicity of mind, are presented with a stone of stumbling and are drawn toward idolatrous practices from which they had [previously] fled. You must curb this [heresy], because it deceitfully calls herself a prophetess, being moved by an evil spirit. COMMENTARY ON THE APOCALYPSE 2.19-20.[15]

---

[7]CCL 107:53. [8]Ex 33:12. [9]Ps 1:6. [10]TEG 8:92. [11]PL 35:2421. [12]Ps 106:39 (105:39 LXX). [13]Jer 3:9. [14]TEG 8:91-93. [15]MTS 1 Sup 1:32. Epiphanius believes these verses refer to the female Montanist prophetesses Priscilla, Maximilla and Quintilla (*Panarion* 2.4.33).

## 2:21 I *Will Throw Her on a Sickbed*

**THE UNREPENTANT WILL RECEIVE JUDGMENT.** APRINGIUS OF BEJA: The Lord promises that a sickness and a weariness will come to this doctrine, and a weakness of the sickbed, that is, the pleasure of this world. And to those who commit adultery through this teaching, he promises that a very great tribulation will come upon them on the Day of Judgment. For Jezebel herself is interpreted as "dung heap" or a "flowing of blood." What else is thought to be in the filth of a dung heap or in blood, unless the evil deed and sin which is committed through fault? Therefore, rightly does he foretell a future condemnation for them, unless they strongly repent of their works. For he also mentions that he will damn her sons, that is, her disciples with the second death. TRACTATE ON THE APOCALYPSE 2.22.[16]

**GOD SOMETIMES GIVES A FALSE SECURITY TO SINNERS.** PRIMASIUS: The bed here is to be understood as that security which sinners often promise to themselves when they have committed disgraceful crimes with impunity. That is, sinners at times do not experience the vengeance of present wrath and so neglect penance until sudden destruction comes upon them like the pain of childbirth and they are not able to escape. They are said to be given over by God to this neglectfulness that this security produces, for they are abandoned to a hidden, although not unjust, judgment. We read of such security also elsewhere: "The little ones are killed by their turning away, and the prosperity of the foolish will destroy them."[17] Another translation renders "mourning" for "bed," whereby is designated the eternal misery that awaits those who do not repent from their works. COMMENTARY ON THE APOCALYPSE 2.22.[18]

**UNION WITH HERETICS IS A SPIRITUAL HARLOTRY.** ANDREW OF CAESAREA: He continues to speak figuratively and compares the union with heretics to that with a harlot, and he threatens to throw her into sickness and death as well as those who have become defiled with her and have committed fornication before God, unless they should turn to him through repentance. COMMENTARY ON THE APOCALYPSE 2.22-23.[19]

## 2:23 I *Will Strike the Children Dead*

**GOD SEES INTO OUR MIND AND WILL.** CYPRIAN: One will not escape and avoid God as his judge, for the Holy Spirit says in the Psalms, "Thine eyes have seen my imperfection and all will be written in thy book,"[20] and again, "Man looks upon the face, but God upon the heart."[21] Let the Lord himself also forewarn and instruct you with these words: "And all the churches shall know that I am he who searches the desires and hearts." He perceives the concealed and the secret and considers the hidden, nor can anyone evade the eyes of God, who says, "Am I a God at hand, and not a God afar off? Shall a man be hid in secret places and I not see him?"[22] He sees the hearts and breasts of each one, and, when about to pass judgment not only on our deeds but also on our words and thoughts, he looks into the minds and the wills conceived in the very recess of a still closed heart. THE LAPSED 27.[23]

**SINNERS WILL DIE A SPIRITUAL DEATH.** TYCONIUS: How is it that before God hands over adulterers to death the churches do not know that God is he who searches mind and heart? How is it that the church is said to know at the end of things and not at the beginning of her faith that God knows all secrets? When he said, "all the churches will know," he was not saying that the church would know only after the event but that the church knows from faith. For the words "I will kill" do not refer to that death that is visible but to spiritual death. Just as his revenge on the mother specifically would become visible, so

---

[16]CCL 107:53-54. [17]See Prov 1:32. [18]CCL 92:34. [19]MTS 1 Sup 1:33. [20]See Ps 139:16 (138:16 LXX). [21]1 Sam 16:7. [22]Jer 23:23-24. [23]FC 36:80-81*.

he here promises that among all the churches it would become clear that the children of the woman, that is, those born of the same spirit, were subject to spiritual death, although they were not [visibly] delivered over to it. David also made this distinction between the particular and the general when he fought Goliath. He said, "I will kill you and all the earth will know that there is a God in Israel."[24] . . . Then he adds the particular when he says, "And all this assembly will know that the Lord saves his people not with sword and spear."[25] He said "all this assembly" because there were persons there who doubted that David could prevail against Goliath. To be sure, there were also spiritual persons who believed that he would defeat [Goliath] in the name of God. Those among whom this event occurred in their presence saw with their own eyes, not by faith. However, through faith we see God at work today, not as they did but in a marvelous way. And so, as with Goliath we see the children of Jezebel, who do not want to be subject to the truth, punished with death. We recognize from the phraseology [of the text] itself that in her children the Lord signifies the woman's posterity. For he threatened the mother with a temporal punishment that he might hand her over to eternal sorrows. However, he did not say, "I kill the children with the sword" but "I will slay them with death." COMMENTARY ON THE APOCALYPSE 2.23.[26]

**THE SINS OF FORNICATION AND IDOLATRY EXIST IN EVEN SMALL SINS.** BEDE: Our works and our words may be made known to people, but what is their intention and what we wish to accomplish through them, only the Lord knows who sees what anyone thinks and in what he takes pleasure. And for what purpose is he who punishes fornication and idolatry, which are manifest sins, said to be one who knows hidden secrets, unless these sins are contained even in the least of transgressions? "You will destroy," he says, "all who commit fornication from you."[27] And when he was discussing about false brothers,

the same apostle John, who had heard this, ended by saying, "Little children, keep yourselves from idols."[28] EXPLANATION OF THE APOCALYPSE 2.23.[29]

### 2:24-25 Hold Fast What You Have

**GOD WILL NOT ACKNOWLEDGE SINNERS.** TYCONIUS: To be sure, the Lord speaks to those who kept their minds from the doctrines of the devil, lest they turn from the dogma of the truth of the church. For they were taught that they should follow no man but rather the truth of the faith, for the Lord said to those who had left the faith, "I never knew you, you evildoers."[30] For just as those who do iniquity do not know God, although they speak of him, so also God does not acknowledge the workers of iniquity, although he knows them all. In this way, the righteous do not know the teaching of Satan, although they might hear it and feel the attraction of his temptations. And so it can happen that the righteous do not hear evil things from which they abstain by righteous living, since it is written, "There must be heresies so that those who are genuine among you may be recognized."[31] And again, "Should they say to you, Lo, Christ is in the inner rooms, do not believe it."[32] COMMENTARY ON THE APOCALYPSE 2.24.[33]

**CHRIST EXHORTS THE SIMPLE TO FAITHFULNESS.** ANDREW OF CAESAREA: To the more simple, the Lord says, "Since on account of your simplicity you are not able to withstand those who are evil and have a facility with words," namely, that you do not know "the deep things of Satan," as you call it, I will not expect from you any war through words, but only that you preserve the teaching which you received until I remove you from there. COMMENTARY ON THE APOCALYPSE 2.24-25.[34]

---

[24]1 Sam 17:46. [25]1 Sam 17:47. [26]TS 2 7:52-53 §§20-23. [27]Ps 73:27 (72:27 LXX). [28]1 Jn 5:21. [29]CCL 121A:161-63. [30]Mt 7:23. [31]See 1 Cor 11:19. [32]Mt 24:26. [33]TS 2 7:54-55 §§29-31. [34]MTS 1 Sup 1:34.

### 2:26-27 *Ruling with a Rod of Iron*

**THE CHURCH POSSESSES WHAT THE SON OF MAN RECEIVED.** TYCONIUS: The church has this power in Christ. Whoever holds fast to his body will be co-heir with the Lord and will have whatever the Son of man received, for "he has given us all things with him."[35] COMMENTARY ON THE APOCALYPSE 2.26-27.[36]

**THE SAINTS WILL JUDGE THE FALLEN ANGELS.** APRINGIUS OF BEJA: God promises that he will give to him power over the nations and kingdoms, so that he might reign over them with an iron rod and destroy them as though they were a clay pot. He refers to the apostate angels who abandoned their own dominion, for they are going to be judged by the saints on the day of judgment and damned and thrown into eternal destruction, as the apostle says.[37] TRACTATE ON THE APOCALYPSE 2.26-27.[38]

**THE BELIEVERS WILL JUDGE THE UNFAITHFUL.** ANDREW OF CAESAREA: "To him who does my works," the Lord says, "I will give authority over five or ten cities," as he said in the Gospel.[39] Or, this passage refers to the judgment of the unfaithful, through which the deceived will be crushed, as though beaten with a rod of iron, and will be judged by those who have believed in Christ. "The men of Nineveh will rise and condemn this generation."[40] The words "as I myself received from the Father" refer to his human nature, which he assumed through the flesh. COMMENTARY ON THE APOCALYPSE 2.26-27.[41]

### 2:28 *The Morning Star*

**THE COMING OF CHRIST SCATTERS THE DARKNESS OF ERROR.** TYCONIUS: It is appropriate that we understand the morning star to represent both Christ and the first resurrection, because his appearance scatters the darkness of error and the worldly shadows of the night are put to flight by the approaching resurrection. For,

as this star brings an end to the night, so also does it mark the beginning of the day. COMMENTARY ON THE APOCALYPSE 2.28.[42]

**JESUS CHRIST IS ETERNAL LIGHT.** APRINGIUS OF BEJA: "And I will give him the morning star," that is, the Lord Jesus Christ, whom evening never overtakes, but who is eternal light, and who is himself always in light. Or, another interpretation: He promises the morning star, namely, the first resurrection; [the resurrection is] the morning star which causes night to flee and announces the light. TRACTATE ON THE APOCALYPSE 2.28.[43]

**SATAN WILL FALL INTO SUBJECTION TO THE SAINTS.** OECUMENIUS: "And I will give him the morning star." It speaks of the Assyrian, namely, of Satan, of whom the prophet speaks, saying, "How has the Day Star, he who rises in the morning, fallen from heaven."[44] And even now the Lord calls him the "Morning Star." And so, he says, I will make Satan to be subject to my servants. The apostle also made a similar statement: "God will trample Satan quickly under your feet."[45] And in another place it says, "You will tread upon the lion and the asp, and you will trample upon the lion and the serpent."[46] COMMENTARY ON THE APOCALYPSE 2.18-29.[47]

**CHRIST IS THE SUN OF RIGHTEOUSNESS.** ANDREW OF CAESAREA: By *morning star* he means either that one of whom Isaiah spoke: "How have you fallen from heaven, O Day Star, O Morning Star?"[48] and of whom it is promised that he will be "crushed under the feet of the saints,"[49] or the Lord means that one of whom the blessed Peter speaks, of the "morning star who rises in the hearts of the faithful,"[50] clearly meaning the illumination of Christ. Both John the Baptist and Elijah the Tishbite were called light bringers. For

---

[35]Rom 8:32. [36]TS 2 7:57 §§37-39. [37]Cf. 2 Thess 1:9; Rev 12:10. [38]CCL 107:54. [39]Lk 19:17. [40]Mt 12:41. [41]MTS 1 Sup 1:34. [42]CCL 92:36. [43]CCL 107:54. [44]Is 14:12. [45]Rom 16:20. [46]Ps 91:13 (90:13 LXX). [47]TEG 8:93. [48]Is 14:12. [49]Rom 16:20. [50]2 Pet 1:19.

the one foretold of the first rising of the "sun of righteousness," and the other is known as the forerunner of the second [rising]. And after these, we believe that those who have conquered the devil will receive their inheritance. Nor is it surprising that we should interpret this in so opposite a fashion. For we learn from the Holy Scriptures that the "lion" from Judah is Christ, while the "lion" from Bashan is the antichrist, the same image signifying both. And so is noted the rising of the coming day, in which the darkness of the present life will be hidden, and the angel proclaims this. For this precedes the "sun of righteousness" which will shine upon the saints and dispel the gloom of the present life, by whose rays may also we be made bright, by the good pleasure of the Father with the all-holy Spirit, to whom be glory forever. Amen. COMMENTARY ON THE APOCALYPSE 2.28-29.[51]

---

[51]MTS 1 Sup 1:34-35.

---

# 3:1-6 TO THE ANGEL OF THE CHURCH IN SARDIS

[1]"And to the angel of the church in Sardis write: 'The words of him who has the seven spirits of God and the seven stars.

"'I know your works; you have the name of being alive, and you are dead. [2]Awake, and strengthen what remains and is on the point of death, for I have not found your works perfect in the sight of my God. [3]Remember then what you received and heard; keep that, and repent. If you will not awake, I will come like a thief, and you will not know at what hour I will come upon you. [4]Yet you have still a few names in Sardis, people who have not soiled their garments; and they shall walk with me in white, for they are worthy. [5]He who conquers shall be clad thus in white garments, and I will not blot his name out of the book of life; I will confess his name before my Father and before his angels. [6]He who has an ear, let him hear what the Spirit says to the churches.'"

**OVERVIEW**: Christ, who as true God gives the Spirit (ANDREW OF CAESAREA), addresses the church at Sardis, where some bear the name of Christian but are empty of good works (VICTORINUS). While one may seem to be alive in bearing the name of Christian, those enslaved to sin are in fact dead (OECUMENIUS). Especially the bishop lacks diligence in the discipline of evildoers, and therefore, although he might seem to be guiltless, he will be regarded as dead unless he strives to enliven those under his care (BEDE). Likewise, there are those who are called Christian but who do not trust Christ and do not hold the correct faith. They too are as though dead, and therefore they are called to repentance of past sins and to the remembrance of the apostolic doctrine (APRINGIUS). If such repentance is not forthcoming, Christ will come to judge suddenly, like a thief. For those who are prepared, judgment will be the end of earthly toil, but for the rest it will be spiritual death (ANDREW OF CAESAREA). Yet there are still some, whom Christ knows by name

(BEDE), who walk with Christ in the whiteness of the purity of the body (APRINGIUS, OECUMENIUS). Those who conquer by preserving the sanctity of their flesh will be clothed with the resurrection of the flesh (TERTULLIAN) and with the white robe of eternal life (OECUMENIUS). This will occur to those who keep their baptism without blemish (BEDE). Christ will also confess such saints as faithful servants before his Father and before his angels (OECUMENIUS).

### 3:1a Write to the Angel of the Church in Sardis

**CHRISTIANS IN NAME ONLY ARE IN DANGER OF DEATH.** VICTORINUS OF PETOVIUM: This fifth class, group or manner of saint refers to those persons who are negligent and behave in a manner other than what they ought in the world, who are vacuous in works and who are only Christian in name. And therefore he exhorts them so that in some way they might reverse themselves from this dangerous negligence and be saved. "Strengthen," he says, "that which is in danger of death. I have not found your work perfect before my God." For it is not sufficient that a tree live but yet not give fruit. Neither is it sufficient that one be called a Christian, confess himself to be a Christian, and yet not do the works of a Christian. COMMENTARY ON THE APOCALYPSE 3.1.[1]

**A BISHOP MUST BE VIGILANT.** BEDE: He says that the angel, that is, the bishop, exercises insufficient diligence in the correction of evil people. Nonetheless, he commends him for having some who walk in white garments, and to these the name of "Sardis" corresponds, namely, "precious stone." ... Indeed, you seem to yourself to be alive, but unless you are vigilant in the correction of the wicked, you will be regarded as already among the dead.... Even though he might seem to people to be guiltless, the works of a ruler are not perfect before God if he does not strive to enliven also others. EXPLANATION OF THE APOCALYPSE 3.1-2.[2]

### 3:1b The Seven Spirits; the Seven Stars

**CHRIST GOVERNS THE ANGELS AND SUPPLIES THE SPIRIT.** ANDREW OF CAESAREA: We have said before that the "seven stars" are divine angels. The "seven spirits" are either the selfsame angels or they are the energies of the life-giving Spirit. Either way, both are in the hand of Christ, for he governs the former as Lord, and as the ὁμοούσιος[3] he is the supplier of the Spirit. COMMENTARY ON THE APOCALYPSE 3.1.[4]

### 3:1c I Know Your Works

**IN SINS, ONE IS DEAD; IN FAITH, ONE IS ALIVE.** OECUMENIUS: I have discussed above the seven stars which he here calls the "spirits of God." But now we must listen to what he says concerning those who live in Sardis. "I know your works," he says, that you possess a name as though you were living a life virtuous in the sight of God, but "you are dead" in sins. For in the holy Scriptures, it is customary that those snared in sins are called "dead," as, for example, in this passage from the most wise Paul concerning those who have passed from disbelief to faith in Christ: "And you, although dead in trespasses, he made alive together with Christ."[5] Likewise, the *Shepherd* says that those who go down into the water of baptism are "dead," but those who come up are "living."[6] COMMENTARY ON THE APOCALYPSE 3.1-6.[7]

### 3:2-3 Be Vigilant, Remember, Obey and Repent

**REPENT OR BE JUDGED.** APRINGIUS OF BEJA: He rebukes those idle persons who do not trust in God with the whole mind and keep the right faith only hypocritically. They are Christians in name only. And so they are said to be living, but

---

[1]CSEL 49:40. [2]CCL 121A:265. Bede follows Tyconius in believing the bishops are addressed in these verses. [3]One who is of one substance with the Father. [4]MTS 1 Sup 1:36. [5]Eph 2:5. [6]*Shepherd of Hermas* 3.9.16 (ANF 2:49). [7]TEG 8:94.

in fact they are dead. For that reason they are rebuked that they might be vigilant and strengthen what remains of that from which they had fallen. And so he urges them, "Remember what you received and heard, and repent." He wishes that they remember the apostolic doctrine, and he warns them to preserve that which they received at the beginning of their faith and to repent of their past sins. And so he threatens whomever does not do this, "If you will not be vigilant, I will come like a thief, and you will not know at what hour I will come upon you." The judgment of God will be sudden, and no one knows the secret hour when he intends to come. TRACTATE ON THE APOCALYPSE 3.2-3.[8]

**LIKE A THIEF.** ANDREW OF CAESAREA: "I will come like a thief." This is reasonably written. For neither the death of any individual nor the common consummation[9] is known to anyone. To those who are prepared, it will be the cessation of toil; however, to those who are unprepared, like a "thief" he will bring on spiritual death. COMMENTARY ON THE APOCALYPSE 3.3.[10]

### 3:4 A Faithful Few

**GOD KNOWS HIS SHEEP BY NAME.** BEDE: He did not say a "few," but a "few names." For he who knew Moses by name calls his own sheep by name and writes the names of his saints in heaven. EXPLANATION OF THE APOCALYPSE 3.4.[11]

**WALKING WITH THE LORD.** APRINGIUS OF BEJA: Everyone who is not soiled with the filth of sin walks with the Lord in white, and he is made worthy so that he might follow the footsteps of the Lamb. TRACTATE ON THE APOCALYPSE 3.4.[12]

**SAINTS WALK IN THE PURITY OF THE BODY.** OECUMENIUS: By the garments that have not been soiled he means the bodies of the saints, just as the patriarch Jacob said, "He will wash his robe in wine."[13] And Isaiah said much the same thing: "Why is your garment red as one who

treads in the wine press, as of one who has completely trodden [the wine press]."[14] And so the white garment signifies the purity of the body. COMMENTARY ON THE APOCALYPSE 3.1-6.[15]

### 3:5 Clothed in White Robes

**THE RESURRECTION OF THE FLESH IS THE ROBE OF HOPE.** TERTULLIAN: We have also in the Scriptures robes mentioned as allegorizing the hope of the flesh. Thus in the Revelation of John it is said, "These are they who have not defiled their clothes with women"[16]—indicating, of course, virgins, and such as have become "eunuchs for the kingdom of heaven's sake."[17] Therefore they shall be "clothed in white raiment," that is, in the bright beauty of the unwedded flesh. In the Gospel even, "the wedding garment" may be regarded as the sanctity of the flesh.[18] And so, when Isaiah tells us what sort of "fast the Lord has chosen," he adds a statement about the reward of good works. He says, "Then shall your light break forth as the morning, and your garments shall speedily arise,"[19] where he has not thought of cloaks or clothing, but means the rising of flesh, of which he declared the resurrection, after its fall in death. ON THE RESURRECTION OF THE FLESH 27.[20]

**THOSE WHO CONQUER THEIR PASSIONS.** OECUMENIUS: "He who conquers" the passions will wear white robes in the age to come, for he has promised in the Gospels that the saints will shine as the sun and the moon. The pure, he says, will be inscribed in the book of the living, for that blessed and eternal life. COMMENTARY ON THE APOCALYPSE 3.1-6.[21]

**WE ARE CALLED TO PRESERVE THE ROBE OF BAPTISM.** BEDE: He calls all to the imitation of those who have preserved the silken robe of bap-

---

[8]CCL 107:55. [9]That is, the general resurrection. [10]MTS 1 Sup 1:37. [11]CCL 121A:267. [12]CCL 107:55. [13]Gen 49:11. [14]Is 63:2. [15]TEG 8:95. [16]Cf. Rev 14:4. [17]Mt 19:12. [18]Mt 22:11-12. [19]Is 58:8. [20]ANF 3:564-65*. [21]TEG 8:95.

tism without blemish. EXPLANATION OF THE APOCALYPSE 3.5.[22]

**THE ANGELS BELONG ALSO TO CHRIST.** OECU-MENIUS: "And I will confess your name before my Father and his angels." He will confess them as his faithful servants and as house slaves who are well-disposed [toward their master], for indeed also in the Gospels he says that whosoever should confess "me before men, him will I also confess before my Father who is in heaven."[23] And that he

speaks of the Father and his angels does not suggest that the holy angels are not also his. For at times he speaks of the angels as the Father's, and at other times he speaks of them as his. For he says in Matthew: "Then the Son of man will send his angels with a loud trumpet sound, and they will gather his elect from the four winds, from one end of heaven to the other."[24] COMMENTARY ON THE APOCALYPSE 3.1-6.[25]

[22]CCL 121A:267. [23]Mt 10:32. [24]Mt 24:31. [25]TEG 8:95.

# 3:7-13 TO THE ANGEL OF THE CHURCH IN PHILADELPHIA

[7]"And to the angel of the church in Philadelphia write: 'The words of the holy one, the true one, who has the key of David, who opens and no one shall shut, who shuts and no one opens.

[8]"'I know your works. Behold, I have set before you an open door, which no one is able to shut; I know that you have but little power, and yet you have kept my word and have not denied my name. [9]Behold, I will make those of the synagogue of Satan who say that they are Jews and are not, but lie—behold, I will make them come and bow down before your feet, and learn that I have loved you. [10]Because you have kept my word of patient endurance, I will keep you from the hour of trial which is coming on the whole world, to try those who dwell upon the earth. [11]I am coming soon; hold fast what you have, so that no one may seize your crown. [12]He who conquers, I will make him a pillar in the temple of my God; never shall he go out of it, and I will write on him the name of my God, and the name of the city of my God, the new Jerusalem which comes down from my God out of heaven, and my own new name. [13]He who has an ear, let him hear what the Spirit says to the churches.'"

**OVERVIEW:** Christ promises to love his church, for Philadelphia means "brotherly love" (BEDE). In this church, the Christians represent the highest form of saintly life, humility and steadfastness even in temptation (VICTORINUS). The Christ who addresses this church is holy and true, for he is sinless and truly is God and man (OECUMENIUS). Christ possesses "the key of David," for he is both the son of David and the one foretold by

David (TYCONIUS). As the one with David's key, Christ rules over physical and spiritual Israel (OECUMENIUS) and reveals through the Holy Spirit the secrets of the law and the psalms (TYCONIUS, ANDREW OF CAESAREA). Through the use of this key, Christ opens and closes, for he reveals the secrets of the law to the faithful alone (PRIMASIUS), judges the hypocrites (TYCONIUS) and in the Holy Spirit gives the power both to speak and to understand (GREGORY THAUMATURGUS).

The preaching of the gospel is an open door throughout the world through which all may enter (TYCONIUS). Those who are faithful to the gospel may have little power, yet they possess strength in their confidence and faith in Christ (OECUMENIUS, PRIMASIUS). Indeed, many who now live in unbelief, especially the Jews, will at the end be gathered from the whole world into the church (TYCONIUS, OECUMENIUS). In the meantime, Christ will deliver his church from every kind of trial and persecution (TYCONIUS, ANDREW OF CAESAREA). Therefore, all the faithful, even confessors, should be aware of the snares of the devil, lest they fall (CYPRIAN). However, God has fixed the number of the elect, so that should someone fall away, another will take his or her crown (AUGUSTINE). But those who retain their love for the Lord and receive the crown of life will see God (OECUMENIUS) and adorn the church now and forever (BEDE). Unlike schismatics who leave the church, those who persevere in love to the end will never go out of the church. Rather, these will possess the new name of Christian, for the Son of man has died, was raised and is ascended (TYCONIUS). These will have eternally the name of the new Jerusalem and immortality (APRINGIUS) and receive blessings which are so sublime that they have never been named anywhere (OECUMENIUS).

### 3:7a Write to the Angel of the Church in Philadelphia

**HUMILITY, SIMPLICITY, STEADFAST FAITH.** VICTORINUS OF PETOVIUM: This sixth class represents the highest manner of life of the elect saints, namely, of those who are humble in the world and are untutored in the Scriptures but hold steadfastly to the faith and in no way withdraw from the faith out of fear. To these he says, "I have set before you an open door," and he further says, "For you have kept the word of my patience"—with such little strength—"and I will save you from the hour of temptation." And that

they might know his glory in this manner, he does not permit them to be handed over into temptation. "He who conquers," he says, "he will become a pillar in the temple of God." A pillar is a decoration of a building, and so he who perseveres will obtain a nobility in the church. COMMENTARY ON THE APOCALYPSE 3.2.[1]

**THE LORD PROMISES TO LOVE HIS CHURCH.** BEDE: Philadelphia is interpreted "brotherly love," and to [that church] is opened the door of the kingdom and he promises that she will be loved by the Lord. EXPLANATION OF THE APOCALYPSE 3.7.[2]

### 3:7b The Holy One, the True One

**CHRIST IS SINLESS, TRUE GOD AND TRUE MAN.** OECUMENIUS: The Holy One is the Son of God. And the seraphim bear witness to this when they ascribe the threefold holiness to the one lordship, as though he possesses nothing earthly nor sinful, and even though the Word became flesh, "He did not sin, nor was any guile found in his mouth," as the prophet Isaiah says.[3] He is said to be "true," for he is, and he truly is what he is said to be. He is said to be God, and the title is not false, for he is truly God, Immanuel, even though the accursed Nestorius does not agree to this. He became man, not because he ceased to be God, but he is truly man, even though Eutyches, hated by God, is displeased with this claim. What he is, he is truly, and there is nothing concerning him which is by way of mere ascription, as the Nestorians say, nor is there anything which is mere appearance and fantasy, as the Eutychians would have it, and also that accursed and despicable race of Manichaeans. COMMENTARY ON THE APOCALYPSE 3.7-13.[4]

### 3:7c The Key of David

**CHRIST IS FROM DAVID.** TYCONIUS: "Who has

---

[1]CSEL 49:40-42. [2]CCL 121A:267. [3]Is 53:9. [4]TEG 8:96-97.

the key of David," that is, royal authority. He says "the key of David" either because Christ was born from his family or because David himself foretold many things concerning Christ. Through the dispensation of Christ, as though by a key, the secrets of the law and of the prophets and of the psalms were made manifest. Christ himself attests to this when he says, "Everything written about me in the law of Moses and the prophets and the psalms must be fulfilled."[5] COMMENTARY ON THE APOCALYPSE 3.7.[6]

**CHRIST HAS THE THRONE OF DAVID.** OECUMENIUS: Since the key signifies the authority, when he says, "he who has the key of David," it is clear that just as David ruled the physical Israel, so in addition to the physical Israel, I also rule the spiritual Israel. However, to be sure, the distinction of authority differs by an incomparable superiority. For, what equality does humankind have with God? And this good news the holy angel, Gabriel, spoke to the Virgin concerning the Lord: "And the Lord God will give to him the throne of David, his father, and he will rule over the house of Jacob forever; and of his kingdom there will be no end."[7] Therefore, since Christ possessed a likeness to the reign of David, it is appropriate that he speak of "him who has the key of David." COMMENTARY ON THE APOCALYPSE 3.7-13.[8]

**THE HOLY SPIRIT OPENS THE TREASURES OF KNOWLEDGE.** ANDREW OF CAESAREA: His kingdom is called "the key of David," for this is a symbol of authority. And, moreover, the Holy Spirit is the key of the book of the Psalms and of every prophecy, for through him the treasures of knowledge are opened. He received the first key according to his humanity, but the second key he possesses according to his deity, which has no beginning. Since in some of the copies there is written "hades" instead of "David," through the image of the "key of hades" the authority of life and death is ascribed to Christ. COMMENTARY ON THE APOCALYPSE 3.7.[9]

## 3:7d Who Opens and No One Shuts

**THE POWER OF SPEAKING AND OF UNDERSTANDING.** GREGORY THAUMATURGUS: These things, moreover, as I judge, he gives forth only and truly by participation in the divine Spirit. There is need of the same power for those who prophesy and for those who hear the prophets. No one can rightly hear a prophet unless the same Spirit who prophesies bestows on him the capacity of grasping his words. And this principle is expressed indeed in the holy Scriptures themselves when it is said that only he who shuts opens, and no other one whatever;[10] and what is shut is opened when that word of inspiration explains mysteries. ORATION AND PANEGYRIC ADDRESSED TO ORIGEN 15.[11]

**CHRIST CLOSES THE DOOR OF LIFE TO HYPOCRITES.** TYCONIUS: "Who opens and no one shall shut, who shuts and no one opens." It is evident that Christ opens [the door] to those who knock, but to hypocrites who knock and say, "Lord, Lord open to us,"[12] he closes the door of life and says to them, "I do not know from where you come; I never knew you, you evildoers."[13] COMMENTARY ON THE APOCALYPSE 3.7.[14]

**CHRIST ALONE OPENS THE SECRETS OF THE LAW.** PRIMASIUS: The secrets of the divine law are disclosed to the faithful by the power of Christ alone, and they are closed to the unbelievers. However, when he loosens, no one shuts, and when he binds, no one loosens. COMMENTARY ON THE APOCALYPSE 3.7.[15]

## 3:8a An Open Door

**THE DOOR OF THE CHURCH.** TYCONIUS: He had said before, "who opens and no one shuts,"

---

[5]Lk 24:44. [6]CCL 92:38. [7]Lk 1:32-33. [8]TEG 8:97. [9]MTS 1 Sup 1:38. [10]Is 22:22. [11]ANF 6:36*. [12]Mt 25:11. [13]Mt 7:23. [14]TS 2 7:63 §§59-60. [15]CCL 92:38.

lest anyone say that the door of the church, which God opens in the whole world, can be closed by anyone in some part of the world. COMMENTARY ON THE APOCALYPSE 3.8.[16]

**CHRIST WILL PRESERVE THE PREACHING OF APOSTOLIC DOCTRINE.** TYCONIUS: The door, which Christ opened, he then began to reveal to the church when he opened the mind of his disciples so that they might understand the Scriptures.[17] This door is never shut, by the power or the effort of anyone, which is already opened to those who preach to the whole world. For this reason the apostle says, "A wide door has opened for us in the Lord, and there are many adversaries."[18] COMMENTARY ON THE APOCALYPSE 3.8.[19]

### 3:8b You Have Little Power

**FAITH KEEPS STRONG THOSE WHO LIVE AMONG THE FAITHLESS.** OECUMENIUS: Philadelphia was a small city and thereby possessed little power. Nonetheless, by keeping the faith of Christ, it rose above its own strength, as one undaunted to live among those who trouble the faithful. Then, as a reward for their genuineness to him, he promises that many on the Jewish registry will come to her and accept the faith in Christ. For this is what it means for them to worship at her feet, namely, in the last days to choose to be enrolled in the church, that is, to be a part of the church. And the prophet also joyfully spoke of this: "I have chosen to be thrown aside in the house of my God, rather than to dwell in the tents of sinners."[20] COMMENTARY ON THE APOCALYPSE 3.7-13.[21]

**TRUE STRENGTH IS IN THE POWER OF CHRIST.** PRIMASIUS: He shows the reason why the church has merited these gifts: because she does not have confidence in her own powers but in the power of Christ the king. And confessing that she has but little power, she is glorified, having been redeemed not in herself but in the Lord. COMMENTARY ON THE APOCALYPSE 3.8.[22]

### 3:9 Bowing Before Your Feet

**GOD WILL GATHER ALSO JEWS.** TYCONIUS: "Behold, those from the synagogue of Satan who say that they are Jews and are not, but lie: behold, I will make them come and bow down before your feet, and learn that I have loved you." At that time he promised to the universal church that there will be "one flock and one Shepherd."[23] We should note that it was not only in Philadelphia that there were believers from the synagogue of the Jews, as we find recorded in the Acts of the Apostles. . . . He said to the second angel, "You have the slander of those who say that they are Jews and are not."[24] Nevertheless, he did not promise that there would be some who would come from them, that is, [fall] at the feet of the body of Christ. We believe that this will happen everywhere, since God will command his church to be gathered from the whole world. Therefore, to the sixth angel, that is the one before the last, he promised what he had indicated to the others without any promise. And so he foretells to the sixth angel what will happen before the final end, that the unbelieving will come as suppliants to the church of God. COMMENTARY ON THE APOCALYPSE 3.9.[25]

### 3:10 Kept from the Hour of Trial

**CHRIST WILL DELIVER THE CHURCH.** TYCONIUS: Although the church is constantly put to the test by both internal and external conflict, and either individuals partially or the whole generally are attacked by various temptations, yet the hour of temptation may also refer to the time of the antichrist who will come in the future. From this hour Christ the Lord promises that he will free every church that remains firm in his [commandments], so that the temptation to ruin

---

[16]TS 2 7:63 §62. Tyconius is speaking against the Donatists. [17]Lk 24:45. [18]1 Cor 16:9. [19]CCL 92.39. [20]Ps 83:11 LXX. [21]TEG 8:98. [22]CCL 92.39. [23]Jn 10:16. [24]Rev 2:9. [25]TS 2 7:64-66 §§65, 67-69. [26]CCL 92.40.

might be recognized to be a deception. COMMENTARY ON THE APOCALPSE 3.10.[26]

**CHRIST WILL NOT ALLOW THE FAITHFUL TO BE TEMPTED BEYOND ENDURANCE.** ANDREW OF CAESAREA: By the "hour of trial" he speaks either of the persecution against the Christians which occurred almost immediately by those who ruled Rome at that time, from which he promised that the church would be freed, or he speaks of the universal coming of the antichrist against the faithful at the end of time. From this coming he pledges to free those who are zealous, for they will beforehand be seized upward by a departure from there, lest they be tempted beyond what they are able [to endure]. COMMENTARY ON THE APOCALYPSE 3.10-11.[27]

## 3:11 Hold Fast

**HOLD FAST TO RIGHTEOUSNESS.** CYPRIAN: For confession [of Christ] does not make one immune from the snares of the devil. Nor does it defend one who is still placed in the world with a perpetual security against worldly temptations and dangers and onsets and attacks. Otherwise we should never have seen afterwards among the confessors the deceptions and debaucheries and adulteries that now with groaning and sorrow we see among some. Whoever that confessor is, he is not greater or better or dearer to God than Solomon. As long as he walked in the ways of the Lord, so long he retained the grace he had received from the Lord. After he had abandoned the way of the Lord, he lost also the grace of the Lord. And so it is written, "Hold what you have, lest another receive thy crown." Surely the Lord would not threaten to deprive of the crown of righteousness unless when righteousness parts, it is necessary that also the crown depart. THE UNITY OF THE CHURCH 20.[28]

**THE NUMBER OF THE ELECT IS FIXED.** AUGUSTINE: I have said all this about those who have been predestined to the kingdom of God, whose number is so fixed that not one can be added to it or taken from it. I have not been speaking of those who, although he had declared and spoken, have been called but not chosen, because they were not called according to his purpose. The fact that the number of the elect is fixed, not to be increased or diminished, is suggested even by John the Baptist, where he says, "Bring forth therefore fruit befitting repentance. And do not think to say to yourselves, 'We have Abraham for our father.' For I say to you that God is able out of these stones to raise up children to Abraham."[29] The words show that those who do not bring forth fruit are to be cut off, in such a way, however, that the number [of children] promised to Abraham will not fall short. However, it is more openly declared in the Apocalypse: "Hold fast what you have, that no one receive your crown." For if another is not to receive a crown, unless someone first lose it, the number is fixed. ADMONITION AND GRACE 13.39.[30]

**GAINING THE CROWN OF LIFE.** OECUMENIUS: "Hold fast what you have, so that no one may take your crown." And what is it which you hold fast? Clearly one's genuine love for the Lord, in which, should one contend unto the end, he will obtain the crown of life. For the victors' prizes go only to those who remain to the end. COMMENTARY ON THE APOCALYPSE 3.7-13.[31]

## 3:12a A Pillar in the Temple of God

**THE ONE WHO CONQUERS WILL SEE GOD.** OECUMENIUS: And I will make him who conquers temptations to rejoice always in the vision of God, for this is what it means to become a pillar of the divine temple. COMMENTARY ON THE APOCALYPSE 3.7-13.[32]

**THOSE WHO PERSEVERE.** BEDE: Whoever has conquered adversity for my sake will be glorious in

---

[27]MTS 1 Sup 1:40. [28]FC 36:115*. [29]Mt 3:8-9. [30]FC 2:293*. [31]TEG 8:98-99. [32]TEG 8:99.

the temple of the church and will never fear any further loss from adversity. These pillars, that is, holy men, now defend the church by supporting it, but then adorn the church by their eminence, just as the two pillars at the entrance of Solomon's temple. EXPLANATION OF THE APOCALYPSE 3.12.[33]

**OUTSIDE THE CHURCH THERE WILL BE NO SALVATION.** TYCONIUS: "And he shall never go out of it." The nations went out from God, and they gave to idols that worship which they owed to God alone. But "all the families of the nations will remember and turn to the Lord and shall worship before him."[34] This refers to those whom he foretold would come "from the synagogue of Satan." For having broken the bond of charity, the schismatics have gone out of the house of God. They are those who have separated themselves from the body of the whole church which is throughout the world and who vainly glory in themselves and firmly believe that they are the whole church, even though they themselves are not everywhere.[35] For when he says that "he shall never go out of it," he shows that at the end of time there will be a struggle. For it will happen that after unity there will be a final struggle in which there will be another separation. And wherever anyone will have been freed, he shall certainly not go out, and he shall remain in the house, not as a slave but as a son.[36] And therefore God allowed those who were saved from the flood in the ark to go out, because until that time there was still time for returning from one's sins. However, at the end of time it will not be allowed one any longer to come out, for whoever at that time will go out, will have not occasion for repentance. COMMENTARY ON THE APOCALYPSE 3.12.[37]

### 3:12b *The New Name*

**THE NEW NAME IS THAT OF THE SON OF MAN.** TYCONIUS: "And I will write on him the name of my God." That is, we are signed with the name of Christian. "And the name of the city of the new Jerusalem which comes down from my God out of heaven." The name of the church that daily comes down from God out of heaven, that is, from the church that is reborn by the Lord. He speaks of it as new because of the newness of the Son of man who is the new Jerusalem. . . . "Indeed, the name which is above every name."[38] However, this name is not new because it refers to the Son of God, who existed before the world and possessed this glory with the Father.[39] Rather, this name is new in regard to the Son of man who died and on the third day rose again and, ascending to the heavens, sits at the right hand of the Father. For it is the Son of man who said "my new name," whom [John] saw "in the midst of the seven lampstands."[40] This Son of man is God "at whose name every knee bows, in heaven and on earth and under the earth."[41] COMMENTARY ON THE APOCALYPSE 3.12.[42]

**THOSE WITH THE NEW NAME.** APRINGIUS OF BEJA: [I will write on him the name of my God] so that he might be signed with the divine name and be adorned with the glory of immortality and might receive the name of the divine city of Jerusalem, which is the vision of peace, and so fully enjoy the society of perpetual quiet and security. This is that city which descends out of heaven from God, so that the saints might dwell and repose within it. "And my new name." In God nothing is old, because he does grow old with age. But the name of the Lord is always new, always fresh. And if any is named by this name, having been changed by the eternal power, he will obtain eternal life. TRACTATE ON THE APOCALYPSE 3.12.[43]

**THE JOY AND BLESSEDNESS OF VICTORY.** OECUMENIUS: Through these names he depicts the joy of God and the blessedness of dwelling in the midst of blessings, which they will have in the coming age. The "new name" has never been

---

[33]CCL 121A:271. [34]Ps 22:27 (21:28 LXX). [35]Tyconius is speaking of the Donatists. [36]Jn 8:35. [37]TS 2 7:71-72 §§85-90. [38]Phil 2:9. [39]See Jn 17:5. [40]Rev 1:13. [41]Phil 2:10. [42]TS 2 7:73-74 §§95-96. [43]CCL 107:57.

heard anywhere, which the saints, who reign with Christ and who are called "friends" and "brothers" and "servants" will obtain. But the new name transcends even these designations. For these names are written in holy Scripture and have been heard by people. But the new name has been unnamed in every place. And that he says "of my God" suggests that he does not deem himself unworthy of the limitations of his condescension or of the humility of his human nature. For if he had disdained these things, who would have compelled him to be personally united to the flesh and so to fashion our salvation? COMMENTARY ON THE APOCALYPSE 3.7-13.[44]

[44]TEG 8:99.

## 3:14-22 TO THE ANGEL OF THE CHURCH IN LAODICEA

[14]"And to the angel of the church in Laodicea write: 'The words of the Amen, the faithful and true witness, the beginning of God's creation.

[15]" 'I know your works: you are neither cold nor hot. Would that you were cold or hot! [16]So, because you are lukewarm, and neither cold nor hot, I will spew you out of my mouth. [17]For you say, I am rich, I have prospered, and I need nothing; not knowing that you are wretched, pitiable, poor, blind, and naked. [18]Therefore I counsel you to buy from me gold refined by fire, that you may be rich, and white garments to clothe you and to keep the shame of your nakedness from being seen, and salve to anoint your eyes, that you may see. [19]Those whom I love, I reprove and chasten; so be zealous and repent. [20]Behold, I stand at the door and knock; if any one hears my voice and opens the door, I will come in to him and eat with him, and he with me. [21]He who conquers, I will grant him to sit with me on my throne, as I myself conquered and sat down with my Father on his throne. [22]He who has an ear, let him hear what the Spirit says to the churches.' "

**Overview**: As the name of Laodicea suggests, the church there was full of lukewarm Christians who possessed status, wealth and knowledge but did not use them for the benefit of the faithful (VICTORINUS, BEDE). Christ speaks to this church as he who is true God, as he who is the Author and Finisher of our faith (PRIMASIUS) and as he who rules all things as the Creator and Maker of all things (OECUMENIUS). However, Christ threatens some with eternal destruction (ANDREW OF CAESAREA), for they have quenched the Spirit given at their baptism through sloth and attention to temporal matters (OECUMENIUS).

This is evident from the tepid use they make of their riches in helping the needy and from their failure to profit others through their study of the Scriptures (PRIMASIUS). Such behavior is hypocrisy and dishonors God, for Christians are worse in transgressions because they ought to be better (SALVIAN). This is especially true of the monk who should excel in meekness, obedience and patience (CAESARIUS OF ARLES). Nonetheless, to such persons Christ exhorts to faith in the word of teaching (ANDREW OF CAESAREA) and to giving to the poor and doing good works (CAESARIUS OF ARLES) so that they might become themselves pure gold with their sins purged away as if by fire (CYPRIAN). In that case, they will be truly rich in the fervor of love and in the understanding of the Scriptures (BEDE), and they will be adorned with the baptism of Christ and with a heart directed toward the divine laws (PRIMASIUS).

The church must also understand that in the world there is suffering and temptation. However, Christians should submit to these with patience and even rejoice at being accounted worthy of God's chastisement (TERTULLIAN). For it is through trials and infirmities that God corrects and teaches us and shows his kindness toward us (FULGENTIUS OF RUSPE). For his part, the priest of Christ must be as a good physician who may even inflict pain for health to be acquired, and therefore he must not reconcile the sinner to the church before adequate repentance (CYPRIAN). The proud and the wicked are often left untroubled in their sins as a sign of the divine judgment against them (CAESARIUS OF ARLES). We should, therefore, open the door of our hearts to Christ that we might govern our flesh aright (JEROME) and make Christ to dwell in our soul through simplicity, temperance, chastity and charity (CAESARIUS OF ARLES). Unlike the devil, Christ possesses a humble and peaceful nature (OECUMENIUS), and so he comes to our hearts through teaching and dwells in our hearts through the grace of his love (BEDE). To those who conquer, Christ will give the kingdom of the coming age, and they will reign with him as he does eternally with the Father (TYCONIUS, ANDREW OF CAESAREA). For Christ possesses this kingdom as an eternal possession, which he determined to share with us through the assumption of the flesh (ANDREW OF CAESAREA).

### 3:14a Write to the Angel of the Church in Laodicea

**FOR THE GOOD OF THE FAITHFUL.** VICTORINUS OF PETOVIUM: This group, the seventh class, speaks of those wealthy persons who are believers placed in positions of dignity and who believe in the manner of wealthy men. Among them the Scriptures are interpreted in their bedchamber, while the faithful are outside and no one understands [the Scriptures]. That is, they boast and say that they know all things and they possess a confidence in the learning of letters, yet they are empty when it comes to works. And so, the Lord says to them that they are neither cold nor hot, that is, that they are neither unbelieving nor believing, for they are all things to all men. And since he who is neither cold nor hot must of necessity be lukewarm, he produces nausea. And the Lord says, "I will vomit him from my mouth." For nausea is hateful and is hidden to no one, and it is the same way with such persons when they are thrown out. But because there is time for repentance, he says, "I counsel you to buy from me gold refined by fire." That is, if in some way you should be able to suffer something for the name of the Lord. And the Lord says, "Anoint your eyes with eye salve." That is, what you freely know through the Scriptures, it is necessary that you desire to do this. And since such persons would be of great benefit not only to themselves but also to many were they in some way to return away from great destruction to a great repentance, he promises to them no small reward, namely, to sit upon the throne of judgment. COMMENTARY ON THE APOCALYPSE 3.3.[1]

**THE REPROACH OF THE LORD.** BEDE: Laodicea is interpreted "tribe beloved of the Lord" or "they were in vomit." For there were some there to whom he had said, "I will begin to spew you out of my mouth," and others to whom he said, "Those whom I love, I reprove and chastise." According to the Greek, [Laodicea] is interpreted "just people." EXPLANATION OF THE APOCALYPSE 3.14.[2]

### 3:14b The Amen, the Faithful and True

**CHRIST IS THE AMEN.** PRIMASIUS: "He who is

---

[1]CSEL 49:42-44. [2]CCL 121A:271.

the Amen says these words, the faithful and true witness." We must consider the meaning here of "is" and "Amen." The term *amen* is certainly said to mean "true" or "faithful." And so, in this passage without question it refers to that essence of the divinity of which God spoke when he said to Moses, "Thus you shall say to the Israelites, 'He who is has sent me to you.'"[3] For he truly is, who is always the same. COMMENTARY ON THE APOCALYPSE 3.14.[4]

### 3:14c *The Beginning of God's Creation*

**CHRIST IS BOTH PATH AND GOAL.** PRIMASIUS: Since in the person of the one Christ humanity is said to have been assumed, he says, "who is the beginning of the creation of God." It is appropriate to regard the Lord Christ as the beginning of God's creation because of the mystery of the incarnation. From his person we read, "The Lord created me as a beginning of his ways."[5] And the apostle said, "Since we have confidence to enter the sanctuary by the blood of Jesus, by the new and living way that he opened for us through the curtain, that is, through his flesh, and since we have a great priest," and following.[6] For he himself is the Way, who is the fatherland, he himself the Author of faith, who is also its fulfiller, he himself both alpha and omega, he himself the beginning whom no ones precedes, he himself the end whom no one succeeds as ruler. COMMENTARY ON THE APOCALYPSE 3.14.[7]

**CHRIST RULES ALL THINGS.** OECUMENIUS: "The beginning of the creation of God," he says. Most likely, that Arian gang of Christ fighters would adduce this passage as though through these words the Son was rendered a creature. But let us not accept these impious words of theirs. Rather, it must be considered whether in any other Scripture such a view is advanced, so that someone might make a judgment by comparing like with like. Writing to the Colossians, the wise apostle spoke of the Son: "Who is first fruit, the firstborn of all creation."[8] He did not say "first-

created." And so, also the prophet says, "From the womb before the morning star, I begot you,"[9] not "I created you." And so also Solomon: "Before all the hills, he brought me forth."[10] In his treatise *Concerning the Son*, the holy Gregory interpreted the passage, "The Lord created me as the beginning of his ways,"[11] to refer to the body of the Lord with its rational soul, but the language "he brought forth" to the divinity.[12] Since they all claim as dogmatic truth the "generation" of the only Word and Son, and not his "creation," what then do these words, "the beginning of the creation of God," mean? Nothing other than that he who possesses the beginning in all things is the "ruler" of the creation of God. For, since the Father made all things through the Son, rightfully does he who is the creator and maker of all things and who brought all things from nonbeing into being rule those things made by him. COMMENTARY ON THE APOCALYPSE 3.14-22.[13]

### 3:15-16 *Neither Hot nor Cold*

**APART FROM GOOD WORKS, WEALTH AND KNOWLEDGE MAKE POOR.** PRIMASIUS: In this passage we recognize persons of nobility in the world, whom he says are neither hot nor cold but lukewarm, because, although they possess an abundance of wealth, they are empty of works of piety, nor are they inflamed by any feeling of compassion toward good works. They are therefore [considered] as poor, said to be neither cold nor hot, for they abound in riches which they use tepidly and so become sluggish, and by not sharing those riches with the needy are rightly regarded as lacking in the desire for good works. But this passage may also refer to those persons who interpret the Scriptures in private while outside it is not known whether they are faithful and being confident in their literary knowledge, they are found to be empty of works. . . . Now they may

---

[3]Ex 3:14. [4]CCL 92:42. [5]Prov 8:22. [6]Heb 10:19-21. [7]CCL 92:42. [8]Col 1:15. [9]Ps 109:3 LXX. [10]Prov 8:25. [11]Prov 8:22. [12]Gregory of Nazianzus *Oration* 30.2 (NPNF 2 7:310). [13]TEG 8:101.

purchase gold for themselves, of which he says, "Receive wisdom as gold and knowledge like chosen silver."[14] And, should they be able to derive something from the sources of the divine Scriptures, as though illumined by the light of wisdom; they might perfect it by works themselves, either the former enkindled by the depths of piety through the largess of their wealth, or the latter informed spiritually through their knowledge of the Scriptures. COMMENTARY ON THE APOCALYPSE 3.15-16.[15]

### LOSS OF THE ZEAL OF THE HOLY SPIRIT.

OECUMENIUS: "I know your works," the Lord says, "you are neither cold nor hot." He who is fervent in the Spirit is "hot," for the holy apostle speaks of those who are "fervent in the Spirit."[16] Likewise, he who lacks the power and indwelling of the Holy Spirit is "cold." But you, he says, "are lukewarm." He calls that person "lukewarm" who in baptism received the communion of the Holy Spirit but has quenched that grace through sloth and attention to temporal matters. And so, this divine directive: "Do not quench the Spirit."[17] Would that you would be either "hot," aglow by the work of the Spirit, or totally "cold," unbaptized and utterly void of the Spirit's grace, but not "lukewarm"! For the person who has the mental fire of the Spirit comes to maturity, since the senses have been trained to distinguish that which is good from that which is evil, and that person is spiritual. And that person who has never received the grace of the Spirit, yet may hope at some time to receive it, and so is not counted among the hopeless. But that person who is "lukewarm" is moribund and moving toward death, and risks losing both baptism and the previous zeal. COMMENTARY ON THE APOCALYPSE 3.14-22.[18]

### HYPOCRISY IN A CHRISTIAN DISHONORS GOD.

SALVIAN THE PRESBYTER: They learn good and do evil who, it is written, confess God by words and deny him by deeds.[19] They, as the apostle says, repose in the law and know its intent and approve of those things that are the more profitable.[20] They have the form of knowledge and of truth in the law. They preach that they must not steal, yet they do steal. They read that they must not commit adultery, yet they commit it. They glory in the law, yet by transgression of the law they dishonor God. Therefore, for this very reason, Christians are worse because they should be better. They do not practice what they preach, and they struggle against their faith by their morals. All the more blameworthy is evil which the label of goodness accuses, and the holy name is the crime of an unholy person. Hence, the Savior also said in the Apocalypse to the lukewarm Christian: "Would that you were cold or hot. But now because you are lukewarm, I will begin to vomit you out of my mouth." THE GOVERNANCE OF GOD 4.19.[21]

### NOT SLACK IN MEEKNESS, OBEDIENCE AND PATIENCE.

CAESAREA OF ARLES: Let us not only beware of serious sins, as I suggested above, but let us also spurn small daily acts of negligence as the poison of the devil. There are some people who are weakened by excessive unconcern after their religious profession, because they seem to have left the world. In such people is fulfilled that sentence of our Lord in which it is said, "How I wish you were one or the other—hot or cold! But because you are lukewarm, I will spew you out of my mouth!" What does it mean that he said, How I wish you were one or the other—hot or cold? This means that it would have been better for you to have remained cold in the world or to be fervent in the monastery. Now because you have withdrawn from the world and still have refused to acquire spiritual warmth because of your carelessness, you have become lukewarm and will be vomited from the Lord's mouth, scarcely ever to be recovered again. For this reason, dearest brothers, with God's help carefully listen to the sentence of sacred Scripture, in

---

[14]See Prov 16:16. [15]CCL 92:42-44. [16]Rom 12:11. [17]1 Thess 5:19. [18]TEG 8:101-2. [19]Tit 1:16. [20]Rom 2:17-18. [21]FC 3:123.

which it is said, "With closest custody guard your heart."[22] There should be rejoicing over the monk who has come to the monastery and, in a meek and humble spirit, wills to practice meekness, obedience and patience. SERMON 235.4, To MONKS.[23]

**THE SEED OF THE DIVINE WORD, THE THISTLES OF WEALTH.** ANDREW OF CAESAREA: Just as that which is lukewarm induces vomiting in those who take it in, so also, he says, I will vomit you out through the word of my mouth into eternal destruction, as though you were rotten food. For mixing together the seed of the divine word with the thistles of wealth, you have become unaware of your poverty in spiritual matters and of the blindness of your spiritual eyes and of your nakedness in good works. COMMENTARY ON THE APOCALYPSE 3.16-17.[24]

### 3:17-18 Buy Gold from Me

**BE YOURSELVES PURE GOLD.** CYPRIAN: You are mistaken and are deceived, whosoever you are, that you think yourself rich in this world. Listen to the voice of your Lord in the Apocalypse, rebuking people of your stamp with righteous reproaches: "You say," says he, "I am rich, and increased with goods, and have need of nothing, and do not know that you are wretched, and miserable, poor, blind and naked. I counsel you to buy gold from me tried in the fire, that you may be rich. And buy from me white clothing, that you may be clothed, and that the shame of your nakedness may not appear in you. Anoint your eyes with eye salve, that you may see." You therefore, who are rich and wealthy, buy from Christ gold tried by fire. Then you may be pure gold, with your filth burned out as if by fire. Buy for yourself white raiment, that you who had been naked according to Adam, and were before frightful and tasteless, may be clothed with the white garment of Christ. You who are a wealthy and rich matron in Christ's church, anoint your eyes, not with the eyewash of the devil but with

Christ's eye salve, that you may be able to attain to see God, by deserving well of God, both by good works and character. WORKS AND ALMSGIVING 14.[25]

**BY YOUR LIFE MERIT TO DIE FOR CHRIST.** CAESARIUS OF ARLES: By the doing of alms and by standing firm in good works you might yourself be made gold. That is, that you might receive understanding from God and through your good behavior you might merit to suffer martyrdom. EXPOSITION OF THE APOCALYPSE 3.18, HOMILY 3.[26]

**THROUGH THE FIRE OF TEMPTATION.** ANDREW OF CAESAREA: If you wish to be rich, he says, with a zealous intent and a willing heart obtain from me, who makes rich, gold that has been purified in fire, namely, the word of teaching that is made brilliant in the fire of temptations. And through this you will have in your heart a treasure that is secure, and you will wear the bright stole of virtue, through which the nakedness, which has come to you by sin, will be clothed. The salve is certainly poverty. For, if "gifts make blind the eyes of those who see,"[27] then certainly that which is incorruptible will open them. COMMENTARY ON THE APOCALYPSE 3.18.[28]

**FAITH PLUS THE FERVOR OF LOVE.** BEDE: Since you are content with mere faith, in vain do you seek to acquire the riches of righteousness. But, should you desire to be truly rich, forsake everything, and buy the fervor of love approved by the flame of afflictions, and anoint the eyes of the mind, not with the antinomy of deceitful boasting but with the eye salve of divine knowledge. To anoint the eyes with eye salve is to acquire an understanding of the holy Scriptures through the performance of a good work. EXPLANATION OF THE APOCALYPSE 3.17.[29]

---

[22]Prov 4:23.  [23]FC 66:206-7.  [24]MTS 1 Sup 1:43.  [25]ANF 5:479-80**.  [26]PL 35:2422.  [27]Sir 20:29.  [28]MTS 1 Sup 1:43-44.  [29]CCL 121A:273.

**CLOTHED WITH WORKS OF RIGHTEOUSNESS.**
PRIMASIUS: He regards those as "naked" who are
destitute of the works of righteousness, whom he
also regards as "blind." However, he is clothed
with white garments who is vested with the baptism of Christ, and he enjoys that faith "working
through love,"[30] for "as many of you as were baptized into Christ have put on Christ."[31] When he
says that the eyes must be anointed with salve, he
advises that the heart be directed toward the
divine testimonies. For "the commandment of the
Lord is clear, enlightening the eyes."[32] COMMEN-
TARY ON THE APOCALYPSE 3.18.[33]

### 3:19 Reproved and Chastened

**BEAR INJURIES WITH PATIENCE AND SELF-
CONTROL.** TERTULLIAN: Let us strive, then, to
bear the injuries that are inflicted by the evil one,
that the struggle to maintain our self-control may
put to shame the enemy's efforts. If, however,
through imprudence or even of our own free will
we draw down upon ourselves some misfortune,
we should submit with equal patience to that
which we impute to ourselves. But if we believe
God strikes some blow of misfortune, to whom
would it be better that we manifest patience than
to our Lord? In fact, more than this, it befits us to
rejoice at being deemed worthy of divine chastisement: "As for me," he says, "those whom I love I
chastise."[34] Blessed is that servant upon whose
correction the Lord insists, at whom he deigns to
be angry, whom he does not deceive by omitting
his admonition! ON PATIENCE 11.3-4.[35]

**A BISHOP MUST BE A PHYSICIAN.** CYPRIAN:
He who consoles the sinner with flattering blan-
dishments furnishes the means for sinning and
does not check transgressions but nourishes
them. But he who rebukes at the same time that
he instructs with firmer counsels urges a brother
on to salvation. "Whom I love," says the Lord, "I
rebuke and chastise." Thus also ought the priest
of the Lord not to deceive by pretended submis-
sions but to provide salutary remedies. A physi-

cian is unskilled who handles the swelling folds of
wounds with a sparing hand and increases the
poison inclosed within the deep recesses of the
vital organs as he cares for it. The wound must be
opened and cut and treated by a sterner remedy
by cutting out the corrupting parts. Although the
sick man, impatient by reason of his pain, cries
out, shrieks and complains, he will give thanks
afterwards, when he has experienced good
health.[36] THE LAPSED 14.[37]

**TRIALS THAT COME FROM GOD.** FULGENTIUS
OF RUSPE: The kindness of God leads us to penance. He afflicts us with trials, he corrects us
with infirmities, teaches us with cares, so that we
who have sinned in the health of the body may
learn to abstain from sins in infirmity. We who
scorned the mercy of God in frivolity, corrected
by the lash of sadness should fear his justice.
Thus it comes about that we who by abusing
health have begotten infirmity for ourselves,
through that infirmity may again procure the
benefits of health. And we who through frivolity
have fallen into trials, through these trials may
regain happiness. Holy Scripture bears witness
that God's love for us is shown more by the lash
and correction. For it says, "My child, do not
despise the Lord's discipline or be weary of his
reproofs, for the Lord reproves the one he loves,
as a father the son in whom he delights."[38] And
the Savior himself says that he loves those he
reproves, saying, "Those whom I love, I reprove
and chastise." The teaching of the apostles does
not cease to proclaim that "it is necessary for us
to undergo many hardships to enter the kingdom
of God."[39] The Lord himself also says that the
road which leads to life is constricted and the gate
narrow. LETTER 7.16, TO VENANTIA.[40]

**A SIGN OF DIVINE JUDGMENT.** CAESARIUS OF

---

[30]Gal 5:6. [31]Gal 3:27. [32]Ps 19:8 (18:9 LXX). [33]CCL 92:44. [34]Prov
3:12. [35]FC 40:212*. [36]Cyprian is criticizing the laxity of some priests
toward those who had fallen in persecution. [37]FC 36:69. [38]Prov 3:11-
12. [39]Acts 14:22. [40]FC 95:362.

ARLES: Do the proud and wicked souls who commit serious sins seem happy to you because they do not suffer evil in this world? Listen to what the Scriptures say about such people: "They are not in the labors of men: neither shall they be scourged with other men. Therefore their pride has held them fast: they are covered with their iniquity and their wickedness. Their iniquity has come forth, as it were from fatness."[41] They are not scourged at all in this world, because they are reserved for eternal punishment due to the excessive number of their sins. They cannot be punished in this short time, for they require endless torture. Now, our Lord and God, who withholds punishment of these people in his justice, does not cease to exercise his children with diverse tribulations, as we read: "God scourges every son whom he receives,"[42] and, "those whom I love I rebuke and chastise." If he scourges every son he receives, then if he does not chastise a person, he does not accept him. If he chastises all whom he loves, he does not love a person if he does not chastise him. The power of God does not effect this, but the wickedness of people merits to suffer it, according to what is written: "He who is filthy, let him be filthy still. He who is just, let him be just still."[43] SERMON 5.3.[44]

### 3:20 I Stand at the Door and Knock

LET CHRIST INTO YOUR HEART. JEROME: On the other hand, God may permit us also to be kings of the earth, "kings of earth" in order to rule over our own flesh. In this connection the apostle says, "Therefore do not let sin reign in your mortal body."[45] In another part of Scripture it is written, "The king's heart is in the hand of God."[46] . . . The kings, therefore, are the saints, and their hearts are in the hand of the Lord. Let us beg God to make us kings that we may rule over our flesh that it be subject to us. The following words of the apostle are appropriate here: "But I chastise my body and bring it into subjection, lest perhaps after preaching to others, I myself should be rejected."[47] May our soul be in

command, our body in subjection; then Christ will come at once to make his abode with us. What does he himself say in the New Testament? "Behold, I stand at the door and knock. If any man listens to my voice and opens the door to me, I will come in to him and will sup with him." Every day, Christ stands at the door of our hearts. He longs to enter. Let us open wide our hearts to him. Then he will come in and be our host and guest. He will live in us and eat with us. HOMILIES ON THE PSALMS 9 (PS 75).[48]

IN GOOD WORKS THE SOUL RECEIVES CHRIST AS GUEST AND RESIDENT. CAESARIUS OF ARLES: If an earthly king or the head of a family invited you to his birthday celebration, with what kind of garments would you endeavor to adorn yourself when you approached? Surely with new and shining ones, costly ones, whose age or cheapness or ugliness could not offend the eyes of the one who invited you. Therefore, with Christ's help, strive as much as you can with a like zeal, so that your soul may with an easy conscience approach the solemn feast of the eternal king, that is, the birthday of our Lord and Savior, if it is adorned with the decoration of various virtues. Let it be adorned with the jewels of simplicity and the flowers of temperance, gleaming chastity, shining charity and joyful almsgiving. For if Christ the Lord recognizes that you are celebrating his birthday with such dispositions, he himself will deign to come and not only visit your soul but also rest and continually dwell in it. As it is written, "I will dwell with them and walk among them";[49] and again, "Here I stand, knocking at the door; if anyone rises up and opens the door, I will enter his house and have supper with him, and he with me." How happy is the soul which, with God's help, has striven to direct his life in such a way that he may merit receiving Christ as his guest and indwelling person. SERMON 187.3.[50]

---

[41]See Ps 73:5-7 (72:5-7 LXX). [42]Heb 12:6. [43]Rev 22:11. [44]FC 31:34-35. [45]Rom 6:12. [46]Prov 21:1. [47]1 Cor 9:27. [48]FC 48:67*. [49]2 Cor 6:16. [50]FC 66:8-9*.

**CHRIST REVEALS A HUMBLE AND PEACEFUL NATURE.** OECUMENIUS: "Behold," he says, "I stand at the door and knock. If anyone hears my voice and opens the door, I will come in to him and dine with him and he with me." Here the Lord reveals his own humble and peaceful nature. The devil with axe and hammer smashes the doors of those who do not receive him, as the prophet said,[51] but the Lord even now in the Song of Songs says to the bride, "Open to me, my sister, my bride."[52] And should someone open to him, he will come in, but if not, he goes away. That supper which is with the Lord signifies the reception of the holy mysteries. COMMENTARY ON THE APOCALYPSE 3.14-22.[53]

**GOD DWELLS WITH HIS ELECT THROUGH HIS LOVE.** BEDE: The Lord stands at the doorway and knocks when he pours into our heart the memory of his will, either through the mouth of a man who is teaching [us] or through his own internal inspiration. When his voice is heard, we open the gate to receive [him] when we willingly present our assent to [his] counsels, whether secret or open, and devote ourselves to accomplishing those things that we recognize are to be done. He comes in order to eat with us and we with him. For he dwells in the hearts of his elect through the grace of his love in order to restore them always by the light of his presence. He lives there so that they may advance more and more to heavenly desires, and so that he himself may feed their zeal for heaven, as it were, with a most pleasing banquet. HOMILIES ON THE GOSPELS 1.21.[54]

### 3:21 Sitting with Christ on His Throne

**WE WILL SHARE WITH CHRIST AS HE DOES WITH THE FATHER.** TYCONIUS: [In the image of the Son] sitting with [the Father], he shows that the Son participates in the power of the Father. For what else does it mean that he is seated on the throne of the Father than that he is of one and the same substance? And just as he conquered the devil and sat at the right hand of the Father, so also he who conquers will sit with him. For God the Son is powerful, who in the Father is everywhere and by his own power fills the heaven and the earth. COMMENTARY ON THE APOCALYPSE 3.21.[55]

**CHRIST WILL SHARE ALL THINGS WITH THOSE WHO CONQUER THE DEVIL.** ANDREW OF CAESAREA: "The throne" indicates the kingdom and the rest of the coming age. Therefore he says that those who have conquered the enemy "will be glorified with me and will rule with me."[56] When he says, "as I myself have conquered," he is speaking in a human manner on account of the assumption [of the flesh]. For God the Word did not acquire the kingdom as a prize for virtue, for he has this essentially as an eternal possession. For if this were not so, he would not be able to share it with others. But according to the Theologian and the "son of thunder," he shared from his fullness with all the saints.[57] For this reason also he promised to his holy apostles that they would sit upon twelve thrones and judge the future twelve tribes of Israel. For when he who is God and the eternal King became man for us, he shared everything which is ours, except only sin, and shared everything of his with those who had conquered the devil, as it was possible for human nature to receive. Therefore, having made a cloud the chariot of his ascension into heaven, he said through the apostle that the saints would be snatched up to meet him on the clouds.[58] And when he, who is the Creator and Lord of creation, shall come as judge, he will allow the saints to judge those who had rebelled against the truly divine and blessed service. COMMENTARY ON THE APOCALYPSE 3.21-22.[59]

---

[51]Ps 74:6 (73:6 LXX). [52]Song 5:2. [53]TEG 8:103-4. [54]CS 110:209*. [55]TS 2 7:78-79 §§110-12. [56]Rom 8:17. [57]Jn 1:16. [58]1 Thess 4:17. [59]MTS 1 Sup 1:45-46.

## 4:1-11 JOHN SEES THE THRONE OF HEAVEN

¹*After this I looked, and lo, in heaven an open door! And the first voice, which I had heard speaking to me like a trumpet, said, "Come up hither, and I will show you what must take place after this."* ²*At once I was in the Spirit, and lo, a throne stood in heaven, with one seated on the throne!* ³*And he who sat there appeared like jasper and carnelian, and round the throne was a rainbow that looked like an emerald.* ⁴*Round the throne were twenty-four thrones, and seated on the thrones were twenty-four elders, clad in white garments, with golden crowns upon their heads.* ⁵*From the throne issue flashes of lightning, and voices and peals of thunder, and before the throne burn seven torches of fire, which are the seven spirits of God;* ⁶*and before the throne there is as it were a sea of glass, like crystal.*

*And round the throne, on each side of the throne, are four living creatures, full of eyes in front and behind:* ⁷*the first living creature like a lion, the second living creature like an ox, the third living creature with the face of a man, and the fourth living creature like a flying eagle.* ⁸*And the four living creatures, each of them with six wings, are full of eyes all round and within, and day and night they never cease to sing,*

*"Holy, holy, holy, is the Lord God Almighty,*

*who was and is and is to come!"*

⁹*And whenever the living creatures give glory and honor and thanks to him who is seated on the throne, who lives for ever and ever,* ¹⁰*the twenty-four elders fall down before him who is seated on the throne and worship him who lives for ever and ever; they cast their crowns before the throne, singing,*

¹¹*"Worthy art thou, our Lord and God,*

*to receive glory and honor and power,*

*for thou didst create all things,*

*and by thy will they existed and were created."*

---

**OVERVIEW:** John sees Christ, who in the body ascended to heaven, is now the open door to heaven, that is, to the church (TYCONIUS). There the preaching of the New Testament occurs which opens the Old Testament (VICTORINUS), and there the faithful are invited also to ascend so that they may be spiritually taught and turn their minds to the mysteries of the Spirit (PRIMASIUS, ANDREW OF CAESAREA). In the spirit John sees the Lord of majesty on the throne of judgment, and he appears as jasper and carnelian. The radiant green of jasper signifies the life-providing nature of God, who sustains all living things through vegetation (OECUMENIUS), and the divine power of the sinless flesh of Christ (APRINGIUS). The fiery, deep red of carnelian indicates the fearsomeness of God, who is severe in his judgments (OECUMENIUS), and the undefiled flesh of Christ taken from the pure and humble Virgin (APRINGIUS). While these two colors also suggest the two judgments of God, that of water and that of fire at the consummation (VICTORINUS), the green jasper is mentioned before the red carnelian to indicate that God is by nature beneficent and gentle and wishes to be our Father and that he becomes severe as a Lord only because of our sins (OECUMENIUS).

Encircling the throne was a rainbow, green like an emerald. Although a natural rainbow is of many colors, this rainbow is of but one color to suggest that the angelic host imitates the good works of their Lord (OECUMENIUS), who is the Sun who illuminates the souls of the saints when he is reconciled to them (PRIMASIUS). Around the throne also sits the entire church, represented by the twelve patriarchs and the twelve apostles (TYCONIUS, VICTORINUS, APRINGIUS), for through them the holy doctrine of God was spoken (APRINGIUS). So also now the leaders and people of the church are called to sit upon the one throne of Christ through whom and in whom the church sits and judges the twelve tribes (TYCONIUS). The twenty-four elders also represent various saints of the Old and the New Testaments (OECUMENIUS).

From the one throne of God the preaching of the gospel is extended through the voices of preachers and the miracle of signs that enlighten the mind as though by lightning and fall on spiritual ears as though thunder (PRIMASIUS, APRINGIUS, ANDREW OF CAESAREA). Before the throne is a sea of glass, for God is surrounded by a multitude of holy spirits who are pure as crystal (OECUMENIUS). Moreover, before the throne is the Holy Spirit, who gives his sevenfold gifts in baptism (PRIMASIUS). Baptism appears as a smooth sea, for it gives the immovable gifts of purity and righteousness (VICTORINUS, APRINGIUS). Unless one is baptized in this sea which is in the presence of God, one is born to destruction (PRIMASIUS).

In addition, four living creatures—like a lion, an ox, a man and an eagle—surround the throne. These indicate the fourfold gospel that proclaims the dispensation of the incarnate Son of God—his divine generation from the Father, his coming which was foretold by the prophetic Spirit, his royal descent from David and his royal power and his priestly, sacrificial death (IRENAEUS, VICTORINUS, AUGUSTINE, APRINGIUS). The church likewise is described by these four creatures, for she too possesses royal dignity and the humble weakness of Christ, since she sacrifices herself to God and is destined to the heights of heaven (PRIMASIUS). The four creatures may also symbolize the providence of God, which extends to all creatures and sustains all creatures (OECUMENIUS). The four creatures each had six wings, indicating that the Old Testament takes flight through the New Testament (VICTORINUS) and that now the church is elevated above earthly affections by the wings of the two Testaments (TYCONIUS). The creatures were perpetually crying, "Holy, Holy, Holy," for they ceaselessly praise and glorify the one, indivisible Trinity (ATHANASIUS) and Christ who is almighty in his dominion over all things (RUFINUS). The church too praises God by word and deed (PRIMASIUS), and in her threefold prayer the faithful learn in this life the duty of their future glory (TERTULLIAN).

Finally, John beholds the elders fall before the throne, for the church ascribes to God alone whatever purity and dignity she possesses (PRIMASIUS). Moreover, in the creation the church recognizes the hidden wisdom of God (TYCONIUS), and in the coming of Christ the prophets exult, knowing that they had rightly preached the word of God (VICTORINUS).

## 4:1a An Open Door in Heaven

**CHRIST IS THE GATEWAY TO THE CHURCH.**
TYCONIUS: "Afterwards," John said, "I saw." After seeing the vision, he remembered that he had seen another. The interval in time belongs not to the events but to the visions. If one were to describe a single event in different ways, it would be the descriptions that differ in time, not what took place at one time. In this way, he retraces the whole span of the church using various figures to describe it. "Behold," he says, "an open door in heaven." The open door represents Christ, who was born, suffered and was raised. Christ is the

gateway, as he himself said, "I am the door."[1] Heaven represents the church because it is the habitation of God where the celestial realities are effected. This is why we pray that the will of God be done on earth even as it is in heaven. Sometimes, however, the church is represented by both heaven and earth, since the earth comes into agreement with heaven, either when the unfaithful are won by the righteous proclamation of the faithful, or when the flesh is subdued by the Spirit, or when the things of the earth are reconciled and united to the things of heaven. COMMENTARY ON THE APOCALYPSE 4.1.[2]

## 4:1b *"Come up Here"*

**THE OLD TESTAMENT IS OPENED BY THE DOOR OF THE NEW TESTAMENT.** VICTORINUS OF PETOVIUM: "There was," he says, "an open door in heaven." John sees the preaching of the New Testament, and it is said to him, "Come up here." When it is shown that the door was opened, it is clear that previously it had been closed to humankind. However, it was sufficiently and perfectly opened when Christ ascended in the body to the Father in heaven. When he says that the voice that he had heard was the voice that spoke with him, without any doubt[3] this proves to the stubborn [unbelievers][4] that he who comes is the very same as he who spoke through the prophets. For John was from the circumcision, and that entire people had heard the preaching of the Old Testament and had been edified by that voice. For "that voice," he says, "which I heard, it said to me, 'Come up here.'" This is Jesus Christ whom a little before he said that he had seen as a son of man among the golden lampstands. And now he recalls that which had been fore-told in the law by means of similitudes, and through this Scripture he joins together all the previous prophets and opens the Scriptures. COMMENTARY ON THE APOCALYPSE 4.1.[5]

**THE FAITHFUL ARE INVITED TO ASCEND TO**

**HEAVEN.** PRIMASIUS: This is, therefore, the voice of prophecy of which it is said, "Lift up your voice like a trumpet."[6] One has gone up and ascended who, having despised the world, is either compelled to come to the church or obtains admission to her. He ascends from the valley of tears to the height of that dignity of which we read, "Come, let us go up to the mountain of the Lord and to the house of the God of Jacob, and he will teach us his ways."[7] However, the faithful are also invited to ascend to heaven when they are commanded to seek and to taste what is in heaven and not what is upon the earth. For when a neophyte in the church is taught that Christ suffered, was raised and has ascended to the Father, and then beyond these things is taught and instructed spiritually to contemplate him in the Father according to the form of God, he is rightly said to ascend, since he will see the secrets of the mysteries in which he has believed. Therefore, the Lord said, "Do not touch me, for I have not yet ascended to the Father,"[8] wishing this touching to be understood as belief. COMMENTARY ON THE APOCALYPSE 4.1.[9]

**THE MYSTERIES OF THE SPIRIT.** ANDREW OF CAESAREA: The opening of the door signifies the revelation of the hidden mysteries of the Spirit. The trumpet represents the sonorous voice of the Revealer. "Come up here" indicates that the mind of the hearer is to turn away completely from the things of the earth and be turned toward heaven. COMMENTARY ON THE APOCALYPSE 4.1.[10]

## 4:2-3 *A Throne in Heaven*

**JOHN SEES THE LORD OF MAJESTY.** APRINGIUS OF BEJA: Who would think that he speaks anything fleshly who reports that he had entered in the spirit? A man so thoroughly tested by his God

---

[1]Jn 10:9. [2]CCL 92:46. [3]Latin *sine contradictione*; French *sans conteste*. [4]Latin *arguuntur contumaces*; French *cela prouve aux incredules*. [5]CSEL 49:44-46. [6]Is 58:1. [7]Is 2:3. [8]Jn 20:17. [9]CCL 92:46-47. [10]MTS 1 Sup 1:47.

receives nothing fleshly, nothing earthly. But he was in the spirit so that he might see the Lord of majesty, whom he perceives in the spirit, but does not behold in the flesh. He thereby fulfilled what the apostle said: "Even though we knew Christ according to the flesh, we know him thus no longer."[11] TRACTATE ON THE APOCALYPSE 4.2.[12]

**Two Testaments Attest God's Judgment.** VICTORINUS OF PETOVIUM: Significantly, there was a "throne set" [in heaven], which is the seat of judgment and of the king, and over this throne he says that he saw something similar to jasper and carnelian. Since jasper has the color of water and carnelian that of fire, it was manifested that these two Testaments have been placed over the tribunal of God until the consummation of the world. And of these judgments one has already been accomplished through water, while the other will be accomplished through fire. COMMENTARY ON THE APOCALPSE 4.2.[13]

**The Undefiled Flesh of Christ.** APRINGIUS OF BEJA: The jasper stone shines with a green and radiant brightness, so that he might know that the flesh of the assumed man, taken up without a hint of sin, shines with the vigor of everlasting sincerity and glows through the indwelling of the divine power. However, the carnelian stone is red and glimmers with a certain darkness, so that you might recognize the integrity of the undefiled flesh assumed from the modest and humble Virgin. TRACTATE ON THE APOCALYPSE 4.3.[14]

**Jasper and Carnelian Analogous to Law and Gospel.** OECUMENIUS: I saw, he says, a throne, and there was upon it God who is spirit, having the appearance of jasper and carnelian. God is not like these things—of course not! — nor is he who is invisible, incorporeal and without form like in any way to the body of any perceptible being. Even the seraphim hide their faces with their wings when they are shown his invisible nature. Similarly, when God was speaking with Moses, he said, "No one will look upon my face and live."[15] And the Evangelist himself, as though contradicting [what he says here], says, "No one has ever seen God."[16] Therefore, since God is similar to nothing in appearance, the vision of him in the Revelation is depicted on the basis of his activities. For the jasper is a green precious stone, something like an emerald and similar to the rust of a shield, from which it receives its name. The carnelian is another precious jewel and is fiery bright and blood red. And so, the jasper depicts the life-bearing and life-providing nature of God, since all food of humankind and of four-footed animals and of birds and of creeping creatures has its beginning and likewise its effective cause in vegetation. For the prophet says, "Who makes the grass to grow for cattle and plants for the service of men, to bring forth bread from the earth. And wine makes glad the heart of man, to make his face cheerful with oil."[17] And again at the creation of the world, God said, "Let the earth bring forth vegetation, bearing seed according to its kind."[18] And so, while the jasper depicts such things concerning God, the carnelian depicts the fearsomeness of God, for the holy Moses said, "Your God is a devouring fire."[19] And the prophet also said, "You are terrible, who will stand before your face,"[20] and the wise apostle wrote in agreement, "It is fearful to fall into the hands of the living God."[21] Since the pure goodness of God is incompatible with those who love to sin and who are scornful, not moving them to repentance but giving them a sense of security for further transgression, with good reason does God desire his severity depicted along with his goodness and beneficence. . . . However, the carnelian is not the first jewel mentioned to describe God. Rather, the jasper is the first. For God's nature is in itself good and beneficent and gentle. And he wishes to be our Father rather than our Lord. But, if it is proper to speak in this way, we force him to become fearsome and

---

[11]2 Cor 5:16. [12]CCL 107:60. [13]CSEL 49:46. [14]CCL 107:60. [15]Ex 33:20. [16]Jn 1:18. [17]Ps 104:14-15 (103:14-15 LXX). [18]Gen 1:11-12. [19]Deut 4:24. [20]Ps 76:7 (75:8 LXX). [21]Heb 10:31.

punishing. And therefore, often he abandons that which is according to his nature, namely, gentleness, and assumes that which is contrary to his nature, namely, severity. COMMENTARY ON THE APOCALYPSE 4.1-3.[22]

## 4:3 A Rainbow Like an Emerald

**A SIGN OF THE CHURCH'S RECONCILIATION TO GOD.** PRIMASIUS: Since the rainbow was given as a sign of safety after the flood, it is now suitably used as a sign of the church's reconciliation to God. For when the storm clouds are irradiated by the splendor of the sun, they produce the form of a rainbow. In comparison to this, when the souls of the saints are illumined by the Sun of righteousness, which is Christ, his deity deigns to be reconciled by their intercession. COMMENTARY ON THE APOCALYPSE 4.2-3.[23]

**THE HOLY ANGELS IMITATE THEIR LORD.** OECUMENIUS: The natural rainbow, which the holy Scriptures call the "bow" of God,[24] occurs from the reflection of the sun's light, which when taken into the thickness of clouds is intercepted and produces multiple and various colors. But this spiritual rainbow that encircles the divine throne is of one color, for it was like an emerald, and this reveals the multitude of holy ministering angels, which surrounds God. And for this reason it is called a "rainbow," even though it is of one color, in order that from the multiple colors of the rainbow we might recognize the distinct orders of the holy angels. And yet, all are bound together into one color since all alike imitate their Lord according to his good works, and therefore the emerald color testifies to their sustaining work, even as the jasper did for God. COMMENTARY ON THE APOCALYPSE 4.1-3.[25]

## 4:4 Twenty-four Thrones and Twenty-four Elders

**THE ELDERS REPRESENT THE CHURCH OF THE OLD AND NEW TESTAMENTS.** VICTORINUS

OF PETOVIUM: And there were twenty-four elders who had twenty-four tribunals. These are the books of the prophets and of the law which give the testimonies of the judgment. However, these twenty-four fathers are also the twelve apostles and the twelve patriarchs. COMMENTARY ON THE APOCALYPSE 4.3.[26]

**SYMBOLS OF THE WHOLE CHURCH.** TYCONIUS: The elders represent the whole church, as we learn through Isaiah, "The Lord has reigned in Zion and in Jerusalem, and he will be glorified in the presence of his elders."[27] However, the twenty-four includes at the same time both leaders and people, as though duplicating the twelve tribes of Israel on account of the two Testaments. For the very same church is established in both the old and in the new, since he shows the church in the twelve apostles, namely, the entire body of leaders. And so we discover Jerusalem in the description of the city descending from heaven. The twenty-four thrones, considered by way of a distribution of offices, are twelve, since also the leaders of the twelve tribes will be advanced. And the twelve thrones, considered by way of a mystical number, is one throne, where from comes the church. For the Lord Christ is alone the one who will sit in judgment. However, the church also will sit and does sit judging the twelve tribes, but she will do this in Christ in whom is the whole [church]. Therefore, the members will sit and judge, but in one head and through one head. COMMENTARY ON THE APOCALYPSE 4.4.[28]

**THE PATRIARCHS AND APOSTLES.** APRINGIUS OF BEJA: Most evidently John has described the chorus of the patriarchs and of the apostles, who sit upon the chair of holy doctrine. These he calls "elders," that is, "fathers," and they are clothed in white garments, that is, they are clothed in works

---

[22]TEG 8:104-6. [23]CCL 92:47. [24]Gen 9:13. [25]TEG 8:106. [26]CSEL 49:50. [27]Is 24:23. [28]CCL 92:48. This passage is based on Tyconius. Primasius adds that the twenty-four may also refer to that perfection that comes by the clear preaching of the gospel, for four sixes make twenty-four.

of righteousness and in purity. They carry upon their heads golden crowns, for they have been made victors in present struggles, since that evil enemy, the devil, has been thrown down, and they have received their crowns from the Lord. Concerning this crown, the vessel of election says: "I have finished the race, I have kept the faith. Henceforth there is laid up for me the crown of righteousness, which the Lord, the righteous judge, will award to me on the day, and not only to me but also to those who love his appearing."[29] TRACTATE ON THE APOCALYPSE 4.4.[30]

**SAINTS OF THE OLD AND NEW TESTAMENTS.** OECUMENIUS: God alone, who knows every mystery, and that person to whom he might reveal it, might know the identity of the twenty-four elders who are seated upon the thrones. But in my own opinion there was Abel, and Enoch and Noah, Abraham and Isaac and Jacob, Melchizedek and Job, Moses and Aaron, Joshua the son of Nun and Samuel, David, Elijah and Elisha, the twelve minor prophets who are accounted as one, Isaiah and Jeremiah, Ezekiel and Daniel, Zachariah and John, James the son of Joseph and Stephen, the two martyrs of the New Testament. One might have mentioned Peter and Paul and James, the brother of John whom Herod killed with the sword, and the rest of the choir of the holy apostles, had not the Lord promised them that not at the present time but at the regeneration they would sit upon twelve thrones, these clearly being different thrones than the ones mentioned above. COMMENTARY ON THE APOCALYPSE 4.4-6.[31]

### 4:5a Flashes of Lightening and Peals of Thunder

**PREACHING THE GOSPEL IS ACCOMPANIED BY SIGNS AND MIRACLES.** PRIMASIUS: In the voices and thunder the proclamation of the gospel is indicated, while the lightning signifies the miraculous signs, as we read in the Gospel, "They went forth and preached everywhere, while the Lord worked with them and confirmed the message by

the signs which followed."[32] And again: "The voice of your thunder was in the whirlwind, and your lightning illumined the whole world."[33] For, as though from the clouds, the world, trembling by the thunderous commandments and astonishing miracles, was brought to fear and made to believe. COMMENTARY ON THE APOCALYPSE 4.5.[34]

**APOSTOLIC PREACHING HAS ONE SOURCE.** APRINGIUS OF BEJA: He desires that we understand that the entire original preaching of the apostles and indeed the heavenly and sacred doctrine proceeds from the judgment and inspiration of God. We interpret therefore the flashes of lightning to be the words of all the saints, and likewise the thunder to be the voices of the preachers. We confess that all these things come forth from one source, namely, God. Concerning these flashes of lightning and sounds of thunder, it is said: "The voice of your thunder was in the whirlwind; your lightnings illumined the whole world."[35] TRACTATE ON THE APOCALYPSE 4.5.[36]

**GOD ENLIGHTENS THOSE WORTHY OF SALVATION.** ANDREW OF CAESAREA: This passage shows how fearful and terrible God is to those unworthy of his long-suffering. However, [the lightning and thunder] become, to those worthy of salvation, their enlightenment. The lightning enlightens the eyes of the mind, and the thunder falls upon spiritual ears. COMMENTARY ON THE APOCALYPSE 4.5.[37]

### 4:5b The Seven Spirits of God

**THE SEVENFOLD SPIRIT IS PRESENT AT BAPTISM.** PRIMASIUS: These seven lamps are the seven spirits of God. Even if he had not explained it, we would have properly under-

---

[29]2 Tim 4:7-8. [30]CCL 107:61. [31]TEG 8:107-8. Andrew of Caesarea mentions the interpretation of Oecumenius, only to reject it. He agrees rather with the interpretation of Apringius: the twelve patriarchs and the twelve apostles are meant. [32]Mk 16:20. [33]Ps 77:18 (76:19 LXX). [34]CCL 92:48-49. [35]Ps 77:18 (76:19 LXX). [36]CCL 107:61-62. [37]MTS 1 Sup 1:49.

stood these seven lamps to represent the Holy Spirit. For we know that at the beginning he had illuminated the apostles in the form of fiery tongues, and [we are aware] of his sevenfold operation. How much more clear is it, when now he himself adds, "which are the seven spirits of God." But where is the Holy Spirit more properly said to be present than at the time of baptism, when we believe that each one of the faithful have properly received him. COMMENTARY ON THE APOCALYPSE 4.5.[38]

## 4:6 A Sea of Glass

**BAPTISM IS AN ENDURING GIFT FROM GOD.** VICTORINUS OF PETOVIUM: And "before the throne there was, as it were, a sea of glass similar to crystal." This is the gift of baptism, which he poured out through his Son during the time of repentance, before he should begin the judgment. And, therefore, it is "before the throne," that is, before the judgment. And since it says "a sea of glass similar to crystal," it shows that it is pure water, smooth, not made rough by the wind nor like a river flowing downhill, but given as an immovable gift from God. COMMENTARY ON THE APOCALYPSE 4.2.[39]

**ONE BAPTIZED OUTSIDE THE CHURCH.** PRIMASIUS: The sea of glass refers to baptism, where "it is believed with the heart unto justification, and there is confession with the mouth unto salvation."[40] And it is likened to glass because of faith. For in glass there is nothing to be seen on the outside than what is true on the inside. Nor is it without reason that baptism is said to be in the presence of the throne, lest heretics believe that they possess this or can bestow this outside [the church]. As so it says that [baptism is] in the presence of the throne, just as we read what was said to Moses, "The place is near me,"[41] or as God himself exhorted in Deuteronomy, "In the place which the Lord your God chooses, to make his name present there."[42] We know that by all these passages the indivisible unity of the church is

declared, where the Trinity may be received by baptism unto salvation, while the one who receives [baptism] outside [the church] is born to destruction. The gift of baptism is not evil but becomes evil when one to whom it is given makes evil use of it, just as was the morsel which was extended to Judas by the hand of the Lord. COMMENTARY ON THE APOCALYPSE 4.6.[43]

**THE FONT OF BAPTISM.** APRINGIUS OF BEJA: The sea of glass is like crystal, that is, it is transparent, indicating that it is infused by a certain whiteness and an uncommon purity. With good reason we think that this is said of the font of baptism and of the grace of regeneration. For [baptism] cleanses and illumines those who have received it and it clothes those who have been led to purity with the splendor of righteousness. These are the waters of which it is written in the prophets: "In those days living waters shall flow out from Jerusalem, half of them to the eastern sea and half of them to the western sea. They shall continue in summer and in winter."[44] TRACTATE ON THE APOCALYPSE 4.6.[45]

**A MULTITUDE OF HOLY SPIRITS SURROUND GOD.** OECUMENIUS: The vision of the sea indicates the multitude, the glass and crystal indicate the purity and utter cleanliness of the holy spirits who are around God, who are as a sea in multitude. For Daniel says, "A thousand thousands stood before him, and ten thousand times ten thousand served him."[46] And, although they be so many, they are all pure, similar to glass and crystal. COMMENTARY ON THE APOCALYPSE 4.4-6.[47]

## 4:6-7 The Four Living Creatures

**IMAGES OF THE DISPENSATION OF THE SON OF GOD.** IRENAEUS: It is not possible that the

---

[38]CCL 92:49. [39]CSEL 49:48. [40]See Rom 10:10. [41]See Ex 33:21. [42]Deut 14:23. [43]CCL 92:49-50. Primasius is probably referring to the Donatists. [44]Zech 14:8. [45]CCL 107:62. [46]Dan 7:10. [47]TEG 8:108-9.

Gospels can be either more or fewer in number than they are. For there are four zones of the world in which we live, and four principal winds, while the church is scattered throughout the world. And the "pillar and ground"[48] of the church is the gospel and the Spirit of life. So it is fitting that she should have four pillars, breathing out immortality on every side and making people alive once more. From which fact, it is evident that the Word, the Craftsman of all things, who sits upon the cherubim and contains all things, who was manifested to humankind, has given us the gospel under four aspects but bound together by one Spirit. As also David says, when praying to the manifestation of the Word, "You, who sit between the cherubim, shine forth."[49] For the cherubim, too, were four-faced, and their faces were images of the dispensation of the Son of God. For, [as the Scripture] says, "The first living creature was like a lion," symbolizing his effectual working, his leadership and royal power. The second [living creature] was like a calf, signifying [his] sacrificial and priestly order. But "the third had, as it were, the face as of a man," an evident description of the Word's advent as a human being. "The fourth was like a flying eagle," pointing out the gift of the Spirit hovering with his wings over the church. And therefore the Gospels are in accord with these things, among which Christ Jesus is seated. For the Word, according to John, relates his original, effectual and glorious generation from the Father, thus declaring, "In the beginning was the Word, and the Word was with God, and the Word was God."[50] Also, "all things were made by him, and without him was nothing made." For this reason, too, is that Gospel full of all confidence, for such is his person. But that according to Luke, the taking up [his] priestly character, commenced with Zechariah the priest offering sacrifice to God. For now was made ready the fatted calf, about to be sacrificed by fire for the finding again of the younger son.[51] Matthew, again, relates his generation of Jesus Christ, "the son of David, the son of Abra-

ham."[52] And also, "the birth of Jesus Christ happened this way."[53] This, then, is the Gospel of his humanity. For which reason it is, too, that [the character of] a humble and meek man is sustained through the whole Gospel. Mark, on the other hand, commences with [a reference to] the prophetic spirit coming down from on high to men. He says, "The beginning of the Gospel of Jesus Christ, as it is written in Isaiah the prophet,"[54] pointing to the winged aspect of the Gospel. On this account he made a compendious and cursory narrative, for such is the prophetic character. AGAINST HERESIES 3.11.8.[55]

**THE FOUR GOSPELS PROCEED FROM ONE MOUTH.** VICTORINUS OF PETOVIUM: The four animals are the four Gospels. "The first," he says, "was similar to a lion, the second similar to a calf, the third similar to a man and the fourth similar to an eagle in flight. And they had six wings all around and eyes within and without, and they did not cease to say, 'Holy, Holy, Holy, Lord God Almighty.'" . . . And that these animals were different in appearance has this explanation. The animal similar to the lion is the Gospel according to John. For while all the Evangelists proclaim that Christ was made man, he proclaims that he was God before he came down and assumed the flesh, saying, "The Word was God,"[56] and since he cried out, roaring like a lion, his preaching took on the appearance of a lion. The likeness of a man refers to Matthew, who strives to tell us the genealogy of Mary, from whom Christ took his flesh. And, therefore, since he numbers [the family of Mary] from Abraham to David and from David to Joseph, he speaks as though of a man, and for this reason his Gospel receives the image of a man. And Luke narrates the sacerdotal service of Zechariah, who offered a sacrifice for the people, and of the angel who appeared to him,

---

[48]1 Tim 3:15. [49]Ps 80:1 (79:1 LXX). [50]Jn 1:1. [51]Lk 15:23. [52]Mt 1:1, 18. [53]Mt 1:18. [54]Mk 1:1-2. [55]ANF 1:428**. Andrew of Caesarea explicitly follows Irenaeus. [56]Jn 1:1.

and on account of the sacerdotal service and the sacrifice, this narrative bears the image of a calf. As the interpreter of Peter, Mark remembered what he had taught publicly and wrote, although not in order, and began with the word of prophecy proclaimed by Isaiah. And therefore, the Gospels begin in the following ways. John says, "In the beginning was the Word and the Word was with God and the Word was God"[57]—these are the face of a lion. Matthew says, "The book of the generation of Jesus Christ, the Son of God, son of David, son of Abraham"[58]—this is the face of a man. Luke says, "There was a priest by the name of Zechariah, of the order of Abia, and his wife was from the daughters of Aaron"[59]—this is the image of the calf. Mark begins, "The beginning of the gospel of Jesus Christ, as was written in Isaiah,"[60] and so he begins with the Spirit in flight and so possesses the image of a flying eagle. However, it is not only the prophetic Spirit but also the very Word of God the Father Almighty, who is his Son, our Lord Jesus Christ, who bore the same images during the time of his coming to us. Indeed, he had been proclaimed as a lion and as a lion's whelp. For the salvation of humankind he was made man for the defeat of death and for the liberation of all. Because he offered himself as a sacrifice to God the Father for us, he is called a calf. And because, when death was conquered, he ascended into the heavens and held out his wings to cover his people, he is called an eagle in flight. And although there are four Evangelists yet there is really but one proclamation, because it proceeds from one mouth, just as the river in paradise was from one source yet was separated into four streams. COMMENTARY ON THE APOCALYPSE 4.3-4.[61]

**EZEKIEL AND JOHN SAW THE FOUR EVANGELISTS.** AUGUSTINE: Both in the prophet Ezekiel and in the Apocalypse of the same John whose Gospel this is, there is mentioned a quadruple beast, having four characteristic faces: a man's, a calf's, a lion's, an eagle's. Very many who have

commented on the mysteries of the holy Scriptures before us have understood the four Evangelists in this animal, or rather in these animals. The lion, [they say], has been put for king, because the lion seems to be, in a way, the king of beasts because of his power and terrifying bravery. This character has been attributed to Matthew because he described in proper order the royal line in the generations of the Lord, how the Lord was through royal descent from the seed of King David. But Luke, because he began from the priesthood of the priest Zechariah, making mention of the father of John the Baptist, is accounted the calf because the calf was the important victim in the sacrifice of the priests. Christ as a man has rightly been assigned to Mark, because neither did he say anything about his royal power nor did he begin from the priestly, but he simply started with Christ the man. All of these have practically not departed from the earthly things, that is, from those deeds that the Lord Jesus Christ performed on earth. They said very few things about his divinity, as if they were walking with him on earth. There remains the eagle: it is John, he who preaches the sublime and who gazes with unflinching eyes upon the internal and eternal light. TRACTATES ON THE GOSPEL OF JOHN 36.5.2.[62]

**THE FOUR GOSPELS ARE CHARACTERIZED BY THE FOUR CREATURES.** APRINGIUS OF BEJA: "The first animal was like a lion." Most of our interpreters say that this signifies the person of Mark, the Evangelist.[63] And indeed this seems most apt and true, for his Gospel begins in this way: "The beginning of the gospel of Jesus Christ, the Son of God. As it is written in Isaiah the prophet, 'Behold, I send my messenger who shall prepare the way before your face.'"[64] Nor is it strange that here Isaiah is mentioned instead

---

[57]Jn 1:1. [58]Mt 1:1. [59]Lk 1:5. [60]Mk 1:1-2. [61]CSEL 49:48-54. [62]FC 88:86-87*. [63]Apringius appears to be following Jerome, who preferred the order man, lion, calf, eagle (*On Ezekiel* 1.1.6-8. Bede follows Augustine). [64]Mk 1:2.

of Malachi, for most certainly this testimony occurs in Malachi. However, "Isaiah" means "the salvation of the Lord," and "Malachi" means "angel." And so at the beginning of the Gospel he prefers to speak of the salvation of the Lord, which is "Isaiah," rather than of the angel, which is "Malachi," in order that through the faith of the gospel he might suggest the immovable perpetuity of the present and future life. And then, to be sure, he mentions the "messenger," which is "angel," and he adds the words of Isaiah: "Prepare the way of the Lord; make straight the highways of our God,"[65] so that, salvation having been both promised and foretold, he might show the messenger of the truth and might prepare the hearts of humankind for the reception of grace. And the form of the lion is in this, that he reports that John was in the desert preaching and enjoying the desert, as he says: "John was in the desert baptizing and proclaiming the baptism of repentance for the forgiveness of sins."[66] The words "the second creature was like an ox" introduce Luke. For a bull is representative of the priesthood, as it is said in Isaiah: "Blessed are you who sow upon all the waters, letting the feet of the ox and the ass go free."[67] And so at the beginning of his Gospel, he speaks of Zechariah the priest: "In the days of Herod, king of Judea, there was a priest named Zechariah."[68] "The third living creature with the face of a man" indicates Matthew, for at the beginning of his Gospel, Matthew wished to report the genealogy of the Lord according to the flesh. The words "the fourth living creature was like a flying eagle" indicate John. For, at the beginning of his Gospel, John did not speak of the humanity of the Lord or of the priesthood or of John preaching in the desert. Rather, desiring like an eagle to reach toward the height of heaven itself, he left behind all things lowly and spoke properly of him as God: "In the beginning was the Word, and the Word was with God, and the Word was God; he was in the beginning with God."[69] TRACTATE ON THE APOCALYPSE 4.7.[70]

**THE PROVIDENCE OF GOD SUSTAINS ALL THINGS.** OECUMENIUS: But what did these creatures shown to the Evangelist signify? That would be good to explain. There was among some of the Jews a certain falsehood, that God exercised providential care among the holy orders in heaven and desired to dwell among them only, while he removed himself from those on the earth on account of Adam's sin and did not care about their well-being. And for that reason, they spoke in Isaiah the following: "Why have we fasted, and you did not know it? Why have we humbled ourselves, and you did not pay attention?"[71] And some such falsehood among them is suggested by this scriptural statement: "Lord, your mercy is in the heavens, and your faithfulness is unto the clouds."[72] It is as though the providence of God did not extend to the earth, regarding that as unworthy on account of sin. And therefore, the vision given to the Evangelist reveals that the providence of God pervades all things, sustaining those who dwell in heaven but also extending to those who dwell upon the earth. And this is what the four living creatures who are around the throne of God symbolize. For every physical and earthly creature is a compound of the four fundamental elements—fire, earth, air and water—and each of the living creatures symbolizes one of these: the lion is a symbol of fire, because of its vigorous ferocity. The ox is a symbol of the earth, because it is a beast that works the earth. The man is a symbol of the air, since he is heavenly and sublime on account of the subtlety of his mind. The eagle is a symbol of water, since the origin of birds is from water. And these creatures are seen to encircle the throne of God, indicating through the four creatures that what is upon the earth is worthy of attention and providential care. COMMENTARY ON THE APOCALYPSE 4.6-8.[73]

---

[65]Is 40:3. [66]Mk 1:4. [67]Is 32:20. [68]Lk 1:5. [69]Jn 1:1-2. [70]CCL 107:62-63. [71]Is 58:3. [72]Ps 36:5 (35:6 LXX). [73]TEG 8:109-10.

**THE CHURCH IS DEPICTED.** PRIMASIUS: The church, therefore, lives and works on the strength and beauty of the royal majesty, because the Lion of the tribe of Judah conquers. "For Judah is a lion's cub,"[74] from whose tribe kings are accustomed to be set over the people. "And the second animal was like a calf." For the same reason, the virtue of the church is indicated in the calf, namely, the first victim, for whenever anyone of the faithful is slain for Christ, he conquers at that moment. "Present your bodies as a living sacrifice, holy and pleasing to God, which is your reasonable worship,"[75] so that what the Head has accomplished on behalf of the body, the body may be worthy to fulfill for the Head. For this reason, [the Gospel of Luke] began with Zechariah the priest. "The third animal had a face like a man." In my opinion, the humility of the church is here commended. For although she has received "the Spirit of the adoption of sons"[76] and possesses "this treasure in clay vessels,"[77] she nevertheless freely prefers to glory humbly in her weaknesses than to be praised in the strengths that she has acquired. In this way she devoutly follows in the footsteps of the Master who was "made obedient even unto death"[78] and who said, "Learn from me for I am gentle and humble of heart."[79] "The fourth animal was like a flying eagle." The celestial church is being described as flying on the spiritual thoughts of her members. For she is free from the heaviness of earthly desires and is drawn into the heights at the direction of the two Testaments. COMMENTARY ON THE APOCALYPSE 4.7.[80]

### 4:8 The Creatures Each Had Six Wings

**THE NEW TESTAMENT REQUIRES THE OLD TESTAMENT FOR FAITH.** VICTORINUS OF PETOVIUM: The wings are the testimonies of the Old Testament, that is, of the twenty-four books, the same number as the elders upon the tribunals. For just as an animal cannot fly unless it has wings, neither can the preaching of the New Testament acquire faith unless its testimony is seen to correspond to those foretold in the Old Testament, through which it rises from the earth and flies. For it is always the case that when something spoken in the past is later found to have happened, that creates an undoubting faith. . . . If the wings do not attach to the animal, they have no source from which to draw their life. And so, unless that which the prophets foretold had been fulfilled in Christ, their preaching would be empty. And therefore the catholic church believes both that which was previously foretold and that which afterwards was fulfilled, and rightly then flies and is lifted from the earth, as though a living animal. Those heretics, however, who make no use of the prophetic testimony are as animals who do not fly, because they are of the earth.[81] And likewise the Jews, who do not accept the preaching of the New Testament, are like wings which have no life, for they offer empty prophecies to people, not allowing the [fulfilling] deeds to correspond to the words [of prophecy]. COMMENTARY ON THE APOCALYPSE 4.5.[82]

**THE TWO WINGS OF THE TESTAMENTS.** TYCONIUS: In the animals the twenty-four elders are indicated, for six wings in four animals amount to twenty-four wings, and moreover he saw the animals around the throne, which is where he said that he had seen the elders. But how could an animal with six wings be like an eagle with two wings unless the four animals were one with twenty-four wings? And in this we recognize the twenty-four elders who are the church, which he likens to an eagle with two wings, that is, the two Testaments, upon which it is borne above, lest it be hindered by earthly affections. COMMENTARY ON THE APOCALYPSE 4.8.[83]

---

[74]Gen 49:9. [75]Rom 12:1. [76]Rom 8:15. [77]2 Cor 4:7. [78]Phil 2:8. [79]Mt 11:29. [80]CCL 92:53-54. Primasius follows the explanation of Augustine but adds this interpretation concerning the church. Following Tyconius, Christ and the church are always mutually implied. [81]Victorinus refers to the followers of Marcion. [82]CSEL 49:54-56. [83]CCL 92:55.

## 4:8 The Creatures Sing, "Holy, Holy, Holy"

**THE DUTY OF OUR FUTURE GLORY.** TERTUL-LIAN: Certainly it is right that God should be blessed in all places and at all times because it is every person's duty to be ever mindful of his benefits, but this wish takes the form of a benediction. Moreover, when is the name of God not holy and blessed in itself, when of itself it makes others holy? To him the attending hosts of angels cease not to say, "Holy, holy, holy!"[84] Therefore, we, too—the future comrades of the angels, if we earn this reward—become familiar even while here on this earth with that heavenly cry of praise to God and the duty of our future glory. ON PRAYER 3.2-3.[85]

**THE FATHER AND THE SON ARE ONE GOD.** RUFINUS OF AQUILEIA: "Almighty" is applied to him on account of the dominion he has over the universe. But the Father governs the universe through the Son, as the apostle himself states: "For through him were all things created, visible and invisible, whether thrones, or dominions, or principalities, or powers."[86] Again, writing to the Hebrews, he states, "Because through him he made the world and appointed him heir of all things."[87] By "appointed" we are to take him as meaning "generated." But if the Father made the world through him, and if through him all things were created and he is the heir of all things, it must be through him that he wields his sway over the universe. Just as light is generated from light and truth from truth, so Almighty is generated from Almighty. So we read in John's Apocalypse about the seraphim: "And they rested not day and night, saying, 'Holy, holy, holy, Lord God of armies, who was, and who is, and is to come, the Almighty.' " He then who is to come is called Almighty. Who else is to come save Christ, the Son of God? COMMENTARY ON THE APOSTLES' CREED 5.[88]

**THE ANGELS GLORIFY THE ONE AND INDIVISIBLE TRINITY.** ATHANASIUS: For what is nearer [God] than the cherubim or the seraphim? And yet they, not even seeing him or standing on their feet, or even with bare, but as it were with veiled faces, offer their praises, with untiring lips doing nothing else but glorifying the divine and ineffable nature with the Trisagion. . . . For the Triad, praised, reverenced and adored, is one and indivisible and without degrees. It is united without confusion, just as the Monad also is distinguished without separation. For the fact of those venerable living creatures offering their praises three times, saying "Holy, holy, holy," proves that the three Subsistences are perfect, just as in saying "Lord," they declare the one Essence. ON LUKE 10:22.[89]

**THE CHURCH CEASELESSLY PRAISES GOD.** PRIMASIUS: Everywhere diffused in its individual members and in those who profess [the faith], the church ceaselessly praises God by word and deed in times of difficulty and in times of prosperity, and she does this throughout a variety of cities, regions, provinces, languages and peoples. Nor does she cease to praise the Lord day and night, while that perpetual praise continues that is given by those rational creatures in the heavens, in the Jerusalem above, after whose likeness the pilgrim church rejoices to be formed. COMMENTARY ON THE APOCALYPSE 4.8.[90]

## 4:10 The Elders Worship

**THE PROPHETS REJOICE AT THE FULFILLMENT OF THEIR WORDS.** VICTORINUS OF PETOVIUM: And when these things occurred, he says, "All the elders fell down and worshiped the Lord, when the animals gave him glory and honor." That is, when the gospel—namely, both the actions and the teaching of the Lord—had fulfilled that word previously foretold by them, [the prophets] worthily and properly exulted, knowing that they had rightly ministered the word of the Lord. And

---

[84]Is 6:3. [85]FC 40:161. [86]Col 1:16. [87]Heb 1:2. [88]ACW 20:36-37*. The text of Rufinus has a final "Almighty" at the end, enabling him to designate Christ as the Almighty. [89]NPNF 2 4:90. Also Andrew of Caesarea believes the Trisagion refers to the "tri-hypostatic deity." [90]CCL 92:57.

finally, because he had come who would conquer death and would alone be worthy to take the crown of immortality, as many as possessed crowns because of the glory of his most excellent deed "threw them under his feet," that is, on account of the greatness of the victory of Christ they threw their victories under his feet. COMMENTARY ON THE APOCALYPSE 4.7.[91]

**THE CHURCH ASCRIBES ITS VIRTUE AND DIGNITY TO GOD.** PRIMASIUS: When the animals resound with praise, that is, when the Evangelists preach and celebrate the dispensation of Christ, . . . the twenty-four elders, that is, the whole church, that is, the leaders and people immediately fall on their faces and adore him who lives forever and ever. . . . By casting their crowns before the throne, they are ascribing to God whatever they possess of virtue and dignity. For whatever good we seek and acquire by right is attributed to him from whom he who conquers receives assistance. A figure of this action

occurred in the Gospel when the people, going before the Lord, cast their garments and palm branches on the road before him, saying,. "Blessed is he who comes in the name of the Lord, the King of Israel."[92] COMMENTARY ON THE APOCALYPSE 4.10.[93]

### 4:11 *Worthy Are You*

**ALL THINGS WERE CREATED TO REVEAL THE WISDOM OF GOD.** TYCONIUS: We also know of another translation: "Because you have created all things, and they exist and are created on account of your will." Indeed, all things existed in the artful wisdom [of God] before they were formed in the act of creation. However, they were created in order that those things might exist also visibly which in their natures are according to the ideas written in the wisdom of God. COMMENTARY ON THE APOCALYPSE 4.11.[94]

---

[91]CSEL 49:58.    [92]Mt 21:9; 23:39.    [93]CCL 92:57-58.    [94]CCL 92:58.

---

## 5:1-5 A SCROLL SEALED WITH SEVEN SEALS

[1]*And I saw in the right hand of him who was seated on the throne a scroll written within and on the back, sealed with seven seals;* [2]*and I saw a strong angel proclaiming with a loud voice, "Who is worthy to open the scroll and break its seals?"* [3]*And no one in heaven or on earth or under the earth was able to open the scroll or to look into it,* [4]*and I wept much that no one was found worthy to open the scroll or to look into it.* [5]*Then one of the elders said to me, "Weep not; lo, the Lion of the tribe of Judah, the Root of David, has conquered, so that he can open the scroll and its seven seals."*

---

**OVERVIEW:** Although the Old Testament was a messenger and a veil of the New Testament, it remained obscure and closed until through his humanity Christ opened and unsealed the Scriptures (APRINGIUS, PRIMASIUS). Through his pas-

sion and resurrection, Christ makes clear a plenitude of mysteries (CAESARIUS OF ARLES) and makes it possible to interpret the whole of Scripture according to its literal and its spiritual meanings (ORIGEN, ANDREW OF CAESAREA). Also, as though all of humankind were registered in a book, God remembers all persons, both those from Israel who followed the law and those from the Gentiles who had been idolaters (OECUMENIUS, ANDREW OF CAESAREA). Moreover, God can perceive the inmost parts of a person even as he knows a person's outward deeds (APRINGIUS).

However, only Christ through the dispensation of his flesh could unseal and open the book. He alone was prophesied by the law as the one who was to die and who was to become God's heir so that he might inherit the human race as his own (VICTORINUS). For such a purpose no angelic creature had either power or right. For such a purpose no one on earth had either power or the needed perfection. For such a purpose no one under the earth, not even one of the departed saints, was worthy (PRIMASIUS, GREGORY THE GREAT). None of these could contemplate the splendor of the New Testament, even as the sons of Israel were not able to look upon the face of Moses (BEDE).

Yet, although no angel, no righteous person, no saint among the dead could open the book, the weeping of the church for her sins and her longing for redemption is not in vain (TYCONIUS, PRIMASIUS). The Lion of Judah was foretold by all the prophets, and their promise gives consolation to the church (TYCONIUS). Christ is the Lion of Judah, and through his death and resurrection he proves himself to be not only a lion but also a lamb. Although he accepted death in innocence, he killed death by power (TYCONIUS, AUGUSTINE). He conquered the devil, who is fierce as a lion. Yet he is a lamb toward the world. He is gentle, lovable and innocent, yet also strong, terrifying and mighty (AUGUSTINE). Although the antichrist will seek to deceive by imitating this Lion of Judah (HIPPOLYTUS), this lion is not only human but also is the Root of David, true God, the Source of all things visible and invisible (OECUMENIUS).

### 5:1 A Scroll Sealed with Seven Seals

**CHRIST REVEALS THE MEANING OF THE SCRIP-**

**TURES.** ORIGEN: And what book does John see, which has writing on the front and back and is sealed? Which book could no one read and loose its seals, except the Lion of the tribe of Judah, the root of David who has the key of David, and who opens and no one will close, and closes and no one will open? For the whole Scripture is what is revealed by the book that has writing on the front because its interpretation is easy, and on the back because it is hidden and spiritual. COMMENTARY ON THE GOSPEL OF JOHN 5.6.[1]

**THE SEVEN STAGES OF CHRIST'S LIFE.** APRINGIUS OF BEJA: This scroll, which is said to be written on the inside and on the outside, is all of the present world which is a creature [of God]. God perceives the inner [thoughts of every creature] and he knows their outer deeds. For, by the virtue of his power he surpasses this world which is contained [by him] and by the clarity of his majesty he searches into the inmost parts. The book is said to be sealed by seven seals, so that the decree and limit of the present seven days, in which the world was made, might be manifested. Another interpretation: This book signifies the teaching of the Old Testament, which was given into the hands of our Lord, who accepted the judgment from the Father. The seven seals are these: First, incarnation; second, birth; third, passion; fourth, death; fifth, resurrection; sixth, glory; seventh, kingdom. These seals, therefore, are Christ. Since he completed all things through his humanity, he opened and unsealed everything which had been closed and sealed in the Scriptures. TRACTATE ON THE APOCALYPSE 5.1.[2]

**THE OLD TESTAMENT VEILS THE NEW AND THE NEW REVEALS THE OLD.** PRIMASIUS: The book is in the right hand because it is in Christ, for he is the arm of God, he is the right hand of the Father, or it means that it was in the highest blessedness. The book written on the inside and the outside is both Testaments, the Old Testa-

---

[1]FC 80:164*. [2]CCL 107:65-66.

ment on the outside because it was visible, and the New Testament on the inside because it lay hidden within the Old.[3] The apostle speaks to the Hebrews of this: "For you have not come to what may be touched, a fire, a storm, and gloom, and a tempest, and the sound of a trumpet, and a voice with words whose hearers entreated that no further word be given to them, for they could not bear what was said," and the following.[4] However, now "comparing spiritual things with spiritual things, we do not contemplate what is seen but what is not seen,[5] for the things that are seen are temporal, but the things that are unseen are eternal."[6] And therefore one book is mentioned, since the New Testament cannot be without the Old, nor the Old without the New. For the Old Testament is the messenger and the veil of the New, while the New is the fulfillment and revelation of the Old. And because the Old Testament was on the outside, it neither disclosed everything nor did it conceal everything. Or, to express this more clearly, every dispensation of the Savior that is either promised or enacted in either Testament is collected here in this book. COMMENTARY ON THE APOCALYPSE 5.1.[7]

**GOD REMEMBERS ALL OF HUMANKIND AS IN A BOOK.** OECUMENIUS: The holy Scriptures depict for us a certain book, in which all of humankind is registered, perhaps calling God's memory of us a "book," except that the prophet calls it a "scroll," saying, "Your eyes saw my unformed substance, and in your scroll shall they all be written."[8] And the most wise Moses, making propitiation for sinful Israel, weeps and cries out to God, "But now, if you will forgive their sin, forgive, but if not, blot me out of your book which you have written."[9] The holy Evangelist saw this book written within and without. That written "within" may be those from Israel who are registered as pious through the guidance of the law, while that "without" would be those from the Gentiles who by a worse fate had been idolaters before they believed in Christ. The

scroll was in the right hand of God. This is, as I certainly think, the ways of the saints who walked uprightly in the old covenant. The scroll was rolled up and sealed with seven seals. As a perfect number, the seven shows how exceedingly securely the scroll is closed and sealed up. COMMENTARY ON THE APOCALYPSE 5.1-7.[10]

**THE DEATH OF CHRIST REVEALS EVERY MYSTERY.** CAESARIUS OF ARLES: "Sealed," it says, "by seven seals." This means that the book was obscured by the plenitude of all mysteries, since until the passion and resurrection of Christ it had remained sealed. For in no way is anything called a "testament," unless those who are about to die make it, and it is sealed until the death of the testator, and after his death, it is opened. And so, after the death of Christ every mystery was revealed. EXPOSITION OF THE APOCALYPSE 5.1, HOMILY 4.[11]

**THE WISDOM OF GOD.** ANDREW OF CAESAREA: We recognize the book to be the most wise memory of God in which, according to David, all people are recorded, as well as the depths of the divine judgments. Those things written on the outside through the letter are more easily comprehended. Those things written on the inside through the Spirit are more difficult to decipher. The "seven seals" signify either the obscurity of the book which is known to no one or the economies of him "who searches the depths of the Spirit of God."[12] No created being is able to open these seals. The "book" also is understood to be the prophecy that Christ himself said to be fulfilled in the Gospel,[13] but the rest of [the prophecy] will be fulfilled in the last days. COMMENTARY ON THE APOCALYPSE 5.1.[14]

### 5:2 *"Who is Worthy to Open the Scroll?"*

---

[3]Primasius uses Tyconius to this point. [4]Heb 12:18-20. [5]1 Cor 2:13. [6]2 Cor 4:18. [7]CCL 92:61-62. [8]Ps 139:16 (138:16 LXX). [9]Ex 32:32. [10]TEG 8:112-13. [11]PL 35:2423. [12]1 Cor 2:10. [13]Lk 4:21. [14]MTS 1 Sup 1:53-54.

**IN HIS DEATH CHRIST INHERITS THE HUMAN RACE.** VICTORINUS OF PETOVIUM: "In the hand of him who is seated on the tribunal there is a book written within, sealed by seven seals." This signifies the Old Testament which was given into the hand of our Lord, who received the judgment from the Father. "A herald cried out," he says, "whether there was anyone worthy to open the book and to loose its seals, and no one was found worthy, neither in heaven, nor on earth, nor under the earth." However, to open the testament is to suffer and to conquer death for humanity. No one was found worthy to do this, neither among the angels in heaven, nor among men on the earth, nor among the souls of the saints who are at rest; only Christ, the Son of God, whom he says that he saw as though a lamb slain, having seven horns. What had been prophesied of him, whatever the law had mediated of him through oblations and sacrifices, it was necessary that he fulfill. And because he himself was the testator who had conquered death, it was just that he himself be appointed God's heir, so that he might possess the property of the one who was dying, that is, the human race. COMMENTARY ON THE APOCALYPSE 5.1.[15]

### 5:3 No One Was Able to Open the Scroll

**THE INCARNATE SON OF GOD ALONE CAN FULFILL ALL THINGS.** PRIMASIUS: When it says that no one in heaven was found worthy, it indicates that [opening the scroll] exceeded the capacities of the angels. This was not because they were ignorant of the future mystery of the Lord's incarnation and work but because this was not to be completed through an angelic creature. For the Son of God, who through the assumption of true humanity was going to redeem humanity, wishes to fulfill all things through himself. Therefore Isaiah said, "Neither an angel nor a messenger but the Lord himself saved them."[16] When it says that no one on the earth was worthy, it means that no one of the just remains perfect in this life, for in order to be re-created man

requires the assistance of him who alone is Creator. And that no one could be found under the earth means that no one among the saints who had died was found worthy to open the scroll or even to see it. Here "to see" means "to comprehend," and therefore Paul says that he preaches the unsearchable riches of Christ to the Gentiles[17] of which the Lord spoke, that is, the glory of the New Testament that was hidden in the law and that Christ reserved for his own presence. And so, no one was able to see this with an adequate sight, so that he might be able to effect it, since Christ had the power to fulfill it by his own dispensation. For [this glory] could only be foreseen by them, but it could not be effected. COMMENTARY ON THE APOCALYPSE 5.3.[18]

**WHY HELL IS UNDER THE EARTH.** GREGORY THE GREAT: But it occurs to me that if we call an object "infernal" because it lies in a lower position, then hell ought to be "infernal" to the earth just as the earth is to the sky. This is perhaps what the psalmist had in mind when he said, "You have freed my soul from the lower infernal regions."[19] The earth then is the "upper infernal," and lying below this is the "lower infernal." The words of John, too, are in keeping with this concept. He says he saw a book sealed with seven seals, and, because no one was found worthy to open the seals, either in heaven or on earth or under the earth, he "was all in tears." Yet, later, he says that the Lion of the tribe of Judah opened the book. This book can refer only to sacred Scriptures, for no one opened it but Christ our Redeemer, who became man, and by his death, resurrection and ascension opened the way to all the mysteries it contained. No one in heaven opened it, because no angel could. No one on earth opened it, because no one living in the flesh had the power of doing so. No one under the earth was found worthy to open it, because souls separated from their bodies do not have such

---

[15]CSEL 49:60-62. [16]Is 63:9. [17]Eph 3:8. [18]CCL 92:83. [19]Ps 86:13 (85:13 LXX).

powers. No one but our Lord could open up the hidden meanings of the sacred word. Since, then, no one under the earth was found worthy to unseal the book, I see no reason why we should not believe that hell is under the earth. DIALOGUES 4.44.[20]

**THE SPLENDOR OF THE NEW TESTAMENT.** BEDE: This vision shows to us the mysteries of the holy Scriptures, which were revealed through the incarnation of the Lord. Its harmonious unity contains, as it were, the Old Testament without and the New Testament within. . . . Neither an angel nor anyone of the righteous who are already freed from the flesh was able to reveal or to search out the mysteries of the divine law or to look into the book, that is, to contemplate the splendor of the grace of the New Testament. Similarly, the sons of Israel had not been able to look upon the face of the giver of the law of the Old Testament, which contains the New. EXPLANATION OF THE APOCALYPSE 5.1-3.[21]

### 5:4 I Wept Much

**THE CHURCH WEEPS AND BESEECHES.** PRIMASIUS: It was the church that wept in John's weeping, for she is weighed down with the burden of sins and beseeches her own redemption, which was shown to exist in the opening of this book. COMMENTARY ON THE APOCALYPSE 5.4.[22]

### 5:5 The Lion of Judah Has Conquered

**THE ANTICHRIST DECEIVES BY IMITATING THE SON OF GOD.** HIPPOLYTUS: Now, as our Lord Jesus Christ, who is also God, was prophesied under the figure of a lion,[23] because of his royalty and glory, in the same way have the Scriptures also previously spoken of antichrist as a lion, because of his tyranny and violence. For the deceiver seeks to liken himself in all things to the Son of God. Christ is a lion, so antichrist is also a lion. Christ is a king,[24] so antichrist is also a king. The Savior was manifested as a lamb;[25] so he too,

similarly, will appear as a lamb, though within he is a wolf. The Savior came into the world in the circumcision, and he too will come in the same way. The Lord sent apostles among all the nations, and he similarly will send false apostles. The Savior gathered together the sheep that were scattered abroad,[26] and he too will bring together a people that is scattered abroad. The Lord gave a seal to those who believed on him, and he too will give one in like manner. The Savior appeared in the form of man, and he too will come in the form of a man. The Savior raised up and showed his holy flesh like a temple,[27] and he too will raise a temple of stone in Jerusalem. ON THE ANTICHRIST 6.[28]

**THE LION OF JUDAH IS THE CONSOLATION OF THE CHURCH.** TYCONIUS: In this one elder we recognize the whole body of the prophets, for their prophecies consoled the church as they foretold that Christ would come from the tribe of Judah and would redeem the world by his own blood. Of him it was foretold: "Judah is a lion's whelp. For prey, my son, you have gone up. You lie in wait as a lion and as a lioness. Who will rouse him up?"[29] Moreover, the same one is taught to be a lamb as well as a lion, for he assumed death with a devout innocence, even as he killed with power the death he had assumed. To death he had long ago truly issued threats, saying through Hosea, "I will be your death, O death, I will be your sting, O hades."[30] And through Isaiah, "Behold, the root of Jesse will rise for the salvation of the people. The nations will entreat him, and his sepulcher will be glorious."[31] For when anyone of the faithful individually and earnestly weeps for his or her own sins and recalls the promises of redemption "through the consolation of the Scriptures,"[32] [that person] will recognize that he or she has the hope of eternal salvation. As I say, by one of the elders this is con-

---

[20]FC 39:252-53.  [21]CCL 121A:287-89.  [22]CCL 92:84.  [23]Gen 49:8-9.  [24]Jn 18:37.  [25]Jn 1:29.  [26]Jn 11:52.  [27]Jn 2:19.  [28]ANF 5:206.  [29]Gen 49:9.  [30]See Hos 13:14.  [31]Is 11:10.  [32]Rom 15:4.

firmed with a similar response. For this reason, he mentions what is past while he is also promising the future, because in the things of the past the Spirit shows future things by way of subtle hints. COMMENTARY ON THE APOCALYPSE 5.5.[33]

**TOWARD THE DEVIL CHRIST IS A LION, TOWARD THE WORLD A LAMB.** AUGUSTINE: So the true victory of our Lord Jesus Christ was achieved when he rose again and ascended into heaven. Then was fulfilled what you heard when the Apocalypse was read, "The lion from the tribe of Judah has conquered." It is he that is called a lion, he that is called a lamb. He is called a lion for courage, a lamb for innocence. A lion because unconquered, a lamb because gentle. And when this lamb was slain, he conquered by his death the lion "who prowls around seeking whom he may devour." The devil, you see, is called a lion for his ferocity, not for any virtue. Thus the apostle Peter says we must be on the watch against temptations, "because your adversary the devil is prowling around seeking whom he may devour"; but he did say how he prowls around: "Like a roaring lion he is prowling around, seeking whom he may devour."[34] Who could avoid encountering the teeth of this lion, if the lion from the tribe of Judah had not conquered? Against the lion fights a lion, against the world a lamb. The devil was exultant when Christ died, and by that very death of Christ was the devil conquered. It's as though he took the bait in a mousetrap. He was delighted at the death, as being the commander of death. What he delighted in, that's where the trap was set for him. The mousetrap for the devil was the cross of the Lord. The bait he would be caught by, the death of the Lord. And our Lord Jesus Christ rose again. SERMON 263.2.[35]

**IN HIS DEATH AND RESURRECTION CHRIST IS LAMB AND LION.** AUGUSTINE: "Like a sheep he was led to be slaughtered, and like a lamb in the presence of his shearer he was without voice, thus he did not open his mouth." Who is this? Obviously the one about whom he goes on to say,

"In humility his judgment was taken away. His generation, who shall relate?"[36] I can see this model of such humility in a king of such power and authority. Because this one, who is like a lamb not opening its mouth in the presence of the shearer, is himself "the lion from the tribe of Judah." Who is this, both lamb and lion? He endured death as a lamb; he devoured it as a lion. Who is this, both lamb and lion? Gentle and strong, lovable and terrifying, innocent and mighty, silent when he was being judged,[37] roaring when he comes to judge. Or perhaps both in his passion lamb and lion, and also in his resurrection lamb and lion. Let us see him as a lamb in his passion. It was stated a moment ago: "Like a lamb in the presence of his shearer he was without voice, thus he did not open his mouth." Let us see him as a lion in his passion; Jacob said, "You have gone up, lying down you have slept like a lion."[38] Let us see him as a lamb in his resurrection. The book of Revelation, when it was talking about the eternal glory of virgins, "They follow the lamb, it is said, wherever he goes."[39] The same book of Revelation says, what I mentioned just now, "The lion from the tribe of Judah has conquered, to open the book." Why a lamb in his passion? Because he underwent death without being guilty of any iniquity. Why a lion in his passion? Because in being slain he slew death. Why a lamb in his resurrection? Because his innocence is everlasting. Why a lion in his resurrection? Because everlasting also is his might. SERMON 375A.1.[40]

**THE INCARNATE LORD IS THE ROOT OF DAVID.** OECUMENIUS: For he said to me, "Behold, the Lion from the tribe of Judah, the Root of David, has conquered, so that he can open its seven seals." He who has conquered our conqueror, the devil, it says, that is the one who has opened the scroll and its seals. And who was

---

[33]CCL 92:84-85. The contrast between Christ as a lion and as a lamb had been made already by Victorinus. [34]1 Pet 5:8. [35]*WSA* 3 7:219-20. [36]Is 53:8. [37]Mk 15:5. [38]Gen 49:9. [39]Rev 14:4. [40]*WSA* 3 10:330.

this "Lion from the tribe of Judah"? Obviously, the Christ, concerning whom the patriarch Jacob spoke: "He lay down and couched as a lion and as a lion's whelp. Who will arouse him?"[41] For the holy apostle is witness that the Lord was from Judah according to the flesh: "It is evident that our Lord Jesus Christ was descended from Judah."[42] Someone might wonder why he was not called "a rod from the root of Jesse" or "flower coming out of the root," as Isaiah said,[43] but rather the "root of David." He says this to show that although according to his humanity he was a rod coming forth from the root of Jesse and David, according to his deity he was the root not only of David but of every visible and invisible creature, since he was the source of them all. COMMENTARY ON THE APOCALYPSE 5.1-7.[44]

---

[41]Gen 49:9. [42]Heb 7:14. [43]Is 11:1. [44]TEG 8:114-15.

---

## 5:6-14 THE LAMB TAKES THE SCROLL

[6]And between the throne and the four living creatures and among the elders, I saw a Lamb standing, as though it had been slain, with seven horns and with seven eyes, which are the seven spirits of God sent out into all the earth; [7]and he went and took the scroll from the right hand of him who was seated on the throne. [8]And when he had taken the scroll, the four living creatures and the twenty-four elders fell down before the Lamb, each holding a harp, and with golden bowls full of incense, which are the prayers of the saints; [9]and they sang a new song, saying,

"Worthy art thou to take the scroll and to open its seals,
  for thou wast slain and by thy blood didst ransom men for God
  from every tribe and tongue and people and nation,
[10]and hast made them a kingdom and priests to our God,
  and they shall reign on earth."

[11]Then I looked, and I heard around the throne and the living creatures and the elders the voice of many angels, numbering myriads of myriads and thousands of thousands, [12]saying with a loud voice, "Worthy is the Lamb who was slain, to receive power and wealth and wisdom and might and honor and glory and blessing!" [13]And I heard every creature in heaven and on earth and under the earth and in the sea, and all therein, saying, "To him who sits upon the throne and to the Lamb be blessing and honor and glory and might for ever and ever!"[14]And the four living creatures said, "Amen!" and the elders fell down and worshiped.

---

**OVERVIEW:** In the Lamb the church beholds the Son of God in his humanity, through which he became the expiation of the whole world (ORIGEN). Although he appears still bearing the trophies of his death (OECUMENIUS), the Lamb stands in the midst of power and the greatness of deity (APRINGIUS). He appears "as though slain," because he trampled death and despoiled hades of

---

all the souls held in it (APRINGIUS, OECUMENIUS). He appears with the symbols of power and of the seven virtues of the Holy Spirit by whom Christ reigns throughout the world in his church (TYCONIUS, APRINGIUS, OECUMENIUS). The Lamb also represents the church, for through her martyrs and through her sacrifice of worldly passions the Lamb is said to be slain (TYCONIUS, CAESARIUS OF ARLES).

Through the economy of the incarnate Word, God is regaining sovereignty over the earth, even as he has sovereignty in heaven (IRENAEUS, APRINGIUS). Receiving power over all things, the Lamb invests humanity with light from the Father and brings it to immortality (IRENAEUS). Likewise, by his death the testament of Moses which was sealed is now unsealed, revealing that Christ has received as his own possession the human race (VICTORINUS). Through his resurrection Christ has made known the mystery of the Trinity that had been hidden from the ages (APRINGIUS), and he has given to his church that same authority that he received from the Father (PRIMASIUS).

Beholding now the Savior of the world, the faithful render to him a harmonious and melodious doxology (ANDREW OF CAESAREA) through their prayers, their public confession, their intercessions, their virtues, and their good deeds (ORIGEN, PRIMASIUS, ANDREW OF CAESAREA). For as the women carried spices to the tomb of Christ, we bear spices and send forth incense when we show to our neighbor the light of a pure life and give to Christ bodies prepared for a martyr's death (BEDE). The praise of the church is a "new song."

Through his life, death and resurrection Christ has fulfilled the Old Testament through the New and leads humankind into the newness of life (VICTORINUS, PRIMASIUS). And so, freed from the antiquity of the letter, every nation and tongue sing the new song of the Spirit, for they have become kings by ruling their passions and priests by offering themselves as a living and holy sacrifice to God (OECUMENIUS, ANDREW OF CAE-

SAREA). This doxology of the faithful is the worship of the whole church, of angels and of men, together with her martyrs (CAESARIUS OF ARLES, ANDREW OF CAESAREA). And to this praise is added that of all existing things, who glorify God in words proper to their own natures (ANDREW OF CAESAREA).

## 5:6 A Lamb As Though Slain

**THE HUMANITY OF CHRIST IS THE EXPIATION OF THE WORLD.** ORIGEN: But if we examine the declaration about Jesus who is pointed out by John in the words, "This is the Lamb of God who takes away the sin of the world,"[1] from the standpoint of the dispensation itself of the bodily sojourn of the Son of God in the life of humankind, we will assume that the lamb is none other than his humanity. For he "was led as a sheep to the slaughter, and was dumb as a lamb before its shearer,"[2] saying, "I was as an innocent lamb being led to be sacrificed."[3] This is why in the Apocalypse, too, a little lamb is seen "standing as though slain." This lamb, indeed, which was slain in accordance with certain secret reasons, has become the expiation of the whole world. In accordance with the Father's love for humanity, he also submitted to slaughter on behalf of the world, purchasing us with his own blood from him who bought us when we had sold ourselves to sins. COMMENTARY ON THE GOSPEL OF JOHN 6.273-74.[4]

**WHEN THE CHURCH MORTIFIES ITSELF, THE LAMB IS SLAIN.** TYCONIUS: The throne, the animals, the elders are all the church. For the church is in the midst, and he continues to describe the scene and says, "A lamb standing as though slain." For as often as Christ is preached in the midst of the church as slain, so often is the same Lamb seen as though sacrificed for the fault of the world, since what is unknown is made known to the uninitiated and the memory

---

[1]Jn 1:29. [2]Is 53:7. [3]Jer 11:19. [4]FC 80:242.

of the faithful is formed by a pious worship. For whenever the church, which Christ has put on, mortifies herself to the world that she might live to God, the Lamb is said to be sacrificed, as though the Head for the body. And so it continues: "Having seven horns and seven eyes which are the seven spirits of God sent out into all the earth." The variety of words teaches but one understanding, for the horns symbolize the most excellent gifts of the Holy Spirit by which Christ reigns throughout the world in his church. It continues, "which are the seven spirits of God." For no one governs with a righteous prominence throughout the world or is especially glorified by the gift of the Holy Spirit spread abroad, except the church. As we know, seven signifies universality and completeness. And this is true, because the horns are upon the head, and so the exaltation of each church is rightly said to be placed upon Christ. For "upon this Rock I shall build my church,"[5] which is as though he said, "I shall build you upon me." COMMENTARY ON THE APOCALYPSE 5.6.[6]

### THE LAMB IS SLAIN IN THE MARTYRS OF THE CHURCH. CAESARIUS OF ARLES: The throne, the animals, the elders and the Lamb as though slain are all the church together with her head. [The church] dies for Christ that she might live with Christ. The martyrs in the church may also be understood as the Lamb slain. EXPOSITION OF THE APOCALYPSE 5.6, HOMILY 4.[7]

### THE LIVING CHRIST GOVERNS WITH GREAT POWER. APRINGIUS OF BEJA: Here he showed even more clearly our Lord, Jesus Christ, whom he declares was not dead but was as though slain because of the suffering and the death which he had undergone. He says that he had seen this [Lamb] in the midst of the throne, that is, in power and in divine majesty. "And among the four living creatures." This is because he is known in the fourfold order of the gospels. "And among the elders." By this he indicates the chorus of the law and the prophets, or of the apos-

tles. He testifies that he saw the Lamb there, not slain but as if slain, that is, even he who had conquered death and had trampled upon the passion. "And he had seven horns and seven eyes." The horns symbolize power and strength. The number seven represents the condition of the world which he rules effectively and which he governs with great power. Moreover, he calls the seven eyes the seven spirits of God, and in this way speaks of the Holy Spirit who remains with our Lord, Jesus Christ, gloriously by the degrees of the seven virtues. Concerning him the apostle says: "We know that God was in Christ reconciling the world to himself."[8] And again: "The Spirit of him who raised Christ from the dead will also vivify our mortal bodies on account of his Spirit who dwells in you."[9] Since "their sound has gone out into the whole world,"[10] he speaks of the Spirit as "those sent," calling to mind the gifts of the Holy Spirit which have been abundantly spread throughout the entire earth. TRACTATE ON THE APOCALYPSE 5.6.[11]

### CHRIST STILL BEARS THE TROPHIES OF HIS DEATH. OECUMENIUS: He has called the Lord a "lamb," because of his innocence in providing what we need. For just as every year the lamb provides by giving of its wool, so also the Lord "opens his hand and satisfies the desire of every living thing."[12] And so, prophecy speaks of him in this way, through Isaiah: "As a lamb that is led to the slaughter, and like a sheep that before its shearer is dumb";[13] and also through Jeremiah: "I was like an innocent lamb led to the slaughter, and I did not know."[14] But the lamb [in the vision] had not been slain, but it was "as though it had been slain." For Christ returned to life, having trampled death and having despoiled hades of all the souls held by it. And so the death of Christ was not a death of inviolate surety; it was as a death cut short by the resurrection. And even

---

[5]Mt 16:18. [6]CCL 92:85. [7]PL 35:2424. [8]2 Cor 5:19. [9]Rom 8:11. [10]Ps 19:4 (18:5 LXX). [11]CCL 107:67. [12]Ps 145:16 (144:16 LXX). [13]Is 53:7. [14]Jer 11:19.

after the resurrection the Lord had carried about the trophies of death—the imprint of the nails, his life-giving body made red by his blood, as Isaiah says in front of the holy angels: "Why is your robe red and your garments like his who treads in a full wine press?"[15]—for this reason he was seen in the vision "as though slain." The seven horns witness to his great power, since the number seven, being perfect, indicates a great amount, as we noted above. And certainly the horns are symbolic of power, as the prophet says, "And all the horns of the sinners I will cut off, and the horn of the righteous will be exalted,"[16] and as Habakkuk says, "His horns are in his hands."[17] And to be sure, Isaiah has interpreted for us the "seven eyes, which are the seven spirits of God sent into all the earth," saying, "And there will rest upon him the spirit of wisdom and understanding, the spirit of counsel and strength, the spirit of knowledge and piety. The spirit of the fear of God will delight him."[18] COMMENTARY ON THE APOCALYPSE 5.1-7.[19]

## 5:7 The Lamb Took the Scroll

**THE INCARNATE WORD BRINGS ALL THINGS TO COMPLETION.** IRENAEUS: The Lord says, "All things are delivered to me by the Father."[20] . . . But in the "all things" [it is implied that] nothing has been kept back [from him], and for this reason the same person is the Judge of the living and the dead; "having the key of David: he shall open, and no man shall shut: he shall shut, and no man shall open." For no one was able, either in heaven or in earth, or under the earth, to open the book of the Father, or to behold him, with the exception of the Lamb who was slain and who redeemed us with his own blood, receiving power over all things from the same God who made all things by the Word, and adorned them by [his] Wisdom, when "the Word was made flesh"; that even as the Word of God had the sovereignty in the heavens, so also might he have the sovereignty in earth, inasmuch as [he was] a righteous man, "who did not sin, neither was there found

guile in his mouth";[21] and that he might have the preeminence over those things that are under the earth, he himself being made "the first-begotten of the dead";[22] and that all things, as I have already said, might behold their King; and that the paternal light might meet with and rest upon the flesh of our Lord, and come to us from his resplendent flesh, and that thus humanity might attain to immortality, having been invested with the paternal light. AGAINST HERESIES 4.20.2.[23]

**THE PASSION OF CHRIST UNCOVERS THE FACE OF MOSES.** VICTORINUS OF PETOVIUM: Therefore, he opens and unseals the testament, which he had sealed. And Moses the lawgiver knew that it was necessary for [the testament] to be sealed and hidden until the coming of his passion, and so [he] covered his face and in that way spoke to the people, revealing that the words of preaching were veiled until the time of Christ's coming. For when he had read this law to the people, he took wool soaked in calf's blood and water and sprinkled all the people, saying, "This is the blood of the testament, concerning which the Lord had commanded you."[24] Therefore, the diligent person ought to be attentive to the fact that the totality of preaching comes together into a unity. For it was not sufficient that it was called "law," since it was also called a "testament." For no law is called a testament, nor is anything called a testament, except that which is made by one who is about to die. And whatever is within the testament is sealed until the day of the death of the testator. And therefore rightly it is unsealed by the Lamb slain who, as a lion, destroyed death and fulfilled that which had been foretold of him, and had freed man, that is, flesh, from death, and had received as a possession the property of him who was dying, namely, of the human race. For as through one body all people had come into the debt of death, so through one body all who believe might rise to

---

[15]Is 63:2. [16]Ps 75:10 (74:11 LXX). [17]Hab 3:4 LXX. [18]Is 11:2. [19]TEG 8:115-16. [20]Mt 11:27. [21]1 Pet 2:22. [22]Col 1:18. [23]ANF 1:488. [24]Ex 24:8.

eternal life. Now the face of Moses is uncovered; now it is revealed, and therefore the apocalypse is called a "revelation"; now his book is unsealed; now the sacrifices of the victims are understood; now the offerings and the duties of the Anointed, the building of the temple and the prophecies are clearly understood. COMMENTARY ON THE APOCALYPSE 5.2.[25]

**CHRIST REVEALED THE MYSTERY OF THE TRINITY.** APRINGIUS OF BEJA: To be sure, the Lamb is the assumed man who for our salvation willingly offered himself over to death. Worthily he received the scroll, that is, the power of all the works of God, and from the right hand of him who is seated on the throne, that is, he received all things from God the Father, as he himself said: "All which the Father has is mine."[26] Then did he receive this scroll, when rising from the dead he showed the mystery of the Trinity, which had been hidden from the ages, and revealed it to the world. TRACTATE ON THE APOCALYPSE 5.7.[27]

**CHRIST IS ALSO THE RIGHT HAND OF GOD.** PRIMASIUS: The Son of man is said to have received the book from the right hand of God as both the dispensation from the Father and an arrangement from himself, for each reigns upon the throne with the Holy Spirit. And also here we ought understand the right hand to represent the blessedness of the victory. Nor ought it be understood in a fleshly manner as though he received the book from another hand of the Father, since the self-same is Son of the Father and the self-same the right hand [of God]. But since he who said, "Rejoice, for I have overcome the world,"[28] always conquers in those who belong to him, he also makes his own church to exist as a conqueror, and it is declared of her that she receives the book. COMMENTARY ON THE APOCALYPSE 5.7.[29]

## 5:8 The Creatures and the Elders Fell Down

**PRAYERS FROM A PURE CONSCIENCE.** ORIGEN: We regard the spirit of every good person as an altar from which arises an incense that is truly and spiritually sweet-smelling, namely, the prayers ascending from a pure conscience. Therefore it is said by John in the Revelation, "The odors are the prayers of the saints";[30] and by the psalmist, "Let my prayer come before you as incense."[31] And the statues and gifts that are fit offerings to God are the work of no common mechanics but are wrought and fashioned in us by the Word of God, to wit, the virtues in which we imitate "the firstborn of all creation," who has set us an example of justice, of temperance, of courage, of wisdom, of piety, and of the other virtues. AGAINST CELSUS 8.17.[32]

**THE FLESH OF CHRIST.** VICTORINUS OF PETOVIUM: The harp, whose strings are stretched out upon wood, signifies the body of Christ, that is, the flesh of Christ bound to his passion.[33] The bowls represent the confession [of faith] and the extension of the new priesthood. COMMENTARY ON THE APOCALYPSE 5.3.[34]

**WHEN WE CRUCIFY OUR PASSIONS.** PRIMASIUS: The bowls that are accepted by God are the pious confession in which no one is hidden with a duplicitous heart but is rather sincere with an open affection. They are also the golden vessels that are in the great house, burning with the sweetness of the pleasant odor of Christ. Moreover, the prayers of the saints are the grateful deeds of those who rejoice over the salvation of the world[35] and their intercessions for the well-being of the helpless. [The apostle] says, "Christ suffered for us, leaving for us an example that we should walk in his footsteps."[36] When, therefore, "those who belong to Christ crucify their own flesh with its passions and desires,"[37] it is as though they are playing to Christ on harps, so that what he has done for them, they might do

---

[25]CSEL 49:62-64. [26]Jn 16:15. [27]CCL 107:68. [28]Jn 16:33. [29]CCL 92:86. [30]Rev 5:8. [31]Ps 141:2 (140:2 LXX). [32]ANF 4:645*. [33]This is the first occurrence of this analogy. [34]CSEL 49:66. [35]Primasius follows Tyconius up to this point. [36]1 Pet 2:21. [37]Gal 5:24.

for him, "looking to Jesus, the pioneer and perfecter of our faith."[38] COMMENTARY ON THE APOCALYPSE 5.8.[39]

THE SACRIFICE OF THE FAITHFUL. ANDREW OF CAESAREA: The harps indicate the harmonious and melodious divine doxology, while the incense indicates the sweet-smelling sacrifice of the faithful that is offered through a most pure life, as the apostle says: "We are the aroma of Christ."[40] The bowls are symbolic of the thoughts from which the sweet aroma of good works and pure prayer come. COMMENTARY ON THE APOCALYPSE 5.7-8.[41]

THE CHURCH RENDERS THANKSGIVING.
BEDE: When the Lord in his passion demonstrated that the proclamation of both Testaments was fulfilled in himself, the church renders thanksgiving and gives herself up to sufferings in order that, as the apostle says, she might fill up that "which is lacking of the sufferings of Christ in its flesh."[42] For the harps represent bodies made ready to die, since the strings are stretched tight on wood. And by the bowls are designated hearts wide open by the breadth of charity. EXPLANATION OF THE APOCALYPSE 5.8.[43]

WE BEAR SPICE TO CHRIST'S TOMB. BEDE: Just as it is proper for us to seek the Lord shining with the light of good works, so also is it proper for us to seek him abundantly provided with the gift of spiritual prayers. Hence it is good that the women who came to the tomb early in the morning are reported to have been carrying with them the spices that they had prepared. Our spices are our voices in prayer, in which we set forth before the Lord the desires of our hearts, as the apostle John attested in the describing mystically the purest inmost longings of the saints, saying, "They had golden bowls full of incense, which are the prayers of the saints." What in Greek is called "spice" in Latin is called "incense." We bear spices to the tomb of the Lord early in the morning when, mindful of the passion and death that he underwent for us, we show to our neighbor out

wardly the light of our good actions and are inwardly aflame in our heart with the delight of simple compunction. We must do this at all times, but especially when we go into church in order to pray and when we draw near to the altar in order to partake of the mysteries of the body and blood of the Lord. HOMILIES ON THE GOSPELS 2.10.[44]

## 5:9-10 They Sang a New Song

THE CHRISTIAN CONFESSION OF FAITH. VICTORINUS OF PETOVIUM: "The twenty-four elders and the four animals had harps and bowls and were singing a new song." The preaching of the Old Testament joined with the New reveals the Christian people singing a new song, that is, the proclaiming of their public confession. It is new that the Son of God became man; it is new that he was given over into death by men; it is new that he rose again on the third day; it is new that he ascended in the body into heaven; it is new that he gives the forgiveness of sins to men; it is new that men are sealed with the Holy Spirit; it is new that they receive the priestly service of supplication and await a kingdom of such immense promises. COMMENTARY ON THE APOCALYPSE 5.3.[45]

CHRIST HAS GIVEN TO THE CHURCH THE NEW SONG. PRIMASIUS: Christ wrote a new song by the harmonious truth of both Testaments. This he did when he, remaining the Word which was in the beginning, was born by a new sort of birth through the Virgin. This he did when he as God put on man in a new manner. This he did when he gave himself over to his killers by his own power. This he did when he was wondrously made alive from the dead and when at a time of his own choosing was ascended beyond the heavens. And this new song he bestowed upon all those who belong to the

[38]Heb 12:2. [39]CCL 92:87. [40]2 Cor 2:15. [41]MTS 1 Sup 1:56. [42]Col 1:24. [43]CCL 121A:291. [44]CS 111:89. [45]CSEL 49:66.

church which he acquired, that it might be sung continually, and that in this [the church] might rest secure as it awaits in hope the coming judge, that "we might walk in the newness of life."[46] As he said, "If any one wishes to be my disciple, let him deny himself and take up his cross and follow me."[47] COMMENTARY ON THE APOCALYPSE 5.9.[48]

**WE HAVE BEEN MADE KINGS AND PRIESTS.**
OECUMENIUS: "And they sang a new song." It was new because it was sung to that God who had become flesh, for this song had formerly never been offered, until the incarnation. And what was the song? "You are worthy," it says, you who were slain for us and who by your blood did acquire an inheritance from the many nations under heaven, to grant this salvation to humanity. And with very good reason he said "from tribe and tongue and people and nation." For while he did not gain all nations—for many have died in unbelief—yet he acquired from every nation those worthy of salvation. And the prophet said something similar: "Arise, O God, judge the earth; for you will inherit [some] from among all the nations,"[49] not to be sure, "all the nations." And he made "them kings and priests for our God, and they will reign upon earth." In addition to the faithful servants of Christ who are kings and leaders of the churches, perhaps you will also be able to understand the "kings" in this passage as those who have ruled their passions and have not been ruled by them, and the "priests" as those who have offered their own bodies as "living sacrifice, holy and pleasing to God," as the Scripture says.[50] COMMENTARY ON THE APOCALYPSE 5:8-12.[51]

**WE SING THROUGH THE SPIRIT.** ANDREW OF CAESAREA: Through this passage it is revealed that the elders, both those in the Old Testament and those in the New Testament, were well-pleasing to God, and that on behalf of the whole world they bring forth a [hymn of] thanksgiving to the Lamb of God who was slain and redeemed us. It is a "new song," which we have been taught to sing, who from every tribe and tongue have been freed from the antiquity of the letter and through the Spirit have received light. He says that these will rule the new earth, which the Lord promised to the humble. COMMENTARY ON THE APOCALYPSE 5.9-10.[52]

### 5:11-13 Wisdom and Honor and Praise

**THE LAMB SLAIN IS CHRIST'S HUMANITY.**
CAESARIUS OF ARLES: This is not said of his Godhead, in which are all the treasuries of wisdom,[53] so that he should receive [wisdom]. Rather, this is said of his assumed manhood, that is, concerning his body, which is the church. Or, it might be said of his martyrs who were slain for his name. For the church receives all things in her Head, as the Scriptures say, "He has given us all things with him."[54] The Lamb himself receives, as he said in the Gospel, "All authority in heaven and on earth has been given to me."[55] However, he receives [this authority] according to his humanity, not according to his divinity. EXPOSITION ON THE APOCALYPSE 5.12, HOMILY 4.[56]

**GOD RECEIVES PRAISE FROM EVERY EXISTING THING.** ANDREW OF CAESAREA: From all beings, whether intelligent or sensible, whether living or simply existing in some way, God, as the Creator of all things, is glorified by words proper to their natures. Also praised is his only begotten and consubstantial Son who graciously renewed humankind and the creation that was made through him. And it is written that, as man, he received authority over all things in heaven and upon the earth. COMMENTARY ON THE APOCALYPSE 5.11-13.[57]

### 5:14 The Elders Worshiped

**ANGELS AND MEN FORM ONE CHURCH.** AN-

---

[46]Rom 6:4. [47]Lk 9:23. [48]CCL 92:88. [49]Ps 82:8 (81:8 LXX). [50]Rom 12:1. [51]TEG 8:118. [52]MTS 1 Sup 1:57. [53]Col 2:3. [54]Rom 8:32. [55]Mt 28:18. [56]PL 35:2424. [57]MTS 1 Sup 1:58.

DREW OF CAESAREA: Through these, one flock and one church from angels and from men is indicated which has been formed through Christ, the God who united that which was separate and has destroyed the partition wall of separation. And so, as we have heard, with the four living creatures who surpass the other angelic ranks, also the [elders], who represent the fullness of those who are being saved, are worthy of the hymn and worship of God. Of which may also we be found worthy in Christ himself, the Giver of peace and our God, with whom together with the Father and the Holy Spirit be glory and might forever and ever. Amen. COMMENTARY ON THE APOCALYPSE 5.14.[58]

---

[58]MTS 1 Sup 1:58-59.

## 6:1-2 THE FIRST SEAL: A WHITE HORSE

[1]*Now I saw when the Lamb opened one of the seven seals, and I heard one of the four living creatures say, as with a voice of thunder, "Come!" [2]And I saw, and behold, a white horse, and its rider had a bow; and a crown was given to him, and he went out conquering and to conquer.*

**OVERVIEW:** The alienation of sinners from God, symbolized by the sealed book, begins to be reversed when the Lamb opens the seals of the book (OECUMENIUS). As the prophecies of the Old Testament are revealed and the events of the last days are made known, the human race is invited to faith (VICTORINUS, PRIMASIUS). The recovery of humanity's free relationship with God was begun when Christ was born of Mary so that we might be born to a confident freedom (OECUMENIUS). When he ascended into heaven to the Father, Christ sent forth the Holy Spirit, who through the preaching of the apostles and of the preachers after them began to conquer the devil, the spirits of the air and human unbelief (VICTORINUS, OECUMENIUS, CAESARIUS OF ARLES, BEDE). As though it were an arrow shot from a bow, the Word of God pierced the hearts of people so that nations were converted to Christ (ANDREW OF CAESAREA) and began to bear the fruits of faith (PRIMASIUS). As Christ had overcome death by dying and received the crown of victory (BEDE), so also the apostles received the crown of victory when they willingly died through torture for the sake of the gospel (ANDREW OF CAESAREA). Likewise, the crown awaits all preachers who speak the word of truth (VICTORINUS, PRIMASIUS).

### 6:1 The Lamb Opened the First Seal

**THE LAMB FORETELLS WHAT WILL HAPPEN.** VICTORINUS OF PETOVIUM: The breaking of the seals is the disclosing of the prophecies of the Old Testament and the foretelling of those things that will happen at the end of time. Although our prophetic writing expresses the events to come by way of the individual seals, it is not until all of the seals have been opened that the announcement is able to run its course.... He said, "one of the living creatures," because all four are one. "Come and see."[1] "Come" is spoken to one who is invited to faith. "See" is spoken to one who has not seen. COMMENTARY ON THE APOCALYPSE 6.1.[2]

---

[1]The text followed by Victorinus has "come and see," following John 1:46. [2]CSEL 49:66-68.

**THE BIRTH OF CHRIST INITIATED OUR RESTORATION TO GOD.** OECUMENIUS: The closing and sealing of the scroll signifies the fearful alienation of those inscribed in it and the closing of their mouths from making any plea for justice before God. Therefore, the gradual opening of the seals reveals the gradual recovery of our free and open relationship with God, which the Only Begotten acquired for us when by his own righteousness he set aright our offenses. It is then to be noted that the loosing of each seal reveals a work done by the Lord for our salvation and effected by him against our spiritual enemies. For the intention of the Lord on our behalf is the destruction of their domination of us. . . . Therefore, the first good work of Christ our Savior toward our race, which loosed the first seal of the scroll, is the physical birth of the Lord. For his birth initiated our restoration from that exile that was occasioned by Adam's sin, and it began the recovery of that closeness of God with us which we had lost and the change of our fearful alienation into a confident freedom. For [his birth] sanctified our birth, so that we might no longer be conceived in transgressions or be born in the sins of our mothers, but that we might have a sanctified birth, Christ having blessed human birth through his own birth. The holy apostle witnesses to this goodness toward humankind when he writes, "Since your children are unclean, but now they are holy."[3] COMMENTARY ON THE APOCALYPSE 6.1-4.[4]

**WITH ONE VOICE.** PRIMASIUS: He said, "I heard one of the four animals say, 'Come and see.'" This one animal is the whole church preaching with a great voice and inviting the church to greater faith, "Come and see!" "If anyone thirsts, let him come and drink."[5] "Approach him and you will be illuminated."[6] "Arise, you who sleep, arise from the dead, and Christ will illuminate you."[7] COMMENTARY ON THE APOCALYPSE 6.1.[8]

**THE APOSTLES ARE CALLED TO A ROYAL STRUGGLE.** ANDREW OF CAESAREA: Indeed, here

is indicated the good order of those in heaven, which descends from the first ranks to the second. And therefore from one figure of the four-formed living creatures, namely, from the lion, he heard the first voice that gave the command, "Come!" to the angel who mystically symbolizes the vision. The first living creature, the lion, seems to me to signify the royal intention of the apostles against the demons. Concerning them it is said, "Behold, the kings of the earth have gathered together."[9] And again: "You will establish them as rulers over all the earth."[10] COMMENTARY ON THE APOCALYPSE 6.1.[11]

## 6:2 A White Horse and Its Rider

**THE HOLY SPIRIT SPEAKS TO THE HUMAN HEART.** VICTORINUS OF PETOVIUM: When the first seal was opened, he says that "he saw a white horse and a rider who was crowned and who had a bow"—for this is what happened at first. For, after our Lord ascended into heaven, he opened all things and sent forth the Holy Spirit. Through preachers, the words of the Holy Spirit penetrate into the human heart as though they were arrows and they conquer unbelief. The crown on the head is promised to the preachers by the Holy Spirit. . . . And therefore, the white horse is the word of preaching when the Holy Spirit was sent into the world. For the Lord has said, "This gospel will be preached in all the world as a witness to the nations, and then the end will come."[12] COMMENTARY ON THE APOCALYPSE 6:1.[13]

**CHRIST CONQUERS THE DEVIL.** OECUMENIUS: The white horse is a symbol of the gospel, since through it good deeds will be done to humanity. The crown is an image of strength and victory. And [the white horse] went out to bring the crown to Christ, who had begun to conquer the devil who had placed our race under bondage.

---

[3]1 Cor 7:14. [4]TEG 8:120-21. [5]Jn 7:37. [6]Ps 34:5 (33:6 LXX). [7]Eph 5:14. [8]CCL 92:94. [9]Ps 47:9 (46:10 LXX). [10]Ps 44:17 LXX. [11]MTS 1 Sup 1:59. [12]Mt 24:14. [13]CSEL 49:68.

"He went out," he says, "conquering and to conquer." Christ was he who was conquering that he might conquer utterly and totally, and he brought the crown as a symbol of victory to him. COMMENTARY ON THE APOCALYPSE 6.1-4.[14]

**PIERCED BY THE WORD OF GOD.** PRIMASIUS: This white horse can be understood as the church of truth, represented in the persons of the apostles and preachers, which was made whiter than snow by grace. The rider upon the horse is Christ. Therefore, it was said to him through the prophet, "For you mounted your horses and your army is salvation."[15] For the same reason he is said to hold an arrow. An arrow is aptly compared with the preaching of the Word of God, for when the hearts of people are pierced, they are able to bear the fruit of faith. And so we read, "Your sharp arrows are very powerful; people fall before you."[16] The crown indicates the reward rightly given to preachers. COMMENTARY ON THE APOCALYPSE 6.2.[17]

**SPEAKING THROUGH THE PROPHETS AND APOSTLES.** CAESARIUS OF ARLES: The white horse is the church, and its rider is Christ. This horse of the Lord with the bow made ready for war was promised beforehand by Zechariah. "The Lord God will visit his flock, the house of Israel, and he will arrange him as a formidable horse in war, and from him he looked, and from him he arranged [the battle order], and from him came the bow in anger, and from him will come out every oppressor."[18] And so we interpret the white horse to be the prophets and the apostles. In the rider who is crowned and has a bow we recognize not only Christ but also the Holy Spirit. For after Christ ascended into heaven, he opened all mysteries and sent the Holy Spirit. Through preachers the word of the Spirit, as though they were arrows, went out to the hearts of people and conquered their unbelief. The crown upon the head are the promises made through the Holy Spirit. EXPOSITION ON THE APOCALYPSE 6.2, HOMILY 5.[19]

**THE APOSTLES GAINED TWO VICTORIES.**

ANDREW OF CAESAREA: We understand the loosing of the first seal to signify the generation of the apostles. For, as though it were a bow, they stretch forth the gospel message against the demons and led to Christ those wounded by the arrows of salvation. And because they conquered the leader of deceit through the truth, they received a crown, and in hope they await a second victory, namely, the confession of the name of the Master unto a violent death. Therefore, it is written, "he went out conquering and to conquer." For, the first victory is the conversion of the nations; the second is the willing departure from the body in persecution for the sake of that conversion. COMMENTARY ON THE APOCALYPSE 6.2.[20]

**BY DYING, CHRIST OVERTHREW THE REIGN OF DEATH.** BEDE: The top of that ark is doubtless properly ordered to be encircled with a golden crown, because when he appeared in the flesh and came to redeem the human race, the Son of God was anticipating a certain time and hour when he would overcome the death he had borne for us (along with the author of death himself) and ascend victorious to the Father in heaven. Of this crown the apostle says, "But we see Jesus, who was indeed made a little lower than the angels, crowned with glory and honor because of the suffering of death."[21] Of this crown John in the Apocalypse says, "And I looked, and behold, a white horse! And the one who was sitting upon it had a bow, and a crown was given to him, and he went out conquering that he might conquer." Surely the white horse is the church. The rider who was commanding it is the Lord. He had a bow because he was coming to make war against the powers of the air; and a crown of victory was given to him because by dying he overthrew the reign of death. ON THE TABERNACLE 1.25.11.[22]

---

[14]TEG 8:121. [15]Hab 3:8. [16]Ps 45:5 (44:6 LXX). [17]CCL 92:94. [18]Zech 10:3-4. [19]PL 35:2424. [20]MTS 1 Sup 1:60-61. [21]Heb 2:9. [22]TTH 18:14. Bede is discussing Numbers 25:11. He may be making a word play on the similar sound of *arca* ("bow") and *archa* ("ark"). The view common to Primasius, Caesarius and Bede that the white horse is the church and its rider is Christ most likely comes from Tyconius.

# 6:3-4 THE SECOND SEAL: A RED HORSE

[3]*When he opened the second seal, I heard the second living creature say, "Come!"* [4]*And out came another horse, bright red; its rider was permitted to take peace from the earth, so that men should slay one another; and he was given a great sword.*

**OVERVIEW:** Through his victory over the temptations of the devil, Christ overcame also our own shame and restored to us the vision of God. Although humankind, once enslaved, may now dismiss the devil like a slave (OECUMENIUS), the devil is still an evil and bloody power against whom the church is forewarned (PRIMASIUS). He will cause much blood to be spilled upon the earth, for he will cause evil people to attack the church (TYCONIUS, CAESARIUS OF ARLES), and he will incite the wicked to perpetual strife and discord even among themselves, so that they even kill each other (CAESARIUS OF ARLES). Yet through such strife that community of evil, which is sinful humanity, will be cut to pieces and its idolatry destroyed (OECUMENIUS). Christ prophesied that such wars would occur also in the future (VICTORINUS). During these evil times God will give permission that those who teach and extend the gospel be martyred and be sacrificed upon the altar of heaven (ANDREW OF CAESAREA). Throughout all of this, the church still possesses an eternal, heavenly peace that passes all understanding and that Christ left behind for us (TYCONIUS, CAESARIUS OF ARLES).

## 6:3 The Lamb Opened the Second Seal

**CHRIST OVERCAME THE TEMPTATION OF THE DEVIL.** OECUMENIUS: The second good work of Christ toward us is the temptation of the Lord and his victory over the tempter. This loosed the second seal of the scroll and granted to us the loosing of our shame and the restoration of the vision of God. And this occurred not only that [Christ] might know victory but that the interloper, beaten down, might no longer "bite the heel of the horsemen" or trip us up in our spiritual walk, but rather that he might fall down and be sent away like a slave, and hear from man whom he had defeated, "Begone, Satan!"[1] (although God was in this man!). And so, he who boasted that he would put his throne upon the clouds and make himself like unto the Most High, as Isaiah dramatically depicted it,[2] departs with shame and now for the first time learns of his own weakness. COMMENTARY ON THE APOCALYPSE 6.1-4.[3]

**THE CHURCH IS WARNED OF FUTURE EVILS.** PRIMASIUS: The same words of exhortation to "come and see" are repeated, but for a different reason. The white horse is portrayed as good, but the red horse is portrayed as evil. Just as in regard to the good, joy is promised for the church's victory, so here there is a warning against evil from a foreknowledge of the future. COMMENTARY ON THE APOCALYPSE 6.3.[4]

**SACRED SACRIFICES.** ANDREW OF CAESAREA: I suppose that the second living creature is the bull to depict the sacred sacrifices of the holy martyrs, since the first [creature] signified the apostolic authority. COMMENTARY ON THE APOCALYPSE 6.3.[5]

## 6:4 A Red Horse and Its Rider

**THERE WILL BE WARS.** VICTORINUS OF PETOVIUM: "And there was a red horse, and he

---

[1]Mt 4:10. [2]Is 14:13-14. [3]TEG 8:121-22. [4]CCL 92:95. [5]MTS 1 Sup 1:61.

who sat upon it had a sword." [This passage] signifies those wars which will occur in the future, as we read in the Gospel: "For nation will rise against nation, and kingdom against kingdom, and there will be earthquakes on the earth."[6] This is the red horse. COMMENTARY ON THE APOCALYPSE 6.2.[7]

**THE CHURCH IS TAUGHT THROUGH BLOODY STRUGGLES.** TYCONIUS: This red horse, gory not with its own blood but with the blood of others, is said to fight against the victorious church when it is sent in to take that peace from the earth that passes all understanding. For [the church] is taught both from deed and from the sword. COMMENTARY ON THE APOCALYPSE 6.4.[8]

**HUMAN CONSENSUS TOWARD EVIL AND IDOLATRY WILL BE DESTROYED.** OECUMENIUS: "A red horse came forth," urged on by one of the living creatures, and authority was given to the rider "to take peace from the earth, that they might kill one another, and a great sword was given to him." The red horse is a figure of blood, and so a sword is given to the rider upon the horse so that he might attack and cut to pieces that consensus of evil that exists among those who dwell upon the earth—for among them there is an agreement to idolatry. "That they might kill one another," that is, that they might slay each other's eagerness toward increased evil. For the Lord did not come "to bring peace to the earth but a sword" and to set "a son against his father and a bride against her mother-in-law" and the young and pious against the old and accused.[9] COMMENTARY ON THE APOCALYPSE 6.1-4.[10]

**STRIFE, DISSENSION AND DEATH.** CAESARIUS OF ARLES: The red horse comes out against the victorious and conquering church. That is, there comes an evil and wicked people, made bloody from its rider, the devil. This is just as we read in Zechariah concerning the red horse of the Lord, except that there it is red from his own blood, while here it is red from the blood of oth-

ers.[11] "And to him a great sword was given, to take peace from the earth." This refers to the peace of the earth, for the church possesses an eternal peace that Christ left behind for himself. As we noted above, the white horse is the church and its rider is Christ or the Holy Spirit in whose hand is a bow that sends forth his commandments, as though they were powerful, sharp arrows, throughout the whole world both to kill sins and to enliven the hearts of the faithful. The crown upon his head is the promise of eternal life. Here, . . . the red horse is an evil people whose rider is the devil. It is said to be red because it has been made red with the blood of multitudes. And a sharp sword was given to it to take peace from the earth. This means that with the devil's connivance and influence evil people join together and do not cease to incite among themselves strife and dissension, even unto death. EXPOSITION ON THE APOCALYPSE 6.4, HOMILY 5.[12]

**GOD PERMITS MARTYRS AND TEACHERS TO SUFFER FOR CHRIST.** ANDREW OF CAESAREA: We suggest that this second seal is to be interpreted as the succession of the apostles that is fulfilled through martyrs and teachers. During this succession, as the proclamation is extended abroad, the peace of the world is taken away, creation being divided against itself, as was spoken by the Lord: "I have not come to bring peace on earth, but a sword."[13] And by this [sword] the sacrifices of the martyrs are offered on the heavenly altar. The "red horse" is symbolic either of the shedding of blood or of the red-hot disposition of those who suffer for Christ. The words "it was permitted to its rider to take peace" show the all-wise permission of God that tests his faithful servants through temptations. COMMENTARY ON THE APOCALYPSE 6.4.[14]

---

[6]Lk 21:10-11. [7]CSEL 49:70. [8]CCL 92:95. [9]Mt 10:34-35. [10]TEG 8:122. [11]Zech 1:8. [12]PL 35:2424-25. [13]Mt 10:34. [14]MTS 1 Sup 1:62.

## 6:5-6 THE THIRD SEAL: A BLACK HORSE

[5]*When he opened the third seal, I heard the third living creature say, "Come!" And I saw, and behold, a black horse, and its rider had a balance in his hand;* [6]*and I heard what seemed to be a voice in the midst of the four living creatures saying, "A quart of wheat for a denarius[a] and three quarts of barley for a denarius[a]; but do not harm oil and wine!"*

a The denarius was a day's wage for a laborer

**OVERVIEW:** Humankind fell into sin through the free exercise of will and still remains inclined toward sin. For this reason, people live in sorrow and apart from faith in Christ (ANDREW OF CAESAREA). Even within the church, there are false brothers who work the works of darkness and cause harm to their fellows (BEDE). In punishment God injures humankind by way of famines, both now and at the time of the antichrist (VICTORINUS). However, through his teaching Christ has loosed us from false worship and restored us to God the Father. The devil is reduced to sorrow and shame, for the Lord has rebuked him and rendered a righteous judgment on our behalf (OECUMENIUS). We should always be aware, therefore, that although some acquire a greater merit than do others, all have been redeemed by the same, one price of the blood of Christ (TYCONIUS, BEDE) and possess a common immortality (PRIMASIUS). For that reason, we must keep from giving offense to our brothers through works of darkness (BEDE) and rather be ready to bring to them the wine of consolation and the oil of compassion so that they might receive the healing of Christ through repentance (ANDREW OF CAESAREA). There will be, however, a time when the teaching of the gospel will be scarce, a famine of the hearing of God's word. Yet, even for those who despise this teaching, there remains hope for them to be gladdened by the preaching of the only begotten Son of God (OECUMENIUS).

### 6:5 The Lamb Opened the Third Seal

**THE LORD PROMISES FAMINE.** VICTORINUS OF PETOVIUM: The black horse signifies famine. For the Lord said, "And there will be famine in many places."[1] However, this passage is also properly extended to the time of the antichrist, that is, to that time when there will be a great famine and people will be injured. COMMENTARY ON THE APOCALYPSE 6.2.[2]

**THE TEACHING OF CHRIST.** OECUMENIUS: The third mercy of Christ toward us opened the third seal and restored us, who had been condemned, to God the Father. This is his salvific teaching and the benefits of his miracles, for these contributed to the dissolution of the devil. For, through these we know who is truly God by nature, so that we may "no longer be children, tossed about by every wind of doctrine"[3] nor honor that which our hands have made but that we might exchange the corrupting demons for the glory of God. As yeast draws flour, the divine teaching of the Lord drew to itself those being taught according to the discourses of the Lord and those who were benefiting from the miracles that were healing souls rather than bodies. And when this occurred, a black horse came out, and the rider had a balance in his hand. The black horse is indicative of shame and sorrow, for the destruction of the devil had received increased intensity by the divine teaching, and therefore he laments his dissolution which lasted for such a long time. The balance . . .

[1]Mt 24:7. [2]CSEL 49:70. [3]Eph 4:14.

is a figure of equality and righteousness, for "he who judges in righteousness sat upon his throne and rebuked the nations of demons,[4] and the impious One who led them was destroyed."[5] The balance is, therefore, a symbol of the righteous judgment of the Lord on our behalf, so that we may speak boldly to him, "You have executed my right and my cause,"[6] and so that we nations might know that we are men, and that we may not be pulled about like beasts with bit and bridle or allowed to be led astray by destructive tyrants. COMMENTARY ON THE APOCALYPSE 6.5-8.[7]

### THE WICKED DECEIVE BY A SHOW OF RIGHT.

CAESARIUS OF ARLES: In the black horse we recognize an evil people which works in concert with the devil. "He had a balance in his hand," which indicates that while evil persons feign to have the scales of justice, they deceive many. EXPOSITION ON THE APOCALYPSE 6.5, HOMILY 5.[8]

### THE SINFUL USE OF FREE WILL BRINGS ON SORROW.

ANDREW OF CAESAREA: I believe that the third living creature here is the man and that [this passage] shows the fall of men and for this reason his punishment because of his inclination toward sin by the power of free will. . . . We think that the "black horse" depicts the sorrow that comes upon those who have fallen away from faith in Christ on account of the abundance of torments. The "balance" is he who tests those who either by inconstancy of mind or by vainglory have fallen from the faith through weakness of the body. COMMENTARY ON THE APOCALYPSE 6.5-6.[9]

### FALSE BROTHERS.

BEDE: This black horse is the troop of false brothers, who have the balance of right confession but harm their fellows through works of darkness. For, when it is said in the midst of the living creatures, "Do not harm," it is clear that there is someone who is doing harm. And, concerning this running horse, the apostle says, "Outside there are wars, inside there are fears."[10] EXPLANATION OF THE APOCALYPSE 6.5-6.[11]

## 6:6 I Heard a Voice

### ALL HAVE BEEN REDEEMED BY ONE PRICE.

TYCONIUS: He is speaking of the church in the figures of the wheat and barley. He speaks either of those who are great and who are least in the church or of those who are leaders and the people. However, one two-pound weight is no less than three two-pound weights, for the same perfection subsists both in the unity and in the trinity. Thus, the Lord said that the leaven was hidden in the three measures of meal,[12] showing the teaching of wisdom that from something small the whole people are consecrated by the mystical number of the undivided Trinity. But this teaches also that there is one price for both the wheat and the barley, that is, that although one person may exceed another in merit, both have nevertheless been redeemed by one price. COMMENTARY ON THE APOCALYPSE 6.6.[13]

### A TIME WHEN THE GOSPEL IS NOT HEARD.

OECUMENIUS: The word of teaching is figuratively called "seed" in the holy Scriptures. In Matthew it is written, "A sower went out to sow," and his most devoted servants say to him, "Sir, did you not sow good seed in the field? Then why are there weeds?"[14] From the seed comes the wheat, that is, the preaching of the gospel, which as a food fit for mature persons trains the minds to distinguish between good and evil. And what is the barley? It is the teaching according to the law of Moses, for barley is less expensive than wheat and when ripe it is food fit for cattle, and so represents that which nourished the child of Israel. Therefore, God speaks from the midst of the four living creatures: "A quart of wheat for a denarius and three quarts of barley for a denarius," symbolizing through this that there would be a famine and a

---

[4]Variant not found. See Ps 95:5 LXX. [5]Ps 9:4-5 (9:5-6 LXX). [6]Ps 9:4 (9:5 LXX). [7]TEG 8:123. [8]PL 35:2425. [9]MTS 1 Sup 1:62-63. [10]2 Cor 7:15. [11]CCL 121A:297-99. [12]Mt 13:33. [13]CCL 92:95-96. [14]Mt 13:3, 27.

scarcity of evangelical teaching among the people at that time, a famine of both the teaching that comes from the Lord and from the law, as is written: "I will give to them not a famine of bread nor a thirst for water, but a famine of hearing the word of the Lord."[15] And if for the most part it is necessary that those who despise all teaching and conversion must suffer so and so, he says, "Do not harm the oil and the wine." Leave them alone and do not bring any destruction upon them. There is still mercy from me for them, God says, since there is hope for them to be gladdened spiritually by the divine preaching of my only begotten. This is the wine which spiritually gladdens the hearts of humanity. COMMENTARY ON THE APOCALYPSE 6.5-8.[16]

**ALL RECEIVE A COMMON IMMORTALITY.** PRIMASIUS: I think that the different numbers of one and three are mentioned on account of the diversity of personal habitations. In the one denarius is indicated eternal life that is common to all even though [they live] among many mansions.[17] And if one is there regarded as more sublime than another according to merits or is given a greater reward, yet no one is thought to be preeminent in comparison with another. For where there is a single immortality to each, there a common eternity exists for all. So also in the wine and oil he prohibits the dishonoring of the power of the sacraments, since that is the chrismation and the precious blood. Therefore we read, "What does he have which is good and beautiful, unless it be the fruit of the elect and producing virgins as wine."[18] And in the psalm: "Wine gladdens the heart of man, and his face is made cheerful in oil."[19] COMMENTARY ON THE APOCALYPSE 6.6, HOMILY 5.[20]

**WINE AND OIL.** CAESARIUS OF ARLES: The wine is to be interpreted as the blood of Christ, and the oil as the unction of chrismation. EXPOSITION ON THE APOCALYPSE 6.6.[21]

**LET US BE PHYSICIANS LIKE CHRIST.**

ANDREW OF CAESAREA: The phrase "a quart of wheat for a denarius" figuratively indicates those who have struggled lawfully and have carefully preserved the divine image given to them. The phrase "three quarts of barley for a denarius" speaks of those who like cattle have through cowardice bowed the neck to persecutors but have later repented and have washed their defiled image with tears. The command "do not harm wine and oil" indicates that the healing of Christ through repentance, which healed him who fell among the thieves, ought not be rejected, nor that those be allowed to be seized prematurely by death who through patience would be retrieved from defeat. Therefore, that we also might possess God as our beneficent physician for the suffering of our souls, let us be zealous to be such to our brothers who have fallen, bringing to them the wine of consolation mixed with the oil of compassion, "so that what is lame may not be put out of joint but rather be healed," as the apostle says.[22] And so becoming fellow workers with God, we may eternally enjoy his blessings by the grace and good will of our Lord, Jesus Christ. COMMENTARY ON THE APOCALYPSE 6.5-6.[23]

**DO NOT OFFEND ONE WHO BEARS THE MARKS OF CHRIST.** BEDE: Beware, he says, lest by an evil example you offend your brother for whom Christ died, for he bears the signs of the sacred blood and the chrism. For whether one has perfect merit or very little, all who have been instructed in the church in the faith of the holy Trinity have been redeemed by the same perfect price of the blood of the Lord. Nor without reason is the perfection of faith or works expressed by the measure of two quarts and not just one, since both at bottom consist of a twofold charity. EXPLANATION OF THE APOCALYPSE 6.5-6.[24]

---

[15]Amos 8:11. [16]TEG 8:124. [17]Jn 14:2. [18]See Zech 9:17. [19]Ps 104:15 (103:15 LXX). [20]CCL 92:96. [21]PL 35:2425. [22]Heb 12:13. [23]MTS 1 Sup 1:63-64. [24]CCL 121A:299.

# 6:7-8 THE FOURTH SEAL: A PALE HORSE

*[7]When he opened the fourth seal, I heard the voice of the fourth living creature say, "Come!" [8]And I saw, and behold, a pale horse, and its rider's name was Death, and Hades followed him; and they were given power over a fourth of the earth, to kill with sword and with famine and with pestilence and by wild beasts of the earth.*

**OVERVIEW:** Through the beatings that Christ endured we are brought closer to God. Condemned by our disobedience, pleasure and quest for sin, we are freed by the obedience and pains of Jesus (OECUMENIUS). However, in the Gentiles, false brothers, heretics and schismatics the devil still possesses his portion of the world (TYCONIUS). Through these, the devil makes war upon the church in body and soul (TYCONIUS, CAESARIUS OF ARLES). Yet the perfect number of the elect will be preserved throughout these attacks (TYCONIUS). God will vindicate his pious, and by his wrath he will devour the souls of the impious should they not repent (VICTORINUS, ANDREW OF CAESAREA). Moreover, God will send death and destruction upon the evil demons, who are responsible for the destruction of humankind (OECUMENIUS). Such destruction will certainly be the fate of heretics, like Arius, who bear death within themselves and lead the spiritually dead to eternal punishment (BEDE). The pestilences arising from the war between the pious and the impious are, indeed, already within the experience of humankind, as we can read in the histories (ANDREW OF CAESAREA).

## 6:7 The Lamb Opened the Fourth Seal

**CHRIST REVEALS OUR FRIENDSHIP WITH GOD.** OECUMENIUS: The loosing of the fourth and of the remaining seals is the beginning of the loosing of sin that was brought about by the transgression of Adam. For the loosing of this seal reveals our friendship with God. For if, as Isaiah says, "our sins have made us separated

from God,"[1] the removal of sins brings us close [to God]. And what is this loosing of the seal? It is the lashes that Christ received and through which we have been freed. For since we were condemned by the pleasure of taste, we have been healed through the opposites. Lashes are the opposite of pleasure, for they give a painful sensation. For Christ has paid in full for us all things through which we were brought down into the corruption of death. And he paid this debt in full through opposites—disobedience through obedience, pleasure through a painful submission, and the hands which lay hold of the forbidden tree through those hands which were valiantly stretched out upon the cross. COMMENTARY ON THE APOCALYPSE 6.5-8.[2]

**THE DIVINE WRATH.** ANDREW OF CAESAREA: The soaring flight and the swiftness upon its prey of the fourth living creature, namely, the eagle, suggests those plagues that come from above, from the divine wrath for the vindication of the pious and for the punishment of the impious, unless these should turn from their sins through improvement. COMMENTARY ON THE APOCALYPSE 6.7.[3]

## 6:8 A Pale Horse and Its Rider

**THE SOULS OF THE IMPIOUS.** VICTORINUS OF PETOVIUM: "And there was a pale horse, and he who sat upon it had the name of death." The Lord had foretold of these very things, along with

---

[1]Is 59:2. [2]TEG 8:125. [3]MTS 1 Sup 1:65.

other catastrophes. For when he said, "And hell follows him," he was speaking of the devouring of the souls of many of the impious. This is the pale horse. COMMENTARY ON THE APOCALYPSE 6.3.[4]

**THE ELECT WILL BE PRESERVED.** TYCONIUS: There are two parts in the world, that which belongs to God and that of the devil. That which belongs to the devil is further divided into three parts, which are both within and outside [the church]. These are the Gentiles, false brothers and those separated by open error or schism. And these three parts are those that war against the one. This one is said to consist of three fourths, either because it believes in the threefold unity or because it is distinguished into orders by the goodly variation of three vocations, that of the virgins, of the widows and of the married. He says that now power is given in these three fourths. He speaks of the church which is one, and because the threefold vocation relates to one head, it consists from the three fourths in the stability of a square. As it says, "built upon the foundation of the apostles and the prophets, Christ Jesus himself being the chief cornerstone."[5] He foretells that the church will be placed into stress by the attacks of evil people, from the Gentiles, from false brothers and by heretical depravity. And this is also to be recognized in the number of the messengers, that the very same good would oppose three evil enemies—the red horse with the sword, the second, black horse with the balance, and the third, pale horse with the sign of death, for the sword signifies war, the black horse famine and the pale horse death. And since he mentions the plagues one by one, he foretells all the future outbreaks of plagues by enumerating them in or through the third, the names of the beasts being added. We may remain undecided whether the speech is literal or figurative. For a visible sword is commonly used against the body, while a spiritual sword is used against the soul. Similarly concerning famine, it can mean here either a famine of the Word of God or a famine that affects the body. And likewise concerning

death, it can here mean either eternal death that affects souls or that temporal death that concerns bodies. Nonetheless, it is clear that the fourth good part, which is opposed by the three evils, is made to struggle in time by all of these visible persecutions. For those who are called according to the purpose of the will of God shall remain in the perfect number of the elect, especially those whom he wills to be preserved by the inviolate sacraments of the wine and oil. For when he said, "Do not harm the wine and oil," he was indicating the price of redemption in the wine and the anointing of baptism in the oil. Indeed, the Lord clearly said in the Gospel, "Father, those whom you have given to me, I have guarded, and none of them is lost but the son of perdition."[6] COMMENTARY ON THE APOCALYPSE 6.8.[7]

**DEMONS WILL BE DEVOURED BY THEIR OWN PASSIONS.** OECUMENIUS: When this happened, at the summons of the fourth holy creature a pale horse came out and its rider's name was Death, and hades followed him. And there was given to them authority over a fourth of the earth. The pale horse is symbolic of wrath, for pale is the color of gall and is so named by physicians. Death and hades were sent to wage spiritual warfare against the wicked demons and to exact vengeance for the destruction of humankind. But since, according to the logic of the vision, the salvific passion of Christ through which he paid for all our sins had not yet happened, the complete destruction of the demons had not yet been effected, but at that time only a fourth part. And this destruction he figuratively calls a "slaughter" and a "famine" brought on those who long ago worshiped them, and "death," revealing the end of their tyranny through death, and "destruction" by the beasts of the earth. For he calls the passions of arrogance and vainglory among the demons "beasts of the earth," which, as they are cast out of their dominion over people, consume and devour them, since they are earthly and as it were

---

[4]CSEL 49:72. [5]Eph 2:20. [6]Jn 17:12. [7]CCL 92:97-98.

revel in the muddied passions of the earth, although they had received incorporeal natures. COMMENTARY ON THE APOCALYPSE 6:5-8.[8]

**WAR, FAMINE AND PESTILENCE.** CAESARIUS OF ARLES: In the pale horse we perceive evil people who never cease to incite persecutions. And these three horses are one, who came out after the white horse and against it. And they have as their rider the devil, who is death. And so, the three horses are interpreted to be war, famine, and pestilence. For in the Gospel, the Lord foretold of these things, and they have already occurred, and as the day of judgment draws nearer will occur even more. EXPOSITION ON THE APOCALYPSE 6.8, HOMILY 5.[9]

**FAMINE AND PESTILENCE IN HUMAN HISTORY.** ANDREW OF CAESAREA: This sequence of events has happened before and reflects also contemporary occurrences. For as Eusebius says in the eighth chapter of the ninth book of his *Ecclesiastical History*, at the height of the persecution, when Maximinus was Roman emperor, both famine and pestilence along with other things fell upon them, so that such an innumerable multitude perished that they could not be buried. At that time indeed the Christians zealously undertook the task of burying the dead and by their love of humanity led those who had been deceived to the recognition of the truth. Moreover, the Armenians resisted the Romans, he says, so that many were killed with the sword and the bodies of the dead were eaten by dogs. Finally, those left alive began to kill the dogs, fearing that they themselves might die and that the living would become their tombs. For it was not impossible that even wild animals shared the same meal with dogs on account of the abundance of food.[10] We know that even in our own times similar things have happened. COMMENTARY ON THE APOCALYPSE 6.8.[11]

**HERETICS ARE THE CAUSE OF DEATH TO THOSE WHO FOLLOW THEM.** BEDE: This image is of the heretics who clothe themselves as though they were Catholics but are worthy to have death abide within them and who draw the army of the lost after themselves. For the devil and his ministers are, by metonymy,[12] called "death" and "hell," since they are for many the cause of death and of hell. The passage may simply be interpreted to mean that eternal punishments there [in hell] follow those who are here spiritually dead. "And there was given to him power over the four parts of the earth." Behold the insanity of Arius, which arose in Alexandria and extended itself even to the Gallic ocean, pursuing the pious not only by a dearth of the word of God but also, as though by beasts, with the physical sword. EXPLANATION OF THE APOCALYPSE 6.8.[13]

---

[8]TEG 8:125-26. [9]PL 35:2425. [10]Eusebius *Ecclesiastical History* 9.8.1-12 (NPNF 2 1:361-62). [11]MTS 1 Sup 1:65-66. [12]That is, exchanging the name of something with a connected concept or thing; e.g., the word *Washington* may be used in place of the U.S. government. [13]CCL 121A:299-301.

# 6:9-11 THE FIFTH SEAL:
# THE SOULS OF MARTYRS UNDER THE ALTAR

[9]*When he opened the fifth seal, I saw under the altar the souls of those who had been slain for the word of God and for the witness they had borne;* [10]*they cried out with a loud voice, "O Sovereign Lord, holy and true, how long before thou wilt judge and avenge our blood on those who dwell upon the earth?"* [11]*Then they were each given a white robe and told to rest a little longer, until the number of their fellow servants and their brethren should be complete, who were to be killed as they themselves had been.*

**OVERVIEW:** The prophet sees under the altar the souls of the slain. This suggests that souls are corporeal yet visible only to the spiritual eye. Those reposing under the altar are martyrs who alone may enter paradise before the resurrection by the key of their own blood (TERTULLIAN). However, it may also be that John saw the righteous dead awaiting the resurrection of their bodies under the "altar" of the earth (VICTORINUS). The saints of the Old Covenant who suffered torment for the holy word cry out in protest against the floggings that they see Christ enduring (OECUMENIUS). The saints and the martyrs of the church now offer praise (BEDE) and rejoice as they repose in the bosom of Abraham and see in the spirit what they await in hope (ANDREW OF CAESAREA). They also pray for the destruction of the demons who destroy people (OECUMENIUS) and for the end of the kingdom of sin and the resurrection of their bodies (PRIMASIUS, BEDE). They do not plead for their vindication from a motive of revenge (PRIMASIUS, CASSIODORUS, BEDE) but for the consummation of the world (ANDREW OF CAESAREA) and that the kingdom of God might come (PRIMASIUS, BEDE), for which all Christians pray (TERTULLIAN). Now the souls of the saints await the vindication of their bodies as they enjoy the bliss and the inexpressible joy of heaven (PRIMASIUS, BEDE) and the consolation of the Holy Spirit (VICTORINUS). As they wait, the saints learn that God is patient and postpones the time of retribution and revenge (FULGENTIUS OF RUSPE) so that those who possess the courage of martyrdom might obtain their deserved crowns (OECUMENIUS) and so that the full number of the elect might be made complete (PRIMASIUS). No one, not even the martyrs, may hasten the time of the remission of sins and the judgment of God (CYPRIAN).

## 6:9 The Lamb Opened the Fifth Seal

**ONLY MARTYRS ARE IN PARADISE UNTIL THE RESURRECTION. TERTULLIAN:** How is it that the region of paradise, which was revealed in the spirit through John as being "under the altar," contains no other souls but those of the martyrs? How is it that Perpetua, that bravest martyr of Christ, on the day of her death saw only the souls of the martyrs in paradise,[1] unless it be that the sword that guarded the entrance allowed none to pass save those that had died in Christ and not in Adam? Those who die this new death for God, and violently as Christ did, are welcomed into a special abode. Here, then, is the difference between pagan and Christian in death: If you lay down your life for God as the Paraclete recommends, then it will not be of some gentle fever in a soft bed but in the torture of martyrdom. You

---

[1]*The Passion of Perpetua* 13:8. Tertullian is mistaken. The vision is that of Saturus, and he sees both martyrs and a multitude of others.

must take up your cross and follow him, according to the precept of Christ.[2] The only key that unlocks the gates of paradise is your own blood. ON THE SOUL 55:4-5.[3]

**THE SOUL IS CORPOREAL, ALTHOUGH INVISIBLE TO THE EYE OF FLESH.** TERTULLIAN: The fact that the soul is invisible flows from the nature of its corporeal substance and is determined by its own nature. Besides, of its very nature it is destined to be invisible to certain things. . . . And so, an object may be invisible to one being and quite clearly seen by another without any prejudice to the corporeality of the object itself that is seen by one and not by the other. The sun is a bodily substance, being made of fire. The eagle gazes at it steadily, but it is invisible to the owl, but the owl does not deny the object seen by the eagle. In such fashion, the bodily substance of the soul may generally be invisible to the eye of flesh, but it is clearly perceived by the spirit. Thus John "in the spirit" saw "the souls of them that were slain for the word of God." ON THE SOUL 8.4-5.[4]

**THE SAINTS REPOSE UNDER THE EARTH.** VICTORINUS OF PETOVIUM: "And he saw the souls of the slain under the altar," that is, under the earth. For both the heaven and the earth are called "altar." And so, the law, prefiguring by way of images the face of the truth, presented two altars, one that is gold within and one that is bronze without.[5] And we understand that this altar is called "heaven," since this testimony was given to us by our Lord. For he said, "When you offer your gift on the altar"—to be sure, our gifts are the prayers that we ought to offer—"and there should remember that your brother has anything against you, leave there your gift,"[6] and most certainly prayers ascend to heaven. And so, heaven is understood to be that altar that was gold within—for even the priest, who had the command of Christ, entered into the temple to the golden altar once a year. The Holy Spirit was signifying that [Christ] was going to do this, that is,

that he would suffer once for all. And parallel to this, the bronze altar is to be understood as the earth, under which exists hades, a region removed from pains and fire, a place for the repose of the saints, in which to be sure the just are seen and heard by the impious, but these cannot go across to those. COMMENTARY ON THE APOCALYPSE 6.4.[7]

**THE SAINTS OF THE OLD COVENANT PROTEST THE BEATINGS OF THEIR MASTER.** OECUMENIUS: The fifth work of salvation that the Lord gave to the human race and that loosed the fifth seal of the Lord and offered to us freedom from sin and friendship with God was the chains and beatings to which the Lord was subjected before he was brought to Pilate and also those that he suffered from Pilate himself because of his timidity. Isaiah spoke of these beatings, when the Lord was asked by the divine angels, "What are these wounds between your hands?" and he said, "Those which I received in my beloved house."[8] For these wounds have healed our wounds that we suffered when we were going down from Jerusalem to Jericho and fell among thieves who beat and wounded us and left us half dead, as the story in Luke says.[9] But he loosed our chains, namely, the bonds of sin that were holding us tightly. For the prophet says, "The cords of the wicked ensnare me."[10] Therefore, while he was working evil, the devil was ignorant concerning him, and through his drunken violence against the Lord thrust a sword into himself and fell from that rule that he had wickedly established. However, when [the fifth seal was opened], the saints who had given witness in the old covenant remained silent. They could recall nothing like this treatment ever having happened to them, and they had not yet seen any such thing done against Christ. For although within the lawless Sanhedrin he had been spit upon, slapped and

[2]Mt 10:38. [3]FC 10:299-300. [4]FC 10:195-96. [5]See Ex 27:2; 30:3. [6]Mt 5:23-24. [7]CSEL 49:72-74. [8]See Zech 13:6. [9]Lk 10:30. [10]Ps 119:61 (118:61 LXX).

beaten, this had occurred in secrecy and only upon the testimony of servants and others summoned to the trial. But when they saw the Lord bound and whipped publicly by Pilate before the crowd of the Jews, they altogether rose up, and regarding that which was happening against their Master as intolerable, remembered also what had happened to them. For it says, "I saw under the altar the souls of those who had been slain for the word of God and for the church which they had." I saw, it says, the souls of the martyrs that had the most exalted place, for they were under the heavenly altar. Then he remarks about these martyrs, namely, that they had been slain for the holy word of the old covenant and for the church or synagogue that they had. For the martyrs die not only for themselves, but they effect a common benefit. Their courage becomes an exhortation to others, and by the blood of the saints the knowledge of God is built up. COMMENTARY ON THE APOCALYPSE 6.9-11.[11]

**THE OFFERING OF PRAISE.** BEDE: Having said that the church was afflicted in many ways in the present age, he also speaks of the glory of the souls after the punishment of their bodies. "I saw them," he says, "under the altar," that is, in the secret place of eternal praise. For the altar that is of gold and is placed within and is near the altar of the Lord's body does not present, as does the altar without, flesh and blood to the Lord, but only the incense of praise. And those who now present their bodies as a living sacrifice, then, when the chains of the body have been broken, sacrifice to him the offering of praise. EXPLANATION OF THE APOCALYPSE 6.9.[12]

## 6:10 "O Lord, How Long?"

**ALL CHRISTIANS JOIN THE MARTYRS IN PRAYING FOR THE KINGDOM.** TERTULLIAN: Our hope is that we may sooner reign and not be slaves any longer. Even if it were not prescribed to ask in prayer for the coming of his kingdom, we would, of our own accord, have expressed this desire in

our eagerness to embrace the object of our hope. With indignation the souls of the martyrs beneath the altar cry aloud to the Lord, "How long, O Lord, will you refrain from avenging our blood on those who dwell on the earth?" For at least from the end of the world vengeance for them is ordained. Indeed, as quickly as possible, O Lord, may your kingdom come! This is the prayer of Christians; this shall bring shame to the heathens; this shall bring joy to the angels; it is for the coming of this kingdom that we are harassed now, or rather, it is for this coming that we pray. ON PRAYER 5.1-4.[13]

**THE SAINTS PRAY AGAINST THE DEMONS.** OECUMENIUS: "And they cried out with a loud voice, saying, 'O Sovereign, both holy and true, how long until you will judge and avenge our blood on those who dwell upon the earth?'" They were not making petition against people but against the demons who like to dwell in earthly things. For it is not according to the love of the saints to rise up against their own kind, but against those who lead people to their own destruction. COMMENTARY ON THE APOCALYPSE 6.9-11.[14]

**A DESIRE FOR THE KINGDOM OF GOD.** PRIMASIUS: This ought not be understood in a carnal manner, as though they were inflamed by animosity and wished revenge. We know that we are to love our enemies through an abundance of love,[15] but it is manifest that they prayed against the kingdom of sin and were praying out of a desire for that kind of kingdom for which we say, "Thy kingdom come!"[16] COMMENTARY ON THE APOCALYPSE 6.10.[17]

**A TEMPORAL VENGEANCE AND A JUST RETRIBUTION.** CASSIODORUS: [The psalmist begs] that the Lord avenge the blood of the faithful, who endured martyrdom for his name. Vengeance is

---

[11]TEG 8:127-28. [12]CCL 121A:301. [13]FC 40:163. [14]TEG 8:128. [15]See Mt 5:44; Lk 6:27. [16]Mt 6:10. [17]CCL 92:99-100.

the means by which force and injustice are repelled by just retribution. But there the prayer seems to be directed toward the conversion of the enemy. For when temporal vengeance is exacted from them in this world, they escape the destruction of eternal damnation; it is in this sense that we read in Revelation that the souls of martyrs under God's altar demand to be avenged by divine decree. This vengeance is to be interpreted as we have defined it, for saintly people do not seek a cruel vengeance since they accept the precept "Pray for your enemies, do good to those that hate you,"[18] and the like. Finally the Lord himself, who executes most powerfully his own commands, spoke these words on the cross: "Father, forgive them, for they know not what they do."[19] EXPOSITION OF THE PSALMS 78.10.[20]

**THE END OF SIN AND THE RESURRECTION OF THE BODY.** BEDE: They do not pray for these things out of hatred of their enemies, for whom they intercede in this world. Rather, they pray out of love of equity, in which as those placed near to the Judge himself and in agreement with him they pray that the day of judgment, in which the kingdom of sin is destroyed and the resurrection of their dead bodies may come. For, also we in the present time, when we are commanded to pray for our enemies, nevertheless say when we pray to the Lord, "May your kingdom come!" EXPLANATION OF THE APOCALYPSE 6.10.[21]

## 6:11 They Were Told to Rest

**TO GRANT REMISSION OF SINS HASTILY IS TO PROVOKE THE WRATH OF GOD.** CYPRIAN: But if anyone with precipitate haste rashly thinks that he can grant remission of sins to all or dares to rescind the precepts of the Lord, not only is this of no advantage to the lapsed but it is even a hindrance. Not to have observed the judgment of the Lord, and to think that his mercy is not first to be implored, but after condemning the Lord to presume on one's own power, is to have provoked his wrath. Under the altar of God the souls of the slain martyrs cry out with a loud voice, saying, "How long, O Lord holy and true, do you refrain from judging and from avenging our blood on those who dwell on earth?" And they are ordered to be quiet and to continue to have patience. Does someone think that anyone can wish to become good by remitting and pardoning sins at random or that he can defend others before he himself is vindicated? The martyrs order something to be done. If just, if lawful, if not contrary to the Lord himself, they are to be done by the priest of God. Let the agreement be ready and easy on the part of the one obeying, if there has been religious moderation on the part of him asking. The martyrs order something to be done. If what they order is not written in the law of the Lord, we must first know, that they have obtained from the Lord what they ask, then do what they order. For what has been assured by man's promise cannot be seen at once to have been granted by the divine majesty. THE LAPSED 18.[22]

**THE SAINTS RECEIVE THE HOLY SPIRIT.** VICTORINUS OF PETOVIUM: He who sees all things willed that we know that these, that is, the souls of the slain, await the vindication of their blood, that is, of their body, from those who dwell upon the earth. However, since at the end of time the eternal reward of the saints and the condemnation of the impious will come, they are told to wait. And for a consolation of their body they received, it says, white robes, that is, the gift of the Holy Spirit. COMMENTARY ON THE APOCALYPSE 6.4.[23]

**THE COURAGE OF MARTYRDOM, THE MARTYR CROWN.** OECUMENIUS: And having said these things, they first receive white robes. This image signifies that they have been cleansed by their own blood and have put off every filth. Then they hear that they ought "rest a little longer, until

---

[18]Mt 5:44. [19]Lk 23:34. [20]ACW 52:281. [21]CCL 121A:301-3. [22]FC 36:72-73*. [23]CSEL 49:74-76.

their fellow servants and their brothers should be completed, who were to be killed as they themselves had been." For it would not be just were those who were similar to them in courage be deprived of their martyr crowns because the demons who were struggling against them had been destroyed prematurely. COMMENTARY ON THE APOCALYPSE 6.9-11.[24]

**The Martyrs Await the Completion of the Saints.** PRIMASIUS: We believe that this was revealed to them by the knowledge of divine wisdom, that since the impious will inevitably be punished with eternal punishment and since the fountain of heavenly grace will flow forth unto the end of the world, many will until then be taken into the company of the holy martyrs. And when they received this response, they were filled with an inexpressible joy, which we believe is aptly symbolized by the white robes. Therefore, each one received a white robe, so that through the perfection of love that is poured out into the hearts of believers through the Holy Spirit, they might be content with this consolation and prefer rather to wait for the completion of the number of other brothers. COMMENTARY ON THE APOCALYPSE 6.11.[25]

**The Time for Vengeance Is Put off by the Divine Patience.** FULGENTIUS OF RUSPE: The Word of God shows that when the time of vengeance comes, conversion will not then help the evil person evade punishment but avenging wrath will destroy him with due damnation. For that will be a time not of remission but of retribution, not of forgiveness but of revenge. This is put off by the divine patience so that the number of the saints can be filled up. The blessed John in the Apocalypse recalls that it is the saints who asked for this vengeance in these words, "How long will it be, holy and true master, before you sit in judgment and avenge our blood on the inhabitants of the earth?" And to teach those who are joined to

this company that the time for vengeance is being put off by the highest ordinance, he adds right away. "Each of them was given a white robe, and they were told to be patient a little while longer until the number was filled of their fellow servants and brothers." ON THE FORGIVENESS OF SINS 2.5.2-3.[26]

**The Saints Pray in Hope.** ANDREW OF CAESAREA: In this passage the saints are shown praying for the consummation of the world. Therefore, they are told to have patience until the completion of the brothers, so that "apart from them they would not be made perfect," as the apostle says.[27] The white robes reveal the brightness that appears on them because of their virtues, in which they are clothed, although they "had not yet received the promises."[28] And so, putting away every dullness, in the hope for these things, which they see in the spirit, they rightly rejoice, resting in the bosom of Abraham. For to many of the saints it is said that each receives a place worthy of the doer of virtue through which they are judged of their future glory. COMMENTARY ON THE APOCALYPSE 6.11.[29]

**The Souls of the Elect.** BEDE: The spirits of the elect who dwell in that heavenly city can be understood as asking in the name of the Savior on their own behalf too, since they clearly desire the coming of the period of universal judgment and the resurrection of their bodies, in which they have striven for the Lord's sake.... Each soul now has a white robe, when each enjoys his bliss alone. They will then receive two, when the number of their brothers has been filled at the end, and they are gladdened by receiving their own immortal bodies. HOMILIES ON THE GOSPELS 2.12.[30]

---

[24]TEG 8:128. [25]CCL 92:100. [26]FC 95:153. [27]Heb 11:40. [28]Heb 11:39. [29]MTS 1 Sup 1:67-68. [30]CS 111:112. Gregory the Great uses this passage for the same argument (*Dialogues* 4.26).

# 6:12-17 THE SIXTH SEAL:
# THE GREAT DAY OF WRATH

$^{12}$*When he opened the sixth seal, I looked, and behold, there was a great earthquake; and the sun became black as sackcloth, the full moon became like blood,* $^{13}$*and the stars of the sky fell to the earth as the fig tree sheds its winter fruit when shaken by a gale;* $^{14}$*the sky vanished like a scroll that is rolled up, and every mountain and island was removed from its place.* $^{15}$*Then the kings of the earth and the great men and the generals and the rich and the strong, and every one, slave and free, hid in the caves and among the rocks of the mountains,* $^{16}$*calling to the mountains and rocks, "Fall on us and hide us from the face of him who is seated on the throne, and from the wrath of the Lamb;* $^{17}$*for the great day of their wrath has come, and who can stand before it?"*

**OVERVIEW:** The death and resurrection of Christ cast the conqueror of humankind down from his throne, and by the ascension of Christ humankind received the way back from death to life. With the opening of the sixth seal the signs that occurred at the time of the crucifixion were seen (OECUMENIUS). These signs also portray the persecutions that shall come upon the church before the arrival of the antichrist (TYCONIUS, ANDREW OF CAESAREA). At that time, the power of Christ will be hidden and the truth of doctrine will be obscured (TYCONIUS). The tribulation and persecution will be as never before (ANDREW OF CAESAREA), and the church will shed her blood more than is usual (BEDE). Even those who seemed excellent and strong will fall away from the church as though they were unripened fruit shaken from a tree (TYCONIUS). Similarly, those who have not experienced the heat of temptation or received the necessary grace will be felled by the wind of the devil (ANDREW OF CAESAREA). At that time, the church will hide herself through a spirit of discretion and avoid persecution through caution (TYCONIUS). The heavenly powers, who could not bear to witness the abuse directed against Jesus (OECUMENIUS), will also grieve for those who fall from faith (ANDREW OF CAESAREA).

During this great conflict at the time of the antichrist, the good will flee, including those who hold office in the church and power in the world (TYCONIUS, ANDREW OF CAESAREA). Those who are evil, however, will by the perversity of their minds become even worse (TYCONIUS). Nonetheless, the arrogant demons and those foolish in their vanity will be overcome. The sinful demons who tyrannized humankind through deceit will seek to hide themselves from the punishment of Christ that is coming upon them (OECUMENIUS). Also those on earth will hide themselves who were rich on earth but poor in heaven and whose faith was as wood and stubble ready for burning (ANDREW OF CAESAREA). However, the saints will find refuge and protection within the church (CAESARIUS OF ARLES) where by example and counsel, by exhortation and prayer, the weaker will find strength in those who are strong. Therefore, when Christ comes, he should find his church not worthy of condemnation but steadfast in faith through the intercession of the saints and the mercy of God (BEDE).

## 6:12 The Lamb Opened the Sixth Seal

**A LIVING WAY.** OECUMENIUS: The loosing of the sixth seal effects the completion of our salvation. It dissolves death and brings back life. It dethrones humanity's conqueror and is openly triumphant in accordance with that which is written: "The Only Begotten ascended on high and led captivity captive and received gifts among men."[1] And what is this loosing of the sixth seal? It is the cross and death of the Lord. The resurrection and the ascension follow after these, and for these every spiritual and physical creature has prayed, for they "renew for us a new and living way,"[2] that is, the way back from death to life through the curtain of his flesh. And he accomplished this good work, not only for the living but also for those who have gone before. For the Lord "went and preached to the disobedient in hades," as the divine apostle Peter says,[3] and he also saved those there who believe, as Cyril thought.[4] COMMENTARY ON THE APOCALYPSE 6.12-17.[5]

### 6:12 Earthquake, Darkness and Blood

**THE POWER OF CHRIST WILL BE HIDDEN.** TYCONIUS: In the sixth seal we recognize the sixth age of the world. Toward the conclusion of this age the last persecution will come, and it says that the vehement shock of this persecution will shake the whole world like an earthquake. The sun and the moon are Christ and the church. The sun is said to become black, because many will be terrified at the last persecution and will deny them. It says, "Even if our gospel is veiled, it is veiled to those who are perishing, for the god of this world has blinded the minds of the unbelievers, so that the brightness of the gospel of the glory of Christ, who is the image of God, might not shine."[6] And therefore it says, "so that even the elect, if possible, are led into error."[7] In this manner is the sun said to become black, when the power of Christ is hidden, or doctrine is obscured for a time, or defense is delayed when the impious are allowed to attack the saints. And therefore the prophet says, "Shall you leave this unnoticed, that the impious swallows the righteous?"[8] And indeed of Christ himself we read, "Behold, this child is set for the fall and resurrection of many, and for a sign that is spoken against."[9] In him some make progress; others, turning away from him, incur ruin. "The moon turned to blood." It is usually foretold that the church will

shed more blood for Christ when the great outbreak of persecutions occurs. Therefore, this speaks of her own blood, not the blood of another as was the case with the red horse, which was described as red with another's blood. COMMENTARY ON THE APOCALYPSE 6.12.[10]

**THE SIGNS OF JUDGMENT.** OECUMENIUS: The vision clearly depicts for us the signs that occurred at the time of the crucifixion: the earthquake and the turmoil of the earth, the darkness of the sun and the transformation of the full moon into blood. And with complete accuracy did he add the word full to the moon. For the moon was fully visible, not merely partially visible on the day of the crucifixion and so greeted the passion in its fullness. . . . And, indeed, the prophet Joel foretold that these things were to happen, "The sun shall turn to darkness, and the moon to blood, before the great and manifest day of the Lord comes."[11] The stars falling from heaven was perhaps a physical occurrence, but if not, the passage indicates that all lights from heaven ceased and everything became darkened. COMMENTARY ON THE APOCALYPSE 6.12-17.[12]

**THE TRIBULATIONS WILL BE BEYOND ANY EXPERIENCE.** ANDREW OF CAESAREA: We think that this passage presents a transition from the times of the persecutions to the time before the arrival of the false Christ. For it has been prophesied that at that time there would be such tribulations, such as we know have never happened before. Indeed, throughout the Scriptures "earthquake" often signifies the change of things. The phrase "once again I will shake" signifies "the removal of what is shaken," as the apostle says.[13] And in the Old Testament it is said concerning the crossing of the Israelites from Egypt, "the earth quaked, the heavens poured."[14] The black-

---

[1]See Ps 68:18 (67:19 LXX); Eph 4:8. [2]Heb 10:20. [3]1 Pet 3:19-20. [4]Cyril of Alexandria *Fragments on the Catholic Epistles*, 1 Pet 3:19-20 (PG 74:1013). [5]TEG 8:129. [6]See 2 Cor 4:3-4. [7]Mt 24:24. [8]See Hab 1:4. [9]Lk 2:34. [10]CCL 92:100-101. [11]Joel 2:31. [12]TEG 8:130. [13]Hag 2:6; Heb 12:26-27. [14]Ps 68:8 (67:9 LXX).

ness of the sun and the dark, bloody appearance of the moon signify the darkness that will come upon those overtaken by the wrath of God, as Cyril often remarked.[15] COMMENTARY ON THE APOCALYPSE 6.12-13.[16]

### THE CHURCH WILL SHED MUCH BLOOD.

BEDE: The church will shed her blood more than is usual. It says "full" moon, because the final earthquake will be in all the earth, while beforehand, as the Scripture says, there will be earthquakes in many places.[17] EXPLANATION OF THE APOCALYPSE 6.12.[18]

### 6:13 The Stars Fell to Earth

EVEN THE MIGHTY FALL. TYCONIUS: The stars signify those in the church who for a time seem, according to human opinion, to stand out from the number of the elect, but who, when the fury of a sharp persecution comes near, are said to fall from their high status as though from heaven. The Lord foretold this in the Gospel, saying, "For then there will be tribulation such as has never been or shall be. And unless those days had been shortened, no flesh would have been saved. But for the sake of the elect, those days will be shortened."[19] The tree represents the church, and the sour fruit, which another translation calls "unripened," represents people. The winds are the turbulent turmoil of persecution by which people are shaken and fall from the church. And it is proper that they are compared with the unripened fruit of the fig tree. For they are either unfaithful and, "twisted like a deceitful bow,"[20] prefer this to the faith that they have abandoned, or because of the immaturity of the time the church suffers in them a tearful miscarriage, although it had sought for a happy birth at their conception. COMMENTARY ON THE APOCALYPSE 6.13.[21]

### FALLING FROM THE WIND OF THE DEVIL.

ANDREW OF CAESAREA: "The stars fell." As has been already written of those deceived by Antiochus,[22] this refers also to those who think themselves to be lights of the world but who will fall, being crushed by the events of that time, as the Lord said, "to lead astray, if it were possible, even the elect by the great tribulation."[23] This is perhaps the reason the fig tree is taken as a parable, for when the wind of the devil shakes it, it casts down its immature fruit that is not yet ripened by the heat of temptations or made sweet by grace. We know that this can be understood in either a good or in a bad sense, whether from the two baskets of good and evil figs that appear in Jeremiah[24] or from the fig tree that Christ made to wither[25] and that mentioned in the Song.[26] But whether these things will occur in a visible manner when Christ comes in glory as judge, only he knows who has the hidden treasures of wisdom and knowledge.[27] COMMENTARY ON THE APOCALYPSE 6.12-13.[28]

### 6:14a The Sky Vanished

THE CHURCH BECOMES CAUTIOUS. TYCONIUS: Rightly does he suggest that the heaven, that is, the church, withdrew like a scroll rolled out rather than as a scroll rolled up. For whatever is rolled up cannot ever be known by anyone, while that which is rolled out is uncovered ever more. And so when these things have been made manifest, [the church] withdraws and prudently avoids persecution, so that concealed from those outside she might not be seen. But through the unity of the Spirit she is wholly known to herself—that is, to her own to whom it is given to believe. And [the church] is cautious towards those who are not known and toward the stranger, and she hides herself through a spirit of discretion, lest becoming known she be betrayed. Therefore, John wrote, "Do not believe every spirit, but test the spirits to see whether they are of God."[29] COMMENTARY ON THE APOCALYPSE 6.14.[30]

---

[15]Cyril of Alexandria *Adoration in Spirit and in Truth* 9 (PG 68:641). [16]MTS 1 Sup 1:68-69. [17]Mt 24:7. [18]CCL 121A:305. [19]Mt 24:21-22. [20]Ps 78:57 (77:57 LXX). [21]CCL 92:101-2. [22]See 2 Macc 4:7—5:27. [23]Mt 24:24. [24]Jer 24:1-5. [25]Mt 21:19-20. [26]Song 2:13. [27]Col 2:3. [28]MTS 1 Sup 1:69-70. [29]1 Jn 4:1. [30]CCL 92:102-3.

### Even the Angels Could Not Bear the Abuse Suffered by Christ. Oecumenius:

By the word *heaven* he speaks of the heavenly powers of the angels who were themselves also thoroughly terrified, not being able to tolerate the abuse directed against their Master, and who were flitting to and fro as a scroll that was unrolled and shaking. Commentary on the Apocalypse 6.12-17.[31]

### The Heavenly Powers Grieve for Those Who Fall from Faith. Andrew of Caesarea:

That heaven is rolled out as a scroll symbolizes either that the second coming of Christ is unknown . . . or that even the heavenly powers grieve for those who have fallen from faith as though they experience a certain rolling out through sympathy and grief. However, this image symbolizes also that the substance of heaven does not disappear, but as though by a kind of unrolling changes into something better. As Irenaeus says, "For neither is the substance nor the essence of the creation annihilated—for faithful and true is he who has established it— but 'the fashion of this world passes away,'[32] within which the transgression occurred, as the elders say."[33] . . . We think that the apostle is using the image of an old custom. For the Hebrews used scrolls rather than codices, which are common among us. To unroll a scroll did not cause anything to disappear but affected the appearance of that written within. So also the opening of the heavenly body shows the revelation of the blessing that lies in wait for the saints. Commentary on the Apocalypse 6.14.[34]

## 6:14b Every Mountain and Island Was Removed

### The Good May Flee, and the Evil May Become Worse. Tyconius:

The church is also symbolized in the mountains and in the islands, for she is a "city set on a hill"[35] on account of "the mountains round about."[36] And we read, "also among the islands of the sea [is] the name of the Lord God of Israel"[37] which foretells that impelled by persecution she will be moved from her place. This is to be applied to both parts [of the church], among the good she is cautious and is moved by flight, among the evil she is moved by a perverse will and is turned into something worse, as it is said, "I shall move your candlestick from its place."[38] Commentary on the Apocalypse 6.14.[39]

### The Arrogant Demons Will Be Moved. Oecumenius:

By "mountains and islands" he means the ranks of the arrogant demons, as it is written of them: "the mountains shake in the heart of the sea."[40] Moreover, by "islands" he speaks of those who in the vain foolishness of their minds think themselves superior and exalted in the fickle and bitter circumstances of the present life. Commentary on the Apocalypse 6.12-17.[41]

### The Powerful in Church and World Will Flee. Andrew of Caesarea:

Our Lord asked the disciples concerning the destruction of the temple and the consummation of the world, and as they were able to receive, he foretold of the coming events. To some extent these events have already happened to the Jews who killed Christ during the siege under Vespasian and Titus, as the Jew Josephus recounts it.[42] But at the end, with a superabundance beyond everything, so to speak, these things will come upon the world at the coming of the antichrist. At that time, the great men, whether those who hold office in the church or those who possess worldly power—here figuratively called "mountains"—and the churches of the faithful—metaphorically called "islands"—which are being renewed to God, as Isaiah said,[43] they will flee from their places, changing from place to place

---

[31]TEG 8:130.  [32]1 Cor 7:31.  [33]Irenaeus *Against Heresies* 5.36.1 (ANF 1:566). See also Tertullian *Against Hermogenes* 24. See Rev 20:11 below.  [34]MTS 1 Sup 1:70-71.  [35]Mt 5:14.  [36]Ps 125:2 (124:1 LXX).  [37]Is 24:15.  [38]Rev 2:5.  [39]CCL 92:103.  [40]Ps 46:2 (45:3 LXX).  [41]TEG 8:130.  [42]Josephus *The Jewish War* 5-6.  [43]See Is 41:1; 45:16.

on account of the false christ. COMMENTARY ON THE APOCALYPSE 6.14-17.[44]

## 6:15-17 *"Fall on Us and Hide Us"*

THE DEMONS SEEK ESCAPE. Oecumenius: By *kings* and *great men* and *generals* and *rich* and *strong* he refers to those sinful demons who tyrannize those on the earth through deceit and guile, and he calls "servants" and "freemen" those among the demons who are of inferior and superior status. That they seek to hide themselves in the caves and among the rocks of the mountains and nevertheless also say "fall upon us and hide us," all of this is spoken figuratively, indicating that they are fugitives who are attempting to escape from the punishment of Christ that is coming upon them. For were there not a certain invisible punishment and retribution coming upon them, what would be the meaning of that spoken by the prophet Isaiah in the person of Christ: "I have trodden the winepress utterly alone, and from the peoples there was none with me, and I have trod them in my anger and trampled them in my wrath, and I have poured out their blood upon the earth,"[45] and what would be the meaning of that spoken by the demons, hated of God, according to Matthew: "What do you have to do with us, O Son of God? Have you come to torment us?"[46] Someone might think that these things reported in the Revelation were not only concerning the sufferings of the demons but also of those lawless Jews who nailed the Lord to the cross and who, accosted by the war with the Romans, became fugitives in the mountains and the caves and the crevices of the earth and from every direction were hemmed in by difficulty and strife. COMMENTARY ON THE APOCALYPSE 6.12-17.[47]

THE REFUGE OF THE SAINTS. Caesarius of Arles: This signifies that the whole world, among the good and the saints, is going to find refuge in the church, so that made firm under [the church's] protection it is able to endure unto eternal life, with the help of our Lord Jesus Christ, who lives and reigns forever and ever. Amen. EXPOSITION ON THE APOCALYPSE 6.15, HOMILY 5.[48]

THE POWERFUL WILL SEEK TO ESCAPE THE DIVINE ANGER. Andrew of Caesarea: "The kings of the earth," that is, those who exert power over it and possess nothing in heaven, they too shall pray with all the great and rich and with the servants of the things below and those free of the service of Christ, that they be hidden by the caves and the rocks and the mountains. For they do not want to experience the divine wrath that with divine consent will pour down upon them either at the coming of the antichrist in the form of punishments from famine and other plagues or in endless torments which are expected after the resurrection. For then the divine anger will burn righteously as a furnace, consuming those who built upon the foundation of faith with wood and chaff and stubble, as though food for the fire. COMMENTARY ON THE APOCALYPSE 6.14-17.[49]

THE WEAK WILL SEEK THE PROTECTION AND COMPASSION OF THE STRONG. Bede: Since all the weak at that time will seek to be strengthened by the examples of the highest in the church, and to be fortified by their counsel, and to be protected by their exhortations and to be sheltered by their prayers, it is as though they entreated the mountains themselves to fall upon them out of compassionate affection. For "the high mountains are a refuge for the deer, and the rocks for the badger."[50] "And hide us from the face of him who is seated on the throne and from the wrath of the Lamb." That is, when he comes, that he should not find us worthy of condemnation but steadfast in faith, our sins being covered by the intercession of the saints and the mercy of God. "And who will be able to stand." Certainly that one will be able to stand who has now taken care to be vig-

---

[44]MTS 1 Sup 1:71-72. [45]Is 63:3. [46]Mt 8:29. [47]TEG 8:130-31. [48]PL 35:2425. [49]MTS 1 Sup 1:72. [50]See Ps 104:18 (103:18 LXX).

ilant, to be steadfast in faith and to live coura-geously. Because, if one refers this earthquake literally to the day of judgment itself, it is not sur-prising if at that time the kings and princes of the earth out of fear seek the refuge of the holy mountains, just as we read has already occurred in the story of the rich man clothed in purple and the poor Lazarus.[51] EXPLANATION OF THE APOC-ALYPSE 6.16-17.[52]

---

[51]Lk 16:19-31. [52]CCL 121A:307.

---

## 7:1-8 144,000 SEALED

[1]*After this I saw four angels standing at the four corners of the earth, holding back the four winds of the earth, that no wind might blow on earth or sea or against any tree.* [2]*Then I saw another angel ascend from the rising of the sun, with the seal of the living God, and he called with a loud voice to the four angels who had been given power to harm earth and sea,* [3]*saying, "Do not harm the earth or the sea or the trees, till we have sealed the servants of our God upon their fore-heads."* [4]*And I heard the number of the sealed, a hundred and forty-four thousand sealed, out of every tribe of the sons of Israel,* [5]*twelve thousand sealed out of the tribe of Judah, twelve thousand of the tribe of Reuben, twelve thousand of the tribe of Gad,* [6]*twelve thousand of the tribe of Asher, twelve thousand of the tribe of Naphtali, twelve thousand of the tribe of Manasseh,* [7]*twelve thou-sand of the tribe of Simeon, twelve thousand of the tribe of Levi, twelve thousand of the tribe of Issachar,* [8]*twelve thousand of the tribe of Zebulun, twelve thousand of the tribe of Joseph, twelve thousand sealed out of the tribe of Benjamin.*

**OVERVIEW:** The suffering of earth and human-kind when the judgment of God comes was indi-cated long ago through the tyranny of the four ancient kingdoms (BEDE). Such suffering was more recently indicated through the suffering of the Jews during the war against the Romans (OECUMENIUS). But such suffering will especially occur at the coming of the antichrist, when the good order of the creation itself will dissolve (AN-DREW OF CAESAREA). Before this happens, how-ever, Elijah will come down to call the Jews to the faith that is spread abroad among the Gentiles (VICTORINUS) so that through the light of the gos-pel those Jews worthy of salvation might be iden-tified and not suffer the same fate as the sinners.

To some extent this happened when those Jews who believed in Christ fled from the siege of Jeru-salem by the Romans. These Jews were very nu-merous (OECUMENIUS, ANDREW OF CAESAREA) and probably included Jews who for whatever reason were not complicit in the plot against Christ and who later were sealed in the faith of Christ (OECUMENIUS).

At the time of antichrist, however, all the faithful will be separated from the faithless by the seal of the life-giving cross, and the creation too will be made clean and freed from its torments (ANDREW OF CAESAREA). The Lord brought this cross with him from heaven when he was born in the flesh. The very shape of the cross reveals the universality of his kingdom and the innumerable multitude of the whole church whose number is perfect and complete (BEDE). The church includes Gentiles and Jews, for had the Jews believed from the first, Christ would not have been crucified, and the Gentiles would have been left bereft of salvation (JEROME). This church possesses in all her members an equal zeal and a unanimity of faith (OECUMENIUS) and possesses virtues that lead her from confession and faith to the right hand of eternal life (BEDE). This way of the church's sojourn is a way of spiritual sight and good works, of blessings and prayer, of hope for things ahead and obedience, of strength in suffering and grace for eternal life. This path upon which the church of the elect walks and that leads to the felicity of Christ's right hand is symbolized by the names of the twelve tribes of Israel (ANDREW OF CAESAREA, BEDE).

### 7:1 Four Angels at the Four Corners of the Earth

**THE JEWS FOUND NO RESPITE.** OECUMENIUS: Here clearly what happened to the Jews during the war against the Romans is shown to the Evangelist, which things occurred to them because of the crucifixion and their blasphemy against the Lord. For the four angels who held the four corners of the land of the Jews were keeping guard lest any of the Jews who were deserving of death should escape. And so they either brought upon them a fear of flight or dissensions or an untimely devotion to the fatherland or to their wives and relatives, and it is these things that are figuratively signified by the four corners of Judea being guarded. And that the four winds are restrained so that they blow neither upon the land nor upon the sea nor against any tree indicates that no respite was found by them in the war nor any consolation from their woes, neither for those who fought on the land, nor for those who fought at sea—for, according to Josephus, there were many sea battles—nor for those whose concern is with farming. For these evils

wholly overpowered everyone, since the cities were destroyed by fire and the land was devastated and wasted. And Josephus accurately relates all of these events in his account of the siege of Jerusalem.[1] COMMENTARY ON THE APOCALYPSE 7.1-8.[2]

**THE ORDER OF CREATION WILL DISSOLVE.** ANDREW OF CAESAREA: Although these things are thought by some to have occurred long ago to the Jews at the hands of the Romans[3] . . . how much more will these things occur at the coming of the antichrist, and not only partially in the land of the Jews but over the whole world at whose four corners the angels stand fulfilling a service assigned to them by God, but unknown to us. The holding back of the winds reveals clearly the dissolution of the good order of creation and the inevitability of evil. For by means of wind the plants of the earth are nourished and ships sail the sea. COMMENTARY ON THE APOCALYPSE 7.1.[4]

**THE FOUR ANCIENT KINGDOMS.** BEDE: [The four angels] refer to the four principal kingdoms, namely, that of the Assyrians, of the Persians, of the Greeks and of the Romans. . . . Suffocating in some way all things by their might, these angels did not allow anyone to breathe freely of his own right. By "the earth" is indicated the various provinces, in "the sea" the various islands, and among "the trees" the various qualities and conditions of people. Another interpretation: These four angels are to be understood as those very four winds of which Daniel speaks in his prophecy: "Behold, the four winds of heaven stirred up the great sea, and the four beasts came up from the sea."[5] EXPLANATION OF THE APOCALYPSE 7.1.[6]

### 7:2-3 An Angel Ascending

**ELIJAH WILL CALL THE JEWS TO THE FAITH**

---

[1]Josephus *The Jewish War* 5-6. [2]TEG 8:132-33. [3]Andrew is referring to Oecumenius. [4]MTS 1 Sup 1:73-74. [5]Dan 7:2-3. [6]CCL 121A:307-9.

**of the Gentiles.** Victorinus of Petovium: "I [saw] an angel descending from the rising of the sun."[7] He is speaking of Elijah the prophet, who was to come before the time of antichrist to restore and to strengthen the churches from the intolerable persecution. We read of these things in the opening of the book both of the Old Testament and of the new preaching. For through Malachi the Lord said, "Behold, I send to you Elijah, the Thesbite, to turn the hearts of the fathers to their children and the heart of man to his neighbor,"[8] that is, to Christ through penitence. "To turn the hearts of the fathers to their children," that is, at the time of the calling to recall the Jews to the faith of that people which follows them. And therefore he shows the number of those from the Jews who will believe and the great multitude of those from the Gentiles. Commentary on the Apocalypse 7.2.[9]

**The Rising of the Sun.** Oecumenius: That the divine angel appears from the rising of the sun and not from its setting which brings on the evening is symbolic of the gospel and the promise of its blessings. For the prophet foresaw in the spirit that sealing that now is when he said, "The light of your face was lifted upon us."[10] Meanwhile he rightly commands that nothing be harmed until those from the Jews who are worthy of being saved should be sealed, so that none of the righteous should suffer any of these calamities along with the sinners. Commentary on the Apocalypse 7.1-8.[11]

**The Faithless Will Be Separated from the Faithful.** Andrew of Caesarea: This was revealed long ago to Ezekiel concerning him who was clothed in a fine linen robe and who sealed the foreheads of those who mourned so that the righteous would not be destroyed along with the wicked,[12] since the virtue of the saints is hidden and is unknown even to the angels. This is shown also here to the blessed [John], that a preeminent holy power encourages the avenging holy angels to do nothing until they might recog-

nize the servants of the truth by virtue of their having been sealed. Although this has happened partially long ago when those who believed in Christ fled from the siege of Jerusalem by the Romans into very many destinations, the great James having showed to blessed Paul their great number,[13] then, as has been said, this will especially occur at the coming of the antichrist when the seal of the life-giving cross will separate from the faithless the faithful who bear without shame and with boldness the sign of Christ before the impious. Therefore, the angel says, "Do not harm the earth of the sea or the trees, until we have sealed the servants of our God upon their foreheads." Just as the creation, created for our sakes, shares in the torments with us who are being chastised, so too it will be made clean with the saints who are being glorified. Through these words we learn that the virtuous will require the power of angelic assistance before the arrival of the trials which come because of the seal of the Spirit which is given to us. [We learn further] that this seal will reveal its power to that extent that we add our own work to it, for everything remains without aid which by its own will wills not to be aided. Commentary on the Apocalypse 7.2-3.[14]

**The Lord Will Seal the Foreheads of His Own.** Bede: This is the Lord born in the flesh, who is the "angel of great counsel,"[15] that is, the messenger of the Father's will, "who has visited us as the dayspring from on high,"[16] carrying the standard of the cross, by which he seals the foreheads of his own.... The great voice of the Lord is that exalted proclamation, "Repent, for the kingdom of heaven has drawn near."[17] ... For this purpose was the rule of the nations destroyed, that the face of the saints might in free-

---

[7]The text of Victorinus appears to have read "descending," not "ascending." Elijah can "descend," because he was, according to ancient understanding, taken directly to paradise. See also Irenaeus *Against Heresies* 5.5.1. [8]See Mal 4:5-6. [9]CSEL 49:80-82. [10]Ps 4:6 (4:7 LXX). [11]TEG 8:133. [12]Ezek 9:2-11. [13]Acts 21:20. [14]MTS 1 Sup 1:74-75. [15]Is 9:6 LXX. [16]Lk 1:78. [17]Mt 4:17.

dom be marked by the sign of faith which they had resisted. For even the figure of the cross itself indicates that the kingdom of the Lord is everywhere extended, as the ancient distich[18] shows:

"Behold, the four-squared world, in distinct
     parts,
   that you might show the sign of faith to
     encompass all things."[19]

Nor in vain was the four-lettered name of the Lord written upon the forehead of the high priest, since this is the sign upon the foreheads of the faithful, about which the psalm "for the wine-vats" sings: "O Lord, our Lord, how majestic is thy name in all the earth," and so on, until he says, "that you may destroy the enemy and the defender."[20] EXPLANATION OF THE APOCALYPSE 7.2-3.[21]

## 7:4 The Number of the Sealed

**MANY THOUSANDS OF JEWS BECAME SERVANTS OF GOD.** OECUMENIUS: And the sealed, it says, was 144,000. For those from the Jews who believed in Christ were numerous and greater than [this] number, and they were accounted worthy to be saved from the common destruction, as those testified who spoke to Paul when he was in Jerusalem: "Do you see, brother, how many thousands there are of the Jews who have believed?"[22] And it was likely that not only the faithful escaped, but also those who were deceived and in ignorance assisted in the crucifixion of the Lord, about whom he said, "Father, forgive them, for they know not what they do."[23] . . . And perhaps not only these [escaped], but also those who were not present at that time or were not living in Jerusalem and so were not complicit in the impious plot of the accursed high priests concerning the crucifixion, and also those who were perhaps present but were not involved in that murderous defilement. Indeed, [Christ] himself blessed everything under heaven, in contrast to what the irreligious council of transgressors had wanted. It is likely that all of these were later sealed in the faith of Christ, otherwise the

angel would not have called them the servants of God. And when these had been rescued, either by flight or by desertion to the Romans, those wicked ones who remained were destroyed in a terrible manner, "having become a spectacle to the world, to angels, and to men,"[24] in a way quite different from what Paul had said of the blessed apostles. And of these things, Josephus is again witness, counting those who were killed by famine as more than ten thousand.[25] COMMENTARY ON THE APOCALYPSE 7.1-8.[26]

**THE CHURCH IS AN INNUMERABLE MULTITUDE.** BEDE: By this finite number is signified the innumerable multitude of the whole church, which is begotten from the patriarchs either by way of the offspring of flesh or by the imitation of faith. For it says, "If you are of Christ, you are the seed of Abraham."[27] And it pertains to the increase of perfection that this twelve is multiplied by twelve and is completed by the sum of a thousand, which is the cube of the number ten, signifying the immoveable life of the church. And for this reason rather often the church is symbolized by the number twelve, since throughout the four-squared world she subsists by faith in the holy Trinity, for three fours make ten and two. And, finally, twelve apostles were elected that they might preach the same faith to the world, signifying by way of the number the mystery of their work. EXPLANATION OF THE APOCALYPSE 7.4.[28]

## 7:5 From Judah, Reuben and Gad

**THE JEWS DID NOT THEN BELIEVE.** JEROME: Someone may ask, Where does one read that all Israel will be saved? First, of course, there is the apostle: "Until the full number of the Gentiles should enter, and thus all Israel should be saved."

[18]A couplet meant to stand alone. [19]Source unknown. [20]Ps 8:1-2 (8:2-3 LXX). [21]CCL 121A:309-11. [22]Acts 21:20. [23]Lk 23:34. [24]1 Cor 4:9. [25]Josephus The Jewish War 5.567-69; 6.420-25. [26]TEG 8:133-34. [27]Gal 3:29. [28]CCL 121A:311-13.

In the second place, John says in his Apocalypse: of the tribe of Judah, twelve thousand shall believe, of the tribe of Reuben, twelve thousand shall believe, and of the remaining tribes, he says the same; and the number of all who believe became 144,000. Then too Psalm 144, which is alphabetical, treats of this number saved. If Israel had believed, our Lord would not have been crucified. If our Lord had not been crucified, the multitude of Gentiles would not have been saved. The Jews are going to believe, but not until the end of the world. It was not the time for them to believe in the cross; for if they had believed, the Lord would not have been crucified. It was not the time to believe. Their infidelity is our faith. By their downfall, we are raised up. It was not their time in order that it might be our time. Homilies on Mark 82 (8).[29]

**All Israel Has an Equal Zeal and an Unanimity of Faith.** Oecumenius: That an equal number from each tribe is said to have been sealed and to have believed indicates the equality of their zeal and unanimity of their faith, although there would have been more from one tribe and less from other tribes of those who were saved and believed on Christ, who although dishonored by the Jews, is worshiped [by us] and by every supernatural creature now and always and forever more. Amen. Commentary on the Apocalypse 7.1-8.[30]

**Confession, Spiritual Sight, Endurance.** Andrew of Caesarea: "From the tribe of Judah, twelve thousand sealed." *Judah* is interpreted "confession,"[31] through which those are manifested who are being saved through the confession to Christ who came forth as a branch from Judah. "From the tribe of Reuben, twelve thousand sealed." *Reuben* is interpreted "son of vision,"[32] through which those are shown who possess spiritual sight through purity of heart.[33] "From the tribe of Gad, twelve thousand." *Gad* is interpreted "temptation,"[34] through which those are shown who through the endurance of tempta-

tions are being crowned, after the example of Job. Commentary on the Apocalypse 7.5.[35]

**The Names of the Tribes.** Bede: It is fitting that he begins with Judah, for from that tribe our Lord came, and he omits the tribe of Dan, from which it is said that the antichrist will come, as it is written: "Let Dan be a serpent in the way, a viper by the path, that bites the horse's heels so that his rider falls."[36] For he does not intend to give the order of earthly generations but to expound the virtues of the church by way of the interpretation of the names, for by its present confession and worship [the church] hastens to the right hand of eternal life—for this is the meaning of the name Judah, which is placed first, and of Benjamin, which is placed last. Therefore, Judah is placed first, who being interpreted means "confession" or "praise." For before the beginning of confession, no one attains the heights of good works, and unless we should renounce evil works through confession, we are not informed by those works which are just. The second name is that of Reuben, who being interpreted means "seeing the son." By *sons* works are indicated, as the psalmist says when speaking of the various blessings of the blessed man: "Your sons will be as olive shoots," and further, "that you may see the sons of your sons."[37] For it is not that he who fears the Lord cannot be blessed unless he beget sons and grandsons, since a greater reward awaits the faithful virgins. But by *sons* is meant works and by *sons of sons* the fruit of works, that is, the eternal reward. For this reason, Reuben comes after Judah, since after the beginning of divine confession there follows the perfection of work. And since "through many tribulations it is necessary that we enter into the kingdom of God,"[38] after Reuben there follows the tribe of Gad, which interpreted means

---

[29]FC 57:177. [30]TEG 8:134. [31]Philo *On Dreams* 2.34. [32]Philo *On the Change of Names* 98; *On Dreams* 2.33. [33]See Mt 5:8. [34]Philo *On Dreams* 2.35. [35]MTS 1 Sup 1:75-76. [36]Gen 49:17. See Hippolytus *On the Antichrist* 14. [37]Ps 128:3, 6 (127:3, 6 LXX). [38]Acts 14:22.

"temptation" or "girt about." For after the beginning of good works, it is necessary that man be tested by greater temptations and be prepared for more serious battles, so that the strength of his faith might be demonstrated. As Solomon says, "Son, if you come forward for the service of God, stand in his righteousness and prepare your soul for temptation."[39] And the psalmist says the same thing: "You did gird me with strength for the battle."[40] EXPLANATION OF THE APOCALYPSE 7.5.[41]

## 7:6 Asher, Naphtali and Manasseh

**THE LORD BLESSES THOSE WHO ARE BOUND TO GOD.** ANDREW OF CAESAREA: "From the tribe of Asher, twelve thousand." *Asher* is interpreted "blessing,"[42] through which are revealed those who are worthy of dominical blessings because of their life and are made worthy of standing at the right hand of Christ[43] and are shown to be sons of the light and of the day. "From the tribe of Naphtali, twelve thousand." *Naphtali* is interpreted "prayer," through which those are characterized who are bound to God through unceasing prayer. "From the tribe of Manasseh, twelve thousand." *Manasseh* is interpreted "forgetfulness,"[44] that is, it refers to those who on account of love for God, have forgotten the things from the past and the homes of their fathers.[45] COMMENTARY ON THE APOCALYPSE 7.6.[46]

**BLESSED ARE THOSE WHO ENDURE TRIALS.** BEDE: And since we bless those who have endured suffering, after Gad is rightfully placed the tribe of Asher, which means "blessed." For blessed is the one who endures trial, for "when he has stood the test, he will receive the crown of life."[47] Because those who are made safe by a sure promise of this blessedness are not placed in distress but rejoicing in hope and patient in tribulation, they sing with the psalmist: "In tribulation you have given me room,"[48] and again, "I have run in the way of your commandments, while you enlarged my heart."[49] And exulting with the

mother of blessed Samuel, they say, "My mouth is made wide over my enemies, for I rejoice in your salvation."[50] And for this reason, Napthali comes next, for it means "breadth."[51] And Manasseh, meaning "forgetting" or "necessity," follows him. For by the mystery of this name we are exhorted that, taught by the troubles of present temptations, we ought to forget that which is behind and as the apostle says, strive for that which is ahead.[52] And in this way we might not make provisions for the flesh in its desires but be constrained by the sole necessity of the human condition, concerning which the psalmist, sighing for better things, prays, "Bring me out of my distresses."[53] EXPLANATION OF THE APOCALYPSE 7.6.[54]

## 7:7 Simeon, Levi and Issachar

**THOSE WHO ARE OBEDIENT LIVE AS TRUE PRIESTS.** ANDREW OF CAESAREA: "From the tribe of Simeon, twelve thousand." Simeon is interpreted "obedience,"[55] clearly referring to those who are becoming righteous through obedience to the divine commandments. "From the tribe of Levi, twelve thousand." Levi is interpreted "having been taken up," through which are indicated those taken up by Christ through a life proper to the priesthood.[56] Levi is listed eighth, since by the eighth day of the resurrection the true priesthood is made known. "From the tribe of Issachar, twelve thousand." Issachar is interpreted "reward,"[57] that is, it refers to those who for the sake of the rewards from God have lived virtuously.[58] COMMENTARY ON THE APOCALYPSE 7.7.[59]

**THOSE WHO REPENT IN SORROW.** BEDE: Simeon is placed next and means "he has heard sor-

[39]Sir 2:1. [40]Ps 18:39 (17:40 LXX). [41]CCL 121A:313-15. [42]Philo *On Dreams* 2.35. [43]See Mt 25:33-34. [44]Philo *On the Change of Names* 99-100. [45]Gen 41:51. [46]MTS 1 Sup 1:76-77. [47]Jas 1:12. [48]Ps 4:1. [49]Ps 119:32 (118:32 LXX). [50]1 Sam 2:1. [51]Philo *On Dreams* 2.36. [52]See Phil 3:13. [53]Ps 25:17 (24:17 LXX). [54]CCL 121A:315-17. [55]Philo *On the Change of Names* 99; *On Dreams* 2.34. [56]Philo *On Dreams* 2.34. [57]Ibid. [58]See Gen 30:18. [59]MTS 1 Sup 1:77.

row" or "the name of dwelling," so that by the character of this name he might more clearly teach what is here to be acquired and what is more advantageously to be awaited. For the joy of the celestial habitation is given to those whose mind is here made sorrowful by a fruitful repentance, of whom indeed it was said, "Your sorrow will be turned into joy."[60] Next listed is Levi, which interpreted means "addition," by which we understand either those who with temporal things purchase eternal things, as Solomon says, "The ransom of a man's life is his own wealth,"[61] or those who by following the counsel of God receive in this world a hundredfold with tribulations, but in the future age [they receive] eternal life. Concerning these it has been written: "He who adds knowledge adds woe."[62] For this reason was the bitterness of tribulations added even to holy Job, that, having been found worthy, he might receive a greater reward. And so not without reason does Issachar follow him in a proper order. Issachar is interpreted to mean "there is a reward," for, as the apostle says, "the sufferings of the present age are not worthy to be compared to the future glory which will be revealed in us."[63] For, indeed, we fight with greater effect when a sure reward is awaited. EXPLANATION OF THE APOCALYPSE 7.7.[64]

## 7:8 Zebulun, Joseph and Benjamin

**A HOLY NUMBER.** ANDREW OF CAESAREA: "From the tribe of Zebulun, twelve thousand." *Zebulun* is interpreted "abode of power" or "fragrance," through which are indicated those who by the indwelling of Christ have been made firm against sufferings and have become his sweet smell, as Paul says.[65] "From the tribe of Joseph, twelve thousand." *Joseph* is interpreted "addition,"[66] that is, those who in addition to the kingdom of heaven receive those things necessary for eternal life, as the Lord says.[67] "From the tribe of Benjamin, twelve thousand." *Benjamin* means "son of sorrow"[68] or "son of day"[69] or "son of my right hand" and refers to those with sorrow in their

heart. This refers either to those believers from the Jews who fled the siege of the Romans and equaled this number, or, what is rather more likely, to those from the Jews who are saved at the consummation when, as the apostle puts it, after "the full number of the Gentiles come in, all Israel will be saved."[70] Either interpretation is acceptable. The exact equality of each tribe seems to me to show the utter fruitfulness of the apostolic seed, since twelve multiplied by twelve and multiplied by the perfect number of a thousand yields the thousands here indicated. For these were the disciples of that seed that out of love for humankind fell upon the earth and brought forth the various fruit of universal salvation. COMMENTARY ON THE APOCALYPSE 7.8.[71]

**THE BODY WILL BECOME INVINCIBLE.** BEDE: However, God works and perfects these things in the "habitation of strength," which is the meaning of *Zebulun*, since "strength is made perfect in weakness."[72] And this God does so that the body, which is regarded as weak by its enemies and through which they strive to wreak destruction upon the soul, might be found, with God's assistance and by the happy addition which will come to it, to be invincible. And this is indicated by the name Joseph, which means the "gifts of grace to be added." By this we must understand either the increase of the spiritual gift from the double return of the talents, or you should think of those offerings which are rendered to God the Redeemer by the devotion of the faithful. And that you might understand that all these, who by sequence and the interpretation of names are placed here in a meaningful way, are those who will in the future judgment be at the right hand of Christ, the eternal king. Benjamin, as we said before, is mentioned in last place. For *Benjamin* means "son of the right hand," because he is at

---

[60]Jn 16:20. [61]Prov 13:8. [62]See Eccles 1:18. [63]Rom 8:18. [64]CCL 121A:317-19. [65]2 Cor 2:15. [66]Gen 30:24; Philo *On the Change of Names* 89-90; *On Dreams* 2.47. [67]Mt 6:33. [68]Gen 35:18; Philo *On the Change of Names* 94-96. [69]Philo *On the Change of Names* 92-93; *On Dreams* 2.36. [70]Rom 11:25-26. [71]MTS 1 Sup 1:77-79. [72]2 Cor 12:9.

the end of the series. For, when the last enemy, namely, death, is destroyed, the felicity of the eternal inheritance will be given to the elect, either each one of the faithful rightfully being named "son of the right hand," or the whole congregation of the church, concerning which we sing, "A queen stood at your right hand dressed in various golden robes."[73] EXPLANATION OF THE APOCALYPSE 7.8.[74]

---

[73]Ps 45:9 (44:10 LXX). [74]CCL 121A: 319-21.

---

## 7:9-17 A GREAT MULTITUDE FROM EVERY NATION

[9]*After this I looked, and behold, a great multitude which no man could number, from every nation, from all tribes and peoples and tongues, standing before the throne and before the Lamb, clothed in white robes, with palm branches in their hands,* [10]*and crying out with a loud voice, "Salvation belongs to our God who sits upon the throne, and to the Lamb!"* [11]*And all the angels stood round the throne and round the elders and the four living creatures, and they fell on their faces before the throne and worshiped God,* [12]*saying, "Amen! Blessing and glory and wisdom and thanksgiving and honor and power and might be to our God for ever and ever! Amen."*

[13]*Then one of the elders addressed me, saying, "Who are these, clothed in white robes, and whence have they come?"* [14]*I said to him, "Sir, you know." And he said to me, "These are they who have come out of the great tribulation; they have washed their robes and made them white in the blood of the Lamb.*

[15]*Therefore are they before the throne of God,*
*and serve him day and night within his temple;*
*and he who sits upon the throne will shelter them with his presence.*
[16]*They shall hunger no more, neither thirst any more;*
*the sun shall not strike them, nor any scorching heat.*
[17]*For the Lamb in the midst of the throne will be their shepherd,*
*and he will guide them to springs of living water;*
*and God will wipe away every tear from their eyes."*

---

**OVERVIEW:** After seeing the 144,000 belonging to the tribes of Israel to whom the gospel had first been preached (BEDE), John sees a multitude without number from every nation and tongue. These are the countless thousands from the Gentiles who received salvation and have been given a place in the choir that stands before the Father's throne (OECUMENIUS, BEDE). Or, in this multitude John sees the same people indicated by the sacred number of 144,000, which is the multitude of the elect. Through the gospel those from the nations are made to be Israel and are rightly called sons of Abraham, for they have been engrafted into the root of Israel

(Primasius, Caesarius of Arles).

Perhaps this multitude is the many martyrs from every tribe who have struggled long ago and will struggle to the end of time (Andrew of Caesarea). By their baptism these are robed in the Holy Spirit (Caesarius of Arles) and in the love given through the Spirit (Primasius) and in the purity of their lives (Oecumenius). The martyrs, too, make white the robes of their deeds through the shedding of their blood (Andrew of Caesarea), and they receive back their bodies glorified through resurrection (Bede). Through the triumph of the cross these share in the victory of Christ against every spiritual foe, and receiving the power to become the sons of God, they persevere in every good work (Oecumenius, Primasius). The martyrs especially, who were companions of Christ in his passion, are received into the heavenly Jerusalem and there praise God for the victory over the demons which he gave to them (Andrew of Caesarea, Bede).

With deep devotion and unceasing praise the multitude praises the holy Trinity who rules on one throne in the power of one nature. To the Trinity the church ascribes the sevenfold virtues in which those participate who have become sons of God (Primasius), and to their praise all the heavenly hosts and the holy angels add their own neverending doxology (Oecumenius).

That John might know this multitude more fully (Oecumenius) and that the faithful might know their future reward (Primasius), one of the elders says, "These have come from the great tribulation and have washed their robes in the blood of the Lamb." To be sure, the martyrs, cleansed by baptism, make their flesh dazzling white and worthy of the light of immortality through their blood (Tertullian, Primasius, Bede). However, all who are baptized have been wiped clean from the filth of sin by the blood of Christ (Oecumenius, Caesarius of Arles) and are made martyrs before God by their inner character. God has promised to dwell among these, for the souls of the righteous are the seat of wisdom (Primasius), and they always hold God in

remembrance (Oecumenius). By suffering with Christ, these have assumed the pleasant and desirable servitude of continuous praise to God (Bede). As they worshiped God in times of prosperity and of adversity (Primasius), they will without end be illumined by the Sun of righteousness and know heavenly mysteries, both those easily acquired and those hidden and deep (Andrew of Caesarea).

This service to God occurs throughout the creation, which is being renewed by the Spirit, but it occurs especially by those who have preserved the gift of the Spirit (Andrew of Caesarea). As in this life they were sheltered from the heat of temptation by the strength of the sacraments (Tyconius), before the throne of God they will be satisfied with countless blessings and be free from every temptation (Oecumenius). Similarly, through baptism the church is led into the joyful life of the Holy Spirit (Tyconius) and through the vision of God becomes the spring of heavenly teaching (Bede). However, after the resurrection, the mourning and sighing that assailed us from the afflictions of soul and body will cease (Tertullian), and we will in infinite joy drink from the abundant stream of the Holy Spirit and possess incorruptibility and perfect knowledge (Andrew of Caesarea).

### 7:9a A Multitude from Every Nation

**All Gentiles Who Received Faith Stand Before the Father's Throne.** Oecumenius: [He sees] the countless thousands from the Gentiles who, having received faith and having attained the blessed portion, have been allotted a place in the glorious choir and stand before the Lord and the throne of his Father. Commentary on the Apocalypse 7.9-17.[1]

**The Elect Are by Right Called Sons of Abraham.** Primasius: By the sign of the sacred number he signifies the multitude of the elect,

[1]TEG 8:136.

"whom God foreknew and predestined to be conformed to the image of his Son."[2] For those who come from the nations are made to be Israel and so by right are called sons of Abraham,[3] not by flesh but by faith in that seed which is Christ, the cornerstone, of whom the apostle said, "He is our peace, who has made us both one, and has broken down the dividing wall of hostility, by abolishing in his flesh the law of commandments and ordinances, that he might create in himself one new man in the place of two, and so make peace, and might reconcile both to God in one body through the cross."[4] COMMENTARY ON THE APOCALYPSE 7.9.[5]

**BY BELIEVING, ALL NATIONS ARE GRAFTED INTO THE ROOT.** CAESARIUS OF ARLES: He did not say, "After this I saw another people," but "I saw a people," that is, the same people that he had seen in the mystery of the 144,000, which he now sees as without number from every tribe and tongue and nation. For by believing, all nations have been engrafted into the root. In the Gospel the Lord showed forth in the [figure of the] twelve tribes the whole church both from the Jews and from the Gentiles. He said, "You will sit on twelve thrones, judging the twelve tribes of Israel."[6] EXPOSITION ON THE APOCALYPSE 7.9, HOMILY 6.[7]

**FROM EVERY TRIBE AND TONGUE.** ANDREW OF CAESAREA: These are the ones of whom David spoke: "I shall number them, and they will be more than the sand."[8] Namely, these are those who long ago struggled as martyrs for the sake of Christ and those from every tribe and tongue who will fight valiantly at the end of time. COMMENTARY ON THE APOCALYPSE 7.9-10.[9]

**JOHN RECALLS THE SALVATION OF THE NATIONS.** BEDE: This can be interpreted to mean that when the tribes of Israel to whom the gospel was first preached have been named, [John] then wishes to recall the salvation of the nations. EXPLANATION OF THE APOCALYPSE 7.9.[10]

## 7:9b Clothed in White Robes, with Palms

**REJOICING IN CHRIST'S VICTORY.** OECUMENIUS: They are clothed in white robes as a sign of the purity of their life, and the palm branches are symbolic of victory and reveal that they rejoice in the victory of Christ against every spiritual and physical foe. COMMENTARY ON THE APOCALYPSE 7.9-17.[11]

**THE SAINTS PERSEVERE IN GOOD WORKS.** PRIMASIUS: By the robes he suggests baptism, and by the palms the triumph of the cross. Since they have conquered the world in Christ, it may be that the robes signify the love which is given through the Holy Spirit. . . . They are said to carry palm branches in their hands. "In their hands" indicates either their perseverance in good works—we read here, "The Lord made strong his arm for a good work,"[12] and "With my hands at night I was before him, and I was not deceived"[13]—or it indicates that power which they received so that they might become sons of God, as is said of Joseph, "And the Lord had placed all things in his hand,"[14] that is, into his power. COMMENTARY ON THE APOCALYPSE 7.9.[15]

**THE GIFT OF THE SPIRIT.** CAESARIUS OF ARLES: By the white robes he means the gift of the Holy Spirit. EXPOSITION ON THE APOCALYPSE 7.9, HOMILY 6.[16]

**THEIR DEEDS ARE WHITE THROUGH BLOOD.** ANDREW OF CAESAREA: By the outpouring of their own blood for the sake of Christ, some have made white and others will make white the robes of their deeds. And they have in their hands palm branches, which are symbolic of victory and which are good, straight and white as are their hearts. And they form a chorus around the divine throne of the godly

---

[2]Rom 8:29. [3]See Gal 3:7. [4]Eph 2:14-16. [5]CCL 92:126. [6]Mt 19:28. [7]PL 35:2427. [8]Ps 139:18 (138:18 LXX). [9]MTS 1 Sup 1:82. [10]CCL 121A:323. [11]TEG 8:136. [12]Source unknown. [13]Ps 77:2 (76:3 LXX). [14]Gen 39:8. [15]CCL 92:126-27. [16]PL 35:2427.

rest, as grateful family members ascribing the victory over the demons to him who provides it. COMMENTARY ON THE APOCALYPSE 7.9-10.[17]

**BODIES GLORIFIED THROUGH RESURRECTION.** BEDE: Let us think attentively about the eternal feast of the martyrs, which is in heaven, and by following in their footsteps insofar as we can, let us also take care to become ourselves participants in this heavenly feast, for as the apostle bears witness, if we have been companions of his passion, we will at the same time be companions of his consolation.[18] Nor should we mourn their death as much as we should rejoice about their attaining the palm of righteousness. Rachel must groan over each of them when, through torments, they are driven away from this life—that is, the church which begot [them] exhorts them with mourning and tears, but when they have been driven out, the heavenly Jerusalem, who is the mother of us all, soon receives them into another life by ministers of gladness who are ready at hand and introduces them into the joy of the Lord to be crowned as his forever. Hence, says John, they were standing before the throne "in the sight of the Lamb, dressed in white robes, and palms were in their hands." For they now stand before God's throne, crowned, who once lay, worn down by pain, before the thrones of earthly judges. They stand in the sight of the Lamb, and for no cause can they be separated from contemplating his glory there, since here they could not be separated from his love through punishments. They shine in white robes and have palms in their hands, who possess the rewards for their works; while they get back their bodies, glorified through resurrection, which for the Lord's sake they suffered to be scorched by flames, torn to pieces by beasts, worn out by scourges, broken by falls from high places, scraped by hoofs and completely destroyed by every kind of punishment. HOMILIES ON THE GOSPELS 1.10.[19]

### 7:10-12 *"Salvation Belongs to God and the Lamb"*

**THE ANGELS ADD THEIR ETERNAL PRAISE.** OECUMENIUS: And they cry out, "Salvation belongs to our God and to the Lamb," confessing that salvation is with them, since, having been sealed as servants of God, they were rescued from the universal destruction of the world. And when they rendered their thanksgiving, all the heavenly hosts, together with the elders, respond with "Amen," adding their own approval to that which had been said. Then the holy angels add their own praise to God, giving him honor with a sevenfold praise, which, as was earlier noted, signifies the neverending praise of the angels, for the number seven suggests perfection. COMMENTARY ON THE APOCALYPSE 7.9-17.[20]

**THE ONE NATURE OF THE TRINITY.** PRIMASIUS: They were confessing with a "loud voice," that is, with a deep devotion and unceasing praise. "Upon the throne," that is, the Father and the Son reign in the Church, with the Holy Spirit ruling equally with them. There is here such an order to the words, "To our God and to the Lamb who sits upon the throne belongs salvation." We find a similar manner of speaking in the Gospel, "That they might know you, the only true God, and Jesus Christ whom you have sent."[21] This is as though he said, "That they might know you and Jesus Christ whom you have sent, the one true God." In the one throne is indicated the power of one nature. However, in the name of the Lamb the personal character of the Father and the Son is designated, just as when the Holy Spirit is alone named, the Father and the Son are there also to be understood. For we read in the Acts of the Apostles, "Take heed to all the flock in which the Holy Spirit has made you overseers," and it immediately adds, "to rule the church of God which he obtained by his own blood."[22] Now, we know that no one has poured out their blood for us except the person of Christ. And so it is sufficiently clear that whenever one alone is

---

[17]MTS 1 Sup 1:82.  [18]2 Cor 1:7.  [19]CS 110:100-101.  [20]TEG 8:136-37.  [21]Jn 17:3.  [22]Acts 20:28.

named, the entire Trinity is to be understood. COMMENTARY ON THE APOCALYPSE 7.10.[23]

**THE MARTYRS GIVE THANKS.** BEDE: With a loud voice [the martyrs] sing of salvation from God, since they recall with great thanksgiving that they have triumphed, not by their own virtue but by his help, in the struggle with the tribulations assailing them. HOMILIES ON THE GOSPELS 1.10.[24]

**THE VIRTUES OF GOD.** PRIMASIUS: Whatever this multitude might be, by expressing these names he indicates the universal church. . . . Through the naming of these seven virtues, we are exhorted to inquire after the reason why he named those things here in which God desires his church to participate. It is for this reason, that when these [virtues] are given to God in praise, they might confess that they have received each of them from him. For we ought not consider that God alone is capable of the [virtues] named here, but that he has found them worthy also to give to the faithful. We rejoice that the church of Christ is allowed to participate in all of these good things: blessing, glory, wisdom, thanksgiving, honor, power and might. It does not mention omnipotence or majesty or eternity, for God alone always rightly possesses these things. But in these seven we recognize all those virtues that could be granted to the faithful from him who gave them power to become sons of God. And so, if we have acquired any of these good things, we shall know with certainty that we have them by the generosity of God. COMMENTARY ON THE APOCALYPSE 7.11-12.[25]

### 7:13 "Who Are These?"

**THE RIGHTEOUS STRUGGLE DURING THE RULE OF ANTICHRIST.** OECUMENIUS: One of the elders asked the Evangelist who those were who were from the nations and were clothed in white robes. He asked this not because he himself did not know but rather to urge the Evangelist to

make them known more fully. And so he says, "These are they who have come out of the great tribulation." For the righteous endured not a small struggle, but indeed an exceedingly great struggle during the rule of the antichrist. COMMENTARY ON THE APOCALYPSE 7.9-17.[26]

**THE FAITH OF THE TEACHER PREACHES TO THE FAITH OF THE HEARER.** PRIMASIUS: This one elder represents either the body of the prophets or the church. It depicts the leaders teaching the other members of the future reward for which the laborers might hope, just as the apostle spoke of the gospel, "In it the righteousness of God is revealed from faith for faith,"[27] that is, from the faith of those who preach, for the faith of those who hear. COMMENTARY ON THE APOCALYPSE 7.13-14.[28]

### 7:14 Out of the Great Tribulation

**THE FLESH IS MADE CLEAN BY BAPTISM.** TERTULLIAN: Then to every conqueror the Spirit promises now the tree of life and exemption from the second death; now the hidden manna, with the stone of glistening whiteness, and the name unknown (to every man except those who receive it); now power to rule with a rod of iron and the brightness of the morning star; now the being clothed in white raiment, and not having the name blotted out of the book of life, and being made in the temple of God a pillar with the inscription on it of the name of God and of the Lord, and of the heavenly Jerusalem; now a sitting with the Lord on his throne, which once was persistently refused to the sons of Zebedee. Who, pray, are these so blessed conquerors, but martyrs in the strict sense of the word? For indeed theirs are the victories whose also are the fights; theirs, however, are the fights whose also is the blood. But the souls of the martyrs both peacefully rest in the meantime under the altar and support their

---

[23]CCL 92:127.  [24]CS 110:101.  [25]CCL 92:127-28.  [26]TEG 8:137.  [27]Rom 1:17.  [28]CCL 92:129.

patience by the assured hope of revenge; and, clothed in their robes, wear the dazzling halo of brightness, until others also may fully share in their glory.[29] For yet again a countless throng are revealed, clothed in white and distinguished by palms of victory, celebrating their triumph doubtless over antichrist, since one of the elders says, "These are they who come out of that great tribulation, and have washed their robes, and made them white in the blood of the Lamb." For the flesh is the clothing of the soul. The uncleanness, indeed, is washed away by baptism, but the stains are changed into dazzling whiteness by martyrdom. SCORPIACE 12.[30]

**BAPTISM AND THE EUCHARIST MAKE WHITE.** OECUMENIUS: And, it says, "they have washed their robes and made them white in the blood of the Lamb." To be sure, one might think that robes dipped in blood would be red, not white. And so, how is it that they have become white? Because, according to the opinion of all-wise Paul,[31] baptism is completed in the death of the Lord and wipes clean from every filth of sin, so that those baptized in him are made white and clean. However, the reception of the life-giving blood of Christ also gives the same grace, for the Lord said concerning his own blood that it was poured out "for many" and "for the sake of many" and "for the forgiveness of sins."[32] COMMENTARY ON THE APOCALYPSE 7.9-17.[33]

**SOME ARE MARTYRS BY THEIR INNER CHARACTER.** PRIMASIUS: When it says that a number of the faithful had come out of the great tribulation, what else is indicated except what we read elsewhere, "Through many tribulations we must enter the kingdom of God."[34] Therefore, the apostle also said, "Brothers, let us not grow weary, for in due time we shall reap."[35] It is through the endurance of struggles that the number of the faithful are sifted out, just as by the weight of the press oil is prepared with diligent care and grain that is to be stored in a barn is collected through the threshing machine. That they wash their

robes in the blood of the Lamb reveals their reward, so that the labor of the aforementioned struggle might be endured with equinimity. And he rightly adds that they made their robes white in the blood of the Lamb. It is as though he said that the robes that some had befouled after the grace of baptism through neglect, ignorance or contempt, these had made white in the blood of the Lamb, that is, in the grace of Christ, or even in undergoing martyrdom. This reward is to be assigned especially to those in the church who have spilled their blood for Christ and have returned the robe of baptism with a greater brilliance by a better service of blood. But if this grace is to refer to all the faithful generally, we must finally conclude that if anyone is cleansed by the font of his Lord, is fed by his flesh and is enflamed by the call of the Spirit, he is in this manner made white as snow. For there are those who are proven to be martyrs before God by their inner character, even though they are not martyrs by way of a public act. COMMENTARY ON THE APOCALYPSE 7.13-14.[36]

**THE PEOPLE OF GOD MADE WHITE BY CHRIST'S BLOOD.** CAESARIUS OF ARLES: These are not, as some think, only martyrs, but rather the whole people in the church. For it does not say that they washed their robes in their own blood but in the blood of the Lamb, that is, in the grace of God through Jesus Christ, our Lord. As it is written, "And the blood of his Son has cleansed us."[37] EXPOSITION ON THE APOCALYPSE 7.14, HOMILY 6.[38]

**THE MARTYRS RENDER THEIR BODIES WORTHY OF IMMORTALITY.** BEDE: Martyrs wash their robes in the blood of the Lamb, while as for their members, which "seem to the eyes of the ignorant"[39] [to be] defiled by the squalor of their pains, they instead have made [these members]

---

[29]Rev 6:9-11. [30]ANF 3:646. [31]See Rom 6:3. [32]Mt 26:28. [33]TEG 8:137. [34]Acts 14:22. [35]Gal 6:9. [36]CCL 92:129-30. [37]1 Jn 1:7. [38]PL 35:2427. [39]Wis 3:2.

clean of all contagion by their blood which is poured forth for Christ. In addition, they have rendered [their members] worthy of the blessed light of immortality, which is [the meaning of] their having made their washed robes white in the blood of the Lamb. HOMILIES ON THE GOSPELS 1.10.[40]

## 7:15 They Serve God Day and Night

CHRISTIANS SERVE GOD AT ALL TIMES. PRIMASIUS: Before the throne of God is the church, in whose "heart he has placed ways to go up in the valley of tears to a place which he has established."[41] They serve him day and night, that is, in times of prosperity and in times of adversity.[42] They are regarded as a "temple" who are said to serve in the temple, just as [they are regarded as] a throne. Therefore, it continues, "And he who sits upon the throne will dwell among them." The soul of the righteous is the seat of wisdom. However, wisdom is Christ, and Christ is truly God. COMMENTARY ON THE APOCALYPSE 7.15.[43]

THE REMEMBRANCE OF GOD BY THE SAINTS. OECUMENIUS: These will serve God forever, while God dwells among them. Indeed, one of the saints said that this dwelling of God is the never-ending remembrance of [God] which remains in the souls of the saints. Rightly, then, does God dwell with those who "serve him day and night." COMMENTARY ON THE APOCALYPSE 7.9-17.[44]

THOSE WHO SUFFER WITH CHRIST WILL ALSO REIGN WITH HIM. ANDREW OF CAESAREA: Blessed are those who through temporary sufferings receive the fruit of eternal rest, and by suffering with Christ also reign with him and serve him continuously. In this passage, the words "day and night" indicate the absence of cessation or end, for then there will be no night. Rather, there will be one day which is illumined by the Sun of righteousness, not by the sun that we see with our eyes. In like manner, *night* refers to the hidden and deep mysteries of

knowledge, while *day* refers to the mysteries that are open and easily obtained. "His temple" is the entire creation, which is being renewed through the Spirit, but especially those who have preserved the living and unquenchable gift of the Spirit, for among them he has promised to dwell and to walk. COMMENTARY ON THE APOCALYPSE 7.14-15.[45]

TO PRAISE GOD. BEDE: To be continuously present at the praises of God is not a laborious servitude but a servitude that is pleasant and desirable. "Day and night," indeed, do not exclusively signify the vicissitude of time, but typologically [they signify] its perpetuity. HOMILIES ON THE GOSPELS 1.10.[46]

## 7:16 They Shall Not Hunger and Thirst

THE SACRAMENTS PRESERVE THE SAINTS. TYCONIUS: They will not hunger because they are fed by the living Bread. He said, "I am the living Bread who comes came down from heaven."[47] Nor will they thirst, for they will drink from a cup so excellent that it will be for them what the Truth said, "Whoever believes in me shall never thirst,"[48] and again, "Whoever drinks from the water that I shall give him, it will become in him a spring of water welling up to eternal life."[49] Nor will the sun strike them, nor will they be burned by the deadly heat of its fire. God promised something similar to his church through Isaiah, "A shelter from the storm, shade from the heat."[50] He proclaims that the strength of his sacraments will be strong in those who belong to him and that they will not be vexed by the heat of temptation. COMMENTARY ON THE APOCALYPSE 7.16.[51]

THE SAINTS WILL NO LONGER BE TEMPTED. OECUMENIUS: "They shall hunger no more, nor

---

[40]CS 110:102. In his commentary, Bede agrees with Caesarius. [41]Ps 83:6-7 LXX. [42]Beginning here, Primasius uses Tyconius. [43]CCL 92:130-31. [44]TEG 8:137. [45]MTS 1 Sup 1:84. [46]CS 110:102. [47]Jn 6:51. [48]Jn 6:35. [49]Jn 4:14. [50]Is 25:4. [51]CCL 92:131.

shall they thirst any more." For, while formerly those from the Gentiles came through every trial, now they will be satisfied with countless blessings. "Nor," it says, "will the sun strike them." The sun is used figuratively by some writers of holy Scripture to refer to temptations. For example, the prophet said, "The sun will not strike you by day, nor the moon by night,"[52] or the Evangelist, who wrote that the shining sun scorched that seed which sprouted on the stony soil, interpreting the sun to be temptations.[53] And so also in this present passage, it says that temptation would no longer harm them. COMMENTARY ON THE APOCALYPSE 7.9-17.[54]

### 7:17 The Lamb Will Be Their Shepherd

**THROUGH FAITH THE TRINITY DWELLS IN THE CHURCH.** TYCONIUS: Earlier he had said that the Lamb seated on the throne received the book. Now he says that the Lamb in the midst of the throne rules them. In this way he teaches that there is one throne for the Father and the Son, since the Father is in the Son, and the Son in the Father, that is, in the midst of the church, in which the one God, the entire Trinity, dwells through faith. COMMENTARY ON THE APOCALYPSE 7.17.[55]

**PERFECT KNOWLEDGE AND INCORRUPTION.** ANDREW OF CAESAREA: They will be led to the pure and clear fountains of divine thoughts, for the image of water already indicates the abundant stream of the divine Spirit. For concerning the one who believes in him in a pure way the Lord said, "Rivers of living water will flow from his belly."[56] From this fount the saints will at that time drink abundantly, and they will be in infinite joy and gladness, possessing perfect knowledge after being rid of partial knowledge, and having become rid of the change which comes with corruption. COMMENTARY ON THE APOCALYPSE 7.17.[57]

**THE SAINTS ARE SPRINGS OF HEAVENLY**

**DOCTRINE.** BEDE: That is, [he will guide them] to the community of the saints, who are the springs of heavenly doctrine. It is possible that he is indicating also the very vision of God, "in whom are hid all the treasures of wisdom and knowledge,"[58] concerning which also David said, "As a deer longs for springs of water, so my soul longs for You, O God."[59] EXPLANATION OF THE APOCALYPSE 7.17.[60]

### 7:17 God Will Wipe Away Their Tears

**AFTER THE RESURRECTION, THERE WILL BE NO AFFLICTION.** TERTULLIAN: "Everlasting joy," says Isaiah, "shall be upon their heads." Well, there is nothing eternal until after the resurrection. "And sorrow and sighing," he continues, "shall flee away." The angel echoes the same to John: "And God shall wipe away all tears from their eyes"; from the same eyes indeed that had formerly wept and that might weep again, if the lovingkindness of God did not dry up every fountain of tears. And again: "God shall wipe away all tears from their eyes; and there shall be no more death,"[61] and therefore no more corruption, it being chased away by incorruption, even as death is by immortality. If sorrow, and mourning, and sighing, and death itself assail us from the afflictions both of soul and body, how shall they be removed, except by the cessation of their causes, that is to say, the afflictions of flesh and soul? Where will you find adversities in the presence of God? Where, incursions of an enemy in the bosom of Christ? Where attacks of the devil in the face of the Holy Spirit, now that the devil himself and his angels are "cast into the lake of fire."[62] ON THE RESURRECTION OF THE FLESH 58.[63]

**SPIRITUAL JOY AND GLADNESS.** TYCONIUS: All of these things will happen to us spiritually when

---

[52]Ps 121:6 (120:6 LXX). [53]Mk 4:5-6. [54]TEG 8:137-38. [55]CCL 92:131. [56]Jn 7:38. [57]MTS 1 Sup 1:85-86. [58]Col 2:3. [59]Ps 42:1 (41:1 LXX). [60]CCL 121A:329. [61]Rev 21:4. [62]Rev 20:10. [63]ANF 3:590.

sins have been forgiven and we rise to life, that is, when the "old man has been stripped off and we have put on Christ"[64] and are filled "with the joy of the Holy Spirit."[65] For this is the life that the Lord promised to his church when he said, "Behold, I create Jerusalem a rejoicing, and my people a joy. I will rejoice over Jerusalem, and be glad in my people; no more will be heard in it the sound of weeping or the cry of distress."[66] COMMENTARY ON THE APOCALYPSE 7.17.[67]

---

[64]See Gal 3:27; Col 3:9. Caesarius of Arles makes explicit that baptism is meant (PL 35:2427). [65]See 1 Thess 1:6. [66]Is 65:18-19. [67]TS 2 7:81-82 §§121-22.

---

## 8:1-6 THE SEVENTH SEAL

[1]When the Lamb opened the seventh seal, there was silence in heaven for about half an hour. [2]Then I saw the seven angels who stand before God, and seven trumpets were given to them. [3]And another angel came and stood at the altar with a golden censer; and he was given much incense to mingle with the prayers of all the saints upon the golden altar before the throne; [4]and the smoke of the incense rose with the prayers of the saints from the hand of the angel before God. [5]Then the angel took the censer and filled it with fire from the altar and threw it on the earth; and there were peals of thunder, voices, flashes of lightning, and an earthquake.

[6]Now the seven angels who had the seven trumpets made ready to blow them.

---

**OVERVIEW:** Just as Christ was crucified on the sixth day and rested on the seventh, the church will enjoy a rest after a period of great affliction (BEDE). The time before the appearance of the kingdom of Christ will be short, for the opening of the seventh seal indicates the dissolution of the earthly city (ANDREW OF CAESAREA) and the beginning of the eternal rest (TYCONIUS). Even though the second coming of Christ is unknown even to the angels (ANDREW OF CAESAREA), when he comes every supernatural power will be silent out of awe over the exceeding greatness of the glory of the king of creation (OECUMENIUS).

At his coming the purpose and intention of his incarnation will be accomplished, when the faithful become co-heirs with Christ and the possessors of perfect glory. The same trumpets that will raise the dead will also announce the coming of the heavenly king, for trumpets are used to signal great occasions (OECUMENIUS). This is the king about whom the church preached as though by a powerful trumpet (TYCONIUS). For made zealous by the Spirit, the church preached the word of power and cast down the pomp of the world and the kingdom of the antichrist as if they were the walls of Jericho (VICTORINUS, BEDE).

This glorious coming of the Lord was prepared by his first coming, when he offered his immaculate and sinless body upon the altar of the cross (TYCONIUS, BEDE). Just as the humanity of Christ was filled with the Holy Spirit like a censer filled with fire (BEDE), so also Christ filled the church, which is his body, with the Spirit so that she might fulfill the will of the Father (TYCONIUS, CAESARIUS OF ARLES). For this reason the church participates in Christ's royal priesthood, for even as Christ takes the tearful prayers of the saints and brings them to God as an acceptable sacrifice, the saints make perfect the sacrifice of God by presenting their own bodies as a living sacrifice (Tyconius, Bede). The prayers of the saints are rendered even more fragrant by the cooperation of the administering angels (Oecumenius). Every high priest is like such angels, for he carries the petitions of the people to God and brings down the blessings of God. The priestly character of the church is also revealed in the sacrifice of the martyrs, which they make upon the altar of Christ (Andrew of Caesarea).

## 8:1 Silence in Heaven

**The Church Is Called "Heaven."** Tyconius: "In heaven" means in the church. The silence for half an hour shows the beginning of the eternal rest. Commentary on the Apocalypse 8.1.[1]

**The Second Coming of Christ Brings Unspeakable Blessings.** Oecumenius: The loosing of the seventh seal effects the most perfect and complete glory for us. No longer is there as before the loosing of sin and our turning to God or God's turning to us. Rather there is now the most unspeakable blessings: to be called "sons of God," to be inheritors of God, to be co-heirs with Christ, to be brothers and friends and children of Christ, also to rule with him and to be glorified with him, and those blessings that "eye has not seen nor has ear heard nor has come into the heart of man."[2] And what is the loosing of the seventh seal? It is the second coming of Christ and the giving of blessings as rewards. For although some are handed over to the punishment of sinners, nonetheless it is the aim of Christ and the intention of the incarnation that everyone become an heir of his kingdom. Therefore, when the seventh seal was loosed, "there was," it says, "silence for about half an hour," since the king of creation was coming and every angelic and supernatural power, astounded at the exceeding greatness of the glory of him who was coming, for that reason became silent. Commen-tary on the Apocalypse 8.1-2.[3]

**The Second Coming Unknown Even to the Angels.** Andrew of Caesarea: Often the number of seven is taken by this saint to correspond to this age and the sabbath rest of the saints. Therefore, also here at the loosing of the seventh seal, the dissolution of the earthly city is signified, the seven angels administering the torments against those people who are deserving of chastisement or punishment. The "silence" reveals the good order of the piety of the angels as well as the fact that the second coming of Christ is unknown even to angels. The "half hour" shows the shortness of time, for when the plagues come and the events of the consummation upon the earth are occurring, the kingdom of Christ will appear. Commentary on the Apocalypse 8.1-2.[4]

**The Church Will Have a Brief Rest after Antichrist.** Bede: It is believed that after the destruction of the antichrist, there will be a short rest in the church. Daniel prophesied of this, "Blessed is he who waits and comes to the thousand three hundred and thirty-five days."[5] The blessed Jerome commented upon this passage [of Daniel]. "Blessed, he says, is he who when the antichrist is killed waits for the forty-five days beyond the thousand two hundred and ninety days, that is, three and a half years. For during them our Lord and Savior will come in his majesty. It is a matter of divine knowledge why there is silence for forty-five days after the death of the antichrist, unless we make the conjecture that the delay of the kingdom of the saints is a test of patience."[6] We should note that the greatest afflictions of the church are envisaged in the sixth period, while a rest is seen in the seventh. For the Lord was crucified on the sixth day, and he rested on the seventh, awaiting the time of the resurrection. Explanation of the Apocalypse 8.1.[7]

[1]CCL 92:132. [2]1 Cor 2:9. [3]TEG 8:139. [4]MTS 1 Sup 1:86. [5]Dan 12:12. [6]Jerome Commentary on Daniel 4.12.12 (CCL 75A:943-44). [7]CCL 121A:329-31.

## 8:2 Seven Angels and Seven Trumpets

**THE PREACHING OF THE CHURCH BRINGS EVERY AGE TO FAITH.** TYCONIUS: In the seven angels we shall recognize again the church according to that rule that indicates that universality is often to be acknowledged in the number seven. [The church] is said to have received a most powerful trumpet of proclamation by which she is strong and by which, we believe, every age comes to faith. For we read, "Life up your voice like a trumpet."[8] COMMENTARY ON THE APOCALYPSE 8.2.[9]

**THE TRUMPETS RAISE THE DEAD AND SIGNAL THE COMING OF CHRIST.** OECUMENIUS: And seven trumpets were given to the seven angels, so that they might sound the signal that the king was arriving. But the sound of these very trumpets will also awaken those who are dead. For, the apostle, who is wise in divine things, wrote in his first letter to the Thessalonians that "the Lord himself will descend at a command, at the call of an archangel, and with the sound of the trumpet of God."[10] And again, "The trumpet will sound, and the dead will be raised incorruptible."[11] COMMENTARY ON THE APOCALYPSE 8.1-2.[12]

## 8:3-4 Incense Mingles with the Prayers of the Saints

**CHRIST OFFERED HIS IMMACULATE BODY AS A SACRIFICE TO GOD.** TYCONIUS: The seven angels received trumpets, and another [angel], it says, came. One might think that this one came after the seven angels, although he saw all of this at one time. As the angel was coming, those seven received their trumpets, that is, when Christ the Lord was coming, his church received the power to preach. And we understand that he himself came over the altar, that is, over the church, which is wholly assumed as the body of the same priesthood and to whom Peter said, "[You are] a holy nation, a chosen race, a royal priesthood."[13] He had a golden censer, which is his immaculate

body that was conceived by the overshadowing of the Holy Spirit and that he offered as an oblation and sweet-smelling sacrifice to God for the redemption of the world and through which he cleansed the conscience of all from dead works. He is also said to have received the prayers of the saints and to have offered them, for through him the prayers of all are able to come to God in an agreeable manner. COMMENTARY ON THE APOCALYPSE 8.3.[14]

**THE ANGELS MAKE OUR PRAYERS MORE FRAGRANT.** OECUMENIUS: He calls the altar a "censer," because it receives incense. When Christ appears, the prayers of the saints, which are by nature fragrant but made even more fragrant by the cooperation of the holy angels, are brought to him by those angels that govern us as though they were his spoils and the first offerings of homage given to him. And for this reason it is said that "much incense was given to him." It is clear that the governance of people was given to the angels from God that they might make our prayers acceptable to him. "And the smoke of the incense rose with the prayers of the saints from the hand of the angel." You see that the prayers of the saints are made more fragrant by the angel and rendered worthy to be offered before God. COMMENTARY ON THE APOCALYPSE 8.3-6.[15]

**THE SACRIFICE OF THE MARTYRS.** ANDREW OF CAESAREA: Although what is revealed to the saints is depicted in material form and with colors, whether it be the altar or the censer or something else, in reality these things are invisible and intellectual. And it is at such an altar that the angel stands and swings the censer (that is, that bowl that receives incense) bearing to God the prayers of the saints as though they were incense. . . . The "altar" is Christ upon which every ministering and holy power is

---

[8]Is 58:1. [9]CCL 92:135. [10]1 Thess 4:16. [11]1 Cor 15:52. [12]TEG 8:139-40. [13]1 Pet 2:9. [14]CCL 92:135-36. [15]TEG 8:140-41.

established and upon which the sacrifices of the martyrs are offered. This altar was prefigured in the altar that was shown to Moses on Mount Sinai together with the tabernacle. The "incense" is the prayers of the saints. . . . He says that the altar, namely, Christ, is "before the throne," that is, before the most eminent and holy of powers who are there because of the abundance of the divine love and of the pure wisdom and knowledge in them. COMMENTARY ON THE APOCALYPSE 8.3.[16]

**CHRIST MAKES THE SORROW OF OUR HEARTS ACCEPTABLE.** BEDE: He "stood before the altar," that is, he appeared in the sight of the church. He was himself made the censer, from which God received the smell of sweet savor and became more favorable toward the world. Another version reads "upon the altar," because for us he offered to the Father upon the altar of the cross his own golden censer, namely, his own sinless body conceived by the Holy Spirit. . . . When Christ offered himself to the Lord as an agreeable and acceptable sacrifice, he made the sorrow of the hearts of the saints acceptable, which arising from the fire within elicits tears, as is usual with smoke. EXPLANATION OF THE APOCALYPSE 8.3-4.[17]

## 8:5 Thunder, Lightning and an Earthquake

**THE SACRIFICE OF GOD IS PERFECTED.** TYCONIUS: The Lord received his body, that is, the church, and filled her with fire from the altar to accomplish the Father's will. This is to say that he filled [the church] with the power of loosing and of binding, which consists in sacrifices and the propitiation of God. Therefore, it is also said, "Who makes the winds his messengers and burning fire his ministers."[18] For in them the church received all power in heaven and on earth, while she perfected the sacrifice of God, first of all the Lord offering up himself and the saints presenting their own bodies as a living and holy sacrifice. And he cast it upon the earth, for through the

preaching of the church knowledge of the future judgment comes to the world, as Zechariah says, "I will place the officers of Judah as a flaming fire."[19] . . . "And there were thunders and voices and lightning and earthquakes." All of these things are spiritual and have to do with the church. The voices are of those who reproach and who threaten, the "broods of vipers"[20] and following. Or, [the voices say], "Repent, for the kingdom of heaven is at hand."[21] The thunder is the proclamation of the Christian faith; the lightning represents the virtues of those have have been made whole; the earthquakes are persecutions that are foretold to come and that are suffered at various times. COMMENTARY ON THE APOCALYPSE 8.5.[22]

**WONDERS AND MARVELS.** OECUMENIUS: Then, it says, the holy angel took and filled the altar with divine fire and "threw it on the earth, and there were voices and peals of thunder and flashes of lightning and an earthquake." Similarly, an angel threw this heavenly fire upon Mount Sinai and there was thunder and voices and trumpets and lightning, and the mountain was covered in smoke, since God had come and was present.[23] Therefore, just as at that time thunder and fearsome wonders preceded him, so also now such wonders occur before the glorious advent of the Lord. COMMENTARY ON THE APOCALYPSE 8.3-6.[24]

**JESUS FILLED THE CHURCH WITH THE HOLY SPIRIT.** CAESARIUS OF ARLES: Jesus received his body, that is, the church, and he filled her with the fire of the Holy Spirit in order that the will of the Father might be fulfilled. "And there were voices and thunder and lightning and earthquakes." All of these things are the spiritual proclamations and virtues of the church. EXPOSITION ON THE APOCALYPSE 8.5, HOMILY 6.[25]

---

[16]MTS 1 Sup 1:87-88. [17]CCL 121A:335. [18]Ps 104:4 (103:4 LXX). [19]Zech 12:6. [20]See Lk 3:7. [21]Mt 3:2. [22]CCL 92:137-38. [23]Ex 19:16-19. [24]TEG 8:141. [25]PL 35:2427

**PRIESTS ARE MEDIATORS BETWEEN GOD AND MAN.** ANDREW OF CAESAREA: The prayers of the saints offered through an administering angel cause the censer filled with the avenging fire to be poured out upon the earth. This is just as it was revealed long ago to Ezekiel by one of the cherubim, that he should receive from such a fire and give it to the angels that they might send the fire for the punishment of the wicked inhabitants of Jerusalem.[26] And every high priest is representative of such an angel, for as a mediator between God and people, he carries up their petitions and brings down God's redemption, and he turns some sinners to repentance either by word or by harsher chastisements. COMMENTARY ON THE APOCALYPSE 8.4-5.[27]

**THE HUMANITY OF CHRIST WAS FILLED WITH THE HOLY SPIRIT.** BEDE: Rightly does he mention the censer as filled with fire. "For God does not give the Spirit in measure,"[28] and we know that this was most especially fulfilled concerning the humanity of Christ, in whom "all the fullness of the Godhead dwells bodily."[29] EXPLANATION OF THE APOCALYPSE 8.5.[30]

### 8:6 The Seven Angels Prepare to Sound the Trumpets

**SEVEN ARCHANGELS WILL ACCOMPLISH GOD'S WILL DURING THE TIME OF ANTICHRIST.** VICTORINUS OF PETOVIUM: He sends these seven great archangels to strike against the kingdom of the antichrist. For the Lord himself said in the Gospel: "Then the Son of man will send his angels and will gather his elect from the four winds, from one end of heaven to the other."[31] And before that he said, "Then there will peace in our land, when in it seven shepherds will arise and eight attacks of men and they will encircle Asshur, that is, the antichrist, in the trench of Nimrod,"[32] that is, at the damnation of the devil. And similarly Ecclesiastes says, "When the keepers of the house tremble."[33] And the Lord himself spoke as follows: "When the servants

came to him and asked him, 'Lord, did you not sow good seed in your field? How then has it weeds?' He answered them, 'An enemy has done this.' They said, 'Do you want us to go and pluck them out?' He said to them, 'No, let both grow together until the harvest, and at that time I will tell the reapers to gather the weeds and throw them into the fire, but to gather the wheat into the barn.' "[34] Here the Revelation reveals that these reapers and laborers are the archangels. The "trumpet" is the word of power. And although there is a repetition of scenes by means of the bowls,[35] this is not as though the events occurred twice. Rather, since those events that are future to them have been decreed [by God] to happen, these things are spoken twice. And therefore, whatever he said rather briefly by way of the trumpets he said more completely by way of the bowls. Nor ought we pay too much attention to the order of what is said. For the sevenfold Holy Spirit, when he has passed in revue [the events] to the last time, to the very end, returns again to the same times and supplements what he had said incompletely. Nor ought we inquire too much into the order of the Revelation. Rather, we ought inquire after the meaning, for there is also the possibility of a false understanding. And therefore, those things written concerning the trumpets and the bowls are either the devastation of the plagues sent to the world, or the madness of the antichrist himself, or the blasphemies of the peoples, or the variety of the plagues, or the hope for the kingdom of saints, or the ruin of cities or the ruin of Babylon, that is, of the city of Rome. COMMENTARY ON THE APOCALYPSE 8.1-2.[36]

**MADE READY TO PREACH.** TYCONIUS: The church, often indicated by the number seven, prepared herself for faithful preaching. COMMENTARY ON THE APOCALYPSE 8.6.[37]

---

[26]Ezek 10:6-7. [27]MTS 1 Sup 1:88. [28]Jn 3:34. [29]Col 2:9. [30]CCL 121A:335-37. [31]Mt 24:31. [32]See Mic 5:5. Asshur and Nimrod were traditional figures for the antichrist or the devil. See Gen 10:8, 10. [33]Eccles 12:3. [34]Mt 13:27-30. [35]See Rev 15:7—16:20. [36]CSEL 49:82-86. [37]CCL 92:138.

**Trumpets Announce the Coming of God.**
Oecumenius: Then angels blew their trumpets to announce the coming of God, for indeed also at that time trumpets were used to announce great occasions. Commentary on the Apocalypse 8.3-6.[38]

**The Preaching of the Church.** Bede: Made zealous by the sevenfold Spirit, the church prepared herself to preach with faithfulness and to cast down the pomp of the world by the heavenly trumpets, even as happened to the walls of Jericho. For even that walking around them for seven days is indicative of the entire time of the church. Explanation of the Apocalypse 8.6.[39]

---

[38]TEG 8:141. [39]CCL 121A:337.

# 8:7 THE FIRST TRUMPET

[7]*The first angel blew his trumpet, and there followed hail and fire, mixed with blood, which fell on the earth; and a third of the earth was burnt up, and a third of the trees were burnt up, and all green grass was burnt up.*

---

**Overview:** At the blowing of the first trumpet, the proclamation of the church concerning the universal judgment of the impious is heard (Bede). As though it were a trumpet initiating a battle, this preaching tells of the wrath of God, which will devour the impious in Gehenna (Tyconius, Bede). This judgment even happens before the consummation and now is occurring by means of the slaughter inflicted by barbarian invaders (Andrew of Caesarea). At the coming of the judgment the impious shall experience distress and a profound grief when they see the saints meeting Christ in the air, while they remain in torment upon the earth (Oecumenius). The torments of divine judgment strike not only human beings but also creatures of every kind (Andrew of Caesarea). Yet through this judgment God separates false brothers, heretics and schismatics from the genuinely pious and in this way reveals those who belong to him and those who belong to the devil (Tyconius).

## 8:7 Hail and Fire Mixed with Blood

**The Wrath of God Devours the Impious.**
Tyconius: By the fire and blood he signifies the wrath of God, which devours the multitude of the impious. Commentary on the Apocalypse 8.7.[1]

**Sinners Will Be Grief-Stricken.** Oecumenius: Since the righteous have been accounted worthy of the blessed portion . . . and so are to be caught up "in the clouds of the air" prior to the coming of the Lord, that they might greet the coming Lord,[2] . . . the vision now finally discusses the fate of the rest of humankind and the punishment of sinners. When the coming destruction occurs, there will necessarily be various kinds of death and various rewards for the wicked. The greater part of these will be consumed by fire, for in his first letter to the Corinthians the holy apos-

---

[1]TS 2 7:90 §150. [2]1 Thess 4:17.

tle wrote that that day will be revealed in fire.[3] For if there are "many rooms" for rest, as the Lord says,[4] there are also different places for torment. And these trumpets that bring death to those upon earth are the same that also raise the dead afterwards. Why does it say that when the first angel blew his trumpet, hail and fire consumed a third of those upon the earth? Were someone to think that this will happen literally, he would not be interpreting this passage incorrectly. But if we understand the passage figuratively, we will also not be wrong, for the passage speaks of "fire" when it refers to the distress and profound grief of the sinners who see the saints "caught up in the clouds to meet the Lord," while they themselves remain dishonorable upon the earth and are not regarded as worthy of any greeting. The passage refers figuratively to sinners as "trees" and "grass" that are on fire because of their folly and the insensitivity of their souls, which are hard as dry wood and so are suitable for burning. COMMENTARY ON THE APOCALYPSE 8.7.[5]

**DIVINE JUDGMENT OCCURS DAILY.** ANDREW OF CAESAREA: Some have interpreted these things to depict the punishment of sinners in Gehenna, which is symbolically described as various kinds of physical torment. However, we think it more likely that the third portion is not of those from the totality of people who will be punished in the coming age, but rather—"for the way which leads to destruction is broad"[6]—this passage shows the plagues that will occur before the consummation. The hail indicates the scourgings that will come from heaven for righteous judgment, and the fire mixed with blood indicates the destruction by fire and slaughter at the hands of the barbarians that will occur daily.[7] COMMENTARY ON THE APOCALYPSE 8.7.[8]

## 8:7 A Third of the Earth and the Trees, All the Grass Was Burned

**THE CHURCH PREACHES THE UNIVERSAL JUDGMENT OF THE IMPIOUS.** BEDE: The first

trumpet of [the church's] preaching reveals the universal destruction of the impious by fire and hail. . . . The foretelling of these plagues is rightly compared with a trumpet, which is the signal for battle. For, the Scripture says, "Lift up your voice as a trumpet; declare to my people their transgressions,"[9] and elsewhere, "Set the trumpet to your lips, as an eagle over the house of the Lord."[10] That the punishment of Gehenna is the reward for works that spill blood is indicated by the voice of the preachers who say, "He will pass from the waters of the snow to very great heat."[11] It is possible that by the word *blood* the spiritual death of the soul is intended. EXPLANATION OF THE APOCALYPSE 8.7.[12]

**THE CHURCH IS OPPOSED BY HERESY AND SCHISM.** TYCONIUS: A third of the earth and the trees and all the grass is said to be burned up. The "earth" represents everything terrestrial, while persons who wave about through unfaithfulness are depicted as "trees." For those blown about by "every wind of doctrine"[13] are mentioned by the apostle Jude, "fruitless trees in late autumn, uprooted, twice dead."[14] The green grass represents flesh fattened with luxury, for "all flesh is grass."[15] Although in an earlier passage three fourths were set against one, that is, the church, this passage confines those opposed to the church to two thirds. One third consists of the false brothers who are mixed in among the good within the church, and another third that is separated by the error of the Gentiles or by heretical depravity or by open schism. And so the church (namely, the one third) must struggle against a double evil, as though it were simplicity resisting duplicity. It is as we read in the Gospel that a king with ten thousand went out to war against twenty thousand.[16] And God did make a promise concerning this through Zechariah, saying, "In the whole land,

---

[3]1 Cor 3:13. [4]Jn 14:2. [5]TEG 8:141-42. [6]Mt 7:13. [7]Andrew may have the A.D. 515 invasion of the "Huns" in mind. [8]MTS 1 Sup 1:90. [9]Is 58:1. [10]Hos 8:1. [11]See Job 24:19. [12]CCL 121A:333, 337-39. [13]Eph 4:14. [14]Jude 12. [15]Is 40:6. [16]Lk 14:31.

says the Lord, two thirds shall be dispersed and perish, and one third shall remain in it; and I shall lead the third part through fire, and I shall refine them as one refines silver, and I shall test them as gold is tested. It shall call my name, and I will answer them and say, 'You are my people,' and they will say, 'The Lord is my God.'"[17] COMMENTARY ON THE APOCALYPSE 8.7.[18]

**GOD WILL REVEAL THE TRUE CHURCH.** TYCONIUS: The "trees" and the "earth" represent people who are the internal enemies of the church and whom [God] shall punish by a future judgment to everlasting punishment. The "grass" represents the flesh, which is fattened through the vices of sins and whose strength and beauty have dried through the heat of the sun. To be sure, the third part which it said was destroyed by being burned up refers to the heretics. For anyone who is found outside of the true church shall be condemned to perpetual torments, along with the devil, who is the author of such division. And so through Zechariah the Lord promised to strike the false shepherds and to free his sheep from their difficulties and to separate the third part, which he says is like the nations and "Sodom,"[19] from the midst of his sheep, that is, from the midst of the pious. "Awake, O sword," it says,

"against the shepherds and those who are next to me, says the Lord Almighty. Strike the shepherds and scatter the sheep," that is, my people. "And I shall test it as gold is tested. It will call me and I will answer it and say, 'You are my people,' and it will say 'You are my God.'"[20] Before this separation occurs, all are regarded as the people of God. However, after the separation has happened, then it will become apparent who are the people of God and who are of the devil. COMMENTARY ON THE APOCALYPSE 8.7.[21]

**CREATURES OF ALL KINDS SUFFER THE TORMENTS OF DIVINE JUDGMENT.** ANDREW OF CAESAREA: By these torments not less than one third of all the creatures on the earth will be physically killed, for wars destroy not only human beings but also everything that is produced upon the earth. And the blessed Joel confirms our understanding of what will come when he says, "Blood and fire and vapor of smoke will come before the great day."[22] COMMENTARY ON THE APOCALYPSE 8.7.[23]

---

[17]Zech 13:8-9. [18]CCL 92:138-39. [19]See Jer 23:14. [20]Zech 13:7, 9. [21]TS 2 7:91-93 §§152-56. [22]Joel 2:30-31 (3:3-4 LXX). [23]MTS 1 Sup 1:90-91.

# 8:8-9 THE SECOND TRUMPET

[8]*The second angel blew his trumpet, and something like a great mountain, burning with fire, was thrown into the sea; [9]and a third of the sea became blood, a third of the living creatures in the sea died, and a third of the ships were destroyed.*

**OVERVIEW:** At the blowing of the second trumpet, the devil is seen cast down from heaven into the "sea" of the world (TYCONIUS, PRIMASIUS, ANDREW OF CAESAREA). There the devil destroys human souls by inflicting upon them spiritual death,

which comes from the wisdom of the flesh, which is hostile to God (PRIMASIUS, BEDE). Such wisdom even blasphemes the Trinity (ANDREW OF CAESAREA). Spiritual death is passed on from one person to another by death-bearing and useless teaching (Tyconius). But many are made filthy in the "sea" of the world by their sins, which are bitter and briny like sea water, and such persons become dissipated over useless remorse for what they did during their lives. The vision may also indicate that the sea, as part of the earth, is presently in bondage but will be freed from corruption and made new by purification (Oecumenius).

### 8:8 A Mountain Cast into the Sea

**The Devil Burns Those Who Are Near to Him.** Tyconius: He speaks of the devil as a burning mountain, for he consumed those near to him as though he were a fire. He is called "great" because he is one angel among others and is himself a creature. . . . He calls the world a "sea," in which he saw the devil who had been cast down from heaven as a burning fire. Commentary on the Apocalypse 8.8-9.[1]

**The Sea Will Be Purified and Made New.** Oecumenius: The holy apostle writes to the Romans that "the creation was subjected to futility, not of its own will but by the will of him who subjected it in hope; because the creation itself will be set free from its bondage to decay and obtain the glorious liberty of the children of God."[2] And when will it be set free? When there will be "new heavens and a new earth according to his promises," as Peter proclaims to us in his second letter.[3] And since the earth changes that it might be freed from corruption and made new, it is necessary that also the sea suffer this same fate, for the sea is on the earth. And how would it also be purified unless by means of purifying fire? And so fire is thrown into it and changes it into blood and kills one third of those in it. This may be interpreted as something that is literal and perceptible. Commentary on the Apocalypse 8.8-9.[4]

**The Devil's Tool for the Destruction of Souls.** Primasius: The burning mountain cast into the sea is the devil, who was sent against the peoples. A third part of the sea became blood. By "blood" he means the wisdom of the flesh, which is hostile to God.[5] For this reason it is said that through such wisdom the human soul is destroyed. And so the apostle said, "To be wise according to the flesh is death,[6] for flesh and blood shall not inherit the kingdom of God."[7] Commentary on the Apocalypse 8.8-9.[8]

**The Devil Is Wrathful Against Us.** Andrew of Caesarea: We are aware that according to the opinion of some this shows the sea with those in it burning by a purifying fire after the resurrection.[9] However, the mention of a third seems to us ill-suited for this interpretation. For, as it is said, those who are being punished are more than those being saved. But according to the anagogical sense[10] there is nothing wrong with thinking that the present life is figuratively called a "sea." . . . As some of our teachers think, we think that the "great mountain" is the devil,[11] who burns with the fire of wrath against us but who will be bound in Gehenna. But during the time allowed to him he will destroy a third of the islands and ships in the sea and that which swims in it, even as long ago he did to Job. For he is an enemy and an accuser against the righteous judgment of God. For "to that which one is submitted, to that one is a slave."[12] And it would not be foreign and contrary to the intention of the passage to say that the death of the soul comes upon those who in the sea of life blaspheme the Trinity through works and words. Commentary on the Apocalypse 8.8-9.[13]

**The Devil Rages Against His Own.** Bede: The second trumpet indicates the expulsion of the devil from the church that he might burn

---

[1]TS 2 7:93 §§158, 160. [2]Rom 8:20-21. [3]2 Pet 3:13. [4]TEG 8:142-43. [5]Primasius has used Tyconius to this point. [6]Rom 8:6. [7]1 Cor 15:50. [8]CCL 92:139-40. [9]Andrew is referring to Oecumenius. [10]Spiritual or mystical interpretation. [11]Andrew is the first Greek commentator to express this interpretation of the mountain. [12]See 2 Pet 2:19. [13]MTS 1 Sup 1:91-92.

more hotly in the sea of the world. . . . As the Christian religion increased, the devil, puffed up with pride and burning with the fire of his own anger, was cast into the sea of the world, as the Lord said: "If you should say to this mountain, 'Be taken up and cast yourself into the sea,' it will be done,"[14] not because he was not there before but because, thrown out of the church, he began to rage even more against his own followers, inflicting upon them spiritual death by the arrogance of fleshly wisdom. For to be wise according to the flesh is death.[15] For flesh and blood did not teach the apostles, but the Father who is in heaven.[16] For they guided the ship of faith upon that sea that had proven itself suitable for walking to the feet of the Lord. EXPLANATION OF THE APOCALYPSE 8.2, 8.[17]

### 8:9 Living Things and Ships Destroyed

**MANY DIE A SPIRITUAL DEATH.** TYCONIUS: Another edition has the reading "[a third of] those who have souls"[18] and shows thereby that they have died a spiritual death, similar to that which the apostle said about the widow, "She who is self-indulgent is dead."[19] And so the passage suggests that one third has killed another third by a poisonous tradition and by imitation of a useless teaching. COMMENTARY ON THE APOCALYPSE 8.8-9.[20]

**THE DEVIL DECEIVES BY TRICKERY.** TYCONIUS: When he speaks customarily of the part that has a soul, he refers to persons who are spiritually dead and separated from the kingdom of God. "And a third of the birds fell to the ground."[21] Therefore, that third that died in the sea destroyed by its own death another third. He is describing the devil and those who are of one mind with the devil, who after the manner of birds fly around and deceive or wish to deceive all by their trickery. COMMENTARY ON THE APOCALYPSE 8.9.[22]

**THE DISTRACTIONS OF LIFE.** OECUMENIUS: According to analogy and rhetorical custom, the "sea" may be regarded as the present life because of its turbulence and its many distractions. And one might interpret the "fish" and the "boats" to be those persons who are made filthy by salty and bitter sins and who are dissipated by anxiety over useless regrets for what they did in life. COMMENTARY ON THE APOCALYPSE 8.8-9.[23]

---

[14]Mt 21:21. [15]Rom 8:6. [16]Mt 16:17. [17]CCL 121A:333, 341. [18]The text of Primasius reads *tertia pars piscium* ("a third of the fish"). He refers here to the reading of the text of Tyconius (*habentium animas*), although Tyconius read a singular, not a plural, *animam*. [19]1 Tim 5:6. [20]CCL 92:140. [21]The text of Tyconius here reads *tertia pars avium* ("a third of the birds"). This no doubt represents a textual error for *tertia pars navium* ("a third of the ships"). [22]TS 2 7:94 §§161-63. [23]TEG 8:143.

## 8:10-11 THE THIRD TRUMPET

[10]*The third angel blew his trumpet, and a great star fell from heaven, blazing like a torch, and it fell on a third of the rivers and on the fountains of water.* [11]*The name of the star is Wormwood. A third of the waters became wormwood, and many men died of the water, because it was made bitter.*

**OVERVIEW:** At the blowing of the third trumpet, the devil was seen to fall (TYCONIUS, ANDREW OF CAESAREA). Through pleasures, the devil brings upon people a bitter destruction, and therefore we ought to examine ourselves so that we might remain spiritually healthy and not be condemned with the world (ANDREW OF CAESAREA). However, persons of good reputation and persons who live the spiritual life within the church sometimes fall like stars from their positions and like animals bend down toward earthly things (TYCONIUS, PRIMASIUS). Similarly, heretics leave the church and pollute the rivers of the holy Scriptures and so make many bitter and corrupt by an evil imitation of their teaching (TYCONIUS, PRIMASIUS, BEDE). As evil teaching makes bitter those who hear it, so too those waters that are used in rebaptisms make dead those who fall into them (CAESARIUS OF ARLES). Finally, as Naomi was called "Bitter" because of her many troubles, so also sinners will become bitter in their sufferings when they see the saints in glory (OECUMENIUS).

## 8:10 A Great Star Like a Torch

**SOME WHO LIVE THE SPIRITUAL LIFE FALL.**
TYCONIUS: The "great star" is the devil, of whom the Lord spoke in the Gospel, "I saw Satan fall from heaven as fire or lightning."[1] It is possible that this passage also refers to ecclesiastical people, who living the spiritual life in the church, have become forgetful of themselves and like animals bend down to the things of the earth and fall from their positions of authority. We read what has been written of such persons: "Although he is in honor, he does not understand; he is compared to the senseless cattle and has become like them."[2] COMMENTARY ON THE APOCALYPSE 8.10.[3]

**SOME OF GOOD REPUTE FALL LIKE STARS.**
PRIMASIUS: It speaks of men who have fallen from heaven as though from the church, that is, of those who have the public reputation of shining brightly with good merits.[4] For that reason they are compared to stars and torches, as did the apostle Jude, who called them "stars of seduction,"[5] since they lead astray by a superficial splendor. And the Lord also compared such people with walls and "whitewashed tombs."[6] COMMENTARY ON THE APOCALYPSE 8.2.10-11.[7]

**THE DEVIL GIVES A BITTER DESTRUCTION TO DRINK.** ANDREW OF CAESAREA: Some say that the bitterness revealed through the wormwood is symbolic of the torment that comes to those sinners being punished in Gehenna, who, on account of their number, are reasonably called "waters."[8] But we think that these depictions signify the sufferings at the time, which has been shown. The star indicates either that these things come upon people from heaven, or it refers to the devil, of whom Isaiah says, "How has the Day Star, which rose in the morning, fallen from heaven."[9] For, through pleasure he gives people a foul and bitter destruction to drink and through this allows punishing torments to come upon them, although not to everyone, but by the long-suffering of God to a third part. . . . It is necessary, therefore, that we examine ourselves lest we be judged. As the holy apostle says, "For if we judged ourselves, we should not be judged, but when we are judged by the Lord, we are chastened,"[10] and we receive the sufferings that come upon us with thanksgiving. For those who are concerned about sicknesses in the body bear patiently the cuts and cauteries of the physician, for they desire to be healed. Therefore, [we should examine ourselves] so that being spiritually healthy and bringing no wood to fuel the fire of Gehenna, we might not be condemned with the world but eternally rule with Christ, to whom be glory, honor and worship, together with the Father and the Holy Spirit forever. Amen. COMMENTARY ON THE APOCALYPSE 8.10-11.[11]

---

[1]Lk 10:18. [2]Ps 48:13 LXX. [3]TS 2 7:94-95 §165. [4]Primasius follows Tyconius to this point. [5]See Jude 13. [6]Mt 23:27. [7]CCL 92:140-41. [8]Andrew refers to Oecumenius. [9]Is 14:12. [10]1 Cor 11:31-32. [11]MTS 1 Sup 1:93-94.

**HERETICS POLLUTE THE WATERS OF THE HOLY SCRIPTURES.** BEDE: The third trumpet shows the heretics apostatizing from the church and corrupting the rivers of the holy Scriptures. . . . The heretics, whom the apostle Jude calls "stars of seduction,"[12] fall from the height of the church and by the flame of their own iniquity endeavor to pollute the fountains of the divine Scriptures, fearing neither to falsify their meaning and often even their words. And so they are worthy of the name Wormwood. For even a small admixture of this is able to make bitter a great sweetness. EXPLANATION OF THE APOCALYPSE 8.2, 10-11.[13]

### 8:11 Many Died of the Bitterness

**TEACHERS OF THE SCRIPTURES SOMETIMES BECOME WAYWARD.** TYCONIUS: The rivers and fountains of waters signify the teachers of the divine Scriptures who instruct others but turn themselves away from the way of truth. Indeed, the name Wormwood indicates either the bitterness or the sweetness of sins, which give a present sweetness to those who desire them but afterwards change themselves into bitterness. COMMENTARY ON THE APOCALYPSE 8.11.[14]

**SINNERS ARE EMBITTERED AT THE GLORY OF THE SAINTS.** OECUMENIUS: Naomi, who lived long ago, was called "Bitter" because of the many troubles she had with her children and with other circumstances of her life.[15] A sample of the extraordinary plagues is that bitterness that we sinners suffer at that time when we are embittered at the glory of the saints. For although such good things have been prepared for humankind, we ourselves have exchanged the things of the present for those which are to come. I think the falling star refers to a certain wrath of God

that makes the waters bitter. He speaks figuratively of people as "waters," according to that spoken by the prophet, "From the voice of many waters, wonderful are the waves of the sea,"[16] and again, "The floods have lifted up, O Lord, the floods have lifted up their voice, the floods lift up their roaring."[17] Although these things are spoken in figurative speech, it is not impossible that these things and things like them will occur at that time. COMMENTARY ON THE APOCALYPSE 8.10-11.[18]

**THE FALL OF GREAT PERSONS CORRUPTS MANY OTHERS.** PRIMASIUS: Since the ruin of those who are great often confuses many, it says that the star fell upon part of the rivers and fountains, and that its name was Wormwood because of its great bitterness. We know that many are weakened by the fall of such persons and are corrupted by an evil imitation of their teaching. [The star] is rightly compared with wormwood, since a small amount of bitterness, when mixed with that which is sweet, will make the whole bitter. Elsewhere the Scriptures make the same point: "I planted you as a chosen vine; how did you turn into the bitterness of the vine of another?"[19] COMMENTARY ON THE APOCALYPSE 8.10-11.[20]

**THOSE WHO ARE REBAPTIZED DIE FROM THE WATERS.** CAESARIUS OF ARLES: A third part of humankind was made like the star that fell upon it. . . . Many die from the waters. This can manifestly be interpreted to refer to those who are rebaptized. EXPOSITION ON THE APOCALYPSE 8.11, HOMILY 6.[21]

---

[12]See Jude 13. [13]CCL 121A:333, 343. [14]TS 2 7:95 §167. [15]Ruth 1:20. [16]Ps 93:4 (92:4 LXX). [17]Ps 93:3 (92:3 LXX). [18]TEG 8:143-44. [19]Jer 2:21. [20]CCL 92:141. [21]PL 35:2428.

## 8:12-13 THE FOURTH TRUMPET

*[12]The fourth angel blew his trumpet, and a third of the sun was struck, and a third of the moon, and a third of the stars, so that a third of their light was darkened; a third of the day was kept from shining, and likewise a third of the night.*

*[13]Then I looked, and I heard an eagle crying with a loud voice, as it flew in midheaven, "Woe, woe, woe to those who dwell on the earth, at the blasts of the other trumpets which the three angels are about to blow!"*

**Overview**: At the blowing of the fourth trumpet, the church was struck and was darkened (Tyconius, Bede). For although the church is bright like the stars, she is darkened by false brothers who fall away (Bede). Similarly, those who are of the devil are darkened when they are given over to their sins (Tyconius). Yet even at the consummation of the age, God's goodness will restrain his judgment so that he might call all to repentance before he brings about a complete destruction (Oecumenius). During the present time the church lives in the heavens out of contempt for earthly things (Primasius), and through her preachers the word of God, which speaks of the evil of heretics, of the antichrist and of the coming plagues of the last times, is freely proclaimed (Tyconius, Bede). By means of such preaching the Holy Spirit forewarns of the imminent wrath so that some might still be saved (Victorinus). The angels in heaven themselves imitate God and look with sorrow and mercy upon those who suffer upon the earth, especially those who are unaware that their suffering is intended for their conversion (Oecumenius, Andrew of Caesarea).

### 8:12 Light Was Darkened

**The Hidden Sins of Sinners Will Be Revealed.** Tyconius: The sun, moon and stars represent the church, a third part of which is struck. This third is a designation, not a quantity. For there are two peoples within the church, that part of God, which is compared with the light, and that part of the devil, which is surrounded by the darkness of shadows, as the Scripture says, "I have compared your mother to the night."[1] And this part was struck so that it might become apparent who is of God and who is of the devil. It has been given over to its own sins and desires, so that their faults that have remained hidden and unknown to all might be revealed. Commentary on the Apocalypse 8.12.[2]

**Out of His Goodness God Calls All to Repentance.** Oecumenius: We have been taught by Joel the prophet that "the sun shall be turned to darkness, and the moon to blood, before the great and glorious day of the Lord comes."[3] . . . And in his second letter, Peter said, "The day of the Lord will come as a thief, on which the heavens will pass away with a loud noise, and the elements will be dissolved with fire."[4] And the Lord himself also says in Matthew, "Immediately after the tribulation of those days the sun will be darkened, and the moon will not give its light, and the stars will fall from heaven."[5] And now we are taught in this Revelation that these things will occur at the consummation of the present age. And why is it said that only a third of what is on the earth and in the sea and rivers and also [a third] of the heavenly bodies

---

[1]Hos 4:5 LXX. [2]TS 2 7:96-97 §§171-74. [3]Joel 2:31. [4]2 Pet 3:10. [5]Mt 24:29.

endure these calamities? This is certainly a proof of the goodness of God toward humankind that he calls to repentance the people [who live at] that time by the partial dissolution of the elements, rather than effecting their total destruction. Upon those who do not repent he finally brings a complete destruction. And the prophet says something similar, "He made a path for his anger; he did not spare them from death."[6] For, since the wrath of God is partial and advances and progresses as though on a road, God is opening a door for repentance and is calling people to a change of heart through fear of that which is coming to pass. COMMENTARY ON THE APOCALYPSE 8.12-13.[7]

**DARKENED BY FALSE BROTHERS.** BEDE: The fourth trumpet shows the defection of false brothers by the darkening of the stars. . . . The glory of the church, which shines like a star, is often darkened by false brothers, who, either in times of prosperity or in times of adversity in the world, cause it to shine less brightly by their defection. EXPLANATION OF THE APOCALYPSE 8.2, 12.[8]

## 8:13 "Woe, Woe, Woe to Those on Earth"

**THE IMMINENCE OF DIVINE WRATH.** VICTORINUS OF PETOVIUM: [This passage] signifies the Holy Spirit who through two prophets proclaims that the great wrath of plagues is imminent. This occurs so that, although it is the end of time, someone might in some manner still be saved. COMMENTARY ON THE APOCALYPSE 8.13.[9]

**THE WORD OF GOD IS FREELY PREACHED.** TYCONIUS: The eagle that he saw flying in mid-heaven is the Word of God, which has free course in the middle of the church and announces openly and publicly the plagues of the last time. COMMENTARY ON THE APOCALYPSE 8.13.[10]

**AN ANGEL LOOKS IN SORROW.** OECUMENIUS: We recognize in the eagle flying in mid-heaven a certain divine angel who looks in sorrow upon the sufferings of those on earth and is sympathetic with humankind in their plight. COMMENTARY ON THE APOCALYPSE 8.12-13.[11]

**THE CHURCH DWELLS IN THE HEAVENS.** PRIMASIUS: He speaks of an eagle that moves through the heavens in swift flight out of contempt for the earth. He speaks of the church flying in mid-heaven, for she is going to possess the whole world, and she says, "Our abode is in the heavens."[12] And he rightly says that she was "in the middle," for "all who are around him offer gifts,"[13] and God works his way in the midst and "works salvation in the midst of the earth,"[14] and "the Lord is round about his people."[15] COMMENTARY ON THE APOCALYPSE 8.13.[16]

**THE ANGELS IMITATE GOD'S MERCY.** ANDREW OF CAESAREA: This passage shows the sympathy and goodness of the holy angels, who, like God, are merciful toward the transgressors who are being chastised, and especially toward those who do not recognize that their suffering is for the purpose of their conversion. For these especially the "woe" is fitting, since they live upon the earth, think earthly thoughts and exhale dust rather than the perfume that has been poured out for us. For those whose citizenship is in heaven,[17] the sufferings become the cause of unfading crowns and rewards. COMMENTARY ON THE APOCALYPSE 8.13.[18]

**THE TEACHERS IN THE CHURCH ANNOUNCE EVILS.** BEDE: The voice of this eagle each day flies through the mouth of the eminent teachers in the church when they announce the evil of the heretics and the rage of the antichrist and the day of judgment, which with all severity will come to those who love the earth, saying, "In the last days

---

[6]Ps 78:50 (77:50 LXX). [7]TEG 8:144-45. [8]CCL 121A:333, 343. [9]CSEL 49:86. [10]TS 2 7:98 §177. [11]TEG 8:145. [12]Phil 3:20. [13]Ps 76:11 (75:12 LXX). [14]Ps 74:12 (73:12 LXX). [15]Ps 125:2 (124:1 LXX). [16]CCL 92:144. [17]Phil 3:20. [18]MTS 1 Sup 1:95.

there will come perilous times, and there will be men who are lovers of self,"[19] and later in the same writing, "Men of corrupt mind and counterfeit faith,"[20] and elsewhere, "Then that evil one will be revealed, who opposes and exalts himself over everything which is called 'god' or is the object of worship."[21] And again: "The day of the Lord will come as a thief in the night; Wwhen people say, 'Peace and security,' then sudden destruction will come upon them."[22] EXPLANATION OF THE APOCALYPSE 8.13.[23]

---

[19]2 Tim 3:1-2. [20]2 Tim 3:8. [21]2 Thess 2:3-4. [22]1 Thess 5:2-3. [23]CCL 121A:345.

## 9:1-12 THE FIFTH TRUMPET

[1]And the fifth angel blew his trumpet, and I saw a star fallen from heaven to earth, and he was given the key of the shaft of the bottomless pit; [2]he opened the shaft of the bottomless pit, and from the shaft rose smoke like the smoke of a great furnace, and the sun and the air were darkened with the smoke from the shaft. [3]Then from the smoke came locusts on the earth, and they were given power like the power of scorpions of the earth; [4]they were told not to harm the grass of the earth or any green growth or any tree, but only those of mankind who have not the seal of God upon their foreheads; [5]they were allowed to torture them for five months, but not to kill them, and their torture was like the torture of a scorpion, when it stings a man. [6]And in those days men will seek death and will not find it; they will long to die, and death will fly from them.

[7]In appearance the locusts were like horses arrayed for battle; on their heads were what looked like crowns of gold; their faces were like human faces, [8]their hair like women's hair, and their teeth like lions' teeth; [9]they had scales like iron breastplates, and the noise of their wings was like the noise of many chariots with horses rushing into battle. [10]They have tails like scorpions, and stings, and their power of hurting men for five months lies in their tails. [11]They have as king over them the angel of the bottomless pit; his name in Hebrew is Abaddon, and in Greek he is called Apollyon[b].

[12]The first woe has passed; behold, two woes are still to come.

b Or Destroyer

---

**OVERVIEW:** At the blowing of the fifth trumpet, an angel is seen descending to earth with the brightness of a falling star (OECUMENIUS, ANDREW OF CAESAREA). This angel leads the evil demons whom Christ had bound at his incarnation up from the pit so that they might do their work before their eternal condemnation (ANDREW OF CAESAREA). Or the star falling from heaven may be understood to be the devil together with his followers who fall from the church through their heresy, blasphemy and disobedience (TYCONIUS, PRIMASIUS, BEDE).

When the devil opens the pit of his own heart and the pit of the hearts of his followers, their sins, like smoke, obscure the sun of the church's faith and the sun of the righteousness of the saints, so that even some among the saints become blind to the truth (TYCONIUS, PRIMASIUS, CAESARIUS OF ARLES). To be sure, those cast into the pit as punishment will experience darkness, for they will no longer see the air and the sun (OECUMENIUS). With the devil and his followers all manners of evil powers are loosed, flying around like locusts to harm humankind (TYCONIUS). Heretics, too, are like smoke that seeks to attain to a high position but is soon dissipated and disappears (PRIMASIUS). Such sinners will experience the unceasing gnawing of the soul as though they were the food of worms (OECUMENIUS).

Yet, God will not allow the army of Satan to harm the elect, which consists of immature, growing and mature Christians (PRIMASIUS). Nonetheless, throughout this age the church will be attacked by heresy and by the temptation to prefer temporal things to eternal blessings (BEDE). In this attack the devil will be like a scorpion who poisons by his tail, for he will poison through sin and many will be handed over to their own desires. Others, however, will be led to the humility of penance (CAESARIUS OF ARLES) and seek to be freed from the chains of sin and so die to the world (TYCONIUS).

The attack of persecution and heresy will be sudden (TYCONIUS). Heretics will feign the truth and mimic the church by their evil teaching, all the while destroying by their mouths and by their wanton morals (TYCONIUS, PRIMASIUS). Running around like horses in battle, the heretics will destroy many as they acquire for themselves fleeting fame as preachers of a foul-smelling doctrine (PRIMASIUS). In all of this, heretics are like the evil demons who make war upon us and who expect to conquer us through their love of luxury and fornication (ANDREW OF CAESAREA). Through their venomous teaching, heretics multiply falsehood and increase the number of those who are deceived (TYCONIUS, PRIMASIUS). For that reason, by a hidden but just judgment God gives such persons a king and ruler who is suitable to them (PRIMASIUS). Therefore, the devil is called the

destroyer or the exterminator, because he destroys those who obey him (PRIMASIUS, ANDREW OF CAESAREA).

At the end of time, we shall see the baneful effects of our evil deeds, for the death of the soul is the end of evil (ANDREW OF CAESAREA). The church does not believe that sinners are purified by temporal punishments so that they escape eternal suffering, for we are taught otherwise by the Lord (OECUMENIUS). Yet it might be the case that after severe punishments now sinners will afterwards be punished less severely (OECUMENIUS). In any case, God uses the bitterness of tribulation to make sinners hate the sin that gave birth to their suffering (ANDREW OF CAESAREA).

## 9:1 The Key to the Bottomless Pit

**TO AGREE WITH THE DEVIL IS TO FALL FROM HEAVEN.** TYCONIUS: In this star he speaks of the body of those many persons who have fallen from heaven through agreement [with the devil]. . . . We ought to understand the key to the pit to be false teachings that confine those within it in such a way that they are not able to look upon the light of truth. And so the devil fell from heaven and received the key to the pit, and [he] opened his mouth in blasphemy and taught his followers not to do the will of God but to do their own will. COMMENTARY ON THE APOCALYPSE 9.1.[1]

**THE JUDGMENT OF SINNERS WILL BE ON THE EARTH.** OECUMENIUS: Until now the vision has explained to us how and by what manner of plagues that upon the earth and in heaven and humankind together with them shall be brought to completion or will be changed. But now, since the consummation has already occurred and the resurrection has been effected, the vision indicates the punishment of sinners. "I saw a star fallen from heaven to the earth," calling an angel

---

[1]TS 2 7:99-100 §§179-82.

of God a "star" because it descends to the earth with brightness. For the judgment of sinners will be on the earth, which was called the "valley of Jehoshaphat" by one of the holy prophets.[2] "And he was given," it says, "the key of the shaft of the bottomless pit." He calls Gehenna "the shaft of the bottomless pit." COMMENTARY ON THE APOCALYPSE 9.1-4.[3]

### THE HUMAN HEART IS AN ABYSS OF INIQUITY. PRIMASIUS: The abyss and the pit are people who are hiding places for error, that is, they hide iniquity in their hearts even though they are in the church. . . . I think that they receive this key to the pit, and through it they open the poisons of their hearts and, once made manifest, burst forth into the open. For, as the apostle says, "There must be factions among you in order that those who are genuine among you may be recognized."[4] Whenever error arises, the truth is preached all the more, and as the integrity of the faith is being defended, that deceptive falsehood that had been hidden for such a long time is at the right time uncovered. For schismatics and heretics frequently arise from those who have fallen, and of these the church truly speaks in the Song of Songs, "The sons of my mother fought against me."[5] COMMENTARY ON THE APOCALYPSE 9.1.[6]

### GOD ALLOWS DEMONS TO DO THEIR WORK. ANDREW OF CAESAREA: The "star" is a divine angel. With God's permission he leads up [from the pit] the evil demons who have been condemned to the pit, namely, those whom Christ bound at his incarnation. [He leads them up] so that they might do their work before the consummation but then attain to neverending torment. COMMENTARY ON THE APOCALYPSE 9.1-5.[7]

### HERETICS ARE FORERUNNERS OF THE ANTICHRIST. BEDE: The fifth trumpet reveals the increased infestation of the heretics who are the forerunners of the time of the antichrist. EXPLANATION OF THE APOCALYPSE 8.2.[8]

## 9:2 The Sun and Air Were Darkened

### HUMAN SIN OBSCURES THE SUN OF FAITH. TYCONIUS: "He opened the shaft of the pit" means that he revealed his own heart and taught people to sin without any fear or shame. "And smoke arose from the pit," that is, from the heart of a blasphemous people which also persecutes the church. "And the sun and air were darkened by the smoke of the pit." The sins that people constantly commit through the world obscure among them the sun of faith and of righteousness and in some produce a blindness so that they do not see the light of truth. "As smoke from a great furnace." This smoke that precedes the fire of the furnace generally refers to the last persecution, for the earlier persecution burns against the church, and then the crowd of hypocrites and unbelievers will be manifested. And outside [the church] the insanity of many caused by this smoke is already advanced. COMMENTARY ON THE APOCALYPSE 9.2.[9]

### THOSE THROWN INTO THE PIT ARE WRAPPED IN DARKNESS. OECUMENIUS: And "smoke rose from the shaft," as though a significant fire was evidently burning in the shaft. So the smoke indicates not only fire but also darkness. For the words of the prophet, "the voice of the Lord divides the flame of fire,"[10] is interpreted by the saints in this way, that the light-giving fire of Gehenna will be divided, so that only the burning heat of the fire along with the darkness remain in it. "And the sun and the air were darkened with the smoke." This does not suggest that these elements were themselves darkened but that those cast into the shaft were filled with darkness because of their punishment and could not any longer see the air and the sun. For, one of the holy prophets said, "The sun will be darkened at midday,"[11] referring by this to the misfortunes of the Jews, even though the sun had not been dark-

---

[2]Joel 3:2 (4:2 LXX). [3]TEG 8:145-46. [4]1 Cor 11:19. [5]Song 1:5 Vg. [6]CCL 92:145. [7]MTS 1 Sup 1:97. [8]CCL 121A:333. [9]TS 2 7:100-101 §§183-89. [10]Ps 29:7 (28:7 LXX). [11]Amos 8:9.

ened. But those who were suffering in this tribulation were not able to see the sun, because the magnitude of misfortune sometimes causes dizziness. COMMENTARY ON THE APOCALYPSE 9.1-4.[12]

**EVIL AND PRIDEFUL PEOPLE DARKEN THE TRUE CHURCH.** CAESARIUS OF ARLES: [The devil] revealed his own heart, which sins without any fear or shame. "And smoke rose from the pit," that is, from a people that covers and obscures the church, so that it is said that "the sun and air were darkened with the smoke." It says that the sun was darkened, not that it fell to the earth. For the sins of evil and prideful persons, which are constantly being committed throughout the world, obscure the sun, that is, obscure the church and sometimes cause darkness for the saints and the righteous. For the number of the evil is so great that it is often with great difficulty that the good among them become evident. EXPOSITION ON THE APOCALYPSE 9.2, HOMILY 7.[13]

### 9:3 Locusts with the Power of Scorpions

**DEMONIC POWERS HARM HUMANKIND.** TYCONIUS: In the locusts he signifies spiritual and adversarial powers that we see flying around in the air in the manner of locusts for the purpose of harming humankind. COMMENTARY ON THE APOCALYPSE 9.3.[14]

**A GNAWING OF SOUL.** OECUMENIUS: I think that he calls "locusts" those worms of which Isaiah spoke: "Their worm will not die, and their fire will not be quenched,"[15] perhaps calling a "worm" that gnawing of the soul and the unceasing, creeping pain that it suffers. COMMENTARY ON THE APOCALYPSE 9.1-4.[16]

**HERETICS RISE HIGH AND THEN ARE DISSIPATED.** PRIMASIUS: The "locusts" signify those who come forth from the smoke. For, like smoke, the heretics desire to rise high, since by their teachings they strive for positions of eminence, yet, again like smoke, they are dissipated. We

read of this smoke, for in the person of those who are evil it was said, "Smoke is the breath in our nostrils, and reason is the sparks for moving our heart."[17] When the impious are said to strive by sin against wisdom, that is, against the Lord Jesus Christ, they are also described as fighting against his church, harming it by their malicious mouth, while they are hindered from harming the green grass and trees. COMMENTARY ON THE APOCALYPSE 9.3.[18]

### 9:4 Those Who Did Not Have the Seal of God

**THOSE WHO SOIL THEIR BAPTISM.** OECUMENIUS: "They were told not to harm the grass of the earth or any green growth or any tree, but only[19] those of humankind who do not have the seal of God upon their foreheads," since by a transformation the earth had become new. Somewhere it says concerning this, "You will send forth your Spirit, and they will be created, and you will renew the face of the earth."[20] It was not yet good for anything that adorns the earth to be stricken, neither a tree nor any plant, only those persons who "do not have the seal of God upon their foreheads." For those persons who were perfectly holy and pure had received that place mentioned above, being always with Christ and gazing upon the throne of God. However, those who have been baptized and bear the sign of Christ upon their foreheads, yet are less holy and have seriously soiled themselves and their baptism by sinful behavior, such persons are, so to speak, halfway between virtue and evil and remain upon the earth, although they experience no further punishment. COMMENTARY ON THE APOCALYPSE 9.1-4.[21]

**IMMATURE, GROWING AND MATURE CHRISTIANS.** PRIMASIUS: By "grass" he refers to those

---

[12]TEG 8:146. [13]PL 35:2429. [14]TS 2 7:102 §191. [15]Is 66:24. [16]TEG 8:146. [17]Wis 2:2. [18]CCL 92:145. [19]Oecumenius adds "only" as an interpretive comment. [20]Ps 104:30 (103:30 LXX). [21]TEG 8:146-47.

small ones who are content with the milk of the Christian faith. By "green vegetation" he refers to those who have begun to live according to the virtues and who are moving not toward dryness but toward a fruitful fertility. By "trees" he refers to those persons in the church who already give spiritual thanks by the production of fruit. Of the first kind, the small ones, we read, "Who spread out the earth upon the waters,"[22] that is, baptism. Of the second type, we read, "It shall rejoice in its drops when it comes forth."[23] And concerning the third kind we read, "I am like a fruitful olive tree in the house of the Lord."[24] The number of the elect is perfected from all of these kinds of persons, which the bite of the locusts cannot harm, except for those who do not have the sign of God upon their foreheads. For the apostle says, "For not all have faith."[25] By such persons, it says, the sun will be darkened, however not extinguished, for although with the increase of iniquity the love of many will grow cold,[26] "God's firm foundation stands," as it is written, "having this seal, 'The Lord knows who are his,' and 'Let every one who calls upon the name of the Lord depart from iniquity.'"[27] COMMENTARY ON THE APOCALYPSE 9.1-4.[28]

## 9:5 Torture Was Like That of a Scorpion

### SINNERS ARE NOW PUNISHED SEVERELY.
OECUMENIUS: Was it not the case that certain fathers deduced the [idea] of restoration from this passage, saying that sinners are punished until now but afterward no longer, since they had been purified through punishment?[29] But what is to be done when the majority of the other fathers and the received Scriptures claim that the torments of those suffering at that time will be everlasting? What should one say, and how should one decide between these two options? One must combine these two opinions. I say this as a kind of exercise and not as an outright assertion. For I agree with the teaching of the church that the punishments in the future age will be everlasting, for this is also what the Lord asserted according

to the Gospel of Matthew: "And they will go away into eternal punishment."[30] And Isaiah also said, "Their worm shall not die, and their fire shall not be quenched."[31] But by way of an exercise this must be said, taking a sort of middle path between the two opinions, that until a certain time, which this Revelation says is "five months," using a certain mystical number, the sinners will be punished with greatest severity as though a scorpion were biting them. But after this, [they will be punished] less severely—for we will not be altogether without punishment—yet to such an extent that they seek death but do not attain it. COMMENTARY ON THE APOCALYPSE 9.5-6.[32]

### THE DEVIL STINGS WITH THE POISON OF SIN.
CAESARIUS OF ARLES: There are two parts in the church, one part of those who are good and one part of those who are evil. The one part is persecuted in order that it might be corrected; the other part is given up to its own desires. A part of those who are good is handed over to humiliation that they might know the righteousness of God and might remember penance, as it is written, "It is good that you have humbled me, that I might know your righteous deeds."[33] [The torture like a sting of a scorpion] occurs when the devil draws near through the poison of transgressions and sins. EXPOSITION ON THE APOCALYPSE 9.4, HOMILY 7.[34]

### THE END OF EVIL DEEDS.
ANDREW OF CAESAREA: That these spiritual locusts sting people after the manner of scorpions shows the baneful death of the soul that lies hidden at the end of evil deeds. Those are subjected to [such a death] who have not signed their forehead with the divine seal and with the enlightenment of the life-

---

[22]Ps 136:6 (135:6 LXX). [23]Ps 64:11 LXX. [24]Ps 52:8 (51:10 LXX). [25]2 Thess 3:2. [26]Cf. Mt 24:12. [27]2 Tim 2:19. [28]CCL 92:146. [29]Oecumenius has in mind the Origenists who believed that at the end, all things would be purified and restored. [30]Mt 25:46. [31]Is 66:24. [32]TEG 8:148. [33]Ps 119:71 (118:71 LXX). [34]PL 35:2429. Caesarius is following Tyconius.

giving cross through the Holy Spirit, so that, as the Lord says, "they may let their light shine before men for the glory of the divine name."[35] We think that the five months of their torment signifies either the shortness of time—"For had those days not been shortened, no flesh would have been saved,"[36] as the Lord says—or a certain five-day period representing the five senses through which sin enters into people, or a determined period that is known to God alone. COMMENTARY ON THE APOCALYPSE 9.1-5.[37]

**SCORPIONS STING FROM THEIR HIND PARTS.** BEDE: Although supported by the secular power, the heretics are for a time allowed to attack those who are good, yet, as the Lord said, they are not able to kill the soul.[38] By the five months he indicates the time of this age on account of the five senses that we use in this life. Another translation has "six months," which agrees with this interpretation on account of the six periods of the age.[39] . . . As a scorpion dispenses its poison from its tail, so the impiety of evil persons injures from their hind parts, when by threats and allurements it causes temporal things, which are behind, to be preferred to that which lies before, that is, to eternal blessings. EXPLANATION OF THE APOCALYPSE 9.5.[40]

### 9:6 People Will Seek Death but Will Not Find It

**SAINTS WISH TO DIE TO THE WORLD.** TYCONIUS: They say that death is a rest. And so, they seek death, not that they may die but that they might have rest from evil things while the evil vices die away. They desired to die, that is, that they might die to the world and, as the apostle says, live again to God.[41] "They seek death but will not find it," it says. They desire to be changed to better things, so that they might have rest after the labor of sins. . . . Therefore, "death will flee" while life is close by and we are truly dying while we are being freed from the chains of sins. COMMENTARY ON THE APOCALYPSE 9.6.[42]

**SUFFERING MAKES SIN HATEFUL TO THE SINNER.** ANDREW OF CAESAREA: Through these words the magnitude of the evils is revealed. For it is common among those in severe troubles to call upon death. But it is from the judgments of God that death does not come to those in the midst of trouble who seek it. For he considers it beneficial to use the bitterness of tribulations to make hateful that sin which was the mother and patron of their torments. COMMENTARY ON THE APOCALYPSE 9.6.[43]

### 9:7-8 Locusts Like Battle Horses

**HERETICS PRESENT A FALSE IMITATION OF THE TRUE CHURCH.** TYCONIUS: In the image of the horses he shows the suddenness of persecution that runs around so that it might oppress the innocent and obstruct [their path] to the celestial kingdom. . . . We recall that it was written that upon the heads of the twenty-four elders, who were a figure of the church, there were crowns of gold. However, these [locusts] do not present a true figure of the church but one only by way of pretense,[44] and so they are not said to have crowns of true gold but crowns similar to gold. . . . Likewise, they are not perfect human beings but like human beings. . . . And by the hair he speaks not only of the effeminacy and laxity of women, but he speaks of those from either sex who are given to wantonness and are stained by every baseness. . . . [By the teeth like lions' teeth] they daily devour the church. COMMENTARY ON THE APOCALYPSE 9.7-8.[45]

**HERETICS DESTROY BY THE FOUL STENCH OF THEIR DOCTRINE.** PRIMASIUS: By the locusts prepared as horses for war he means those who originate evil teachings. For just as locusts which

---

[35]See Mt 5:16. [36]Mt 24:22. [37]MTS 1 Sup 1:97. [38]Mt 10:28. [39]The text of Primasius reads "six months." [40]CCL 121A:349. [41]See Rom 6:11. [42]TS 2 7:105-6 §§205-7, 210. [43]MTS 1 Sup 1:98. [44]Caesarius of Arles makes explicit that heretics are meant (PL 35:2429). [45]TS 2 7:106-8 §§212-20.

destroy by their mouth, so also these persons tear asunder by their preaching. It is as we read, "fierce wolves not sparing the flock."[46] Moreover, they are like horses running around aimlessly and so destroy in such a war many whom they lead astray.... And if false doctrine is indicated by the mouth, by the hair of women he aptly describes their effeminate morals and their souls that are open to seduction. And so the apostle says, "These are those who make their way into households and capture weak women, burdened with sins and swayed by various impulses."[47] By these images he suggests both leaders and those whom they have led astray, so that he shows them to be not only deceitful in their faith but also hateful in their morals. The historical record shows that some of both sexes exhibit [these characteristics]. For women gave their support to many heretics, such as Priscilla and Maximilla to Montanus and Lucilla to Donatus.... It is natural for the teeth of lions not only to mangle but also to give off a natural stench. And since [the heretics] run around like horses to acquire for themselves fleeting fame as preachers, their opinion is rightly regarded as a stench. For in a good sense the apostle said, "We are the good aroma of Christ."[48] This bad odor, therefore, is derived from their evil doctrine and is by comparison like the odor of a lion's mouth. COMMENTARY ON THE APOCALYPSE 9.7-8.[49]

**EVIL DEMONS EXPECT TO CONQUER THROUGH PLEASURE.** ANDREW OF CAESAREA: Some have interpreted these words and those which come afterward to indicate that the locusts are angels who administer the divine punishment and who are metaphorically described through each of the various images.[50] These images would then describe either their fearsomeness and the panic they arouse, or their swiftness, or the destruction that comes upon those worthy of condemnation in Gehenna. However, I think that the image of these locusts depicts rather evil demons who are prepared for war against us and who wear upon their heads crowns as of gold in

expectation of victory against us. Whenever we submit to these demons and win an evil victory through pleasure, we believe ourselves also to be crowned with such crowns. That their hair is like that of women reveals their love of luxury and their arousal to fornication. The teeth like those of a lion signifies their murderous and poisonous character. COMMENTARY ON THE APOCALYPSE 9.7-9.[51]

### 9:9-10 *Having Power to Hurt Humankind*

**FALSE TEACHERS ARE "TAILS."** TYCONIUS: By the "tails" he speaks of the leaders who have fallen away from the Head of the church, that is, from the Lord, and so those who were the first have become the last. This is as God thought it worthy to say through Isaiah, "The elders who are honored and admired are the head; and the prophet who teaches iniquity is the tail."[52] Therefore, the "power" of the locusts refers to the character of the false prophets who never desist from attacking the true church by their lying and venomous doctrines. COMMENTARY ON THE APOCALYPSE 9.10.[53]

**HERETICAL LEADERS INCREASE THE DIVERSITY OF NOVEL OPINIONS.** PRIMASIUS: [The noise of their wings was like the sound of chariots] signifies that the few who were in the lead as the horses have now been multiplied in the chariots [that follow]. This suggests either an increase in the diversity of new opinions or the increase in the number of those who have been led astray. Moreover, they rush into battle because the preachers of error rebel against the truth and fight against unity. The apostle described such persons in a similar fashion, "As Jannes and Jambres opposed Moses, so these men also oppose the truth, men of corrupt mind and counterfeit faith," and following.[54] ... [That they had power

---

[46]Acts 20:29. [47]2 Tim 3:6. [48]2 Cor 2:15. [49]CCL 92:149-50. [50]Andrew refers to Oecumenius. [51]MTS 1 Sup 1:98-99. [52]Is 9:15. [53]TS 2 7:109-10 §§226-28. [54]2 Tim 3:8.

in their tails] reminds us of what Isaiah wrote, "The elder and the honored man is the head, and the prophet who teaches falsehood is the tail, and those who bless my people will lead them astray, and those who are blessed have fallen."[55] It is clear from this that these persons wish to rule that which every saint and teacher of the truth desires at all costs to avoid, namely, the glory of the world and the error of a destructive preaching. That they have power in their tails for five months indicates again the present life where falsehood can be strong and can either capture the useless or torment the spiritual for a short period of time. COMMENTARY ON THE APOCALYPSE 9.9-10.[56]

**DEMONS PRODUCE SPIRITUAL DEATH.**
ANDREW OF CAESAREA: Their iron breastplates show their hardness of heart. . . . We think that the sound of the wings of these spiritual locusts is said to resemble the sound of war chariots because of their speed in the air. For, as the blessed David says, "They make war upon us from on high."[57] And their tails which are like those of scorpions symbolize the result of sins, the producing of spiritual death. For "sin when it is perfected brings forth death."[58] COMMENTARY ON THE APOCALYPSE 9.9-12.[59]

## 9:11 Abaddon and Apollyon

**THE DEVIL HAS GREAT POWER IN THE WORLD.** TYCONIUS: [The angel of the bottomless pit] is the devil, who possesses his great power among the kings of the world. COMMENTARY ON THE APOCALYPSE 9.11.[60]

**A SUITABLE KING FOR THOSE WHO SERVE HIM.** PRIMASIUS: ["As king they have over them

the angel of the bottomless pit, whose name in Hebrew is 'Armageddon,' whose name in Greek is 'Apollion,' and whose name in Latin is 'Exterminans.' "] Although God is supremely good, by hidden yet just judgments he nevertheless allows an angel suitable for such persons to rule over them. For a person is awarded as servant to the one who conquered him. And so the apostle said that they had been handed over "to every wicked deception because they refused to love the truth and so be saved. Therefore, God sends upon them a strong delusion that they might believe what is false and that all who did not believe the truth but consented to iniquity might be condemned."[61] The kind of work he did, therefore, was befitting to the character of his name, that is, the "exterminator." COMMENTARY ON THE APOCALYPSE 9.11.[62]

**THE DEVIL DESTROYS THOSE WHO OBEY HIM.** ANDREW OF CAESAREA: It follows that the devil is to be regarded as their king, for he certainly destroys those who obey him. COMMENTARY ON THE APOCALYPSE 9.9-12.[63]

## 9:12 Two Woes Still to Come

**WOE COMES TO THE WORLD.** BEDE: Since he had foretold that three woes were to come, he now mentions that one woe has already come in the deceit of heresy. However, he says that two woes remain which will come against the perverse during the time of the antichrist and at the day of judgment. EXPLANATION OF THE APOCALYPSE 9.12.[64]

---

[55]Is 9:15-16.  [56]CCL 92:150-51.  [57]Ps 56:2 (55:3 LXX).  [58]Jas 1:15.  [59]MTS 1 Sup 1:99-100.  [60]TS 2 7:110-11 §230.  [61]2 Thess 2:10-12.  [62]CCL 92:151-52.  [63]MTS 1 Sup 1:100.  [64]CCL 121A:353.

## 9:13-21 THE SIXTH TRUMPET

$^{13}$*Then the sixth angel blew his trumpet, and I heard a voice from the four horns of the golden altar before God,* $^{14}$*saying to the sixth angel who had the trumpet, "Release the four angels who are bound at the great river Euphrates."* $^{15}$*So the four angels were released, who had been held ready for the hour, the day, the month, and the year, to kill a third of mankind.* $^{16}$*The number of the troops of cavalry was twice ten thousand times ten thousand; I heard their number.* $^{17}$*And this was how I saw the horses in my vision: the riders wore breastplates the color of fire and of sapphire$^c$ and of sulphur, and the heads of the horses were like lions' heads, and fire and smoke and sulphur issued from their mouths.* $^{18}$*By these three plagues a third of mankind was killed, by the fire and smoke and sulphur issuing from their mouths.* $^{19}$*For the power of the horses is in their mouths and in their tails; their tails are like serpents, with heads, and by means of them they wound.*

$^{20}$*The rest of mankind, who were not killed by these plagues, did not repent of the works of their hands nor give up worshiping demons and idols of gold and silver and bronze and stone and wood, which cannot either see or hear or walk,* $^{21}$*nor did they repent of their murders or their sorceries or their immorality or their thefts.*

c Greek *hyacinth*

---

**OVERVIEW**: With the blowing of the sixth trumpet, the sixth age of the world is initiated. At that time, the church will send forth her preachers against the antichrist and his lies and against his followers (TYCONIUS, CAESARIUS OF ARLES, BEDE). The church will despise the words and commands of the antichrist and separate herself from those who have apostatized with him (CAESARIUS OF ARLES). Yet this time will be a time of severe trial, for God will command that an evil people be loosed to persecute the church (TYCONIUS, PRIMASIUS). This people will be the embodiment of Satan and of his will and, as Esau persecuted Jacob, it will attack the church (TYCONIUS). For at all times the devil and his wicked angels are prepared and eager to harm the church and to inflict death upon the human race (PRIMASIUS, BEDE). This evil horde will persecute through heresy that is promoted by irreligious kings and worldly prelates, for apart from such the devil is rendered harmless (CAESARIUS OF ARLES). These heretics will be of large number and will claim for themselves the sacraments of the church. Like a concubine who unites herself to a man by way of an illegitimate union, they desire only influence and human praise. However, they bear within themselves their own punishments (PRIMASIUS). As the heretics are of the devil through falsehood, the pagans are of the devil through their wickedness and unbelief. They too will die (BEDE).

At the end of time, the most preeminent of the angels will leave the bliss of the vision of God and be sent to earth for the punishment of the wicked. These avenging angels are fearsome and will accomplish their task irresistibly. Therefore, during the present life we should confess our sins and with contrition in our souls turn to that which is good. For in the future life the time for prudent choice is over; then one only receives the reward for the life one has lived (OECUMENIUS). At that time too, also the antichrist and a multitude of demons will be loosed by divine command to trouble the nations. These will attack not only the Christians but also each other, and in the struggle some will be shown to be faithful and worthy, like ripened wheat, while others will be manifested as wicked and unrepentant and, like chaff, will receive a harsh condemnation. The demons are swift and do their beastly work through evil people who, like horses, are governed and led by their demonic riders. Sinners who have allowed the fruits of their hearts to be consumed by the assaults of the demons invite upon themselves the universal wrath of God. For divine wrath results from idolatry, murder, fornication and theft. And the frenzy that these vices visit upon the nations may perhaps be seen in the devastation of fire and blood inflicted on cities by the barbarians (ANDREW OF CAESAREA).

### 9:13a The Sixth Angel Blew His Trumpet

**THE FINAL PREACHING OF THE CHURCH.**
TYCONIUS: When it says that the first woe has passed and the trumpet of the sixth angel has sounded, it announces the final preaching, that of the sixth age. COMMENTARY ON THE APOCALYPSE 9.13.[1]

**THE LIES OF THE ANTICHRIST UNCOVERED.**
BEDE: The sixth trumpet shows the appearance of the antichrist and the war that his followers will wage against the church, and after an insertion reviewing again the [time from] the coming of the Lord, the sixth trumpet indicates the destruction of the same enemy.... The sixth angel indicates the preachers of the final struggle, who, as the gospel warns, uncover the lies of the antichrist. EXPLANATION OF THE APOCALYPSE 8.2, 9.13.[2]

### 9:13b A Voice from the Golden Altar

**THE ANGELS OFFER SPIRITUAL SACRIFICES TO GOD.** OECUMENIUS: By the "horns of the altar" he refers to those preeminent among the angels and who are superior to all the others. He says that the altar is "golden," for in mentioning that element that is of great value among us, he describes the altar as precious and holy and wondrous. And since we understand "the horns of the altar" to refer to the leaders of the angels, it follows that we interpret the altar itself to refer to all the ministering spirits on account of the spiritual sacrifice they bring to God. COMMENTARY ON THE APOCALYPSE 9.13-19.[3]

**THE CHURCH SEPARATES FROM ALL APOSTASY.** CAESARIUS OF ARLES: In the altar that is in the sight of God we are to understand the church. In the time of the last persecution she will despise the words and commands of that most inhumane of kings and will separate from those who have submitted to him. EXPOSITION ON THE APOCALYPSE 9.13, HOMILY 7.[4]

**THE GOSPELS ARE PREEMINENT IN THE CHURCH.** BEDE: Certainly the horns of the golden altar are the Gospels, which are preeminent in the church. EXPLANATION OF THE APOCALYPSE 9.13.[5]

### 9:14 "Release the Four Angels Bound at the Euphrates"

**GOD WILL LOOSE AN EVIL PEOPLE FOR THE TESTING OF THE CHURCH.** TYCONIUS: In these four angels that are bound at the Euphrates River we understand those adversaries that God will command to be loosed for the testing of his church. To be sure, this passage shows that the winds and the angels are the same thing, for it said that the winds were held back by the angels[6] and now that the angels are to be loosed by an angel. "Loose," it says, "the four angels at the great river Euphrates." Those whom above it said were at the "four corners of the earth" it now says are bound "at the river Euphrates." The river Euphrates indicates a people that persecutes [the church]. In this people, Satan and his will are bound, lest he should accomplish whatsoever he desires before it is time. The Euphrates is in the

---

[1]CCL 92:152. [2]CCL 121A:333, 353-55. [3]TEG 8:150-51. [4]PL 35:2429-30. [5]CCL 121A:355. [6]Rev 7:1.

land of Babylon, of which the prophet Jeremiah testifies as follows, "This says the Lord" concerning this Euphrates, "This is the day of the Lord God of hosts, so that he might avenge himself on his foes, and the sword shall devour and be sated and drink its fill of their blood. For the sacrifice to the Lord of hosts is in the north country by the river Euphrates."[7] He speaks of sacrifice, but that of strangled animals, not of praise. And Isaiah said, "The sword of the Lord is sated on blood, it is gorged with the fat of goats and rams, for the sacrifice of the Lord is in Bosor and a great slaughter in Idumea."[8] Bosor and Idumea are cities of Esau, who by persecution forced his brother, Jacob, to flee from his father's lands. COMMENTARY ON THE APOCALYPSE 9.14.[9]

## ANGELS LEAVE THE VISION OF GOD TO PUNISH THE WICKED. OECUMENIUS:

The divine Scriptures sometimes represents to us the apostate angel—by which I mean Satan and those who fell along with him—as having been bound in darkness by eternal chains. At other times it represents him as having been condemned to the depths of the sea. In his second letter Peter says, "For if God did not spare the angels when they sinned but cast them into Tartarus and to the pits of gloom, to be held for judgment,"[10] and in his letter Jude said, "The angels that did not keep their own rule but left their proper dwelling, he kept in gloom by eternal chains for the judgment of the great day."[11] Also in the book of Job it says that the apostate was cast into the sea, in many ways speaking figuratively of the form, size and bitterness of his abode, saying also that "the angels of God make sport of him."[12] . . . But there is no tradition among us that they are bound at the river Euphrates or will ever be loosed, or that people will be punished through them. For when Jude says that they are bound by "eternal chains," he excludes the idea that they will ever be released. . . . How, therefore, should someone understand the present claim that they are bound "at the river Euphrates" and that they will be released and that they themselves will

punish sinners? I think that he is speaking figuratively, as is customary in visions. I think he means to say that the angels are bound to the vision of God, which gladdens the soul. For that which is divine is figuratively called a "river" by Isaiah, "Behold, I will extend peace to them like a river and the wealth of nations like an overflowing stream,"[13] and by the prophet, "The streams of the river make glad the city of God."[14] And in section twenty-two of the Gospel of John, the Lord himself speaks of the Holy Spirit: "He who believes in me, as the Scripture says, rivers of living water will flow from his belly."[15] It says that he loosed these [angels] from the vision of God and sent them for the punishment of the wicked, for these have been set apart for the coming day. What kind of angels are these? Perhaps they are those mentioned in the Scripture—Michael, Gabriel, Uriel and Raphael.[16] When this happens, they went out with an army of cavalry of a great, indeterminate size. This indicates the invincible power of the angels of God, whom he compares to a very large cavalry. COMMENTARY ON THE APOCALYPSE 9.13-19.[17]

## DEMONS WILL BE LOOSED TO TROUBLE THE NATIONS. ANDREW OF CAESAREA:

I think that these [angels] are the most evil of the demons who were bound at the coming of Christ and who, according to a divine command that comes from the heavenly altar (whose image was the ancient tabernacle), will be loosed by a divine angel so that they might trouble the nations. They will fight not only against the Christians but also against each other, so that while some, like ripe wheat, might be made manifest as approved and faithful and worthy of the best rewards and of the highest mansions and dwellings, others, like chaff, namely, the wicked and the gross sinners and those unrepentant, might

---

[7]Jer 46:10. [8]Is 34:6. [9]TS 2 7:113-16, §§238-45. [10]2 Pet 2:4. [11]Jude 6. [12]See Job 40:14. Oecumenius also quotes Is 27:1; Ps 104:26 (103:26 LXX); Ezek 32:2. [13]Cf. Is 66:12. [14]Ps 46:4 (45:5 LXX). [15]Jn 7:38. [16]Cf. Jude 9; Dan 8:16; 4 Ezra 4:1; Tob 3:17. [17]TEG 8:151-53.

be here justly punished but receive at the judgment an even harsher condemnation. It is not strange that they are bound at the Euphrates.[18] For according to the ordinance of God, some [demons] were condemned for a time to the abyss, others to the swine, and others to other places, so that after the conclusion of their warfare against humankind they might receive eternal punishment. And perhaps the mention of "Euphrates" indicates that the antichrist will come from those regions. And we have no reason to doubt concerning the multitude of demons, for all the saints say that the air is replete with them. COMMENTARY ON THE APOCALYPSE 9.13-16.[19]

### 9:15 The Four Angels Released

THE DEVIL ALWAYS PREPARED TO HARM THE CHURCH. Primasius: "The four angels were released" indicates the beginning of the persecution.... He indicates by an apt expression the four times during which the persecution will be continuing, that is, [he indicates] three years and six months. He said "for the hour, the day, the month, and the year," since a day is gradually filled with hours, and months with days, and finally years with months. It says that they were "prepared" in order to indicate the character of the devil and his angels. For they entangle themselves in ongoing hostilities against the church and constantly desire to do it harm. However, divine power restrains them, lest they wreak havoc as much as they want. Rightly did he previously say that the locusts were similar to horses arrayed for battle,[20] for now when he says that the angels were loosed, he says that he saw horses. COMMENTARY ON THE APOCALYPSE 9.15.[21]

WICKED SPIRITS DESIRE THE DEATH OF HUMANKIND. Bede: He spoke of four angels, since the persecution will rage in the four parts of the world. These are the same angels whom the seer previously saw standing at the four corners of the earth and restrained from harming the earth and the sea so that the servants of God

might be sealed.... [They were ready for the hour, the day, the month, and the year] for the wicked spirits desire the death of humankind at every hour and moment of time. These will be permitted to rage more freely so that the church might be made stronger, but at the proper time, they themselves will be destroyed. And what do you think [such spirits] will do when they are released, when they work such devastation even now when they are bound? EXPLANATION OF THE APOCALYPSE 9.15.[22]

### 9:16 Twice Ten Thousand Times Ten Thousand

HERETICS BOAST ONLY A FRAUDULENT UNION WITH CHRIST. Primasius: "The number of that cavalry was eighty thousand." ... He again uses different ways to suggest the whole body of evil persons. Here it says eighty thousand. Just as through the perfection of the number six, he signifies for us the form of sixty good people, so that we read "there were sixty queens,"[23] so sometimes the number eighty is used in a bad sense. [Eighty] arises from that which is fourfold, on account of the four well-known qualities of the body—cold and heat, moisture and dryness—or on account of the four passions that often vex humans in life—dread, desire, pain and joy. When these four are doubled because of the two sexes, they become eight. This number similarly increasing by way of tens makes eighty, and in some way this shows that portion of evil persons who as cavalry fight against the body of Christ, which is the church. Therefore, that verse continued, "there are eighty concubines,"[24] as though they were not united by a legitimate union but by a fraudulent one. And this is characteristic of all heresies that lay hold of the sacraments of faith for a time while they are clothed in the name of Christ. Yet just like concu-

---

[18]Andrew is probably responding to Oecumenius on this point. [19]MTS 1 Sup 1:101-2. [20]Rev 9:7. [21]CCL 92:153-54. [22]CCL 121A:355. [23]Song 6:7. [24]Song 6:7.

bines who do not remain permanently in the home, they desire to profit from the name of Christ by gaining influence or advantage or authority or human praise.... Tyconius comments upon another translation, "And the number of soldiers was twice ten thousand times ten thousand." ... It seems to us that also in this translation the portion of the people of perdition are aptly indicated. For twice ten thousand is twenty thousand, and this is the number which the Lord in the Gospel placed against the king who had ten thousand,[25] so that, as it were, the duplicity of those who are evil opposes the simplicity of the Christians. COMMENTARY ON THE APOCALYPSE 9.16.[26]

### 9:17 Horses and Riders

**FEARSOME AND IRRESISTABLE.** OECUMENIUS: The fire is symbolic of wrath and punishment. The hyacinth reveals that these who are sent are of heaven, for the sky is similar to hyacinth. The sulfur indicates that they are pleasing to God, since they are delightful to God—for to delight is to please. And who would please God more than the holy angels? Then the vision changes imagery and exalts the power of the holy angels, comparing them with lions and to fire, smoke and brimstone and snakes. In all of these analogies their fearsomeness and irresistibility is signified. COMMENTARY ON THE APOCALYPSE 9.13-19.[27]

**HERETICS ARE APTLY DESCRIBED.** PRIMASIUS: The horses are men, and their riders are evil spirits. Just as we could say in a good sense "You mounted upon your horses," referring to preachers, "and your victorious cavalry,"[28] so here in an evil sense [these horses] are joined to iniquitous spirits.... And although little similarity can be found between locusts and horses, the same is true concerning lions. Yet each of these is suitable for symbolizing the persons of heretics.... The description of the breastplate signifies the punishments of the impious, for we read that those who worship the beast are promised fire and sul-

phur, and "the smoke of their torments goes up for ever and ever."[29] COMMENTARY ON THE APOCALYPSE 9.17.[30]

**EVIL DEMONS USE EVIL PEOPLE.** ANDREW OF CAESAREA: I think that these "horses" are either men who, like beasts, lust after women, or they are those who are submitted to demons and are ruled by them. For those who sit upon others are those who also govern them. It is common for these to use not only each other as servants but also to use evil people as instruments for plotting against people of similar kind. We interpret "the breastplates of fire and of smoke and of sulfur" to signify the aerial nature of the evil demons and of their destructive work, and that the heads of lions show their murderous and beastly nature. COMMENTARY ON THE APOCALYPSE 9.17-19.[31]

### 9:18-19 A Third of Humankind Was Killed

**THE DEVIL DOES HARM THROUGH IMPIOUS KINGS AND WORLDLY PRELATES.** CAESARIUS OF ARLES: [The smoke, fire, and sulphur from their mouths] are the blasphemies that proceed from their mouths against God. "Their tails are like serpents." The leaders [of the heretics] we call "tails," and the rulers of the world we call "heads." It is through these that the devil does his harm, and without these he is not able to do harm. For either irreligious kings do harm by an evil exercise of authority, or worldly prelates do harm by teaching badly. EXPOSITION ON THE APOCALYPSE 9.18-19, HOMILY 7.[32]

**SIN CONSUMES THE FRUIT OF THE HEART.** ANDREW OF CAESAREA: "The fire that proceeds with smoke and sulfur from their mouths," through which one third of humankind is killed, signifies those sins that consume the fruits of the heart by means of the poisonous assaults and

---

[25]Lk 14:31. [26]CCL 92:154-55. Caesarius of Arles and Bede follow the reading of Tyconius. [27]TEG 8:153. [28]See Hab 3:8. [29]Rev 14:11. [30]CCL 92:156-57. [31]MTS 1 Sup 1:103. [32]PL 35:2430.

instigations of the demons. Or the fire signifies the devastation of cities by fire and by the shedding of blood, which God allows to be done through the hands of the barbarians. COMMENTARY ON THE APOCALYPSE 9.17-19.[33]

## 9:20-21 Humankind Did Not Repent of Idolatry or Immoralities

**THE PRESENT LIFE IS FOR REPENTANCE.** OECUMENIUS: The prophet had described for us the fate of those being punished in hades, saying to God, "In death there is no one who remembers you; in hades who will confess you?"[34] He thus indicates that they are deprived of both joy with God and repentance. For spiritual joy comes from the remembrance of God—for somewhere else he says, "I remembered God and was made glad"[35]—and through confession there is repentance. Confession is the declaration of faults out of sorrow and a conversion that comes from contrition in the soul. Indeed, God has set before us two kinds of life, the present one and the future one. In the present one we are to live according to prudent judgment and authority, while in the future life there are rewards for how one has lived. The present life is not one of judgment, unless someone should perhaps be beneficially reminded and urged toward repentance. Nor is the future life one of works and habits, so that indeed we may be changed from a life filled with accusations into something better. This being the case, how is it then that this verse says of those being punished there, "and the rest of humankind, who were not killed by these plagues, did not repent of the works of their hands?" He did not say this for those who did not repent in the life there but for those who are still living and have not repented from such and such evil deeds out of obedience or from the sight of that which will occur then. And by this present plague they will not die the spiritual death—calling punishment "death"— since they endure forever with the wicked, unless they will be punished in another, harsher manner, which he attempted to explain but wisely kept secret. May it be that all of us remain free from such things by the grace and goodness of our Lord, Jesus Christ, with whom be glory to the Father with the Holy Spirit forever. Amen. COMMENTARY ON THE APOCALYPSE 9.20-21.[36]

**UNIVERSAL WRATH.** ANDREW OF CAESAREA: The rest of humankind, who were spared and did not suffer these things, yet remained unrepentant. They will suffer these same things, since they did not keep themselves from idolatries and murders and fornications and thefts and works of magic. It is clear that the universal wrath comes from such things as these. These various deceits effect a frenzy in those nations that do not acknowledge the truth and that worship idols and the creature rather than the creator. And this is certainly so among those who confess to know God but deny him by their works and who wrap themselves up in the form of piety but deny the power of it. . . . May it be that we display the purity and authenticity of our faith in Christ by deeds so that we never hear those terrible words, "Truly, truly I say to you, I do not know you."[37] "Depart from me, you workers of iniquity."[38] Rather, may we hear this blessed invitation, "Come, you blessed of my Father, inherit the kingdom prepared for you from the foundation of the world."[39] COMMENTARY ON THE APOCALYPSE 9.20-21.[40]

**PAGANS WILL DIE IN THEIR UNBELIEF.** BEDE: Since he had described the false Christians and the heretics, now that he might fully describe the whole body of the devil, he mentions also the error of the pagans. For it in no way profited them not to be killed by these plagues, since it is clear that they continue in their pagan wickedness. Nor in that persecution will the pagans be coerced to consent by those things mentioned above, but rather they will die in their unbelief. EXPLANATION OF THE APOCALYPSE 9.20.[41]

---

[33]MTS 1 Sup 1:103. [34]Ps 6:5 (6:6 LXX). [35]Ps 76:4 LXX. [36]TEG 8:153-54. [37]Mt 25:12. [38]Lk 13:27. [39]Mt 25:34. [40]MTS 1 Sup 1:104-5. [41]CCL 121A:359.

# 10:1-7 A MIGHTY ANGEL WITH A LITTLE BOOK IN HIS HAND

¹*Then I saw another mighty angel coming down from heaven, wrapped in a cloud, with a rainbow over his head, and his face was like the sun, and his legs like pillars of fire. ²He had a little scroll open in his hand. And he set his right foot on the sea, and his left foot on the land, ³and called out with a loud voice, like a lion roaring; when he called out, the seven thunders sounded. ⁴And when the seven thunders had sounded, I was about to write, but I heard a voice from heaven saying, "Seal up what the seven thunders have said, and do not write it down." ⁵And the angel whom I saw standing on sea and land lifted up his right hand to heaven ⁶and swore by him who lives for ever and ever, who created heaven and what is in it, the earth and what is in it, and the sea and what is in it, that there should be no more delay, ⁷but that in the days of the trumpet call to be sounded by the seventh angel, the mystery of God, as he announced to his servants the prophets, should be fulfilled.*

**OVERVIEW:** The seer sees the Lord as a mighty angel sent from the almighty Father coming down from heaven. With the signs of his resurrection and his judgment (VICTORINUS) he comes wearing in the form of a cloud his own holy flesh and his church, which is his body. In his coming he bears the symbols of the promise of salvation and perseverance that he gave to his church, and in his face he shows the future brightness of the saints (TYCONIUS, PRIMASIUS). This "messenger of great counsel" carries an open scroll, for he reveals the grace of the New Testament, which is announced throughout the world by his apostles (VICTORINUS, TYCONIUS, PRIMASIUS). Although all things have been placed under his feet (VICTORINUS), many will nonetheless be martyred in his name before his final advent (PRIMASIUS). These are the strong members of the church who suffer the attacks of persecution (TYCONIUS, PRIMASIUS). Others, however, have not yet received the sign of faith (TYCONIUS), nor have they been tempted by great dangers. Such persons will be spared by God, who will not allow us to be tempted beyond our strength to endure (PRIMASIUS).

During this time of repentance, the church interprets the Old Testament through her prophets (VICTORINUS) and proclaims her message in various manners befitting the various readiness of her hearers (PRIMASIUS). But the church will not make known her mysteries to the unworthy and the faithless, so that they might remain mired in their wickedness (TYCONIUS). And after the time of the preaching of repentance, there will be no future hope for the sinner (VICTORINUS). The saints, however, will then undergo no further testing or cleansing but rather experience the end of all persecution and perpetual peace (TYCONIUS).

Or, the seer sees an angel descend from heaven for the punishment of the impious and the unrepentant (OECUMENIUS). Attending him are the symbols of the formlessness and the invisibility of the angels and of the brightness and virtue of their angelic nature (OECUMENIUS, ANDREW OF CAESAREA). The angel brings with him a little book in which are written the names of the wicked who have sinned upon the land and upon the sea. This angel expresses his wrath against the impious, for he and the other angels agree that the verdict of God against the sinners is just and right (OECUMEnius). Much of this will remain unrevealed until the clear interpretation of all things is given at the end of time (OECUMENIUS, ANDREW OF CAESAREA). Then that eternity will begin which has no temporal measure and in which God is worshiped and praised (ANDREW OF CAESAREA).

## 10:1 A Mighty Angel Came from Heaven

**THE SIGNS OF RESURRECTION AND JUDGMENT.** VICTORINUS OF PETOVIUM: And by this "mighty angel" . . . he signifies our Lord. By the words "his face was as the sun" he indicates the resurrection. By the "rainbow over his head" the seer indicates the judgment, which has occurred or will occur. COMMENTARY ON THE APOCALYPSE 10.1.[1]

**CHRIST COMES WEARING HIS CHURCH LIKE A CLOUD.** TYCONIUS: In this angel the person of our Savior is indicated. On his body he wears the church as though she were a cloud. For the church was constituted in the body of Christ and is often described in diverse manners. At times we read of her as a cloud, as a robe, as the sun, as the moon and as clothes white as snow. And even the saints are compared with clouds, as we read in the prophet Isaiah, "These are they who will fly as the clouds."[2] To be sure, the cloud with which he is clothed is his body, which was conceived by the Holy Spirit. The "rainbow over his head" indicates the promise and the perseverance of his church. "His face was like the sun, and his feet as pillars of fire." There is here a great and marvelous plan, so that at the beginning of this book he might show the fire of the last persecution and afterward might indicate the future brightness of the saints as a fire. For at first he spoke of "his feet as refined in a furnace,"[3] and afterward he describes his face "as the shining in full strength."[4] That he might show how great is the brightness of the church, he now mentions the face before the feet, which are refined, and afterward compares his feet with pillars of fire. COMMENTARY ON THE APOCALYPSE 10.1.[5]

**ANGELS ARE INVISIBLE, BRIGHT AND FULL OF VIRTUE.** OECUMENIUS: He says, "I saw an angel descending from heaven." The angel comes with various forms of punishment against those who were still alive and even though they had heard or seen the torments of the sinners had nonetheless not repented but had remained in their wickedness. His appearance and equipment were as follows. He was wrapped in a cloud. The cloud signifies the formlessness and invisibility of the holy angels, for the cloud is a symbol of invisibility, as the prophet clearly indicates when he speaks of the invisibility of God, saying, "A cloud and deep darkness were around him."[6] "And a rainbow was over his head." This is as though he had said, "The primary and distinctive feature of the good angels is brightness," for they are angels of light. "And his face was as the sun," it says. This is a demonstration of unmixed brightness. While the rainbow grants a brightness and is indicative of that brightness that comes through virtues—for that reason, the brightness of the rainbow is not uniform but is varied, signifying all the virtues of the angels—the sun is symbolic of their natural brilliance. Therefore, he was wrapped in a rainbow—for the virtues are around us—but his face resembled the sun, for in us there is every natural excellence. "And his feet were like pillars of fire." Fire symbolizes that punishment that he brought against the impious. COMMENTARY ON THE APOCALYPSE 10.1-4.[7]

**CHRIST COMES WITH THE CHURCH, MARTYRS AND APOSTLES.** PRIMASIUS: He sees the Lord Christ coming down from heaven dressed in a cloud, which is the church. Or, he is clothed by the cloud of his flesh, which is elsewhere said to be a new bride who descends from heaven,[8] or as Daniel says, the Son of man has come on the clouds of the heavens.[9] The arc above his head represents the promise of propitiation, which

---

[1]CSEL 49:88. [2]Is 60:8. [3]Rev 1:15. [4]Rev 1:16. [5]TS 2 7:126-28 §§284-91. [6]Ps 97:2 (96:2 LXX). [7]TEG 8:155-56. [8]See Rev 21:2. [9]Dan 7:13.

remains among those who are good, but it signifies also those who will be decorated with martyrdom before the advent of the Lord, as Abel and others. . . . And his face was as the sun, since the Lord Jesus Christ was made manifest through the glory of the resurrection,[10] of which we read, "In the sun he has set his tabernacle,"[11] that is, where he is revealed so that he might no longer be hidden. For by his face is indicated the revelation of the present, which the prophet awaited and said, "Show your face, and we shall be saved."[12] His feet are the apostles who were enflamed by the words of God and by the Holy Spirit and were sent out to preach. As it says, "Did not our hearts burn within us while he talked to us on the road and opened to us the Scriptures?"[13] They are called "pillars" on account of the stability of the church, and of them the prophet said, "I have strengthened its pillars,"[14] and "How beautiful upon the mountains are the feet which announce and declare peace."[15] Finally, the apostle said, "Who [Peter, James, John] were reputed to be pillars of the church."[16] COMMENTARY ON THE APOCALYPSE 10.1.[17]

### ANGELS POSSESS VIRTUE AND ALL KNOWLEDGE.

ANDREW OF CAESAREA: The cloud, the rainbow and the light like the sun show how we are to understand this holy angel. For through these [symbols] the manifold character of its virtues and the brightness of the angelic nature and understanding is revealed. COMMENTARY ON THE APOCALYPSE 10.1.[18]

## 10:2 A Little Scroll

### CHRIST IS THE MESSENGER OF THE FATHER.

VICTORINUS OF PETOVIUM: The "open book" is the Revelation that John received. As we explained earlier, "his feet" are the inspired apostles. That he stands upon both the sea and the land signifies that all things have been placed under his feet. He speaks of him here as an "angel," for he is the messenger of the almighty Father and is called the "messenger of great coun-

sel."[19] COMMENTARY ON THE APOCALYPSE 10.1.[20]

### THE REVELATION OF CHRIST ADVANCES.

TYCONIUS: With reason did his face shine "as the sun in full strength," for he opened the book that had been sealed in mystery. "He placed his right foot upon the sea and his left foot upon the land," so that he might confirm the precept of his law by land and by sea. Nor was it without reason that he placed his right foot on the sea and his left foot on the land. In the right foot he signifies the stronger members who have been made firm through great dangers. In the left foot he indicates the crowd of candidates[21] who have not yet received the sign of the faith. COMMENTARY ON THE APOCALYPSE 10.2.[22]

### THE ANGEL OPENS THE RECORD OF THE WICKED.

OECUMENIUS: "And he had in his hand," it says, "a little scroll opened." Daniel recalled such scrolls when he said, "The tribunal sat before him, and books were opened."[23] It was the little scroll in which were written both the names and the transgressions of the severely wicked who are going to be punished. And therefore he used the diminutive "little scroll," since there is a book or a scroll—both are mentioned in holy Scripture—in which the names of all people are written. But here he speaks of a little scroll in which the names of the exceedingly wicked are written. For those who worship idols and are marked by murders and sorceries and are enfeebled in other ways that he reports would not be sufficient to fill an entire book. "And he set his right foot upon the sea and his left foot upon the land." On the one hand, this is an indication of the multitude of the saints, but on the other hand this indicates that he was carrying the instruments of punishment for those who transgressed

---

[10]Primasius uses Tyconius to this point. [11]Ps 19:4 (18:5 LXX). [12]Ps 80:19 (79:20 LXX). [13]Lk 24:32. [14]Ps 75:3 (74:4 LXX). [15]Is 52:7. [16]Gal 2:9. [17]CCL 92:159-60. [18]MTS 1 Sup 1:106. [19]Is 9:6. [20]CSEL 49:88-90. [21]Tyconius uses *competentes*, perhaps referring to those enrolled to be baptized but not yet baptized. [22]TS 2 7:128-29 §§293-96. [23]Dan 7:10.

upon the land and upon the sea, in that they were drowned in it, and who had otherwise done evil. COMMENTARY ON THE APOCALYPSE 10.1-4.[24]

**THE STRONG SUFFER PERSECUTION; THE WEAK ARE SPARED.** PRIMASIUS: If earlier the deep secrets of the Old Testament were recognized to have been hidden in the sealed book, it is appropriate that the revealed grace of the New Testament is believed to be disclosed here in the opened book. Therefore, the apostle confidently says, "And we, with unveiled face, beholding the glory of the Lord, are being changed into his likeness from glory to glory, as though by the Spirit of the Lord."[25] Indeed, this is why his face is said to shine like the sun. Moreover, the right foot upon the sea represents those members who are strong so that they might suffer the attacks of persecution. . . . The left foot upon the land represents those who are not exposed to the greater dangers. For God does not allow us to be tempted beyond what we are able, but with temptation [he] provides also a way, so that we might endure.[26] It is certain, nonetheless, that the proclamation is extended by way of land and sea. COMMENTARY ON THE APOCALYPSE 10.2.[27]

## 10:3 Seven Thunders Sounded

**AFTER THE TIME FOR REPENTANCE.** VICTORINUS OF PETOVIUM: That he "cried out with a loud voice" signifies that great voice of heaven, which announces the words of the almighty God to people that when the time of repentance is closed there will afterward be no future hope. COMMENTARY ON THE APOCALYPSE 10.1.[28]

**GOD'S PUNISHMENT IS JUST.** OECUMENIUS: That the holy angel roars like a lion is symbolic of his wrath against the impious. "And when he called out," it says, "the seven thunders sounded their voices." He calls the seven ministering spirits "seven thunders." They were mentioned earlier. Here he mentions them by way of the

definite article, "the seven thunders," referring to those seven spirits who bear the offering. What does it mean that the seven spirits cry out? It means that these also concur fully with the punishments against the sinners and bring forth a hymn of thanksgiving to God, that all that he has done is just. And they cried out together revealing the forms of the punishments. COMMENTARY ON THE APOCALYPSE 10.1-4.[29]

**THE CHURCH ADAPTS PREACHING TO THE HEARERS.** PRIMASIUS: [The loud voice] indicates that through his servants he was proclaimed faithfully and with strength. As the prophet says, "And he made firm the glory of his strength."[30] "When he called out, the seven thunders sounded." Because of the known use of the number seven, I think that the seven thunders signify the various manners of the church's preaching.[31] The apostle Paul spoke of this concerning his service to others, "As babes in Christ, I fed you with milk, not solid food,"[32] however to others, "solid food is for the perfect,"[33] yet also to others, "avoid the heretical man after the first and second admonition."[34] Therefore, the church is said to proclaim rightly through its usual offices of preaching. COMMENTARY ON THE APOCALYPSE 10.3.[35]

## 10:4 "Seal Up What the Seven Thunders Said"

**THE CHURCH INTERPRETS THE OLD TESTAMENT THROUGH HER PROPHETS.** VICTORINUS OF PETOVIUM: "The seven thunders uttered their voices." The Spirit of sevenfold power announced through the prophets all things that were to come and by his voice has given witness in the world. But since he said that he was going to write whatsoever the thunders had said, that is, whatever

---

[24]TEG 8:156-57. [25]2 Cor 3:18. [26]See 1 Cor 10:13. [27]CCL 92:160-61. Primasius is following Tyconius, who apparently gave also this interpretation of the left foot. Bede repeats this interpretation. [28]CSEL 49:90. [29]TEG 8:157. [30]Source unknown. [31]Primasius follows Tyconius to this point. [32]1 Cor 3:1-2. [33]Heb 5:14. [34]Tit 3:10. [35]CCL 92:161.

had been obscurely foretold in the Old Testament, he was forbidden to write but told to keep it [sealed]. For he was an apostle, and it was not good that the grace of the second rank should be given to the person in the first rank, "for the time is already near."[36] For the apostles overcame unbelief by powers and signs and wonders and mighty deeds. And after them the comfort of having the prophetic Scriptures interpreted was given to the churches which were confirmed in the faith. These interpreters [the apostle] calls prophets, for he says, "He has appointed in the church first apostles, second prophets, third teachers" and following.[37] In another place he says, "Let two or three prophets speak and let the others weigh what is said."[38] And he says, "Any woman who prays or prophesies with her head unveiled dishonors her head."[39] When he said, "Let two or three prophets speak and let the others weigh what is said," he is not speaking of some unheard of and unknown orthodox prophecy but of that prophecy which is already spoken.[40] They weigh what is said to ensure that the interpretation conforms with the witness of the sayings of the prophets. It is clear that John, armed with a superior power, had no need of this, while the church, which is the body of Christ, is adorned by her own members and ought to respond from her own rank.[41] COMMENTARY ON THE APOCALYPSE 10.2.[42]

**THE CHURCH DOES NOT REVEAL MYSTERIES TO THE UNWORTHY.** TYCONIUS: It was said to him, "Do not write" that which you have heard, so that what is in mystery and is reserved to the church would not be revealed to those who are unworthy and faithless.... [Elsewhere] he says, "Do not seal up the words of the prophecy of this book, for the time is near."[43] He shows that there are those to whom the mystery ought to be sealed and those to whom it ought to be opened. As the Lord himself said, "To you"—he is speaking to his disciples—"it has been given to know the secret of the kingdom of God, but for others it is in parables."[44] It says, "Let him who continues to

do evil, do evil still, and him who is filthy, be filthy still, and let him who is righteous still perform more righteous deeds, and likewise the holy more holy deeds."[45] This is to say, "This is why I speak to them in parables, that they who do not see may see and they who see might become blind."[46] And again, "Blessed are your eyes, for they see, and your ears, for they hear."[47] Daniel likewise said, "Seal the book until the time of the consummation."[48] And [John] explains why he was commanded to seal the book in the following words, "Let the unrighteous transgress so that all the wicked and the sinners might not know, but let those who understand understand."[49] COMMENTARY ON THE APOCALYPSE 10.4.[50]

**COMPLETE UNDERSTANDING.** ANDREW OF CAESAREA: This shows that what is now undisclosed is to be explained through experience and the course of the events themselves. And from the heavenly voice the Evangelist learned that the voices are to be imprinted on the mind but that the final understanding and the clear interpretation of them is reserved for the last times. COMMENTARY ON THE APOCALYPSE 10.4.[51]

### 10:5-6 The Angel on the Sea

**ETERNAL LIFE.** ANDREW OF CAESAREA: God swears by himself, since there is none greater than he. But the angels, being creatures, swear by the Creator, for due to our untrustworthiness, they are the guarantors of what is said by them. They swear either that in the coming age there will no longer be time which is measured by the sun, since eternal life is transcendent to temporal measure, or they swear that there is not much

---

[36]Rev 1:3; 22:10. [37]1 Cor 12:28. [38]1 Cor 14:29. [39]1 Cor 11:5. [40]The Christian prophet does not give new prophecy but interprets the prophecies of the Old Testament. [41]The man who speaks with head uncovered is the apostle; the woman who speaks with head covered is the church speaking through her interpreter prophets. [42]CSEL 49:90-92. [43]Rev 22:10. [44]Lk 8:10. [45]Rev 22:11. [46]Mt 13:13; Jn 9:39. [47]Mt 13:16. [48]Dan 12:4. [49]Dan 12:10. [50]TS 2 7:130-34 §§302-7. [51]MTS 1 Sup 1:107-8.

time after the six voices of the angel before the prophecies are fulfilled. COMMENTARY ON THE APOCALYPSE 10.5-6.[52]

### 10:7 The Mystery of God Should Be Fulfilled

THE FUTURE PEACE EXCLUDES ALL FURTHER TESTING. TYCONIUS: The seventh trumpet signifies the end of the persecution and the advent of the Lord, our Savior. For this reason the apostle Paul said that the resurrection of the dead would occur "at the last trumpet."[53] Therefore, he affirms that in the time of the future peace the time of the church would no longer be one of cleansing. For the final persecution will cleanse the church until the seventh trumpet. COMMENTARY ON THE APOCALYPSE 10.7.[54]

EVERY MYSTERY RECEIVES ITS FULFILLMENT. OECUMENIUS: This is said in the manner of an ellipsis. For it says, "When the seventh angel was about to blow his trumpet," all the various and different punishments against the impious will be fulfilled. He does not say that this will occur now when he blows his trumpet in this vision, since the other [woes] have not yet occurred. Rather, this will happen when he blows his trumpet at the appointed time. And when this has happened, "the mystery of God as he proclaimed it to his servants, the prophets" will receive its completion. For the prophets prophesied until the judgment and the recompense of the good and the wicked, but after that [they prophesied] no longer. Therefore, when the seventh angel blows his trumpet at that [seventh] age, every mystery and every prophetic foretelling will receive its fulfillment. COMMENTARY ON THE APOCALYPSE, 10.5-7.[55]

---

[52]MTS 1 Sup 1:108. [53]See 1 Cor 15:52. [54]TS 2 7:135 §§309-10. [55]TEG 8:158.

## 10:8—11:2 JOHN TAKES THE LITTLE BOOK

[8]Then the voice which I had heard from heaven spoke to me again, saying, "Go, take the scroll which is open in the hand of the angel who is standing on the sea and on the land." [9]So I went to the angel and told him to give me the little scroll; and he said to me, "Take it and eat; it will be bitter to your stomach, but sweet as honey in your mouth." [10]And I took the little scroll from the hand of the angel and ate it; it was sweet as honey in my mouth, but when I had eaten it my stomach was made bitter. [11]And I was told, "You must again prophesy about many peoples and nations and tongues and kings."

11 Then I was given a measuring rod like a staff, and I was told: "Rise and measure the temple of God and the altar and those who worship there, [2]but do not measure the court outside the temple; leave that out, for it is given over to the nations, and they will trample over the holy city for forty-two months.

**OVERVIEW:** In the open book the church receives the truth of the law and the prophets that has been made manifest in Christ. For Christ is the truth and the end of the law (PRIMASIUS). This truth is sweet to the mouth, for it concerns the highest precepts, the promised salvation, divine justice and the knowledge of future things (PRIMASIUS, ANDREW OF CAESAREA). However, those who preach this truth will find that through suffering the gospel is necessarily bitter even to themselves and to their hearers who persevere in the commandments (VICTORINUS, BEDE). Moreover, the precepts of Christ are sweet to pious and spiritual persons who delight in the divine law, but they are bitter and harsh to the impious and carnal minded whose god is the belly and who bear a bitter hatred toward the preachers of Christ (AUGUSTINE, PRIMASIUS, CAESARIUS OF ARLES).

In a way the preaching of divine judgment is bitter also to the pious, for they are turned to a better life by the bitterness of penance (PRIMASIUS). John, however, was a holy and chaste man and did not know how bitter are the sins of people. By eating the book that recorded the names and sins of serious sinners, John gained a sort of spiritual experience of the bitterness of sin and its consequences (OECUMENIUS). Compassion on those who receive the punishment of divine judgment will also be bitter to those who are of Christ (ANDREW OF CAESAREA). The church has never ceased to preach the truth among the tribes, tongues and nations, and it will do so again and again so that the whole world will be filled with its preaching (TYCONIUS). John especially was called to preach to the end of time through his Gospel, his catholic letters and this Revelation (VICTORINUS, OECUMENIUS, ANDREW OF CAESAREA).

Indeed, it may be that John will appear again at the end of time to preach against the antichrist (ANDREW OF CAESAREA). Through his writings John gave to the church a "measure" or yardstick of the faith by which the various heretical sects of Satan were excluded from the worship of the

Father and the Son (VICTORINUS). However, outside the church and her faith are also the Jews and unbelieving Gentiles (PRIMASIUS, ANDREW OF CAESAREA) and those who appear to be in the church but who are in reality outside (TYCONIUS). Yet, the church of the New Testament will be immeasurably greater than the Israel of the Old Testament, for the church is out of the nations and is the fulfilling reality of the shadow of the old covenant. Although there is but little time for citizenship in the city of the church (OECUMENIUS), this time will be replete with attacks and persecutions by hypocrites, heretics, Jews and the antichrist (TYCONIUS, PRIMASIUS, ANDREW OF CAESAREA).

## 10:8 *"Take the Scroll"*

**THE CHURCH RECEIVES THE TRUTH OF THE LAW AND THE PROPHETS.** PRIMASIUS: The voice from heaven is the command of God, who breathes into the heart of the church and orders her to receive from the open book that which the church is to preach before the future peace.[1] For it seems to us that to accept the open book from the hand of the angel is to understand the truth of the law and the prophets, which has been made manifest in Christ. And for that reason it says that [the church] should take the open book, which is no longer, as above, the sealed [book]. "For Christ is the end of the law unto righteousness for everyone who believes."[2] Christ, who is the truth, wished then to be born from the earth, that is, from Mary, when "Righteousness looked down from heaven."[3] That is why I think that it is said, "I heard a voice from heaven speaking with me," just as [Christ] himself said, "I am the Beginning who is also speaking to you."[4] COMMENTARY ON THE APOCALYPSE 10.8.[5]

## 10:9-10 *Sweet in the Mouth but Bitter in the Stomach*

---

[1]Primasius follows Tyconius to this point. [2]Rom 10:4. [3]Ps 85:11 (84:12 LXX). [4]See Jn 8:25. [5]CCL 92:162-63.

**SUFFERING MAKES BITTER THE FRUIT OF PREACHING.** VICTORINUS OF PETOVIUM: That he "received the little scroll and ate it" indicates that he committed to memory what had been shown [to him]. "And it was sweet in the mouth." The fruit of preaching is very sweet to the speaker and to those who hear, but through suffering it becomes very bitter to the preacher and to those who persevere in the commandments. COMMENTARY ON THE APOCALYPSE 10.3.[6]

**THE COMMANDS OF CHRIST GIVE INDIGESTION TO THE CARNAL.** AUGUSTINE: "Our belly stuck to the ground."[7] They mean that "our belly" consented to the impious persuasion of that dust [i.e., godless persecutors]; for that is what the expression "stuck to" implies. . . . To cling to God is to do his will. It makes sense, then, to say of the belly that it clung to the earth, when we mean those people who could not hold out under persecution but yielded to the will of the wicked; for this is how they "stuck to the earth." But why are they called "the belly"? Because they are carnal. It suggests that the church's mouth is to be found in the saints, in spiritual people, and the church's belly in the carnal. This is why the church's mouth is plainly visible, but its belly is covered up, as befits something weaker and more vulnerable. Scripture supports this interpretation in the passage where someone says he was given a book to eat, "and the book was sweet in my mouth but bitter in my stomach." What can that mean? Surely that the highest precepts, which spiritual persons accept, are unacceptable to the carnal, and that commands that delight the spiritual only give the carnal indigestion. What is in that book, brothers and sisters? "Go and sell all you possess, and give the money to the poor."[8] How sweet is that command in the church's mouth! All the spiritual have obeyed it. But if you tell any sensual person to do that, he or she is more likely to walk sadly away, as the rich man in the Gospel walked away from the Lord, than to fulfill the injunction.[9] Why does a carnal person walk away? Because that book, so sweet to the mouth, is bit-

ter in the belly. EXPLANATION OF PSALM 43.25.[10]

**THE HOLY APOSTLE LEARNS OF THE BITTERNESS OF SIN.** OECUMENIUS: When I took it, it says, I ate it and "it was sweet in my mouth," but after the eating, it was bitter to my stomach. Then the blessed Evangelist saw and heard the torments against the wicked that he might learn by experience, and not only by report, how bitter and abominable are the transgressions of people that are brought to God. He was taught this through this vision—for as a holy and chaste man himself, he did not know this from [his own] experience—and through the vision he came to know that the wrath of God against the wicked is just. For the book contained the names and the sins of those who were especially serious transgressors, as we noted above. He is therefore commanded to eat it, and as though by taste and a sort of spiritual experience of the bitterness of sin that comes through his vision, he found that what had been sweet to the mouth was, when eaten, bitter to the stomach afterward. For such it is with every sin. It is sweet in the doing but bitter in its consequences. COMMENTARY ON THE APOCALYPSE 10.8-11.[11]

**DIVINE REPROOF.** PRIMASIUS: [I told the angel to give me the book.] The church is moved by divine inspiration to be thoroughly instructed about this mystery. "And he said, 'Take and eat it.'" This means that he was to store [the book] in his secret inward parts. "And it will be bitter to your stomach but sweet as honey in your mouth." This means that when you receive it, you will be delighted by the sweetness of the divine speech and by the hope of the promised salvation and by the sweetness of the divine justice; however, you will then sense bitterness when you begin to preach this to the pious and to the impious.[12] For when the preaching of the divine judgment is heard, some are turned by the bitterness of penance and

---

[6]CSEL 49:92.  [7]Ps 44:25 (43:26 LXX).  [8]Mt 19:21.  [9]See Mk 10:22.  [10]*WSA* 3 16:278.  [11]TEG 8:159.  [12]Primasius follows Tyconius to this point.

are changed for the better, while others are offended and become yet more hardened and bear a bitter hatred toward the preachers. "Reprove a wise man, and he will love you; refute a foolish man, and he will hate you."[13] But the preacher takes in bitterness from either of these two persons. For he either sheds tears with the penitents out of a feeling of compassion, or he is tormented by the bitterness that comes from their failure. For this reason the apostle said, "I have great sorrow and unceasing anguish in my heart; for I wished that I myself were accursed from Christ for the sake of my brothers."[14] But I think it more apt that the bitterness mentioned here be attributed to the impious alone and the sweetness to the pious. For the spiritual person can say, "How sweet are your words to my taste, sweeter than honey and the honeycomb to my mouth!"[15] COMMENTARY ON THE APOCALYPSE 10.9.[16]

**Sweet to the Spiritual but Bitter to the Carnal.** CAESARIUS OF ARLES: "It will be sweet in your mouth but bitter in your stomach." By the *mouth* we are to understand the good and spiritual Christians, while by the *stomach* we understand the carnal and dissolute. And so it is that when the word of God is preached, it is sweet to the spiritual, but to the carnal, whose "god is the belly" as the apostle says,[17] it seems bitter and harsh. EXPOSITION ON THE APOCALYPSE 10.10, HOMILY 8.[18]

**Out of Compassion for the Wicked.** ANDREW OF CAESAREA: He says that although the knowledge of future things will be sweet to you, at the same time it will be bitter to your stomach, that is, to your heart, which is the dwelling place of spiritual foods. For you will have compassion on those who receive punishments given according to God's judgment. COMMENTARY ON THE APOCALYPSE 10.9.[19]

## 10:11 Prophesy Again

**John Prophesies Again.** VICTORINUS OF

PETOVIUM: "It is necessary that you again preach," that is, to prophesy, "among peoples and tongues and nations." When John saw this revelation, he was on the island of Patmos, having been condemned to the mines by Caesar Domitian. There, it seems, John wrote the Revelation, and when he had already become aged, he thought that he would be received [into bliss] after his suffering. However, when Domitian was killed, all of his decrees were made null and void. John was, therefore, released from the mines, and afterward he disseminated the revelation that he had received from the Lord. That is what it means when it says, "You must prophesy again." COMMENTARY ON THE APOCALYPSE 10.3.[20]

**The Church Fills the World with Preaching.** TYCONIUS: In the one angel he clearly shows the body of the church. Although he speaks of one, he shows many. "He says to me, 'You must preach again.'" When did the church ever cease from its preaching, so that she should preach again what she had preached before? However, in the whole world [the church] is commanded to preach again among the peoples, tribes, tongues and in many regions what she had preached before. For there is one church diffused throughout the whole world, which she has filled with its preaching. COMMENTARY ON THE APOCALYPSE 10.11.[21]

**John Prophesies to the End.** OECUMENIUS: "It is necessary that you prophesy again about many peoples and nations and tongues and kings." This is as though he had said, "Although you have seen the consummation of the age and the wrath against the wicked in this vision, do not think that the day of fulfillment has in fact come. There remains much time yet for you to prophesy to many nations and to kings." And so

[13]Prov 9:8. [14]Rom 9:2-3. [15]Ps 119:103 (118:103 LXX). [16]CCL 92:163-64. [17]Phil 3:19. [18]PL 35:2432. [19]MTS 1 Sup 1:109-10. [20]CSEL 49:92-94. [21]TS 2 7:138-39 §§321-23. Tyconius has the Donatist schism in mind.

it is that up to the present time the blessed Evangelist prophesies through his Gospel and his catholic epistles and this Revelation. For all things have been spoken and prophesied to him by the Spirit. COMMENTARY ON THE APOCALYPSE 10.8-11.[22]

**JOHN WILL PROPHESY AGAINST THE ANTICHRIST.** ANDREW OF CAESAREA: This passage indicates either that after the vision of the divine Revelation, that which was seen will not immediately receive its fulfillment, but that the saint must prophesy to those who read his Gospel and his Revelation until the consummation. Or the passage indicates that [John] would not yet taste death, but that at the end he would come to hinder the acceptance of the deceit of the antichrist.[23] COMMENTARY ON THE APOCALYPSE 10.11.[24]

**PREACHING THE GOSPEL IS BITTER WORK.** BEDE: He indicates that when he ate the book sweetness would be mixed with bitterness. That is to say, that when he is released from exile, he was to preach the gospel to the nations. This would be a sweet task as regards love, but it would be a bitter work on account of the persecutions that he would endure. EXPLANATION OF THE APOCALYPSE 10.11.[25]

## 11:1-2 A Measuring Rod

**THE CREED OF THE CHURCH IS THE MEASURE OF FAITH.** VICTORINUS OF PETOVIUM: "He received a measuring rod like a staff, that he might measure the temple and the altar and those who worship in it." In this passage he speaks of that authority that [John] afterward exercised in the churches after his release. For he later also wrote a Gospel. And when Valentinus and Cerinthus and Ebion and other sects of Satan had spread throughout the world, bishops from the neighboring cities gathered to him and persuaded him to write his testimony concerning the Lord. The "measure" of the faith,[26] however, is the com-

mandment of our Lord, namely, that we must confess the Father Almighty, as we have been taught, and his Son, our Lord Jesus Christ, who was spiritually begotten from the Father before the beginning of the world, who was made man, and when he had conquered death was received with his body by the Father into heaven, holy Lord and pledge of immortality; he was foretold by the prophets, he was described by the law, and through the hand of God and the word of the Father Almighty he is also the creator of the whole world.[27] This is the rod and measure of the faith, so that no one worships at the holy altar except him who confesses this, "the Lord and his Christ." "The court on the inside leave outside." The court is called an "atrium," an open area between walls. He commands that such as these are to be thrown out of the church, for they are unnecessary. "It is given over to be trampled by the nations." This means that such persons are to be trampled either by the nations or with the nations. He mentions then again the destruction and the slaughter of the last times and says, "and they will trample the holy city for forty-two months." COMMENTARY ON THE APOCALYPSE, 11.1-2.[28]

**NOT ALL ATTACHED TO THE CHURCH ARE IN THE CHURCH.** TYCONIUS: When he says "Rise," he arouses the church, for John, who is an image of the church, did not hear these things sitting down but standing up. "Measure," it says, "the temple and the altar and those who worship there." He did not command that everyone be measured; rather, he commanded that a portion be prepared unto the end [time], so that what is

---

[22]TEG 8:160. [23]See Jn 21:23. The tradition that John would come at the end to fight the antichrist appears first in the fourth century. Augustine reports the tradition that John is buried alive at Ephesus and that the ground above his grave heaves at his breathing (*Tractates on the Gospel of John* 124.2). See also Rev 11:3 below. [24]MTS 1 Sup 1:110-11. [25]CCL 121A:367. [26]Victorinus takes *mensura* to be the equivalent of *regula* (*fidei*). [27]Jerome's rendering of Victorinus has *hunc esse manum dei et verbum patris*, identifying Christ to be the "hand of God and the Word of the Father." [28]CSEL 49:94-98.

said in the Gospel might be fulfilled, "Many are called, but few are chosen."[29] "But do not measure the court outside the temple, leave that out." The court, which is outside the temple, although it seems to belong to the temple, in fact is not the temple, for it has no relation to the holy of holies. These are those persons who appear to be in the church but are outside of it. . . . Those persons who are outside the temple are also the nations who have never believed the gospel of the Lord. Both groups will trample his church. COMMENTARY ON THE APOCALYPSE 11.1-2.[30]

**ISRAEL IS IMMEASURABLY INCREASED BY THE GENTILES.** OECUMENIUS: The blessed John had earlier seen a vision of the multitude of saints who are with Christ and who behold the throne of God. Among these there were many more Gentiles than there were those from Israel.[31] The present vision now reveals something else to John. It reveals how many were pleasing [to God] at the time of the Old Testament and how many at the time of the New Testament. And note how cleverly this is sketched out for him. He is given a measuring stick that he might measure "the temple of God and the altar" in the temple (clearly the one in Jerusalem) "and those worshiping in it." And he measured. Those who pleased God during the time of the Old Testament were easily measured because there were so few of them. "But do not measure the court outside the temple; leave that out, for it is given over to the nations." When he had measured the temple and the altar and those sacrificing within, he heard that it was necessary to place the court on the outside and to widen it, but definitely not to measure it, since it was to attain to greater things than measuring. The court, it says, is given over to the nations, and it is adjacent to and lies outside the temple. Likewise, the New Testament follows immediately upon the Old, for the New fulfills spiritually and in reality that which has but shadow in it. And realities of a different kind arise next to [the Old Testament], as Jeremiah says, "Behold, the days are coming, says the Lord,

and I will make a new covenant with the house of Israel and the house of Judah, not like the covenant which I made with their fathers when I took them by the hand to bring them out of the land of Egypt."[32] For this reason he calls the New Testament the "court of the temple." And so, the vision indicates in a mystical manner that he who in the New Testament is named "Christ" and "Beginning" was Lord of the Old Testament . . . and he calls the New Testament the "court" of the Old Testament. For the court is the beginning and entrance to God, but it is not the temple. Therefore, he did not measure the court by which both the [New Testament] and those in it are signified. For both the New Testament and those justified in it are beyond comprehension, these because of their unspeakable magnitude and the New Testament because of its subtlety and the sublimity of its teachings. For it says, "it was given over to the nations." The blessings of the New Testament were given also to Israel, but since the Gentiles in it are greater in number than those who were pleasing from Israel, it indicates the whole from the greater part, saying that the court was given to the nations. "And they will trample upon the holy city for forty-two months." It speaks of "the city," not of the temple, calling the church a "city," about which it says, "Glorious things are spoken of you, O city of God, the heavenly Jerusalem, the mother of the firstborn who are enrolled in heaven."[33] And what does it mean that the measuring will be for forty-two months? It indicates that there is little time remaining upon the earth for the citizenship given in the New Testament and that afterward the end will come. For the number forty, the sum of four tens, is not complete, nor is the number two. By these numbers the verse shows that the duration of the New Testament does not last long in the present life, and so the Scripture calls the time of the New Testament the "last" hour or the "eleventh" hour, at which time the Only Begotten became

---

[29]Mt 22:14. [30]TS 2 7:140-42 §§325-31. [31]Rev 7:9. [32]Jer 31:31-32. [33]See Ps 87:3ff (86:3ff LXX); Gal 4:26; Heb 12:22-23.

man. But he will endure forever in the coming life. COMMENTARY ON THE APOCALYPSE 11.1-2.[34]

**THOSE OF A FALSE FAITH AND A SINFUL LIFE ARE TO BE EXPELLED.** PRIMASIUS: He commands that the teaching of a false faith and the contagion of a sinful way of life among the heretics, Jews and Gentiles be expelled, for it is not right that such persons approach the holy of holies. For the apostle says, "What have I to do with judging outsiders? Is it not those inside whom you are to judge?"[35] When all the Jews, heretics, and Gentiles incessantly attack the church by all means available, it is as though they are trampling upon the church. The number of the months signifies not only the time of the last persecution but also the entire time of Christianity. For there are six ages of the world and seven days by which all time moves by passing away and returning. Six times seven makes forty-two, and I believe that the passage refers to both of these [numbers]. COMMENTARY ON THE APOCALYPSE 11.2.[36]

**UNBELIEVING GENTILES AND JEWS.** ANDREW OF CAESAREA: We think that the church is called the "temple of the living God," for in it we offer spiritual sacrifices to God. And I think that the "court outside" is the assembly of the unbelieving Gentiles and Jews, and so by virtue of their impiety they are unworthy to be measured by the angel. "For the Lord knows those who are his,"[37] as it says, but he who knows all things is said not to know the transgressors. That the holy city, whether that be the new Jerusalem or the catholic church, will be trampled by the nations for forty-two months signifies, I believe, that at the appearance of the antichrist those who are faithful and trustworthy will be trampled and persecuted for three and a half years. COMMENTARY ON THE APOCALYPSE 11.1-2.[38]

**WE ARE TO MEASURE OUR SPIRITUAL PROGRESS.** BEDE: He said, "Rise," not because John was sitting when he heard these words, but because by this word the heart of each person is aroused to measure the words and deeds of the Gospel. For there each will discover to what extent he has progressed and to what extent he is in agreement with the divine rule. EXPLANATION OF THE APOCALYPSE 11.1.[39]

---

[34]TEG 8:160-62. [35]1 Cor 5:12. [36]CCL 92:166. Primasius is basing himself upon Tyconius. [37]Mt 7:23. [38]MTS 1 Sup 1:112. Andrew mentions the opinion of Oecumenius but offers his own. [39]CCL 121A:367-69.

# 11:3-10 THE TWO WITNESSES

[3]*And I will grant my two witnesses power to prophesy for one thousand two hundred and sixty days, clothed in sackcloth."*

[4]*These are the two olive trees and the two lampstands which stand before the Lord of the earth.* [5]*And if any one would harm them, fire pours from their mouth and consumes their foes; if any one would harm them, thus he is doomed to be killed.* [6]*They have power to shut the sky, that no rain may fall during the days of their prophesying, and they have power over the waters to turn them into blood, and to smite the earth with every plague, as often as they desire.* [7]*And when they have*

*finished their testimony, the beast that ascends from the bottomless pit will make war upon them and conquer them and kill them, ⁸and their dead bodies will lie in the street of the great city which is allegorically[d] called Sodom and Egypt, where their Lord was crucified. ⁹For three days and a half men from the peoples and tribes and tongues and nations gaze at their dead bodies and refuse to let them be placed in a tomb, ¹⁰and those who dwell on the earth will rejoice over them and make merry and exchange presents, because these two prophets had been a torment to those who dwell on the earth.*

d Greek *spiritually*

**OVERVIEW:** Just as the coming of Christ in humiliation was announced by John the Baptist, so his coming in the glory of the Father will be announced by Elijah and Enoch (OECUMENIUS). It may be, however, that John also will return at the end along with Elijah and Enoch (PSEUDO-HIPPOLYTUS), or that it will be Jeremiah who along with Elijah returns to announce the Lord's coming (VICTORINUS). The sending of forerunners reveals the Lord's kindness to humanity and his care for mortal sinners (PSEUDO-HIPPOLYTUS). Through them humankind will be instructed about the deception of the antichrist and the wrath of God (PSEUDO-HIPPOLYTUS, TYCONIUS, OECUMENIUS), and by their example the forerunners will show the way of repentance to sinners (TYCONIUS).

The two witnesses symbolize as well the two Testaments by which God governs and rules his church (TYCONIUS). At the same time, there are two kinds of witness, that which is private and in the heart and that which is public and known to all (PRIMASIUS). The two witnesses are said to be two olive trees and two lampstands, for they represent the one church, which is formed from the two peoples of the Jews and the Gentiles (OECUMENIUS, PRIMASIUS) and is illuminated by the two Testaments which pour the oil of knowledge into the church (TYCONIUS, PRIMASIUS). Were anyone to harm the church, the prayers of the church would consume them, either that they might be corrected or that they might be punished (TYCONIUS, CAESARIUS OF ARLES). All that God has done for the church, he has given to the church. There-

fore, the church has the power of binding and loosing so that she can cause the rain of blessing to cease to fall upon the earth (TYCONIUS, PRIMASIUS).

Similarly, at the end of time God will give great power to his two prophets, for they will promote truth and light by signs and wonders, even as the antichrist by false signs advances the cause of deceit and darkness (OECUMENIUS, ANDREW OF CAESAREA). The preaching of the two witnesses will be met with great resistance by the antichrist, who will exalt himself and glorify himself as God (PSEUDO-HIPPOLYTUS). As many texts claim, the antichrist will arise by God's allowance as a kingdom among kingdoms and from among the Caesars (VICTORINUS). Yet tradition says that the antichrist will arise from the tribe of Dan and hence from the iniquitous hearts of the Jews (TYCONIUS). More likely yet, however, the antichrist will arise from the unstable substance of our sinful human nature. In any case, he will be savage, inhuman and bloodthirsty as is a beast (OECUMENIUS). And so the antichrist will slay those who confess Christ and will slay spiritually those who are deluded by his deceit (TYCONIUS, BEDE). Suitably, he will set up his kingdom in Jerusalem, where the prophets were killed and the Christ was crucified (TYCONIUS, ANDREW OF CAESAREA).

In this way the antichrist imitates David, whose son was the Christ (ANDREW OF CAESAREA). Yet the Jerusalem of the antichrist will be as Sodom and Egypt because it will enslave and abuse the servants of Christ and will be noted for its licentiousness (OECUMENIUS). Moreover, that spiritual Sodom and Egypt will possess neither the light of faith nor the sound of confession (BEDE). Rather, in it the wicked will rejoice over the death of the righteous (OECUMENIUS) as they strive to destroy the church and remove her from the world (PRIMASIUS). May we, therefore, turn to the Lord of our salvation when we are chastened, so that we might escape eternal punishment, unlike those who rejoiced that they were free from the sufferings intended for their correction (ANDREW OF CAESAREA).

## 11:3 Power to Prophesy

**SENT FOR OUR INSTRUCTION.** PSEUDO-HIPPOLYTUS: Through the Scriptures we are instructed in two advents of the Christ and Savior. The first after the flesh was in humiliation, because he was manifested in lowly estate. So then his second advent is declared to be in glory, for he comes from heaven with power and angels and the glory of his Father. His first advent had John the Baptist as its forerunner, and his second, in which he is to come in glory, will exhibit Enoch and Elijah and John the Theologian.[1] Behold, too, the Lord's kindness to humankind; how even in the last times he shows his care for mortals and pities them. For even then he will not leave us without prophets but will send them to us for our instruction and assurance and to make us give heed to the advent of the adversary, as he intimated also of old in Daniel. For he says, "I shall make a covenant of one week, and in the midst of the week my sacrifice and libation will be removed." For by one week he indicates the showing forth of the seven years, which shall be in the last times. And the half of the week the two prophets, along with John, will take for the purpose of proclaiming to all the world the advent of antichrist, that is to say, for a "thousand two hundred and sixty days clothed in sackcloth." ON THE END OF THE WORLD, THE ANTICHRIST AND THE SECOND COMING 21.[2]

**JEREMIAH WILL COME WITH ELIJAH AT THE END.** VICTORINUS OF PETOVIUM: Many think that either Elisha or Moses was with Elijah. However, both of these died. However, the death of Jeremiah was never discovered. Our ancients have handed over the opinion that [the other witness] was in every respect Jeremiah.[3] For the very word, which was given to him, is witness of this: "Before I formed you in the womb of your mother, I knew you; and I appointed you prophet to the nations."[4] However, he was never a prophet among the nations, and so, since the two words are divine, it is necessary that what God promised, that he also demonstrate, namely, that he be a prophet among the nations. COMMENTARY ON THE APOCALYPSE 11.3.[5]

**TO PROCLAIM THE WRATH OF GOD.** TYCONIUS: He had earlier said that "you must prophesy again." Now he desires to show this in his two witnesses. In the two witnesses, he wants us to understand the two Testaments by which his church is governed and ruled. For he did not say, "I make witnesses for myself," as though they did not yet exist. Rather, he said, "I shall give to my witnesses," who were with me from the beginning and have never at all departed from me. The 1,260 days are not a time of peace but of the last persecution, during which time the devil shall break out against the Christians, namely, when he receives power to test the church. And just as before the flood, when the sins of humankind raised their head to the heavens, there was not absent someone who might proclaim the wrath of God to those who were perishing, so also at that time there will be those who will announce the kingdom of God and the last day and by their own example will show the way of repentance to sinners. [The witnesses] were "clothed in sack-

---

[1]On the basis of Jn 21:23, John was associated with Elijah and Enoch as one who had not died and would come at the end to fight the antichrist. See Rev 10:11 above.  [2]ANF 5:247.  [3]For the view that Jeremiah would return to earth at the end of time, see 2 Esdr 2:17-18 (with Isaiah) and [Ps.] Tertullian *Carmen adversus Marcionem* 3.179-89 (CCL 2.1439; on Elijah, 3.149-50).  [4]Jer 1:5.  [5]CSEL 49:98.

cloth," it says, that is, they were established in confession. As the prophet said, "When they troubled me, I clothed myself in sackcloth."[6] And Job said, "They have sewed sackcloth upon my skin."[7] COMMENTARY ON THE APOCALYPSE 11.3.[8]

### FORERUNNERS OF THE SECOND COMING.

OECUMENIUS: Since the vision outlined for the Evangelist the entire economy of the Lord's incarnation—his birth, the temptation, his teachings, the beatings, also the cross and resurrection, the second coming and the reward of both the holy and the sinners—it had left unmentioned any information about the forerunners of his second coming. Now, as though by a sharp U-turn, [the vision] teaches him about them. When Malachi said, "Behold, I will send you Elijah the Tishbite before the great and terrible day of the Lord comes, who will turn the heart of a father to the son and the heart of a man to his neighbor, lest I come to trample the land utterly,"[9] the holy Scripture with great clarity foretold that Elijah the Tishbite will come. And in Matthew, the Lord spoke of the Baptist: "And if you are willing to accept it, this is Elijah who is to come."[10] Concerning other forerunners we have heard nothing with clarity except that Genesis said concerning Enoch that "having pleased God, he was taken,"[11] and the wise apostle said concerning him, "By faith Enoch was taken up so that he should not see death; and he was not found, because God had taken him."[12] An old, traditional saying is prevalent in the church, that with Elijah the Tishbite also Enoch will come as a forerunner of the second coming of Christ and at the coming of the antichrist.[13] This passage says that they come and proclaim beforehand that the signs performed by [the antichrist] are deceptive and that it is not necessary to believe the sinful one. Using either a figurative number or a literal description of what will be, the vision now reports of these [forerunners] that they will prophesy so many days. They will prophesy "clothed in sackcloth," for they will lament over the disobedience of those who live at that time. COMMENTARY ON THE APOCALYPSE 11.3-6.[14]

### THE CHURCH'S WITNESS.

PRIMASIUS: While he had said that "you must prophesy again," here it is that "I will grant to my two witnesses and they will prophesy." As there he spoke of John, here of the two witnesses, that is, of the church that preaches and prophesies on the basis of the two Testaments.[15] There is another interpretation. The Truth proposes that there are two kinds of witness. On the one hand, there is the witness by way of one's manner and character. This witness occurs in the heart and is known to God alone, also when there is but minimal approval during times of suffering. On the other hand, there is the witness by way of deed, which is accomplished publicly in the view of all when the opportunity of persecution arises. For sometimes witness seems to fail the soul, while at other times the soul in some seems to fail the witness. Therefore, the blessed Cyprian said, "The first title to victory is for him who has fallen at the hands of the Gentiles confessing the Lord; the second step to glory is to make a cautious withdrawal and then to keep himself for God. The one is a public confession; the other private. The former conquers the judge of the world; the latter satisfied with God as his judge guards a conscience pure by integrity of heart."[16] But the point is also very clearly demonstrated in the two sons of Zebedee. James, who was killed by Herod,[17] is accounted a martyr because of his public confession, while his brother, John the Evangelist, is crowned because of his secret witness [as one who was] with Jesus. Moreover, it is clear that earlier the Lord had said to both, "You will drink

---

[6]Ps 35:13 (34:13 LXX). [7]Job 16:16. [8]TS 2 7:142-44 §§ 333-40. [9]Mal 4:4-5 (3:22-23 LXX). [10]Mt 11:14. [11]Gen 5:24. [12]Heb 11:5. [13]From the second century onward it was common opinion that Enoch would accompany Elijah as forerunners of Christ at the end of time (see Tertullian *On the Soul* 50; Hippolytus *On the Antichrist* 43; perhaps already Irenaeus *Against Heresies* 5.5.1). [14]TEG 8:163-64. [15]Primasius follows Tyconius to this point. [16]Cyprian *The Lapsed* 3 (FC 36:59). [17]Acts 12:2.

my cup."[18] That is, one would give witness by way of deed, the other by way of his manner and practice. They are clothed in sackcloth. This means that they were both established in confession, for the humility of confession is characteristic to both kinds of witness. COMMENTARY ON THE APOCALYPSE 11.3.[19]

## 11:4 Two Olive Trees and Two Lampstands

THE CHURCH IS PROTECTED BY THE TWO TESTAMENTS. Tyconius: "These are those who stand," it says, not those who shall stand as though they were not able to stand. In the two lampstands he signifies the church, which is fortified by the protection of the two Testaments. For in the seven angels and in the seven lampstands he designated the one church, so that when he spoke of one, he had also spoken of the others. When Zechariah who prophesied of our figure was awakened from sleep that he might behold the light of the church, he saw a single sevenform lampstand in which was declared the mystery of the sevenform church. For the two olive trees are the two Testaments, which pour out the oil of knowledge into the lampstand. And therefore the same prophet said, "He waked me, like a man that is wakened out of his sleep. And he said to me, 'What do you see?' I said, 'Behold, I see a lampstand all out of gold, with torches upon it, and seven lamps on it, with seven lips of light which are upon it, and two olive trees upon it, one on the right of the torch and one on the left.' "[20] And I asked what these might be. And the angel answered and said, these seven lights are seven spirits which are "the seven eyes of the Lord that range through the whole earth."[21] And when I inquired of the two olive trees, he said to me, "These are the two anointed sons who are with the Lord of the whole earth."[22] COMMENTARY ON THE APOCALYPSE 11.4.[23]

THE TWO OLIVE BRANCHES. Oecumenius: That the two olive branches have been interpreted as the two peoples, that from the Jews and that from the nations, is not unknown to the saints. However, it is also possible that these two of whom the present passage speaks are two prophets. COMMENTARY ON THE APOCALYPSE 11.3-6.[24]

THE ONE CHURCH. Primasius: He shows now that he is speaking not of future realities but of present things when he says, "These are the two olive trees and the two lampstands that stand before the Lord of the earth." This refers to the church, which is illuminated and made strong by the light of the two Testaments and is equipped by the two kinds of witness that by divine inspiration is allowed in various of its members. The two lampstands represent the [one] church, but he has spoken of two because of the two Testaments or because [the church] is gathered from the circumcision and uncircumcision and exists in union with the chief cornerstone. COMMENTARY ON THE APOCALYPSE 11.4.[25]

## 11:5 If Any Harm Them, Fire Kills Their Foes

RECEIVING THE SAME HARM. Tyconius: This means that should anyone wish to harm the church, as one condemned he is consumed by a fire, which harms in the very same manner as a sort of reciprocal judgment. That is, he receives justly that very thing which he desired to inflict unjustly. Or, in a good sense this means that through the prayers of the church's mouth one is consumed spiritually by fire so that one might be changed for the better, since when one is turned away from error, error ceases and one is saved. COMMENTARY ON THE APOCALYPSE 11.5.[26]

THOSE WHO HARM THE CHURCH. Caesarius of Arles: Should anyone harm the church or wish to harm her, through the prayers of her

---

[18]Mt 20:23. [19]CCL 92:166-67. [20]Zech 4:1-3. [21]Zech 4:10. [22]Zech 4:14. [23]TS 2 7:145-47 §§ 343-48. [24]TEG 8:164. [25]CCL 92:167-68. [26]CCL 92:168

mouth he shall be consumed by a divine fire either in the present age for his correction or in the future age for his damnation. EXPOSITION ON THE APOCALYPSE 11.5, HOMILY 8.[27]

## 11:6 Power to Shut the Sky

**THE CHURCH EXERCISES POWER FROM GOD.**
TYCONIUS: It says, "they have," not "they will have." For whoever remains in the faith of the one church of God will in no way be wanting in that power conferred upon him by God. "They have power to turn the waters into blood and to smite the earth with every plague as often as they desire." We have often said that everything that God is said to have done for the sake of his church is attached to the powers of the church. The Lord gives power to the church so that what is bound on earth is also bound in heaven.[28] Heaven is spiritually closed "that no rain fall," that is, that no rain of blessing fall upon the dry land. The Lord spoke of this concerning the vineyard of the Jews: "I shall also command the clouds that they rain no rain upon it."[29] And not only did they suspend the rain but even made useless that rain which had fallen. For the water was changed into blood, even as the very earth was struck with every plague. Nor did these things occur by way of accident or fortuitously. Rather, "as often as they desired," that is, as often as he desired who conceded to them such power. As the apostle says of the Holy Spirit, "apportioning to each one individually as he wills."[30] And again, "As God assigns to each one a measure of faith." COMMENTARY ON THE APOCALYPSE 11.6.[31]

**THE TWO FORERUNNERS.** OECUMENIUS: Such is [the power] of these very persuasive individuals. For if one of them, Elijah the Tishbite, had such power even before he fulfills the service of Christ, how would he remain unpersuasive as the precursor of Christ? "And they had power," it says, "over the waters to turn them into blood, and to strike the earth with every plague as often

as they wish." For since "the coming of the antichrist will be by the activity of Satan with all power and with deceitful signs and wonders," as Paul says in his second letter to the Thessalonians,[32] these signs will lead to agreement and faith. And for this reason these two prophets who refer to him as a deceiver and a cheat will also make use of various signs, so that they might attract those who hear to faith. COMMENTARY ON THE APOCALYPSE 11.3-6.[33]

**THE CHURCH DISPENSES LIFE AND DEATH.**
PRIMASIUS: Not only do they suspend the rain, but also they make useless that rain that falls. That is, they turn the waters into blood on account of those who judge in a carnal way those things which the church gives to be discerned in a spiritual manner. Therefore, they deservedly die, being struck by the church with a just condemnation. And so they incur the defect of death from that source which for others brings forth spiritual life. For the apostle says that to think according to the flesh is death.[34] "The good aroma of Christ," which rises up from the church, is "to some a fragrance of death to death, to others a fragrance of life to life."[35] And so [the church] is said to strike the earthly with plagues when by the power of binding and loosing that she has she assigns to each a proper penalty for the variety of their merits and sins. COMMENTARY ON THE APOCALYPSE 11.6.[36]

**THE FORERUNNERS CORRECT BY THEIR TEACHING.** ANDREW OF CAESAREA: How deep is the divine goodness! For he brings a healing that is commensurate with the wound. For since he has received the full operation of the devil, the antichrist will come with every false sign and wonder and will be more wondrous than every sorcery and enchantment. And so in the power of true signs and wonders, God will equip these

---

[27]PL 35:2432. [28]See Mt 18:18. [29]Is 5:6. [30]1 Cor 12:11. [31]TS 2 7:149-51 §§353-60. [32]2 Thess 2:9. [33]TEG 8:164-65. [34]See Rom 8:6. [35]2 Cor 2:16. [36]CCL 92:168-69.

saints for the promotion of truth and light, and they will expose the lies and darkness [of the antichrist], and to those who have been deceived they will give correction through the word of their teaching and through chastising scourges (drought, fire, changes in the elements and the like), and they will make an example of the deceiver, while until the completion of their prophesying they will remain uninfluenced either by him or by someone other. COMMENTARY ON THE APOCALYPSE 11.5-6.[37]

## 11:7-8 The Beast Will Make War

**THE ANTICHRIST WILL MAKE WAR.** PSEUDO-HIPPOLYTUS: When they have proclaimed all these things, they will fall on the sword, cut off by the accuser. And they will fulfill their testimony, as Daniel also says; for he foresaw that the beast that came up out of the abyss would make war with them, namely with Enoch, Elijah and John, and would overcome them and kill them, because of their refusal to give glory to the accuser, that is, the little horn that sprang up. And he, being lifted up in heart, begins in the end to exalt himself and glorify himself as God, persecuting the saints and blaspheming Christ. ON THE END OF THE WORLD, THE ANTICHRIST AND THE SECOND COMING 21.[38]

**ATTESTED BY MANY WITNESSES.** VICTORINUS OF PETOVIUM: "These are the two olive trees and the two lampstands that stand in the presence of the Lord of the earth,"[39] that is, in paradise. It is necessary that after many plagues have come to the world these be killed by the antichrist, who, it says, is "the beast that ascends from the bottomless pit." That he will ascend from the pit is attested by many witnesses. For Isaiah says, "Behold, Assyria is a cypress on Mount Lebanon."[40] "Assyria" is a deeply rooted "cypress," high and full of branches, that is, [Assyria possesses] a numerous people. It is "on Mount Lebanon," that is, a kingdom among kingdoms. It is "beautiful in its offshoots," that is, it is strong in its armies.

"Water nourishes it," it says[41]; that is, there are many thousands of persons who will be submitted to it. "The abyss increased him," that is, it vomited him forth. Ezekiel often speaks in such words. Paul also gives witness that antichrist is in a kingdom among kingdoms and was among the Caesars. He writes to the Thessalonians, "If only he restrains, who is seen [to be restraining], until he be taken from the way. And then he will appear whose coming is like the activity of Satan with signs and deceptive works."[42] And that they might know that he who was to come was then emperor, he adds, "he is already working the mystery of wickedness."[43] That is, he is working in a mysterious way that wickedness which he will do. But he will not be aroused [to this work] by his own strength or by that of his father but by the command of God. And for this reason Paul said, "Therefore, since they did not receive the love of God, God sends upon them a spirit of error, that all of them might be persuaded by delusion, who were not persuaded by the truth."[44] Isaiah says, "Darkness arose upon them who were awaiting the light."[45] COMMENTARY ON THE APOCALYPSE 11.4.[46]

**ANTICHRIST COMES BEFORE THE LAST PERSECUTION.** TYCONIUS: When he says, "when they have finished their witness," he clearly explains that these things will take place before the last persecution, at least that which they relate until the revelation of the beast who will ascend from the abyss, that is, from the depths of the iniquity of the hearts of the Jews. For, according to tradition, the antichrist will arise from the tribe of Dan. And "he will conquer them," namely, in those who will have succumbed. However, "he will kill them," indicating those who for the name of Christ will have been killed by a praiseworthy suffering. "And he will lay their

---

[37]MTS 1 Sup 1:113-14. [38]ANF 5:247. [39]See Zech 4:11-14. [40]Ezek 31:3. Victorinus wrongly attributes this passage to Isaiah. [41]Ezek 31:4. [42]2 Thess 2:7-9. [43]2 Thess 2:7. [44]See 2 Thess 2:10-12. [45]See Is 59:9. [46]CSEL 49:100-102.

bodies in the middle of that great city which is spiritually called Sodom, where also their Lord was crucified." Another translation renders it [in the singular] "body." And so it speaks of one body of the two, while elsewhere in subsequent verses it speaks of the "bodies." In this way, he preserves the number of the Testaments, while the two witnesses demonstrate the one body of the church. This body—he speaks not only of those killed but also of those who are living—is thrown down, that is, it is despised, as [the psalmist says], "You have cast my words behind you."[47] [He casts them down] "in the middle," that is, openly and visibly. This is, to be sure, that "Jerusalem which killed the prophets," according to the words of the Lord who reproached it, saying, "and stoned those who were sent to you."[48] Rightly was [Jerusalem] reproved, nor did it deserve to be restored. COMMENTARY ON THE APOCALYPSE 11.7-8.[49]

**SAVAGE AND BLOODTHIRSTY.** OECUMENIUS: [The prophets] will testify that the one who is present is not the Christ but a certain rogue, a deceiver and a destroyer. He will in no way come as the Son of God in whom one must believe as Savior and as God and who came for the benefit of humankind both in his appearance long ago and in his present appearing. It speaks of "the beast that ascends from the bottomless pit." He calls the antichrist a "beast" because of his savagery, his inhumanity and his thirst for blood. He calls the life of people a "bottomless pit," for it is bitter and distasteful on account of sins and unstable because it is buffeted about by evil spirits. For the sinful one will not arise out of any other substance but out of our own human nature, for he will be a man "whose coming is in the activity of Satan," as was just now said. This beast, it says, will kill the two witnesses and will cast their dead bodies unburied in the streets of Jerusalem. For in it he will rule as king of the Jews whom he will deceive, and he will come to those who assist and trust him in every thing. As the Lord said in [the Gospel of] John: "I have come

in my Father's name, and you do not receive me; if another comes in his own name, him you will receive."[50] He calls Jerusalem "Sodom," not in a literal sense but in a spiritual sense on account of the licentiousness and ill-repute it possessed at that time. And he calls it "Egypt" because it had enslaved and abused the servants of Christ, just as the actual Egypt did to Israel. And it was there "where also their Lord," that is, [the Lord] of the two witnesses, "was crucified." COMMENTARY ON THE APOCALYPSE 11.7-10.[51]

**ANTICHRIST WILL ESTABLISH HIS KINGDOM IN JERUSALEM.** ANDREW OF CAESAREA: After [the two witnesses] have witnessed and urged escape from this deceit, the beast, that is, the antichrist, comes forth from the dark and deep recesses of the earth to which the devil had been condemned. And, with God's allowance, he will kill them and leave their unburied bodies in Jerusalem itself, no doubt the ancient one which is now in ruins and in which the Lord also suffered. As it seems, he will establish his kingdom in Jerusalem in imitation of David, whose son is Christ, our true God, who is come in the flesh. In this way [the antichrist] intends to prove that he is the Christ who is fulfilling the prophetic word that says, "I will raise up the booth of David that is fallen and rebuild its ruins."[52] And having been deceived at his coming, the Jews will accept this. COMMENTARY ON THE APOCALYPSE 11.7-8.[53]

**THE CITY OF ANTICHRIST.** BEDE: He clearly shows that all this will happen before the final persecution, for he says, "when they have finished their testimony." At least that will happen which they show until the revelation of the beast who will emerge from the hearts of the wicked. They will strive at that time valiantly to resist the enemy with the same testimony; however, it is believed that at that time the church will be made destitute of the gift of miracles, while the adver-

---

[47]Ps 50:17 (49:17 LXX). [48]Mt 23:37. [49]CCL 92:169-70. [50]Jn 5:43. [51]TEG 8:165-66. [52]Amos 9:11. [53]MTS 1 Sup 1:114-15.

sary will be openly active with deceptive signs. As the Lord says, "Want will go before his face."[54] "And he will conquer and kill them." He will conquer in those who will have succumbed, and he will kill those who by a praiseworthy suffering for the name of Christ will be slain. Or, should he conquer and kill in a spiritual manner, we understand this to refer to a portion of the witnesses, as it says in the Gospel, "They will deliver you up to tribulation and put you to death."[55] And the Evangelist Luke indicates that this was spoken of a part, saying, "Some of you they will put to death."[56] "And they will throw their bodies onto the streets of the great city." "If they persecuted me, they will also persecute you," it says.[57] Therefore, it is not surprising if the city of the wicked, which did not fear to crucify the Lord, should also hold his servants in derision, even if they are dead. The history of the church relates that such things often occurred. "Which is spiritually called Sodom and Egypt." "Sodom" and "Egypt" mean "silent" and "dark," for this city possesses neither the light of faith nor the sound of confession. For "man believes with his heart and so is justified, and he confesses with his lips and so is saved."[58] As a sign of spiritual punishment, these regions were oppressed with these plagues, that is, [Sodom] by a ravaging fire and [Egypt] by water turned into blood. EXPLANATION OF THE APOCALYPSE 11.7-8.[59]

## 11:9-10 People Rejoice over the Witnesses' Bodies

**THE SIGHT OF THE RIGHTEOUS VEXES THE UNRIGHTEOUS.** TYCONIUS: Since they do not allow their bodies to be gathered in a suitable place, they prevent a day for their memory to be indicated by a sacred celebration of the living. . . . It is no wonder that the earthly minded rejoice over the deaths of the righteous. For in addition to the plagues that beset the human race on account of the testaments of God, even the very sight of the righteous oppresses the unrighteous, as it is written, "Even the sight of him is a burden

to us."[60] Not only does it oppress, it also causes him to melt away, and so the psalm says, "The sinner will see and be angry; he will gnash his teeth and melt away."[61] COMMENTARY ON THE APOCALYPSE 11.9-10.[62]

**THE WICKED DELIGHT IN THE DEATH OF GOD'S WITNESSES.** OECUMENIUS: And seeing the destruction of the witnesses, those from every nation who have been deceived by the antichrist will rejoice over them, as though their own king had conquered. That they exchange gifts is another indication of their glee and delight. It says, "Because the two prophets had been a torment to those living on the earth." [The prophets] will not torment them with any physical torment, but spiritually by mocking and reproving them for their sins and by making utterly clear their deceit. COMMENTARY ON THE APOCALYPSE 11.7-10.[63]

**THE IMPIOUS STRIVE TO REMOVE THE CHURCH FROM THE WORLD.** PRIMASIUS: The intentions are expressed by which the impious strive to remove the church of Christ from the world, as the psalmist says, "Let the name of Israel be remembered no more!"[64] And although they are unable to fulfill their desire, yet they make their evil intention known. COMMENTARY ON THE APOCALYPSE 11.9.[65]

**LET US PRAY THAT GOD REPROVE US.** ANDREW OF CAESAREA: Those Jews and Gentiles, who once were overpowered by the false wonders of the antichrist and who had indelibly engrafted that abominable name upon their hearts, prohibited the holy bodies from being buried, and they rejoiced because they were free from the torments that [the prophets] gave for their correction. For they did not acknowledge that "the Lord reproves him whom he loves,"[66]

---

[54]See Job 41:13. [55]Mt 24:9. [56]Lk 21:16. [57]Jn 15:20. [58]Rom 10:10. [59]CCL 121A:373-75. [60]Wis 2:15. [61]Ps 112:10 (111:10 LXX). [62]CCL 92:170. [63]TEG 8:166. [64]Ps 83:4 (82:5 LXX). [65]CCL 92:170. [66]Prov 3:12.

and that "he scourges every son whom he receives" and "by muzzle and bridle he will pull and tug at those who are not near to him."[67] And God works in this way so that they might turn from necessity into the straight way from which they turned aside when they were deceived. We must make petition of the Lord and pray, "It is good for me that I was afflicted, that I might learn your statutes,"[68] and "Turn us, O God of our salvation, that you do not enter into judg-ment with your servant."[69] "When we are judged by you, our beneficent master, we are chastened so that we may not be condemned along with the world"[70] but may rather through a few torments escape an eternal punishment. COMMENTARY ON THE APOCALYPSE, 11.9-10.[71]

---

[67]Ps 32:9 (31:9 LXX). [68]Ps 119:71 (118:71 LXX). [69]Ps 85:4 (84:5 LXX); cf. Ps 143:2 (142:2 LXX). [70]1 Cor 11:32. [71]MTS 1 Sup 1:115-16.

# 11:11-14 THE TWO WITNESSES RECEIVE THE BREATH OF LIFE

[11]*But after the three and a half days a breath of life from God entered them, and they stood up on their feet, and great fear fell on those who saw them.* [12]*Then they heard a loud voice from heaven saying to them, "Come up hither!" And in the sight of their foes they went up to heaven in a cloud.* [13]*And at that hour there was a great earthquake, and a tenth of the city fell; seven thousand people were killed in the earthquake, and the rest were terrified and gave glory to the God of heaven.*

[14]*The second woe has passed; behold, the third woe is soon to come.*

---

**OVERVIEW**: After three and a half days the two witnesses came alive through the breath of God. They rose up and ascended into heaven on the dominical chariot of the clouds (ANDREW OF CAESAREA). Their rising symbolizes the general resurrection at the time of the second coming of Christ, when those still alive are shaken at the sight of the rising of the dead. The rising of the two witnesses indicates also the separation of the just from the unjust at that time (TYCONIUS). Although at the end of time there may be a natural earthquake and the physical death of thousands, more likely these things are symbols of the change of the world's substance into something more secure and stable and of the eternal judg-ment of those who remained attached to the present life (ANDREW OF CAESAREA). It is also likely that the whole time of the church is indicated, for the church always suffers the earthquakes of persecution and the fall of perverse doctrine within it. Within the church there are two buildings, one laid upon the Rock and the other laid upon the sand. Those built upon the sand crumble at the violence of present dangers and are given over to punishment. Those built upon the Rock rejoice that they are free of the torments of punishment and increase in their obedience to the commandments (TYCONIUS).

### 11:11-12 A Breath of Life from God

**THE RISING OF THE WITNESSES.** TYCONIUS: "And they went up to heaven in a cloud." The apostle spoke of this, saying, "We will be caught up in the clouds to meet Christ in the air."[1] It is written that this cannot happen to anyone before the coming of the Lord,[2] since at his coming all flesh is approved to arise from their graves. And so the faulty idea of those is excluded who think that these two witnesses are only two men who ascend on the clouds before the coming of Christ. For how could those "who dwell on the earth" rejoice at the death of two men if they died in only one city? Or how do they "exchange presents" if in a short period of time those who threw their bodies in the streets were disquieted by their resurrection although shortly beforehand they were rejoicing at their death? Their courage and reason were stupefied because throughout the earth the announcement came not of their death but of their resurrection. What kind of joy would it be, or what kind of pleasure for those who are feasting would it be, if along with the feast there was the stench of the dead? "And a great fear fell on those who saw them." He says this of those who are alive when they see the resurrection of those who sleep and are shaken by a horrible fear. "And their enemies saw them [ascend]." Here he separates the unrighteous from the righteous and those who were steadfast in faith from those who were timid. COMMENTARY ON THE APOCALYPSE 11.11-12.[3]

**THE WITNESSES ASCEND.** ANDREW OF CAESAREA: Being dead for as many days as there were years of their prophecy, they will rise up and ascend into heaven on a cloud, that dominical chariot. And fear and perplexity will seize those who see it. COMMENTARY ON THE APOCALYPSE 11.11-12.[4]

## 11:13 The Rest Feared and Glorified God

**THE DEATH OF SINNERS.** TYCONIUS: "In that hour there was a great earthquake." By mentioning again the persecution, he confirms what he

had said above. The Lord also expressed an opinion that is in harmony with this passage. He said, "In that hour let him who is on the housetop not come down to take whatever is in the house, nor let him who is in the field turn back."[5] When he says "in that hour," he is indicating all time. "And a tenth of the city fell; seven thousand were killed in the earthquake." The number ten and the number seven are perfect. Even were it not the case, it would be fitting to understand the whole from the part. He says that a tenth of the city, that is, all of it, fell, along with its builders who allowed the construction of perverse doctrine in the temple of their hearts. For there are two kinds of structures in the church. One structure is laid upon the Rock. The other structure is founded upon the sand and is not able to withstand the onslaught of present dangers. Rather, it crumbles straightway and topples with it whoever had not kept the faith of the true church with a pure heart.[6] "The rest were terrified and gave glory to the God of heaven." These are those who have been laid upon the Rock. When the unrighteous are dying from the earthquake, these fear lest they also become partakers with the unrighteous in this punishment. And through the confession of the Christian name and by the despising of their souls, they glorify the Lord, since they have been spared the torments of the unrighteous. The saint sang of this when he said, "The righteous will rejoice when he sees vengeance; he will wash his hands in the blood of the sinner."[7] For when the righteous sees the death of the sinner, he increases all the more in obedience to the commandments and does them with greater joy and purity, since he is himself being freed from the punishments of the wicked. As it is written, "When a just man sees the wicked punished, he becomes wise."[8] COMMENTARY ON THE APOCALYPSE 11.13.[9]

---

[1]1 Thess 4:17. [2]Caesarius of Arles, who closely follows Tyconius, quotes here 1 Cor 15:23 (PL 35:2435). [3]TS 2 7:163-66 §§397-405. [4]MTS 1 Sup 1:117. [5]Mt 24:17-18; Lk 17:31. [6]See Mt 7:24-27. [7]Ps 58:10 Vg (LXX reads "he sees the vengeance of the ungodly"). [8]Prov 21:11. [9]TS 2 7:166-71 §§406-19.

**THE SECOND DEATH.** ANDREW OF CAESAREA: It is possible that these things will happen at that time in a physical way. But we think that the "earthquake" symbolizes the transposition of those things that are shaking and tottering to something more firm and secure. That a "tenth of the city" falls refers to the corpse of impiety, which was not wise in the seizing of those prophets. The "seven thousand" who are killed signify those who remained attached to the seven days of

the present life but did not wait for the eighth day of the resurrection and who must also be killed with "the second death" in Gehenna, namely, eternal punishment. Or, perhaps the seven thousand will be those Jews who were persuaded by the antichrist. COMMENTARY ON THE APOCALYPSE 11.13.[10]

---

[10]MTS 1 Sup 1:117-18.

---

## 11:15-18 THE SEVENTH TRUMPET

[15]Then the seventh angel blew his trumpet, and there were loud voices in heaven, saying, "The kingdom of the world has become the kingdom of our Lord and of his Christ, and he shall reign for ever and ever." [16]And the twenty-four elders who sit on their thrones before God fell on their faces and worshiped God, [17]saying,

"We give thanks to thee, Lord God Almighty, who art and who wast,
that thou hast taken thy great power and begun to reign.
[18]The nations raged, but thy wrath came,
and the time for the dead to be judged,
for rewarding thy servants, the prophets and saints,
and those who fear thy name, both small and great,
and for destroying the destroyers of the earth."

**OVERVIEW**: The seventh trumpet announces the day of judgment, the eternal sabbath and the dominion of the true King (BEDE). Although God is always king and is maker of all things, yet the voices in heaven proclaim him King because every rule upon the earth by people or by demons has ceased (OECUMENIUS). During the first coming of Christ, the nations raged and the wicked were in rebellion. But with the seventh trumpet, the day of divine wrath has come when God will reward the saints according to their merits and the evil according to their deeds (TYCONIUS, BEDE). While

in the past God exercised patience and long-suffering toward the unbelieving nations, they did not use God's kindness (OECUMENIUS, ANDREW OF CAESAREA). In the day of judgment, recompense is given to them and to the lesser saints and to the more eminent saints (ANDREW OF CAESAREA). At the sound of the seventh trumpet the neverending praise of the Holy Trinity by the church and the heavenly hosts is heard. (OECUMENIUS, TYCONIUS).

**11:15 The Seventh Angel Blew His Trumpet**

**GOD ALONE WILL RULE.** OECUMENIUS: By way of digression the vision related the attacks upon the two witnesses or prophets and discussed everything about them. The vision now returns to the previous narrative from which it departed. It has spoken of the future reward of the saints and that those from the nations were more numerous than those from Israel, and those who pleased God in the New Testament more numerous than those who pleased him in the Old Testament. And, it says, when the seventh angel blew his trumpet "there were voices in heaven saying, 'The kingdom of the world has become the kingdom of God and of his Christ.'" To be sure, God always is king and has never begun nor indeed shall ever cease to rule the heaven and the earth and that which is visible and invisible in them, for he is without beginning and without ending Master and Lord of all things. However, since also people take the title of "king" upon earth and after a manner God has those who reign with him, when the earthly kingdom of people is dissolved at the consummation of the present age, God alone will rule. And for this reason it says that "the kingdom of the world has become the kingdom of God and of his Christ," because those people who rule on the earth and the tyrannical demons have been destroyed and brought to an end. COMMENTARY ON THE APOCALYPSE 11.15-19.[1]

**ETERNAL SABBATH AND THE RULE OF THE TRUE KING.** BEDE: The seventh trumpet reveals the day of judgment in which the Lord will reward his own followers and banish those who have corrupted the earth. . . . The six previous trumpets, corresponding to the periods of the present age, proclaimed the course of the various struggles of the church. This seventh trumpet is the messenger of the eternal sabbath and of the victory and dominion of the true King. EXPLANATION OF THE APOCALYPSE 8.2, 11.15.[2]

## 11:16-18 The Elders Worship God

**ONE WHO CORRUPTS BAPTISM WILL BE**

**CORRUPTED.** TYCONIUS: He speaks of the beginning and the end. When he says, "You have begun to reign and the nations raged," he indicates the first coming, for at his birth Herod and the people of Jerusalem were troubled.[3] However, the time of the second coming is declared by wrath and judgment. . . . "Behold, the third woe has come," it says. By the sound of the trumpet of the seventh angel he refers to nothing other than the church, which is praising the Lord and is in the sound of the trumpet giving thanks to him without end. And from this we understand that the rewarding of those who are good is not without the punishment of the wicked. "To reward your saints and to corrupt the corrupters of the earth," it says. This means that [the Lord] gives to the righteous a recompense proper to their merits and to those who were corrupters he gives evil proper to their [wicked] deeds. For whoever has corrupted in himself the temple of the Lord, that is, the church of the body of Christ in baptism, he will without doubt be subjected to corruption. As the apostle said, "If anyone destroys God's temple, God will destroy him."[4] COMMENTARY ON THE APOCALYPSE 11.16-18.[5]

**THE REWARD OF THE GOOD.** TYCONIUS: He is now mentioning both the beginning and the end of the dispensation of Christ. For when he says, "You have begun to reign and the nations raged," he is speaking of the first coming of Christ. But, indeed, when it follows that "your wrath has come and the time of the dead," or as another translation has it, "at which time he will judge concerning the dead," he is speaking of the second coming, when the saints and the prophets and those who fear his name, the small and the great and the old and the young, will receive their reward. As it says, "Your eyes beheld my imperfection, and in your book everything will be written."[6] And lest the wicked think that they may act with impunity, he subjects to destruction whom-

---

[1]TEG 8:168. [2]CCL 121A:333, 383. [3]See Mt 2:3. [4]1 Cor 3:17. [5]TS 2 7:173-75 §§425-31. [6]Ps 139:16 (138:16 LXX).

ever has corrupted the earth. As the psalmist says, "The face of the Lord is against those who do evil."[7] It says that the third woe comes at the sound of the seventh angel, and when he sounded [his trumpet], only the church is mentioned as she praises the Lord and gives him thanks. And from this we learn that the recompense of the good is not apart from the woe of the wicked. And so the psalmist said, "When his wrath is quickly kindled," certainly upon the wicked, "blessed are all those who trust in him."[8] And so now the church herself says, "Your wrath has come and the time for death, to reward your servants," and following. This is the final woe. Since the bodily nativity of the Lord has been nicely recapitulated, he suggests that he is about to speak of the same things but in a different and more extensive manner. COMMENTARY ON THE APOCALYPSE 11.15-19.[9]

THE ELDERS PRAISE THE TRIUNE GOD. OECUMENIUS: When the voice was heard, "the elders worshiped God," bringing their own thanksgiving and saying, "We give you thanks, O God, the Almighty, who is and who was." The phrases *who is* and *who was* are fitting to be used of the holy Trinity, although usually *who is* is used of the Father and *who was* of the Son. For "to be" is true of the Father and of the Son and of the Holy Spirit, and we speak rightly when we say "was" of the Father and Son and Holy Spirit. Therefore, the thanksgiving of the elders is ascribed to the holy Trinity. For it says, "You have taken your great power" from those on the earth, and you have taken your rule which you gave to them, and you now alone rule. And since the earthly kingdom is destroyed, naturally "the nations raged," for they had been deprived of their dominion— by *nations* he speaks of the ranks of the demons and of unfaithful people. "But your wrath has come," it says, "and the lot of the nations to be judged and to give reward to your servants the prophets and the saints." Although, it says, you exercised great long-suffering toward them in the past, they made no use of your kindness, and

now, that is, in the day of judgment, you have brought your wrath against them, and that fate that has been determined for the nations has come and is present. And what is this? This, that they are judged and that recompense is given to the saints who had suffered evil from them, and that they who had corrupted the earth by polluting it with their sins be destroyed by the recompense of punishment. COMMENTARY ON THE APOCALYPSE 11.15-19.[10]

PRAISE TO CHRIST. ANDREW OF CAESAREA: Here again he says that the holy angels and those who live as do the angels send a hymn of thanksgiving to God, because for our sake he has become worthy to receive as man that kingdom that as God he possessed from the beginning. And having been patient with the unbelieving nations who were enraged at this as though it were a new and strange teaching, at the end he brings judgment upon them.... "The time of the dead" is the time of the resurrection of the dead, at which time recompense will be given to each, one after the other. In the "prophets and saints and those who fear God" we are perhaps to recognize the three orders of those who produce fruit a hundredfold, sixtyfold and thirtyfold.[11] However, certainly the apostles will receive the first place and sit upon the twelve thrones. We think that the "small and great" are either the lesser saints and those who are rather more preeminent than they, or the "small" are the sinners who are subjects of contempt and the "great" are the righteous. COMMENTARY ON THE APOCALYPSE 11.15-18.[12]

ALL THE NATIONS WILL BE GATHERED FOR JUDGMENT. BEDE: To be sure, from eternity you have reigned, although the wicked are in rebellion, but now their anger is suppressed and ceases to exist. For "the Lord reigns, let the people be angry."[13] "And the time for the dead to be judged

---

[7]Ps 34:16 (33:17 LXX). [8]Ps 2:12. [9]CCL 92:176-77. [10]TEG 8:168-69. [11]Mt 13:23. [12]MTS 1 Sup 1:119-20. [13]Ps 99:1 (98:1 LXX).

and for the rewarding of your servants," et cetera. This corresponds to the order we have in the Gospel narrative. First, all the nations are to be gathered before the judge; then those on the right will be placed in many mansions in the kingdom of the Father, while those on the left will be

tossed outside the limits of the kingdom and cast into the flames of their condemnation. EXPLANATION OF THE APOCALYPSE 11.16-18.[14]

[14]CCL 121A:383.

## 11:19 — 12:6 THE WOMAN WITH CHILD AND THE FIERY DRAGON

[19]*Then God's temple in heaven was opened, and the ark of his covenant was seen within his temple; and there were flashes of lightning, voices, peals of thunder, an earthquake, and heavy hail.*

12 *And a great portent appeared in heaven, a woman clothed with the sun, with the moon under her feet, and on her head a crown of twelve stars;* [2]*she was with child and she cried out in her pangs of birth, in anguish for delivery.* [3]*And another portent appeared in heaven; behold, a great red dragon, with seven heads and ten horns, and seven diadems upon his heads.* [4]*His tail swept down a third of the stars of heaven, and cast them to the earth. And the dragon stood before the woman who was about to bear a child, that he might devour her child when she brought it forth;* [5]*she brought forth a male child, one who is to rule all the nations with a rod of iron, but her child was caught up to God and to his throne,* [6]*and the woman fled into the wilderness, where she has a place prepared by God, in which to be nourished for one thousand two hundred and sixty days.*

**OVERVIEW**: The temple of God was opened when Christ the Lord was born, for the body of Christ is the temple of God (VICTORINUS, TYCONIUS, BEDE). When he came, Christ revealed the ark of the new covenant (TYCONIUS, BEDE), which is the preaching of the gospel and mercy for sins (VICTORINUS). Such preaching is done by the church which, as the body of Christ, holds within herself the ark of Christ's incarnation (TYCONIUS, BEDE). Revealed also are those blessings prepared for the saints which are now hidden in Christ (OECUMENIUS, ANDREW OF CAESAREA). At the same time heaven emits the thunder and the lightning of the punishments that will come upon the lawless

who like hail break themselves apart when they strike the faith of Christ (TYCONIUS, OECUMENIUS, ANDREW OF CAESAREA).

The mother of God is depicted in heaven, for she is pure in soul and body and wholly worthy of heaven. Yet the Virgin is fully human as we are and is clothed with the spiritual sun whom she bore in her womb (OECUMENIUS). The church too is adorned with heavenly glory, for she is clothed with the brightness of the Word (HIPPOLYTUS, METHODIUS) and carries the hope and promise of the resurrection to glory (VICTORINUS, CAESARIUS OF ARLES). The church stands upon the faith of those whom she has purified from corruption by

170

baptism (METHODIUS). She clings to the immoveable good and so by her love overcomes all that is changeable (PRIMASIUS). Crowned with the twelve apostles (HIPPOLYTUS, TYCONIUS), the church places under her feet all heretics (TYCONIUS, PRIMASIUS), hypocrites and fallen believers (CAESARIUS OF ARLES). Bearing within herself the incarnate Wisdom of God (PRIMASIUS), the church never ceases to preach the Word to an unbelieving world (HIPPOLYTUS) and to gather together the nations of the Gentiles (TYCONIUS). At the same time she gives spiritual birth to many through water and the Spirit (TYCONIUS, ANDREW OF CAESAREA), even as she excludes from herself, as though by miscarriage, those who fall from the true Light (ANDREW OF CAESAREA). In her own way, too, Mary was in anguish, for she blushed before Joseph and was faint of heart until the holy angel revealed to him that the child in her womb was of the Holy Spirit (OECUMENIUS).

Opposed to Christ and his church is Satan, who has fallen from heaven and who is full of murder, bloodthirstiness and oppression (VICTORINUS, OECUMENIUS). It was he who enflamed the envy of Herod (TYCONIUS), and he remains always in hostile opposition to the Spirit and to the law (ANDREW OF CAESAREA). Satan caused many other angels to fall with him from heaven (VICTORINUS, OECUMENIUS), and he now causes many to fall away from the brightness of their baptism (METHODIUS, ANDREW OF CAESAREA). Such persons become false prophets who cause the simple to fall (TYCONIUS), or they become heretics who pervert the doctrine of the Trinity (METHODIUS) or bring others to the falsehood of a second baptism (CAESARIUS OF ARLES). Murderous from the beginning, Satan incited Herod to kill the baby Jesus (TYCONIUS, OECUMENIUS, PRIMASIUS), and he attempted to subject Jesus to death by tempting him (VICTORINUS). As Christ suffered through the work of Satan, so now his church suffers that which her Head has suffered (TYCONIUS), and in the suffering of his church Christ continues also to suffer (ANDREW OF CAESAREA). Yet in these sufferings the church brings

forth Christ (TYCONIUS) even as she does through the sacred washing of baptism. As Mary remained virginal in the birth of Christ, the church too remains inviolate in her giving birth in baptism and in the sufferings of her members (QUODVULTDEUS). As the Christ child was saved from Herod by the Father's providential care (OECUMENIUS), the saints are preserved in the midst of temptations lest they succumb to difficulties (ANDREW OF CAESAREA).

The church also participates in the ascension of Christ. For as Christ ascended into heaven and rules the nations (VICTORINUS), the church brings forth heavenly kings and becomes the instructor of the nations (HIPPOLYTUS). Through baptism the church gives birth to children who bear the image and the virility of Christ (METHODIUS), for they conquer the devil (TYCONIUS) and are not weakened by unworthy desires (ANDREW OF CAESAREA). The church sits in heavenly places (PRIMASIUS), and for that reason she tramples upon the scorpions of impiety and the serpents of arrogance (TYCONIUS, CAESARIUS OF ARLES). Moreover, the church dwells in the garden of virtue, where she lives in the perfect knowledge of the holy Trinity (METHODIUS), and she sends monks into the desert, where they escape the assaults of evil people and demons (ANDREW OF CAESAREA), just as once Mary escaped Herod by fleeing to Egypt (OECUMENIUS).

## 11:19 Lightning, Voices, Thunder, Earthquake, Hail

**THE GOSPEL AND MERCY FOR SINS.** VICTORINUS OF PETOVIUM: That "the temple of God which is in heaven was opened" signifies the appearance of our Lord. For the temple of God is his Son, as he said, "Destroy this temple and in three days I will raise it up." And when the Jews said, "It was built in forty-six years," the Evangelist said, "He was speaking of the temple of [his] body."[1] The "ark of the covenant" is the preaching

---

[1]Jn 2:19-21.

of the gospel and mercy for sins and everything whatsoever which will have come with him. That, he says, appeared. COMMENTARY ON THE APOCALYPSE 11.6.[2]

### THE CHURCH BEARS THE MYSTERY OF THE INCARNATION OF CHRIST. TYCONIUS: When

Christ the Lord was born, the temple of God was manifested in heaven, that is, in the church. The temple of God can be understood as the body of Christ, as the Lord himself said, "Destroy this temple and in three days I will raise it up."[3] . . . Although the ark often signifies the church, here the ark is said to have appeared in the temple, and by adding the "ark of the covenant," he indicates that there is something more exalted to be comprehended. Moreover, by saying "in heaven" he urges us to penetrate some mystery, so that this might be understood: the temple is the church, and the ark of the covenant is the mystery of the incarnation of Christ, who, like that ark, bore the tablets of the covenant within himself. For he came not to destroy the Law but to fulfill it,[4] . . . as God promised through Jeremiah that the ark of the covenant would be taken from human hearts, certainly referring to that ark of the Hebrews, which was in Jerusalem. That is, [he promises] that the church will be called the throne of the Lord. He says, "When you have multiplied and increased in the land, says the Lord, they will no longer say 'the ark of the covenant of the Lord,' nor will it come to mind. In those days and at that time they will call Jerusalem the throne of the Lord, and all nations will be gathered to her in the name of the Lord."[5] . . . The lightning is those virtues by which Christ the Lord makes his apostles to shine. The voices and the thunder are the preaching of the apostles, who thunder to the peoples as though they were clouds. Hail always harms itself when it dashes against fruit and breaks apart, and it diminishes itself even as it causes ruin. So also the fierce multitude of the Gentiles persecutes the faith of Christ, yet afterward are themselves broken apart and become smaller or nonexistent. COMMEN-

TARY ON THE APOCALYPSE 11.19.[6]

### THE SAINTS RECEIVE KNOWLEDGE PREVIOUSLY HIDDEN. OECUMENIUS: "And the temple

of God in heaven was opened," it says, "and the ark of his covenant was seen in his temple." When this had been said, those good things, which had been hidden, and in addition certain new mysteries were seen by the saints. For this is the significance of the ark of the covenant being opened. And [Paul] shows that the good things of the coming age are hidden from people at the present time by saying, "What no eye has seen, nor ear heard, nor the heart of man conceived, that God has prepared for those who love him."[7] And that there will be certain mysteries and another knowledge that is now unknown, the Lord shows when he said, "I shall not drink again of this fruit of the vine until that day when I drink it new with you in my Father's kingdom."[8] While the saints have been thought worthy of these things, for the sinners "there were flashes of lightning, voices, and thunder, earthquakes and heavy hail." This is the third woe. From that which is familiar to us, the passage depicts those punishments and terrors from God that come upon the wicked. COMMENTARY ON THE APOCALYPSE 11.15-19.[9]

### PUNISHMENT WILL FALL ON THE LAWLESS.

ANDREW OF CAESAREA: By the opening of heaven and the vision of the covenant is shown the revelation of those blessings that have been prepared for the saints. According to the apostle, these blessings are hidden in Christ in whom the fullness of deity dwells bodily.[10] And these things will be revealed when the punishments of Gehenna rain down upon the lawless and impious like terrifying voices and lightnings and thunder and hail. The earthquake signifies the transposition of present things. COMMENTARY ON THE APOCALYPSE 11.19.[11]

---

[2]CSEL 49:104. [3]Jn 2:19. [4]See Mt 5:17. [5]Jer 3:16-17. [6]CCL 92:177-78. [7]1 Cor 2:9. [8]Mt 26:29. [9]TEG 8:169-70. [10]Col 2:3, 9. [11]MTS 1 Sup 1:120-21.

**CHRIST'S DIVINITY WAS HIDDEN IN HIS BODY.** BEDE: Formerly the temple of the Lord on the earth contained the ark of the covenant hidden behind the mystical veil. However, since the veil of the ancient temple and the wall of partition have now been torn asunder by the sword of the blood of the Lord, in the church, the temple of the living God whose citizenship is in heaven, the ark of his incarnation is laid open to all the world. For just as the manna from heaven was in a pure gold [container], so is his divinity in his holy body. EXPLANATION OF THE APOCALYPSE 11.19.[12]

### 12:1 A Woman Clothed with the Sun

**THE CHURCH IS ADORNED WITH HEAVENLY GLORY.** HIPPOLYTUS: By the "woman clothed with the sun," he meant most manifestly the church, endued with the Father's Word, whose brightness is above the sun. And by "the moon under her feet," he referred to [the church] being adorned, like the moon, with heavenly glory. And the words "upon her head a crown of twelve stars" refer to the twelve apostles by whom the church was founded. ON THE ANTICHRIST 61.[13]

**THE ANCIENT SAINTS WILL RISE.** VICTORINUS OF PETOVIUM: This is the ancient church of the fathers and the prophets and the holy apostles. For they experience the groans and torments of their desire until that which was long since promised was fulfilled out of their own people and according to their own flesh. That [the woman] was "clothed with the sun" signifies the hope of the resurrection and the promise of glory. The "moon" refers to the fall of the bodies of the saints on account of their irreversible debt to death which can never fail. For just as the life of people is diminished and so again is increased, so also the hope of the sleeping is never utterly extinguished, as some think, but in their darkness they will have light as of the moon. The "crown of twelve stars" indicates the [crown] of the fathers[14] from whom the spirit[15] was to

assume flesh, according to the birth of the flesh. COMMENTARY ON THE APOCALYPSE 12.1.[16]

**THE CHURCH LABORS TO BRING FORTH A PERFECT NEW BIRTH.** METHODIUS: The woman who "appeared in heaven clothed with the sun" and crowned with "twelve stars" and with the moon as her footstool, "travailing in birth and in pain to be delivered," . . . is properly and in the exact sense of the term our mother, a power in herself distinct from her children, whom the prophets have, according to the aspect of their message, sometimes called Jerusalem, sometimes the Bride, sometimes Mount Zion, and sometimes the Temple and God's Tabernacle. She is the force mentioned by the prophet, whom the Spirit urges to be enlightened, crying out to her, "Be enlightened, O Jerusalem, for your light is come, and the glory of the Lord is risen upon you. Behold, darkness and storm clouds shall cover the earth, they shall cover the people; but the Lord shall appear upon you, and the Lord's glory shall be seen upon you. And kings shall walk in your light, and nations in your brightness. Lift up your eyes round about, and see your children gathered together. All your sons have come from afar, and your daughters shall rise up at your side."[17] It is the church whose children by baptism will swiftly come running to her from all sides after the resurrection. [The church] it is who rejoices to receive the light that knows no evening, clothed as she is in the brightness of the Word as with a robe. Surely, having light for its garment, what was there more precious or more honorable for [the church] to be clothed in as befitted a queen, to be led as a bride to the Lord, and thus to be called on by the Spirit? Continuing therefore, I beg you to consider this great woman as representing virgins prepared for marriage, as she gleams in pure and wholly unsullied and abiding beauty, emulating the brilliance of the lights.

---

[12]CCL 121A:385. [13]ANF 5:217. [14]Presumably the twelve patriarchs. [15]Victorinus-Jerome reads "Christ." "Spirit" here probably refers to the deity of Christ. [16]CSEL 49:106. [17]Is 60:1-4.

For her robe, she is clothed in pure light; instead of jewels, her head is adorned with shining stars. For this light is for her what clothing is for us. And she uses the stars as we do gold and brilliant gems; but her stars are not like those visible to us on earth, but finer and brighter ones, such that our own are merely their copies and representations. And her standing on the moon, I think, refers by way of allegory to the faith of those who have been purified from corruption by baptism; for moonlight is rather like lukewarm water, and all moist substance depends upon the moon. Thus the church stands on the faith and our adoption—signified here by the moon—"until the fullness of the Gentiles shall come in,"[18] laboring and bringing forth natural people as spiritual people, and under this aspect is she indeed their mother. For just as a woman receives the unformed seed of her husband and after a period of time brings forth a perfect human being, so too the church, one might say, constantly conceiving those who take refuge in the Word, and shaping them according to the likeness and form of Christ, after a certain time makes them citizens of that blessed age. Hence it is necessary that she should stand upon the laver as the mother of those who are washed. So too, the function she exercises over the laver is called the moon because those who are thus reborn and renewed shine with a new glow, that is, with a new light; and hence too they are designated by the expression "the newly enlightened," and she continues to reveal to them the spiritual full moon in her periodic representation of his passion,[19] until the full glow and light of the great day shall appear. Sym-posium 8.5-6.[20]

**THE CHURCH OF THE HERETICS IS NOT GLO-RIFIED BY CHRIST'S PRESENCE.** TYCONIUS: "And a great sign was seen in heaven." We now see that which has occurred in the church, God has taken form in man. "A woman," it says, "clothed with the sun, and the moon under her feet." We have already noted that a genus may divide into many species. For what [in one pas-sage] is heaven, here signifies the temple placed in heaven. In the woman he indicates the church who in the purification of baptism puts on Christ, the "sun of righteousness,"[21] as the apostle Paul testifies, "As many as were baptized into Christ have put on Christ."[22] However, in this passage the moon is described as placed under the feet of the woman and so indicates the church of the heretics that the "sun of righteousness," that is, Christ, does not allow to be illumined by his presence. Yet, since everything which is found in the Scriptures concerning the church may be interpreted in a twofold way, we can also interpret the moon in a good sense and compare it with the church. As it is written in the psalms, "Once I have sworn by my holiness; I will not lie to David. His seed shall endure forever. His throne [will endure] as the sun before me and as a full moon forever. The witness in the skies is sure."[23] And again, "Bright as the sun and fair as the moon in her beauty."[24] "And on her head a crown of twelve stars." He is indicating the twelve apostles whom Christ placed as a crown over the twelve tribes of Israel upon the head of his church and adorned her with spiritual gems. COMMEN-TARY ON THE APOCALYPSE 12.1.[25]

**THE MOTHER OF GOD PORTRAYED AS A CITI-ZEN OF HEAVEN.** OECUMENIUS: The vision intends to describe more completely to us the cir-cumstances concerning the antichrist. . . . How-ever, since the incarnation of the Lord, which made the world his possession and subjected it, provided a pretext for Satan to raise this one up and to choose him [as his instrument]—for the antichrist will be raised to cause the world again to fall from Christ and to persuade it to desert to Satan—and since moreover his fleshly concep-tion and birth was the beginning of the incarna-tion of the Lord, the vision gives a certain order

---

[18]Rom 11:25. [19]This refers to the celebration of the Eucharist, or, more specifically, to the liturgy of Holy Week. [20]ACW 27:110-12*. In his commentary, Andrew of Caesarea follows Methodius and quotes him extensively. [21]See Mal 4:2. [22]Gal 3:27. [23]Ps 89:35-37 (88:36-38 LXX). [24]Song 6:10. [25]TS 2 7:178-80 §§440-49.

and sequence to the material that it is going to discuss and begins the discussion from the fleshly conception of the Lord by portraying for us the mother of God. What does he say? "And a sign appeared in heaven, a woman clothed with the sun and the moon was under her feet." As we said, it is speaking about the mother of our Savior. The vision appropriately depicts her as in heaven and not on the earth, for she is pure in soul and body, equal to an angel and a citizen of heaven. She possesses God who rests in heaven —"for heaven is my throne," it says—yet she is flesh, although she has nothing in common with the earth nor is there any evil in her. Rather, she is exalted, wholly worthy of heaven, even though she possesses our own human nature and substance. For the Virgin is consubstantial with us. Let the impious teaching of Eutyches, which makes the fanciful claim that the Virgin is of another substance than we, be excluded from the belief of the holy courts together with his other opinions. And what does it mean that she was clothed with the sun and the moon was under her feet? The holy prophet, Habakkuk, prophesied concerning the Lord, saying, "The sun was lifted up, and the moon stood still in its place for light,"[26] calling Christ our Savior, or at least the proclamation of the gospel, the "sun of righteousness."[27] When he was exalted and increased, the moon—that is, the law of Moses—"stood still" and no longer received any addition. For after the appearance of Christ, it no longer received proselytes from the nations as before but endured diminution and cessation. You will, therefore, observe this with me, that also the holy Virgin is covered by the spiritual sun. For this is what the prophet calls the Lord when concerning Israel he says, "Fire fell upon them, and they did not see the sun."[28] But the moon, that is, the worship and citizenship according to the law, being subdued and become much less than itself, is under her feet, for it has been conquered by the brightness of the gospel. And rightly does he call the things of the law by the word *moon*, for they have been given light by the sun, that is, Christ,

just as the physical moon is given its light by the physical sun. The point would have been better made had it said not that the woman was clothed with the sun but that the woman enclothed the sun, which was enclosed in her womb. However, that the vision might show that the Lord, who was being carried in the womb, was the shelter of his own mother and the whole creation, it says that he was enclothing the woman. Indeed, the holy angel said something similar to the holy Virgin: "The Spirit of the Lord will come upon you, and the power of the Most High will overshadow you."[29] For to overshadow is to protect, and to enclothe is the same according to power. COMMENTARY ON THE APOCALYPSE 12.1-2.[30]

**THE CHURCH OVERCOMES ALL THAT IS MUTABLE.** PRIMASIUS: This is what now appears in the church, namely, that by the operation of the Holy Spirit the human nature is joined to the Wisdom of God and that from the two the selfsame Christ becomes the mediator of God and humanity and is so proclaimed and believed. As he himself said, "Destroy this temple, and in three days I will raise it up,"[31] and the Evangelist said, "He was speaking of the temple of his body."[32] "A woman clothed with the sun, with the moon under her feet." It is frequently said that a genus is divided into many species which are the same thing. For what was heaven itself is now a temple in heaven and now is the woman clothed with the sun and having the moon under her feet. Namely, this is the church who has put on Christ and on account of her love is trampling upon every mutable thing. For [the church] is not enraptured by these changeable things who, clinging to the immoveable good, says truthfully, "But for me it is good to be near to God."[33] From this fact comes those expressions which we read concerning the church, "fair as the moon, bright as the sun,"[34] and again, "as the full moon forever, and the witness in the heaven is

---

[26]Hab 3:11. [27]Mal 4:2. [28]Ps 57:9 LXX. [29]Lk 1:35. [30]TEG 8:170-72. [31]Jn 2:19. [32]Jn 2:21. [33]Ps 73:28 (72:28 LXX). [34]Song 6:10.

true."[35] He aptly says that the church is a sojourner, for after the human birth of Christ we see many false opinions expressed by heretics. For concerning this temple the heresiarchs, falsifying as they willed, taught variously, Valentinus saying one thing and Bardesanes another, Apollinaris yet another and Nestorius another, Eutyches another and Timothy Aelurus another. It was as though truth sprang from the earth and controversies followed. And from all of this the orthodox and faithful acquired their reward, while by evil ideas concerning the incarnation of Christ, the heretics incurred the punishment of eternal damnation. COMMENTARY ON THE APOCALYPSE 12.1.[36]

**HYPOCRITES AND EVIL CHRISTIANS.** CAESARIUS OF ARLES: [The moon under her feet] refers to the hypocrites and evil Christians which the church has under her feet. . . . The twelve stars are to be interpreted as the twelve apostles. That the woman is clothed in the sun signifies her hope in the resurrection. For this reason it is written, "then the righteous will shine like the sun in the kingdom of their Father."[37] EXPOSITION OF THE APOCALYPSE 12.1, HOMILY 9.[38]

## 12:2 She Cried Out in Childbirth

**THE CHURCH WILL NOT CEASE TO PREACH THE WORD.** HIPPOLYTUS: [The words that she was with child and cried out in anguish for delivery] mean that the church will not cease to bear from its heart the Word that is persecuted by the unbelieving in the world. ON THE ANTICHRIST 61.[39]

**THE CHURCH GATHERS THE NATIONS.** TYCONIUS: "She was with child and cried out in pangs of birth." This means that by her preaching [the church] desires to gather together the nations of the Gentiles. "She is in anguish for delivery" as long as [the church] is either gathering together the multitude of the Gentiles or is excluding the hypocrites from its womb. COMMENTARY ON THE APOCALYPSE 12.2.[40]

**THE CHURCH SUFFERS FOR HER CHILDREN.** TYCONIUS: "She was with child," not in her womb but in her mind, "and she cried out, groaning (in the valley of tears) and was in anguish that she might deliver." The church spiritually gives birth to those with whom she is in the pangs of childbirth, but she also never ceases to be in the pangs of childbirth with those to whom she has already given birth. For this reason the apostle says, "My little children, with whom I am again in travail until Christ be formed in you."[41] COMMENTARY ON THE APOCALYPSE 12.2.[42]

**MARY BLUSHED BEFORE JOSEPH.** OECUMENIUS: "And she was with child," it says, "and she cried out in her pangs of birth, in anguish for delivery." Clearly Isaiah speaks concerning her: "Before she was in labor she gave birth; before the pain of her labor she fled and gave birth to a son."[43] Also in his thirteenth homily on the Song concerning the Lord, Gregory says, "whose pregnancy remains without union, and the childbirth without defilement, and the labor free of pain."[44] If according to such a prophet and to such a teacher of the church the Virgin escaped the pain of childbirth, how is it that here it says "she cried out in her pangs of birth, in anguish for delivery"? What is said is not contradictory. By no means! For there would be nothing contradictory said by the same Spirit who was speaking through both. Rather, you will understand the present phrase "she cried out and was in anguish" is this way. Until the holy angel said to Joseph that that which was borne in her womb was of the Holy Spirit, she was faint of heart, as is natural for a virgin, and she blushed before her betrothed and thought that perhaps from the secrecy of the marriage he might think that she was in labor. And so, according to the rules of figurative language, he calls this faintheartedness and sorrow a

---

[35]Ps 89:37 (88:38 LXX). Primasius follows Tyconius to this point. [36]CCL 92:179-80. [37]Mt 13:43. [38]PL 35:2434. [39]ANF 5:217. [40]TS 2 7:180 §§450-51. [41]Gal 4:19. [42]CCL 92:180. [43]Is 66:7 LXX. [44]Gregory of Nyssa Homilies on the Song of Songs 13 (PG 44:1053).

"crying out" and "anguish." Nor is this unusual. For even to the blessed Moses, when he was spiritually conversing with God and losing heart—for he saw Israel in the desert surrounded by the sea and the enemy—God said, "Why are you crying to me?"[45] So also here, the vision calls the troubled disposition of the Virgin in her mind and heart a "crying out." But may you, who by your unspeakable birth did bring to an end the faintheartedness of your undefiled servant, your mother according to the flesh, but my mistress, the holy mother of God, also forgive my sins. For it is proper to give you glory forever. Amen. COMMENTARY ON THE APOCALYPSE 12.1-2.[46]

**THOSE WHO FALL FROM CHRIST ARE MIS-CARRIAGES.** ANDREW OF CAESAREA: We say that the church is in birth pangs for each one of those who are being born anew through water and the Spirit, "until Christ is formed in them," as the apostle says.[47] Those who have fallen from the true light of Christ are regarded as miscarriages and experience death at the end of their life because of unfaithfulness. COMMENTARY ON THE APOCALYPSE 12.2.[48]

## 12:3 A Red Dragon

**RED FROM MURDER AND OPPRESSION.** VICTORINUS OF PETOVIUM: It says that [the dragon] was the color of red, that is, of scarlet, for the fruit of his work has given him such a color. For he was a murderer from the beginning,[49] and everywhere he has oppressed the whole race of people, not so much by the debt of death as through all kinds of miseries. The "seven heads" are the seven Roman kings from whom the antichrist comes; . . . the "ten horns" are the ten kings at the end of time. COMMENTARY ON THE APOCALYPSE 12.3.[50]

**THE DEVIL INFLAMED HEROD WITH ENVY.** TYCONIUS: [The red dragon] is the devil. He says that there was "another portent" to indicate the hostile opposition of the devil. It was he who inflamed Herod with the fire of envy so that he would feign to adore the Christ even while seeking with all his power to kill Christ whom he knew was to be born king of the Jews. . . . The "seven heads" are kings, and the horns are kingdoms. . . . For in the seven heads and seven diadems he signifies the rule of all kings, while in the ten horns we have the number of the ten persecutors who will fan the fires of persecution against the whole church in the last times. COMMENTARY ON THE APOCALYPSE 12.3.[51]

**SATAN CAST FROM HEAVEN.** OECUMENIUS: The vision now intends to depict more fully the events around the coming of the antichrist, starting with an event even prior to those mentioned earlier (I refer to the birth of the Lord). It speaks now of the casting of Satan down of heaven. . . . "And another sign appeared in heaven." As though rebuking Satan, that author of evil, who although a heavenly being became base because of his pride, the passage shows him first in heaven, so that the apostate might know from what heights to what depths he has fallen. "Behold, a great red dragon," it says. He calls Satan a "dragon" because of his deceitful ways. Isaiah also speaks of him in this way, saying, "against the dragon, that twisting serpent."[52] He is said to be red because of his thirst for blood and his angry nature. He had "seven heads and ten horns and seven diadems upon his heads." The prophet also knew that he had many heads, and therefore he says to God, "You have crushed the heads of the dragon; you did give him as food to the people of Ethiopia."[53] It refers to him as having many heads, since, as we have often noted, seven signifies many, for he exercises many dominions and performs many crafty plots against people by which he enslaves them. The diadem too is a symbol of tyranny, and the ten horns signify his very great power, for the number ten is perfect and the horn

---

[45]Ex 14:15. [46]TEG 8:172-73. [47]Gal 4:19. [48]MTS 1 Sup 1:123. [49]Jn 8:44. [50]CSEL 49:110. [51]TS 2 7:181-82 §§453-57. [52]Is 27:1. [53]Ps 73:14 LXX.

is a symbol of power. For it is said, "My horn will be exalted like that of a wild ox."[54] And one may learn that he is powerful by reading the book of Job. Commentary on the Apocalypse 12.3-6.[55]

### Opposed to the Spirit and the Law.

Andrew of Caesarea: Here we think that "heaven" signifies the air, and that the "red dragon" is that creature that was deceived and mocked by the angels of God, as it is written in Job.[56] He is "red" either because of his murderous and bloodthirsty character or because of the fiery nature of his angelic essence, since he did fall from the angels. The seven heads that he has are seven powers more wicked than himself and that are opposed to the [seven] powers of the Spirit. Or perhaps they correspond to the seven spirits of whom Christ spoke in the Gospels and that established themselves in the man who had a heart swept clean and emptied of good thoughts and deeds.[57] Or perhaps they are the seven evils that Solomon says are in the heart of the evil one, who with a great voice deceitfully seeks followers for himself.[58] The horns signify either those sins that are in opposition to the Ten Commandments of the law, or they signify the divisions of the kingdom that bring credit to him who rejoices in seditions. And there are "seven diadems upon his heads," since those who conquer the demonical powers receive again the crowns of victory, since they have gained victory with toils and sweat. Commentary on the Apocalypse 12.3.[59]

## 12:4a His Tail Swept Down a Third of the Stars

### The Dragon Causes Heretics to Fall.

Methodius: The great red dragon, cunning, wily, with seven heads, and horned, that drags down the third part of the stars and lies in wait to devour the child of the woman in labor, is the devil, who lies in ambush to abuse the mind of the illumined faithful who are Christ's possession and to destroy the clear image and representation of the Word that has been begotten in them. But

he misses and loses his prey, for the reborn are snatched up on high to the throne of God: that is, the minds of those who have been renewed are raised up to the divine throne and to the irrefragable foundation of truth, being taught to try to see and to picture to themselves the things of that world and not to be tricked by the dragon who tries to prevail over them. For he is not permitted to destroy those who look upwards and are turned toward heaven. The stars that he touches with the tip of his tail and draws down to earth are the seditious groups of heresies. For the dark, faint and low-circling stars are to be explained as the assemblages of the heretics. They too, of course, profess to be proficient in heavenly things and to believe in Christ, to have the abode of their soul in the heavens and to draw near to the stars as children of light. But they are swept down and driven away by the dragon's coils, because they did not abide within the triangular forms of religion and were mistaken with regard to its orthodox practice. Thus, too, are they called a "third part of the stars," because they have gone astray with respect to one of the numbers of the Trinity: as, for example, with regard to the Father, a man like Sabellius, who claimed that it was the almighty Father himself who suffered; with regard to the Son, such as Artemas and those who claimed that he was manifested in appearance only; and with regard to the Spirit, such as the Ebionites, who contend that the prophets spoke only by their own power. Indeed, there is Marcion, Valentinus, Elchasai and his disciples, and the rest. Symposium 8.10.[60]

### The Devil Seduced Many Angels to Fall.

Victorinus of Petovium: That "the tail of the dragon swept down a third of the stars" may be understood in a twofold way. Many understand this to mean that he was able to seduce a third of the believers. However, this may be more truthfully understood to mean that he [seduced] a

---

[54]Ps 92:10 (91:11 LXX). [55]TEG 8:174-75. [56]Cf. Job 40—41. [57]Mt 12:43-45. [58]Prov 26:25. [59]MTS 1 Sup 1:123-24. [60]ACW 27:115-16.

third of the angels who were subordinated to him while he was yet prince and [fell] when he toppled from his position. COMMENTARY ON THE APOCALYPSE 12.7.[61]

### FALSE PROPHETS DESTROY SIMPLE PERSONS.

TYCONIUS: The "tail" is the iniquitous prophets who throw down to earth the stars of heaven, namely, those simple persons who join themselves to them. When he speaks of "a third part of the stars," he is speaking of the Jews and their leaders who rejected Christ and with impious voices cried out that they did not want Christ to be over them but rather Caesar, and therefore they killed him. COMMENTARY ON THE APOCALYPSE 12.4.[62]

### THE ARROGANCE OF SATAN. OECUMENIUS:

"And his tail swept down a third of the stars of heaven and cast them to the earth." Along with himself, [the devil] cast down a very great number of angels. For he had persuaded them to apostatize from God and so made those who were heavenly to become earthly and those who were bright as stars to become dark. "By his tail" is as though to say "by his rear parts and his hindermost transgressions," for at first devising rebellion and apostasy, he thoroughly reviewed this in the arrogance of his mind and so came also to the corruption of the others. COMMENTARY ON THE APOCALYPSE 12.3-6.[63]

### FALSE PROPHETS CAUSE MANY TO FALL. CAE-

SARIUS OF ARLES: The tail symbolizes the evil prophets, that is, heretics who threw down to earth those stars of heaven who joined them through a repeated baptism. They are under the feet of the woman. Many believed that these are persons whom the devil made his companions since they were of the same mind as he. Many believe that these are angels who were thrown down with him when he fell. EXPOSITION ON THE APOCALYPSE 12.4, HOMILY 9.[64]

### THE DEVIL CAUSES MANY TO FALL. ANDREW

OF CAESAREA: It is our opinion that this passage refers either to the former fall of [the devil] from heaven which through a final movement of envy—for elevation was first—brought down with him the apostate angels, or to that movement of his tail which, after the crushing of his head, drags down those who have moved from their heavenly minds. They are figuratively called "stars" because of the brightness of their baptism. COMMENTARY ON THE APOCALYPSE 12.4.[65]

## 12:4b *That the Dragon Might Devour Her Child*

### THE DEVIL COULD NOT SUBJECT CHRIST TO

DEATH. VICTORINUS OF PETOVIUM: "The red dragon stood expecting to devour her son when she had delivered him." This is the devil, namely, that fugitive angel who thought that the destruction of all people could be equally accomplished through death. However, he who was not born from seed owed no debt to death, and for this reason [the devil] was not able to devour him, that is, to subject him to death. For, indeed, [the devil] had come to him intending to tempt him as man. But when he had discovered that he was not whom he thought, "he departed from him," it says, "until an opportune time."[66] COMMENTARY ON THE APOCALYPSE 12.2.[67]

### EVERY CHRISTIAN SUFFERS WHAT THE HEAD

HAS SUFFERED. TYCONIUS: Whenever the Holy Spirit promises and tells of future events, he foretells and shows the future in the church as past event. For in her misfortunes the church is always bringing forth Christ, for which reason he promises the coming of the Son of man always in the reality of similar sufferings. The devil in heaven is always seeking to devour that person who is being born through heavenly things and who is

---

[61]CSEL 49:116. [62]TS 2 7:183 §§459-60. [63]TEG 8:175-76. [64]PL 35:2434. [65]MTS 1 Sup 1:125-26. [66]Lk 4:13. At the temptation in the desert, Satan learns of Christ's true identity (also Irenaeus *Against Heresies* 5.21-22). [67]CSEL 49:106-8.

born to God and is caught up to his throne. Indeed, every Christian suffers that which the Head has suffered, who after the third day was going to be raised in glory. For in the person of Herod the whole company of persecutors is revealed. Although Herod alone had died, nonetheless all are indicated, for the Evangelist said, "All who sought the child's life are dead."[68] The Lord spoke similarly also to Moses, "All those who were seeking your life are dead,"[69] when another had succeeded [that] pharoah who had sought his life and that of the people. COMMENTARY ON THE APOCALYPSE 12.4.[70]

### WHAT EVE BOUND THROUGH DISOBEDIENCE, MOTHER CHURCH LOOSENS THROUGH OBEDIENCE.

QUODVULTDEUS: Our holy mother church has received you in her womb through the most sacred sign of the cross and with the greatest joy will give birth spiritually as she did also with your brothers. As new and future offspring of such a mother, until she restores to the true Light those born anew through the sacred washing, she feeds in her womb those whom she is carrying with suitable food, and she who is joyful leads those who are joyful to the day of their birth. She does not possess the mind and thought of Eve, who in sadness and in groaning brings forth sons who are themselves without joy but full of lamentation. What that [mother] bound, this [mother] has loosened, so that as [Eve] gave over to death her offspring through her disobedience, this [mother] restores to life through her obedience. All the mysteries that have been done and are being done among you through the ministry of the servants of God—the exorcisms, prayers, spiritual songs, insufflations,[71] the coarse garment, the bowing of the neck, the humility of the feet—all of these things, as I have said, are food that refreshes us in the womb and makes us strong, so that when we have been reborn through baptism, our mother might bring us happy to Christ. And you have received the symbol, the protection of her who desires to bring you to birth against the poison of the serpent. It

is written in the Apocalypse of the apostle John that the dragon stood before a woman who was about to give birth, so that when she gave birth, he might devour her child. We all know that the dragon is the devil and that that woman signifies the Virgin Mary, who remaining intact gave birth to our Head who was complete. She herself presents in herself a figure of the holy church, so that just as she remained a virgin while giving birth to a son, so also [the church] at all times brings forth his members without losing her virginity. ON THE SYMBOL 3.1.1-6.[72]

### SATAN ATTEMPTED TO KILL THE BABY JESUS THROUGH HEROD.

OECUMENIUS: "And the dragon stood before the woman who was about to bear a child, that he might devour her child when she brought it forth." He is speaking of events in the Lord's life. Since he who was to destroy his [i.e., Satan's] dominion was going to be born, [Satan] watched with close attention, so that when the Virgin gave birth, he might kill the child. And so, too, he took no chances but incited Herod, a lascivious man with a harem of women, to destroy the male and manly child. For Isaiah proclaims to us, "Before the child knows how to cry 'father' or 'mother,' he will take the power of Damascus and the spoils of Samaria before the king of Assyria."[73] COMMENTARY ON THE APOCALYPSE 12.3-6.[74]

### THE APOSTATE PERSECUTES CHRIST.

ANDREW OF CAESAREA: The apostate always arms himself against the church, desiring to make those food for himself who are being born anew from her. Rather, through the church he persecutes Christ himself, since he is [the church's] head, and he makes his own what belongs to the faithful. And therefore [Christ] said to Saul, "Why are you persecuting me?"[75] COMMENTARY ON THE APOCALYPSE 12.4.[76]

---

[68]Mt 2:20. [69]Ex 4:19. [70]TS 2 7:184-85 §§462-65. [71]A Christian ceremonial rite of exorcism performed by breathing on a person. [72]CCL 60:349. [73]Is 8:4. [74]TEG 8:176. [75]Acts 9:4. [76]MTS 1 Sup 1:126.

## 12:5 She Bore a Male Child Who Will Rule the Nations

**THE INSTRUCTOR OF ALL THE NATIONS.** HIPPOLYTUS: "And she brought forth," he says, "a man child who is to rule all the nations." By this is meant that the church, always bringing forth Christ, the perfect manchild of God, who is declared to be God and man, becomes the instructor of all the nations. And the words "her child was caught up unto God and to his throne" signify that he who is always born of her is a heavenly king and not an earthly; even as David also declared of old when he said, "The Lord said unto my Lord, Sit thou at my right hand, until I make thine enemies thy footstool."[77] ON THE ANTICHRIST 61.[78]

**THE CHURCH LABORS.** METHODIUS: Someone might take objection [that the woman who is with child is the church who baptizes], when the Apocalypse explicitly states that the church brings forth a "male child." . . . Remember that the mystery of the incarnation of the Word was fulfilled long before the Apocalypse, whereas John's prophetic message has to do with the present and the future. And Christ, who was conceived long before, was not the child who "was taken up" to the throne of God for fear that he might be injured by the serpent; rather he descended from the throne of his Father and was begotten precisely so that he might remain and check the dragon's assault on the flesh. And so, you must admit that it is the church that is in labor, and it is those who are washed in baptism that are brought forth. And the Spirit tells us this too somewhere in Isaiah: "Before she was in labor and before her time came to be delivered, she escaped and brought forth a male child. Who has heard such a thing? And who has seen anything like this? Shall the earth be born in one day, or a nation brought forth at once? For as soon as Zion was in labor, she brought forth her male child."[79] From whom then did she not flee except, of course, the dragon, in order that she, the spiritual

Zion, might bring forth her male child, that is, a people that would return from its feminine passions and immorality to the unity of the Lord and would be made strong in spiritual endeavor? . . . I think that the church is here said to bring forth "a male child" simply because the enlightened spiritually receive the features and image and virility of Christ. The likeness of the Word is stamped on them and is begotten within them by perfect knowledge and faith. Thus Christ is spiritually begotten in each one. And so it is that the church is with child and labors until Christ is formed and born within us, so that each of the saints by sharing in Christ is born again as Christ. This is the meaning of a passage of Scripture that says, "Do not touch my anointed; and do no evil to my prophets,"[80] those who are baptized in Christ become, as it were, other Christs by a communication of the Spirit, and here it is the church that effects this transformation into a clear image of the Word. SYMPOSIUM 8.7-8.[81]

**CHRIST RULES ALL HIS ENEMIES.** VICTORINUS OF PETOVIUM: "And he was caught up to the throne of God." We read of this in the Acts of the Apostles. For as he was speaking with the disciples, he was caught up into heaven. "And he is to rule all nations with a rod of iron," which is the sword. For under the subterfuge of the antichrist all the nations are going to be arrayed against the saints. By the sword, it says, both will fall. COMMENTARY ON THE APOCALYPSE 12.3.[82]

**THE DEVIL CEASED TO BE CONQUEROR.** TYCONIUS: "And she brought forth a male child." The church brings forth Christ who, although he was God, deigned to be born as man. He speaks of a "male child," because through his victory the devil, who had conquered a woman, ceased to be a conqueror. "Who is to rule the nations with a rod of iron." Indeed, [he speaks here] of his whole body. For the same Lord said of this, "He who

---

[77]Ps 110:1 (109:1 LXX). [78]ANF 5:217. [79]See Is 66:7-8. [80]Ps 105:15 (104:15 LXX). [81]ACW 27:112-13. [82]CSEL 49:108-10.

conquers and keeps my works until the end, I will give him power over the nations, and he shall rule them with a rod of iron, as when earthen pots are broken in pieces, even as I myself have received power from my Father."[83] "And her son was caught up to God and his throne." This means that whoever shall be resurrected in Christ will sit with him on the throne of God at the right hand of the Father.[84] Commentary on the Apocalypse 12.5.[85]

**Through the Father's Providence the Child Escaped Herod.** Oecumenius: Reveal to us more clearly, O John, who this is who was born, this male child! He says, "who is to rule all the nations with a rod of iron." O inspired one, you have declared clearly to us that he is our Savior and Lord, Jesus, the Christ. For his own Father promised him, "Ask of me, and I will give to you the nations as your inheritance and the ends of the earth as your possession. You will shepherd them with a rod of iron, and you will dash them like a potter's vessel."[86] "But her child was caught up to God and to his throne." The poisonous dragon lay in wait and incited Herod to kill the children in Bethlehem, thinking that certainly among them he would locate the Lord.[87] But by the providence of the Father the child escaped the plot. For Joseph heard a warning from heaven and took the child and its mother and fled into Egypt, since Herod was seeking the life of the child. Commentary on the Apocalypse 12.3-6.[88]

**What Is of the Head Corresponds to His Church As to His Body.** Primasius: Rightly is Christ, the Head of the church, said to be born in each [of his] members, who is known to rule [in them]. For he himself is both the Author and the Finisher of faith in whom we shall accomplish virtue. He reigns among the good with a rod of iron, that is, with an inflexible righteousness, but he breaks the evil into pieces. What is from the head is joined also to his church as to his body, "for all who have been baptized

have put on Christ,"[89] and "the two shall be one flesh," because whatever is to be understood "in Christ," the apostle says is also "in the church."[90] "Her child was caught up to God and to his throne." Although Christ, when his work was completed, went on before as the Head and so ascended to the Father, this nonetheless also corresponds to the church. For this reason the apostle can speak like this: "He who raised us up, made us to sit in the heavenly places,"[91] and "Our citizenship is in heaven,"[92] and "If you have been raised with Christ, seek the things that are above, where Christ is, seated at the right hand of God."[93] Should you wish to interpret [this passage] as referring especially to the person of Christ, you can appropriately gather other stories together and consider the treacheries of the red dragon to be all those persecutions that Christ had to face from his cradle because of Herod even unto death on the cross to which he willed to submit. For although the dragon sought his death, as it were, with gaping mouth, yet he was brought to naught by his resurrection. However, we must except from these agonies his birth from the blessed Mary, for we know that in conceiving she experienced no sin of sexual desire. Commentary on the Apocalypse 12.5.[94]

**The Fullness of Spiritual Maturity.** Andrew of Caesarea: Through those who are baptized, the church is always giving birth to Christ, since in them he is being formed unto the fullness of spiritual maturity, as the apostle says.[95] The "male child" is the people of the church who are not effeminate in their desires, through whom Christ, our God, as though an iron rod has already ruled the nations by the mighty hands of the powerful Romans. However, also after the resurrection of the dead he will establish those strong in the faith as judges and will rule as with

---

[83]Rev 2:26-27. [84]See Eph 2:6; Col 3:1. [85]TS 2 7:188-89 §§475-81. [86]Ps 2:8-9. [87]See Mt 2:1-18. [88]TEG 8:176-77. [89]See Gal 3:27. [90]Gen 2:24; Eph 5:32. [91]Eph 2:6. [92]Phil 3:20. [93]Col 3:1. [94]CCL 92:181-82. [95]See Eph 4:13.

iron the nations who are crumbling and weak vessels. For by their unfaithfulness they did not possess the mystical new wine. "But her child was caught up to God and to his throne." The saints are caught up in midst of temptations, lest they be subdued by difficulties beyond their powers. And "they will be caught up in the clouds to meet the Lord in the air,"[96] and they will be with God and his throne, that is, with the most excellent of the angelic powers. COMMENTARY ON THE APOCALYPSE 12.5.[97]

## 12:6 The Woman Fled to the Wilderness

**THE LOVELY PLACE OF VIRTUE.** METHODIUS: Now the woman who has brought forth and continues to bring forth "a male child," the Word, in the hearts of the faithful, and who went forth into the desert undefiled and unharmed by the wrath of the beast, is our mother the church. And the wilderness into which she comes and where she is nourished for "a thousand two hundred sixty days" is a wilderness truly bare of evil, unfruitful and sterile in what is corruptible, difficult to reach and hard for the majority to pass through. But it is fruitful and abounding in pasture, blossoming and easy of approach to the holy, full of wisdom and flowering with life. And this is none other than the lovely place of virtue, full of fair trees and gentle zephyrs, where the south wind rises and the north wind blows and the "aromatical spices flow."[98] . . . The "thousand two hundred sixty days" we sojourn here, my dear maidens, signify the direct, clear and perfect knowledge of the Father, Son and Spirit, in which as she grows our mother rejoices and exults during this time until the restoration of the new ages, when, entering into the heavenly assemblage, she will contemplate Being, now no longer through abstract knowledge but with clear intuition, entering in with Christ. For the thousand, consisting of one hundred times ten, contain the full and perfect number and is a symbol of the Father himself, who by his own power has cre-

ated and rules over all things. Two hundred consists of two perfect numbers added together and so is a symbol of the Holy Spirit inasmuch as he produces our knowledge of the Father and the Son. And the number sixty is ten times six and is thus a symbol of Christ, because the number six, if we proceed from one, is composed of its own proper parts, so that nothing in it is excessive or deficient. Thus it is complete when it is resolved into its components, such that when six is divided into equal parts by equal parts, it must result in the same number again from its divided segments. For first, if it is divided by two it makes three; then divided by three, it makes two; and again, divided by six it makes one, and is again completed in itself. For when it is divided into two times three, and three times two, and six times one, when three and two and one are added, they make up six again. Now a thing is necessarily perfect when it needs nothing further for its completion beyond itself and never has anything left over. . . . And thus it is that the number six has taken on a relationship with the Son of God, who came into this world from "the fullness of the Godhead." For, having "emptied himself" and "taking the form of a slave,"[99] he was restored once again to the fullness of his perfection and dignity. For having been made smaller in himself and divided into his parts, from his smallness and his parts he was restored again to his former fullness and grandeur without ever losing anything of his perfection. . . . The church, then, comes to this spot that is a wilderness and, as we have said before, is barren of evil, and [the church] receives nourishment; borne on the heaven-traversing wings of virginity, which the Word has called the pinions of a mighty eagle,[100] she has crushed the serpent and driven away the storm clouds from the full light of the moon which the church possesses. SYMPOSIUM 8.11-12.[101]

---

[96]1 Thess 4:17. [97]MTS 1 Sup 1:126-27. [98]Song 4:16. [99]Phil 2:7. [100]Ezek 17:3. [101]ACW 27:116-18.

### The Church Walks Among Every Power of Satan.

Tyconius: "The woman fled into the wilderness, where she has a place prepared by God where she might be nourished." . . . It says "into the wilderness," for in the apostles the church has received authority to walk among scorpions, serpents and every power of Satan. The Lord said to the apostles, "Behold, I have given you authority to tread upon serpents and scorpions and over all the power of the enemy."[102] As a figure of the whole church, the people of Israel were fed and led in the desert among the serpents of this world. "All these things happened as a figure for us upon whom the ends of the ages have come."[103] Furthermore, as a figure of the church sings and says, "[Those] whom he has redeemed from the hands of their enemies he has gathered from the lands, from the east and from the west, from the north and from the sea. They wandered in the desert and dry places."[104] To be sure, he is describing Israel in the wilderness, for she was not gathered from those places mentioned but from the stock of Abraham, who was in Mesopotamia. Commentary on the Apocalypse 12.6.[105]

### Mary Was Saved from the Plot of Herod.

Oecumenius: "And the woman fled into the wilderness, where she has a place prepared by God, that there they might nourish her for one thousand two hundred and sixty days." And so was the child saved from the plot of the dragon but the woman given over to destruction? Indeed not. But she too was saved by the flight into Egypt, which is a desert, and there was free from the plot of Herod. And there she was hid away and was nourished for one thousand two hundred and sixty days, which equals three and a half years, more or less. Thus, for some such length of time the mother of God remained in Egypt, until the death of Herod, after which another message from an angel brought them to Judea. Commentary on the Apocalypse 12.3-6.[106]

### The Church Tramples the Impious and Haughty.

Caesarius of Arles: We understand the wilderness to be this world where Christ feeds and leads the church unto the end. In this world the church herself tramples under foot through the help of Christ haughty and impious persons as though they were scorpions and vipers and all the power of Satan. Exposition on the Apocalypse 12.6, Homily 9.[107]

### Monks and Hermits Flee to the Desert.

Andrew of Caesarea: When the devil through the antichrist in whom he works arrays himself for battle against the church, those in the church who are elect and preeminent will spit upon the tumults of life and the desires of the world and flee into that desert devoid of every evil, that life which bears every virtue, as Methodius says,[108] and these escape the assaults of people and demons who war against them. It is likely that the physical desert will also save those who flee from the plot of the apostate to the mountains and caves and holes in the earth, as was recently the case with the witnesses, for in the three and a half years are reckoned the 1,260 days during which the apostasy will rage. During this time the great judge will not think to tempt us beyond what we are able to bear, but freeing us will present to us a strong mind free from any weakness against the onslaughts upon it. And so we, fighting against the principalities and powers of darkness,[109] may be decorated with the crown of righteousness and receive the rewards of victory. For to him who through those who are weak puts to flight the mighty principalities of the air, it is proper to ascribe victory and might, together with the Father and the life-giving Spirit forever and ever. Amen. Commentary on the Apocalypse 12.6.[110]

---

[102]Lk 10:19. [103]1 Cor 10:11. [104]Ps 107:2-4 (106:2-4 LXX). [105]TS 2 7:189-92 §§482-89. [106]TEG 8:177. [107]PL 35:2434. [108]Andrew refers to *Symposium* 8.11 (see p. 183). [109]Cf. Eph 6:12. [110]MTS 1 Sup 1:127-28.

# 12:7-12 A WAR IN HEAVEN

[7]*Now war arose in heaven, Michael and his angels fighting against the dragon; and the dragon and his angels fought,* [8]*but they were defeated and there was no longer any place for them in heaven.* [9]*And the great dragon was thrown down, that ancient serpent, who is called the Devil and Satan, the deceiver of the whole world—he was thrown down to the earth, and his angels were thrown down with him.* [10]*And I heard a loud voice in heaven, saying, "Now the salvation and the power and the kingdom of our God and the authority of his Christ have come, for the accuser of our brethren has been thrown down, who accuses them day and night before our God.* [11]*And they have conquered him by the blood of the Lamb and by the word of their testimony, for they loved not their lives even unto death.* [12]*Rejoice then, O heaven and you that dwell therein! But woe to you, O earth and sea, for the devil has come down to you in great wrath, because he knows that his time is short!"*

**OVERVIEW:** When Satan exalted himself against God and made plans to bring others into his rebellion, Michael and the other angels banished him from their ranks. Intolerant of his arrogance and insolent pride, the angels threw him from heaven (OECUMENIUS, ANDREW OF CAESAREA). When Satan later warred against Christ, the angels served Christ and rendered him assistance after the temptation (ANDREW OF CAESAREA). Also now Satan continues to war against the church, which is protected by Michael, the helper of God. But Satan is again thrown out of heaven when the faithful renounce him and no longer do his will (PRIMASIUS). At the end of time too the dragon and all his apostate angels will be thrown out of heaven (VICTORINUS). Deprived of his heavenly rank, Satan departs from spiritual realities and sinks down to an earthly mind (OECUMENIUS, PRIMASIUS). After the coming of Christ, Satan increased his blasphemy and slanders even the virtues and all who love them (ANDREW OF CAESAREA). And so cast out of the virtuous saints, he enters those who love and hope in earthly things (CAESARIUS OF ARLES).

At the banishment of Satan the angels sing a hymn of triumph, for the accuser has departed from the saints and has been conquered by them

(OECUMENIUS, ANDREW OF CAESAREA). They conquered the dragon by the efficacious and precious blood of Christ and now are called "brothers" by the angels, even as they are by Christ (OECUMENIUS). The victory of Christ grants authority to the church which in Peter received the keys of binding and loosing. And the angels rejoice in divine grace and judgment, for in the redeemed they behold God's mercy and goodness, while in the lost they see his equity and judgment (PRIMASIUS). To be sure, when Satan was cast down to earth, many suffered harm. However, for the sober and wise, trials and temptations serve as a gymnastics instructor who through exercise makes them to become approved and hardened as iron. The slothful and weak, by contrast, are unstable of mind and fall to the tyranny of Satan (OECUMENIUS). For such as these the angels grieve and lament, for they imitate God in his mercy (PRIMASIUS, ANDREW OF CAESAREA).

## 12:7-8 The Angels Fight the Dragon

**THE DEVIL WILL BE CAST OUT OF HEAVEN.** VICTORINUS OF PETOVIUM: This is the beginning of the coming of the antichrist. However, beforehand Elijah must preach and there must be peaceful times. And when the three years and six months of the preaching of Elijah is ended, the [dragon][1] along with all the apostate angels is to be thrown out from heaven, where he had the power of ascent until that time. And that the antichrist is to be aroused from hell, also Paul the apostle says, "Unless the man of sin shall come first, the son of perdition, the adversary, who will exalt himself over everything which is called and is worshiped as God."[2] COMMENTARY ON THE APOCALYPSE 12.6.[3]

**SATAN WAS BANISHED BY THE ANGELS.**
OECUMENIUS: The vision that is to explain the events concerning the antichrist refers to a beginning earlier than the beginning just described. This earlier beginning . . . is the fall of Satan from heaven. The Lord also spoke of this, "I saw Satan fall like lightning from heaven."[4] Why, then, does it say, "And there was war in heaven"? The holy Scripture says that Satan exalted himself against God, that is, he lifted up a stiff and insolent neck to him and devised an apostasy. Although God, who is by nature good and forbearing, was patient with him, the holy angels did not tolerate the arrogance of their master and banished him from their ranks. This passage speaks of this event. Michael, one of the great leaders of the angels, made war against Satan and his followers, and Satan did not prevail in this war against him. COMMENTARY ON THE APOCALYPSE 12.7-9.[5]

**MICHAEL IS THE HELPER OF GOD.** PRIMASIUS: We must not think that the devil and his angels dared to fight in heaven, since he could not even tempt Job without God's permission.[6] Rather by "heaven" he quite manifestly indicates the church, where each one of the faithful constantly contends against spiritual evils. Therefore the apostle says, "Our struggle is not against flesh and blood but against the principalities and powers and against the world rulers of this present darkness."[7] And so he says here that Michael with his angels fights against the devil, because by praying according to the will of

God for the church in this world and by granting her his aid, he is properly understood to be fighting for her. And so the apostle says, "Are not all ministering spirits sent forth to serve for the sake of those who are to obtain salvation?"[8] Indeed, the name of Michael himself is interpreted to mean "the helper of God," and so this work is properly assigned to him. Also Daniel said that in the last distress [Michael] would come for the succor of the church: "At that time shall arise Michael, the great prince who stands for the children of your people. And there shall be a time such as has never been since the nations first began to be. And in that time your people shall be delivered, everyone who shall be found written in the book."[9] The angels are said to be his by a certain manner of speaking, such as we read, "For their angels always behold the face of my Father who is in heaven."[10] And so it speaks of those who by believing began to be citizens in Christ and thus are his angels, because they are regarded as protected by one guardian king and as made glad by one life-giving spirit.[11] . . . The devil and his angels are not only those who are similar to him in nature and will. They are also as men, who after being caught in his traps, became pursuers of such things. Indeed, because of the qualities of his will it is said about the devil, "An evil man has done this,"[12] and about Judas, "[One of you] is a devil."[13] The devil is said to express himself by way of a twofold body. When he is conquered, he is said to be thrown out by those who have renounced him and have received faith in Christ and so no longer do his errors. Rather, in them "love [remains] from a pure heart and a good conscience and sincere faith."[14] Or, since the church is already separated from any admixture of evil

---

[1]Some manuscripts read here "antichrist," but for Victorinus the dragon is not the antichrist but the devil. [2]2 Thess 2:3-4. [3]CSEL 49:114. [4]Lk 10:18. [5]TEG 8:177-78. [6]Primasius is following Tyconius to this point. [7]Eph 6:12. [8]Heb 1:14. [9]Dan 12:1. [10]Mt 18:10. [11]Caesarius explicitly identifies Michael with Christ: "Understand Michael to be Christ and his angels to be holy persons" (PL 35:2434). [12]Mt 13:28. [13]Jn 6:70. [14]1 Tim 1:5.

and is glorified by the future blessedness, no place is given to the devil and to his angels to seduce the evil or to tempt the good. The psalm refers to him and says, "I passed by, and lo! he was not; and I sought him, but his place was not found."[15] COMMENTARY ON THE APOCALYPSE 12.7-8.[16]

**THE ANGELS COULD NOT TOLERATE THE PRIDE OF THE DEVIL.** ANDREW OF CAESAREA: These words can refer to the first fall of the devil from his angelic rank because of his pride and envy, or it can refer to his destruction through the cross of the Lord, when, as the Lord says, "the ruler of this world is judged," cast out of his ancient tyranny.[17] It is probable that the holy angels, together with their chief leader, Michael, could not tolerate the pride of the devil and previously threw him out of any association they had with him, since they found in him a lack of righteousness. As Ezekiel says, he was cast out by the cherubim "from the midst of the stones of fire,"[18] that is, as I think, from the angelic ranks. When Christ came, they served him after the temptation, since the slave, although dishonored, was once more being loathsome. We should note that, as the fathers thought, after the creation of the physical world, [the devil] was thrown down because of his arrogance and envy, although he had at first been entrusted as the prince of the air, as the apostle says.[19] Papias also speaks of this passage: "To some of them, clearly the holy angels of that time, he gave dominion over the arrangement of the earth, and he commissioned them to exercise their dominion well." And then he says, "But it happened that their arrangement came to nothing."[20] COMMENTARY ON THE APOCALYPSE 12.7-8.[21]

## 12:9 The Dragon Was Thrown Down

**SATAN THINKS HE IS HARMING GOD.** OECUMENIUS: "And there was no longer any place" either for refuge or, indeed, for dwelling "in heaven, and he was thrown down to the earth."

[The dragon] either experienced this in a physical way, or, having been deprived of his heavenly and angelic position, he was cast down to an earthly mind. Then, as though avenging himself on God because of his fall, he harms his servants and deceives people and tempts them to apostatize from God. Since he could not harm God himself, he thinks that in this way he is harming the Master. COMMENTARY ON THE APOCALYPSE 12.7-9.[22]

**THE DEVIL CONFINED TO EARTHLY THINGS.** PRIMASIUS: The wise tend to understand the "earth" here to refer to those earthly things in which by the strength of that curse the devil is known to inhabit. For it says, "Earth you shall eat all the days of your life."[23] Having been exiled from spiritual realities, he assailed those of the earth who were suitable to his own strengths. This is what it means that he was cast out of heaven and was thrown down to the earth. COMMENTARY ON THE APOCALYPSE 12.9.[24]

**THE DEVIL GOES TO THOSE WHO HOPE IN EARTHLY THINGS.** CAESARIUS OF ARLES: The devil, as well as every unclean spirit along with their leader, were expelled from the hearts of the saints to the earth, that is, to persons who are wise only in earthly things and have their entire hope in earthly things. EXPOSITION ON THE APOCALYPSE 12.9, HOMILY 9.[25]

**THE DEVIL BECAME EVEN MORE OF A BLASPHEMER.** ANDREW OF CAESAREA: This is most proper. For heaven has nothing to do with a base, earthly mind, since darkness has nothing in common with the light. If the term *the Satan* occurs here with the definite article, it does not suggest that he is someone other than the devil . . . rather he is named with two names. He is called "devil" because he accuses and slanders the virtues and those who love them, and he has even slandered

---

[15]Ps 36:36 LXX. [16]CCL 92:183-85. [17]See Jn 16:11. [18]Ezek 28:16. [19]See Eph 2:2. [20]Papias, from an unknown work. [21]MTS 1 Sup 1:129-30. [22]TEG 8:178. [23]Gen 3:14. [24]CCL 92:185. [25]PL 35:2434.

God himself to people, as he did when he suggested to Adam that God was envious.[26] He is called "Satan" because he opposes himself against the Master and his servants. It is therefore to be noted that the downfall of the devil did not only occur after the cross, as though he were inactive in former times. Rather, as he himself confessed to Anthony, the saying of the psalm is fulfilled in him, "The swords of the enemy have come to their end."[27] Therefore, his banishment is the abolition of all his evil enterprises along with his total exclusion from heaven and from his rank. The blessed Justin Martyr noted that after the coming of Christ and after the devil's sentence to Gehenna, the devil especially became a blasphemer, while in former times he did not blaspheme God so brazenly.[28] And so it is accurately said about him, "His heart is hard as stone,"[29] since he is unyielding in his evil. And if the expectation of punishment makes him even more evil, how would punishing either him or his followers in Gehenna through fire wash out the filth of sin? And not attaining to this, how would there be a cessation of punishment against those who think vain thoughts?[30] COMMENTARY ON THE APOCALYPSE 12.9.[31]

## 12:10-11 *The Kingdom of Our God and the Authority of Christ Have Come!*

**THE HOLY ANGELS CALLED PEOPLE THEIR BROTHERS.** OECUMENIUS: The holy angels hint at the joy they received at the banishment of Satan by singing a triumphal hymn to God, saying, "Now have the salvation and the kingdom and the power of God appeared, and the authority of his Christ," since he is all-powerful. For by the assistance [of Christ's authority], it says, we have conquered the enemy, and "the accuser of our brothers, who accuses them day and night before God," has departed from us. O, the moderation of the holy angels! How much like their own Master they are! They call people their "brothers." But why should this seem so marvelous, when even our common Master did not think it improper to call them by this name, saying, "I will proclaim your name to my brothers, in the midst of the congregation I will praise you"?[32] But why does it say that Satan has departed? Because he has been deprived of his rank and there is no longer a place for him to accuse people before God. But these gained their revenge in equal measure, for they defeated him who seemed so unconquerable when he had even dared to rise up against God. They conquered by the efficacious and beneficial and precious blood of Christ and the word of witness about him, which they regarded as more precious than their own lives. COMMENTARY ON THE APOCALYPSE 12.10-12.[33]

**THE WHOLE CHURCH RECEIVED AUTHORITY TO BIND AND TO LOOSE.** PRIMASIUS: Quite clearly he is showing in which heaven we are to understand that these things occur. For in the church we know that salvation is accomplished by the victory of Christ. Through this she has also received that authority to bind what is loose and to loose what is bound, since by way of a universal sign all in the one Peter heard, "Whatever you bind on earth shall be bound in heaven, and whatever you loose on earth shall be loosed [in heaven]."[34] And about this the Lord says, "All authority in heaven and on earth has been given to me."[35] He is not speaking of that authority that he always possessed but of that authority in the church that [Jesus] began to have from the time he wished to be the Head among the members. ... Using a manner of speech he speaks from the person of the angels and says "the accuser of our brothers." That is, he speaks of those who in the future will be fellow citizens [of the angels] but who now are sojourners [on the earth]. For, to be sure, the faithful now are wending their way to that city, the celestial Jerusalem, in which the

---

[26]See Gen 3:5. [27]Ps 9:7 LXX. See Athanasius *Life of St. Anthony* 41 (NPNF 2 4:207). [28]See Irenaeus *Against Heresies* 5.26.2; Eusebius *Ecclesiastical History* 4.18.9. [29]Job 41:24. [30]Against the Origenist doctrine of the restoration of all things, condemned at the Fifth Ecumenical Council at Constantinople, 553. [31]MTS 1 Sup 1:130-31. [32]Heb 2:12. [33]TEG 8:179. [34]Mt 16:19. [35]Mt 28:18.

angels now dwell in happiness. However, since [the devil] has been thrown out of heaven and sent to the earth, they are depicted as joyful and as rejoicing together for the redemption of those whom the Lord had deigned to prepare to inhabit as a temple for himself. For the souls of the righteous are the seat of wisdom. And the angels also give praise concerning the earthly into whom [the devil] is said to have descended, for the angels peer into the depths of the divine justice and the blessed always sing to him of his mercy and judgment, for in the redeemed they recognize his goodness and in the lost they behold his equity. Since they conquered through the blood of the Lamb, they are said to have been able to overcome the devil. And there follows, "For they loved not their lives even unto death." We must believe that they received that love that "is poured out into our hearts," to be sure, not from ourselves but "through the Holy Spirit which has been given to us."[36] COMMENTARY ON THE APOCALYPSE 12.10-11.[37]

**THE SAINTS HAVE CONQUERED THEIR ACCUSER.** ANDREW OF CAESAREA: Because of his accusations and calumny against people, he has been called "accuser," which he is. The angels rejoice at his downfall, for faith has nothing to do with faithlessness. And although the saints have been accused and slandered by him, as was also Job, yet by their sufferings for the sake of Christ they have conquered him as well as all those who trusted in him. COMMENTARY ON THE APOCALYPSE 12.10-12.[38]

## 12:12 Rejoice, O Heaven, but Woe to Earth and Sea

**TRIALS TRAIN THE FAITHFUL FOR APPROVAL.** OECUMENIUS: When these events occurred, it says, "Rejoice all you angels of God, for you have been delivered from the bitter association with Satan." But "woe to the earth and to the sea, for the devil has come down to you in great wrath, for he knows that his time is short." Someone

might ask, "If by his coming down Satan was intending to do evil upon the earth and sea, why [was he allowed] to come down?" Because, for those who are sober and have hope in God, this did not occur for their harm but rather for their benefit. It trained them, as though by a gymnastics instructor, so that by these trials they might be made more approved and hardened to be like iron. But this does harm the slothful and the weak, who, since the one urging them on is himself without foundation, would quickly become evil out of themselves and exchange any hardship for what they are by nature. When he says "woe to the earth and to the sea," he is not saying "woe to those who live upon the earth and sail upon the sea." Rather, he calls those "earth" and "dust" who are earthly in thought and, moreover, fickle, without direction and unstable in mind. Against such as these, our common enemy makes war and enslaves the weak who are willing to submit to his tyranny. "Knowing," it says, "that his time is short." The time from the downfall of Satan until his judgment and condemnation, when he will be thrown aside into unending ages, is short. COMMENTARY ON THE APOCALYPSE 12.10-12.[39]

**EXULTATION FOR THE REDEEMED BUT LAMENTATION FOR THE PERISHING.** PRIMASIUS: As above, in angels the church is recognized to be "heaven," and it is proper to both to rejoice harmoniously in the Lord, for people are said to be the associates of angels and in Christ the angels serve the human nature. But there follows, "Woe to you, O earth and sea." Just as there was exultation for those who are redeemed, there is lamentation for those who are perishing. Therefore, Ezekiel said that he saw a book having written within a lament, a song and a woe.[40] In the lament he refers to the wailing of the penitent; in the song he refers to the joyfulness of the saints; in the woe he properly manifests the condemnation of the wicked. It is to these last that here [John]

[36]Rom 5:5. [37]CCL 92:185-86. [38]MTS 1 Sup 1:131-32. [39]TEG 8:179-80. [40]See Ezek 2:9-10.

alludes when he says, "Woe to you, earth and sea and the rest, for he knows that there is little time left to him." And so, moved by an unconquered power he confesses to the Lord and says, "Have you come to destroy us before the time."[41] Commentary on the Apocalypse 12.12.[42]

**The Saints Become Heaven.** Caesarius of Arles: It says "come down" to preserve the allegory. As all are in "heaven," that is, in the church, which is rightly called heaven, when the devil is thrown out of the saints, he "comes down" to his followers who are the "earth" because of their earthly affection. He is said to be thrown out of heaven, not so that he might come to those who have already been made heaven but because of those who have not become what they might be. For the saints cannot become heaven, unless the devil has been expelled. Exposition on the

Apocalypse 12.12, Homily 9.[43]

**Angels Grieve for Those Who Cling to Earthly Things.** Andrew of Caesarea: In imitation of God, it follows that the powers above rejoice at his downfall but grieve over those who by his plot cling to earthly things. But woe to those who dwell upon the earth, that is, clearly to those who have no citizenship in heaven but only on earth. For many upon the earth do defeat the enemy and will continue to do so, although because of the nearness of his punishment he now is especially enraged against those who fight him. And so it is necessary to think that those are unhappy who have an earthly mind and are buffeted about by the sea of life. Commentary on the Apocalypse 12.11-12.[44]

[41]Mt 8:29. [42]CCL 92:186-87. [43]PL 35:2434-35. [44]MTS 1 Sup 1:132.

## 12:13-17 THE WOMAN IS SAVED FROM THE DRAGON

[13]And when the dragon saw that he had been thrown down to the earth, he pursued the woman who had borne the male child. [14]But the woman was given the two wings of the great eagle that she might fly from the serpent into the wilderness, to the place where she is to be nourished for a time, and times, and half a time. [15]The serpent poured water like a river out of his mouth after the woman, to sweep her away with the flood. [16]But the earth came to the help of the woman, and the earth opened its mouth and swallowed the river which the dragon had poured from his mouth. [17]Then the dragon was angry with the woman, and went off to make war on the rest of her offspring, on those who keep the commandments of God and bear testimony to Jesus. And he stood[e] on the sand of the sea.

e Other ancient authorities read And I stood, connecting the sentence with 13.1

**Overview:** Having fallen from his angelic rank, the devil persecuted the Virgin Mary, who had given birth to the Savior of humankind. He was envious of humankind, for it would ascend to heaven while he had been expelled from heaven (Oecumenius). And so the devil's hatred against

Christ and the apostles and the church knows no bounds (PRIMASIUS), for condemned to eat the dirt of earthly thoughts, he pursues all the more those who bear the virility of Christ and are free from desire (PRIMASIUS, ANDREW OF CAESAREA).

Although pursued by Satan, Mary was saved by an angel who told Joseph to flee to the wilderness of Egypt (OECUMENIUS). To be sure, the virginity of Mary is symbol of that wilderness which is barren of all evil and desire and which all true virgins imitate and so receive the crowns of virtue (METHODIUS). Mary perhaps even escaped death, but she never had carnal relations (EPIPHANIUS). And this is an image of the church, which escapes earthly thoughts and desires by her love for God and for the neighbor (PRIMASIUS, ANDREW OF CAESAREA). Taught by the two Testaments, the church escapes the world by the affection of her mind, the absence of lust and the vision of God in a pure heart (PRIMASIUS, ANDREW OF CAESAREA, BEDE). Even as the heart of Mary was made glad when the earth took the body of Christ and gave it back again (OECUMENIUS), so is the church made sure through the teachings of Christ and through the victory of his human nature, which swallowed death in the fullness of its life (PRIMASIUS). Even now monks swallow up the temptations of the devil through their humility and sincerity of heart (ANDREW OF CAESAREA). Having failed to kill the Lord incarnate or to sap the apostles of their confidence, the devil now persecutes the offspring of Mary through earthly tyrants, for the faithful confess the child born of Mary to be God and keep the commandments of God by faith in Jesus Christ (OECUMENIUS, BEDE).

## 12:13 The Dragon Pursued the Woman

**SATAN ENVIES HUMANKIND ITS SALVATION.** OECUMENIUS: When the dragon saw himself in these bad circumstances and that he had fallen from his angelic rank, he became exceedingly bitter against humankind and persecuted the woman who had given birth to the Savior of humankind, in order that he might kill her. "He

pursued the woman," for he knew that her child was too great to be captured, and he envied people their salvation from the Lord, for he could not tolerate such a change that while he had been expelled from heaven, people would ascend from earth to heaven through virtue. COMMENTARY ON THE APOCALYPSE 12.13-17.[1]

**THE DEVIL'S HATRED IS BOUNDLESS.** PRIMASIUS: As we said before, the devil carries on a hatred against the church that is without bounds and with all means. For the more he is defeated and is expelled, the more sharply does he try to multiply his deceptions. COMMENTARY ON THE APOCALYPSE 12.13.[2]

**THE DEVIL PERSECUTES THE CHURCH.** ANDREW OF CAESAREA: When the devil wrestled with Christ after his baptism, he was overcome. Then arming himself against the holy apostles, he was again shamed when he saw that they found life through death, while as a snake he had been condemned to crawl upon the ground and to eat dirt, that is, earthly thoughts. He then began to persecute the church, for it has borne and continues to bear the masculine people of God which is not womanly because of desire. COMMENTARY ON THE APOCALYPSE 12.13-14.[3]

## 12:14 The Woman Was Given Two Wings

**A VICTORIOUS VIRGIN WINS THE SEVEN DIADEMS OF VIRTUES.** METHODIUS: The church comes to this spot, which is a wilderness, and, as we have said before,[4] is barren of evil, and she receives nourishment; borne on the heaven-traversing wings of virginity, which the Word has called the pinions of a mighty eagle,[5] she has crushed the serpent and driven away the storm clouds from the full light of the moon which is [the church's]. My fair virgins, [we wish that you] imitate your mother as best you can and not to be

---

[1]TEG 8:181. [2]CCL 92:187. [3]MTS 1 Sup 1:133. [4]See Rev 12:6 above. [5]See Ezek 17:3.

disturbed by the pains, afflictions and reverses of life. . . . Do not then lose heart at the deceits and the slanders of the beast, but equip yourselves sturdily for battle, arming yourselves with the helmet of salvation, your breastplate and your greaves.[6] For if you attack with great advantage and with stout heart you will cause him untold consternation; and when he sees you arrayed in battle against him by him who is his superior, he will certainly not stand his ground. Immediately the hydra-headed, many faced beast will retreat and let you carry off the prize for the seven contests. . . . With sober and virile heart, then, take up your arms against the swollen beast; do not on any account yield your ground, and do not be terrified by his fury. Endless glory will be yours if you defeat him and carry off his seven diadems, for this is the prize of our contest, as our teacher Paul tells us.[7] The virgin who first overcomes the devil and destroys his seven heads wins seven diadems of virtue,[8] after engaging in the seven great contests of chastity. One of the dragon's heads is luxury and incontinence; whoever crushes it wins the diadem of temperance. Another head is weakness and cowardice; whoever tramples on this wins the diadem of martyrdom. Another is folly and disbelief, and so on through all the other fruits of wickedness. Whosoever overcomes and destroys these will carry off the respective rewards, and in this way the dragon's power is uprooted in various ways. Symposium 8.12-13.[9]

**Mary Never Had Carnal Relations.**
Epiphanius of Salamis: When the Savior was on the cross, the Lord turned, as the Gospel according to John tells us, "and saw the disciple whom he loved, and said to him of Mary, 'Behold thy mother.' And to her he said, 'Behold thy son.'"[10] If Mary had children and her husband was alive, why did he entrust Mary to John and John to Mary? Why not rather entrust her to Peter? Why not to Andrew, Matthew and Bartholomew? But it is plain that he entrusted her to John because of virginity. For he says, "Behold thy mother," even though physically she was not

John's mother; he says this to show that as the originator of virginity she was his mother, since the life began with her. . . . For if she had not truly been the mother who bore him, he would not have taken care to entrust the Ever-virgin to John—his mother because of the incarnation, but in his honor undefiled and the wondrous vessel. But the Gospel says, "And from that day he took her unto his own home."[11] But if she had a husband, a home, children, she would return to her own home and not to someone else's. . . . Indeed, when this had been done and John had taken her to himself, she did not yet live with him. If any think I am mistaken, moreover, let them search through the Scriptures and neither find Mary's death, nor whether or not she died, nor whether or not she was buried—even though John surely traveled throughout Asia. And yet, nowhere does he say that he took the holy Virgin with him. Scripture simply kept silence because of the overwhelming wonder, not to throw people's minds into consternation. For I dare not say—though I have my suspicions, I keep silent. Perhaps, just as her death is not to be found, so I may have found some traces of the holy and blessed Virgin. In one passage Simeon says of her, "And a sword shall pierce through your own soul also, that the thoughts of many hearts may be revealed."[12] And elsewhere the Revelation of John says, "And the dragon hastened after the woman who had born the man child, and she was given the wings of an eagle and was taken to the wilderness, that the dragon might not seize her." Perhaps this can be applied to her; I cannot decide for certain, and [I] am not saying that she remained immortal. But neither am I affirming that she died. For Scripture went beyond human understanding and left it in suspense with regard to the precious and choice vessel, so that no one would suspect carnal behavior of her. Whether she died, I don't know; and even if she was buried, she never had carnal

---

[6]Eph 6:13-17. [7]See Eph 6:12-17. [8]See Rev 12:3. For Methodius, the "heads" of the dragon are seven vices; the seven "diadems" are seven virtues. [9]ACW 27:118-19. [10]Jn 19:26-27. [11]Jn 19:27. [12]Lk 2:35.

relations, perish the thought! PANARION 7.78.10.9-11.5.[13]

**MARY ESCAPED ON EAGLE'S WINGS.** OECUMENIUS: And so, the woman did not come into the control of Satan but fled into the desert. This is Egypt. For this reason the prophet sought "wings like a dove, so that flying away, he might take rest . . . in the desert."[14] But to the all-holy Virgin even more powerful wings were given, the wings of the great eagle. By the phrase "wings of an eagle," he refers to the visitation of the holy angel who urged Joseph to take the boy and his mother and flee into Egypt. By means of this visitation, as though by means of the wings of an eagle, they arrived in Egypt. And since the dragon failed in this plot, which he had devised through Herod, he developed another one against the Virgin, namely, the death of her son. Consequently, the remaining portion of the narrative relates the cross and death of the Lord. COMMENTARY ON THE APOCALYPSE 12.13-17.[15]

**THE CHURCH FLEES IDOLATRY.** PRIMASIUS: As though they were wings, the church uses the two Testaments, for taught by them and instructed in their precepts, she strives to avoid the snares of the enemy, and being fashioned to followed their examples, she overcomes.[16] Moreover, [the church] is guided by the twofold love of God and the neighbor. The place of solitude is this place of our earthly sojourn, for "while we are in the body, we are away from the Lord."[17] And this is especially true of the heart that does not go away from the world by way of place but by way of affection, as the prophet says, "Behold, I fled afar off and remained in solitude; I awaited him who might save me."[18] It is proper that here he used the image of the eagle, for it can fly to greater distances than can other birds, yet when it sees its prey from afar, moved by its natural needs, it immediately swoops to low levels. Such is the church also, for although in her spiritual members she seeks and ponders in her mind that which is above, yet burdened by the weakness of

the body, she submits to the requirements of bodily needs. Because of this, "she groans in travail until now, for the creation is subjected to futility, not of its own will but on account of him who subjected her in hope."[19] And again, "For either we are beside ourselves for God, or in our right mind for you."[20] The period of three years and six months signifies that time up to the end of world during which the church increases and flees the worship of idols and every error of the serpent. COMMENTARY ON THE APOCALYPSE 12.14.[21]

**THE CHRISTIAN FLEES FROM UNWORTHY DESIRES.** ANDREW OF CAESAREA: From the beginning love for God and for the neighbor and a mind receptive of him who was crucified for us was given to [the church], as were the two Testaments. All of these things are symbolized by the wings of the eagle, and they were given to [the church] so that taking flight by them into the desert, that is, into a citizenship devoid of every desire, she might be nourished. To be sure, this occurs always, but it will especially be so at the coming of the antichrist, who will rule everywhere, it is written, for the designated time of three and a half years. It may be that during that time even those who have hid themselves in the mountains and caves of the literal, physical desert will flee him. COMMENTARY ON THE APOCALYPSE 12.13-14.[22]

**THE CHRISTIAN SEES GOD WITH A PURE HEART.** BEDE: Supported by the two Testaments, the church avoids the poisonous tumults of the world, and by the affection of the mind each day seeks the solitude of a quick and gentle spirit. And so in joy she sings, "Behold, I have gone far away in flight and remain in solitude."[23]

---

[13]NHMS 36:608-609. This is from a letter of Epiphanius to Arabia against the "Antidicomarians," who said that Mary had relations with a man after Christ's birth. [14]See Ps 55:6-7 (54:7-8 LXX). [15]TEG 8:181-82. [16]The idea that the two wings are the two Testaments most likely derives from Tyconius. [17]2 Cor 5:6. [18]Ps 55:7-8 (54:8-9 LXX). [19]See Rom 8:20-22. [20]2 Cor 5:13. [21]CCL 92:187-88. [22]MTS 1 Sup 1:133. [23]See Ps 55:7 (54:8 LXX).

Nor is it contradictory that [in the psalm] she asked for the wings of a dove while here she received the wings of an eagle. For, just as the church, whose youth will be renewed as the eagle's, is represented in the former because of the gift of the Holy Spirit, so in the latter she is symbolized because of the lofty flight and sublime sight by which she sees God with a pure heart. "Where she is to be nourished for a time, and times, and half a time." He is speaking of the whole time of the church, which is comprehended in the number of days mentioned previously. For a "time" signifies one year, "times" signifies two years, and "half a time" signifies six months. EXPLANATION OF THE APOCALYPSE 12.14.[24]

## 12:15-16 The Serpent Poured a River of Water

THE EARTH GAVE AID TO MARY. OECUMENIUS: The holy Scripture figuratively speaks of temptation as a "river." Jonah said, "You have cast me into the deep, into the heart of the sea, and the rivers encircled me,"[25] and the Lord spoke similarly: "The rain fell, and the rivers came, and the winds blew, but they did not blow that house down, because it was built upon the rock."[26] And so here the trial of the Lord's passion is called a "river," and it says that through this [the dragon] intended to drown the Virgin. And truly, since they [the rivers] did bring her to this [the cross] and to very great grief, the dragon was able to fulfill his intention. For why did Simeon say to her, "And a sword will pierce through your own soul also, that the thoughts of many hearts might be revealed"?[27] "But the earth came to the help of the woman, and the earth opened its mouth and swallowed the river that the dragon had poured out of its mouth" upon the woman. That the earth swallowed the river signifies that it received the trial into itself, that is, it received the Lord, who had been crucified. But the help that the earth rendered was not simply in this. Rather, its help was in this, that it gave the Lord back again. For on the third day he came to life again, having

trampled on death, since it was not strong enough to hold him who was the Author of life, as the blessed Peter says.[28] And that the whole narrative might be told, one must know the ending to the words "the earth came to the help of the woman." Consequently, as though responding to a question after the manner of this aid, it says, "it swallowed the river," that is, it received in itself the Lord, who had been betrayed, and gave him back again, and in this way [the earth] rendered its assistance. COMMENTARY ON THE APOCALYPSE 12.13-17.[29]

CHRIST'S HUMAN NATURE SWALLOWED DEATH. PRIMASIUS: It is possible to interpret the "earth" here to refer to the church, as in the psalm, "He who set the earth on its foundations, so that it should never be shaken."[30] That is, he [set the earth] on the saints whose prayers and teachings and the working of salvation [which they have received] dispels the uncovered intrigues of the enemy. However, it would be better to interpret the "earth" to be the human nature in Christ, for it is itself the "truth" that "has sprung up from the earth,"[31] and that always appears before the face of God and so, as the apostle says, "intercedes for us."[32] When it swallowed death, which it took to itself, this earth is said to have opened its mouth when it gulped down the author of death by the abundance of its own life. And no less was he swallowed when Christ taught sitting upon the mountain and opening his mouth gave greater precepts to his disciples, "abolishing the law with its commandments and ordinances."[33] COMMENTARY ON THE APOCALYPSE 12.16.[34]

THE DEVIL SENDS DEMONS AFTER THE MONKS. ANDREW OF CAESAREA: When the church fled to inaccessible places where the deceiver makes his approach, out of his mouth,

---

[24]CCL 121A:397. [25]Jon 2:3. [26]See Mt 7:25. [27]Lk 2:35. [28]Acts 3:15. [29]TEG 8:182. [30]Ps 104:5 (103:5 LXX). [31]See Ps 85:11 (84:12 LXX). [32]See Heb 9:24. [33]Eph 2:15. [34]CCL 92:188-89.

that is, clearly by his command, came water like a river after her. That is, he sent out against her a host of godless people and evil demons and all kinds of temptations that he might enslave her. But the earth, it says, came to [the church's] aid. This may refer to the very great distances of travel in the desert and the aridity and dryness of those places, and in this way the river of temptations were swallowed up.[35] Or [the demons and their temptations were overcome] by the humility of the saints who say with utter sincerity, "I am earth and dust" and so bring to naught all the snares of the devil, even as the angel said to the holy Anthony.[36] COMMENTARY ON THE APOCALYPSE 12.15-16.[37]

## 12:17 The Dragon Made War on the Woman's Offspring

**THE DRAGON PERSECUTES THE FAITHFUL.** OECUMENIUS: And since the dragon had failed also in his second plot [i.e., to kill the male child], what further is there for him to do? He has persecuted those called sons and brothers of the Lord, that is, the faithful—for it says that these are the offspring of the woman, since the faithful are the sons and brothers of the Lord, as it is written, "I will proclaim your name to my brothers,"[38] and again, "Behold, I and the children which God has given to me."[39] Therefore, they are relatives of his mother—and [the dragon] made war with them, persecuting them and plotting against them and killing them through the tyrants and powers of the earth, since they were giving witness that the one born of the Virgin was God. COMMENTARY

ON THE APOCALYPSE 12.13-17.[40]

**BY OBEDIENCE THE FAITHFUL FIGHT THE DEVIL.** BEDE: The [dragon] saw that he could no longer continue the persecutions since they were stopped by the mouth of the holy earth [i.e., Christ], and so he armed himself all the more with the mystery of wickedness, so that he might be able to continue his plotting. "Who keep the commandments of God and bear testimony to Jesus." To keep the commandments of God by faith in Jesus Christ is to fight against the devil and to provoke him to war. But thanks be to God who has brought to naught all that the evil dragon has begun! For, behold, although he tried to kill the Lord incarnate, he was frustrated in this by the Lord's resurrection. And afterward, he worked to take from the apostles the confidence of their teaching, and this was as though he had given himself the task of taking the woman, that is, the whole church, from human affairs. But since he has failed to accomplish this, he fights against the faithful in every age. "And he stood on the sand of the sea." This means that he stood upon the multitude of the people, "which the wind drives away from the face of the earth."[41] For when he wishes to excite plots and wars, he stands upon that multitude that is in the habit of adopting his plans. EXPLANATION OF THE APOCALYPSE 12.17-18.[42]

---

[35]The very remoteness of the hermits shielded them from outside temptations. [36]This scene is not found in the *Life of St. Anthony*. [37]MTS 1 Sup 1:134. [38]Heb 2:12. [39]Is 8:18. [40]TEG 8:182-83. [41]See Ps 1:4 LXX. [42]CCL 121A:399.

## 13:1-10 A BEAST RISES OUT OF THE SEA

¹*And I saw a beast rising out of the sea, with ten horns and seven heads, with ten diadems upon its horns and a blasphemous name upon its heads. ²And the beast that I saw was like a leopard, its feet were like a bear's, and its mouth was like a lion's mouth. And to it the dragon gave his power and his throne and great authority. ³One of its heads seemed to have a mortal wound, but its mortal wound was healed, and the whole earth followed the beast with wonder. ⁴Men worshiped the dragon, for he had given his authority to the beast, and they worshiped the beast, saying, "Who is like the beast, and who can fight against it?"*

⁵*And the beast was given a mouth uttering haughty and blasphemous words, and it was allowed to exercise authority for forty-two months; ⁶it opened its mouth to utter blasphemies against God, blaspheming his name and his dwelling, that is, those who dwell in heaven. ⁷Also it was allowed to make war on the saints and to conquer them.ᶠ And authority was given it over every tribe and people and tongue and nation, ⁸and all who dwell on earth will worship it, every one whose name has not been written before the foundation of the world in the book of life of the Lamb that was slain. ⁹If any one has an ear, let him hear:*

¹⁰*If any one is to be taken captive,*
      *to captivity he goes;*
   *if any one slays with the sword,*
      *with the sword must he be slain.*
*Here is a call for the endurance and faith of the saints.*

f Other ancient authorities omit this sentence

**OVERVIEW:** At the end of time God will send a man as antichrist to deceive those who shunned the light and separated themselves from God. This apostate in whom all apostasy is concentrated (IRENAEUS) will arise from the tumultuous and unstable life of this world (OECUMENIUS, ANDREW OF CAESAREA). He will exercise a powerful lordship through cunning tricks and deceits (OECUMENIUS), and his blasphemy may be observed in the Roman emperors, Julian and Valens, who slandered Christ (ANDREW OF CAESAREA). However, his blasphemy and apostasy may be seen in all impious and evil persons who as followers of him are his body (TYCONIUS, CAESARIUS OF ARLES). This beast from the sea may, however, be a powerful demon called the devil, whose fa-

ther is Satan. Like a leopard the devil is quick to form plots, and in his deception he is sturdy like a bear, for Satan is his teacher and the author of his works (OECUMENIUS). Likewise too the antichrist will have the power of Satan and as a king of the Romans will destroy kingdoms through false signs and wonders (ANDREW OF CAESAREA).

The kingdom of the antichrist will be a mixture of nations whose nature is malice and madness and whose desire is blood (VICTORINUS, CAESARIUS OF ARLES). Even now we see his power in the heretics who devastate the church as the pagans did formerly (CAESARIUS OF ARLES). Although the heretics are wounded, however, by catholic confession and the testimony of Scripture, yet they, as it were, are revived again in their ongoing blasphemy (CAESARIUS OF ARLES). In them the devil has his throne and his rule, for through them he seduces others to follow and to worship him (TYCONIUS). At the coming of the antichrist he will raise the dead through sorcery, as happened at the time of Simon Magus (ANDREW OF CAESAREA). The antichrist will even seduce the Jews, for he will come as a christ who defends circumcision and the law (VICTORINUS), and through their idolatry of him the Jews will heal the wound they inflicted by their reverent worship. Through those who follow and worship him the devil is given a mouth to speak his slanders (OECUMENIUS). Therefore, it is by heretics and apostates that the devil blasphemes the Word made flesh (PRIMASIUS, ANDREW OF CAESAREA), the saints (CAESARIUS OF ARLES, ANDREW OF CAESAREA) and the holy angels (OECUMENIUS, ANDREW OF CAESAREA). Yet some from both the Gentiles and from Israel will remain free from the devil's wiles, for they will remain pious and pure in the manner of their lives (OECUMENIUS). Those who place themselves under his destructive lordship, however, will be his slaves and will die a spiritual death of the soul by the satanic sword (OECUMENIUS, ANDREW OF CAESAREA). In the meantime, the church continues to suffer the devil's hostility, for as Christ allowed to his persecutors power over him, so the church temporarily is submitted to arrogance by God's permission (PRIMASIUS).

## 13:1 A Beast Rising from the Sea

### A HABITATION OF DARKNESS FOR THOSE WHO SHUN THE LIGHT. IRENAEUS: Since then in this world some persons come to the light, and by faith unite themselves to the light and by faith unite themselves with God, but others shun the light and separate themselves from God, the Word of God comes preparing a fit habitation for both. For those indeed who are in the light, that they may derive enjoyment from it and from the good things contained in it; but for those in darkness, that they may partake in its calamities. . . .

For this reason the apostle says, "Because they did not receive the love of God, that they might be saved, therefore God shall also send them the operation of error, that they may believe a lie, that they all may be judged who have not believed the truth, but consented to unrighteousness."[1] For when [antichrist] arrives, and of his own accord concentrates in his own person the apostasy, and accomplishes whatever he shall do according to his own will and choice, sitting also in the temple of God, his dupes will adore him as the Christ. Therefore he shall deservedly "be cast into the lake of fire,"[2] [and this will happen according to divine appointment], God by his prescience, foreseeing all this at the proper time sending such a man, "that they may believe a lie, that they all may be judged who did not believe the truth, but consented to unrighteousness."[3] AGAINST HERESIES 5.28.1-2.[4]

### THE PEOPLE OF THE DEVIL WEAR A BLASPHEMOUS NAME. TYCONIUS: Here a "sea" is mentioned, which above was called a "bottomless pit" from which this beast would ascend.[5] In both instances a people is indicated. Indeed, he sees a people arising from a people, namely, a beast coming forth from a people. Normally "beast" is a designation of that which is hostile to the Lamb, but in a narrative one must determine from passage to passage what aspect of the beast is signified. For sometimes the devil is the beast, elsewhere the beast is his body or one of the heads of that beast such as the one which rises up although he seemed wounded unto death, which is a false imitation of the true faith. In other passages the beast might signify only the leaders. In this present passage the beast that rises from the sea refers to the body of the devil, which has ten horns and seven heads and diadems upon its horns and a blasphemous name upon its heads. And rightly is he said to be named with a name of

---

[1]2 Thess 2:10-12. [2]Rev 19:20. [3]Irenaeus continues by quoting Rev 13:2-10 as a description of the coming of the antichrist. [4]ANF 1:556-57*. [5]Rev 11:7.

blasphemy, since he desires to be regarded as God. COMMENTARY ON THE APOCALYPSE 13.1.[6]

**SATAN IS THE FATHER OF THE DEVIL.** OECU-MENIUS: In the previous vision the holy Evangelist saw "a sign in heaven, and behold," it says, "a red dragon."[7] But now he says that he saw "a beast rising out of the sea, like a leopard." Moreover, in the following vision he sees "another beast which rose out of the earth," and it had "two horns like a lamb." Therefore, we have three beasts altogether, the first is in heaven, the second is from the sea, and the third is from the earth. Who the first and the third beast are is clear to everyone. The first is the dragon who was the author of evil, namely, Satan, who became apostate and exalted himself against God Almighty. The third is the antichrist. But this second beast who now lies before us in the vision, who is he? I think that he comes after the apostate dragon, that is, Satan who was the leader of the other demons—for many fell with Satan and were cast down to earth—and from this it is clear that the holy Scripture says that this leader of all the demons is condemned to the sea and to tartarus. And perhaps it speaks of him in this figurative way because of the disorder and turmoil in which he exists, recognizing also from whence he has fallen and into what condition he has come, and that "he is kept for the judgment of the great day," as it is written.[8] ... But this second beast which now appears to us is introduced in the book of Job, conversing with God and seeking Job and bringing upon him many trials and even saying that he is come "walking to and fro upon the earth under heaven."[9] But it is not only the book of Job that speaks of him, but the Lord too makes mention of him when in the Gospel of John he says to the Jews, "You are of your father the devil, and your will is to do your father's desires. He was a murderer from the beginning and has nothing to do with the truth, because there is no truth in him. When he lies, he speaks according to his own nature, for he is a liar and as is his father."[10] He

calls the apostate dragon the "father of the devil," namely, of this one who is present in this vision. For [Satan] is "father" as their leader and the author of the apostasy, even as the holy Abraham was called "father of nations," since he was progenitor of the faith before them, as it was said of to him," I have made you the father of many nations."[11] "I saw a beast rising out of the sea, with ten horns and seven heads, with ten diadems upon his horns." He saw him coming out of the sea. For him it is an ascent, since he is elevated from the troubled, unstable life of people who have elected him to be their master. The ten horns testify to his powerful lordship, even as the seven heads suggest his various cunning deceits and tricks. For the numbers ten and seven are perfect numbers. The diadems upon his horns reveal that he has become a powerful force against humankind, since through deception we have willingly given ourselves over to him. "And blasphemous names were upon his heads." Rightly does it say "upon his heads," for he rages against himself and his own head and is insulting to God. And stripping worship from God, he grants it to himself. COMMENTARY ON THE APOCALYPSE 13.1-4.[12]

**ALL THE UNGODLY ARISE FROM THE DEVIL.** CAESARIUS OF ARLES: "I saw a beast rising out of the sea," that is, out of an evil people. That he was "rising out" means that he was coming into existence, even as the blooming flower comes forth from the root of Jesse. In the beast coming forth from the sea he signifies all impious who are the body of the devil. EXPOSITION ON THE APOCALYPSE 13.1, HOMILY 10.[13]

**ANTICHRIST ARISES FROM THE SEA OF HUMAN LIFE.** ANDREW OF CAESAREA: Some have interpreted this beast to be a certain power, a leader of the other demons, who is second to Satan, and that after this beast the antichrist

[6]CCL 92:193. [7]Rev 12:3. [8]Jude 6. [9]See Job 1:7. [10]Jn 8:44. [11]Gen 17:5. [12]TEG 8:183-85. [13]PL 35:2435.

arises from the earth.[14] However, according to holy Methodius and holy Hippolytus and others this beast is to be interpreted as the antichrist who comes from the tumultuous and rough sea of this life.[15] The ten horns with the diadems and the seven heads signify the unity that the devil has with him—for these characteristics were interpreted above as also belonging to him.[16] The ten horns and seven heads also signify the division of the earthly government at the end of time into ten, and the earthly government corresponds to this world, which is calculated as consisting of seven days and is divided into seven successive kingdoms. For this reason, Satan, who operates in him, is called "the ruler of this age."[17] "A blasphemous name is upon its heads" clearly refers to his supporters. For from the beginning these never ceased from blaspheming Christ until the accession of Constantine. But after him, [the emperors] Julian and Valens again slandered against Christ. COMMENTARY ON THE APOCALYPSE 13.1.[18]

## 13:2 The Dragon Gave Power to the Beast

**STRONG, FILTHY AND BLOODY.** VICTORINUS OF PETOVIUM: "And I saw a beast rising out of the sea, like a leopard." This passage indicates that the kingdom of that time, the kingdom of the antichrist, will be commingled with a variety of nations and peoples. "Its feet were like the feet of a bear," that is, they were of a strong and utterly filthy beast. He speaks of the leaders [of this kingdom] as his "feet." And "its mouth was like the mouths of lions." This means that the beast is armed by teeth intended for blood.[19] For the "mouth" is his command and his tongue which proceed only for the purpose of the shedding of blood. COMMENTARY ON THE APOCALYPSE 13.1.[20]

**THE DEVIL IS QUICK TO DECEIVE.** OECUMENIUS: "And the beast that I saw was like a leopard," because, I think, of his ability to turn quickly and quickly to form devious plans. "And its feet were like a bear's," it says, since they are

sturdy and steadfast, that he might "walk to and fro upon the earth under heaven,"[21] plotting against humankind. "And its mouth was like a lion's," for "our adversary, the devil, prowls around like a lion, seeking someone to devour," as it is written.[22] "And to it the dragon gave his power." Without question the power of the apostate dragon inhabits these deceptions and wiles, for he has become for [the devil] both the instigator and the teacher of his works. COMMENTARY ON THE APOCALYPSE 13.1-4.[23]

**HERETICS POSSESS THE DEVIL'S POWER IN THIS WORLD.** CAESARIUS OF ARLES: The beast is like a leopard because of the variety of nations; he is like a bear because of his maliciousness and madness; he is like a lion because of the strength of his body and the haughtiness of his mouth.[24] At the time of the antichrist his kingdom will be [as a leopard], for it will contain a commixture of various nations and people; it will have feet as a bear in its leaders, and its commanding authority will be as the mouth [of a lion]. "And the dragon gave him his power," for we see how the heretics, who have the power of the devil, are powerful in this world. For just as formerly it was the pagans who devastated the church, so now it is the heretics. EXPOSITION ON THE APOCALYPSE 13.2, HOMILY 10.[25]

**THE RUIN OF THE WEAK AND UNSTABLE.** ANDREW OF CAESAREA: The kingdom of the Greeks is signified by the leopard; the Persians are signified by the bear; the Babylonians are signified by the lion. The antichrist, who will come as a king of the Romans, will rule over them and destroy their empires, when he beholds the clay

---

[14]Andrew is referring to Oecumenius. [15]This view cannot be found in the literary remains of Methodius. Hippolytus interprets the dragon to be the Roman Empire and the beast from the earth as antichrist (see *On the Antichrist* 49). Andrew follows the view of Irenaeus (*Against Heresies* 5.28.2). [16]Rev 12:3. [17]See Jn 12:31. [18]MTS 1 Sup 1:135-36. [19]Adopting the reading of Dulaey (SC 423:104). Hausleiter reads "armed and wet with blood" (CSEL 49:116). [20]CSEL 49:116. [21]Job 1:7. [22]1 Pet 5:8. [23]TEG 8:185-86. [24]Caesarius received these meanings from Tyconius. [25]PL 35:2435.

toes of their feet, by which is indicated the destruction of a weak and brittle kingdom. Satan, that spiritual dragon, will give all of his authority to the antichrist, who through false signs and wonders will work for the ruination of those who are weak and unstable. COMMENTARY ON THE APOCALYPSE 13.2.[26]

### 13:3-4 The Earth Followed the Beast and Worshiped the Dragon

**ANTICHRIST WILL POSE AS A DEFENDER OF THE LAW.** VICTORINUS OF PETOVIUM: "One of its heads was mortally wounded, but its mortal wound was healed."[27] He is referring here to Nero. For it is a well-known fact that when the army sent by the Senate was following him, he cut his own throat. And he is the one whom, when he has been brought to life again, God will send as a king worthy of those who are worthy of him, namely, the Jews and those who persecute Christ, and he will send him as a christ such as the persecutors and the Jews deserve. And since he will bear another name, he will also undertake another life, so that they [the Jews] might receive him as the Christ. For Daniel said, "he will not know the desire of women"—he who himself is the most impure!—"and he will know no god of his fathers."[28] To be sure, he would not be able to seduce the people of the circumcision were he not to pose as a defender of the law. Finally, he will urge the saints, if he proves able to seduce them, to accept nothing other than circumcision. And so at last he will create a trust in himself, so that he will be called "Christ" by them. That he will come forth from hades, we have already mentioned through the words of Isaiah, "water nourished him and the deep set him on high."[29] COMMENTARY ON THE APOCALYPSE 13.3.[30]

**THE DEVIL'S THRONE.** TYCONIUS: One of its heads refers to the antichrist, because there are seven heads not in regard to number but as a sign of the universality of that earthly kingdom that is hostile to the Lamb. It is evident that the dragon,

that is, the devil, will give his authority and his throne to [the antichrist]. As in a good sense the soul of a righteous person is the seat of wisdom, so in an evil sense the enemy is said to give his throne to those whom he especially possesses and whom he uses for the seduction of others. Moreover, with God's permission he frequently does amazing things through them, and he proceeds to so great a rashness that in imitation of the true Head and in order to delude the souls of [God's] children, he claims that one of the seven heads resurrected as if it had died before and that he should be accepted instead of Christ, who actually accomplished this deed. "And the nations which inhabit the earth wondered at the beast." . . . By "earth" he refers to those who are earthly and who desire to follow and to worship him, that is, those who in the antichrist are said to worship the dragon as in an image. COMMENTARY ON THE APOCALYPSE 13.3.[31]

**ISRAEL HEALED THE WOUND OF THE TEMPTER.** OECUMENIUS: The inspired Evangelist himself would know the meaning of this. But, as it seems to me, the meaning is something like this. The death-bearing wound which the devil received on one of its heads was because of the reverent worship of Israel. But this was healed through their subsequent idolatry. "And the whole earth followed the beast with wonder." How would this not be the case, since even the pious people of Israel came to worship him? And this is indicated in Isaiah, who in the person of God speaks to Israel: "Because of you, my name is forever blasphemed among the nations."[32] But with the beast they worshiped also the dragon who is the instigator and cause of such deception and deleterious wiles. . . . Those from Israel whom he conquered devise for him songs of praise, saying, "Who is like the beast, and who can fight against it?" COMMENTARY ON THE APOCALYPSE 13.1-4.[33]

---

[26]MTS 1 Sup 1:136-37. [27]Victorinus reads *occisum*, not *quasi occisum*. He believed that Nero had once died but was to be revived in the future. [28]Dan 11:37. [29]Ezek 34:4. [30]CSEL 49:120-22. [31]CCL 92:194. [32]Is 52:5. [33]TEG 8:186-87.

**HERETICS WOUNDED BY THE SOUND TESTI-
MONIES OF SCRIPTURE.** CAESARIUS OF ARLES:
That which "seemed wounded" are the heretics
who hypocritically seem to confess Christ and
blaspheme since they do not believe as the catholic faith has it. They prophesy that he who was
wounded is also raised again, for even Satan himself transfigures himself into an angel of light.[34]
Another interpretation might be that heresies are
wounded by the catholics, for they are suppressed
by the testimonies of the Scriptures. Yet, as
though a wound of Satan they are revived and
accomplish the works of Satan and do not cease
from blaspheming and attracting whomever they
can to his teachings.... [The dragon gave his
power to the beast], for indeed the heretics possess power, especially the Arians.[35] ... "And they
adored the beast, saying, 'Who is like the beast,
and who can fight against it?'" To be sure, the
heretics flatter themselves that no one believes
better than they and that no one can conquer
their people who are marked by the name of the
beast. And it will be given to him by the devil
himself, although with God's permission, that he
should speak haughty things and blasphemies, as
the apostle says, "There must be heresies in order
that those who are genuine among you may be
manifested."[36] EXPOSITION ON THE APOCALYPSE
13.3-4, HOMILY 10.[37]

**THE DEVIL WILL DECEIVE THROUGH FALSE
RESURRECTIONS.** ANDREW OF CAESAREA: That
he had a head that was wounded indicates that
one of his lieutenants, having been put to death,
deceptively seems to be raised again by him
through his sorcery, in a way similar to Simon the
magician, who, in light of his magic tricks, was
unmasked by the chief of the apostles.[38] Or the
phrase could indicate that the Roman Empire,
having suffered a kind of wound through division, seems to be healed by a unified rule, as
occurred at the time of Augustus Caesar.... The
wonder directed at the antichrist will be transferred to the devil, who is working through him.
For through him the devil will be worshiped, and

through him he will seem, to those blinded in the
eyes of the mind, to raise the dead and perform
signs. COMMENTARY ON THE APOCALYPSE 13.3-
4.[39]

### 13:5-6 The Beast Blasphemed God and His Dwelling[40]

**THOSE WHO WORSHIP THE DEVIL.** OECUME-
NIUS: Since all were vanquished and placed
under his feet, "he was given a mouth uttering
haughty and blasphemous words." By whom
was it given? By those persons who had been
deceived and had come to worship him. For such
boasting comes from arrogance. And what is
more haughty than saying, "I will ascend to
heaven; I will set my throne above the stars of
heaven"?[41] And a little further down: "I will
make myself like the Most High."[42] Isaiah here is
lampooning him, since such claims are blasphemies against God. "And it was allowed to exercise authority for forty-two months." We earlier
noted that "forty-two months" indicates a short
period of time, for compared with the unending
ages, all time is short, even if it should seem to
be very long. [He blasphemes God's name and
his dwelling] for such are the blasphemies
against God spoken by the apostate. The "dwelling" of God is the holy angels, since God dwells
among them. For if it is said concerning people,
"I will dwell among them and I will walk among
them,"[43] how should one speak of the heavenly
powers among whom God dwells? COMMEN-
TARY ON THE APOCALYPSE 13.4-8.[44]

**THE DEVIL BLASPHEMES THE GLORIFIED
JESUS AND HIS CHURCH.** PRIMASIUS: With
these months there is completed the three years
and six months, which above were understood

---

[34]See 2 Cor 11:14. [35]Caesarius probably has in mind the Arian Visigoths, who ruled in south Gaul. [36]See 1 Cor 11:19. [37]PL 35:2435-36.
[38]See *Acts of Peter* 25-26. [39]MTS 1 Sup 1:137-38. [40]Dionysius of
Alexandria applies these verses to events during the persecution under
Valerian (Eusebius *Ecclesiastical History* 7.10.2-9). [41]Is 14:13. [42]Is
14:14. [43]2 Cor 6:16. [44]TEG 8:187.

to refer to the quality of the present age. However, here the severity of the final persecution is especially foretold.[45] For were one to consider the four familiar directions of the earth and multiply four times the ten sayings of the law, which is the symbol of perfection, one would have forty. Were the performance of the two commandments of love added to this, the number forty-two would be completed. That which is commanded in words achieves no favor if it is not perfected by works. And the church is said to be protected by these [commandments] as though by the wings of an eagle, and she flees from the treachery of the dragon into the wilderness to be nourished there for 1,260 days, which is equal to the forty-two months, so that the calculation of the same number may not render a useless meaning. . . . [The beast blasphemed] against God and the church, which dwells in heaven, because "our citizenship is in heaven,"[46] and "now you are not in the flesh."[47] I think that here the temple might also signify the glorified trophy of the body of Christ against whom the antichrist is said then to blaspheme, when he has dared assign to himself that honor which is especially due to [Christ]. Concerning this the Lord said in the Gospel, "That they might lead astray, if possible, even the elect,"[48] and just earlier, "But for the elect those days will be shortened."[49] COMMENTARY ON THE APOCALYPSE 13.5-6.[50]

**APOSTATES BLASPHEME GOD.** CAESARIUS OF ARLES: The forty-two months are to be interpreted as the time of the last persecution. "It opened its mouth to blaspheme against God."[51] It is clear that this refers to those who have left the catholic church, for while earlier they seemed to be within the church as though they held the right faith, in time of persecution they openly blaspheme God with the mouth. [The dwelling of God] is the saints who are contained within the church, which is called "heaven," for they are the habitation of God. EXPOSITION ON THE APOCALYPSE 13.5-6, HOMILY 10.[52]

**THE DEVIL WILL BLASPHEME THE WORD MADE FLESH.** ANDREW OF CAESAREA: With the allowance of God, it says, he will have authority for three and a half years to blaspheme against God and to harm the saints. The "dwelling of God" is the dwelling of the Word in the flesh, that is, his incarnation, as well as his repose among the saints, against whom, as also against the holy angels, he will fully direct his blasphemy. COMMENTARY ON THE APOCALYPSE 13.5-6.[53]

### 13:7-8 War on the Saints

**SOME KEEP PURE FROM THE DEVIL'S CULT.** OECUMENIUS: He received his authority from those persons who had willingly placed themselves under his destructive lordship. And so it correctly says that "all who dwell on the earth will worship it." For with the exception of faithful Israel, the rest of humankind worshiped idols, and since even Israel suffered from this, it finally says that every clan and tribe of people had come to worship the wicked one. "Every one whose name is not written in the book of the life of heaven of him who was slain before the foundation of the world." With great care does the vision place limits on this. For although it says that all who dwell on the earth worshiped the apostate devil, there were a few persons from both the Gentiles and from Israel who kept themselves pure from his cult, such as Job and his four friends, and Melchizedek, and from Israel the holy prophets and they who gave a pious witness in the Old Testament. It means that all worshiped him except those who through their piety and through the pure and perfect manner of their lives are inscribed in heaven and are protected by God. For this is the significance of the fact that the book is sealed. Therefore, according to Luke, the Lord speaks of this book when he says to his

---

[45]Primasius follows Tyconius to this point. [46]Phil 3:20. [47]Rom 8:9. [48]Mt 24:24. [49]Mt 24:22. [50]CCL 92:195. [51]Bede (CCL 121A:405) explains that *ad deum* ("to God") means *adversus deum* ("against God"). [52]PL 35:2436. [53]MTS 1 Sup 1:138.

disciples, "Nevertheless, do not rejoice in this, that the spirits are subject to you; but rejoice that your names are written in heaven."[54] COMMENTARY ON THE APOCALYPSE 13.4-8.[55]

**IT IS NO WONDER THAT THE CHURCH SUFFERS.** PRIMASIUS: By saying that he opened his mouth, it shows that he spoke with that damnable bravado that while before he blasphemed secretly, he will at that time do so publicly. For he will have dared to attribute to himself that honor that especially belongs to [Christ]. And he speaks his inquities arrogantly, for he is hostile to Christ and wishes to be accepted instead of Christ, either by the use of force or by supplanting him with fraudulent means. For a time he will attain power, which he will use in an evil way to harm the body of Christ, so that as Christ suffers, the persecutors praise [the beast] all the more since [Christ] is crucified more cruelly with his [saints]. Of this power the Lord said, "You would have no power over me unless it had been given you from above."[56] If, therefore, at the time of his passion Christ had temporarily given power to his persecutors, although the prince of this world could find in him nothing worthy of death, why is it surprising that in his church he allows evil persons to attack, so that one might say that [the beast] has defeated them? Even we must understand the part from the whole, namely, that part which he is able to conquer. COMMENTARY ON THE APOCALYPSE 13.7.[57]

## 13:9-10 A Call for Endurance and Faith

**THE DEVIL'S INSTRUMENTS.** OECUMENIUS: If any one has a mind able to understand what is being said, it says, "let him hear" what is being spoken and let him know that whoever is ready to bring others into captivity will be captured by the beast and will desert willingly to him. For having no defense from God, he will be carried away into utter evil. And should anyone be prepared for murders, he will die a spiritual death by worshiping the devil. "Here is a call for the endurance and faith of the saints." In this manner is one free from the servitude of the evil one. May it be that we all be found free from such servitude by the grace of God, who has called us to his knowledge. To him be glory forever. Amen. COMMENTARY ON THE APOCALYPSE 13.9-10.[58]

**SPIRITUAL DEATH BY THE SATANIC SWORD.** ANDREW OF CAESAREA: Every one will receive a recompense worthy of his deeds. Those who are willing to harm their neighbor will be captured by the devil and will undergo the death of his soul by the satanic sword. For, as the great James says, they are made slaves of that one by whom they have been conquered through their works.[59] But those who have a pure faith and unshakeable endurance in trials will be indelibly written in the book of life. With such may the all-merciful God also find us partakers who consider "that the sufferings of this present time are not worth comparing with the glory that is to be revealed" to the saints[60] and who walk valiantly the narrow way, so that, finding at the end of it glory in the coming age and rest and paradise, we might reign with Christ, with whom to the Father be all thanksgiving and worship with the Holy Spirit forever. Amen. COMMENTARY ON THE APOCALYPSE 13.9-10.[61]

---

[54]Lk 10:20. [55]TEG 8:188. [56]Jn 19:11. [57]CCL 92:195-96. [58]TEG 8:189. [59]See Jas 3:3. [60]Rom 8:18. [61]MTS 1 Sup 1:139-40.

# 13:11-17 ANOTHER BEAST
# COMES OUT OF THE EARTH

[11]*Then I saw another beast which rose out of the earth; it had two horns like a lamb and it spoke like a dragon. [12]It exercises all the authority of the first beast in its presence, and makes the earth and its inhabitants worship the first beast, whose mortal wound was healed. [13]It works great signs, even making fire come down from heaven to earth in the sight of men; [14]and by the signs which it is allowed to work in the presence of the beast, it deceives those who dwell on earth, bidding them make an image for the beast which was wounded by the sword and yet lived; [15]and it was allowed to give breath to the image of the beast so that the image of the beast should even speak, and to cause those who would not worship the image of the beast to be slain. [16]Also it causes all, both small and great, both rich and poor, both free and slave, to be marked on the right hand or the forehead, [17]so that no one can buy or sell unless he has the mark, that is, the name of the beast or the number of its name.*

**OVERVIEW:** The beast from the earth is the antichrist, who has earth as his source of origin as does all of humankind (OECUMENIUS). Or this beast is the false prophet who is the armorbearer of the antichrist and by sorcery and deceit prepares the way for the antichrist (VICTORINUS, ANDREW OF CAESAREA). He will arise from an earthly and groveling manner of life (ANDREW OF CAESAREA) and will set himself up as the Son of God and a king (HIPPOLYTUS). Although at first he will assume the form of a righteous and pious man (VICTORINUS, ANDREW OF CAESAREA) and will use the two Testaments as though he were the true Lamb (TYCONIUS), he will afterward show himself to be full of malice, a deceiver and murderous within like a wolf (HIPPOLYTUS, VICTORINUS, ANDREW OF CAESAREA). Although he is neither the devil nor the Christ, he does the work of the devil while he imitates the Christ (OECUMENIUS). As John the Baptist led those who believe to the Savior, this false prophet deceives many to believe that the antichrist is God (ANDREW OF CAESAREA). Yet he attacks the body of the Lamb and drives from the truth those whom he has deluded (TYCONIUS).

Like a magician, the false prophet will seem to raise the dead (VICTORINUS) and to cause fire to fall from heaven (ANDREW OF CAESAREA). However, he is merely imitating the church of the Lamb, which alone possesses the Holy Spirit who came upon the apostles in the form of fiery tongues. The Holy Spirit will frustrate this prophet even as he did the magicians who competed against Moses (PRIMASIUS). Nonetheless, the power of the beast's seduction is great, for it brings both body and soul of people to destruction (TYCONIUS) and leads many heretics to leave the church through a false worship (CAESARIUS OF ARLES). His rule will be great and glorious, for he will govern in the manner of Augustus (HIPPOLYTUS) and will erect the image of antichrist in the temple as did Nebuchadnezzar (VICTORINUS). However, he will be harsh to the servants of God who do not obey him, and just as Antiochus Epiphanes tortured the righteous Jews, he will slaughter the faithful (HIPPOLYTUS). Many will, nonetheless, be deceived by him and will, as though one city, confess the antichrist with a uniform confession (PRIMASIUS). This beast represents the city of confusion, Babylon, which lives by fakery and imitation (CAESARIUS OF ARLES).

Given up to sorcery as were those tricked by the magicians of Pharaoh and by Simon Magus (Oecumenius, Andrew of Caesarea), the citizens of this city are unfaithful and live the life of infidelity, even though they might confess the catholic faith (Caesarius of Arles).

## 13:11 Another Beast Rises Out of the Earth

**A Kingdom of Deceit.** Hippolytus: By the beast coming up out of the earth, he means the kingdom of antichrist; and by the two horns he means him and the false prophet after him. And in speaking of "the horns being like a lamb," he means that he will make himself like the Son of God and set himself forward as king. The term "he spoke like a dragon" means that he is a deceiver and not truthful. On the Antichrist 49.[1]

**The Form of Righteousness but Full of Malice.** Victorinus of Petovium: "Another great beast rose out of the earth." This is the false prophet who will do signs and portents and false prodigies before him in the presence of people. It says that he has "horns like a lamb" because he has the form of a righteous man and that he "speaks like a dragon" because he is full of the malice of the devil. Commentary on the Apocalypse 13.4.[2]

**The Antichrist Will Beguile.** Tyconius: It has two horns that are like those of a lamb. These are the two Testaments that belong to the true Lamb but that the beast tried to usurp for himself by feigning to be a lamb. Nevertheless, it is said to speak like a dragon, because by the hypocrisy of a false truth it beguiles those whom it can lead astray. For it would not be like a lamb were it to speak openly as a dragon. It now pretends to be the Lamb so that it might assail the Lamb, that is, the body of Christ.[3] It speaks against God, since it drives away from the way of truth those whom he has deluded and who now seek after him. Commentary on the Apocalypse 13.11.[4]

**The Antichrist Arises from the Earth.** Oecumenius: "Then I saw," it says, "another beast which rose out of the earth." The earth is the source of origin for all humankind, for the antichrist is a man "whose coming will be by the activity of the devil," as the all-wise Paul says.[5] "And it had two horns like a lamb, and it spoke like a dragon." Rightly does it say that it had two horns "like a lamb," not the horns of a lamb, and that it spoke "like a dragon," not that it was a dragon. For since the wicked one makes himself out to be the Christ but is not, he has given to him horns "like a lamb." And since through every kind of unholy work he spreads what is similar to the devil but in fact is not the devil, it does not say that he is a dragon but that he speaks like a dragon. And since such is the case, the discourse has preserved for him an image also in the vision, and it gives to him a form, not that of a lamb but like a lamb, and not that of a dragon but like a dragon. For Christ is said to be a lamb, and the devil is said to be a dragon, but this one is neither one nor the other. Commentary on the Apocalypse 13.11-13.[6]

**The Skin of a Lamb but a Wolf Within.** Andrew of Caesarea: Some say that this beast is the antichrist, while to others its two horns signify the antichrist and the false prophet. But since also the false prophet is thought to come in his own person, it is proper to think that the dragon is to be interpreted as Satan, the beast that arises from the sea as the antichrist, and this beast that comes up from the earth as the false prophet, which is the opinion of the blessed Irenaeus. That he comes up from the earth symbolizes that he arises from an earthly and groveling manner of life. That he has two horns like a lamb indicates that in the skin of a lamb he cloaks the murderousness of the wolf hiding within[7] and that at the beginning he will have the form of

[1]ANF 5:214. [2]CSEL 49:126-28. [3]Caesarius of Arles will simply call this beast the "heretical church" (PL 35:2436). [4]CCL 92:197-98. [5]2 Thess 2:9. [6]TEG 8:190-91. [7]See Mt 7:15.

piety. Concerning him Irenaeus says, "Concerning his armorbearer, whom he also calls the false prophet, he says, 'he spoke like a dragon.' "[8] The authority of signs and wonders was given to him, so that going before the antichrist, he might prepare the way of destruction for him. We say that the healing of the wound of the beast is either the apparent, short-lived unity of the divided empire, or the temporary restoration by the antichrist of the tyranny of Satan that had been destroyed, or the fraudulent resurrection of one of his associates who had died. It says that he speaks like a dragon, because he will do and say the things of the devil, who is the author of evil. COMMENTARY ON THE APOCALYPSE 13.11.[9]

## 13:12-13 It Makes Fire Fall from Heaven

**THE ANTICHRIST WILL RULE EVERYTHING.**
HIPPOLYTUS: In regard to the words "he exercised all the power of the first beast before him and caused the earth and those who dwell within it to worship the first beast, whose deadly wound was healed," this signifies that, after the manner of the law of Augustus, by whom the empire of Rome was established, he too will rule and govern, sanctioning everything by it and taking greater glory to himself. ON THE ANTICHRIST 49.[10]

**IN THE MANNER OF A MAGICIAN.** VICTORINUS OF PETOVIUM: He will perform [his works] in the presence of people, so that even the dead seem to rise again, for through apostate angels even magicians do such things in front of people. COMMENTARY ON THE APOCALYPSE 13.4.[11]

**FALSE LEADERS DO THE WILL OF THE DEVIL.**
TYCONIUS: It exercised all the power of the first beast on the earth. He spoke of that earlier beast that he had seen rising from the sea and to which the dragon had given his own great power. He said that the beast exercised this power before the beast. For all the power of the people is in their leaders, which he described, just as the power of the locusts and the horses is in their tails.[12] In

front of the people, the leaders do what is useful to the will of the devil under the cover of an imitation of the church. Clearly, in both beasts there is one body, and they practice the worship of one iniquity, so that the mimicry of the latter beast may be said to work to the advantage of that earlier beast.... "So that those who dwell on the earth worship the first beast." ... Or as another translation renders, "so that the earth and those who inhabit it." ... And he mentioned the earth and those who inhabit the earth with good reason. For it might have sufficed to mention either the earth or those who inhabit the earth. However, he shows the force of [the beast's] seduction which has given both body and soul to him as property. For whoever falls by force without being enticed away is made captive in the body alone. However, whoever falls to seduction is made captive both in the body and in the mind, and for this reason he said, "He caused the earth and those who inhabit it to worship the beast whose mortal wound was healed." COMMENTARY ON THE APOCALYPSE 13.12.[13]

**ONLY THE CHURCH POSSESSES THE HOLY SPIRIT.** PRIMASIUS: "And he did great signs, even making fire come down from heaven in the sight of people." Although it says that he would do many signs, he mentions only this remarkable sign. This translation speaks as though of the past, while it announces the future, although indicating that the future will also be different. And so it says, "so that he also makes fire come down from heaven." That he causes fire to descend from heaven to the earth, that is, from the church to those who are earthly, indicates that whether from a variety of peoples or by the wiles of a falling enemy he causes his servants to speak in new and multiple tongues. In this manner they prattle as though they had received the gift of the Holy Spirit who in the form of fiery tongues had once truly shined upon the individ-

[8]Irenaeus *Against Heresies* 5.28.2. [9]MTS 1 Sup 1:140-41. [10]ANF 5:214*. [11]CSEL 49:128. [12]See Rev 9:9, 19. [13]CCL 92:198-99.

ual disciples of Christ.[14] And, indeed, the Lord especially commended this sign of those who believe, saying, "These signs will accompany those who believe: in my name they will cast out demons, they will speak in new tongues,"[15] and the like. It is not surprising, therefore, if that beast which by imitation usurped the name of the Lamb who had been killed and now is living should also fraudulently lay claim by mimicry to that great gift of the Holy Spirit and feign that gift also for his servants, even as we recall what once Simon boasted but was unable to do.[16] For when the very ministers of Satan listed their expulsions of demons and their various wonders and said, "Did we not cast out demons in your name?" and the like, the Lord did not approve of their boasting but reproved them as arrogant and worthy of damnation.[17] And therefore, perhaps by emphasizing this sign [of fire], which represents the Holy Spirit, he wished to indicate especially that which is superior to all else. For although heresies seem to have some things in common with us, only the church of Christ can boast that she especially is possessed of this gift. Although the magicians of Pharaoh performed wonders similar to those of Moses, we are told that they were frustrated by the Holy Spirit. When they gave up on their own claims and were defeated, they spoke a true confession and said, "This is the finger of God."[18] The Gospel testifies that the Holy Spirit is called "the finger of God" when one Gospel says, "By the Spirit of God I cast out demons,"[19] while another says, "By the finger of God I cast out demons."[20] And so the sheer force of the seduction is indicated, that the beast is thought to possess that Spirit that resisted the magicians and brought their deceptions to nothing. COMMENTARY ON THE APOCALYPSE 13.13.[21]

**FIRE FALLS FROM HEAVEN.** CAESARIUS OF ARLES: Since the church is "heaven," what is this fire that falls from heaven other than heresies that fall from the church? As it is written, "They went out from us, but they were not of

us."[22] For fire falls from the church whenever heretics leave the church as though fire and persecute the church. Therefore, the beast with the two horns causes the people to worship the image of the beast, that is, the devices of the devil. EXPOSITION ON THE APOCALYPSE 13.12-13, HOMILY 11.[23]

**THIS BEAST LEADS MANY TO THE FALSE CHRIST.** ANDREW OF CAESAREA: The forerunner of the apostate false christ will do all things through sorcery for the deception of humankind, so that the antichrist will be regarded as God. And, since [the antichrist] receives the witness of the worker of such marvels, he receives undisputed honor, in imitation of the Baptist, who led those who believed to the Savior. For falsehood is zealous to imitate the truth for the deception of humankind. Therefore, it is not remarkable that to the eyes of those deceived, fire is seen coming down from heaven. For somewhere in the story of Job we are taught that, with the permission of God and by the activity of Satan, fire came down and consumed his flock.[24] COMMENTARY ON THE APOCALYPSE 13.12-13.[25]

### 13:14-17 Marks on the Right Hand and the Forehead

**THE ANTICHRIST WILL PERSECUTE THOSE WHO DO NOT OBEY.** HIPPOLYTUS: Being full of guile and exalting himself against the servants of God, with the wish to afflict them and persecute them out of the world because they do not give glory to him, he will order incense pans to be set up by all everywhere, that no one among the saints may be able to buy or sell without first sacrificing. This is what is meant by the mark received upon the right hand. And the words "on their forehead" indicate that all are crowned and put on a crown of fire, and not of life but of death.

---

[14]Acts 2:1-4. [15]Mk 16:17. [16]Acts 8:9-24. [17]See Mt 7:22-23. [18]Ex 8:19. [19]Mt 12:28. [20]Lk 11:20. [21]CCL 92:200-201. [22]1 Jn 2:19. [23]PL 35:2436. [24]Job 1:16. [25]MTS 1 Sup 1:142.

For in this way, too, did Antiochus Epiphanes the king of Syria, the descendant of Alexander of Macedon, devise measures against the Jews. He, too, in the exaltation of his heart, issued a decree in those times that "all should set up shrines before their doors and sacrifice, and that they should march in procession to the honor of Dionysus, waving chaplets of ivy,"[26] and that those who refused obedience should be put to death by strangulation and torture. But he also met his due recompense at the hand of the Lord, the righteous Judge and all-searching God; for he died devoured by worms. ON THE ANTI-CHRIST 49.[27]

**AN IMAGE OF ANTICHRIST WILL BE ERECTED.** VICTORINUS OF PETOVIUM: [The beast] will even see to it that a golden image of the antichrist is placed in the temple at Jerusalem, and the apostate angels will enter there and from there issue prophesies and oracles. And he himself will cause "both slave and free to receive a mark on their foreheads or on their right hands"—namely, the number of his name—"so that no one can buy or sell unless he has the mark." Daniel had already spoken of this destruction of people and this contempt of God and this abomination, saying, "And he will place [an image] in his temple between the mountain of the sea and the two seas,"[28] that is, at Jerusalem, and then he will place here his golden image, just as King Nebuchadnezzar had done. And the Lord recalls this to all the churches when he speaks of the last times: "When you see the contempt of turning away[29] spoken of by the prophet Daniel, standing in the holy place, where it ought not, let the reader understand."[30] It is said to be "contempt" when God is provoked because idols are being worshiped. On the other hand, it is said to be a "turning away" when unstable people, seduced by false signs and wonders, are turned away from their salvation. COMMENTARY ON THE APOCA-LYPSE 13.4.[31]

**LED BY THE SAME DEMON.** OECUMENIUS: "And

by signs he deceives those who dwell on earth." He does signs, beguiling the eyes of those who look on, even as the magicians did in front of Pharaoh, for both they and this one are led by one and the same deceitful demon. And it rightly says that he does signs in the presence of the beast. For since he will set up an image for him, which he will compel all to worship, he will actually perform signs before it, and as though regarding the image as divine, claim that from it he has the power to do these things. "And it was allowed to give breath to the image." They say that many statues both perspire and seem to speak by the activity of the devil. COMMENTARY ON THE APOCALYPSE 13.14-18.[32]

**THE DECEIT OF ANTICHRIST.** PRIMASIUS: It is as though he had said that the deception had succeeded to such an extent that the earthly, led astray by the wonders of the beast, gave their full miserable assent to the beast and by a mutual devotion encouraged each other to make an image of the beast in the fraudulence of their hearts. And so they believe that there is no room for doubt but are convinced by the evidence of the fire that [the beast] is indeed the Christ, although the devil is in the antichrist and the same malignant spirit has taken the form of the Spirit and, with divine permission, lays down such seductive snares. Therefore, he is said "to give breath to the image of the beast so that the image of the beast should even speak." This may be interpreted in two ways. Either the whole body of evil persons are persuaded by the demonstrations of power, since the devil is working and the leaders are urging the people, so that there is for everyone the same confession and that all are to proclaim it by a uniform formula, so that should anyone not speak this through the image of the beast, that is, through a mutual imitation, he should be killed. . . . Or, just as

---

[26]See 2 Macc 6:7; also 1 Macc 1:51-64. [27]ANF 5:214. [28]Dan 11:45. [29]Latin *aspernationem eversionis* (cf. *Vetus Latina*). [30]Mt 24:15. [31]CSEL 49:128-30. [32]TEG 8:192.

through conversation with a woman the first man was led astray by the mouth of a serpent, so then he deludes many by a similar fraud, when he causes his followers to receive messages by consulting an image, that is, the antichrist, to whom they believe honor is due, as to a god, although he is "the man of sin and the son of perdition."[33] . . . "And he causes all . . . to be marked on the right hand or the forehead." He here distinguishes the individual members, although more often he includes them as a whole in the body or the person of the beast. The "hand" indicates works, and it is the right hand to simulate the truth. The "forehead" symbolizes the confession of faith. Since they are defrauded in regard to both of these good things, they are said to be marked on both. COMMENTARY ON THE APOCALYPSE 13.14-16.[34]

## THIS BEAST IS THE CITY OF THE IMPIOUS.

CAESARIUS OF ARLES: "That he give them a mark on the right hand or on the forehead." He speaks of the mystery of deception. For the saints who are in the church receive Christ in the hand and on the forehead. The hypocrites, however, receive the beast under the name of Christ. "Those who do not worship the beast . . . will be slain." It is not inconsistent with the faith that the beast be understood as the city of the impious itself, that is, as the congregation or conspiracy of all those who are impious or filled with hubris. This city is called "Babylon," which is interpreted as "Confusion," and to it belong all who desire to work that which is worthy of confusion. He himself is the citizenry of unfaithful persons who are the opposite of the faithful people, that is, the city of God. His image is an imitation, that is, among those people who confess the catholic faith but live the life of infidelity. For they feign to be what they are not, and they are called Christians, not by way of the true image but by way of a false image. Of such persons the apostle wrote, "holding the form of religion but denying the power of it."[35] Not a small number of these persons are within the catholic church. However, the righteous do

not worship the beast, that is, they do not assent to him, nor do they submit to him, nor do they receive his mark, the mark of sin, on their forehead, on account of the confession, and on their hand, on account of works. EXPOSITION ON THE APOCALYPSE 13.15-16, HOMILY 11.[36]

## THIS ARMORBEARER OF ANTICHRIST WORKS THROUGH DEMONS.

ANDREW OF CAESAREA: [The beast] deceives those who continually dwell upon the earth in their hearts. For those who possess their citizenship in heaven are not deceived by fake appearances, since they have been sufficiently fortified by the prediction of his coming. . . . It is reported that demons often speak by sorcery through images and statues and trees and streams, also through Apollonius and others, and I think, even through dead bodies. For example, in the presence of Peter, Simon the Magician showed the Romans a dead body that he was moving. However, the apostle unmasked his deception by showing through those whom he himself raised how the dead were raised [by Simon].[37] And so there is nothing strange in the fact that working through demons, this standard-bearer of the antichrist should make an image for the beast and contrive to show it speaking and see to it that those who did not worship it were killed. And he will eagerly strive to place the mark of the ruinous name of the apostate upon everyone. He will make the mark upon their right hands to bring to an end the doing of good works, and upon their foreheads in order to teach those deceived to be bold in their deception and darkness. But those who have had their faces sealed with the divine light will not receive the mark. He will undertake to spread the mark of the beast everywhere through buying and selling, so that a violent death might come to all who do have the mark from the lack of necessities. COMMENTARY ON THE APOCALYPSE 13.14-17.[38]

---

[33]2 Thess 2:3. [34]CCL 92:201-3. [35]2 Tim 3:5. [36]PL 35:2436-37. [37]See *Acts of Pilate* 28. [38]MTS 1 Sup 1:142-44.

**The Antichrist Will Deceive the Senses Through Phantasms.** Bede: "By the signs which it is allowed to work, it deceives those who dwell on earth." "For his coming," it is said, will be "by the activity of Satan with all power and false signs and wonders."[39] It may be that these are called "false signs and wonders" because he will deceive the senses of people through phantasms, so that he seems to do what in fact he does not do. Or it may be that these signs, even though they will be astonishing wonders, will

lead those to falsehood who, unaware of the power of the devil, will think that such things could not be accomplished apart from divine power. For it was not by a fake fire or storm that the devil destroyed the whole family of the saintly Job together with all of his flocks, but by a real fire and a real whirlwind. Explanation of the Apocalypse, 13.14.[40]

---

[39]2 Thess 2:9. [40]CCL 121A:411.

## 13:18 THE NUMBER OF THE BEAST IS 666

[18]*This calls for wisdom: let him who has understanding reckon the number of the beast, for it is a human number, its number is six hundred and sixty-six.*[g]

g Other ancient authorities read *six hundred and sixteen*

**Overview:** The name of antichrist is not given in the divine book. Time and experience will reveal the significance of the name to the sober-minded (Andrew of Caesarea). However, the number 666 suggests completion and perfection, for the world was finished in six days (Bede). Indeed, as the stories of Noah and the image of Nebuchadnezzar indicate, this evil man will concentrate in himself all apostasy, wickedness and deception so that shut up in him, all apostate power may be cast into the lake of fire (Irenaeus). Attempts at the name may be made, however, according to Greek calculation (Primasius). Although many shameful names and titles correspond to the number (Oecumenius), "Titan" is especially probable because the antichrist will be fierce and will claim for himself royal dignity (Irenaeus). Since the antichrist will usurp the honor due to God alone and will deny the true Christ, the names "Antemos" and "Arnoume" are

also appropriate (Primasius). The antichrist is, in any case, shameless and will revel in being called names of wickedness.

### 13:18 The Number of the Beast

**All Apostasy and Wickedness Is Concentrated.** Irenaeus: There is in this beast, when he comes, a recapitulation made of all sorts of iniquity and of every deceit, in order that all apostate power, flowing into and being shut up in him, may be sent into the furnace of fire. Fittingly, therefore, shall his name possess the number 666, since he sums up in his own person all the commixture of wickedness that took place previous to the deluge, due to the apostasy of the angels. For Noah was six hundred years old when the deluge came upon the earth, sweeping away the rebellious world, for the sake of that most infamous generation that lived in the times of

Noah. And [antichrist] also sums up every error of devised idols since the flood, together with the slaying of the prophets and the cutting off of the just. For that image that was set up by Nebuchadnezzar had indeed a height of sixty cubits, while the breadth was six cubits; on account of which Ananias, Azarias and Misael, when they did not worship it, were cast into a furnace of fire,[1] pointing out prophetically, by what happened to them, the wrath against the righteous that shall arise towards the [time of the] end. For that image, taken as a whole, was a prefiguring of this man's coming, decreeing that he should undoubtedly himself alone be worshiped by all people. Thus, then, the six hundred years of Noah, in whose time the deluge occurred because of the apostasy, and the number of the cubits of the image for which these just men were sent into the fiery furnace, do indicate the number of the name of that man in whom is concentrated the whole apostasy of six thousand years, and unrighteousness, and wickedness and false prophecy, and deception.[2] AGAINST HERESIES 5.29.2.[3]

**THE NAME OF ANTICHRIST.** IRENAEUS: It is therefore more certain and less hazardous to await the fulfilment of the prophecy than to be making surmises and casting about for any names that may present themselves, inasmuch as many names can be found possessing the number mentioned; and the same question will, after all, remain unsolved. For if there are many names found possessing this number, it will be asked which among them shall the coming man bear. It is not through a want of names containing the number of that name that I say this, but on account of the fear of God, and zeal for the truth. For the name *Euanthas* (ΕΥΑΝΘΑΣ) contains the required number, but I make no allegation regarding it. Then also *Lateinos* (ΛΑΤΕΙΝΟΣ) has the number 666; and it is a very probable [solution], this being the name of the last kingdom [of the four seen by Daniel]. For the Latins are they who at present bear rule; I will not, however, make any boast over this [coincidence]. *Teitan*

(TEITAN, the first syllable being written with the two Greek vowels ε and ι) too, among all the names that are found among us, is rather worthy of credit. For it has in itself the predicted number and is composed of six letters, each syllable containing three letters; and [the word itself] is ancient and removed from ordinary use; for among our kings we find none bearing this name Titan, nor have any of the idols that are worshiped in public among the Greeks and barbarians this appellation. Among many persons, too, this name is accounted divine, so that even the sun is termed "Titan" by those who do now possess [the rule].[4] This word, too, contains a certain outward appearance of vengeance and of one inflicting merited punishment because he (antichrist) pretends that he vindicates the oppressed. And besides this, it is an ancient name, one worthy of credit, of royal dignity, and still further, a name belonging to a tyrant. Inasmuch, then, as this name Titan has so much to recommend it, there is a strong degree of probability, that from among the many [names suggested], we infer that perchance he who is to come shall be called "Titan." We will not, however, incur the risk of pronouncing positively as to the name of antichrist; for if it were necessary that his name should be distinctly revealed in this present time, it would have been announced by the one who beheld the apocalyptic vision.[5] AGAINST THE HERESIES 5.30.3.[6]

**THE ANTICHRIST WILL REJOICE TO BE CALLED SHAMEFUL NAMES.** OECUMENIUS: "This calls for wisdom." Let anyone search for the name of the beast and through this search let him find it. For it says, I will not speak of a reckoning that is strange and unusual, nor will I present a name that is secret and unclear, but I will give a

---

[1]See Dan 3. [2]Irenaeus is aware of manuscripts that have the number 616, although he thinks this reading occurred "through the fault of the copyists" (*Against Heresies* 5.30.1). [3]ANF 1:558*. [4]Cicero and Ovid say that the sun is called Titan. [5]Hippolytus clearly follows the discussion of Irenaeus but seems to favor the name *Latinus* (*On the Antichrist* 50). [6]ANF 1:559.

calculation that is oft-used and known to people, which adds up to 666. While to be sure this number signifies also many other names, both proper names as well as titles, it signifies also these following. Among the proper names it can render "Lampetis," and "Benedict" and "Titan." "Titan" is written with an iota, but it can be written with a diphthong. For if "Teitan" is derived from τεῖσις [stretching]—the verb is τείνω and the future is τενῶ—then it is correctly written with the diphthong, even as φθείρω is from φθερῶ and σπείρω is from σπερῶ. Among the titles, the number can render ὁ νικητής [the Conqueror]—for perhaps he named himself this when he warred against the three horns or three kings and rooted them out. See what Daniel says about them in his eighth vision: "I considered his horns (that is, those of the fourth beast) and behold, there came up among them another little horn, and three of the former horns were rooted out before it; and, behold, in this horn were eyes like the eyes of a man, and a mouth speaking haughty things."[7] And then there are also these titles, ὁ ἐπίσαλος [Unstable], κακὸς ὁδηγός [Evil Guide], ἀληθὴς βλαβερός [Truly Harmful], πάλαι βάσκανος [Ancient Slanderer], ἀμνὸς ἄδικος [Unjust Lamb]. Perhaps he was called these names by those who opposed him. But this one will not be at all ashamed to be called these things; he will rather even rejoice in such appellations, since he is not ashamed even to call himself such things. Rebuking such wicked and vile choices, the wise apostle says, "Whose glory is in their shame."[8] Therefore, since many names have been found, anyone who wishes has the right to bestow a more suitable name on the accursed. COMMENTARY ON THE APOCALYPSE 13.14-18.[9]

**DISHONOR AND DENIAL GIVE THEIR NAME TO THE ANTICHRIST.** PRIMASIUS: This calls for wisdom. Whoever has understanding, let him reckon the number of the beast, for the number of the beast, it says, is that of a man. Let us reckon the number that is to be received, so that in the number we might also learn the name and

the mark. And the number, it says, is 666, which we will reckon according to the Greek, especially since he was writing to Asia and said according to the manner of their own language, "I am the alpha and the omega." Having already described as much as he could the fraudulence of the adversarial party by which the devil attempts to usurp for himself the honor of deity that he does not merit, so that he might exhibit the antichrist who is the opposite to divine honor, he instructs us to investigate the character of the beast, whether by the mark or by the number of his name, that is, of the will and the work of that most wicked beast. The name is ΑΝΤΕΜΟΣ, which, if you compute the numbers that correspond to these Greek letters, fulfills the number 666 (I + L + CCC + V + XL + LXX + CC). This name is interpreted as "contrary to honor," and so he is said to be contrary to that honor that belongs to God alone, and for this reason he is said to be inept, insolent and inconstant, for no honor pertains to him, but only anathema.[10] And so through the number a name is found and from the name a number is computed, and from the interpretation of this name the character of his works is learned. There is another name that gives the sum of the same number and that might rightfully be advanced, and that is ΑΡΝΟΥΜΕ, which also renders 666 (I + C + L + LXX + CCCC + XL + V). The interpretation of this is "I deny." And it is not surprising that the antichrist is worthy of this name, that is, of denial, since the name of belief is proper to Christ, as he himself indicated, saying, "This is the work of God, that you believe in him whom he has sent,"[11] and also, "You believe in God, believe also in me."[12] And so, whether one would speak of ΑΝΤΕΜΟΣ, that is, "contrary to honor," or ΑΡΝΟΥΜΕ, that is, "I deny," either can aptly refer to the antichrist, so that as through two parts of speech, that of the

---

[7]Dan 7:8. [8]Phil 3:19. [9]TEG 8:193. [10]Primasius seems to interpret ΑΝΤΕΜΟΣ as the equivalent of ΑΝΤΙ + ΤΙΜΟΣ ("contrary to honor"). However, the name might refer to Antemos, emperor of the west from 467-472, who was much disliked in Italy. [11]Jn 6:29. [12]Jn 14:1.

name and that of the word itself, both the character of his person and the severity of his work is suggested. COMMENTARY ON THE APOCALYPSE 13.18.[13]

**IT IS NOT NECESSARY TO KNOW THE NAME.**
ANDREW OF CAESAREA: For the sober-minded, time and experience will reveal the actual significance of the number and the truth of whatever has been written about it. For, were it necessary, as some of the teachers say, that such a name be clearly known, the seer would have revealed it. But the divine grace did not consent that the name of the destroyer be noted in the divine book.[14] COMMENTARY ON THE APOCALYPSE 13.18.[15]

**THIS SEDUCER KING WILL EXACT A TAX.**

BEDE: Another interpretation[16]: Who is unaware that the number six, the number of days in which the world was created, is symbolic of a completed work? Or, that this number whether in simple form or multiplied by ten or by a hundred signifies the fruit of the same perfection to be thirty-fold, sixtyfold or a hundredfold? "Now the weight of gold that came to Solomon in one year was 666 talents."[17] Therefore, this seductor tyrant will attempt to exact for himself that tax that is rightfully due and paid to the true king. EXPLANATION OF THE APOCALYPSE 13.18.[18]

---

[13]CCL 92:203-5. [14]Andrew adduces, "as though by way of a verbal exercise," suggestions given in Hippolytus and Oecumenius. [15]MTS 1 Sup 1:145. [16]Bede earlier gave the name Titan and those suggested by Primasius, ANTEMOC and APNOYME. [17]1 Kings 10:14. [18]CCL 121A:417.

---

## 14:1-5 THE LAMB STANDS ON MOUNT ZION

[1]*Then I looked, and lo, on Mount Zion stood the Lamb, and with him a hundred and forty-four thousand who had his name and his Father's name written on their foreheads.* [2]*And I heard a voice from heaven like the sound of many waters and like the sound of loud thunder; the voice I heard was like the sound of harpers playing on their harps,* [3]*and they sing a new song before the throne and before the four living creatures and before the elders. No one could learn that song except the hundred and forty-four thousand who had been redeemed from the earth.* [4]*It is these who have not defiled themselves with women, for they are chaste[h]; it is these who follow the Lamb wherever he goes; these have been redeemed from mankind as first fruits for God and the Lamb,* [5]*and in their mouth no lie was found, for they are spotless.*

h Greek *virgins*

---

**OVERVIEW:** Although the Romans had devastated the ancient city of Jerusalem because of the insanity of the cross (OECUMENIUS), Christ is seen standing on Mount Zion. In the last days the Jews will come to faith and the Lord will once again make them his own possession and bring them to himself (VICTORINUS, OECUMENIUS). It may also be, however, that Christ is standing upon the new city of the living God. With him are that infinite number who believed the apostolic preaching and were chaste in the inner and the outer person (ANDREW OF CAESAREA) and who love God with heart and soul and mind (BEDE).

From the church comes the voice of the saints who with a divine and melodious euphony (OECUMENIUS, ANDREW OF CAESAREA) celebrate the struggles of Christ by praise and imitation (BEDE). Their song is like the harmony of many harps, for they crucify their flesh with its vices and desires and with united breath praise God with psalter and harp (ANDREW OF CAESAREA, BEDE). The new song that they sing can be sung only by those taught by virtue and deemed worthy by chastity and purity (OECUMENIUS, ANDREW OF CAESAREA). Knowledge of this song is for those purchased by the blood of Christ (OECUMENIUS), and this knowledge is given according to their behavior and good will (ANDREW OF CAESAREA).

Those who sing this new song are especially those who have kept their flesh incorrupted and who eternally rejoice with Christ before the other elect (BEDE). The 144,000 follow Christ wherever he goes. Christ became the Archvirgin of the church when he was made man and preserved his flesh incorrupt in virginity (METHODIUS). The church possesses a spiritual virginity in those who hold to the rule of the catholic faith and are not corrupted by any adulterous commixture with heretics (FULGENTIUS OF RUSPE, CAESARIUS OF ARLES). She possesses a spiritual virginity also in those who preserve their marital chastity and in the devoted widows (AUGUSTINE, FULGENTIUS OF RUSPE). However, in those who keep their flesh untouched by any sexual intercourse, the church receives a fuller, more perfect virginity (FULGENTIUS OF RUSPE). Therefore, those whose virginity of body remains undefiled sing a new song that none but they will be able to sing (AUGUSTINE).

Such virgins are firstfruits, with the widows and those continent in marriage accompanying them in due order (JEROME, AUGUSTINE). The true virgin follows the Lamb by a full imitation and alone follows him wherever he goes; other Christians follow the Lamb so far as they can and are able. The virgins will have, therefore, a joy more blessed and a dominion more sweet (AUGUSTINE), for they will enjoy a closer vision of him in the life to come (BEDE). The martyr, too, follows the Lamb by a special imitation. Yet virgins, married people and widows need not despair over their vocation, for Christ suffered for all, and his garden includes not only the roses of martyrs but also the lilies of virgins, the ivy of married people and the violets of widows (AUGUSTINE). He who overcame the devil and unlocked the underworld by his resurrection returned as victor to heaven, where the Father has placed him at his right hand. To that exalted place the unsullied flock will follow their unsullied leader (MAXIMUS OF TURIN).

### 14:1 On Mount Zion Stood the Lamb

**MANY JEWS WILL COME TO FAITH.** VICTORINUS OF PETOVIUM: Concerning this [first] resurrection he says, "I saw the Lamb standing and with him—that is, standing with Christ—144,000." He is speaking of those from the Jews who at the end of time will come to faith through the preaching of Elijah, and of these the Spirit testifies that they are virgin not only in body but also in language.[1] COMMENTARY ON THE APOCALYPSE 20.1.[2]

**THE JEWS WILL AGAIN BECOME THE LORD'S POSSESSION.** OECUMENIUS: In the Gospels the Lord is depicted speaking to the lawless people of the Jews, "Behold, your house is desolate."[3] For after the insanity of the cross, they were no longer worthy of the divine visitation. How is it, then, that the Lord, as though through a change of mind, is shown by the vision "standing on Mount Zion"? For that their city and temple and entire populace was left wholly desolate, the

---

[1]Victorinus is commenting on Rev 14:4-6. [2]CSEL 49:140. [3]Mt 23:38.

Romans have clearly shown, having burned the temple and having torched the cities, having laid waste to the entire land and having enslaved the capital city itself. But that now the Lord is shown having come to Mount Zion represents the conversion of Israel by faith in the last days, when indeed the Lord will make them his own possession and bring them to himself. For this was proclaimed through Isaiah, saying, "The Redeemer will come from Zion and will remove ungodliness from Jacob, says the Lord."[4] And both the prophet and the apostle stand in agreement with Isaiah. For the one sings, "You will make them turn their back; among those who remain you will prepare their face,"[5] and the other writes, "When the full number of the Gentiles come in, then all Israel will be saved."[6] . . . In a previous section he said that the 144,000 were those from Israel who had come to faith, 12,000 from each of the tribes.[7] Does he now also again refer to these? I do not think so. For he does not designate them here with a definite article—he did not say "the 144,000" but only "144,000"—let alone indicate that they had vigilantly practiced virginity. For virginity was in no way eagerly practiced in Israel, just as later the Gentiles were not interested in it. Therefore, we must regard those mentioned to be a mixture of persons from Israel and from the Gentiles, and the greater part from the Gentiles. COMMENTARY ON THE APOCALYPSE 14.1-5.[8]

**CHRIST STANDS ON THE NEW CITY.** ANDREW OF CAESAREA: Without any doubt whatsoever, the "Lamb" is Christ. He is standing on Mount Zion, not the ancient city, but the new city of the living God. These thousands indicate either the full harvest of the apostolic seed, the grace in each being completed twelve times a thousand, the perfect fruit of the faith of those being saved, or they signify those from the New Testament who are chaste in both the inner and the outer person. For among the ancients the virtue of virginity was rare, found only in a very few, and from this fact one must suppose that these are different from those mentioned earlier who were introduced

with the names of the tribes of Israel, to whom he did not attribute virginity. The foreheads of all of these are sealed with the light of the divine countenance, by which they are revealed as holy to the avenging angels. COMMENTARY ON THE APOCALYPSE 14.1.[9]

**THE CHURCH REJOICES IN BODY, SOUL AND MIND.** BEDE: By the example of his power and the safety of his protection the Lord Christ guarded his church, which was toiling under the burden of its struggles. For although the body which had been confounded by the power of the devil and marked by his brand was shown,[10] lest you fear that the body of the Lamb had been overcome by the furor of the beast, he showed also the church rejoicing with its usual brightness and number. Note as well that the beast stands on the sand of the sea,[11] while the Lamb stands upon Mount Zion. This finite number [144,000] should be regarded as representing an infinite number and by the meaning of a hidden mystery suitable for that virginal throng that loves God with all its heart, all its soul and all its mind, and by the integrity of the body, which consists of four qualities, is consecrated to him. For three times three makes nine, and four times four makes sixteen, and sixteen times nine completes the number of 144,000, so that there should be no doubt concerning the remaining members of the church when such a perfect multitude is seen from those who in the midst of a more difficult life are seen with the Lamb, having been deservedly placed upon Mount Zion. [His name and the name of his Father on their foreheads] stands in analogy with the mark on the forehead of the body of the beast,[12] for it says that God and Christ were written upon the foreheads of the church. EXPLANATION OF THE APOCALYPSE 14.1.[13]

### 14:2 A Voice Like Harpers Playing Harps

---

[4]Is 59:20. [5]Ps 20:13 LXX. [6]Rom 11:25-26. [7]Rev 7:4-8. [8]TEG 8:194-95. [9]MTS 1 Sup 1:146-47. [10]That is, in Rev 13:11-17. [11]See Rev 12:17. [12]See Rev 13:16. [13]CCL 121A:419.

**THE SINGING OF THE RIGHTEOUS.** OECUME-
NIUS: That the sound was like that of harpists
indicates the divine euphony and harmony of the
song. For if "praise is not seemly in the mouth of
a sinner," as it is written,[14] it is certainly seemly
and fitting in the mouth of the righteous. COM-
MENTARY ON THE APOCALYPSE 14.1-5.[15]

**THE MELODIOUS SONG OF THE SAINTS.**
ANDREW OF CAESAREA: The voice of many
waters and of thunder and of the harpers indicates the penetrating clarity of the singing of the
saints and of the harmonious and melodious
euphony of their song, which resounds throughout "the assembly and festal gathering of the firstborn who are enrolled in heaven"[16] and which,
just as in the harmony of strings, sounds forth
with the united breath of the saints and is accomplished by the dying of the desires of the body.
COMMENTARY ON THE APOCALYPSE 14.2-3.[17]

**ALL SAINTS ARE HARPS.** BEDE: The loud voice
of the saints is the great devotion of love, which
he says he heard from heaven. When he said that
those who uttered the voice stood on Mount
Zion, it was to indicate that by *Mount Zion* he
referred to nothing other than the church who,
encouraged toward overcoming the distresses of
her afflictions by the sublime joy of the contemplation of her king, celebrates [his] struggles at
the same time by praise and by imitation. This is
truly to sing to the Lamb who is standing [on
Mount Zion].... Although all the saints are
harpists of God, who crucify their flesh with its
vices and lusts and praise him with psalter and
harp, how much more are they who, by the privilege of an angelic purity, render themselves totally
a sacrifice to the Lord and in a particular way
deny themselves and, taking up their cross, "follow the Lamb wherever he goes." EXPLANATION
OF THE APOCALYPSE 14.2.[18]

## 14:3 *They Sing a New Song*

**ONLY THOSE PURIFIED BY CHRIST'S BLOOD**

**KNOW THE NEW SONG.** OECUMENIUS: "And no
one," it says, "could learn this song except the
144,000 who had been redeemed from the earth."
I think that no one is strong enough even to hear
the mysteries of the new song except for those
who are thought worthy to sing them. For knowledge is given to each according to the measure of
his purity. For "there are many rooms," says the
Lord, or rewards of good things, "with my
Father."[19] He calls those "redeemed" who had
been purchased by the blood of Christ. For the
precious blood of Christ was poured out on
behalf of all humankind. Yet for some it was without profit, namely for those who willingly robbed
themselves of the salvation that came from it—
indeed, through the prophet the Lord reproached
these, saying, "What profit is there in my blood,
when I go down into destruction?"[20] But for those
who have been saved and made righteous, of
whom these, of whom the passage now speaks,
are the first fruit and the first offering, it was
immensely profitable, more than anyone could
say. COMMENTARY ON THE APOCALYPSE 14.1-5.[21]

**KNOWLEDGE OF THE NEW SONG BELONGS TO
THE FAITHFUL.** ANDREW OF CAESAREA: No one
else, it says, can learn this song except these, for
the knowledge [of the song] is co-extensive to the
measure of their behavior, just as the servants of
people are allowed to know their master's secrets
in proportion to their good will.... We think
that, after the twenty-four elders, these are leaders of the rest who because of their chastity and
purity in word and deed have, after the sojourn of
Christ, come to possess the brightness of the virtues. Taught by the virtues, they sing the new
song, which remains unknown to most, not only
in this life but in that to come. For although when
"the perfection of knowledge will come, then the
imperfect will cease," as the apostle says,[22] the
appearance of the divine mysteries will be propor-

---

[14]Sir 15:9. [15]TEG 8:195. [16]Heb 12:23. [17]MTS 1 Sup 1:147. [18]CCL
121A:421. [19]See Jn 14:2. [20]Ps 30:9 (29:10 LXX). [21]TEG 8:195-96.
[22]1 Cor 13:10.

tionate to the life of the saints here. For "in my Father's house are many rooms,"[23] and "star differs from star in glory,"[24] just as also there is a difference of torments. Redeeming us from these, may the Lord of all count us among those who are being saved through his own goodness, not regarding the multitude of our sins but his own mercies, on account of which he came to the earth and shed his precious blood for us, that washing away our stains and spots, he might bring us to the Father, with whom glory, power and honor are due to him, the Leader of our salvation, together with the all-holy Spirit, now and forever and ever. Amen. COMMENTARY ON THE APOCALYPSE 14.3-5.[25]

## ONLY VIRGINS SING THIS SONG ETERNALLY TO THE LAMB.

BEDE: The old song was this: "Blessed is he who has his seed in Zion and his household in Jerusalem."[26] However, the new song is this: "Rejoice, O barren one, who did not bare,"[27] and again, "To eunuchs in my house and within my walls, says the Lord, I shall give a place and a name better than sons and daughters."[28] ... To sing the song to the Lamb is to rejoice with him for eternity before all the faithful, especially from the incorruptibility of the flesh. Nevertheless, the other elect are able to hear the song, although they cannot sing it, because through love they have been made glad in their high status, although they do not rise to their rewards. EXPLANATION OF THE APOCALYPSE 14.3.[29]

## 14:4 They Are Virgins Who Follow the Lamb

## THE LORD PROMISES THE GRACE OF CONTINENCE ALSO TO WOMEN.

CYPRIAN: Nor is this an empty precaution and a vain fear that takes thought of the way of salvation, that guards the life-giving precepts of the Lord, so that those who have consecrated their lives to Christ, and, renouncing the concupiscent behaviors of the flesh, have dedicated themselves to God in body as well as in spirit, may perfect their work, des-

tined as it is for a great reward, and may not be solicitous to adorn themselves or to please anyone except their Lord, from whom in truth they await the reward of virginity, since he himself says, "All do not accept this word but those to whom it is given; for there are eunuchs who were born so from their mother's womb, and there are eunuchs who were made so by men, and there are eunuchs who have made themselves eunuchs for the kingdom of heaven."[30] Again, too, by these words of the angel the gift of continence is made clear, virginity is extolled: "These are they who were not defiled with women, for they have remained virgins. These are they who follow the Lamb wherever he goes." And indeed not to men only does the Lord promise the grace of continence, disregarding women; but since woman is a part of man and was taken and formed from him, almost universally in the Scriptures God addresses the first formed because they are two in one flesh, and in the man is signified likewise the woman. But if continence follows Christ, and virginity is destined for the kingdom of God, what have such maidens to do with worldly dress and adornments, whereby in striving to please men they offend God? THE DRESS OF VIRGINS 4-5.[31]

## THE WORD INCARNATE PRESERVED HIS FLESH INCORRUPT.

METHODIUS: What then did the Lord, the Truth and the Light, accomplish on coming down to the world? He preserved his flesh incorrupt in virginity with which he had adorned it. And so let us too, if we are to come to the likeness of God, endeavor to aspire to the virginity of Christ. For becoming like God means to banish corruptibility. Now we are told that the Word incarnate became the Archvirgin as well as Archshepherd and Archprophet of his church, by John in the book of the Apocalypse where, filled with Christ, he says, "And I beheld, and lo the Lamb stood upon Mount Zion, and with him 144,000, having his name, and the name of his

---

[23]Jn 14:2. [24]1 Cor 15:41. [25]MTS 1 Sup 1:147-49. [26]Is 31:9 LXX. [27]Is 54:1. [28]Is 56:5. [29]CCL 121A:421-23. [30]Mt 19:11-12. [31]FC 36:34-35.

Father, written on their foreheads. And I heard a voice from heaven, as the noise of many waters and as the voice of great thunder; and the voice which I heard was as the voice of harpers harping on their harps. And they were singing as it were a new canticle, before the throne, and before the four living creatures and the ancients; and no man could say the canticle, but those 144,000, who were purchased from the earth. These are they who were not defiled with women; for they are virgins. These follow the Lamb wherever he goes"—thus showing that the Lord is leader of the choir of virgins. And notice, again, how excellent is the dignity of virginity in God's sight. "These were purchased from among men, the firstfruits to God and to the Lamb; and in their mouth was found no lie; for they are without spot; these follow," he says, "the Lamb wherever he goes." Here it is also clear that he wishes to teach us that the virgins were restricted to this number, that is, 144,000, from above, whereas the multitude of the rest of the saints is beyond counting. Note what he teaches us as he considers the others: "I also saw a great multitude that no man could number, of every tongue and tribe and of every nation."[32] Obviously, then, as I have said, he introduces an untold number in the case of the other saints but only a very small number in the case of the virgins, as though he deliberately intended a contrast with the larger, uncounted number. SYMPOSIUM 1.5.[33]

**VIRGINS ARE FIRSTFRUITS.** JEROME: Out of each tribe, except the tribe of Dan, the place of which is taken by the tribe of Levi, twelve thousand virgins who have been sealed are spoken of as future believers, who have not defiled themselves with women. And that we may not suppose the reference to be to those who have not had relations with harlots, he immediately added, "for they continued virgins." Whereby he shows that all who have not preserved their virginity, in comparison with pure and angelic chastity and of our Lord Jesus Christ himself, are defiled. "These are they who sing a new song that no man can

sing except him that is a virgin. These are first-fruits unto God and unto the Lamb and are without blemish." If virgins are firstfruits, it follows that widows and the continent in marriage come after the firstfruits, that is, are in the second and third rank; nor can a lost people be saved unless it offer such sacrifices of chastity to God and with pure victims reconcile the spotless Lamb. AGAINST JOVINIAN 1.40.[34]

**THE WHOLE FLOCK OF GOD WILL BE GATHERED.** MAXIMUS OF TURIN: The man Jesus Christ, who overcame the devil by his suffering and unlocked the underworld by his resurrection, returning to heaven like a victor after having accomplished a great deed, hears from God the Father: "Sit at my right hand."[35] And it is not to be wondered at that it is given to the Son to sit on the same seat as does the Father, since by nature he is of one substance with the Father. But perhaps someone is puzzled that the Son is said to be on the right. For although there are no degrees of dignity where the fullness of divinity is concerned, nonetheless the Son sits on the right not because he is preferred to the Father but so that he not be believed to be inferior. And the Son is on the right because, according to the Gospel, the sheep will be gathered on the right but the goats on the left. It is necessary, therefore, that the first lamb occupy the place of the sheep and that the unsullied leader come before the unsullied flock that will follow him, as John says in the Apocalypse: "These are the ones who follow the Lamb of God wherever he goes, who have not defiled themselves with women." Therefore the prophet David says, "The Lord said to my Lord: Sit at my right hand." That is to say, the Lord who is Father offers the lofty seat of his throne to the Lord God Christ, who is his Son, and for the sake of honor he places him at his right on an eternal seat. SERMON 40.2.[36]

---

[32]Rev 7:9. [33]ACW 27:47-48. [34]NPNF 2 6:378. See also *Letter* 48.10-11 (NPNF 2 6:71). [35]Ps 110:1 (109:1 LXX). [36]ACW 50:99-100.

**THOSE FAITHFUL IN MARRIAGE HAVE HOPE.**
AUGUSTINE: And we too, brothers and sisters, if we truly love him, let us imitate him. After all, we won't be able to give a better proof of love than by imitating his example. "For Christ suffered for us, leaving us an example, so that we might follow in his footsteps."[37] In this sentence the apostle Peter appears to have seen that Christ suffered only for those who follow in his footsteps and that Christ's passion profits none but those who follow in his footsteps. The holy martyrs followed him, to the shedding of their blood, to the similarity of their sufferings.[38] The martyrs followed, but they were not the only ones. It's not the case, I mean to say, that after they had crossed, the bridge was cut; or that after they had drunk, the fountain dried up. What, after all, is the hope of the good faithful, who either bear the yoke of matrimony in chastity and concord in the wedded state, or tame the allurements of the flesh by living continently as widows, or even raise the standard of a loftier sanctity, and flourishing in a new kind of virginity, "follow the Lamb wherever he goes"? What hope, I repeat, is there for these, what hope for all of us, if the only ones who follow Christ are those who shed their blood for him? So is mother church going to lose all those children of hers, whom she has brought forth all the more abundantly, the more secure she has been in the time of peace? In order not to lose them, is she to pray for persecution, pray for trials and temptations? Perish the thought, brothers and sisters! How, I mean to say, can anyone pray for persecution who cries out every day, "Do not bring us into temptation"?[39] That garden of the Lord's brothers and sisters, includes, yes it includes, it certainly includes not only the roses of martyrs but also the lilies of virgins, and the ivy of married people and the violets of widows. There is absolutely no kind of human beings, dearly beloved, who need to despair of their vocation; Christ suffered for all. It was truly written, it is he "who wishes all men to be saved and to come to the acknowledgment of the truth."[40]
SERMON 304.2.[41]

**TRUE VIRGINS FOLLOW THE LAMB.** AUGUSTINE: Marriages are to possess their own good, not because they bring forth children but because they bring them forth honorably, lawfully and chastely, for the good of society; and once they are begotten, they likewise bring them up in a wholesome and purposeful way. Marriage is a good also because the partners preserve for each other the fidelity of the marriage bed, and because they do not violate the sacrament of marriage. All these, however, are duties of human obligation, whereas unsullied virginity and abstention from all intercourse by devoted continence is a role assigned to angels, the intention to preserve enduring incorruption while in the corruptible flesh. All physical fertility, all marital chastity must yield precedence to this, for the first does not lie within human power, and the second does not abide in eternity; free will does not control bodily fertility, and there is no marriage, however chaste, in heaven. It is certain that those who already in the flesh possess something not of the flesh will attain a grandeur beyond the rest in that immortality that is shared by all....

So there is no commandment of the Lord that binds virgins. However, in the eternal life that is to be attained by avoidance or forgiveness of sins, there is an illustrious glory that is to be assigned not to all who will dwell in eternity, but to certain individuals there, and to obtain this it is not sufficient to have been freed from sins; some vow must also be made to him who has delivered us. It is not a sin to have failed to make such a vow, but it is praiseworthy to have made and delivered it. ... But because in that eternal life the lights of their merits will shine differently, "There are many dwelling places"[42] in the Father's house. Accordingly, since the value of the denarius remains the same, one of us will not live longer than another, but in those numerous dwelling

---

[37]1 Pet 2:21. [38]In the *Letter of the Lyons Martyrs*, Vettius Epagathus is said to be "a genuine disciple of Christ, following the Lamb wherever he goes" (Eusebius *Ecclesiastical History* 5.1.10). [39]Mt 6:13. [40]1 Tim 2:4. [41]*WSA* 3 8:316-17. [42]Jn 14:2.

places one will obtain brighter glory than another.

So press on, holy ones of God, boys and girls, males and females, unmarried men and women; press on unremittingly to the end. Praise the Lord in tones sweeter as your thoughts center on him more fruitfully. Hope in him more blessedly as you serve him more urgently; love him more glowingly as you please him more diligently. With loins girded and lamps alight, await the Lord's arrival from the wedding. You will bring to the marriage of the Lamb a new song to play on your harps—not indeed one such as the whole earth sings when it is bidden, "Sing a new song to the Lord, sing to the Lord, the whole earth,"[43] but one such as none but you will be able to sing. For in the Apocalypse this is how you were seen by the man beloved of the Lamb before all others, who was wont to recline on his breast, who imbibed and vomited forth God's description of the wonders of heaven. That man saw you, twelve times twelve thousand blessed harpists, your virginity of body undefiled, your truth of heart inviolate, and he wrote these words about you because you follow the Lamb wherever he goes. Where do we imagine this Lamb goes, when no one but you presumes or is able to follow him there? Into what glades and meadows? Where, I believe, the pasture is one of joys—not the empty joys of this world for they are deceitful lunacies, nor those joys in God's kingdom that accrue to the rest who are not virgins, but joys distinct from the portion of those allotted to all the rest. These are the joys of Christ's virgins, issuing from Christ, in Christ, with Christ, following Christ, through Christ, because of Christ. The joys peculiar to Christ's virgins are not the same as those of nonvirgins, though these too are of Christ; for there are different joys for different persons, but no others obtain such as these.

Advance towards them, follow the Lamb, for the Lamb in the flesh is assuredly virginal as well; for this he preserved for himself when he was full-grown, and he did not deprive his mother of it when he was conceived and born. Follow him

as you deserve, because of your virginity in heart and flesh, wherever he goes, for what does "follow" mean but "imitate"? For as the apostle Peter says, "Christ suffered for us, leaving us an example to follow in his steps."[44] Each of us follows him in as much as we imitate him, not as the Son of God through whom alone all things were made, but as the Son of man who revealed in himself all that we must imitate. Many things in him are revealed for all to imitate, but bodily virginity is not set forth for all, for those who have already lost their virginity have not the means of being virgins. So the rest of the faithful, who have lost their virginity, must follow the Lamb not wherever he goes, but so far as they themselves can go. They can in fact follow everywhere except where he has advanced into the glory of virginity. "Blessed are the poor in spirit";[45] imitate him who became poor for your sake, when he was rich. "Blessed are the meek."[46] But what is beyond doubt is that married people too can walk in his footsteps. Though they do not plant their feet perfectly in the same traces, they none the less tread the same paths. But see, that lamb treads the virgin's path, so how will those who have lost it follow him when they never recover it? So you who are his virgins, you must follow him on that path as well, for it is on this score alone that you follow him wherever he goes. We can encourage those who are married to advance toward any other gift of sanctity to which they can follow him, excepting when they have lost this path beyond hope of recovery.

Follow him therefore, maintaining with constancy the course that you vowed with burning zeal to take. While you can, ensure that you do not lose the good of virginity, for you can do nothing to regain it. The rest of the crowd of the faithful who cannot follow on this path will observe you. They will observe you, but they will not envy you, and by sharing the joy with you they will possess in you what they do not possess in themselves. They will not be able to sing that

---

[43]Ps 96:1 (95:1 LXX).  [44]1 Pet 2:21.  [45]Mt 5:3.  [46]Mt 5:5.

new song that belongs to you alone, but they will be able to hear it and to take delight in that good of yours that is so surpassing. But you who are virgins will both sing and hear it, for you will also hear it from your own lips as you sing it; your joy will be the more blessed and your dominion sweeter. Those who do not attain your greater joy will experience no grief, for the Lamb whom you follow wherever he goes will not abandon those either who cannot follow him where you can. The Lamb of whom we speak is almighty; he will both go before you yet not desert them, for he will be the God who is "all in all."[47] HOLY VIRGINITY 12, 14, 26-29.[48]

**IN HER VIRGINS THE CHURCH GAINS A FULLER VIRGINITY.** FULGENTIUS OF RUSPE: [The church], though she has in her diverse members different gifts, according to the grace that has been given to her, still she has received the greater grace of a gift in those members in whom she is spiritually called a virgin, so that she also gains the integrity of bodily virginity. For in other faithful members, who believe in God correctly according to the rule of the catholic faith and observe conjugal and widow's chastity, who are not splattered by any stain of any act of fornication and remain exempt from any illicit sexual act of infidelity, the church gains a spiritual virginity only; but in those members in whom she guards the correct faith in such a way that they keep the flesh untouched by any sexual intercourse, the more the church has a fuller virginity, the more perfectly she possesses the name of the same virginity. In the former she has nothing less of its life; in the latter, however, she acquires something more for glory, because just as Paul says, "The brightness of the sun is one kind, but the brightness of the moon another, and the brightness of the stars still another. For star differs from star in brightness. So also is the resurrection of the dead."[49] Finally, under the name of eunuchs (who also in the Gospel the Lord affirms have castrated themselves for the sake of the kingdom of heaven) the Lord through Isaiah again promises virgins a better place in his house and within his walls. For so it is written: "For thus says the Lord, 'To the eunuchs who keep my sabbaths, who choose the things that please me and hold fast my covenant, I will give in my house and within my walls, a monument and a name better than sons and daughters; I will give them an everlasting name that shall not be cut off.' "[50] Also in the Apocalypse of blessed John, they are the ones who "follow the Lord wherever he goes" who have remained virgins. LETTER TO PROBA 10.[51]

**THE CHURCH HOLDS TO THE PURITY OF THE FAITH.** CAESARIUS OF ARLES: In this passage we do not understand the "virgins" to be only those who are chaste in the body. Rather, we have especially in mind the whole church that holds to the pure faith, as the apostle says, "I betrothed you to one husband, to present you as a pure virgin to Christ."[52] For she is not corrupted by any adulterous commixture of the heretics, nor to the end of its life is it hindered by the alluring yet deadly desires of this world or by an infelicitous perseverance in them without the remedy of penance. EXPOSITION ON THE APOCALYPSE 14.4, HOMILY 11.[53]

**A CLOSER VISION OF CHRIST.** BEDE: The elect are doubtless imbued with one true faith, even if their merits differ in rank; for they will come to one light of eternal truth in heaven, even though the ones who endeavor to cleave to Christ higher up in this life will enjoy a closer vision of him in that life. Accordingly, it is said of certain ones on account of the merit of their great virtue, "These are those who follow the Lamb wherever he goes"; just before, it is said of others, as if of the nearby branches on the lampstand, "And they were singing a new song, as it were, before the

---

[47]1 Cor 15:28. [48]ABC 79, 81, 101-5. Primasius quotes these passages of Augustine as his commentary on Rev 14:2-4 (CCL 92:211-14). Bede quotes from *Holy Virginity* 27 for his commentary on Rev 14:4 (CCL 121A:423-25). [49]1 Cor 15:41-42. [50]Is 56:4-5. [51]FC 95:316-17. [52]2 Cor 11:2. [53]PL 35:2437.

throne and before the four living creatures and before the elders." By this it is shown that all the saints throughout the streets of that heavenly city sing a new song of gladness to God, but those who in this life transcended the common life of the faithful by the special privilege of sacred virginity are there raised up into a special position above the others in the joy of song.[54] ON THE TABERNACLE 1.25, 32.[55]

## 14:5 They Are Spotless

**BEYOND HUMAN NATURE.** OECUMENIUS: The language of the vision relays how surpassingly excellent and beyond human nature are those who are in Christ. COMMENTARY ON THE APOCALYPSE 14.1-5.[56]

**PHYSICAL VIRGINITY UNWORTHY WITHOUT PURITY OF HEART.** CAESARIUS OF ARLES: Truly, dearest brothers, of what profit is it for a man or woman, whether cleric or monk or religious, if bodily virginity is preserved, as long as purity of the heart is violated by evil desires? Of what benefit is it to show chastity in one member and to keep corruption in all the rest? For if you notice carefully, those virgins who follow the Lamb do not do so merely because of the fact that they have preserved only bodily virginity. Finally, when he had said, "These are they who did not defile themselves with women," he continued and added, "and in their mouth there was found no lie; they are without blemish." Listen carefully that if anyone boasts about bodily virginity alone, as long as he loves deceit he will not be able to follow Christ along with those holy virgins. For this reason let no virgin presume only upon her physical virginity, because if she is disobedient or gossiping she knows that she will have to be excluded

from the bedchamber of her heavenly Spouse. Although a virgin possesses a hundredfold and a married woman the thirtyfold, still a chaste and humble married woman is better than a proud virgin. SERMON 155.3.[57]

**BAPTISM AND PENANCE.** CAESARIUS OF ARLES: It does not say "there was no [lie in their mouth]," but "no lie was found in their mouth." For whatever the Lord finds when he calls forth from here, that is what he judges. For whether through baptism or through penance we are able to be made both virgins and without falsehood in the interior person. EXPOSITION ON THE APOCALYPSE 14.5, HOMILY 11.[58]

**THE WHOLE CHURCH IS VIRGIN.** BEDE: Virgins are not joined to the divine following because of chastity only, unless they also lead a life unblemished by any infection of sin. Tyconius does not interpret this vision to refer especially to virgins, but generally to the whole church, which the apostle betroths "to one husband, to present a pure virgin to Christ,"[59] and he concludes in this way: "He did not say 'no lie was in their mouth' but 'no lie was found.'" As the apostle says, "And such were you, but you have been washed,"[60] and "the iniquity of the unjust will not harm him on the day he will have turned from his iniquity,"[61] and he will be able to be a virgin, and deceit will not be found in his mouth. For those who are chaste and pure he calls "virgins." EXPLANATION OF THE APOCALYPSE 14.5.[62]

---

[54]In his *Homily on the Gospels 1.13*, Bede presents a long application of Rev 14:4 to Benedict Biscop, founder of the monasteries of Wearmouth and Jarrow and teacher of Bede (CS 110:130-31). [55]TTH 18:35. [56]TEG 8:196. [57]FC 47:346. [58]PL 35:2437. [59]See 2 Cor 11:2. [60]1 Cor 6:11. [61]See Ezek 33:12. [62]CCL 121A:425.

## 14:6-7 THE EVERLASTING GOSPEL

*[6]Then I saw another angel flying in midheaven, with an eternal gospel to proclaim to those who dwell on earth, to every nation and tribe and tongue and people; [7]and he said with a loud voice, "Fear God and give him glory, for the hour of his judgment has come; and worship him who made heaven and earth, the sea and the fountains of water."*

**OVERVIEW:** The seer sees an angel flying in midheaven. This angel is a preacher, perhaps Elijah, whose preaching will precede the kingdom of the antichrist (VICTORINUS). Or perhaps this single angel represents the many preachers who in the church preach of eternal life (PRIMASIUS, BEDE). These preachers are said to be preaching an eternal gospel, for they look forward to the eternal salvation (PRIMASIUS), and they carry about the gospel of the eternal kingdom through which the earthly minds of the hearers are lifted up from their sluggishness (BEDE). It may be, however, that this angel possesses an especially loftly, exalted and sublime nature (OECUMENIUS, ANDREW OF CAESAREA) and in imitation to God is a mediator who leads the body of Christ to unity with its Head (ANDREW OF CAESAREA). He declares the eternal teaching that one should fear God who possesses the power of judgment rather than the antichrist, who has no power to kill the soul with the body (OECUMENIUS, ANDREW OF CAESAREA). The eternal rewards that the saints will enjoy in the glory of the Father were prefigured by the coming of the Savior in humility, even as his coming was the fulfillment of the law given through Moses (ORIGEN).

### 14:6 An Angel Flying with an Eternal Gospel

**THE LAW OF THE ETERNAL GOSPEL.** ORIGEN: It is Moses who hears from God all that is written down in the law of Leviticus, whereas in Deuteronomy it is the people who are represented as listening to Moses and learning from him what they could not hear from God. This indeed is

why it is called Deuteronomy, meaning the second law; a fact that some will think points to this, that when the first law given through Moses came to an end, a second legislation was apparently composed, and this was specially delivered by Moses to his successor Joshua; and Joshua is certainly believed to be a figure of our Savior, by whose second law, that is, by the precepts of the Gospels, all things are brought to perfection. We must also see, however, whether the Scriptures may not perhaps indicate this further truth, that just as the legislation is presented with greater clearness and distinctness in Deuteronomy than in those books that were written at the first, so also we may gather from that coming of the Savior that he fulfilled in humility, when he "took upon him the form of a servant,"[1] an indication of the "more splendid and glorious second coming in the glory of the Father,"[2] at which coming, when in the kingdom of heaven all the saints shall live by the laws of the "eternal gospel," the figure of Deuteronomy will be fulfilled. And just as by his present coming he has fulfilled that law which was a "shadow of the good things to come,"[3] so also by that glorious coming the shadow of his first coming will be fulfilled and brought to perfection. For the prophet has spoken of it thus: "The breath of our countenance is Christ the Lord, of whom we said that under his shadow we shall live among the nations,"[4] that is, at the time when he shall duly transfer all the saints from the temporal to the eternal gospel, to use a

---

[1]Phil 2:7. [2]See Mt 16:27. [3]Heb 10:1. [4]Lam 4:20.

phrase employed by John in the Apocalypse, where he speaks of the "eternal gospel."[5] ON FIRST PRINCIPLES 4.3.12-13.[6]

**THE ANGEL IS ELIJAH.** VICTORINUS OF PETOVIUM: The "angel flying in mid-heaven" which he said that he saw we have interpreted above[7] to be that very Elijah who precedes the kingdom of the antichrist. COMMENTARY ON THE APOCALYPSE 14.1.[8]

**THE BEGINNING OF WISDOM IS FEAR OF THE LORD.** OECUMENIUS: "Mid-heaven" signifies the exalted and sublime nature of the holy angel. He had "an eternal gospel." The saving teaching that one should fear the Lord is from eternity, since the "beginning of wisdom is the fear of God, and its end is love."[9] On the other hand, it says, the harsh beast who works spiritual death, the antichrist, is not to be feared, even though he may threaten and do the most amazing feats. For "the hour of his judgment has come," and he who is fearful to those who live upon the earth will punish him in a way wholly unprecedented. Rather, [we should] "worship him who made" every creature rather than worship the wicked devil who is hated by God. COMMENTARY ON THE APOCALYPSE 14.6-7.[10]

**THE ANGEL LEADS PEOPLE TO HEAVEN.** ANDREW OF CAESAREA: The phrase "in mid-heaven" indicates that the angel that here appears is exceedingly lofty and heavenly. It has been sent from above to people, who come from the ground, so that through this middle position it might be a mediator and lead them, in imitation of God, to heaven. And so the body of the Church will be united to Christ, our Head. The "eternal gospel," which from eternity was foreordained by God, says, "Fear God, but have no fear of the antichrist who cannot kill the soul with the body;[11] rather, fervently stand opposed to him who has power but for a short time, for the time of his judgment and the reward for what he has done is near." COMMENTARY ON THE APOCALYPSE 14.6-7.[12]

**PREACHERS PROCLAIM A SINGLE MESSAGE.** PRIMASIUS: He refers to the messenger who runs throughout the church, which is spread far and wide and is to be extended even more. He uses the singular for the plural, or in the one [messenger] he is suggesting the unity of the single church; yet, at the same time, he is alluding to the [many] preachers of eternal life. It rightly says that he preaches an eternal gospel, by which the preacher is taught to look forward to eternal salvation. And so the one who preaches is indicated by that which is preached. Therefore the psalm says, "He who makes the winds his messengers and burning fire his ministers."[13] COMMENTARY ON THE APOCALYPSE 14.6.[14]

**THROUGH PREACHING, EARTHLY MINDS ARE LIFTED UP.** BEDE: Since he had described the anticipated and diverse battles that the church in the world wages against the dragon, it remains now to assign to either army the appropriate prize, showing what penalty will follow those who are evil and what reward will follow those who are good. For this reason, the preacher who runs about within the church carries the gospel of the eternal kingdom. . . . It is appropriate that those who are lifted up by celestial flight should also, through preaching, lift their earthly minds from the place of their [present] sluggishness. . . . "This gospel," it says, "will be preached throughout the whole world, and then the end will come."[15] EXPLANATION OF THE APOCALYPSE 14.6.[16]

### 14:7 Fear God and Worship Him

**CHRISTIAN PREACHING BRINGS THE END NEAR TO THE HEARER.** PRIMASIUS: Although

---

[5]As the law was a shadow of Christ's first coming, his first coming was a shadow of the "eternal gospel" of the heavenly kingdom. See also *On First Principles* 3.6.8; *Commentary on the Gospel of John* 1.40 (FC 80:42). [6]OFP 309-10. [7]Apparently referring to his comments on Rev 12:7. [8]CSEL 49:130. [9]See Prov 1:7. [10]TEG 8:196-97. [11]See Mt 10:28. [12]MTS 1 Sup 1:149-50. [13]Ps 104:4 (103:4 LXX). [14]CCL 92:214-15. [15]Mt 24:14. [16]CCL 121A:425-27.

from the beginning of the Christian faith we have learned that the kingdom of heaven is said to be approaching, here, however, he proclaims that the hour of his judgment will come very soon and is virtually here already. And therefore he maintains that preaching of this kind must necessarily be made known to all people, as also the Lord said, "This gospel will be preached throughout the world, and then the end will come."[17] And to show that that moment of time takes place, when

the adversity of the last persecution will draw near, he has rather added that the temporal power of the beast should best be regarded as insignificant and that the Lord rather be feared, whom every one of his creatures, whom he mentions, acknowledges to be eternal. COMMENTARY ON THE APOCALYPSE 14.7.[18]

---

[17]Mt 24:14. [18]CCL 92:215.

## 14:8 BABYLON IS FALLEN!

[8]*Another angel, a second, followed, saying, "Fallen, fallen is Babylon the great, she who made all nations drink the wine of her impure passion."*

**OVERVIEW:** "Babylon" means "confusion" and refers to the random trials and troubled disorders of this present life (OECUMENIUS, ANDREW OF CAESAREA). Babylon also refers to the city or people of the devil that works through vice for the ruin of the human race. This city, made drunk by error and idolatry, will inevitably fall (TYCONIUS). Those who are frenzied by idol worship possess a darkened mind, for they worship wood and stone and call forth the wrath of God, which leads to everlasting fire (OECUMENIUS, ANDREW OF CAESAREA). Indeed, all sin is a form of drunkenness and derangement (ANDREW OF CAESAREA).

### 14:8 *"Fallen, Fallen Is Babylon the Great!"*

#### THE CITY OF THE DEVIL WILL INEVITABLY FALL. TYCONIUS: Babylon is interpreted as confusion.[1] By it the city and the people of the devil are signified, as is also the entire seduction of the vices that it always exercises for its own ruin and for the ruin of the human race. It says that this

city, which is hastening toward its fall, has already fallen. This is a common way of speaking in the Scripture, which often refers to events as past when they are yet in the future, especially when it knows that what it predicts will inevitably be fulfilled. Here is an example of this way of speaking: "They divided my clothes among themselves,"[2] and other similar statements. However, it may also speak in this manner because it was already well known then that the haughty fall whenever they dare to become proud. Therefore the psalm says, "You have cast them down when they were lifted up,"[3] for, to be sure, they were then thrown down when they were lifted up. According to this habit of speaking, then, the Scripture has said, "All nations have fallen because of the wine of their fornication," because this city, which is drunk and is constructed from all nations that it gathers to itself, itself has

---

[1]See Gen 11:9; already in Methodius *Symposium* 4.3. [2]Ps 22:18 (21:19 LXX); Mt 27:35. [3]Ps 72:18 LXX.

drunk from the wine of fornication. For all the nations, made drunk by errors, constitute the city itself,[4] but the Scripture, according to its style, talks only of the one [city]. Commentary on the Apocalypse 14.8.[5]

**Idolatry and Apostasy Darken the Mind.** Oecumenius: By "Babylon" he is referring to the confusion and arbitrarily random trials of the present life—for *confusion* is the meaning of Babylon—and to the manic stupefaction of those who worship idols. And the city is magnified with names, being called by them the "inspired" city. But were you to consider the physical Babylon itself, you would not fall down before the sight before you. By the "wine of the wrath of her fornication" he refers to [the city's] apostasy from God, as it is written, "You have destroyed every one that goes a whoring from you."[6] Such fornication entails a darkness of the mature reason, for who, possessing a sound mind, would choose to worship wood and stones and call forth the wrath of God? Therefore, concerning this wine it is said, "Their wine is the wrath of serpents and the incurable wrath of asps."[7] Babylon itself at first drank of this deadly wine,

and then it compelled all the nations that it ruled to drink. Commentary on the Apocalypse 14.8.[8]

**The Derangement That Comes from Sin.** Andrew of Caesarea: He speaks of "Babylon," which refers to the confusion of the world and the troubled disorder of this life, which in no way has abated. By "the wine of the wrath of her fornication" he means not only the frenzy that attends to idol worship and the ecstasy of their minds, but also to the drunkenness and derangement that attends all sin, by which everyone who whores against God is wholly destroyed, as the saying of the psalm goes.[9] As it were, pulled up by its roots, such a Babylon falls completely at the appearance of the Jerusalem that is above, for those who have been workers of iniquity are sent to the everlasting fire. Commentary on the Apocalypse 14.8.[10]

---

[4]Caesarius of Arles expressly contrasts this city with the city of God, which is "the church and that manner of life that is heavenly" (PL 35:2437). [5]CCL 92:215-16. [6]Ps 73:27 (72:27 LXX). [7]Deut 32:33. [8]TEG 8:197-98. [9]Cf. Ps 73:27 (72:27 LXX). [10]MTS 1 Sup 1:150.

## 14:9-13 WORSHIP OF THE BEAST REAPS WRATH

[9]*And another angel, a third, followed them, saying with a loud voice, "If any one worships the beast and its image, and receives a mark on his forehead or on his hand,* [10]*he also shall drink the wine of God's wrath, poured unmixed into the cup of his anger, and he shall be tormented with fire and sulphur in the presence of the holy angels and in the presence of the Lamb.* [11]*And the smoke of their torment goes up for ever and ever; and they have no rest, day or night, these worshipers of the beast and its image, and whoever receives the mark of its name."*

[12]*Here is a call for the endurance of the saints, those who keep the commandments of God and the faith of Jesus.*

[13]*And I heard a voice from heaven saying, "Write this: Blessed are the dead who die in the Lord*

*henceforth." "Blessed indeed," says the Spirit, "that they may rest from their labors, for their deeds follow them!"*

---

**OVERVIEW:** Those who worship the beastlike antichrist and lead an ungodly life like his will drink a cup of judgment that is devoid of divine mercy and that brings darkness and derangement to those under the wrath of God (OECUMENIUS, ANDREW OF CAESAREA). Among these are included the heretics who withdraw from the church because of their evil belief, those who live according to a depravity of morals, and the arrogant Jews who condemned the Lamb (PRIMASIUS). The angels and the saints will witness this torment and give thanks to their Redeemer for his mercy (PRIMASIUS, BEDE). The variety of punishments delivered from this cup will correspond to the variety of evils freely chosen by those who did them (ANDREW OF CAESAREA). Nonetheless, the goodness of God is many times greater than is his wrath; otherwise no one would stand before his righteous anger. God's mercy hems in the exercise of his justice, and, therefore, those who suffer this eternal torment do not suffer in a physical manner but suffer the absence of the blessings of God (OECUMENIUS). For this reason, their weeping and lamentation rise forever like smoke. In view of this eventual punishment of the wicked, the saints are exhorted to keep inviolate the commandments of God and to remain steadfast in their faith and love of God (OECUMENIUS, ANDREW OF CAESAREA). By persevering in this momentary suffering, they will escape eternal fellowship with the beast (PRIMASIUS) even as they behold the eternal penalties of their persecutors (BEDE). Just as the impious never have rest, so the martyrs and all who have died to the world will rest eternally from the time of their deaths (OECUMENIUS, PRIMASIUS, ANDREW OF CAESAREA, BEDE). This is also true of those priests and bishops who have labored faithfully in the vineyard of God (PRIMASIUS). Since we must endure to the end in contests with invisible powers, it is necessary that we pray unceasingly to God, "Incline

our hearts, O Lord, and turn our eyes from every vanity" (ANDREW OF CAESAREA).

### 14:9-10 A Third Angel Followed

**GOD'S RIGHTEOUSNESS IS CONSTRAINED BY HIS MERCY.** OECUMENIUS: The third angel forbids people to worship the beast and to receive its mark. For to worship any other as God rather than he who really and truly is God is most unholy. "And he also shall drink the wine of God's wrath poured unmixed into the cup of his anger." The holy David mentioned this cup and this wine when he said, "There is a cup in the hand of the Lord, full of unmixed wine; and he has turned it from side to side, but its dregs have not been wholly poured out; all the sinners of the earth shall drink [them]."[1] He calls the wrath of God "wine," not using this metaphor because of the gladness elicited by wine but because of the darkness and the derangement that oppress those brought under the wrath of God. And, it says, it is "poured out unmixed," that is, utterly poured out. For the wrath of God is poured out along with his benevolence and goodness, wholly poured out. For there is not an equal measure of wrath and goodness, but the benevolence of God is many times greater. Indeed, were the righteous anger and the goodness of God in equal measure, no one would be able to withstand it. Aware of this, the prophet said, "If you, O Lord, should mark iniquities, Lord, who could stand?"[2] And the same writer indicated that goodness is much greater in the cup of God than is his righteous anger, when he said, "Merciful is the Lord, and righteous; yea, our God is merciful."[3] In this passage he placed God's righteousness in the middle, so that hemmed in by mercy on either side, his righteousness would not work its way without

---

[1] Ps 74:9 LXX.  [2] Ps 130:3 (129:3 LXX).  [3] Ps 116:5 (114:5 LXX).

constraint. For it is characteristic of justice to meet each according to his merit. Having mentioned wine, and by this referring to God's wrath, he continues the metaphor and calls the "cup" what is given from the hand of God to sinners. COMMENTARY ON THE APOCALYPSE 14.9-12.[4]

**MERITING THE WINE OF DIVINE WRATH.** PRIMASIUS: Certain heretics withdraw from us because of their evil belief, while with a different depravity of morals, others turn aside from our traditions, and in addition there are yet others ordained to perish from both faith and morals. Here in summary fashion he includes all those among the living who have the inscription of the beast on their forehead or on their hand. Here the cup of wrath must not only be understood as the one of which the Lord spoke, "He must endure God's wrath"[5] showing original sin, but also the cup that he mentions to the arrogant Jews, when he says, "You will die in your sin,"[6] indicating the merit obtained through their accursed actions. . . . It says that they will be tormented in the sight of the Lamb for whose condemnation they suffer, whom they haughtily condemned and over whose members they inappropriately pretended to be masters. They will also be tormented in the sight of his angels who know by God's revelation that they are paying a just penalty. COMMENTARY ON THE APOCALYPSE 14.9-10.[7]

**SHARING THE CUP DEVOID OF DIVINE MERCY.** ANDREW OF CAESAREA: It says that should anyone bow down to the beastlike antichrist and pursue an ungodly life like his, and should anyone proclaim him to be God in word and deed—for the mark given on the forehead and upon the hand would show this—that person will share with [the antichrist] in the drinking of the revenge-filled cup, which is unmixed and devoid of any divine mercy because of the justice of the judgment. And this cup is of wine poured from different punishments because of the diversity and variety of evils that were freely

chosen. He aptly calls this torment the "wine of wrath," since it follows upon the wine of godlessness, which inebriates those who drink of it, for "in that way by which one sins shall one also be punished."[8] COMMENTARY ON THE APOCALYPSE 14.9-10.[9]

**THE SAINTS WILL GIVE PRAISE TO THEIR REDEEMER.** BEDE: [He will be tormented in the sight of the holy angels.] The saints who reign with the Lord are always able to observe the punishment of the wicked, so that they might give the greater thanks to their Redeemer and sing forever of the mercies of the Lord. For the torments of the wicked that are seen do not distress those who are in agreement with the just Judge, just as the rest of Lazarus that was seen was able to give no refreshment to the rich man who was buried in the flames.[10] EXPLANATION OF THE APOCALYPSE 14.10.[11]

### 14:11 No Rest Day or Night

**DEPRIVED OF THE BLESSINGS OF GOD.** OECUMENIUS: Perhaps someone might say, "How can you say that the mercy of God is many times greater in the judgment at that time, when the vision tells us that the torments of those who are punished are little short of everlasting?" For why does it say, "And the smoke of their torment goes up forever and ever, and they have no rest day or night?" To such a person one might respond, "O, sir, what is suffered is indeed eternal, but it is not suffering according to merit. If someone is deserving of fire and darkness, why is he condemned to the darkness? Such a one is tormented only in this, that he does not share in the good things of God, and he suffers only this, but he is not also tormented physically." By the phrase "the smoke of their torment goes up" he refers to the heaving breath of the sinners that they exhale from below in their lamentations

---

[4]TEG 8:198-99. [5]Jn 3:36. [6]Jn 8:21. [7]CCL 92:216-17. [8]Wis 11:16. [9]MTS 1 Sup 1:151. [10]Lk 16:23-24. [11]CCL 121A:429.

over their situation. COMMENTARY ON THE APOCALYPSE 14.9-12.[12]

**EVERLASTING BLISS OR EVERLASTING TORMENT.** ANDREW OF CAESAREA: We must understand this smoke to be either the sighing of those being tormented, which arises from below along with their lamentation, or the smoke that comes from the fire that torments the fallen. It says that it "goes up forever and ever," and by this we learn that even as the bliss of the righteous is everlasting, so also is the torment of the sinners. . . . He says "day and night," not as though the condition of the future age in which the ungodly will have no rest will be measured by the sun, but he rather accommodates himself to the custom in the present time, which is reckoned in nights and days. Or it might be that the "day" is to be regarded as the life of the saints and the "night" as the torment of the impure, which those who do the works of the devil and blaspheme against Christ in the manner of the apostate beast will attain. For through the doing of these things they make an image [of the beast] and engrave his name upon their hearts as though it were precious. COMMENTARY ON THE APOCALYPSE 14.11.[13]

**THE ANTICHRIST INFLICTS SUFFERING.** BEDE: They say that a lion will spare a man who is lying on the ground. But this beast is more ferocious than a lion, for the more he is adored, the more he inflicts sufferings. EXPLANATION OF THE APOCALYPSE 14.11.[14]

## 14:12 A Call for the Endurance

**THE SAINTS WILL ENDURE.** OECUMENIUS: "Here is a call for the endurance of the saints," it says. This will be manifested at this time of the antichrist and in this ordeal. For however great is the danger and the tribulation at that time, so great is the need for endurance. Then the passage continues as though in response to a question. And who are those, it says, whom you call holy and patient? "Those who keep the command-

ments of God and the faith of Jesus." For when the tribulations and death have come, such persons as these will regard all things as second in importance to faith and to the love of God. COMMENTARY ON THE APOCALYPSE 14.9-12.[15]

**THOSE WHO ENDURE ESCAPE FELLOWSHIP WITH THE BEAST.** PRIMASIUS: The Lord says, "He who endures to the end will be saved,"[16] and the apostle says, "You have need of endurance."[17] So also in this passage it says that the endurance of the saints consists in this, that those who persevere to the end escape the fellowship of the beast and the mark of its name. COMMENTARY ON THE APOCALYPSE 14.12.[18]

**THE SAINTS ENDURE IN FAITH.** ANDREW OF CAESAREA: While the impious will be tormented eternally in the coming age, the saints here below show their patient endurance, keeping inviolate the commandments of God and their faith in Christ during the present time, which is quickly passing away. COMMENTARY ON THE APOCALYPSE 14.12.[19]

**MOMENTARY SUFFERING.** BEDE: Although the beast will be ferocious, nonetheless this momentary suffering, which will be rewarded with eternal bliss, will not distress the saints. For the saints will see their persecutors, who were arrogant for a short while, suffering eternal penalties along with the beast. EXPLANATION OF THE APOCALYPSE 14.12.[20]

## 14:13 "Blessed Are the Dead Who Die in the Lord"

**THE CROWN OF MARTYRDOM.** OECUMENIUS: He blesses those who did not choose to worship the image of the beast or to receive the mark on their foreheads and upon their hands, and who

[12]TEG 8:199. [13]MTS 1 Sup 1:152. [14]CCL 121A:429. [15]TEG 8:199-200. [16]Mt 10:22. [17]Heb 10:36. [18]CCL 92:217. [19]MTS 1 Sup 1:153. [20]CCL 121A:431.

for this reason were killed. Being crowned with the crown of martyrdom, these attain to the same lot with the martyrs. COMMENTARY ON THE APOCALYPSE 14.13.[21]

**FAITHFUL CLERGY WILL RECEIVE A SPECIAL REST FROM THEIR LABORS.** PRIMASIUS: Those are said to die in the Lord who showed themselves approved in both their faith and their life. And for that reason they deserved to be called out from there. And so the text continues: "'Yes,' says the Spirit, 'they will rest from their labors.'" As . . . he says that those impious have no rest day or night, now he says that the faithful deserved the rest from their good works. Indeed, since he had made mention of the wicked, it was necessary also to mention the fullness of the bliss of those who are good. And since this [bliss] exists among the leaders and the people, he in summary fashion includes both, speaking first in an indefinite manner, "Blessed are the dead who die in the Lord." However, on behalf of those who work in the vineyard, he says they rest from their labors and so manifestly declares happiness to all so that he might promise to those who work in the vineyard a special fruit of rest after their labor. Therefore the apostle says, "We beseech you that you respect those who labor among you and are over you in the Lord and admonish you and that you esteem them more highly in love because of their work."[22] And he speaks even about himself, "I worked harder than any of them."[23] "For their deeds follow them," it says. Concerning these the prophet says, "Establish the works of our hands over us."[24] COMMENTARY ON THE APOCALYPSE 14.13.[25]

**A REST FROM THEIR LABORS.** ANDREW OF CAESAREA: The voice from heaven does not bless all the dead, but only those who die in the Lord, who have died to the world and so carry about the dying of Jesus in the body and suffer with Christ. For these persons the departure from the body is truly a rest from their labor. Moreover, the obedience of their works is the reason for

their unfading crowns and the rewards of glory that are the prizes given in great measure to those who prevail in the contests that the contestants of Christ, our God, endure to the end against invisible powers. "For the sufferings of the present time are not worth comparing with the glory that is to be revealed" to those who please God, as the apostle says.[26] It is necessary also that we who yearn for such glory should pray unceasingly to God, saying, "Incline our hearts, O Lord, to your testimonies, and turn our eyes from every vanity," and "enter not into judgment with your servants, for no living creature will be righteous before you."[27] Rather, visit us with your bountiful mercies, for the might and the kingdom and the power and the glory are yours, namely, of the Father and of the Son and of the Holy Spirit, now and forever and unto the ages of ages. Amen. COMMENTARY ON THE APOCALYPSE 14.13.[28]

**THE VOICE FROM HEAVEN AND THE SPIRIT ARE HARMONIOUS.** BEDE: The harmony of those who speak is beautiful. For observe how the one announces that the kingdom of the Lord is come, the other announces the fall of the city of the devil. One indicates the flames of the wicked, while another announces the rest of the blessed. This last one projects his voice from heaven and commands that it is worthy to be committed to writing to be eternally remembered. For the righteous rejoice that their names are written in heaven, while the impious are blotted out of the book of the living. "Blessed are the dead who die in the Lord." I thank you, Jesus, that you bless those in heaven who on earth die in you. How much more, then, those who place their happy souls both in you and in your faith? . . . Just as he had said that the impious never have any rest, so he teaches . . . that the faithful, assisted by their previous works, will rest "from henceforth," that is, from the

---

[21]TEG 8:200. [22]1 Thess 5:12-13. [23]1 Cor 15:10. [24]Ps 90:17 (89:17 LXX). [25]CCL 92:217-18. [26]Rom 8:18. [27]Cf. Ps 143:2 (142:2 LXX). [28]MTS 1 Sup 1:153-54.

time of death. For "when he shall have given sleep to his beloved, this is the inheritance of the Lord."[29] However, "the sluggard would not plow in the cold, therefore he will beg at the

time of harvest, but nothing will be given him."[30] EXPLANATION OF THE APOCALYPSE 14.13.[31]

---

[29]Cf. Ps 127:2-3 (126:2-3 LXX).  [30]Cf. Prov 20:4.  [31]CCL 121A:431-33.

---

# 14:14-16 ONE LIKE A SON OF MAN PUTS IN HIS SICKLE

[14]*Then I looked, and lo, a white cloud, and seated on the cloud one like a son of man, with a golden crown on his head, and a sharp sickle in his hand.* [15]*And another angel came out of the temple, calling with a loud voice to him who sat upon the cloud, "Put in your sickle, and reap, for the hour to reap has come, for the harvest of the earth is fully ripe."* [16]*So he who sat upon the cloud swung his sickle on the earth, and the earth was reaped.*

---

**Overview:** Christ is seen seated on the "cloud" of his flesh (PRIMASIUS). The mother of God may also be called a "cloud," for she is pure and blameless and not even one sin weighed her down (OECUMENIUS). Christ also rides upon his own body, which is the church made white through persecution (PRIMASIUS, CAESARIUS OF ARLES). Although Christ ascended upon a visible cloud into heaven (ANDREW OF CAESAREA) and rides now upon the angelic powers who are sublime and exalted in nature and rank (OECUMENIUS, ANDREW OF CAESAREA), Christ will come for judgment covering his divinity with the cloud of his flesh so that the wicked will see him whom they pierced (BEDE). Christ governs both the visible and invisible powers (ANDREW OF CAESAREA) and is crowned with the glory of his kingdom (OECUMENIUS). The church, too, is crowned with the twelve apostles whose preaching the church has preserved from the beginning (PRIMASIUS). The same Christ who came in the flesh possesses power over the world's consummation (OECUMENIUS, ANDREW OF CAESAREA), and through his judgment the impious will be separated from the pious and the heretics from the catholics (PRIMA-

SIUS, CAESARIUS OF ARLES, BEDE). At that time, there will be a plentiful harvest, and whatever chaff remains among humankind will be given over to fire (OECUMENIUS, PRIMASIUS). The church also, when it has completed her spiritual warfare, will more clearly discern those who are truly the faithful and those who are not (PRIMASIUS). The angels in heaven pray for the coming of this separation when what is transient will give way to what is immoveable and enduring (ANDREW OF CAESAREA).

## 14:14 One Like a Son of Man

**CHRIST CAME ON THE "CLOUD" OF HIS PURE AND BLAMELESS MOTHER.** Oecumenius: He sees the Lord who was worthy to become the Son of man and who is riding upon a cloud. This is either in reality a cloud, for the Gospel also speaks of this, whose witness we have referred to in an earlier discussion,[1] or the cloud is a certain angelic power, for it is written, "He mounted on cherubim and flew, he flew on the

---

[1]See Rev 1:7; Mk 13:25-26.

wings of the winds."[2] He calls the angels a "cloud" on account of their sublimity and their exalted nature and rank. Or rather, he calls the mother of God a "cloud" on whom he rode, honoring her who is his mother according to the flesh. For, indeed, Isaiah foresaw her in this manner, saying, "Behold, the Lord is seated on a swift cloud, and he will come to Egypt, and the idols of Egypt will tremble at his presence."[3] Interpreting this saying, Aquila says that the cloud is a "light material." "Material," as I think, because she was a human being and flesh, and "light" because of her purity and blamelessness and because not even one sin weighed her down, yet also because of the excellence and heavenward character of her soul. You will consider the "cloud" in this manner. It is white because of the purity and radiance of those things that are here seen. To be sure, the crown signifies the kingdom of our Lord, Jesus Christ. For Christ is king of things both unseen and seen. The crown is of gold to depict the glory of the kingdom by means of that which among us has great value. That he has a sickle in his hand signifies that the consummation of the age rests in his power. COMMENTARY ON THE APOCALYPSE 14.14-16.[4]

**CHRIST COMES ON THE CHURCH.** PRIMASIUS: By the cloud he indicates the incarnation of our Head, Jesus Christ. Or he shows the body of the church that Christ put on after the fires of persecution were cooled as with snow. [The church] has a golden crown on her head. This is the [twenty-four] elders with their golden crowns,[5] or the [crown is] the twelve apostles whom the beginning of the preaching of the faith acquired at the beginning.[6] Therefore we read, "You set a crown of precious stone on his head."[7] The sharp sickle is symbolic of the judicial sentence against the impious by which they are to be separated [from the pious], and this sentence is more justly inflicted upon them by divine judgment for the sake of the church, for whose defense Christ, the Shepherd, is always vigilant. Therefore, Zechariah said, "This is the curse that goes out over the face of the whole land."[8] COMMENTARY ON THE APOCALYPSE 14.14.[9]

**SEPARATING THE CATHOLICS FROM THE HERETICS.** CAESARIUS OF ARLES: [The one like a son of man] is Christ. He is describing the church in her glory, especially since she is white after the flames of persecution. [The gold crown] is the elders with their golden crowns, and the sickle in his hand is that which separates the catholics from the heretics and the saints from the sinners, just as the Lord speaks concerning the reapers. EXPOSITION ON THE APOCALYPSE 14.14, HOMILY 11.[10]

**HE GOVERNS THE VISIBLE AND INVISIBLE POWERS.** ANDREW OF CAESAREA: We think that this cloud is either the visible cloud that took our Lord Jesus Christ from the eyes of the apostles, or that it is a certain angelic power [here called a "cloud"] because of its purity and sublimity, for the psalmist says, "He rode on a cherub and flew."[11] For this reason, we believe that the one seen upon the cloud similar to a son of man is Christ, and that the crown upon his head signifies his governance over both the visible and the invisible powers. The crown is gold because of the value of this substance among us. The sickle indicates the consummation, for indeed the Lord himself called the end of the world a "harvest."[12] COMMENTARY ON THE APOCALYPSE 14.14.[13]

**CHRIST COMES WITH THE CLOUD OF HIS FLESH.** BEDE: Until now we have heard the voices of the heralds. However, now the person of the judge himself is revealed, who, when he comes for judgment, covers the glory of his divinity with a cloud of flesh so that the wicked might behold him whom they pierced. . . . What kind of crown this is was described above concerning the

---

[2]Ps 17:11 LXX. [3]Is 19:1. [4]TEG 8:200-201. [5]See Rev 4:4. [6]This interpretation of the gold crown comes from Tyconius. [7]Ps 20:4 LXX. [8]Zech 5:3. [9]CCL 92:218. [10]PL 35:2437-38. [11]Ps 18:10 (17:11 LXX). [12]Mt 13:30. [13]MTS 1 Sup 1:154-55.

adornment of the woman, "And on her head a crown of twelve stars."[14] But perhaps it may signify the victory of the King.... [The sharp sickle] refers to the judicial sentence of separation, and we can in no way avoid this judgment. We are most definitely within it, no matter where we might try to flee, for whatever is felled by a sickle falls within. EXPLANATION OF THE APOCALYPSE 14.14.[15]

## 14:15-16 He Reaped the Earth

AT THE HARVEST OF ALL HUMANKIND. OECUMENIUS: And why does the angel say to him, "Put in your sickle and reap, for the hour to reap has come, for the harvest of the earth is fully ripe"? "And he swung his sickle," it says, "and the earth was reaped." A "plentiful harvest" is mentioned in the Gospels, while "the laborers are few."[16] However, in that passage the harvest signified the gathering of the faithful, while here the harvest represents the consummation of humankind, so that, should there be any chaff or impurities in them which is worthy of fire, it might be given over to fire. COMMENTARY ON THE APOCALYPSE 14.14-16.[17]

THE CHURCH WILL RECEIVE JUDICIAL POWER FROM GOD. PRIMASIUS: From the explanation of the Lord, we know that the angels will be the reapers and that the end of the world is signified by the appearance of a ripe harvest. Moreover, it is known that after the harvesting of the crop there is chaff in the straw and fragile ears, while the wheat is in the grains. And so, we see with greater clarity in this passage that when it says that the sickle must be used on the ripe crop, the fate merited by the good and by the evil are symbolized. And to whom more appropriately than to the church is this said? ... At the time of the last judgment, when she has concluded her spiritual warfare against the beast, the church will possess a greater illumination and will be able to know whom she must consider as her own and whom as outside. To sit on the cloud means that when she has received the judicial power from God, [the church] will distinguish between the good and the evil: "You will also sit on twelve thrones, judging the twelve tribes of Israel."[18] COMMENTARY ON THE APOCALYPSE 14.15-16.[19]

ALL HEAVENLY POWERS PRAY. ANDREW OF CAESAREA: The cry of the angel symbolically represents the supplications of all the heavenly powers who desire to see both the honoring of the saints and the separation of the transgression of the sinners. At that time, that which is changeable and transient will cease to exist and that which is immovable and enduring will be manifested. That the harvest is ripe indicates that the time of the consummation has come when the seed of piety, having matured as ripe wheat, will be regarded as ready for the heavenly granaries and will yield for the husbandman thirtyfold, sixtyfold and a hundredfold. COMMENTARY ON THE APOCALYPSE 14.15-16.[20]

---

[14]See Rev 12:1. Bede interpreted the crown to be either the twelve apostles or Christ (CCL 121A:387). [15]CCL 121A:433. [16]Mt 9:37. [17]TEG 8:201-2. [18]Mt 19:28. [19]CCL 92:218-19. [20]MTS 1 Sup 1:155-56.

## 14:17-20 THE WINEPRESS OF THE WRATH OF GOD

*[17] And another angel came out of the temple in heaven, and he too had a sharp sickle. [18] Then another angel came out from the altar, the angel who has power over fire, and he called with a loud voice to him who had the sharp sickle, "Put in your sickle, and gather the clusters of the vine of the earth, for its grapes are ripe." [19] So the angel swung his sickle on the earth and gathered the vintage of the earth, and threw it into the great wine press of the wrath of God; [20] and the wine press was trodden outside the city, and blood flowed from the wine press, as high as a horse's bridle, for one thousand six hundred stadia[i].*

i About two hundred miles

**OVERVIEW:** At the consummation Christ will also reap a harvest in his church, which is both his field and his vineyard (CAESARIUS OF ARLES, BEDE). He will also be assisted by ministering angels who will serve in cutting off those who are the most wicked (OECUMENIUS, ANDREW OF CAESAREA). The church daily prays with a fervent desire that the kingdom of the Lord come. And when the sins of the wicked are completed (BEDE), then the impious and serious transgressors will receive the wrath of demons in the place prepared for the devil and his angels (ANDREW OF CAESAREA). These sinners will be regarded as not even worthy of a defense, but they will rather go immediately to their banishment (OECUMENIUS). Those who had become like horses full of lust and eager for sin will be overtaken themselves by tortures equal to their unbridled passions (ANDREW OF CAESAREA). Likewise, the devil and his accomplices will be requited for the blood of the saints that they spilled and for the wars begun by the heretics (PRIMASIUS). The angels, too, who administer the final judgment will wreak such a vengeance that they figuratively are said to be soaked in blood (OECUMENIUS). The judgment will destroy all that is useless and vain but will prove worthy that which is incorruptible (PRIMASIUS, BEDE). There is, however, a great chasm between the godly and the ungodly so that the rewarding of the sinners will occur neither in the church (PRIMASIUS) nor in the heavenly Jerusalem. Therefore, the bliss of the saints will not be spoiled by those who are being justly punished (OECUMENIUS).

### 14:17 Another Angel Came Out of the Temple

**AN ANGEL WILL SERVE AS A MINISTER OF GOD.** OECUMENIUS: The angel that has the sickle and comes out of the heavenly temple is in [God's] service and the same will also be a servant of the coming consummation. Since he is heavenly and a minister of God, he is described as one who has come out of the temple in heaven. COMMENTARY ON THE APOCALYPSE 14.17-20.[1]

**THE THREE ANGELS RIGHTLY DIVIDE THE WORD OF TRUTH.** CAESARIUS OF ARLES: If we must understand the reaper seated on the white cloud to be Christ himself, who is this vintager, unless it is the Selfsame, only in his body which is the church? Perhaps we would not be far wrong were we to understand those three angels who come out[2] to represent the threefold sense of the Scriptures, namely, the historical, the moral and the spiritual senses. The sickle would then be the difference [between them]. EXPOSITION ON THE

---

[1]TEG 8:202. [2]That is, in Rev 14:15, 17, 18.

Apocalypse 14.17, Homily 11.[3]

**Cutting Off the Impious.** Andrew of Caesarea: Although Christ is called the "angel of great counsel" of the Father, nonetheless from the following words the present angel is shown to be one of the ministering angels, for he comes out of the heavenly temple with a sharp sickle in order to accomplish the cutting off of those who are the most impious. Commentary on the Apocalypse 14.17.[4]

**The Caretakers of the Church.** Bede: If Christ was seen on the white cloud as a reaper, who is this vintager, unless he be the Selfsame, the repetition nicely occurring because of the twofold fruit of the church? For he who sowed good seed in his field is also he who planted a vineyard in a fertile place. However, both plantings have come to ruin because of the neglect of the caretakers.[5] Explanation of the Apocalypse 14.17.[6]

## 14:18 Another Angel Came from the Altar

**An Angel Appointed for the Punishment of Sinners.** Oecumenius: I think that this angel has been appointed for the punishment of the ungodly. Therefore, he says, "Put in [the sickle] and gather the clusters of the vine of the earth." The harvest mentioned above described the righteous and the sinners being brought to completion together. Their separation will be accomplished through "the winnowing fork of the Lord, by which he will clear his threshing floor and gather the wheat into the granary, but the chaff he will burn with unquenchable fire," according to the words of the Gospels.[7] However, this vintage of the clusters of grapes refers especially to the serious transgressors, for the vision depicts them lifelike as drunken and deranged. It is clear from the passage that their Lord did not regard them as worthy to be gathered in as were the first ones. Rather, a certain angel casts them immediately outside "into the winepress of the wrath of God," since they were thought worthy for neither a defense nor an interrogation. They come straightway to judgment, just as sinners are prosecuted in the Gospels, for whom exclusion and banishment become an occasion for punishment. I think that the prophet spoke of these persons when he said, "The wicked will not stand in the judgment."[8] Commentary on the Apocalypse 14.17-20.[9]

**The Angel Commands the Judgment of the Impious.** Andrew of Caesarea: From this passage we learn that angelic powers have been placed over the creatures, one is over water, another is over fire, and another is over some other part of creation. We learn of the fearsomeness of this particular angel because he is placed over fire. It says that he is of the highest angels, for with a cry he commands the one having a sickle to gather grapes of the vine of the earth. The "grapes" indicate the impious and the transgressors who have filled the cup of the wrath of the Lord and who receive as harvest the wrath of demons and of asps instead of the wine of gladness from the good husbandman. Commentary on the Apocalypse 14.18.[10]

**The Church Prays Daily That the Kingdom of the Lord Come.** Bede: As Jerome says, "The duty of the angels is twofold. Some assign rewards to the righteous; others preside over the various torments."[11] As it is said, "Who makes the winds to be his messengers and the flaming fire his ministers."[12] The two angels who announce that the harvest is dry and that the vineyard is ripe can be understood to represent the prayers of the church, which with a loud voice, that is, with a fervent desire, daily prays that the kingdom of the Lord come, saying: "Put in your sharp sickle, and gather the clusters of the

---

[3]PL 35:2438. [4]MTS 1 Sup 1:156. [5]For Bede this would refer to the pastors and bishops. [6]CCL 121A:435. [7]Mt 3:12. [8]Ps 1:5. [9]TEG 8:202-3. [10]MTS 1 Sup 1:156-57. [11]See *Commentary on Daniel 7:10* (CCL 75A:846). [12]Ps 104:4 (103:4 LXX).

vine of the earth." As it was with the harvest, so also the vintage is partly of the earth and partly of heaven. But the maturation of both indicates the end of the age. "For its grapes were ripe." This means that their sins are completed, although the perfection of that which is good can also be called "ripeness." EXPLANATION OF THE APOCALYPSE 14.18.[13]

## 14:19 *The Angel Gathered the Vintage of the Earth*

**THE PLACE OF TORMENT IS WIDE AND SPACIOUS.** ANDREW OF CAESAREA: The "wine press of God" is the place of torment prepared for the devil and his angels. Because of the multitude of those who are to be punished, it is "great." For the "way of destruction is wide" and spacious.[14] COMMENTARY ON THE APOCALYPSE 14.19.[15]

## 14:20 *The Winepress Was Trodden*

**THE BLISS OF THE SAINTS.** OECUMENIUS: And he has called the punishment a "winepress," fittingly extending the metaphor of the grape clusters and the vintage. "And the winepress was trodden outside the city." It would not be seemly were those punished to receive the rewards of their evil deeds in the heavenly Jerusalem allotted to the saints or if the happiness of the saints was spoiled by any experience with those who are justly being punished. Moreover, there is a "great chasm" that separates the godly from the ungodly, as the patriarch Abraham said when he spoke to the rich man in the Gospels. "And blood flowed from the winepress," it says. He speaks rightly of "blood," to show that he was speaking figuratively when he spoke of "clusters of grapes." For, to be sure, it is real persons who are being trampled up and cut up, so that [their blood flowed] "as high as a horse's bridle, for one thousand and six hundred stadia." In the holy Scriptures there is a common usage whereby God has certain horses with himself as the rider, these horses symbolizing an angelic power. For in the Song of Songs

the heavenly bridegroom says to the bride, "I have compared you, my love, my love, to my horse in the chariot of Pharaoh,"[16] and Habakkuk the prophet sings to God, "You will mount upon your horses, and your chariots are salvation."[17] The Apocalypse says that the bridles of these horses are soaked with the blood of sinners, not only of those close by but also of those standing far away. The passage is wholly figurative, intending to show the great amount of blood. For those who walk in the wide road are much more numerous than those who walk in the straight and narrow path, so that they soak the bridles of the horses responsible for punishment, even though these be angels. COMMENTARY ON THE APOCALYPSE 14.17-20.[18]

**THE BLOOD OF THE SAINTS.** PRIMASIUS: [The winepress is trodden] outside the city, that is to say, outside of the church. This will obviously take place when the future separation has been accomplished, for then every person of sin will be outside. This trodding of the winepress or the threshing of the field will destroy all that is useless, but it will prove that which is incorruptible, for the trials of tribulations test the righteous,[19] just as a vase is tested by fire.[20] The blood flowing as high as horses' bridles represents the vengeance that reaches even to the leaders of the nations. When the devil, together with his accomplices, begin to pay the penalties for the persecutions that they initiated, it is aptly said that the blood of the saints, which was once spilled, reaches as far as him and his princes, that is, those horses which in the person of the heretics started wars, as well as those who followed their errors. As it had been foretold, in the blood of sin "also the blood shall pursue you"[21] for 1,600 stadia, that is, into all the four corners of the world. For four is multiplied by four, as in four square-shaped faces and in wheels. Four times

---

[13]CCL 121A:435-37. [14]See Mt 7:13. [15]MTS 1 Sup 1:157. [16]Song 1:9. [17]Hab 3:8. [18]TEG 8:203-4. [19]See Sir 27:5-7. [20]Primasius follows Tyconius to this point. [21]See Ezek 35:6.

four hundred gives 1,600. COMMENTARY ON THE APOCALYPSE 14.20.[22]

**OVERTAKEN BY TORTURES.** ANDREW OF CAESAREA: However, it is possible to understand this another way.[23] For since those who transgressed by giving themselves over to pleasure have become horses full of lust, they will be overtaken by tortures up to their bridles, for they knew no bridle in their pleasures. By the "1,600 stadia" we learn of the great chasm that separates the righteous from the sinners. For these were perfect in evil and did that which is abominable, and therefore ten times one hundred signifies the complete magnitude of their evil, while the six hundred suggests their eager engagement in sin through the misuse of the creation, which was created in six days, and also in the six hundredth year of Noah all land was inundated by water.[24] COMMENTARY ON THE APOCALYPSE 14.20.[25]

**TRIALS TEST WHAT IS USEFUL.** BEDE: Should this harvest and vintage pertain only to the evil, the winepress signifies punishment. However, should they also pertain to the good, then the treading of the winepress and the threshing of the floor grinds down that which is useless and tests that which is useful. For it is as the apostle said, precious metals are tested by fire, but wood, hay and stubble are consumed by fire. And both are accomplished outside the heavenly Jerusalem. The winevat of wrath is so called by a manner of speaking, as it is said: "On the evil day the Lord delivered him."[26] . . . Tyconius interprets the harvester and the vintager to be the church, which shines after the fires of persecution and holds the power of binding and loosing. He says that the angels from the temple and the altar announce the kingdom of the Lord, not with an audible voice but by the suggestion of the Holy Spirit who works in [Christ's] body and teaches that now is the time for the evil to be accursed. And he has power over the fire, that is, that which comes out of the mouth of the witnesses and consumes their enemies. EXPLANATION OF THE APOCALYPSE 14.20.[27]

---

[22]CCL 92:220. [23]Andrew first repeats the interpretation of Oecumenius that the horses are angels. [24]Gen 7:11. [25]MTS 1 Sup 1:158. [26]See Ps 41:1 (40:2 LXX). [27]CCL 121A:437-39.

---

## 15:1-8 THE SONG OF THE LAMB

[1]*Then I saw another portent in heaven, great and wonderful, seven angels with seven plagues, which are the last, for with them the wrath of God is ended.*

[2]*And I saw what appeared to be a sea of glass mingled with fire, and those who had conquered the beast and its image and the number of its name, standing beside the sea of glass with harps of God in their hands.* [3]*And they sing the song of Moses, the servant of God, and the song of the Lamb, saying,*

*"Great and wonderful are thy deeds,*
*O Lord God the Almighty!*
*Just and true are thy ways,*
*O King of the ages* [j]

*⁴Who shall not fear and glorify thy name, O Lord?*
*For thou alone art holy.*
*All nations shall come and worship thee,*
*for thy judgments have been revealed."*
*⁵After this I looked, and the temple of the tent of witness in heaven was opened, ⁶and out of the temple came the seven angels with the seven plagues, robed in pure bright linen, and their breasts girded with golden girdles. ⁷And one of the four living creatures gave the seven angels seven golden bowls full of the wrath of God who lives for ever and ever; ⁸and the temple was filled with smoke from the glory of God and from his power, and no one could enter the temple until the seven plagues of the seven angels were ended.*

j Other ancient authorities read *the nations*

---

**OVERVIEW**: Filled with a sevenfold grace, the church will survive the final persecution (BEDE). Then God will bring his wrath to an end (OECUMENIUS) by smiting utterly and completely the rebellious people who practiced injustice throughout the seven days of the present age (BEDE, ANDREW OF CAESAREA). Made holy by the fiery water of their baptism, the righteous are immoveable in their faith and unshaken by every wind of doctrine (PRIMASIUS). Yet those who are being saved must also be cleansed and purified from all filth, for even the righteous are in need of purification (OECUMENIUS, ANDREW OF CAESAREA). Thus baptized and purified by the life-giving Spirit, the righteous will possess divine knowledge (ANDREW OF CAESAREA) and will live a life in harmony with the virtues (OECUMENIUS, ANDREW OF CAESAREA). As the flesh of Christ was stretched upon the cross like strings on a harp, the righteous put to death their members (ANDREW OF CAESAREA) and live according to the harmonious truth of the two Testaments (PRIMASIUS). The euphonious hymn to God sung by those who live in holiness after the coming of Christ (ANDREW OF CAESAREA) is in agreement with the song sung by Moses upon the destruction of Pharaoh. As Israel was victorious over horse and rider, so Christ has judged the wicked (OECUMENIUS) and given victory to the faithful (PRIMASIUS) so that they give thanks to Christ for his gifts and benefactions (ANDREW OF CAESAREA).

With the incarnation of Christ the mysteries of God once enclosed in one city are now opened spiritually to the whole world. The teachers of the church and all the faithful mortify the flesh and gird their minds with divine wisdom (PRIMASIUS, BEDE), for they have put on Christ, the elect chief Cornerstone (BEDE). Whoever is clothed with this stone is free from every desire that is destructive of the soul (OECUMENIUS). At the consummation, seven angels, also clothed in Christ as a pure, bright Stone, will come from heaven in the brightness of their virtues (OECUMENIUS, ANDREW OF CAESAREA). These seven angels will pour out the wrath of God, which will bring salvation to the righteous and vengeance to the wicked (OECUMENIUS, PRIMASIUS). Until that wrath-filled day, the church sends up a pious confession of sins, so that she might be aglow with faith and love and truth. For when the wrath of God is outpoured, the hidden mysteries of divine judgment will be opened (PRIMASIUS, BEDE) and the terrible and tormenting character of God's anger will be known (ANDREW OF CAESAREA), and no one will be able to confront it or withstand it (OECUMENIUS).

### 15:1 *The Wrath of God Is Ended*

**THE WRATH OF GOD WILL REACH ITS END.** OECUMENIUS: "And I saw," it says, "seven angels with seven plagues." He speaks of "seven" to indicate the many [plagues] prepared for the sinners through which the wrath of God will reach its end. COMMENTARY ON THE APOCALYPSE 15.1-4.[1]

**INJUSTICE WILL BE RESTRAINED.** ANDREW OF CAESAREA: Everywhere he uses the number seven, signifying that the injustices done brazenly during the seven days of the present age will be held back by the seven plagues and the seven angels. After these, the future life of the saints, symbolized by the glass sea, will commence. COMMENTARY ON THE APOCALYPSE 15.1.[2]

**THE WRATH OF GOD.** BEDE: The "seven angels" are the church full of the sevenfold grace. . . . He calls [the seven plagues] the "last," because the wrath of God always smites a rebellious people with seven plagues, that is, he smites them utterly and completely, as it is often stated in Leviticus, "I will smite you with seven plagues."[3] These will be the final [persecutions], since the church will come out from the midst of them. EXPLANATION OF THE APOCALYPSE 15.1.[4]

## 15:2 A Sea of Glass Mixed with Fire

**EVEN THE RIGHTEOUS NEED PURIFICATION.** OECUMENIUS: Somewhere the most wise Paul says, "Should anyone build upon this foundation gold, silver, precious stones, wood, hay, straw, fire will test the quality of the work of each, for it will be revealed by fire."[5] Will then not only sinners, who bring loads of kindling wood through their sins, but also the righteous, who offer gold and precious materials, be tested by fire? He says as much when he here says that those who have in every way defeated the beast stand on the sea of glass mixed with fire. For [the sea] is glass because of the brightness and purity of the righteous in it. However, it is mixed with fire because of the cleansing and purification from all filth, for there is need of purification even for the righteous. "For we all make mistakes," as it is written,[6] and "Who is clean from filth, even if his life upon the earth is

but one day?"[7] As has been frequently noted, the "harps" are a figure for the euphonious hymn to God sung by the saints. COMMENTARY ON THE APOCALYPSE 15.1-4.[8]

**THE SAINTS IMMOVEABLE IN THE FAITH OF THEIR BAPTISM.** PRIMASIUS: [He saw] the water of baptism made holy by the fire of the Holy Spirit. Or, in view of the character of fire, this water has been made red through martyrdom. For this reason we read, "The kiln tests the clay vessels, and the trial of tribulation the righteous."[9] "And I saw those standing upon [the sea] who had conquered the beast and his image." The term *standing upon*[10] indicates that they are immoveable in the faith. The psalm describes them in virtually the same way. For after it says, "who made by understanding the heavens," indicating no doubt those who are spiritual and fully enjoy the clear understanding of the heavenly truth, it adds, "who founded the earth upon the waters,"[11] namely, those who are immoveable upon their baptism. And although they seem to be nourished by milk, nonetheless they are not carried about "by every wind of doctrine."[12] And so here they are said to conquer the beast and his image.[13] [The harps] refer to their hearts, which are devoted to the praise [of God] and which are in full harmony through the harmonious truth of the two Testaments. Or this image speaks of the flesh of the passion, which is extended upon the wood, where not only the sound of the voice but also the effect of a good work is signified.[14] For this reason he includes also mention of that great man, Moses, to whom God bears witness, saying, "My ser-

[1]TEG 8:204. [2]MTS 1 Sup 1:159. [3]Lev 26:24. [4]CCL 121A:441. [5]1 Cor 3:12-13. [6]Jas 3:2. [7]Job 14:4. [8]TEG 8:205. [9]Sir 27:5. [10]The text of Primasius reads *superstantes* ("standing upon"). [11]Ps 136:6 (135:6 LXX). [12]Eph 4:14. [13]Caesarius of Arles states explicitly that they conquer the beast "in their baptism" (PL 35:2438). [14]The interpretations of the harps come from Tyconius. The contrast between the "sound of the voice" and the "good work" is that between the prophecy of the law and the fulfillment of it in the death of Jesus.

vant, Moses, who is faithful in all my house."[15] Commentary on the Apocalypse 15.2.[16]

**The Saints Radiate Brightness.** Andrew of Caesarea: We think that the "sea of glass" signifies the multitude of those who are being saved, the purity of the coming reward and the brightness that the saints will radiate by the sparkling of their virtue. The fire that is mixed with it may be understood from what was written by the apostle, "Fire will test the work of each, whatever it is."[17] Although this fire does not harm the pure and the undefiled, it is divided without mixture into two energies, according to the word of the psalmist:[18] it burns the sinners, and, as the great Basil understood, it illumines the righteous.[19] It is possible that the "fire" indicates both the divine knowledge and the grace of the life-giving Spirit. For God appeared to Moses in fire, and the Holy Spirit descended upon the apostles in the form of tongues of fire. The "harps" suggest the dying of members and the harmonious life in the symphony of virtues, plucked with the plectrum of the divine Spirit. Commentary on the Apocalypse 15.2.[20]

## 15:3-4 Great Are the Deeds of Almighty God

**All Nations Will Come and Worship Christ.** Oecumenius: "And they sing," it says, "the song of Moses," clearly indicating that song that Moses sang when Pharoah was drowned along with his entire army: "Let us sing to the Lord, for he has triumphed gloriously; the horse and the rider he has thrown into the sea. He has become for me a helper and protector for salvation."[21] This present song of triumph is because of the punishment of the wicked and the victory over the devil and the son of lawlessness, the antichrist. "And the song of the Lamb," it says, referring to the agreement [of Moses] with the Lord and his just judgment against the wicked. And therefore, indeed, they marvel at the truth and righteousness of the Lord. It says, "the king of the nations." To be sure, Christ is the king of

everyone. However, since it is said by Isaiah, "And there will be a root of Jesse, and he who arises to rule over the nations, upon him shall the nations hope,"[22] the prophecy [of the Revelation] says that he is "the king of the nations" and that all the nations will come and worship him and in this way [this passage] fittingly foretells the call of the nations and the faith which they will have in the Lord. Commentary on the Apocalypse 15.1-4.[23]

**The Elect Are Taught and Perfected in Both Testaments.** Primasius: He expresses here more fully the purpose and goal of the elect, who say from the heart, "Put the way of iniquity far from me, O Lord, and graciously teach me your law,"[24] or, "For the sake of your law I have endured for you, O Lord,"[25] and things similar to these. [By this scene] he wishes to make clear that these are in the number of the faithful in that they are participants in the victory mentioned. In Moses the Old Testament is signified as the New Testament is signified in the Lamb, and by this it teaches us that the elect were all equipped from both and perfected in both. . . . By a harmonious truth the pages of both Testaments testify to us concerning [their song], for "all the paths of the Lord are mercy and truth."[26] He is more aptly called the king of the nations, because he was a God not only known among the Jews, nor did the dew from heaven moisten only one fleece.[27] But as Malachi said, "From the rising of the sun to its setting my name is great among the nations, and in every place a pure offering is sacrificed and offered to my name."[28] Commentary on the Apocalypse 15.3.[29]

**The Holy Give Thanks for Christ's Gifts and Benefits.** Andrew of Caesarea: From the song of Moses we learn the hymn sent

---

[15]Num 12:7. [16]CCL 92:221. [17]1 Cor 3:13. [18]See Ps 29:7 (28:7 LXX). [19]*Homilies on the Psalms* 28:6 (PG 29:297). [20]MTS 1 Sup 1:160. [21]Ex 15:1-2. [22]Is 11:10. [23]TEG 8:205-6. [24]Ps 119:29 (118:29 LXX). [25]See Ps 129:5 LXX. [26]Ps 25:10 (24:10 LXX). [27]See Judg 6:37. [28]Mal 1:11. [29]CCL 92:221-22.

up to God by those who were justified by the law before [the coming of] grace. From the song of the Lamb we learn the thanksgiving of those who lived in holiness after the coming of the Christ. This thanksgiving is for those benefactions and gifts from him that have come to our race, since through the holy apostles he has called all nations to the knowledge of him. COMMENTARY ON THE APOCALYPSE 15.3-4.[30]

## 15:5-6 Seven Angels with the Seven Plagues

**THE ANGELS HAVE NATURES GIVEN OVER TO THE GOOD.** Oecumenius: In the holy Scriptures it is customary to call the tent constructed in the desert by Bezalel, the architect of the things made at that time, the "tent of witness" because it was the tent of the testimonies and ordinances of God. There was in it the ark of the covenant, the mercy seat, the table, the altars either for incense or for fruit offerings, the lampstand and whatever else God commanded holy Moses to provide, saying, "According to all that I show you on the mountain you shall make for me."[31] Therefore, in view of the image of the ancient tabernacle he has called also the supercelestial temple, which is always a "tent of witness." From there, it says, "the seven angels came out." Why was it necessary that the heavenly ministers of God be seen coming out from there rather than from the heavenly temple? They had in their hands, it says, seven plagues that they were going to release against the earth. For at the time of the consummation there will be many signs on the earth of which also Christ made mention in the Gospels when he was teaching about the end. That the angels are clothed in a pure, bright stone is indicative of their rank, purity and brightness, and that they possess a nature wholly given to the good, since they have put on Christ. For the Lord is called "stone" by the divine Scriptures. For example, Isaiah said, "Behold, I am laying for the foundations of Zion a costly and select stone,"[32] and the prophet said, "The stone which the builders rejected, he has become the head of the

corner."[33] The all-wise Paul also exhorts us to put on this stone, saying, "Put on our stone, Jesus Christ, and make no provision for the flesh to gratify its desires."[34] And whoever is enclothed with this [stone] is free from every desire destructive of the soul. COMMENTARY ON THE APOCALYPSE 15.5-16.1.[35]

**THE CHURCH WILL BE MADE WHITE BY THE GLORY OF GOD.** Primasius: The hidden secrets of the testimonies foretold concerning Christ and the church are now revealed. [The seven angels with the seven plagues] are the church against which a hostile portion rebelled through unending treacheries. Therefore it says that plagues come out, either for the defense of the saints in whom the Lord Christ earlier had suffered abuse, as he said to Paul, "Saul, Saul, why do you persecute me?"[36] or, as James noted, the time of judgment begins with the household of God.[37] To be sure, persons will be scourged in a twofold manner, so that the just God might punish their sins, as in the case of Pharaoh, or that he might test their virtues by a greater trial, as in the case of Job. And therefore we read concerning him, "The Lord has tested me, as gold that passes through fire; I have kept his ways, and I have not departed from the commandments of his lips."[38] The number of the angels and the plagues prefigures the universal extent of the consummation, as it says often in Leviticus, "I will smite you with seven plagues."[39] "They are clothed in pure white linen." Mortification is often indicated by a linen garment. If, then, the blameless judgments of God are recognized in that which is white, the sense is aptly applied also to these pure linen garments, so that those who are mortified are made snow-white by this whiteness, when they behold the glory of God at the revelation of his judgments. "They were girded with golden girdles." Scripture teaches that gold signifies wisdom, as it

---

[30]MTS 1 Sup 1:161. [31]Ex 25:9. [32]Is 28:16. [33]Ps 118:22 (117:22 LXX). [34]Rom 13:14. [35]TEG 8:206-7. [36]Acts 9:4. [37]See 1 Pet 4:17. [38]Job 23:10-12. [39]Lev 26:24.

says, "Receive wisdom as gold."[40] And it is rightly around the breast, where according to the law the priest is often commanded to wear the *logium*, that is, what is intellectual, so that his mind is well aware of divine things and does not despise them but rather praises the divine judgments and by the brightness of the gold on him also urges others to praise them unhesitatingly. COMMENTARY ON THE APOCALYPSE 15.5-6.[41]

**THE ANGELS ARE PURE IN NATURE.** ANDREW OF CAESAREA: The seer says that a "tent" was in heaven, and it was according to the likeness of this tent that God commanded Moses to build the tabernacle below. He says that from this temple angels proceeded out, dressed in "pure linen" or, as some copies have it, in a "pure stone." Their dress indicates the purity of their natures and the proximity that they have to Christ, the Cornerstone, and the brightness of their virtue. The phrase "girded with golden girdles" refers to the power and the purity and the honor of their nature and to the freedom they have in their works of service. COMMENTARY ON THE APOCALYPSE 15.5-6.[42]

**BEAUTIFUL IN THEIR VIRTUES.** BEDE: This vision corresponds to the hymn. For in order that the Lord might be adored by all nations, the temple of the mysteries of God, once enclosed in the walls of one city, now begins to be opened spiritually to the whole world. "Out of the temple came the seven angels with the seven plagues." This is what Mark spoke about, "And they went forth and preached everywhere."[43] They are "robed in a pure white stone," for as the apostle says, "For as many of you as were baptized into Christ have put on Christ."[44] Christ himself is the elect chief Cornerstone. Or, if one should understand the singular [stone] to represent a plural, the stone signifies the various beauties of the virtues. Another rendering has "white linen." This would indicate the mortification of the flesh that our teachers endure. It says, "I pommel my body and subdue it to servitude, lest

after preaching to others, I myself should be disqualified."[45] "Their breasts were girded with golden girdles." Whoever desires to preach mighty things, let him not only mortify the body but also bind his breast with the gold of wisdom. Or, to bind the breast with golden girdles is to bind every movement of our changeable thoughts by the chain of love alone. EXPLANATION OF THE APOCALYPSE 15.5-6.[46]

### 15:7 Seven Golden Bowls Full of the Wrath of God

**THE WRATH OF GOD IS GOOD, BENEFICIAL AND JUST.** OECUMENIUS: Their girdles are symbolic of the fact that they are effective and well equipped for their task. For concerning them it is said, "Mighty in strength are those who do his word."[47] These seven angels take from one of the four living creatures, concerning whom we have said much, the wrath of God in seven golden bowls. And aptly did he say "golden," for the wrath of God is worthy, bearing within itself that which is good and beneficial rather than just, even though those who are tormented might experience distress. COMMENTARY ON THE APOCALYPSE 15.5-16.1.[48]

**SALVATION TO THE RIGHTEOUS, RUIN TO THE IMPIOUS.** PRIMASIUS: Previously [the seer] mentioned seven angels with the same number of bowls containing the prayers of the saints.[49] Now he says that they are full of the wrath of God. The very same bowls are said to hold both the sweetness of supplication and the wrath of destruction, for [prayers] are poured out from the saints for the coming of the kingdom of God, at which time the judgments of God will no longer be hidden as in an abyss but will be open as in bowls. Moreover, they will bring salvation to the righteous but will inflict ruin upon the impious, as the apostle says, "For we

---

[40]Prov 16:16. [41]CCL 92:222-23. [42]MTS 1 Sup 1:161-62. [43]Mk 16:20. [44]Gal 3:27. [45]1 Cor 9:27. [46]CCL 121A:443-45. [47]Ps 103:20 (102:20 LXX). [48]TEG 8:207. [49]Rev 5:8.

are the good aroma of Christ among those who are being saved and among those who are perishing, to some a fragrance of death to death."[50] For if it was said of our Lord, "Behold, this [child] is set for the ruin and resurrection of many,"[51] why would it be surprising were the bowls to bring sweetness to the righteous but inflict the vengeance of the plagues upon the impious. COMMENTARY ON THE APOCALYPSE 15.7.[52]

THE ANGELS SHARE KNOWLEDGE OF GOD'S PLANS. ANDREW OF CAESAREA: The angels take the golden bowls filled with the wrath of the Lord from the four living creatures, as it also says in Ezekiel.[53] This shows that eternally in heaven the knowledge of God's plans is shared by those who are preeminent to those who are of second rank, even as the great Dionysius says.[54] COMMENTARY ON THE APOCALYPSE 15.7.[55]

## 15:8 The Glory and Power of God

NO ONE CAN CONFRONT OR WITHSTAND THE WRATH OF GOD. OECUMENIUS: The smoke of the divine anger is a sign, for it is written, "Smoke went up in his wrath."[56] This fiery smoke is symbolic, but so was the smoke that the holy Isaiah saw when he said, "and the lintel shook at the voice which the holy seraphim uttered, and the house was filled with smoke."[57] That smoke revealed the wrath of God against [the temple] of Jerusalem. He speaks periphrastically when he says that the smoke was from the glory of God and from his power. It is as though he said, "It was filled with smoke from the wrath of God," for God is himself power and himself glory, and who can withstand his wrath? [No one could enter the temple], for who will confront the wrath of God, or who will live when enveloped by it? For if no one has "stood in the counsel of the Lord," as it is written,[58] one could hardly be able to endure the wrath of God. COMMENTARY ON THE APOCALYPSE 15.5-16.1.[59]

CONFESSION OF SINS PRECEDES FAITH AND LOVE. PRIMASIUS: The smoke indicates that no

one can penetrate the secrets of the judgments of God. Rather, the minds of mortals grow dark and tremble at the thought of the plagues that are inflicted, which he now begins to narrate, and he says that the smoke will remain in the temple until the plagues are completely ended. Rightly, then, there follows, "No one could enter the temple," that is, that innermost secret, "until the seven plagues of the seven angels were ended." Therefore, also the psalm says, "It seemed to me a wearisome task, until I went into the sanctuary of God and I understood their ends."[60] Another interpretation might be that in the smoke we are to understand confession, as is often the case. As smoke precedes fire, so the confession of sins precedes the flame of faith and of love. And the psalm indicates such things when it says, "Who looks on the earth and makes it to tremble, who touches the mountains and they smoke."[61] "And the Lord looked at Peter,"[62] and he washed away his confession in tears, because when he denied, he was reduced to a fearful trembling. And so this is the meaning: No one could enter the temple until the seven plagues were ended, that is, no one shall ever be able to say, "I will walk in the innocence of my heart in the midst of your house,"[63] and "the king brought me into his chambers,"[64] except he who shall have taken care to efface by confession all iniquitous behavior that he has previously committed. "The thought of man will confess you," behold, the smoke, "and the remainder of his thoughts will celebrate solemn feasts for you,"[65] as a certain praise for the righteousness that has been obtained. And so, until all the plagues are ended, the church remains in the lament of confession, both in those who, as we said, pay the fruitful penalty for previous faults and in those who it will become clear are

---

[50]2 Cor 2:15-16. Primasius follows Tyconius to this point.   [51]Lk 2:34.   [52]CCL 92:223-24.   [53]Ezek 9:8; 20:8, 13, 21; passim.   [54]See Celestial Hierarchy 8.2; 13:2 (PG 3:240-41, 300).   [55]MTS 1 Sup 1:162.   [56]Ps 18:8 (17:9 LXX).   [57]Is 6:4.   [58]Jer 23:18.   [59]TEG 8:208.   [60]Ps 73:16-17 (72:16-17 LXX).   [61]Ps 104:32 (103:32 LXX).   [62]Lk 22:61.   [63]Ps 101:2 (100:2 Vetus Latina).   [64]Song 1:4.   [65]Ps 75:11 LXX.

approved by a better worship. COMMENTARY ON THE APOCALYPSE 15.8.[66]

**FRIGHTFUL, TERRIBLE AND TORMENTING.** ANDREW OF CAESAREA: From the smoke we learn of the frightful, terrible and tormenting character of the wrath of God. We are taught that the temple is filled with this wrath, which comes at the time of judgment against those who are worthy of it, and especially against those who obey the antichrist and do the works of apostasy. COMMENTARY ON THE APOCALYPSE 15.8.[67]

**THE MYSTERIES OF GOD'S JUDGMENT.** BEDE: When she is about to preach to the nations, the church herself is first set aglow with the fire of love and emits the smoke of a pious confession, "giving thanks to God for his inexpressible gift."[68] "No one could enter the temple until the seven plagues of the seven angels were ended." No one

may be incorporated among the members of the church except one who hears the mysteries of the faith and is taught by our teachers that Jesus is "ordained by God to be the Judge of the living and the dead."[69] However, if one interprets the smoke to be the hidden mysteries of the judgments of God, these remain impenetrable and closed to mortal beings until the plagues of the present age are ended and the Lord then shall come, who both illumines what has been hidden in the darkness and makes manifest to what extent the coming of the antichrist will be useful either for the testing of the faith of the church or just for the blinding of the Jews, who have not received the love of the truth that they might be saved. EXPLANATION OF THE APOCALYPSE 15.8.[70]

---

[66]CCL 92:224-25. [67]MTS 1 Sup 1:162-63. [68]2 Cor 9:15. [69]Acts 10:42. [70]CCL 121A:445-47.

# 16:1-2 THE FIRST BOWL

[1]*Then I heard a loud voice from the temple telling the seven angels, "Go and pour out on the earth the seven bowls of the wrath of God."*

[2]*So the first angel went and poured his bowl on the earth, and foul and evil sores came upon the men who bore the mark of the beast and worshiped its image.*

---

**OVERVIEW:** The exodus of Israel from Egypt was a type or model of the exodus of the church. This exodus takes place as the church is formed from the Gentiles, but it will take place completely at the end, when Christ will lead the church out of the world into the everlasting inheritance (IRENAEUS). At the present time the wrath of God is poured out by the church, for she judges those who are to be damned. However, even as God mercifully gives to the church authority to forgive

sins (TYCONIUS), so he now scourges sinners through calamities and wars so that he might moderate and lessen the unending torments that are to come (ANDREW OF CAESAREA). The wrath of God is poured out through preaching, for preaching makes manifest the impious (BEDE). Already in the preaching of Christ an incurable sore was inflicted upon the unbelieving Jews who rejected Jesus. Like a sore that infects the whole body, the apostasy of the Jews will find its imitation in the nations that accept and follow the antichrist (PRIMASIUS). Sinners who received no chastisement in the present age but rather themselves inflicted suffering will at the end suffer grievous spiritual sores in their souls (CAESARIUS OF ARLES). At the end, tribulations and rumors of wars will vex the souls of people (OECUMENIUS). As though it were puss from a sore, the grief of apostates will throb in their hearts; yet antichrist, whom they have made to be their god, will not heal them (ANDREW OF CAESAREA).

## 16:1 "Pour Out the Bowls of the Wrath of God"

**THE PLAGUES OF EGYPT ARE TYPES.** IRENAEUS: The whole exodus of the people out of Egypt, which took place under divine guidance, was a type and image of the exodus of the church that should take place from among the Gentiles; and for this reason he leads [the church] out at last from this world into his own inheritance, which Moses the servant of God did not give but which Jesus the Son of God shall give for an inheritance. And if anyone should pay close attention to those things that are stated by the prophets concerning the [time of the] end and to those that John the disciple of the Lord saw in the Apocalypse, he will find that the nations [are to] receive the same plagues universally, as Egypt once did particularly. AGAINST HERESIES 4.30.4.[1]

**THE CHURCH INFLICTS JUDGMENT AND GIVES ABSOLUTION.** TYCONIUS: The inevitable outcome of the divine command is here revealed. However, also revealed is that authority which the church especially merited to receive by divine inspiration, namely, to inflict judgment upon those who are to be damned and to grant mercifully absolution to those who have changed their ways. COMMENTARY ON THE APOCALYPSE 16.1.[2]

**PRESENT SUFFERING MODERATES ETERNAL TORMENTS.** ANDREW OF CAESAREA: From this we are led to think that until the divine vexation

with the wicked distinguishes who the righteous are, the saints in no wise obtain the lot of the Jerusalem above or the priesthood in the temple of God or the [final] rest. "It is necessary," it says, "that the plagues be completed." By way of the plagues the wages of sin are brought to light for those who are worthy to receive them, and these obtain the judicial sentence that has been determined for them. Then the habitation in the metropolis above will be awarded to the saints. I think that no one who considers each of the plagues in relation to those persons who are found at the consummation shall make an error concerning what is fitting and right. For being beneficent to humankind, God will determine that the unending torments in the coming age be lessened, but that in the present life the avenging scourges be brought upon those who deserve them, either through the prophets, Enoch and Elijah, or through the change of the elements or through the sufferings which occur from wars. Through such scourges there will be a moderation in the payment for sins. However, let us pray that we be chastised in a fatherly manner and not be scourged with harsh treatment by the wrath that comes from the Lord—"for there is no health in our flesh because of his anger"[3]—so that having cleansed through the tears of repentance our robes which have been stained by sins, and being dressed as for a wedding, we might enter into the bridal chamber of Christ, our God, to whom belong all glory, honor and worship together with the Father and the Holy Spirit forever and ever. Amen. COMMENTARY ON THE APOCALYPSE 16.1.[4]

## 16:2 Sores Upon Those with the Mark

**RUMORS OF WARS.** OECUMENIUS: We can interpret these things in a twofold manner. Either these events will occur literally at the time of the consummation, or they are to be understood alle-

---

[1]ANF 1:504. [2]CCL 92:225. [3]Ps 38:3 (37:4 LXX). Andrew reflects a slight variant reading. [4]MTS 1 Sup 1:163-64.

gorically. When the Lord addressed his disciples about the signs of the end, he spoke openly about the evil events that will happen at that time, saying, "And you will hear of wars and rumors of wars; and nation will rise against nation, and kingdom against kingdom, and there will be famines and plagues and earthquakes in various places. All of this is the beginning of the birth pangs."[5] And a little later he said, "For then there will be great tribulation, such as has not been from the beginning of the world until now, no, and never will be."[6] As each of the seven bowls is poured out, the events said to have occurred in the present passages should be interpreted in the light of those things [the Lord said]. In this case, the sores that come from the first bowl would symbolize the tribulations and distresses that vex the souls of people at that time because of the rumors of wars. COMMENTARY ON THE APOCALYPSE 16.2-7.[7]

**MANY FROM THE NATIONS WILL FOLLOW THE ANTICHRIST.** PRIMASIUS: The character of a mortal wound is such that the smaller the area on the body that is infected, the greater the likelihood that the remaining healthy part of the body can serve for the restoration of the health of the person. And although the preaching of the Lord, Jesus Christ, assists toward the salvation of those who believe yet is a witness of condemnation for those who do not believe, it is possible that from this spot the terrible wound is regarded as inflicting the whole body of those who are lost. For we read about Christ, "Behold, this [child] is set for the ruin and resurrection of many, and for a sign that is spoken against."[8] This is especially true of the people of the Jews, from whom it is said the antichrist is going to arise. By this one sin they lost the righteous ordinances of the law, if they were able to obey them, and they themselves perished without recourse to cure. For they did not wish to accept the Christ whom had been promised to them, and representing them the elder brother says to his father, "Lo, these many years I have served you, and I never disobeyed your command; yet you never gave me a kid, that I might make merry with my friends," and following.[9] He represents a people who despised the Lamb, disdaining as it were what is more on the right, for the place of the lambs is on the right, and who favored the kid goat, deviating as it were to the left to be damned, which is to say, they despised the Christ and accepted the antichrist. Therefore, it probably means here that a huge and terrible sore has come upon those persons who have the mark of the beast's name and who worship its image, so that confounded by the singular guilt of this wound, they are sentenced to the punishment of eternal torments. Concerning this sin, as if of a most terrible sore, the Lord said, "If I had not come and spoken to them, they would not have sin; but now they have no excuse for their sin. If I had not done among them the works that no one else did, they would not have sin; but now they have seen and hated both me and my Father."[10] This is an incurable sore. To be sure, [the Jews] will have many who follow them by a most wicked imitation, and therefore he has spoken indefinitely about those persons who have the mark of the beast's name, lest someone think that he was speaking only about the people of the Hebrews. For in a good sense the law calls those peoples the sons of Abraham who imitate him by faith, not that they were born of him according to the flesh but because they confessed Christ, who was from the tribe of Judah and who had victoriously resurrected from the dead. So, in a similar yet bad sense the Jews will have disciples from the nations who by accepting and following the antichrist, who will come from the tribe of Dan, will be marked as their accomplices by the mark of their transgression and will likewise be their partners in the penalties of an eternal damnation. COMMENTARY ON THE APOCALYPSE 16.2.[11]

**THE SINS OF THE HAUGHTY ARE SORES IN THEIR SOULS.** CAESARIUS OF ARLES: All of

---

[5]Mt 24:6-8. [6]Mt 24:21. [7]TEG 8:209. [8]Lk 2:34. [9]Lk 15:29. [10]Jn 15:22, 24. [11]CCL 92:225-26.

these plagues are spiritual, and they occur in the soul. For at that time the whole people of the impious will be unharmed by any plague of the body, because they were undeserving to be chastised in the present age, and it was as though they had received all the power of causing pain. However, spiritually all who are impious and haughty are going to suffer, for their sins of will and their mortal sins are sores in their souls. EXPOSITION ON THE APOCALYPSE 16.2, HOMILY 12.[12]

**GRIEF OOZES FROM THE HEARTS OF APOSTATES.** ANDREW OF CAESAREA: The bowl here, just as the cup, is to be interpreted as a tormenting activity that, when poured out by the angel, produces an evil sore, which here is symbolic of grief that throbs in the heart even as puss oozes from a sore. This grief occurs in the hearts of apostates, for since they are punished by plagues sent from God, they receive no healing from the antichrist whom they have made their god.

Perhaps also their bodies are physically wounded as a reproach to their souls, which have been wounded by the arrows of that deceitful rogue, the devil. COMMENTARY ON THE APOCALYPSE 16.2.[13]

**THE IMPIOUS RECEIVE THE PUNISHMENTS THEY GAVE TO THE FAITHFUL.** BEDE: Those who preach pour out the bowls of the wrath of God in a twofold manner. By a spiritual judgment, they inflict the punishments [given out by] the impious upon those very same impious, as Peter said to Simon, "May your money perish with you."[14] Or they reveal [the impious] to the church by preaching, as Peter said, "From of old their condemnation has not been idle, and their destruction has not been asleep."[15] EXPLANATION OF THE APOCALYPSE 16.2.[16]

---

[12]PL 35:2438. [13]MTS 1 Sup 1:164-65. [14]Acts 8:20. [15]2 Pet 2:3. [16]CCL 121A:447-49.

# 16:3 THE SECOND BOWL

[3]*The second angel poured his bowl into the sea, and it became like the blood of a dead man, and every living thing died that was in the sea.*

**OVERVIEW:** Those among the Jews who interpreted the law in a fleshly manner thought of the law as though it were a salty and bitter sea, and so, not recognizing Christ in the law, they crucified him. They will be led to condemn themselves and will be led to the further filth of worshiping the antichrist (PRIMASIUS). Those who attack the church by waves of persecution will be bloodied by a spiritual revenge (BEDE). As through Moses God exposed the hardheartedness of Pharaoh and revealed his own power, God will manifest

the weakness of the antichrist and the instability of those whom he deceived (ANDREW OF CAESAREA). It may be, too, that the wars during the final days will bloody the seas by sea battles and the rivers and streams by land battles (OECUMENIUS, ANDREW OF CAESAREA).

### 16:3 The Sea Became Like Blood

**BLOODY RIVERS, STREAMS AND SEA.** OECUMENIUS: The blood in the sea suggests those who are killed in naval battles, while the blood in the rivers and streams would refer to, most likely, the deaths of those who were killed in battles while encamped alongside such waters. COMMENTARY ON THE APOCALYPSE 16.2-7.[1]

**WORSHIPING THE ANTICHRIST.** PRIMASIUS: [It says that] water turned to blood. It is easy to turn the soul from spiritual matters and think after the manner of the flesh, which we knew without difficulty to be symbolized in that first of the plagues that we read was inflicted upon the Egyptians.[2] For then it reports that the fresh waters were turned to blood, whether the rivers of Egypt or the rain waters, as some translations have it, saying, "And their rain waters [were turned] to blood." . . . However, the present passage raises a question, because here it says that the second bowl was poured into the sea, that is, into waters that are bitter and salty. And [the waters] became blood, it says, and every living thing in the sea died. It seems to me that this passage signifies those among the Jews who did not interpret the law spiritually but understood it in a fleshly manner, and therefore they could not discern Christ in it. As the apostle says, "Had they recognized [him], they would not have crucified the Lord of glory."[3] But in addition to this, they are led by the burden of their deserts to such an extent, as though struck by the second wound of an even worse plague, that they desire the image of the beast and, possessing the mark of its name, think that they ought worship the beast rather than Christ. And so, perhaps in this passage what is described in the exodus to have happened in the first plague is placed in the second bowl, in that from the sterile waters [of the sea] they also move to the filth of blood, through which it says that every living thing in the sea, that is, [every soul] in this world, has been killed,[4] referring to the part from the whole, as in this passage, "There is no one who does good, no, not one."[5] To be sure, those are characterized by a manifest sterility of whom it is said, "I looked for it to yield grapes, but it yielded thorns."[6] And these are those whose tongues became so enfeebled[7] that they said to their own condemnation, "his blood be on us and on our children."[8] COMMENTARY ON THE APOCALYPSE 16.3.[9]

**THE CREATOR WILL REVEAL HIS POWER THROUGH ENOCH AND ELIJAH.** ANDREW OF CAESAREA: It is not surprising that to expose the weakness of the antichrist and the light-mindedness of the deceived, the divine power would through the holy prophets, Enoch and Elijah, change the sea into "blood as of a dead man," that is, as of one who had been slain, and would effect the corruption of all in it, just as long ago in Egypt he worked through Moses to expose the hardheartedness of Pharaoh and to demonstrate his own power. And therefore, those who were of secure faith were strengthened and the unstable were made fearful, seeing the creation arrayed against those who fought for the honor of the destroyer. It is also possible that through these words the slaughters that will happen in wars at the coming [of the antichrist] are indicated. For when Gog and Magog will move against each other in the four parts of the world and, in addition, the kings who had not obeyed will be annihilated with their whole armies and there will be slaughter in every place, then the sea will be defiled by sea battles, and the rivers will be mingled with the blood of those who were killed there. COMMENTARY ON THE APOCALYPSE 16.3.[10]

**BLOODIED BY A SPIRITUAL REVENGE.** BEDE: Those who are marked not only by the sign of the beast but also attack the steadfast servants of Christ by the waves of persecution will be punished by a spiritual revenge, which here he calls "blood." And those who boasted that they are alive will be proved to have served the author of death. EXPLANATION OF THE APOCALYPSE 16.3.[11]

---

[1]TEG 8:209. [2]Ex 7:17-21. [3]1 Cor 2:8. [4]There has been a play on words throughout this citation: *anima* ("living creature"); *anima* ("soul"). [5]Ps 14:3 (13:3 LXX). [6]Is 5:2 LXX. [7]Primasius carries on the image of the wound and its effects. [8]Mt 27:25. [9]CCL 92:227-28. [10]MTS 1 Sup 1:165-66. [11]CCL 121A:449.

## 16:4-7 THE THIRD BOWL

⁴*The third angel poured his bowl into the rivers and the fountains of water, and they became blood.* ⁵*And I heard the angel of water say,*
>"*Just art thou in these thy judgments,*
>*thou who art and wast, O Holy One.*

⁶*For men have shed the blood of saints and prophets,*
>*and thou hast given them blood to drink.*
>*It is their due!*"

⁷*And I heard the altar cry,*
>"*Yea, Lord God the Almighty,*
>*true and just are thy judgments!*"

---

**OVERVIEW**: God is good. Therefore, he has desired that the holy angels also assist him in the providential succor and aid of those on earth who are in need of everything. So God gives to the angel set over the water the task of providing water to those in need of it because they are caught in drought and famine and sickness (OECUMENIUS). However, as though it were water turned to blood, the teaching of the nations contains within itself both natural error and impure lusts that have captured people's minds in death and hostility toward God (PRIMASIUS). Persons who give foul teaching to the innocent and unaware will themselves be smitten by revenge (BEDE). Such persons have shed the blood of the prophets and have understood the spiritual law only in a fleshly way. Rightly, then, they are handed over to the corruptions of flesh and blood (PRIMASIUS). It is as though God had given them blood to drink, for those who turn from the prophets become participants in their murder (ANDREW OF CAESAREA). Those who serve at the heavenly altar give thanks to God for his righteous judgments (OECUMENIUS). Indeed, while angels above give thanks to God, a divine angel attends to each one of us. This angel converses with our minds and rejoices when those who have been darkened by sin become contrite and confess to God. May our man-

ner of life give cause for joy among the angels (ANDREW OF CAESAREA).

### 16:4 Waters and Fountains Become Blood

**NATURAL ERROR LEADS THE NATIONS TO DEATH.** PRIMASIUS: [This bowl] contains all of the other nations who have been so overcome by natural error and enmeshed in impure lusts that they even think of divine things in a carnal manner. And so, by these waters one may understand the teachings of the Gentile nations. Therefore, it says, "They became blood," just as it says in Genesis, "My spirit shall not abide in these people, for they are flesh,"[1] and also in the book of Wisdom, "stirred up by filthy blood for rebuke."[2] In addition, the apostle says, "To set the mind on the flesh is death" and "the wisdom of the flesh is hostile to God."[3] COMMENTARY ON THE APOCALYPSE 16.4.[4]

**SMITTEN BY CONTINUAL PLAGUE.** BEDE: Those who feign to offer that which is sweet so that they might pour out their poison upon the unaware will be smitten by the deserved revenge of continual plague. EXPLANATION OF THE APOCALYPSE 16.4.[5]

---

[1]Gen 6:3. [2]Wis 11:6-7. [3]Rom 8:6-7. [4]CCL 92:228. [5]CCL 121A:449.

## 16:5-6 Blood to Drink

**ANGELS ASSIST GOD IN THE PROVIDENTIAL CARE OF THE WORLD.** OECUMENIUS: "And I heard the angel of the waters saying," it says. To be sure, God is all-powerful and provides for his creatures and is sufficient for the beneficial care of all things, and so he has need for no one to assist him in this task. For since his willing a work is for it at the same time to be effected, and since by the movement of his will all things were brought into being, how is it that he should be in need of a coworker and an assistant for his providential care? But since he is good, he wishes that also the holy angels be benefited through the succor which goes to those in need—for the one who aids another in need benefits not so much the other as he does himself, and there is none in the angelic ranks who is wanting for and in need of the aid of any other. And so God has ordained that the holy angels provide aid and succor to those on the earth who are in need of every good thing. For indeed, in earlier sections we noted that angels were placed as benefactors of the churches, and the all-wise Daniel wrote that the leader of the angels, Michael, looked after the race of the Jews.[6] And now the Apocalypse explains to us that an angel is set over the waters. For although the world is constituted out of the four elements of air, fire, earth and also water—although some think that the heavenly things are established from some fifth element that they say is ethereal and moves in a circle—the three elements of fire, earth, and air are richly abundant for the purpose of breathing and for other common necessities, . . . water alone is not present to everything in abundance, whether it be fresh water in wells, springs, cisterns or rivers, or that water of the air that moves in the sky in clouds and gives to us timely rain by the command of God and nourishes every living thing on the earth. Therefore, since water is not everywhere abundant, one of the holy angels is set over it, so that when sufficiently abundant for what is needed he might provide to those who are in need of it that water which often is sparse and lacking due to our vices, causing drought and famine and the sickness that follows them. Most certainly it is this angel who is placed by the providence of God over the waters whom, he says, "I heard saying, 'Righteous are you, who is and was, the holy One.'" The phrase *who is* shows the endlessness of God, and *who was* that he is without beginning. The *Holy One* refers to the fact that he is righteous in all things on behalf of all things. For it says, "You have judged these things," so that those who have spilled the blood of the saints might drink blood. And it is necessary that those who encamped and fought by streams and rivers drink the water polluted by the blood of the dying being carried away downstream. COMMENTARY ON THE APOCALYPSE 16.2-7.[7]

**UNDERSTANDING THE SPIRITUAL LAW IN A FLESHLY WAY.** PRIMASIUS: The angels of the waters[8] are the messengers of the peoples who by an affection of the heart raise up together loud praises to God. . . . To be sure, both the Jews and the nations have in a bodily manner shed the blood of the saints, which the Lord says must be exacted "from the blood of Abel to the blood of Zachariah."[9] However, this plague might also be interpreted as a plague of that blindness so that they might even recognize that they have shed the blood of the prophets.[10] For while they were abusing them [the prophets], they turned their minds to other things. It is as though he said, whoever understood the spiritual law in a fleshly way, they are justly handed over to the corruptions of the flesh and of blood when both the sins and the punishment for sins is recognized. Therefore, the apostle said, "For they did not receive the love of truth so that they might be saved; therefore, God shall send upon them a work of error to make them believe what is false,

---

[6]See Dan 10:13, 21. [7]TEG 8:209-11. [8]The text of Primasius reads the plural, "angels." [9]Mt 23:35. [10]The thought seems to be that there is a blindness in which sinners see their sin but do not see it as a guilty deed or do not feel guilt as they ought.

so that all may be condemned who did not believe the truth but had consented to iniquity."[11] Commentary on the Apocalypse 16.5-6.[12]

**Those Who Turn from the Prophets.**
Andrew of Caesarea: Here also it is shown that angels are placed over the elements. One of these, who is over the waters, sings a hymn to God for the just condemnation that has come upon the transgressors. For since they soiled their hands in the blood of the saints, God has given them blood to drink. By means of these words, it is shown either that at that time many are accounted worthy of the prophetic grace because of their remaining steadfast in faith, those, namely, who are killed by the henchmen of the devil, or that those who turn from the preaching of the prophets of God and justify their murder at the hands of the hardhearted Jews, become purposefully participants in their slaughter, as the Lord said to the Jews, "for although you build the tombs of the prophets, you consent in their murder."[13] Commentary on the Apocalypse 16.4-6.[14]

## 16:7 God's Judgments Are Just

**The Angels Praise the Justice of God.**
Oecumenius: Those who stand around the heavenly altar send up a thanksgiving in agreement with that of the angel, for when he says, "I heard the altar saying" something, it signifies thereby those who minister at the altar. May it be that, being delivered from all the sufferings described above, we send up to Christ a hymn of thanksgiving, to whom be glory forever. Amen. Commentary on the Apocalypse 16.2-7.[15]

**Each Christian Has a Personal Angel.**
Andrew of Caesarea: Sometimes "the altar" signifies Christ, for in him and through him are brought to the Father our spiritual offerings and living sacrifices, which the apostle has instructed us to render.[16] At other times "the altar" signifies the angelic powers who, we read, "are sent forth to serve for the sake of those who are to obtain salvation,"[17] and so they carry upward our intercessions and spiritual sacrifices. From this ministering altar, it says, a voice proceeded, commending as just all the judgments of God that surpass both thought and expression. We have learned from the Gospels that the intellectual powers are glad and rejoice over the salvation of those who turn through repentance but grieve over those who leave the straight way and yet give thanks to God for the punishment of those who transgress the divine commandments. So let us hasten to bestow upon them joy and gladness for our repentance, recognizing that a divine angel attends each one of us and by a certain unutterable word implants in us what must be done, in as much as his mind imperceptibly converses with our mind and he intends to rejoice over that which is heeded, but like God to grieve over that which is disregarded. And so from this converse that profits the soul we should understand that the angel, sad and from afar, follows a person who has been darkened by many sins and enters into the church. But if this person has been made contrite and confesses from the heart to him who delights in mercy that he has rejected his former life and has converted to a better one, when he departs [from the church], the angel leads the way cheerfully and joyfully, while the wicked demon, having been shamed, follows behind at a distance. May it be, then, that our holy manner of life give cause for dejection to the demons but cause for joy to the angels, so that together with them, rejoicing with a shout of gladness and the sound of confession, we might give thanks to Christ, our God, for his victory over the evil powers, with whom glory is due to the Father together with the Holy Spirit, now and always and forever and ever. Amen. Commentary on the Apocalypse 16.7.[18]

---

[11]2 Thess 2:10-12. [12]CCL 92:228-29. [13]See Lk 11:47. [14]MTS 1 Sup 1:166-67. [15]TEG 8:211. [16]Rom 12:1. [17]Heb 12:1. [18]MTS 1 Sup 1:167-68.

## 16:8-9 THE FOURTH BOWL

[8]*The fourth angel poured his bowl on the sun, and it was allowed to scorch men with fire;* [9]*men were scorched by the fierce heat, and they cursed the name of God who had power over these plagues, and they did not repent and give him glory.*

**OVERVIEW:** The devil and his followers are tormented by the constancy of the saints and are aroused to further blasphemy against God. While the saints and the elect are moved by the error of their sins, the wicked and the weak are rather inflamed by temporal desires (PRIMASIUS, BEDE). Although the devil glories in his own followers and what they do, the Holy Spirit defines this glory to be nothing but plagues and sorrows (BEDE). Although God attempts to draw such persons to repentance, many have fallen to such depravity of their minds that they prefer rather to blaspheme. By suffering the heat of temptations they might have come to hate sin. But they rather "sharpen their tongues" against God (ANDREW OF CAESAREA). At the end they and the persecutors of the church will be burned up by the fires of Gehenna (BEDE). Similarly, those who continue to live during the wars at the end could pray to God for release from their woes. Yet they will not repent but will rather curse God (OECUMENIUS). It is the habit of blasphemers to blame God for their iniquities and struggles rather than to blame themselves. Inflamed by envy when they see the church struggling with a tireless constancy, they exhale fires of hatred from their hearts (PRIMASIUS). Therefore, God sends plagues upon their souls. Nonetheless, they continue to persecute the saints (CAESARIUS OF ARLES).

### 16:8-9 A Fierce Heat

**THOSE AT THE END WILL CURSE GOD.** OECUMENIUS: It is not difficult to interpret this passage according to the figures of speech. That the

sun scorches people could be the drought, affliction and distresses of those remaining in war. Although they are pressed by evils and find it needful to petition God, who is powerful, for help and release from those who are oppressing them with sorrows, yet they cursed [God] and did not repent. It is clear that the plagues are for this purpose, to bring those to acknowledge God through torments, who did not acknowledge their Master through his beneficent work. COMMENTARY ON THE APOCALYPSE 16.8-11.[1]

**THE DEVIL BLASPHEMES GOD.** PRIMASIUS: It is not given to the sun, but to that angel who poured out [the bowl] on the sun [to scorch people]. This fire is not to be regarded as that of Gehenna, for there no opportunity for blasphemy remains for anyone, when for the damned any attempt at repentance will be fruitless. And so the law says that they will say, "What has our arrogance profited us? And what good has the boast of our wealth brought to us?"[2] Therefore, I think that in this passage the fire and the heat ought be interpreted to mean that the body of the devil is irremediably tormented by the steadfastness of the saints, and aroused by the heat, [he] is led to blasphemy. For perhaps it says "on the sun" in the sense of "by the sun," as if he had put the sun in the ablative case, referring in this case to the "sun of righteousness." We have such readings; for example, "I shall watch over my word to perform it,"[3] and in Daniel, "Let us seek mercy from God Almighty

---

[1]TEG 8:212. [2]Wis 5:8. Primasius follows Tyconius to this point. [3]Jer 1:12.

over this mystery."[4] And so, from where the elect receive the steadfastness of their illumination, from there the wicked are said to obtain fire. COMMENTARY ON THE APOCALYPSE 16.8-9.[5]

**THROUGH SUFFERING SOME LEARN TO HATE SIN.** ANDREW OF CAESAREA: Perhaps humankind will literally be burned by the fierce heat of the sun. While God in his goodness "curbs them with bit and bridle who do not draw near to him"[6] so that they might look toward repentance, some have fallen to such depths of evil that by the depravity of their minds they will not turn to conversion but rather to blasphemy. Perhaps, however, the image of the sun signifies the course of the day that burns those worthy of scourging by the heat of temptations, so that by the experience of sufferings they might learn to hate the mother of these things, namely, sin. However, those who are mindless concerning any knowledge of their own faults will "sharpen their tongue"[7] against God, just as even now we see many who are distressed by the unspeakable horrors that encompass us at the hands of the barbarians and who blame the goodness of God, since he has held such evils for our own generation. COMMENTARY ON THE APOCALYPSE 16.8-9.[8]

**THE WISE REPENT OF THEIR EVIL.** BEDE: The persecutors of the church, who like a burning sun attempt to dry up the seed of the word of God, will be burned in the future fire by the flames of Gehenna. Or, if one interprets the sun to be the splendor of the wise, it is not given to the angel to pour out upon the sun, but it is given to the sun itself to punish people with heat and fire. For while wise people, conquered by torments, are affected by the error of having done evil, the weak, persuaded by their example, are inflamed by temporal desires. However, the heat may also be understood to be that by which the person of the devil is incurably tormented by the steadfastness of the saints and is incited to blasphemy. The prophet has spoken concerning this [fire], "Zeal overcomes a people without understanding, and now fire consumes

the adversaries."[9] It says "and now" because the fire of the last judgment is reserved. "And people were scorched by the fierce heat." In the present time, so far as it is permitted, the devil glorifies his own followers, although the Holy Spirit has defined such glorification and joy to be nothing but plagues and sorrows. For we also read above that the army of the devil has killed people with fire, smoke and sulphur. Not that he killed them openly, but rather that with these plagues he binds to himself those who were in agreement with him. EXPLANATION OF THE APOCALYPSE 16.8-9.[10]

## 16:9 They Did Not Repent and Give Him Glory

**IT IS THE HABIT OF BLASPHEMERS TO BLAME GOD.** PRIMASIUS: It is the habit of blasphemers that they prefer to blame God for wickedness and iniquity rather than themselves, and therefore [they] do not seek penance after plagues but, even though tormented, continue to throw insults. For just as a bronze vase, when subjected to a great fire, brings up bubbles from the inside that boil up on the outside and exceed its own capacity, so also those who belong to the beast, resisting the Unconquered, see the church of Christ struggle with a tireless constancy, and inflamed by the flames of an intolerable envy, exhale a fire conceived in the heart through the blasphemies of an impure mouth. COMMENTARY ON THE APOCALYPSE 16.9.[11]

**THE PLAGUES FROM GOD HARDEN THE SOUL.** CAESARIUS OF ARLES: These plagues from God do not strike them in the body but in the soul. And, therefore, they do not consider God but progress toward greater evil and for that reason blaspheme [God] and persecute his saints. EXPOSITION ON THE APOCALYPSE 16.9, HOMILY 12.[12]

---

[4]Dan 2:18. Primasius thinks that "over" (*super*) can sometimes be rendered as though it were introducing an ablative of means. Hence here, *super solem = sole.* [5]CCL 92:229-30. [6]See Ps 32:9 (31:9 LXX). [7]See Ps 64:3 (63:4 LXX). [8]MTS 1 Sup 1:169. [9]See Is 26:11. [10]CCL 121A:451-53. [11]CCL 92:230. [12]PL 35:2439.

## 16:10-11 THE FIFTH BOWL

[10]*The fifth angel poured his bowl on the throne of the beast, and its kingdom was in darkness; men gnawed their tongues in anguish* [11]*and cursed the God of heaven for their pain and sores, and did not repent of their deeds.*

**OVERVIEW**: At the coming of the Lord in glory, the impious tyranny of the antichrist will come to an end (OECUMENIUS, ANDREW OF CAESAREA). Bereft of the light of the "sun of righteousness" (ANDREW OF CAESAREA), his subjects will become darkened in their minds and confused (OECUMENIUS). The plagues sent from God will give such pain that some will gnaw on their tongues in the hope that the tribulation might cease (OECUMENIUS, ANDREW OF CAESAREA). Even now the kingdom of the antichrist is darkened, for many rejoice and make merry in their earthly happiness and do not remember their sins (PRIMASIUS, BEDE). Exalted by the arrogance of their temporary prosperity, they do not recognize the wrath of God and continue to curse God by reveling in their sins (PRIMASIUS, BEDE).

### 16:10-11 People Gnawed Their Tongues and Cursed

**WHEN THE LORD COMES IN GLORY.** OECUMENIUS: The bowl of the fifth angel was poured out, it says, "on the throne of the beast, and its kingdom was in darkness." The apostle wrote concerning the antichrist: "whom the Lord will slay with the breath of his mouth,"[1] and Isaiah said, "Let the ungodly be taken away, that he see not the glory of the Lord."[2] By *glory* Isaiah is referring to the coming of the Lord in glory. Therefore when it says here that the bowl was poured out "on the throne of the beast," it shows that the impious tyranny of the antichrist will receive its end and that he will be mercifully taken away, while by the unexpected retribution of the accursed, darkness will seize all those who allowed themselves to become his subjects. For they will endure a darkness of their reason, becoming befuddled by what is happening. "And they gnawed their tongues in anguish," it says. This often happens in the most serious of afflictions when people are wont to cut off their tongues or some other part of the body with their teeth, thinking that this will bring the tribulation to naught. And it is necessary that these themselves repent, if for no other reason than because of the destruction of the antichrist whom they chose to be their king and god. But they continue to blaspheme the true God because of the destruction of the wicked one. COMMENTARY ON THE APOCALYPSE 16.8-11.[3]

**SINNERS REJOICE RATHER THAN REPENT.** PRIMASIUS: The throne of the beast, or his kingdom, as it were, his judicial authority, is said to be darkened, because [its followers] are darkened by the joy of earthly happiness. And although they heartily rejoice in their present good rather than in the possessing of the highest blessedness, they "suppress the truth by wickedness,"[4] and so gnaw at their own tongues. The psalm adds its voice to this understanding when it says, "whose mouths speak lies and whose right hand is a right hand of iniquity,"[5] and "they spoke iniquity from on high."[6] Just like smoke, they rise by the arrogance of their temporary prosperity, from which they ought to turn in repentance, and although they are in the dark, they rejoice. As Job said, "They spend their days in prosperity, and in a moment

---

[1]2 Thess 2:8.  [2]Is 26:10.  [3]TEG 8:213.  [4]Rom 1:18.  [5]Ps 144:8 (143:8 LXX).  [6]Ps 73:8 (72:8 LXX).

they go down to hell."[7] COMMENTARY ON THE APOCALYPSE 16.10-11.[8]

### BEREFT OF THE "SUN OF RIGHTEOUSNESS."

ANDREW OF CAESAREA: Pouring the bowl on the throne of the beast signifies the pouring out of a great wrath upon the kingdom of the antichrist. This kingdom is shown to be in darkness, that is, it is bereft of the light of the "sun of righteousness." The gnawing of tongues reveals the intensity of the pain that those who have been deceived by him will have when they are struck by these plagues sent from God. These things will occur so that they might recognize that he whom they have worshiped as God is a fraud and so might want to be free from their deception. However, they will not turn from this to repentance. Rather, they will turn to further blasphemy. COMMENTARY ON THE APOCALYPSE 16.10-11.[9]

### SINNERS CURSE GOD BY REVELING IN THEIR SINS.

BEDE: The throne of the beast, or his kingdom, as it were, his judicial authority is darkened by plagues of this kind, that is, by the false joy of earthly happiness. It became dark by being deprived of light, as the psalmist says, "You did cast them down even while they were being lifted up."[10] He did not say, "after they had been lifted up" [they gnawed their tongues.] Just as a righteous person will eat the fruit of his labors, so also an ungodly person, given punishments worthy of his blasphemy, is sated, as it were, with his own tongue. Therefore, those who blaspheme are simply hurting themselves, thinking that the wrath of God by which they are impaled is in fact gladness. [And they cursed God.] He does not refer to their hardness [of heart] but to the righteous indignation of God, who gave [to them] such a plague that in it they cannot remember. For when afflicted by a bodily torment, who does not feel the hand of God, as did Antiochus?[11] It says, "they cursed," not that they did this openly, but in that they reveled in their sins. EXPLANATION OF THE APOCALYPSE 16.10-11.[12]

---

[7]Job 21:13. [8]CCL 92:230-31. [9]MTS 1 Sup 1:170. [10]Ps 72:18 LXX. [11]2 Macc 9:5-12. [12]CCL 121A:453.

## 16:12-16 THE SIXTH BOWL

[12]*The sixth angel poured his bowl on the great river Euphrates, and its water was dried up, to prepare the way for the kings from the east.* [13]*And I saw, issuing from the mouth of the dragon and from the mouth of the beast and from the mouth of the false prophet, three foul spirits like frogs;* [14]*for they are demonic spirits, performing signs, who go abroad to the kings of the whole world, to assemble them for battle on the great day of God the Almighty.* [15]*("Lo, I am coming like a thief! Blessed is he who is awake, keeping his garments that he may not go naked and be seen exposed!")* [16]*And they assembled them at the place which is called in Hebrew Armageddon.*

---

**OVERVIEW:** At the end of time, divine providence will cause the Euphrates River to diminish in size (ANDREW OF CAESAREA), perhaps by drying up some of its tributaries (OECUMENIUS). In this way the path is made easy for the kings of the east, who most likely will come from Scythia or from the eastern part of Persia (ANDREW OF CAESAREA). They will gather together for war against each other (OECUMENIUS) and to inflict bodily and spiritual death upon the rest of humankind (ANDREW OF CAESAREA). Christ, too, will come as a king from the east for the judgment of those who like a dry river have nothing living remaining in it (PRIMASIUS).

From the mouths of the devil, the beast and the false prophet come foul spirits like frogs. They are likened to frogs because of their filthy nature (ANDREW OF CAESAREA) and because they love foul mud and live in sewers and because they rejoice in the life of those who likewise live in slime and filth (OECUMENIUS, PRIMASIUS, CAESARIUS OF ARLES). Even as frogs emit an annoying croaking, so teachers of error make a great noise by their damnable rantings (PRIMASIUS). Hypocrites, too, are like frogs, for they leave the waters of penance and baptism to wallow in the mud of their sins and vices (CAESARIUS OF ARLES). From such persons saints and teachers of truth are as distant as they are from frogs (PRIMASIUS). Yet, as the magicians of Pharaoh earlier did marvels, these foul spirits will also perform wonders and signs. During the time of the present life they make nations captive to their superstitions and so enroll them in the army of Satan (TYCONIUS). At the time of the consummation they will gather the kings together for war against God, but they will be utterly defeated (OECUMENIUS, ANDREW OF CAESAREA).

It is necessary, therefore, that in our present life we do not stain the garment of our baptism with sins (TYCONIUS), for our good works become for us a garment of a holy body and a virtuous life. Apart from this garment we will stand naked at the last judgment (OECUMENIUS, ANDREW OF CAESAREA). Since the covering of good works can clothe the dishonor of an earlier life (BEDE), we should ask the Lord to wash the robes of our souls so that we might enter the bridal chamber to meet the pure and blameless Bridegroom. The kings will gather at a place called "cutting," for the devil delights in human blood (ANDREW OF

CAESAREA). The place is also called "general uprising in former things," for the devil will resume his previous activity of plotting against the Lord (BEDE).

## 16:12 The River Euphrates Dried Up

**THE WAY TO WAR IS MADE EASY.** OECUMENIUS: The sixth angel made the Euphrates River passable, perhaps by drying up some of its tributaries, so that the crossing of it would be easy for the many kings who by the work of the devil and the allowance of God were gathered together for war against each other. For . . . the Lord said that there would also be wars near the time of the consummation.[1] COMMENTARY ON THE APOCALYPSE 16.12-16.[2]

**CHRIST IS COMING FOR THE JUDGMENT.** PRIMASIUS: [The waters dried up to prepare the way for the coming king from the east], that is, for Christ,[3] concerning whom we read, "Behold a man, whose name is East,"[4] for him who is coming a way is prepared so that he might judge. Moreover, in the name of the river, Euphrates, as in the sea, the rivers, the springs of water, the sun and the throne of the beast, over all of which the angels are said to have poured out their bowls, those peoples who are impure are indicated. And its waters were made dry, it says. This means that these peoples will possess nothing which is green or living within themselves, for what they have will be fit for the fire of the approaching judgment.[5] Just as it said above that the crop was withered[6] in its ripeness and that the vintage was harvested, so in this passage it says metaphorically that the water of the river had become dry

---

[1]Mt 24:6-8. [2]TEG 8:214. [3]The text of Primasius has a singular ("king"), not a plural ("kings"). [4]Zech 6:12. The LXX reads ἀνατολή ("East") = oriens, which is the Latin rendering Primasius gives for Zech 6:12. The Greek has the idea of rising up, which may be why it is the word for the usual translation ("branch"). [5]This interpretation comes from Tyconius. [6]See Rev 14:16, 19. The text of Primasius reads aruisse ("dried up") instead of messum est ("was reaped").

so that nothing at all living remained in it, but rather that everything was to be destroyed by the fire of divine judgment, by which either the wicked are consumed as straw or the saints are made approved as gold. COMMENTARY ON THE APOCALYPSE 16.12.[7]

### FROM THE REGION OF THE SCYTHIANS OR FROM EAST PERSIA.

ANDREW OF CAESAREA: Perhaps by divine providence the Euphrates River will diminish in size and provide passage to the kings of the nations for their wars of destruction against each other and the rest of humankind. According to what is adduced in subsequent portions of the Revelation, we think that the mention of Gog and Magog suggests that these kings will arise out of the region of the Scythians. But it is also possible that the antichrist, coming out of the eastern regions of Persia, where the Hebrew tribe of Dan resides, will cross the Euphrates with other kings or with strong men who have received a royal name, and [they will] inflict upon humankind either bodily death to some on account of their faith and perseverance or spiritual death to others because of their cowardice and faintheartedness. COMMENTARY ON THE APOCALYPSE 16.12.[8]

## 16:13 Three Foul Spirits Like Frogs

### DEMONS ARE LIKE FROGS.

OECUMENIUS: He calls the devil, that originator of evil, a "dragon." But by the title of "false prophet" he refers either to a certain other who prophesies through the operation of the devil or to the antichrist. However, should he be speaking completely of the antichrist whom above he introduced as one slain by the breath of the Lord and whom now he depicts as still alive—he pours out demons through his mouth—let not the reader be amazed. For that which is seen is a vision, and the Evangelist often shows that which comes first as last, and contrariwise that which is last as first. . . . He calls the demons "frogs" because they rejoice at that life of people that is muddy and

slimy. Moreover, they take pleasure in the life of sinners, which is moist and without constraint, rather than in the life of the righteous, which is steadfast and austere, being also very envious and joyful at the destruction of the living. COMMENTARY ON THE APOCALYPSE 16.12-16.[9]

### TEACHERS OF TRUTH DIFFER FROM FALSE PROPHETS.

PRIMASIUS: In view of the various passions in all of the vexations and vices they cause, evil spirits are said to possess a diversity of characteristics. And so, rightly did [Jesus] say somewhere in the Gospel, "deaf and dumb spirit,"[10] and elsewhere, "unclean spirit,"[11] and elsewhere the prophet said, "a spirit of harlotry had led them astray,"[12] for no other reason than that those under its control perform the uncleanliness of its own vice. Here, however, he includes all three unclean spirits, because he indicates that the one body of the devil is made up of its habitual differences, mentioning those [spirits] that possess the greater power, starting with the devil as the dragon; then the beast, which is the antichrist with his followers; and the false prophet, who represents the leaders and teachers of noxious doctrines. Therefore, he sees one spirit but mentions three for the number of the parts of the one body, so that every one of the lost is shown to be led by one malign spirit.[13] Perhaps for this reason he adds the horrible filthiness of frogs as a comparison with their impudence. For like frogs living in the sewers at night, these false prophets make a great noise through the damnable ranting of their error. Just as frogs are loathsome in the places they inhabit, in their appearance and in their annoying croaking, so the devil with his followers is recognized to be abominable to the truth and is deservedly and justly damned to eternal fire. The blessed apostle says something similar when he says, "Do not be mismated with unbelievers. For what partnership have righteousness and iniquity? Or what fellowship has

---

[7]CCL 92:231. [8]MTS 1 Sup 1:173-74. [9]TEG 8:214-15. [10]Mk 9:25. [11]Lk 9:42. [12]Hos 4:12. [13]This interpretation comes from Tyconius.

light with darkness? What accord has Christ with Belial? Or what has a believer in common with an unbeliever? What agreement has the temple of God with idols?"[14] And so here, when it says that from their mouths came forth unclean spirits similar to frogs, it is as though it said, why do you compare filth to heaven when it is fitting as a habitation of frogs even as it is of the horrible blasphemies of the false prophets? He is claiming that the teachers of the truth are as far removed [from such persons] as frogs are from holy persons, so that those who are not able to recognize that their frauds must be refuted by the power of discretion, may at least, when confronted by the ugliness of frogs, attempt to avoid such persons who, like frogs, are a hindrance to the ignorant lest they receive the truth in the quiet practice of devotion. COMMENTARY ON THE APOCALYPSE 16.13.[15]

**LIKE FROGS IN MUD, HYPOCRITES WALLOW IN SIN.** CAESARIUS OF ARLES: In addition to their ugly appearance, frogs are unclean also in their places of habitation. Although they seem to be native to the waters, they cannot endure it when the waters recede or dry up, and they roll around in the waters themselves and in the mud and filth of the waters. The hypocrites likewise do not spend their time in the waters, as they seem to, but in filthy acts that those who believe lay aside in the water. Similar to frogs are such persons who are not ashamed to wallow in sins and vices, which others put aside through penance or baptism. Whenever someone converts to God and repents that he had been arrogant, adulterous, drunken or lustful, such a person imitates these sins that another has relinquished by confessing and thinking to himself says, "I do what I want and later I will do penance as that one has done penance." But suddenly the last day overtakes him, and any confession is lost and his damnation remains. Such is that person who wishes to imitate others, not in that which is good but in that which is evil, and like frogs cover themselves and roll around in that muck and mire from

which others have been liberated. Frogs, therefore, signify the spirits of demons who do signs and wonders. EXPOSITION ON THE APOCALYPSE 16.13-14, HOMILY 13.[16]

**EVIL SPIRITS HAVE A FILTHY NATURE.** ANDREW OF CAESAREA: This passage mentions individually the devil as a dragon, the antichrist as a beast, and the false prophet as another figure distinct from the other two. It says that spirits similar to frogs come out from these, for they are characterized by a poisonous and filthy nature, and these evil powers love the mud and creep toward foul and moist pleasures. By the commands of the devil and of the antichrist and of the false prophet, they will use their mouths to show false signs and wonders to humankind. COMMENTARY ON THE APOCALYPSE 16.13.[17]

### 16:14 The Demonic Spirits Gather the Kings of the World

**CAPTIVE TO SUPERSTITIONS.** TYCONIUS: We are to believe that these will do wonders even as was the case through the magicians of Pharaoh. Not without reason did he recollect their deeds at the mention of the frogs, so that he might foretell that the ministers of Satan will themselves do similar wonders. For until the sign of the frogs the magicians had been allowed to prevail through their incantations. "They go out to the kings to gather them for war." This does not mean that there will be an assembly from every place on the earth to one location but that each and every nation made captive in its own place to its own superstitions will wish to serve in the army [of Satan]. . . . The "day of the Lord" must be interpreted according to various situations and contexts. Sometimes it refers to the whole time from the passion of the Lord, so that those who are going to be condemned to the last judgment are said now to be gathered together, as though to

---

[14]2 Cor 6:14-16. [15]CCL 92:231-33. [16]PL 35:2439. [17]MTS 1 Sup 1:174.

say, prepared. At other times "day of the Lord" can be understood to refer to the day of judgment itself, and at other times the phrase refers to the time of persecution, in which case it is clear that people of this kind are gathered together throughout the whole time of the present life. COMMENTARY ON THE APOCALYPSE 16.14.[18]

**THE TIME OF CONSUMMATION.** OECUMENIUS: One form of the wonders [worked by] the demons is that they gather the kings for war against each other at the time of the consummation. And he calls this day or that time "great," for it is truly great and fearful and is so called also by Joel, who says, "before the great and terrible day of the Lord comes."[19] COMMENTARY ON THE APOCALYPSE 16.12-16.[20]

**THOSE WHO FIGHT AGAINST GOD.** ANDREW OF CAESAREA: The false signs produced by the demons will cause those who follow them to make war on the "great and terrible day of God, the Judge of the living and the dead."[21] On that day, those who fight against God will be utterly defeated and, although they lament over their former deception, they will weep in vain. COMMENTARY ON THE APOCALYPSE 16.14.[22]

### 16:15 "I Am Coming Like a Thief!"

**NOT STAINING THE VESTMENT OF BAPTISM WITH SIN.** TYCONIUS: The apostle also says, "He will come like a thief in the night."[23] ... [The apostle] says, "As many of you as were baptized into Christ have put on Christ."[24] I think that here he urges that these vestments be preserved so that they will not be torn asunder by repeated baptism or besprinkled and stained by the spots of sins. In either case the ugliness of their treachery is uncovered which might have been avoided had their intention been preserved with a greater vigilance. COMMENTARY ON THE APOCALYPSE 16.15.[25]

**KEEPING THE BODY PURE AND HOLY.** OECU-

MENIUS: "Lo, I am coming like a thief," says the Lord. He says "like a thief" because of the suddenness and unexpectedness of his second coming. "Blessed is he who is awake and keeps his garments that he may not go naked." He continues the image of the thief. Therefore, he said that it is necessary to preserve one's garments that they not be lost. By the term *garments* he refers either to that virtuous and decent life through which we become worthy of God's protection, or he refers to the body, that it be pure and holy. For he who does not keep [his garments] will be ashamed in front of the divine throne of the angels and of people, harried by the judgment at that time and left "naked" of divine succor. COMMENTARY ON THE APOCALYPSE 16.12-16.[26]

**GOOD WORKS ARE THE GARMENTS OF THE SAINTS.** ANDREW OF CAESAREA: "To be awake and to keep one's garments" means to remain vigilant and always concerned with good works. For [good works] are the garments of the saints, and were one to be without these, one would necessarily be made ashamed as one naked and full of shamefulness.... We are taught in this passage that it is a terrible thing to be naked of the garments of virtue, and ... we have learned from the Gospel parable that he who is without this is thrown out of the bridal chamber. And ... we have learned from the apostolic saying that speaks of incorruptibility, "that putting this on, we shall not be found naked,"[27] that is clearly of good works. [Therefore] let us earnestly beseech the Lord that he wash the robes of our souls, so that, as the word of the psalm says, "they may be made whiter than snow,"[28] lest we hear, "Friend, how did you get in here without a wedding garment?" and "having our hands and feet bound, be cast into outer darkness."[29] Rather, as the wise Solomon says, let us "always have our garments

[18]CCL 92:233-34. [19]Joel 2:31. [20]TEG 8:215. [21]See Joel 2:11; Mal 4:5 (3:22 LXX). [22]MTS 1 Sup 1:175. [23]1 Thess 5:2. [24]Gal 3:27. [25]CCL 92:234. [26]TEG 8:215. [27]2 Cor 5:3. [28]Ps 51:7 (50:9 LXX). [29]Mt 22:12-13.

white"[30] and wear [robes] bright and white from a virtuous life, decorated with sympathy. And so [let us] enter into the bridal chamber with the pure and blameless Bridegroom of holy souls, Christ our God, with whom glory, might and honor is due to the Father, together with the Holy Spirit, now and always, and forever and ever. Amen. COMMENTARY ON THE APOCALYPSE 16.15-16.[31]

**THE GOOD WORKS OF THE FAITHFUL.** BEDE: "Blessed are those whose sins are covered,"[32] who before the eyes of the saints cover the dishonor of a reprehensible life at the judgment with the covering of subsequent good works. EXPLANATION OF THE APOCALYPSE 16.15.[33]

**16:16 Assembled at a Place Called "Armageddon"**

**MANY WILL BE "CUT UP."** ANDREW OF CAESAREA: Armageddon is translated as "cutting" or "being thoroughly cut up." And so we should think that the nations gathered and led for battle there by the devil will be slaughtered, since the devil rejoices in human blood. COMMENTARY ON THE APOCALYPSE 16.16.[34]

**THE DEVIL RESUMES HIS FORMER PLOTS.** BEDE: Elsewhere he mentions this place and says, "He gathered them for battle, and they surrounded the camp of the saints and the beloved city,"[35] that is, the church. [Or] the place of the ungodly can be understood to be the devil, who in the man of perdition, puffed up with an usurped deity, will be glad to resume his former plots, which were formerly forbidden by the Lord. For Armageddon is interpreted to mean "a general uprising in former things" or "a spherical mountain." EXPLANATION OF THE APOCALYPSE 16.16.[36]

---

[30]Eccles 9:8. [31]MTS 1 Sup 1:175-76. [32]Ps 32:1 (31:1 LXX). [33]CCL 121A:457. [34]MTS 1 Sup 1:175. [35]Rev 20:8-9. [36]CCL 121A:457-59.

---

## 16:17-21 THE SEVENTH BOWL

[17]The seventh angel poured his bowl into the air, and a loud voice came out of the temple, from the throne, saying, "It is done!" [18]And there were flashes of lightning, voices, peals of thunder, and a great earthquake such as had never been since men were on the earth, so great was that earthquake. [19]The great city was split into three parts, and the cities of the nations fell, and God remembered great Babylon, to make her drain the cup of the fury of his wrath. [20]And every island fled away, and no mountains were to be found; [21]and great hailstones, heavy as a hundredweight, dropped on men from heaven, till men cursed God for the plague of the hail, so fearful was that plague.

---

**OVERVIEW:** When the commandment and will of God are accomplished (OECUMENIUS, ANDREW OF CAESAREA) and the last enemy, death, is destroyed (BEDE), an angelic voice from heaven will say, "It is done!" At that time when the Christ comes, there will be alarm, terror and turmoil on the earth (OECUMENIUS, ANDREW OF CAESAREA). The greatest of all tribulations and wondrous signs, whether from the good or from the bad, will occur (BEDE) similar to those that announced the descent of God upon Sinai (ANDREW OF CAESAREA). This time will also commence the transformation of the visible world (OECUMENIUS, ANDREW OF CAESAREA).

Moreover, at that time cities will fall and the peoples will be divided. This will include Jerusalem, which is great not because of its buildings but because of the sufferings of Christ in it. This city will be divided into Christians, Jews and Samaritans, for at the present time the Jews and the Samaritans do not dare to separate themselves from the Christians. But when the cleansing fire of temptation comes, they will be unmasked and a division will take place, for the sinners will gather together with those of like habit (ANDREW OF CAESAREA).

This division similarly will distinguish those who remained steadfast in faith, those who defiled their baptism with filthy deeds, and the Jews who did not receive the proclamation of the gospel (ANDREW OF CAESAREA). Rome also will fall at this time, as will those who seize it. Indeed, all cities will fall at the end, for when the earth is becoming new, no city befouled by the habitation of sinners can stand (OECUMENIUS), nor will the pagan manner of life remain at the coming of the kingdom of God (ANDREW OF CAESAREA).

The great city may also be understood to be the city of all the haughty and arrogant people who will be divided into Gentiles, heretics and Jews, and the false brothers (PRIMASIUS). Or the great city may represent all people upon the earth, for at the end these will be divided into Gentiles, heretics and false brothers, and the catholic church (CAESARIUS OF ARLES). During the great tribulation the church will be established in stability like islands and mountains (PRIMASIUS, BEDE), and especially the Gentile churches will rejoice, for like islands they rose above their distasteful idolatry (OECUMENIUS). Yet the church will flee at the coming of these terrible occurrences. For wisely she will hide from her persecutors (BEDE) and will seek refuge

among the mountains and caves to preserve her piety (ANDREW OF CAESAREA) and to avoid all contact with evil persons so that there be no longer any mixture of the wicked with the church (PRIMASIUS).

Despite all of this, some will continue to curse God, even in the midst of their torments. They will prove to be even more intransigent than was Pharaoh, who at least to some extent relented of his hardness of heart (ANDREW OF CAESAREA). Such ongoing blasphemy will be both sin and a punishment of sin, for these impious become worse and more demented when they are being corrected (PRIMASIUS).

### 16:17-18 It Is Done!

**THE FULFILLMENT OF GOD'S WILL.** OECUMENIUS: He poured out the bowl in the air, and the voice said, "It is done!" What is done? To be sure, the commandment of God and his will. And when from the air the voice said, "It is done," there were flashes of lightning and voices, lightning from on high and voices from those on the earth who were alarmed by the lightning. "And peals of thunder and an earthquake." By "earthquake" he means either the turmoil of the earth, since this also is included in the signs of the end, or he means the transformation of the visible world, as it is said in Haggai: "Once again I will shake not only the heaven but also the earth and the sea and the dry land; and I will shake all nations."[1] Therefore, he also indicated that there had never been such an earthquake. COMMENTARY ON THE APOCALYPSE 16.17-21.[2]

**THE FUTURE COMING OF CHRIST WILL BE TERRIFYING.** ANDREW OF CAESAREA: The angelic voice from heaven said, "It is done!" That is, the commandment of God has been accomplished. The flashes of lightning and the voices and the thunders are symbolic of the terrifying nature of these occurrences and of the future

[1]Hag 2:6-7. [2]TEG 8:216.

coming of Christ, just as long ago they announced the descent of God upon Mount Sinai.[3] The earthquake signifies the transformation of that which exists, as the apostle explained: "Yet once more I will shake not only the earth but also the heaven."[4] COMMENTARY ON THE APOCALYPSE 16.17-18.[5]

**A TRIBULATION SUCH AS NEVER BEFORE.** BEDE: Just as above[6] the blood of vengeance goes out as far as the bridles of the horses, that is, to the unclean spirits, so also here, when the final revenge was poured over the same powers of the air, it is said, "It is done." That is, the end is come, when, as the apostle says, "the last enemy, death, will be destroyed."[7] . . . When at the end of time there will be such a tribulation as has never been from the beginning, the greatest signs will similarly be evident. However, whether they come from the side of the good or from the side of the evil or come from both sides, as was the case with Moses and the magicians, is in this passage not sufficiently made clear. EXPLANATION OF THE APOCALYPSE 16.17-18.[8]

## 16:19 The Great City Split into Three Parts

**ALL CITIES, DEFILED BY SIN, WILL FALL.** OECUMENIUS: By the words "the great city" he speaks of Jerusalem, and it is clear that in this way he distinguishes it from the cities of the nations. For it is customary in the holy Scriptures to call the rest of humankind apart from Israel by the term *nations*. And he speaks of it as "great," as though it were famous. But all the cities fell. For when the earth is being transformed and is becoming new, how could it be that the cities in it would stand, having been defiled by the habitation of sinners? "And God remembered great Babylon, to give to it the cup of the wine of the wrath of his anger." In a foregoing passage it says, "And a second angel followed, saying, 'Fallen, fallen, is Babylon the great.'"[9] But in this present passage, he intends for us to think of another Babylon, not that one, and he assigns to it

another sense. I think that he is speaking of Rome and of those who will capture it at that time, as the narrative will teach further on. And, therefore, he says, "God remembered great Babylon," that is, God remembered its former sins, when they persecuted and killed the saints. COMMENTARY ON THE APOCALYPSE 16.17-21.[10]

**THE REPROBATE POPULATION DIVIDED INTO THREE PARTS.** PRIMASIUS: The city that was great because of the size of its population and that was haughty and arrogant because of its immodest enterprises shall fall into three parts. One part will be of the Gentiles, another of the heretics and the Jews, and the third part which is of the false brothers is rejected, for they "confess to know God, but they deny him by their deeds; they are detestable, disobedient, unfit for any good deed."[11] The passage continues, "The cities of the nations fell," that is, all the strength and confidence of the nations fell. "And that great Babylon was remembered and came under the sight of God." This indicates that the multitude of all of the damned were confused. "And he gave to her from the wine of the fury of his wrath." It describes the wicked receiving the retribution of that revenge that they merited. COMMENTARY ON THE APOCALYPSE 16.19.[12]

**ALL PEOPLE DIVIDED INTO THREE PARTS.** CAESARIUS OF ARLES: This great city is to be understood as in general every people that is under heaven and that is seen to be in three parts when the church is divided [into three parts]. And so, the Gentiles are considered to be one part, the heretics and false Christians [are] another part, and the catholic church [is] the third part. EXPOSITION ON THE APOCALYPSE 16.19, HOMILY 13.[13]

---

[3]See Ex 19:16-19. [4]Heb 12:26. [5]MTS 1 Sup 1:177. [6]Cf. Rev 14:20. [7]1 Cor 15:26. [8]CCL 121A:459-61. [9]Rev 14:8. [10]TEG 8:216-17. [11]Tit 1:16. Primasius follows Tyconius to this point. [12]CCL 92:235. [13]PL 35:2440.

## THE CLEANSING FIRE OF TEMPTATION.

ANDREW OF CAESAREA: We understand Jerusalem to be a "great city" not because of the number and size of its buildings but as that which is the most ancient and greatest in regard to godliness, in as much as it was made great by the sufferings of Christ and is to be distinguished from the cities of the nations. We think that the division of this city into three parts suggests the division between the Christians and the Jews and the Samaritans who live in it. Or the division is of those who are steadfast in faith and those who have defiled their baptism with filthy works and the Jews who have in no way received the proclamation.... For at the present time the Jews and Samaritans hide their real intentions out of fear of our pious rulers, and they seem to be associated with us, not daring to separate themselves with their own people. It is similar to the fact that those who are truly Christians are intermingled with those who possess the name [of Christian] alone. But when the cleansing fire of temptations will unmask them, then there will occur the division of these people into the three groups of the impious, the pious and the sinners,[14] and these will gather together with those of like habits and be associated with their own kind. The falling of the cities of the nations indicates either their destruction or the cessation of the pagan manner of life at the coming of the kingdom of God, which, according to Daniel, the saints will possess.[15] "And God remembered great Babylon, to make her drain the cup of the wine of the fury of his wrath." The thronging multitude, confounded by the meaningless distractions of life and made great by the wealth of their injustices, will drink the cup of the wrath of God. It is as though they went from a merciful forgetfulness [of God] to a remembrance and now faced the retribution for their trampling of the righteous One and for the impiety of their words and deeds. COMMENTARY ON THE APOCALYPSE 16.19.[16]

## 16:20 Islands and Mountains Vanish

## THE RANKS OF DEMONS WILL BE OBLITERATED.

OECUMENIUS: By *islands* he speaks of the Gentile churches, as the prophet says, "The Lord has reigned; let the earth be glad, and let the many islands rejoice."[17] He calls them "islands" because they lifted their heads and rose above their bitter and distasteful idolatry. Someone might also think otherwise and interpret the "islands" to refer to the impure orders of the demons, since they wallow in this briny and turbulent life. But that he refers to demons when he mentions the "mountains," even the holy psalmist shows, singing, "The mountains melt like wax before the Lord, for he is coming,"[18] Therefore, this passage transmits to us that the ranks of the demons at that time will be wiped out and obliterated. And, where might the wretched flee from God, in whose hand are the corners of the earth and who measured the heaven with a span and the earth with his hand[19]—unless those who are smitten by these events should attempt a futile flight and escape? When these things take place and there is a violent hailstorm, it is necessary that people at that time turn to prayers and entreaties—for these signs against them might have ceased, but they rather cursed God and therefore these evils even intensified against them. COMMENTARY ON THE APOCALYPSE 16.17-21.[20]

## THE CHURCH WILL BE ESTABLISHED.

PRIMASIUS: It is my view that by the terms *islands* and also *mountains* the church is signified on account of the greatness of its stability. Isaiah spoke about these: "In [your] teachings give glory to the Lord; in the islands of the sea [give glory] to the name of the Lord, the God of Israel,"[21] and again: "And in the latter days that mountain of the house of the Lord will be established upon the tops of the mountains."[22] This flight will occur when the

---

[14]Or *unrighteous, the righteous and the sinners.* [15]See Dan 7:18, 22, 27. [16]MTS 1 Sup 1:177-79. [17]Ps 97:1 (96:1 LXX). [18]See Ps 97:5 (96:5 LXX). [19]See Ps 95:4 (94:4 LXX); Is 40:12. [20]TEG 8:217-18. [21]See Is 24:15. [22]See Mic 4:1.

society of evil persons is at last avoided to such an extent that there will be no confusion or mixture of the church with the wicked. Therefore, the prophet said, "Flee from the midst of Babylon, let every one save his life."[23] Babylon will fall at that time when at the end it has received the power to persecute the saints. For this reason [Scripture] says, "The heart is proud before destruction, and the spirit is humbled before glory."[24] COMMENTARY ON THE APOCALYPSE 16.20.[25]

**FLEEING TO MOUNTAINS AND CAVES.** ANDREW OF CAESAREA: The holy Scriptures have taught us that "islands" refer to the churches and "mountains" refer to those who are leaders in them. That they flee at the time of the arrival of the aforementioned occurrences, we have heard from the Lord, who said, "Then they will flee from the east to the west and from the west to the east. For there will be a great tribulation, such as has not been from the foundation of the world, nor will ever be."[26] At that time some will be tormented for their sins, and others will endure misfortunes for the testing of their virtue. Such misfortunes will not only be those torments from the antichrist which they suffer for the sake of Christ, but also their flights and their sufferings among the mountains and caves. For they will prefer the mountains and caves to living in the cities for the sake of preserving their piety. COMMENTARY ON THE APOCALYPSE 16.20.[27]

**THE CHURCH WILL HIDE.** BEDE: The church, which is compared with islands and to mountains because of its excellent stability, wisely hides herself from the attacks of the persecutors. EXPLANATION OF THE APOCALYPSE 16.20.[28]

## 16:21 Great Hailstones

**BOTH SIN AND THE PUNISHMENT FOR SIN.** PRIMASIUS: The hail represents the wrath of [God's] revenge, of which we read, "The wrath of

the Lord descends as hail."[29] The Lord desires to protect his followers from this, for he says through the apostle, "[Jesus] delivers us from the wrath to come."[30] Nor is it without reason that he mentions the weight of a talent. For [the punishment] inflicted on each person by the equity of the divine judgment is due to a diversity of sins. Among the Greeks the talent is regarded as a certain weight and among the Romans as a certain different weight. Indeed, some things are sins, while other things are the punishments, and yet other things are both sins and punishments. . . . In this passage the blaspheming of God for the hail is recognized to be both sin and the punishment of sin by which the impious are so blinded that they do not come to their senses even when corrected, and so by these punishments [they] become even worse and more demented.[31] COMMENTARY ON THE APOCALYPSE 16.21.[32]

**EVEN MORE HARDENED THAN PHARAOH.** ANDREW OF CAESAREA: We think that the hail that comes down from heaven is the wrath from God, which also comes from above. That this hail weighs a hundredweight indicates the completeness [of its fearful torment] on account of the extremity and seriousness of the sins, which the image of the talent suggests and as Zechariah saw.[33] That those who are smitten by this hail are moved to blasphemy rather than to repentance reveals the unyielding hardness of their hearts. And so they will be like Pharaoh,[34] or rather they will be even more intransigent than he was. For he at least to some extent was softened by the plagues sent from God and confessed his own ungodliness, but these persons will blaspheme even in the midst of being tormented. COMMENTARY ON THE APOCALYPSE 16.21.[35]

---

[23]Jer 51:6. [24]See Prov 16:18. [25]CCL 92:235-36. [26]See Mt 24:21. The first part of this quotation is not in the Gospel. [27]MTS 1 Sup 1:179. [28]CCL 121A:463. [29]See Ezek 13:13. [30]1 Thess 1:10. [31]This interpretation of the blasphemy is from Tyconius. [32]CCL 92:236. [33]Zech 5:7-8. [34]See Ex 4:21; 7:3; 9:12. [35]MTS 1 Sup 1:179-80.

## 17:1-5 THE GREAT HARLOT

¹*Then one of the seven angels who had the seven bowls came and said to me, "Come, I will show you the judgment of the great harlot who is seated upon many waters,* ²*with whom the kings of the earth have committed fornication, and with the wine of whose fornication the dwellers on earth have become drunk."* ³*And he carried me away in the Spirit into a wilderness, and I saw a woman sitting on a scarlet beast which was full of blasphemous names, and it had seven heads and ten horns.* ⁴*The woman was arrayed in purple and scarlet, and bedecked with gold and jewels and pearls, holding in her hand a golden cup full of abominations and the impurities of her fornication;* ⁵*and on her forehead was written a name of mystery: "Babylon the great, mother of harlots and of earth's abominations."*

**OVERVIEW:** Old Rome was a harlot, for she was an apostate from God and compelled others to follow in her idolatry (OECUMENIUS). Moreover, the Senate of Rome and its kings from Domitian to Diocletian were guilty of the blood of the saints (VICTORINUS). However, old Rome has lost its former dominion, and it is unlikely that it will ever regain its ancient status. It is more likely, therefore, that the harlot is the earthly kingdom in general which will be condemned at the end (ANDREW OF CAESAREA). Indeed, the multitude of the lost are aptly called "harlot," for they have allowed themselves to be ravished by demons and are abandoned by the Creator (PRIMASIUS, BEDE). They are corrupted by wickedness and made mad by impiety and are called "great" because of the enormity of their transgressions (PRIMASIUS). The faithful, however, are betrothed to one husband and are presented as a pure bride to Christ (BEDE).

Not surprisingly, the woman has the image of the devil and is a murderess (VICTORINUS) and sits upon the devil, who is himself a murderer and scarlet with the blood of the saints (OECUMENIUS). Sitting upon the beast who is always arrayed against the Lamb, the woman sits as one exalted by the pride of presumption (PRIMASIUS) and, like the devil, she delights in blood and becomes a coworker with him in his blasphemies

against God (ANDREW OF CAESAREA). Void of the paradise of God's presence (PRIMASIUS), the woman is seen in the desert, that is, with those who are deserted by God and dead in their souls (CAESARIUS OF ARLES).

The earthly dominion of the beast claims universality and so assails the faithful by open aggression and desires to ensnare them by a fraudulent truth. Nothing indicates more the bogus power of this kingdom than the claim of the antichrist to be the Christ and so to seduce humankind by imitation, fraud and deceit. Against this vain and unclean spirit Christ gives his own Holy Spirit, the Spirit of wisdom, of understanding, of counsel, of fortitude, of knowledge, of piety and of the fear of God (PRIMASIUS). The kingdom of the devil and of the antichrist is arrayed with jewels and gold as though it were rich, beautiful and royal. However, it is all deceit, for it is full of pretense and false allurements (TYCONIUS), of idolatries and defilements (OECUMENIUS).

This harlot desires to multiply her own fornication, and as a mother gives birth to her own children (OECUMENIUS), so she gives birth to transgressions that are loathsome to God (ANDREW OF CAESAREA, BEDE). As a display of their piety, therefore, chaste and modest virgins ought to shun the adornments of the harlot and the allurements of beauty, since these are the insignia of brothels (CYPRIAN).

## 17:1-2 *The Judgment of the Great Harlot*

**ROME HAS GIVEN LAWS FOR PERSECUTING THE FAITH.** VICTORINUS OF PETOVIUM: He says, "Come, I will show you the damnation of the harlot who is seated upon many waters." And I saw, it says, "a woman drunk from the blood of the saints and from the blood of the witnesses of Jesus Christ."[1] For all the saints have suffered martyrdom because of a decree of the Senate of this city,[2] and although tolerance is proclaimed, it is she who has given to all nations every law against the preaching of the faith. COMMENTARY ON THE APOCALYPSE 17.2.[3]

**ROME SOMETIMES COMPELLED APOSTASY FROM GOD.** OECUMENIUS: Having completed its discourse about the consummation of the present age and what will happen at that time, the vision now reveals to the Evangelist what will befall Rome. He said to me, it says, "Come, I will show you the judgment of the harlot who is seated upon many waters." By *judgment* he means that way of life and conduct in which, he has judged, she lived and which she pursued. He calls [Rome] a "harlot" because she had fornicated, that is, apostatized from God. For this is called "fornication" by the divine Scriptures, as in the saying by the prophet to the God of all things: "You have destroyed every one who fornicates from you."[4] By *many waters* he refers to the nations that [Rome] rules and governs, as he says later on. "With whom the kings of the earth have committed fornication," it says. These are those who ruled among them [the nations]. For these kings of the earth are those who participated in her fornication and the madness of her idolatry. "Those who dwell on the earth have become drunk with the wine of her fornication," it says. For indeed also the rest [of humankind], over whom she was ruling, apostatized from God along with her. She was sometimes compelling the rest and some-

times leading the way. COMMENTARY ON THE APOCALYPSE 17.1-5.[5]

**PROSTITUTION WITH THE DEMONS.** PRIMASIUS: Isaiah speaks of the devil in a similar manner when he foretells the fall [of the devil] under the figure of the leader of Babylon. "How you are fallen from heaven, O Lucifer, who has risen in the morning."[6] Speaking of the body of all the lost, which he often calls by various yet suitable names, the Holy Spirit considers that it always moves to a greater variety of excesses and is corrupted by its wickedness and is hooked on its errors and is made mad by such a level of impiety that it is opposed by the gentle. And so [the Holy Spirit] depicts this body which is perishing with a suitable description, calling it a "harlot." For being forsaken by the Creator, she has given herself over to prostitution, allowing herself to be ravished by demons. She is called "great" because of the enormity of her transgressions through which she has offended the saints for a long time. She sits upon many waters, that is, upon many nations. COMMENTARY ON THE APOCALYPSE 17.1.[7]

**IDENTIFICATION OF THE HARLOT.** ANDREW OF CAESAREA: Some consider this harlot to be old Rome, since she sits on seven hills, and the seven heads of the beast that carries [the harlot] to be the more ungodly kings from Domitian to Diocletian who persecuted the church. However, we are guided as much as possible by the sequence of events and think that she is either the earthly kingdom generally, depicted as in one body, or that city that is ruled until the arrival of the antichrist. For old Rome lost the power of dominion a long time ago, and we do not suppose that the ancient status will again return to it. But should we grant this, the power that governs today will have been destroyed beforehand. For the Revela-

---

[1]Rev 17:6. [2]Victorinus is probably referring to the persecution under Decius. See also Commodian *Carmen Apologeticum* 823, 851. [3]CSEL 49:130-32. [4]Ps 73:27 (72:27 LXX). [5]TEG 8:218-19. [6]See Is 14:12. [7]CCL 92:237.

tion says, "The woman that you saw is the great city that has dominion over the kings of the earth."[8] COMMENTARY ON THE APOCALYPSE 17.1-3.[9]

**THE SAINTS ARE BETROTHED TO ONE HUSBAND.** BEDE: The multitude of the lost, who, abandoned by the Creator, gave themselves over to the corruption of demons are said to sit upon the waves, that is, upon the seditious discord of the nations. "The company of those who believed were of one heart and soul,"[10] whom the apostle betrothed "to one husband, to present her as a pure bride to Christ."[11] "The kings of the earth have committed fornication [with the harlot], and with the wine of her fornication the dwellers on earth have become drunk." The whole is greater than the parts. For the kings and the inhabitants of the earth each seek arrogantly after the things of the earth, and through the lust of vice they are corrupted by the allurements of the world and are made drunk by the madness of their minds. EXPLANATION OF THE APOCALYPSE 17.1-2.[12]

## 17:3 A Woman on a Scarlet Beast

**THE WOMAN HAS THE IMAGE OF THE DEVIL.** VICTORINUS OF PETOVIUM: [The woman is] she who is responsible for murders, and she has the image of the devil. . . . Because of the dispersion of the peoples, in the Apocalypse she is called "Babylon," as does Isaiah.[13] However, Ezekiel calls her "Sor."[14] And if one would compare what is said of Sor and what the Apocalypse and Isaiah say about Babylon, one would discover that they are the same. COMMENTARY ON THE APOCALYPSE 17.2.[15]

**THE WOMAN IS RED FROM THE BLOOD OF THE SAINTS.** OECUMENIUS: The wilderness symbolizes her coming desolation. "And I saw," it says, "a woman sitting on a scarlet beast." The "beast" is the devil on whom she was resting and by whom she was being commanded, and it is "scarlet"

because she has become red by the blood of the saints. And the beast was full of blasphemous names, for by attributing to himself that worship due to God, the devil sinned against God. "He had seven heads and ten horns," it says. The Evangelist will explain this later on, saying that the heads and the horns are kings who have ruled in [the harlot] and those who will rule.[16] COMMENTARY ON THE APOCALYPSE 17.1-5.[17]

**RAISED HIGH BY PRIDE.** PRIMASIUS: The desert refers to the absence of God, for his presence is paradise. [He was led] in the spirit, because these realities can [only] be seen in the spirit. In whose image does the divine word most depict her, if not the image of the woman "from whom is the beginning of sin, and because of her," as it is written, "we all die."[18] She is said to sit on a beast, since from it she is raised up high by the pride of presumption. [The beast is] scarlet, since it is a bloody beast, as we said, and it is a body arrayed against the Lamb. At times we are to recognize the devil in this beast, at other times the head which appears as though slain, at other times the people of the beast, which is the whole of Babylon, that is, confusion. And so, it is scarlet because it is bloody in its impiety, and it was drunk by its corruptions as though they were blood. "It was full of blasphemous names." Although it is worse to perform blasphemy by way of deeds than to be called blasphemous, here he nevertheless says that it fully abounds with names so that it might not be thought that it is lacking in any excess.[19] And because it is one thing to sin before God and another thing to sin against God, he who blasphemes against God is guilty of the greater offense. COMMENTARY ON THE APOCALYPSE 17.3.[20]

**THOSE WHO ARE DEAD IN THEIR SOULS.**

[8]Rev 17:18. [9]MTS 1 Sup 1:181. [10]Acts 4:32. [11]2 Cor 11:2. [12]CCL 121A:463-65. [13]Is 21:9. [14]Ezek 26—28. "Sor" (LXX Σόρ) is the Hebrew name for "Tyre." [15]CSEL 49:132. [16]Rev 17:12. [17]TEG 8:219. [18]Sir 25:24. [19]"She is said to sit upon the beast . . . lacking in any excess" is from Tyconius. [20]CCL 92:237-38.

CAESARIUS OF ARLES: In the beast the whole people who are evil is recognized, and in the woman its corruption is revealed. It says that the woman sits [on the beast] in the desert, because she sits on the impious, those who are dead in their souls and those who are deserted by God. [He was led] in the spirit, it says, because a desertion [by God] of this kind cannot be seen except in the spirit. EXPOSITION ON THE APOCALYPSE 17.3, HOMILY 13.[21]

**EVERY CITY IS A WILDERNESS.** ANDREW OF CAESAREA: It is necessary to say what we think concerning the wilderness into which he says he was led in the spirit. We think that in spiritual matters every city or populated place is a "wilderness" that is blameworthy because of a drunkenness of soul and fornication from God and of other such activities. It is also to be noted that in the vision that the spirit gives, the apostle sees the devastation of the harlot, whom he saw as a woman because she was softened for sin and unmanly. She was seated upon a scarlet beast because through evil deeds she reposed on the devil, who is murderous and delights in blood. Through such evil deeds she becomes a co-worker with the apostate in his blasphemies against God. The beast with its scarlet appearance is an indication of its cruelty and savagery and murderous intention. COMMENTARY ON THE APOCALYPSE 17.1-3.[22]

## 17:3 Seven Heads and Ten Horns

**THE MONARCHY OF THE EARTHLY KINGDOM.** PRIMASIUS: The prophecy of holy Daniel says that as the final persecution approaches, there will be ten kings.[23] This book often symbolizes them in the seven heads and ten horns of the beast, as it does here. Earlier it is said that diadems are worn by them, for when all the kingdoms have been overthrown, they only will reign in the whole world. Indeed, the diadems are signs of the conquered kingdoms, which are displayed as trophies upon the arrogant heads [of these

kings]. Therefore, through a mind of wisdom [this book] also says that the seven heads must be understood to be seven hills, so that it might signify Rome, which sits upon seven hills.[24] For since Rome once exercised an absolute monarchy in all the world, [this prophecy] has adduced it as a similitude for the kingdom of those [ten rulers], and in the name of Rome symbolizes the power of the entire earthly kingdom. In the number seven this passage intends to indicate the universality of its domination, since from the number three and from the number four, that is, from an odd and an equal number it is seen to consist of diverse members and so its universality is suggested.... In the seven churches we have indicated that [this universality] is indicated in the good sense, since it is foretold that the one church of Christ will possess the whole world. In this passage the same number is used in the contrary sense to refer to those seven heads that are in opposition and in which that universal power is said to have everywhere dominion. For holy Scripture frequently uses the number seven in both a good and in a bad sense. In view of his sevenfold work, the prophet Isaiah testifies that the Holy Spirit is to be regarded as sevenfold,[25] and here seven is used in the good sense. Similarly, however, an evil spirit is often described as sevenfold. Since the monarchy of these kings, which is often placed in opposition to the church of Christ, not only assails the faithful by way of open aggression but also desires to ensnare them by a bogus form of the truth, this passage indicates its manifest power by the ten horns and its fraudulent truth by the seven heads. Therefore, this future persecution is predicted to be violent, during which the practice of this deceiving power is supported and what is lacking to the deceit is supplemented by power. The illusory nature of this fraud was earlier indicated when it was said that "one head of the seven heads seemed to have been wounded unto death, but its mortal wound was healed."[26]

---

[21]PL 35:2440. [22]MTS 1 Sup 1:181-82. [23]See Dan 7:24. [24]See Rev 17:9-10. [25]Is 11:2-3. [26]Rev 13:3.

That is to say, one head from that universal rule of the worldly kingdom that opposes the church, namely the antichrist, who seeks to be received as though he were the Christ, will claim that he is resurrected, as though he had been dead, for he impiously seeks to separate the incautious from Christ, who really did die and truly did rise again. Concerning this [head] it has already been said that the dragon, that is, the devil, has given to him his own power and throne and authority, and so it says that he is full of blasphemous names, even as it said that "a blasphemous name was upon its head."[27] And there cannot be a more grievous blasphemy than as one who is opposed to Christ, which is what the name antichrist indicates, to wish to be regarded as Christ, so that he might seduce by a skewed truth those whom he was unable to break by violent terrors, and that he might lead those to adopt an imitation of the truth who had refused manifest error. COMMENTARY ON THE APOCALYPSE 17.3.[28]

**THE LORD FORETOLD THE COMING OF THE UNCLEAN SPIRIT.** PRIMASIUS: The Lord taught in the Gospel that we should be on our guard for this plague, saying, "When the unclean spirit has gone out of a man, he passes through waterless places seeking rest, but he finds none. Then he says, 'I will return to my house from which I came.' And then he goes and brings with him seven other spirits more evil than himself, and they enter and dwell there, and the last state of that man becomes worse than the first."[29] Did he not speak above of one unclean spirit? Why then did he mention seven others more wicked than himself, unless the unclean spirit is sevenfold in such a way that through his hidden evils he is discovered to be seven times more despicable?

And that what we say may be become more plain and clear, it is well that the reader be attentive. The good Spirit is a Spirit of wisdom, to which is opposed the evil spirit who is a spirit of foolishness and who is worse because it *feigns wisdom*. The good Spirit is a Spirit of understanding, while the evil spirit is a spirit of silliness and is

worse because it *feigns discipline*. The good Spirit is a Spirit of counsel, while the evil spirit is a spirit of imprudence and is worse because it *feigns prudence*. The good Spirit is a Spirit of fortitude, to which is opposed the evil spirit who is spirit of open *cowardliness* and who is worse because its weakness deceives by the appearance of strength. The good Spirit is a Spirit of knowledge, to whom the spirit of ignorance stands in opposition and is worse because it *steals knowledge* [for its own use]. The good Spirit is a Spirit of piety, while the evil spirit is a spirit of impiety and is worse because it is covered with a *false piety*. The good Spirit is a Spirit of the fear of God, to whom the spirit of recklessness is opposed, and this one is worse because it deceives through a *fake religiosity*.[30] I have extended a little my discussion of the deception of this adversary, so that this exposition might contribute to our understanding of many passages. The apostle too announced this future persecution, which will be so characterized by force and cunning, when he said, "Then the lawless one will be revealed, and the Lord Jesus will slay him with the breath of his mouth and destroy him by his appearing and his coming. The coming of the lawless one by the activity of Satan will be with all power and with pretended signs and wonders, and with every wicked seduction for those who are to perish."[31] By "power" he indicates its violent force, and by "seduction" he means its lying hypocrisy. COMMENTARY ON THE APOCALYPSE 17.3.[32]

## 17:4 A Gold Cup Full of Impurities

**SHUN THE INSIGNIA OF BROTHELS.** CYPRIAN: Showy adornments and clothing and the allurements of beauty are not becoming in any except prostitutes and shameless women, and of none, almost, is the dress more costly than those whose modesty is cheap. Thus in holy Scripture, by which the Lord has wished us to be instructed

---

[27]Rev 13:1. [28]CCL 92:238-40. [29]Mt 12:43-45. [30]For these virtues, see Is 11:2-3. [31]2 Thess 2:8-10. [32]CCL 92:240-41.

and admonished, a harlot city is described, beautifully attired and adorned, and with her adornments, and rather because of those very adornments, destined to perish.[33] . . . Let chaste and modest virgins shun the attire of the unchaste, the clothing of the immodest, the insignia of brothels, the adornment of harlots. THE DRESS OF VIRGINS 12.[34]

**JEWELS AND GOLD SYMBOLIZE THE DECEIT OF HYPOCRISY.** TYCONIUS: The purple symbolizes the pretense and deceit of her false rule, and the scarlet indicates the bloody disposition of her impiety. . . . [The jewels] symbolize all the allurements of that which deceitly claims to be true. . . . And then he discloses what is really on the inside of this beauty, saying, "She had in her hand a gold cup full of abominations and the impurities of the fornication of the whole world." The gold symbolizes the hypocrisy, for as the Lord said, on the outside they appear to everyone as righteous, but on the inside they are full of every form of uncleanness. COMMENTARY ON THE APOCALYPSE 17.4.[35]

**THE CAUSE OF EVIL AND IDOLATRY.** OECUMENIUS: "The woman was arrayed in purple and scarlet," purple because of her sovereignty and scarlet because she had shed the blood of many saints. She was "bedecked with gold and a precious stone and pearls." The passage appropriately describes her as a queen in royal garb. "She held in her hand a golden cup full of abominations." It was gold because of the rank of her sovereignty but yet full of idolatries and defilements by which she was nourished and by which she offered a libation to her own demons. "And the impurities of the fornication of the earth," it says. It ascribes to her the idolatries also of other nations, since she was the primary cause of their own evils and of the madness of their idolatry. COMMENTARY ON THE APOCALYPSE 17.1-5.[36]

**NOT SATED BY HER EVILS.** ANDREW OF CAESAREA: She is clothed in scarlet and purple, for

these are symbols of her dominion and rule over all. Therefore, she is decorated with precious stones and pearls. The "cup" indicates the sweetness of evil deeds before they are tasted, and it is gold because such deeds seem precious, as someone said of Job, "who drinks scoffing like water."[37] Moreover, the cup demonstrates that she is not sated by her evil but pursues further evil with a thirst for her own destruction. Therefore, she multiplies abominations for herself, that is, [she demands] practices that are abominable to God and that she makes the multitude who love the martyrs to drink. In this way she draws, as though it were a sweet drink, the abominable stupor of sin and the pollution of fornication from God. COMMENTARY ON THE APOCALYPSE 17.4.[38]

## 17:5 A Name of Mystery

**THE NATIONS REMAIN LOYAL TO THE ERRORS OF THEIR FOREFATHERS.** OECUMENIUS: And there was written upon her forehead, as though inscribed upon a public monument, as I might put it, that she was "Babylon, the mother of harlots." She is "Babylon" because of the terror and confusion in her and the persecutions of the saints—for the name Babylon means "confusion," as we have said—and she is mother because of her fornication, that is, her apostasy from God. For how is she not mother and teacher who persecutes the gospel and those who preach it and persuades the nations to remain loyal to the error traditional to their forefathers? COMMENTARY ON THE APOCALYPSE 17.1-5.[39]

**TRANSGRESSIONS LOATHSOME TO GOD.** ANDREW OF CAESAREA: The writing on the forehead indicates the shamelessness of the fullness of sins and of the confusion of the heart. She is mother because for those cities ruled by her she is

---

[33]Cyprian continues with a loose quote of Rev 17:1-5. [34]FC 36:41-42. Also Tertullian *The Apparel of Women* 2.11-12 (ANF 4:24). [35]CCL 92:241. [36]TEG 8:219-20. [37]Job 34:7. [38]MTS 1 Sup 1:182-83. [39]TEG 8:220.

the teacher of their spiritual fornication, giving birth to transgressions that are loathsome to God. COMMENTARY ON THE APOCALYPSE 17.5.[40]

**THE WOMAN IS THE NURTURER OF VICES.**
BEDE: This corrupter is immediately shown in her very face to be the nurturer of vices. How-

ever, since she is recognized only by the wise mind, for she is dressed in precious clothing, he indicates that this name is that of a mystery. EXPLANATION OF THE APOCALYPSE 17.5.[41]

[40]MTS 1 Sup 1:183. [41]CCL 121A:467.

## 17:6-18 THE BEAST RECEIVES ALL EARTHLY POWER

[6]And I saw the woman, drunk with the blood of the saints and the blood of the martyrs of Jesus.

When I saw her I marveled greatly. [7]But the angel said to me, "Why marvel? I will tell you the mystery of the woman, and of the beast with seven heads and ten horns that carries her. [8]The beast that you saw was, and is not, and is to ascend from the bottomless pit and go to perdition; and the dwellers on earth whose names have not been written in the book of life from the foundation of the world, will marvel to behold the beast, because it was and is not and is to come. [9]This calls for a mind with wisdom: the seven heads are seven mountains on which the woman is seated; [10]they are also seven kings, five of whom have fallen, one is, the other has not yet come, and when he comes he must remain only a little while. [11]As for the beast that was and is not, it is an eighth but it belongs to the seven, and it goes to perdition. [12]And the ten horns that you saw are ten kings who have not yet received royal power, but they are to receive authority as kings for one hour, together with the beast. [13]These are of one mind and give over their power and authority to the beast; [14]they will make war on the Lamb, and the Lamb will conquer them, for he is Lord of lords and King of kings, and those with him are called and chosen and faithful."

[15]And he said to me, "The waters that you saw, where the harlot is seated, are peoples and multitudes and nations and tongues. [16]And the ten horns that you saw, they and the beast will hate the harlot; they will make her desolate and naked, and devour her flesh and burn her up with fire, [17]for God has put it into their hearts to carry out his purpose by being of one mind and giving over their royal power to the beast, until the words of God shall be fulfilled. [18]And the woman that you saw is the great city which has dominion over the kings of the earth."

**OVERVIEW:** All cities that rejoice in murder and bloodshed and possess the power of the earthly kingdom are analogous to such a harlot. This is true of old Rome, of new Rome and of the Persians (ANDREW OF CAESAREA). Such cities are part of the one body that opposes the church and through a unity of spirit persecutes the church within and without (CAESARIUS OF ARLES).

The beast, which is the devil, was and is not. He "was" before the foundation of the world when he had not yet acted arrogantly against God. He "is not" in view of his ungodliness and the judgment of God, which will send him into fire at the consummation (Oecumenius). He also "was" before the cross, when he was powerful. But after the cross he "is not," for he has been deprived of his authority and power (Andrew of Caesarea, Bede). The devil will, to be sure, "ascend" at the end when the antichrist arises out of the abyss of this present life with the depth of its sin (Andrew of Caesarea) and when the antichrist is exalted by the false worship of those whom he has deceived (Oecumenius). In the meantime, the city of the devil, as it were, "was and is not" because through the coming and the going of the generations wicked children copy and replace their wicked parents (Primasius, Caesarius of Arles, Bede). At the end, when the beast ascends, many who are untaught in the prophecies of Christ will be amazed that the devil has regained his ancient strength (Andrew of Caesarea).

When the beast goes to perdition, those who trusted in him will be amazed at his sudden collapse as his power is stripped away (Oecumenius). These persons will realize too late that the beast is a false Christ, and in amazement they will learn that our Christ is the true judge (Primasius). Since the devil's ascent will accompany his judgment, wisdom and spiritual discernment is required (Oecumenius, Andrew of Caesarea). The beast has seven heads, which are mountains. This signifies Rome, for Rome is the city of seven hills (Oecumenius). Or perhaps the seven mountains are those most excellent and powerful kingdoms that have succeeded themselves from the Assyrians in Nineveh to the royal power of new Rome, which is favorable to Christ (Andrew of Caesarea).

The seven heads are also seven kings. This might refer to the six weeks of the present age, which will be followed by the seventh week of the sabbath rest (Hippolytus). Perhaps, however, the seven kings refer to the full duration of the earthly dominion whose final period, that of

antichrist, has not yet come (Bede). Or perhaps the seven kings refer to actual kings. In this case they may be the seven Caesars from Galba to Nerva who reigned during the time when the Revelation was written (Victorinus), or they may be the seven greatest persecuting emperors of Rome (Oecumenius), or they may be those kings who ruled first in the seven successive kingdoms from Assyria to new Rome (Andrew of Caesarea).

We must also be aware that the beast guides and rules our five senses as though he were their king, and he keeps many now in error before the final appearance of the evil spirit (Primasius). The beast belongs to the seven kings because he has been the ruling power hidden behind all persecutors (Oecumenius), and therefore he shares in their evil (Primasius). Yet the beast is said to be an eighth because he will arise after the seven to deceive and to devastate the earth (Andrew of Caesarea) and because he will excel them in a worse hypocrisy (Primasius).

The ten horns on the beast also symbolize ten kings. These kings will arise at the end to confront the antichrist. From Rome they will march against a resurrected Nero who will march against Rome from the east (Victorinus). In any case, these kings will rule only for a very short time, for they will soon submit themselves to the antichrist (Oecumenius, Andrew of Caesarea). This short time will experience a more acute and intense exercise of the arrogance and boasting of the kingdoms of this world (Primasius, Bede). The ten kings are said to receive power "as kings," for they oppose the kingdom of Christ (Bede). As Christ even now triumphs in his elect (Primasius), so then Christ will hand the ten kings over to the antichrist for death (Oecumenius) so that he might share with his elect the kingdom that he possesses as God (Andrew of Caesarea).

Astonishingly, the harlot will become the object of hatred and will be made desolate by the kings and by antichrist. In this God will use the devil and his followers as instruments of his own vengeance (Andrew of Caesarea). God will inform the hearts of the impious to do what is pleasing to him (PRIMASIUS), and they will lay waste that city that abandoned the laws of God (ANDREW OF CAESAREA). Perhaps Rome will be ravaged by the brutalities of warfare and be seized as a prize of victory (OECUMENIUS).

Yet even now the life of luxury plunders the lives of many, causing many to become dissolute and full of lust and bringing persecution on the saints. Such wicked people make the world a desert (CAESARIUS OF ARLES) and they themselves can be compared with the ruins of a deserted city (BEDE). May we who in the eucharistic cup are now united to Christ as the water is to the wine (CYPRIAN) be redeemed from such terrors by him who will recline with us and serve us in the Jerusalem which is above (ANDREW OF CAESAREA).

## 17:6-7 The Mystery of the Woman and the Beast

**UNITY OF SPIRIT AMONG THOSE WHO PERSECUTE THE CHURCH.** CAESARIUS OF ARLES: There is one body that opposes the church within and without. For within the church there are false Christians, and outside the church there are heretics and pagans. And although this body might seem to be separated in terms of place, yet when it persecutes the church there is working a unity of spirit. For it is impossible that a prophet perish away from Jerusalem, which persecutes the prophets.[1] That is to say, it is impossible for good Christians to suffer any persecution without evil Christians. And so the descendants of their ancestors are accused of consenting to the stoning of Zachariah, even though they themselves did not do it.[2] EXPOSITION ON THE APOCALYPSE 17.6, HOMILY 14.[3]

**EVERY CITY THAT SHEDS THE BLOOD OF THE SAINTS IS A HARLOT.** ANDREW OF CAESAREA: From many examples we learn that descriptive names can be ascribed to cities because of their reputations. Ancient Babylon is named in this way and is called a "pleasant harlot, skilled in

sorcery,"[4] and ancient Jerusalem is named "you had a whore's face,"[5] and in the letter of Peter the older Rome is called "Babylon."[6] More recently, she who held power among the Persians is called "Babylon" and a "harlot," as well as any other city that rejoices in murder and blood. And so, when the Evangelist saw one of these cities polluted with the blood of the saints, he was perplexed and learned about it from the angel, inasmuch as one who bears the power of the earthly kingdom at the end of time must suffer for its trespasses. And this is so whether one believes it to be the power of the Persians, or old Rome or new Rome, or whether the kingdom is taken generically as in one body. For we know that in each of these there are different sins and the shedding of innocent blood, sometimes more, sometimes less. Indeed, who could reckon the blood of the martyrs shed until Diocletian, or the torments of these at the hands of the Persians?[7] Moreover, for those who read them, the histories relate the perfidies done secretly under Julian and those done in new Rome against the orthodox during the time of the Arians. COMMENTARY ON THE APOCALYPSE 17.6-7.[8]

## 17:8a The Beast Will Go to Perdition

**THE UNGODLY DO NOT EXIST IN THE MEMORY OF GOD.** OECUMENIUS: "The beast that you saw," it says, "was, and is not, and is to ascend from the bottomless pit." For the devil "was" before the foundation of the visible world, having been created by God for good works, even as were also the other holy angels. But he "is not" in respect to the events surrounding the consummation of the age which are shown to the Evangelist, in which he will go "into the fire prepared for him and his angels." For it is certainly so that he is among them and not among them. Accordingly, since by his activity the antichrist will be mani-

---

[1]See Lk 13:33-34. [2]Mt 23:35. [3]PL 35:2442. [4]Nahum 3:4. [5]Jer 3:3. [6]1 Pet 5:13. [7]See Sozomen *Ecclesiastical History* 2.9-14 (NPNF 2 2:264-68). [8]MTS 1 Sup 1:183-84.

fested around the days of the end, it says that "he will ascend from the bottomless pit and go to perdition." For through the antichrist the devil will experience an ascent and a kind of increase, since the antichrist will deceive humankind and persuade them to worship, as the many predictions above have indicated. Or you might interpret the phrase "he was and is not" in this way. Writing to the Philippians, the apostle says, "to all the saints in Christ Jesus who are at Philippi,"[9] calling the saints those "who are" because they are in Christ and in the possession and memory of God. If, therefore, the saints are those "who are," the wicked devil "is not" now, although he "was" before he acted arrogantly against God and fell from his rank. It is similar also with the ungodly. Although they appear to exist so far as their substance and essence are concerned, yet they do not exist in regard to the judgment and memory of God. And since this is the case, the book of Genesis gives no genealogy of those who descended from Cain, because they "were not" because of their ungodliness.[10] Rather, it speaks of "perdition" to which he is destined to go, namely, to the just punishment of Gehenna against him. For in Matthew the Lord says that those condemned in it are destroyed: "Rather fear him who can destroy both soul and body in Gehenna."[11] COMMENTARY ON THE APOCALYPSE 17.6-9.[12]

**THE DEVIL ARISES AND PASSES AWAY.** PRIMASIUS: The holy Scriptures teach that from the beginning of the world there has been the rise and the advance to the present time of two cities. Of these, one is of God and the other is of the devil, and in this passage [the city of the devil] is indicated by the beast as [representing] altogether the whole body of the wicked. And so it says that it was and is not, because in the passing away of generations that succeed one another, it is built up and supplemented. And, therefore, it follows that it is going to ascend from the abyss as well as go to destruction. For by the hidden yet just judgment of God, it is brought to its end, so that the psalm says, "Your judgments are like the

great deep."[13] Or it claims that [the beast] will come forth from the hearts of the impious, of which the psalm speaks, "The deep calls forth the deep."[14] COMMENTARY ON THE APOCALYPSE 17.8.[15]

**THE WICKED ARE BORN OUT OF THE WICKED.** CAESARIUS OF ARLES: We understand this to mean that an evil people is born out of an evil people. And so we can say the beast comes out of the beast and the abyss out of the abyss. And what does it mean that the beast comes out of the beast, unless an evil people is born out of an evil people? This is so because wicked children copy and replace their wicked parents, and while some are dying, others succeed to them. Therefore, those who from the beginning have always plotted against the church are never lacking, whether they be few or many, whether they be hidden or manifest. And although in this world we can never be separated from having some contact with them, let us beseech the mercy of God, that we might be so separated in our conduct that we do not go with them to an eternal punishment. Rather, when they hear, "Depart from me, you cursed, into the eternal fire," may we be worthy to hear, "Come, blessed of my Father, inherit the kingdom."[16] EXPOSITION ON THE APOCALYPSE 17.8, HOMILY 14.[17]

**THE DEVIL "WAS" BUT "NO LONGER IS."** ANDREW OF CAESAREA: The beast is the devil who is always seeking someone to devour. He was killed by the cross of Christ, but, it is said, he will live again at the end, effecting the denial of salvation through the deceit of the antichrist in signs and wonders. In this way he "was" and was powerful before the cross, but he "no longer is" after the salvific sufferings, for he has become powerless and is deprived of his authority that he had over the nations on account of idolatry. And at the end he will come, in the way we have indicated, arising from the abyss or from wherever he

---

[9]Phil 1:1. [10]Gen 5:1—6:1. [11]Mt 10:28. [12]TEG 8:221-22. [13]Ps 36:6 (35:7 LXX). [14]Ps 42:7 (41:8 LXX). [15]CCL 92:242. [16]Mt 25:41, 34. [17]PL 35:2442.

was condemned and where the demons, thrown out by Christ, begged him not to send them, but rather into the swine.[18] Or he will come out of the present life, which is figuratively called "abyss" because of the depth of sin that lives in it and that is blown about and agitated by the winds of passion. From this place the antichrist, having Satan in himself, will come for the destruction of men, going himself to perdition in the age to come. COMMENTARY ON THE APOCALYPSE 17.8.[19]

**WHEN THE LORD WAS CRUCIFIED, THE DEVIL WAS CAST OUT.** BEDE: The devil ruled in the world at one time, but when the Lord was crucified, he was cast out. However, at the end of the world, when he has been released from the confinement of his prison, he will perish for eternity by the breath of the mouth of the Lord. Tyconius interprets the beast to be the entire body of the devil, which is supplemented by the course of generations that pass away and succeed themselves. And especially for this reason he shows the woman seated on the beast whom he had promised to show seated upon the many waters, that is, upon the people. EXPLANATION OF THE APOCALYPSE 17.8.[20]

## 17:8b Those on the Earth Will Marvel

**THOSE WHO TRUSTED THE BEAST WILL MARVEL AT HIS FALL.** OECUMENIUS: And, it says, "the dwellers on earth will marvel." Not all dwellers, but those whose names are not in the Book of Life. And why will they marvel? Because the beast was and is not and will come and be destroyed. For those who trusted in him will be amazed at the great change that has come upon him. For desiring to be ruler of the world and manifesting himself in this way, he will not only be stripped of his power but he will also receive a fate corresponding to his depravity. COMMENTARY ON THE APOCALYPSE 17.6-9.[21]

**THOSE SEDUCED BY THE BEAST.** PRIMASIUS: He is referring to those very same people from

whose members the body destined to damnation is built up. And should the names make for some ambiguity, in his epistle [John] has spoken of the same thing in the singular: "As you have heard that antichrist is coming, so now there are many antichrists."[22] And shortly thereafter he says, "They went out from us, but they were not of us; for if they had been of us, they would have continued with us."[23] Therefore, those whose names are not written in the Book of Life and who will still be living at the end of the world and who will experience the destruction of their own damnation, these will realize too late that he whom they had thought to be the Christ is not. And they will be amazed, for they had been deceived by the hidden seduction of the beast. Rather, when they have been most justly condemned, they [will realize that the Christ] is our Christ whom they will realize is indeed the judge. Therefore, since the foundation of the world, as "the Lord knows those who are his,"[24] so he has also promised that he would say to them, "Come, blessed of my Father, inherit the kingdom prepared for you from the foundation of the world."[25] And so also, those who are not his, he has not written in the Book of Life from the foundation of the world. But as those unknown to him and foreknown from afar he will condemn to the punishment of that eternal fire "which is prepared for the devil and his angels."[26] "For the Lord is high and regards the lowly, but the haughty he knows from afar,"[27] and so he says, "I never knew you; depart from me, you evildoers."[28] COMMENTARY ON THE APOCALYPSE 17.8.[29]

**THOSE UNTUTORED IN THE PROPHECIES OF CHRIST.** ANDREW OF CAESAREA: On account of the false miracles, those whose names are not written in the book of those who live forever and who have not been sufficiently taught in the prophecies of Christ concerning him will be

---

[18]See Lk 8:30-33. [19]MTS 1 Sup 1:185. [20]CCL 121A:467-69. [21]TEG 8:222. [22]1 Jn 2:18. [23]1 Jn 2:19. [24]2 Tim 2:19. [25]Mt 25:34. [26]Mt 25:41. [27]Ps 138:6 (137:6 LXX). [28]Mt 7:23. [29]CCL 92:242-43.

astonished at his coming and wonder how he had regained his ancient power. COMMENTARY ON THE APOCALYPSE 17.8.[30]

### 17:9 "This Calls for Wisdom"

#### THE DEVIL'S REEMERGENCE WILL DEMAND WISDOM. OECUMENIUS: "This calls for a mind with wisdom," it says. Here is a mind made crafty and cunning, it says. Let it understand the riddle how "he was and is not and will ascend from the bottomless pit." For even though he is passing from being into nonbeing, his re-emergence from the bottomless pit seems to indicate the opposite, only it is not so if one understands according to the words here stated. . . . "The seven heads are seven mountains," it says, "on which the woman is seated." From this it is clearly evident that the passage refers to Rome, for it and no other city is reported to be on seven hills.[31] COMMENTARY ON THE APOCALYPSE 17.9-14.[32]

#### THE SEVEN HEADS OR MOUNTAINS. ANDREW OF CAESAREA: Since what is to be interpreted is spiritual, there is need, it says, for a spiritual wisdom, not a worldly wisdom to understand what is being said. . . . We believe that the seven heads and the seven mountains are to be interpreted as seven places that excel the rest in excellence and worldly power. In these places we recognize that at various times the kingdom of the world is established, such as at first the rule of the Assyrians in Nineveh. Second, in Ecbatana there was the power of the Medians who from the time of Arbakes seized power from the Assyrians whose king, Sardanapal, Arbakes is said to have destroyed. After these there was the power of the Chaldeans in Babylon, whose king was Nebuchanezzar. Then after their fall the rule of the Persians in Susa was initiated by Cyrus. And after the destruction of this kingdom by Alexander, there was the rule of the Macedonians. After these there was in old Rome the power of the Romans that was sovereign under Augustus Caesar and its recent emperors and consuls and

was possessed by wicked men until Constantine. After the fall of these, the royal powers of emperors favorable to Christ were transferred to new Rome. COMMENTARY ON THE APOCALYPSE 17.9.[33]

### 17:10 Seven Kings

#### THE SEVEN KINGS ARE THE TIMES FROM ADAM. HIPPOLYTUS: The times are noted from the foundation of the world and are reckoned from Adam. . . . For the first appearance of our Lord in the flesh took place in Bethlehem, under Augustus, in the year 5500; and he suffered in the thirty-third year. And it is necessary that six thousand years be accomplished, in order that the sabbath may come, the rest, the holy day "on which God rested from all his works."[34] For the sabbath is the type and emblem of the future kingdom of the saints, when they "shall reign with Christ,"[35] when he comes from heaven, as John says in the Apocalypse: "For a day with the Lord is as a thousand years."[36] Since, then, in six days God made all things, it follows that six thousand years must be fulfilled. And they are not yet fulfilled, as John says, "five are fallen; one is," that is, the sixth; "the other is not yet come." In mentioning the "other," moreover, he specifies the seventh, in which there is rest. COMMENTARY ON DANIEL 2.4-5.[37]

#### THE CAESARS FROM GALBA TO NERVA. VICTORINUS OF PETOVIUM: This must be understood in terms of the time when the Apocalypse was written, for Domitian was Caesar at that time. However, before him there was Titus, his brother, and Vespasian, their father, also Otho, Vitellius and Galba. These are the five who have fallen. "One is," it says. This is Domitian, in whose reign the Apocalypse was written. "The other has not yet come." This refers to Nerva,

---

[30]MTS 1 Sup 1:185-86.  [31]Also Victorinus, who simply comments, "that is, the city of Rome" (CSEL 49:118).  [32]TEG 8:222-23.  [33]MTS 1 Sup 1:186-87.  [34]Gen 2:2.  [35]See 2 Tim 2:12.  [36]2 Pet 3:8; cf. Ps 90:4 (89:4 LXX).  [37]ANF 5:179.

who "when he comes, he must remain only a little while," for he did not complete even two years [as Caesar]. Commentary on the Apocalypse 17.2.[38]

### The Seven Kings Are Seven Persecuting

Emperors. Oecumenius: It is appropriate that he recognizes kings in the heads, for the kings exercise the fullness of Roman hegemony. However, why, when so many kings have ruled for Rome, did he mention only seven heads on the beast? He mentions these seven only, since they especially have represented the beast, that is, the devil and have caused it to raise its head against the Christians by initiating persecutions against the church. Of these the first was Nero, the second was Domitian, then Trajan, after him Severus, Decius, Valerian and Diocletian. Of those who ruled Rome, these constantly persecuted the church, as Eusebius reports in his *Chronicle*. He says that five of these seven have fallen by death—Nero, Domitian, Trajan, Severus, Decius—while one is, namely, Valerian. "The other has not yet come, and when he comes he must remain only a little while." He identifies the "other" as Diocletian, after whom the government seated in Rome ceased and was transferred to the city named for pious Constantine when Constantine moved the seat of government there. All these things were with great accuracy announced to the Evangelist, especially the information about Diocletian that "when he comes he must remain only a little while." By "remain" he means the persecution directed against the Christians. For although he reigned for twenty years, he instigated his persecution in the final two years and then forfeited his imperial power. Commentary on the Apocalypse 17.9-14.[39]

### Leaders, Kings and Subjects. Primasius:

As we have said frequently, in each member of a species the whole genus is indicated. Hence when we indicate what the whole beast is, there are the seven heads, and again the heads are called seven mountains and seven kings. That is to say, they are the entire reality of wicked people, which consists in the leaders as well as in kings and their subjects.[40] It is called by the various names on account of the different actions by which it either exercises force or deceives by fraud. For whenever it creeps with smooth movements, it seizes people by the delights of sensual things. As we read in the Scripture, "Death has entered through our windows."[41] And I think that this can rightly be understood to refer to our fivefold senses: sight, hearing, smell, touch and taste. And for that reason, the Lord said to the Samaritan woman, "You have had five husbands, and he whom you now have is not your husband."[42] What there is called "husbands," understand here as the "kings," by whose governance, as we know, the basic realities of human life are guided and administered. And the beasts appear to have these things in common with us. And what is said there, "And he whom you now have is not your husband," namely, that she was not living with a legitimate husband, that is, [she was living with] error, here is expressed in this way, "Five have fallen, one remains." And when it says, "Another has not yet come," he means that there remains outstanding another part of that same evil body that will succeed the generation that is passing away, and . . . it will similarly possess the same malignant spirit that we have noted consists in a sevenfold form. For it says that five have fallen, and that one still is, and that another is yet to come, and that makes seven in all. Commentary on the Apocalypse 17.9.[43]

### Those Who Ruled First in the Seven

Successive Kingdoms. Andrew of Caesarea: We think that the seven kings display the same idea [as the seven mountains], for the change of peoples in no way damages the identity of the notion, even though there the seven heads are shown in the form of a woman and the seven mountains in a neutral way. Here he showed

---

[38]CSEL 49:118. [39]TEG 8:223-24. [40]Primasius follows Tyconius to this point. [41]Jer 9:21. [42]Jn 4:18. [43]CCL 92:243-44.

seven kings. For often in the Scripture male names indifferently are given in the place of female names, and vice versa. For example, "Ephraim is a heifer made mad,"[44] or again, "Ephraim is a dove having no heart."[45] According to the theologian, "There are three who witness to Christ, the blood and the water and the Spirit,"[46] and according to Solomon, "There are three, the goat and the rooster and a king who is speaking publicly."[47] Therefore, through the seven heads he shows the cities after the manner of a woman, and through the seven mountains he depicts in neutral form seven majestic powers that at various times rise up over the rest of the earth, not by any geographical placement among the nations but because of their position of glory. And, as we said, we have interpreted the kings to be either those places made glorious by their royal prominence, or those kings who have ruled first in each of the aforementioned kingdoms, by periphrasis each standing for the entire kingdom—so, Nines for Assyria, Arbakes for Media, Nebuchanezzar for the Babylon, Cyrus for Persia, Alexander for Macedonia, Romulus for old Rome and Constantine for new Rome. COMMENTARY ON THE APOCALYPSE 17.10.[48]

**A SHORT PERIOD OF AFFLICTION.** BEDE: It says that the heads of the beast are kings of the world. For because of the swelling of their pride, they are compared with high mountains on which wanton ungodliness rests, so that they oppress by force and deceive by fraud. . . . Since the number seven indicates the full [duration] of earthly dominion, whose final period, that of the kingdom of the antichrist, has not yet come; it accordingly indicates that five have passed away, the sixth now exists, and the seventh is yet to come. "When he comes, he must remain only a little while." Since the Lord considers us, both the proud and the weak, it says that those days that he will inflict on us and that will be especially evil will be made short for mercy's sake. [This will be] so that he might terrify their arrogance by the adversities of that time yet might revive their

weakness because of its brevity. EXPLANATION OF THE APOCALYPSE 17.10.[49]

## 17:11 The Beast Goes to Perdition

**A RESURRECTED NERO WILL COME FROM THE EAST.** VICTORINUS OF PETOVIUM: [The beast belongs to the seven], for before the reign of these kings, Nero reigned. "But it is an eighth," since it will soon come and is reckoned to the eighth place. And since with him the consummation will occur, it adds, "and it goes to perdition." For "ten kings have received royal power." When [Nero] moves from the east, these will be sent by the city of Rome with their armies.[50] He calls these "ten horns" and "ten diadems." And Daniel also reveals this: "three of the first will be rooted up,"[51] that is, three of these chieftains will be killed by the antichrist. And the remaining seven will give him "glory and honor and kingdom and power." Concerning these it says, "these will hate the harlot," speaking here of the city, "and they will devour her flesh with fire." COMMENTARY ON THE APOCALYPSE 17.2.[52]

**THE GUIDING POWER OF ALL PERSECUTORS.** OECUMENIUS: He has ranked the devil first and last as a persecutor and one of like mind with the seven. For how would this one not be ranked with the seven, when he in fact had been their guiding power? COMMENTARY ON THE APOCALYPSE 17.9-14.[53]

**THE EIGHTH SHARES EVIL WITH THE SEVEN KINGS.** PRIMASIUS: Lest we should think him of

---

[44]Hos 10:11; 4:16. [45]Hos 7:11. [46]1 Jn 5:8. [47]Prov 30:29, 31. [48]MTS 1 Sup 1:187-88. [49]CCL 121A:469. [50]According to Victorinus, the eighth is Nero, who would be resurrected from the dead and march on Rome from the East. See the comment of Victorinus on Rev 13:3 above. The idea that Nero would return and seek revenge on his enemies was held also by the Romans. See Dio Chrysostom *Oration* 21.10; Tacitus *Histories* 1.2; 2.8; Suetonius *Nero* 57.1-4. That he would come from the East is attested in *The Sybilline Oracles* 4.115-39; 5.363-70. According to Jerome, some Christian chiliasts believed the antichrist would come from the Assyrians (*Commentary on Isaiah* 5; CCL 73:200). [51]Dan 7:8. [52]CSEL 49:118-20. [53]TEG 8:224.

a different kind, it adds that the one whom it calls the eighth is from the seven and goes to perdition. In this way it shows that he is of the same evil genus, and by going beyond the number seven, it indicates that he is even a worse hypocrite. As the Lord was speaking of one unclean spirit and mentions seven, he suddenly adds, "And he brings with him seven other spirits more evil than himself."[54] So in this passage, beginning with seven it indicates the other seven in one of the same genus, that is, in the eighth. Therefore, it says that he is from the seven and goes to perdition, in order to show that he merits the same punishment due to his singular genus. COMMENTARY ON THE APOCALYPSE 17.11.[55]

**THE ANTICHRIST ARISES FROM ONE OF THE SEVEN KINGDOMS.** ANDREW OF CAESAREA: The "beast" is the antichrist. He is the "eighth" because he arises after the seven kingdoms for the deception and devastation of the earth. He is "from the seven" because he arises from one of these. For he will not come forth from a nation other than those mentioned before, but as a king of the Romans for the defeat and destruction of those who believed in him. And after this he will go into the destruction of Gehenna. COMMENTARY ON THE APOCALYPSE 17.11.[56]

## 17:12 The Ten Horns Are Ten Kings

**THE REIGN OF THE TEN KINGS.** OECUMENIUS: The all-wise prophet, Daniel, remarked concerning these ten kings or horns that they would arise in the last times out of the Roman rule.[57] And the antichrist will rise up in the middle of them. And for this reason it says that "they have not yet received royal power, but they are to receive authority as kings." It rightly says "as kings" because of the rapid demise and fleeting nature of their reign. Then it continues, "they receive it for one hour, together with the beast." Here it calls the antichrist "beast" as it had also in earlier passages, saying, "I saw another beast coming up from the earth, and it had two horns like a lamb."

That they rule for one hour signifies either the short duration of their rule, or it is a figure of speech indicating by one hour one year. COMMENTARY ON THE APOCALYPSE 17.9-14.[58]

**THE ARROGANCE OF EARTHLY KINGDOMS.** PRIMASIUS: He is speaking again of every kingdom of the world, which just above he indicated in the kings and their subjects.[59] "The kings receive power with the beast for one hour." Here the hour is to be interpreted as referring to the time from the passion of the Lord, as the apostolic voice says, "It is the last hour."[60] Therefore, until all the future is fulfilled, it says that they have not yet received the kingdom. For although they indeed now rule over many, yet the insane power of that arrogance will be more intense when it also deceives many by signs. COMMENTARY ON THE APOCALYPSE 17.12.[61]

**THE KINGS WILL SUBMIT TO THE ANTICHRIST.** ANDREW OF CAESAREA: Daniel also saw these ten horns that precede the antichrist.[62] After rooting out three of them, the accursed one will subdue the others. The "one hour" indicates either the brevity of time or the one hour of the year, or by way of figure of speech, clearly meaning a three-month period, after which they will submit themselves to the antichrist as to their leader. COMMENTARY ON THE APOCALYPSE 17.12.[63]

**THE PERSECUTION OF THE CHURCH.** BEDE: In persecuting the church, the kingdoms of the world have not yet fully demonstrated their power. For although now they indeed rule over most, nevertheless the power of their insane boasting will be the more acute when they will deceive most through signs. Some interpret this to mean that when the last persecution draws near, there will be ten kings who divide the

---

[54]Mt 12:45. [55]CCL 92:244. [56]MTS 1 Sup 1:189. [57]See Dan 7:7-12. See Irenaeus *Against Heresies* 5.26.1 (ANF 1:554-55). [58]TEG 8:224-25. [59]See Rev 17:8. [60]1 Jn 2:18. [61]CCL 92:244-45. [62]See Dan 7:7-12. [63]MTS 1 Sup 1:190.

world among themselves, according to the prophecy of Daniel, who said concerning the fourth beast: "It had ten horns, and behold, there came up among them another horn, a little one, before which three of the first horns were plucked up."[64] [These interpreters further say] that the antichrist would arise from Babylon and would overcome the kings of Egypt, Africa and Ethiopia, and that when these had been killed, seven other kings would submit their necks to the conqueror.[65] However, others say that the antichrist is placed as the number eleven, as an indication of his collusion. For they think that eleven is a departure from the number ten, which is perfect. [They receive power] "as kings," for those who oppose the kingdom of Christ rule as though in a dream. EXPLANATION OF THE APOCALYPSE 17.12.[66]

## 17:13-14 They Give Power to the Beast

CHRIST WILL HAND THE EVIL KINGS OVER FOR DEATH. OECUMENIUS: Although these future ten kings have no agreement among themselves, yet they are of one mind in this, that they give their power and authority to the beast, that is, to the antichrist. For they will be defeated by him, and he alone will finally rule over all things. Although they will be defeated against their will, it is said nonetheless that they have one mind, since the ten suffer the same experience of defeat and ruin. It is as though he had said, "The ten agreed and consented to be defeated by the antichrist." "These will make war on the Lamb," it says. For before they are wholly destroyed by the antichrist, these kings, about whom the passage is speaking, will persecute the church. However, Christ will triumph, for he will hand these evil men over to the yet more evil antichrist for death. And Christ will triumph in another way also, since his servants struggle unto death for their faith in him. For it says, "they are called and chosen and faithful," that is, the servants of Christ. COMMENTARY ON THE APOCALYPSE 17.9-14.[67]

CHRIST WILL TRIUMPH IN HIS FOLLOWERS. PRIMASIUS: It now says clearly that that power that they had received with the beast they will hand over to the beast, that is, to that head that seemed to have died and to have come to life again. For by a common consent and will they will give to him every worship of their desire and effort and exhibit their servitude. . . . Although it is describing the power of this adversarial body, it now rightly foretells the victory of the Lamb. And to indicate that he will triumph in his followers, it adds, "And those with him, the elect, the faithful and the called." And with good reason does it mention the elect first, for the Lord said, "Many are called, but few are chosen."[68] COMMENTARY ON THE APOCALYPSE 17.13-14.[69]

PARTICIPATING IN CHRIST'S RULE. ANDREW OF CAESAREA: Indeed! For "no one can serve two masters."[70] And so those who conspire together with an evil agreement and ally themselves with the antichrist will oppose themselves to Christ. However, the Lamb of God who was slain for us will conquer them. For he was not deprived of his kingdom and lordship over all things when he became man, so that he might acquire even his elect as participants in his own rule. COMMENTARY ON THE APOCALYPSE 17.13-14.[71]

## 17:15-18 Until the Words of God Are Fulfilled

ROME MAY BE RAVAGED. OECUMENIUS: It says that the waters on which the harlot sits are the peoples and nations, clearly those over which the city exercises its rule. But how will these kings lay waste to Rome, for we see that the Revelation depicts it so? Perhaps it will be the object of warfare among the kings, as a queen who is both strong and populous and the recipient of tribute.

---

[64]Dan 7:7-8. [65]See Jerome Commentary on Daniel 2.7.7-8 (CCL 75A:844). [66]CCL 121A:471. [67]TEG 8:225. [68]Mt 22:14. Primasius is here following Tyconius. [69]CCL 92:245. [70]Mt 6:24. [71]MTS 1 Sup 1:190.

Thus, in the war for it, it will be necessary that it, lying open as the prize of victory, suffer terribly at the hands of all, being ravaged by fire and made desolate. "For God has put it into their hearts to carry out his purpose." Through God's allowance of these things, those who oppose it and desire to capture it follow along. And he causes them to be of one mind and to give their royal power to the beast, just as they agreed to be handed over to the antichrist as subjects, as we explained above. "Until the words of God shall be fulfilled." They will become subject to the beast, it says, until the punishment of the antichrist overtakes him and all the words spoken by God through the prophets against him receive their fulfillment. And wishing to indicate even more clearly what will befall the city, the passage continues, "The woman is the great city which has dominion over all." COMMENTARY ON THE APOCALYPSE 17.15-18.[72]

**THE DEVIL IS AN INSTRUMENT OF GOD'S VENGEANCE.** ANDREW OF CAESAREA: Since the angel explained these things clearly, a more detailed explanation of them is superfluous. It is remarkable to me how the devil is both enemy and avenger. For he will work through the ten horns, who are guided by him, to oppose that lover of good and virtue, Christ our God, and to lay waste that populous city that has abandoned the divine laws and become servant to his pleasures, and like a bloodthirsty beast they will glut themselves on its blood. He will regard its conflagration as an occasion for rejoicing and the mutilation of human flesh as proper food, and he who always rejoices in duplicity will grant harmony to those ten apostate horns. That which continues makes very clear that the woman who was seen is the great city that exercises power over the kings of the earth, and the sufferings of that power that is ruling during those times is prophesied. From these trials the beneficent God will redeem us and enlist us in the heavenly city, namely, in the Jerusalem above. In this city "he will be everything to everyone," as the apostle says,[73] "when he shall destroy every rule," clearly every apostate

rule, "and every authority and power."[74] In addition, he will recline with and serve those who have served him here faithfully and wisely, that is, he will give them the enjoyment of the eternal blessings that have been "prepared from the foundation of the world."[75] Of this bliss may also we be found worthy in Christ, the Savior and Redeemer of our souls, with whom be glory and power to the Father, together with the Holy Spirit forever and ever. Amen. COMMENTARY ON THE APOCALYPSE 17.15-18.[76]

**IN THE EUCHARISTIC CHALICE THE NATIONS ARE UNITED TO CHRIST.** CYPRIAN: Christ, who teaches and shows that the people of the Gentiles were coming into that place that the Jews had lost and that we were arriving afterward through the merit of faith, made wine from water, that is, he showed that the people of the Gentiles rather would resort together and come to the nuptials of Christ and of his church when the Jews were leaving. For the divine Scripture declares in the Apocalypse that the waters signify the peoples, saying, "The waters that you saw on which that harlot sits are peoples and crowds and nations of the heathen and tongues." We perceive that this is actually also contained in the sacrament of the chalice. For because Christ, who bore our sins, also bore us all, we see that people are signified in the water, but in the wine the blood of Christ is shown. But when water is mixed with wine in the chalice, the people are united to Christ, and the multitude of the believers is bound and joined to him in whom they believe. This association and mingling of water and wine are so mixed in the chalice of the Lord that the mixture cannot mutually be separated. Whence nothing can separate the church, that is, the multitude established faithfully and firmly in the church, persevering in that which it has believed, from Christ as long as it clings and remains in undivided love. But thus, in the con-

---

[72]TEG 8:226. [73]1 Cor 15:28. [74]1 Cor 15:24. [75]Cf. Mt 25:34. [76]MTS 1 Sup 1:191-92.

secrating of the chalice of the Lord, water alone cannot be offered, nor can wine alone. For if anyone offers wine alone, the blood of Christ begins to be without us. If, in truth, the water is alone, the people begin to be without Christ. But when both are mixed and, in the union, are joined to each other and mingled together, then the spiritual and heavenly sacrament is completed. LETTER 63.12-13.[77]

**ARROGANT AND DISSOLUTE PERSONS.** CAESARIUS OF ARLES: The harlot is the life of luxury that is lived by plunder and pleasures. It says that they would hate the harlot, for dissolute persons who are also proud, lustful and arrogant not only persecute the saints, but they also hold themselves in hatred. And in another way do those hate themselves in whom the word of Scripture is fulfilled, "Those who love iniquity hate their own soul."[78] "And they will make her desolate and naked." Through the wrath of God and his just judgment by which they are abandoned by him, they themselves will make the world a desert, since they have been given over to it and use it unrighteously. "And they will devour her flesh." This is so, because as the apostle says, "They will bite and eat one another."[79] EXPOSITION ON THE APOCALYPSE 17.16, HOMILY 15.[80]

**IN THE HEARTS OF THE IMPIOUS.** PRIMASIUS: What the apostle said, "God gave them up to a base mind to do what they ought not,"[81] that is also now said. For God has placed in their hearts to do that which is pleasing to him. Righteousness is pleasing to God, through which we know that retribution is visited upon the impious. Moreover, [it is according to God's will] that they who have given their kingdom to the beast pay

their just penalties with the beast, until the words of God be fulfilled, which, to be sure, consist of justice and mercy. For "all the paths of the Lord are mercy and truth."[82] COMMENTARY ON THE APOCALYPSE 17.17.[83]

**THE WOMAN SHARES FULLY IN CORRUPTION.** PRIMASIUS: This woman is the very one who was given over to the corruptions of flesh and blood and who had prospered through the power of the earthly kingdom. And since she consists of those very kings over whom she is said to reign according to her habit, [the text] has divided the very same one into parts, as though separating a genus into its species, so that the words of the Lord will be fulfilled in the woman, in the city, in the kings, on the kings and on [the woman], when he redeems his own by his mercy and by his justice condemns the insolent. COMMENTARY ON THE APOCALYPSE 17.18.[84]

**THE GODLESSNESS OF THE WICKED.** BEDE: Later, when the seer is commanded to behold the wife of the Lamb, he sees the holy city coming down from heaven, and he says concerning her, "The kings of the earth carried their glory into her."[85] For in the world there are two cities, one that arises from the abyss and the other that comes down from heaven. And so now he compares the same ungodliness, which he had described in the form of a harlot made naked and burned up, with the ruins of a deserted city. EXPLANATION OF THE APOCALYPSE 17.18.[86]

---

[77]FC 51:210-11. [78]Ps 11:5 (10:5 LXX). [79]Gal 5:15. [80]PL 35:2443. [81]See Rom 1:28. [82]See Ps 25:10 (24:10 LXX). [83]CCL 92:246. [84]CCL 92:246-47. [85]Rev 21:24. [86]CCL 121A:475.

# 18:1-24 THE JUDGMENT OF THE GREAT BABYLON

[1]*After this I saw another angel coming down from heaven, having great authority; and the earth was made bright with his splendor.* [2]*And he called out with a mighty voice,*

*"Fallen, fallen is Babylon the great!*
*It has become a dwelling place of demons,*
*a haunt of every foul spirit,*
*a haunt of every foul and hateful bird;*
[3]*For all nations have drunk[k] the wine of her impure passion,*
*and the kings of the earth have committed fornication with her,*
*and the merchants of the earth have grown rich with the wealth of her wantonness."*
[4]*Then I heard another voice from heaven saying,*
*"Come out of her, my people,*
*lest you take part in her sins,*
*lest you share in her plagues;*
[5]*for her sins are heaped high as heaven,*
*and God has remembered her iniquities.*
[6]*Render to her as she herself has rendered,*
*and repay her double for her deeds;*
*mix a double draught for her in the cup she mixed.*
[7]*As she glorified herself and played the wanton,*
*so give her a like measure of torment and mourning.*
*Since in her heart she says, 'A queen I sit,*
*I am no widow, mourning I shall never see,'*
[8]*so shall her plagues come in a single day,*
*pestilence and mourning and famine,*
*and she shall be burned with fire;*
*for mighty is the Lord God who judges her."*
[9]*And the kings of the earth, who committed fornication and were wanton with her, will weep and wail over her when they see the smoke of her burning;* [10]*they will stand far off, in fear of her torment, and say,*

*"Alas! alas! thou great city,*
*thou mighty city, Babylon!*
*In one hour has thy judgment come."*
[11]*And the merchants of the earth weep and mourn for her, since no one buys their cargo any more,* [12]*cargo of gold, silver, jewels and pearls, fine linen, purple, silk and scarlet, all kinds of*

scented wood, all articles of ivory, all articles of costly wood, bronze, iron and marble, [13]cinnamon, spice, incense, myrrh, frankincense, wine, oil, fine flour and wheat, cattle and sheep, horses and chariots, and slaves, that is, human souls.

[14]"The fruit for which thy soul longed has gone from thee,

    and all thy dainties and thy splendor are lost to thee, never to be found again!"

[15]The merchants of these wares, who gained wealth from her, will stand far off, in fear of her torment, weeping and mourning aloud,

[16]"Alas, alas, for the great city

    that was clothed in fine linen, in purple and scarlet,

    bedecked with gold, with jewels, and with pearls!

[17]In one hour all this wealth has been laid waste."

And all shipmasters and seafaring men, sailors and all whose trade is on the sea, stood far off [18]and cried out as they saw the smoke of her burning,

    "What city was like the great city?"

[19]And they threw dust on their heads, as they wept and mourned, crying out,

    "Alas, alas, for the great city

    where all who had ships at sea grew rich by her wealth!

    In one hour she has been laid waste.

[20]Rejoice over her, O heaven,

    O saints and apostles and prophets,

    for God has given judgment for you against her!"

[21]Then a mighty angel took up a stone like a great millstone and threw it into the sea, saying,

    "So shall Babylon the great city be thrown down with violence,

        and shall be found no more;

[22]and the sound of harpers and minstrels, of flute players and trumpeters,

        shall be heard in thee no more;

    and a craftsman of any craft

        shall be found in thee no more;

    and the sound of the millstone

        shall be heard in thee no more;

[23]and the light of a lamp

        shall shine in thee no more;

    and the voice of bridegroom and bride

        shall be heard in thee no more;

    for thy merchants were the great men of the earth,

        and all nations were deceived by thy sorcery.

[24]And in her was found the blood of prophets and of saints,

        and of all who have been slain on earth."

k Other ancient authorities read *fallen by*

**Overview:** The holy powers in heaven are brighter than the stars (Andrew of Caesarea). But this angel from heaven is himself the Light, whose coming expelled the false wisdom of this world by the true light of his own wisdom (Primasius). This wisdom now brightens the earth through the preachers of the church (Bede). The angel openly declares the condemnation of Babylon (Oecumenius). As Isaiah once foretold the fall of Babylon to Cyrus (Andrew of Caesarea, Bede), so now the angel announces the fall of the city in which all arrogant, dissolute and wicked people dwell (Caesarius of Arles). As the city of the devil (Bede), Babylon is full of every impure spirit and unclean soul (Caesarius of Arles). Collapsing under the weight of its own sins (Primasius), Babylon becomes the abode of the demons who hate humankind but love human blood (Oecumenius, Andrew of Caesarea). The fallen city was the location of every sin, especially the sins of avarice, licentiousness and gluttony (Primasius). In it, many were corrupted by insatiable greed and the love of money (Oecumenius). Trading their souls for temporal abundance (Primasius), its citizens were wealthy in sins (Caesarius of Arles), but they were wanton and uncaring for those in need (Andrew of Caesarea). As long ago Lot fled from sinful Sodom (Oecumenius), so now righteous Christians are to flee from the sins of the world (Oecumenius, Primasius). Whenever one abandons a profligate and evil manner of life, one is abandoning that Babylon that loves only the things of the earth (Caesarius of Arles). Such are the monks and virgins who leave the wealth and flattery of the world for the simplicity and silence of Christ's manger stall (Jerome).

When God out of his goodness punishes less than the penitent deserves, it is a double blessing (Oecumenius). Yet the impenitent pagan city does receive double for its deeds. For although it persecuted the church, now its idols lie broken and the word of reproach moves to sorrow those who once worshiped them (Augustine). However, those who remain in their self-confidence and do not repent will suddenly, as though in one day, be judged (Apringius, Andrew of Caesarea), for they remain bound to their temporal delights (Primasius, Bede), and so they will be condemned in body and soul to eternal sufferings (Primasius, Andrew of Caesarea, Bede). From such a fate God alone can save, for he is mighty and desires to keep those who please him free from such plagues (Oecumenius, Primasius, Andrew of Caesarea).

However, when the carnal and sensual pleasures of this world cease (Caesarius of Arles, Bede), sinners will be terrified at the sudden change (Andrew of Caesarea), and they will fear for themselves, seeing the ruin of their hope and the sufferings of others (Caesarius of Arles). At that time, only penitence remains for the impious (Bede). All such persons will weep inconsolably and will suffer the reproach of their consciences (Andrew of Caesarea). Those stricken by contrition will submit to conversion through a fruitful penance. Then those who converted will be made glad (Primasius) and will join in jubilation with all the souls of the righteous (Oecumenius) and with all the angels at the vindication of the saints and the martyrs (Apringius, Oecumenius). Christ instructed his disciples to be glad when the end of the world comes (Bede). Therefore, the prophets and the apostles rejoice at the chastisement of the wicked, not because of the sufferings but because God has brought sin to an end (Andrew of Caesarea).

And so it will happen that the harlot city that Cain established with the blood of his brother and that persecuted the saints to the end of time (Caesarius of Arles) will suddenly disappear, like a great stone sinking out of sight beneath the water (Andrew of Caesarea, Bede). Like a heavy stone, the church remains stable and firm, withstanding every wave of temptation and persecution (Bede).

## 18:1 Another Angel Came from Heaven

**Christ Brought Power and Wisdom.** Pri-

MASIUS: This angel possesses great power. For it is speaking of the destruction of the world's wisdom, which is also signified by the destruction of Jericho, and of the ruin of the earthly kingdom. By indicating that a stronger one has come against the strong one in order to expel the false appearance of truth and by covering over the faintness of the world's wisdom, it gives witness that now the true light of wisdom has come. Moreover, to the wise of this world and to the kings of the earth who rely upon their own strength it further demonstrates that [this light] is unconquered in both power and wisdom. . . . I think that this signifies the coming of our Lord, Jesus Christ, who in Isaiah is called the angel of great counsel.[1] In his first advent, he said, "Repent, for the kingdom of heaven is at hand,"[2] and brought to naught the work of worldly power. And the earth was made bright by his splendor, for he is himself "the true Light that enlightens everyone coming into this world."[3] COMMENTARY ON THE APOCALYPSE 18.1.[4]

### THE HOLY POWERS OUTSHINE THE STARS.

ANDREW OF CAESAREA: This passage reveals the brilliance and brightness of the holy powers, which greatly surpasses the light of the stars and the heavenly bodies. COMMENTARY ON THE APOCALYPSE 18.1.[5]

### THE TEACHERS OF THE CHURCH ARE BRIGHT LIGHTS.

BEDE: This angel who is strong and brightens the earth may be regarded as both the Lord incarnate himself as well as the teachers of the church who, granted heavenly light, preach the fall of the world, saying, "The kingdom of heaven is at hand."[6] EXPLANATION OF THE APOCALYPSE 18.1.[7]

## 18:2 "Fallen, Fallen Is Babylon!"

### THE HAUNT OF EVERY FOUL SPIRIT.

OECUMENIUS: "Fallen is Babylon," it says. He openly announces the sentence of condemnation that God has rendered against it. He has decreed, it says, that it should suffer these things. "It has become a dwelling place of demons." For as those who hate humankind and are desirous of blood, these wicked demons search out places in which the blood of people killed in warfare or in some other manner has been shed, and as though rejoicing at what has happened, they make their abode in such places. Therefore, since most will be killed in the city, as we have said, it finally becomes the "dwelling place of demons and a haunt of every foul spirit," since the place safeguards the hedonistic lifestyle of the demons in it. "And a haunt of every foul bird and every unclean beast," it says. For such animals flee the abode of people and take possession of abandoned places, keeping them free from those who intend them harm and hunt wild animals. The prophet Isaiah also said something like this concerning Babylon: "And sirens will rest there, and demons will dance there, and satyrs will dwell there, and hedgehogs will make their nests in their houses."[8] COMMENTARY ON THE APOCALYPSE 18.1-3.[9]

### COLLAPSED FROM THE HEINOUSNESS OF ITS TRANSGRESSIONS.

PRIMASIUS: If [the city] has fallen, how can it be said to be a habitation and refuge for demons and for unclean spirits and birds? Because by collapsing from the great heinousness of its transgressions, it showed itself to be worthy as a habitation for demons.[10] . . . In addition, that city that in the sea of this world repeatedly rose up against the faith of Christ through the forceful waves of persecutions, now groans in the restraint of more narrow limits and growls as though enclosed in a wineskin. For this reason, we sing in the psalm, "He gathered the waters of the sea as in a bottle; he put the deeps in storehouses."[11] . . . That iniquitous spirits can be symbolized by birds is indicated in that passage of the book of Genesis, which reports that Abraham drove away birds that were swooping

---

[1]See Is 9:6. [2]Mt 4:17. [3]Jn 1:9. [4]CCL 92:251. [5]MTS 1 Sup 1:192. [6]Mt 4:17. [7]CCL 121A:475. [8]Is 13:21-22. [9]TEG 8:227. [10]Primasius follows Tyconius to this point. [11]Ps 33:7 (32:7 LXX).

down upon the carcasses [of sacrificial animals].[12] COMMENTARY ON THE APOCALYPSE 18.2.[13]

**BABYLON IS THE CITY OF CONFUSION.** CAESARIUS OF ARLES: Can the ruins of a single city contain every unclean spirit or every foul bird, or at the time when a city falls, is the whole world made devoid of impure spirits and birds so that they inhabit the ruins of a single city? There is no city that contains every unclean soul except the city of the devil, in which every uncleanness dwells in wicked persons throughout the whole earth. Those whom it calls "kings" because they persecute Jerusalem are evil people who persecute the church of God. . . . Whenever you hear the name Babylon, do not think of it as a city made of stones, for "Babylon" means "confusion." Rather, understand that the name signifies those people who are arrogant, robbers, dissolute and impious, and who persevere in their wickednesses. . . . Whenever you hear the name Jerusalem, which refers to the vision of peace, understand that it refers to persons who are holy before God. EXPOSITION ON THE APOCALYPSE 18.2, HOMILY 15-16.[14]

**IMPURE SPIRITS INHABIT PLACES OF DESOLATION.** ANDREW OF CAESAREA: Something similar to this was foretold in Isaiah about the Chaldean capital city of Babylon when it was captured by Cyrus and the Persians, namely, that it would be filled with beasts and impure spirits on account of its utter desolation.[15] For it is the habit of beasts and of evil demons to stalk in arid places. This is due both to the divine economy, which frees people from their harm, and their own dislike of humankind. COMMENTARY ON THE APOCALYPSE 18.2-3.[16]

**THE CITY OF THE DEVIL CONTAINS EVERY UNCLEAN SPIRIT.** BEDE: "O Jerusalem," it says, "do not fear the power of the earthly city, which collapses from that very thing by which it subjugated you through the hatred of its wicked citizens." Isaiah also describes Babylon as inhabited by impure monsters.[17] For there is no other city

than that of the devil, which receives every unclean spirit and in which every impurity remains throughout the world. EXPLANATION OF THE APOCALYPSE 18.2.[18]

## 18:3 Impurity and Wealth

**MANY HAVE BECOME RICH FROM A SLOTHFUL WAY OF LIFE.** OECUMENIUS: "For all the nations have drunk from the wrath of her fornication." By *fornication* he means their insatiable greed and their love of money, for such is the manner of harlots. For those in the city of which we speak have clung close to all nations, since they have placed them in subjection and commanded that they pay tribute. "And the kings," it says, namely, those who have become partners with it and companions in its love of money. "And the merchants" who have traded in it "have grown rich from her wantonness." That is, they have become rich from its arrogance and from its unconstrained, prodigal and slothful way of life, since they put out for sale in it every kind of merchandise. COMMENTARY ON THE APOCALYPSE 18.1-3.[19]

**AVARICE, LICENTIOUSNESS AND GLUTTONY.** PRIMASIUS: This passage refers to three kinds of sins, and it also mentions the same number of those persons who transgress by them. It refers to avarice, which according to the apostle is also called a "servitude of idols"[20]; licentiousness by the word *fornication*; and gluttony in that which pleases. Against this the Lord forewarned, saying, "Do not allow your hearts to be weighed down in dissipation and drunkenness."[21] It says that the kings of the earth have committed fornication with it. For merchants are enriched, as it says, by avarice, although some [interpreters] prefer to interpret this to mean that they are rich in sins rather than in wealth. By *nations* it desig-

---

[12]See Gen 15:11. [13]CCL 92:251-52. [14]PL 35:2443. [15]See Is 13:21-22. [16]MTS 1 Sup 1:193. [17]See Is 13:21-22. [18]CCL 121A:475-77. [19]TEG 8:227-28. [20]See Col 3:5. [21]Lk 21:34.

nates that promiscuous multitude of the lewd crowd; by *kings* it refers to those among them who appear for a time to succeed; and by *merchants* it refers to those who in their desire for earthly riches trade their souls by an unhappy barter for temporal abundance. Such persons act wholly contrary to the words of the Lord: "What shall a man give in return for his life?"[22] COMMENTARY ON THE APOCALYPSE 17.3.[23]

### THE PROFLIGATE CORRUPT EACH OTHER.

CAESARIUS OF ARLES: [The kings of the earth fornicated] with each other. For it would be impossible for all kings to commit fornication with a single harlot. Rather, since the evil and profligate, who are members of the harlot, corrupt each other, they are said to commit fornication with the harlot, that is, by a sinful manner of life. Then it says that "all the merchants of the earth were made rich by the wealth of her wantonness." Here it speaks of those who were wealthy in their sins. For excess in luxury makes for poverty rather than for wealth. EXPOSITION ON THE APOCALYPSE 18.3, HOMILY 16.[24]

### BABYLON WAS WANTON TOWARD THE NEEDY.

ANDREW OF CAESAREA: And how did the present Babylon cause the nations to drink the wine of its fornication? By becoming in every way their leader in every transgression and by sending gifts to obedient cities making their rulers enemies of truth and righteousness. It says that because of the abundance of the riches of its injustice, it gave the merchants of the earth opportunities for profit because it consumed well beyond its needs and was wanton toward those in need. COMMENTARY ON THE APOCALYPSE 18.3.[25]

## 18:4-5 "Come Out, My People"

### THE INN OF BETHLEHEM CONTRASTED WITH THE FALLEN CITY. JEROME: Of all the ornaments of the church our company of monks and virgins is one of the finest. . . . Let us pass now to the cottage inn that sheltered Christ and Mary. . . . The

stall where he cried as a babe can best be honored by silence, for words are inadequate to speak its praise. Where are the spacious porticoes? Where are the gilded ceilings? . . . Behold, in this poor crevice of the earth the Creator of the heavens was born; here he was wrapped in swaddling clothes; here he was seen by the shepherds; here he was pointed out by the star; here he was adored by the wise men. . . . Read the Apocalypse of John, and consider what is sung therein of the woman arrayed in purple and of the blasphemy written upon her brow. . . . "Come out of her, my people," so the Lord says, "that you be not partakers of her sins and that you receive not of her plagues." . . . It is true that Rome has a holy church, trophies of apostles and martyrs, a true confession of Christ. The faith has been preached there by an apostle, heathenism has been trodden down, the name of Christian is daily exalted higher and higher. But the display, power and size of the city, the seeing and being seen, the paying and the receiving of visits, the alternate flattery and detraction, talking and listening, as well as the necessity of facing so great a throng even when one is least in the mood to do so—all these things are alike foreign to the principles and fatal to the repose of the monastic life. . . . But in the cottage of Christ all is simple and rustic, except for the chanting of psalms everything is completely silent. LETTER 46.10-12.[26]

### CHRISTIANS MUST FLEE FROM THE SINS OF THE WORLD. OECUMENIUS: When the angels of God took hold of the city of the Sodomites and on that occasion exacted punishment on its inhabitants and the surrounding cities—or rather, as it would seem to the saintly Cyril, when the Son of God and the Holy Spirit visited there, for "the Father judges no one," as it is written, "but has given all judgment to the Son,"[27] the life-

---

[22]Mt 16:26. [23]CCL 92:252-53. [24]PL 35:2443. [25]MTS 1 Sup 1:193. [26]NPNF 2 6:64-65*. On behalf of Paula and Eustochium, Jerome writes to Marcella in the hope that she will leave Rome and join them in the monastic life at Bethlehem. [27]Jn 5:22.

giving Spirit clearly being with him according to nature and essence[28]—then the angels said to holy Lot, "Save your own life. Do not look back nor remain in all the country round about; escape to the mountain, lest you be overtaken together with them."[29] This is what the Revelation now is also teaching us. For although the servants of Christ are not in one large and populous city, Rome, it says to them, "Come out of her, my people, lest you take part in their sins, lest you share in her plagues." For to partake of sins is also to partake of the plagues, since the plagues come on account of sins. "For her sins are heaped high as heaven," it says. This is as though he had said, "And they polluted the air all around with their sins." And so it says, although God is in every way longsuffering, he has now arisen to give to [the city] its due. COMMENTARY ON THE APOCALYPSE 18.4-8.[30]

**THE RIGHTEOUS SEPARATE FROM THE SINFUL.** PRIMASIUS: What the heavenly voice said was this, "Those whom he foreknew he also predestined to be conformed to the image of his Son,"[31] and, "The Lord knows those who are his,"[32] or something similar to this. There follows, "Come out of her, my people, lest you take part in her sins." To this point I think that [the narrative] has been of the first coming, when until the end of the world the good [people] allow the wicked to be intermingled with them, so that [the wicked] do not think that the good are to be abandoned on their behalf or that they are to be followed by a noxious imitation. For the prophecy, "Go out from her, my people, lest you touch any unclean thing,"[33] is fulfilled in this way— when the righteous no longer commingle with the sinful, not so much by the separation of the body but by the difference of their fully sound will. COMMENTARY ON THE APOCALYPSE 18.4.[34]

**TO "COME OUT" MEANS TO ABANDON AN EVIL LIFE.** CAESARIUS OF ARLES: We see from this passage that Babylon is divided into two parts. For as long as God allows, the wicked are converted to the good, so that Babylon is divided, and that part that departs from it is the making of Jerusalem. For as long as some are moved from Babylon to Jerusalem and others are seduced from Jerusalem to Babylon, so long are the wicked converted to the good and those who seem through hypocrisy to be good are openly revealed to be wicked. And, therefore, through Isaiah Scripture speaks to the good, "Go out from their midst and touch no unclean thing; go out from their midst and be separated from them, you who bear the vessels of the Lord."[35] The apostle also mentions this separation, saying, "The firm foundation of the Lord remains; and the Lord knows those who are his, and let every one who names the name of the Lord depart from iniquity."[36] "Lest you take part in her sins," it says, "and lest you share in her plagues." Although it is written, "Whatever righteous man shall be taken by death, he will be at rest,"[37] how can a righteous person, whom the fall of the city affects along with the impious, partake of sin? Except perhaps in this way. When the good leave the city of the devil, that is, abandon a profligate and impious life, should any one of them choose to remain and to enjoy the pleasures of Babylon, such a one would certainly share in its plagues. But whenever it says "Come out," do not understand this in a bodily sense but in a spiritual sense. For one comes out of Babylon whenever one abandons an evil manner of life. Babylonians are with Jerusalemites in each house and in the one church and in each city. Nonetheless, as long as the good do not consent with the wicked and the wicked do not convert to the good, Jerusalem is recognized in the good and Babylon is recognized in the wicked. Although they live together in the body, they are far from each other in the heart, for the life of the wicked is always in the things of the earth, for they love the earth and they place their entire hope and the entire intention of their soul

---

[28]Cf. Cyril of Alexandria *Adoration in Spirit and in Truth* 1 (PG 68:169-76). [29]Gen 19:17. [30]TEG 8:228-29. [31]Rom 8:29. [32]2 Tim 2:19. [33]Is 52:11. [34]CCL 92:253. [35]Is 51:11. [36]2 Tim 2:19. [37]Wis 4:7.

in the earth. But according to the apostle, the mind of the good is always in the heavens, since they are wise in that which is on high.[38] EXPOSITION ON THE APOCALYPSE 18.4, HOMILY 16.[39]

## 18:6-8 *"Repay Her Double for Her Deeds"*

**THE WITNESS OF THE SAINTS REPAYS THE PAGAN TWOFOLD.** AUGUSTINE: Now, brothers, you see the saints armed.[40] Observe the slaughter, observe their glorious battles. . . . What have these done who had in their hands swords sharpened on both sides? "To do vengeance on the nations." See whether vengeance has not been done on the nations. Daily is it done; we do it ourselves by speaking. Observe how the nations of Babylon are slain. She is repaid twofold. . . . How is she repaid double? The saints wage war, they draw their "swords twice sharpened." From there come defeats, slaughters, severances. How is she repaid double? When she had the power to persecute the Christians, she slew the flesh indeed, but she crushed not God. Now she is repaid double, for the pagans are extinguished and the idols are broken. . . . And lest you should think that people are really smitten with the sword, blood really shed, wounds made in the flesh, he goes on and explains "chastisements on the peoples."[41] What is "chastisements"? Reproof. Let the two-edged sword go forth from you. Do not delay. Say to your friend, if you have yet a friend [among the pagans] left to whom to say it, "What kind of man are you, who have abandoned him by whom you were made, and worship what he made? Better is the workman than that which he makes." When he begins to blush, when he begins to feel compunction, you have made a wound with your sword, it has reached his heart, he is about to die that he may live. EXPLANATION OF PSALM 149.9.[42]

**STERILITY AND WIDOWHOOD.** APRINGIUS OF BEJA: In Isaiah it is said to her, "Come down and sit in the dust, O virgin daughter of Babylon; sit on the ground, for there is no throne for the daughter of the Chaldeans, because you shall no longer be called tender and delicate."[43] And shortly thereafter: "Sit, be silent, go into the darkness, for you shall no more be called the mistress of kingdoms."[44] And again: "You said, 'I shall be mistress forever,' so that you did not lay these things to heart, nor did you remember your name. Now therefore, hear this, you delicate one who dwells in confidence, who says in your heart, 'I am, and there is no one besides me; I shall not sit as a widow or know the loss of children.' These two things shall come to you suddenly, in one day, sterility and widowhood."[45] Who would not understand these things together to be one prophecy and that they were said of one, universal event? TRACTATE ON THE APOCALYPSE 18.6-8.[46]

**GOD DESIRES TO PUNISH LESS THAN IS DESERVED.** OECUMENIUS: Therefore, it says, "repay her double for her sins." It is true that through wise Moses God has commanded us, "You will not take vengeance twice at the same time."[47] How, therefore, does God repay "double"? The word *double* does not mean twofold or twice. Rather, since God is a lover of humankind and good and punishes to a much lesser degree than is deserved, he deems that he has given back double, and indeed not only double but even sevenfold, whenever he gives back only a part. And knowing this, the prophet said, "Repay to your neighbors sevenfold into their bosom the reproach with which they have reproached you, O Lord."[48] In this petition for the punishment of their enemies according to their deserts, they implore God to give back sevenfold. Similar to these words, it says, "give back to her," who was exalted and lived wantonly during this present life, giving no thought to the divine will. For [Babylon] said, I will never lose my rule or see any evil—for by

---

[38]See Col 3:2. [39]PL 35:2444. [40]Augustine is referring to Ps 149:6. [41]Ps 149:7. [42]NPNF 1 8:680. [43]Is 47:1. [44]Is 47:5. [45]Is 47:7-9. [46]CCL 107:69. [47]Nahum 1:9. [48]Ps 79:12 (78:12 LXX).

"widow" it means to be deprived of rule. Therefore, on account of her arrogance utter evil will come on her all of a sudden. For it says, God is mighty, and he will be hindered by no one from bringing upon her judgment and torment. From this [judgment] may we all be free by the grace of him who has called us into his knowledge and into the hope of Christ, to whom be glory forever. Amen. COMMENTARY ON THE APOCALYPSE 18.4-8.[49]

### WHOEVER TOOK PLEASURE IN TRANSIENT DELIGHTS. PRIMASIUS: All of these future events are appropriate for the second advent, when upon the inquiry of the final judgment the society of the impious will be excluded and will suffer its just reward, so that those who sinned in time might be punished in perpetuity. This is what is meant when it says, "Repay her double" and "a double draught is mixed for her," that whoever took pleasure in transient delights might suffer eternal torments. By way of the psalm the Lord foretells that he frees his own from such payments: "From usury and injustice he will redeem their souls."[50] In addition, they are said to burn in a perpetual fire and to be afflicted by a famine, namely, then when those who now hunger and thirst after righteousness shall receive an incorruptible abundance. Moreover, they suffer death, since God has abandoned them. For just as when the soul leaves, the body dies, so when God abandons the soul, it is thought to die. This mourning is that of which Christ speaks in the Gospel, "Woe to you that laugh now, for you shall mourn and weep."[51] To show that God desires to keep his followers unharmed by these plagues, it says, "Lest you share in her plagues." This is as though it said, since you were turned away from their will and were not like them in their sins, you will not receive an equal punishment. Nor can we by our own strength avoid these plagues, since this can be granted to us only by the goodness of God. But keeping to the proper order, the Holy Spirit declares that those who were not made captive in their heart by an

assent to impiety would in no way suffer the torments of the impious, saying, "The souls of the righteous are in the hand of God, and no torment will ever touch them."[52] COMMENTARY ON THE APOCALYPSE 18.6-8.[53]

### SINNERS WILL SUFFER IN BODY AND IN SOUL. ANDREW OF CAESAREA: These words may refer to those who, although innocent in [Babylon], yet suffered the most terrible things at the hands of those who ruled her and through their endurance of these agonies were the reason for the punishment of their tormentors. Or these words may refer to a change of persons and circumstances, from those who were tormented to certain holy powers that have acquired the power of punishment and through love of God exercise those torments that had been done by her against their fellow servants. He speaks of the cup as "double," either because sinners and transgressors are punished both here and in the age to come, or because both the soul and the body are punished for their common deeds, or because of the depth of divine benevolence that is reckoned as double which is lacking of pure justice on account of sin, and punishment is often endured in the conscience. "In her heart she says, 'A queen I sit, I am no widow, and mourning I will never see.'" If there is no fear of God in them, it is the habit of those in prosperity to say, "I shall never be moved."[54] This is what [the city] has spoken to herself.... By a "single day" he means either the suddenness and shortness of the time in which mourning will come to her either from the sword or from famine, and she will be wasted from pestilence and will be consumed by fire. Or it refers to the course of the day itself in which [the city] will experience these things that are prophesied. For after the enemies gain control of the city, only one day will suffice to bring every evil and every form of death upon those who have been defeated. For God is strong both to save those who please him and to punish

---

[49]TEG 8:229-30. [50]Ps 72:14 (71:14 LXX). [51]Lk 6:25. [52]Wis 3:1. [53]CCL 92:254-55. [54]See Ps 30:6 (29:7 LXX).

those who are unrepentant sinners. COMMEN-
TARY ON THE APOCALYPSE 18.6-8.[55]

**THE CITIZENS OF JERUSALEM DO NOT WANT
FUTURE JOYS IN THE PRESENT TIME.** BEDE:
[When the angel says, "Repay her double for her
deeds," he is praying] that [the city] that took
delight in temporal enjoyments might be tortured
with eternal sufferings. Since she took delight in
the luxury of the present time, she took no effort
to prevent the coming retribution. Therefore, in a
short time she will be punished with both spiritual and bodily disaster. . . . The citizens of the
heavenly land, who place Jerusalem before their
own happiness, do not want to sing the Lord's
song in a foreign land, that is, to receive in the
present time that joy that pertains to the future
age.[56] EXPLANATION OF THE APOCALYPSE 18.6-8.[57]

## 18:9-10 *"Thy Judgment Has Come"*

**SINNERS WILL FEAR FOR THEMSELVES.** CAE-
SARIUS OF ARLES: With this repentance, the
kings are not bewailing the evil of wealth, because
they sinned with [the harlot]. Rather, they recognize that they are losing the prosperity of the
world through which they became subject to its
pleasures. Or, since those things in it were beginning to come to an end that because of their luxury were previously pleasing to them, these
profligates fight and consume one another. . . .
They are said to stand afar off, not physically but
in their souls, since each one will fear for himself
when he sees what another suffers through the
maliciousness and power of the haughty. "They
say, 'Alas, alas, thou great city, Babylon!' " . . . The
Spirit speaks the name of the city. Indeed, they
lament the world, which is overtaken by punishment in such a short time and all of whose indus-
try has come to an end so violently. EXPOSITION
ON THE APOCALYPSE 18.9-10, HOMILY 16.[58]

**THE RULERS ARE TERRIFIED.** ANDREW OF
CAESAREA: We think that in this passage the
"kings" refer to the rulers, as the psalmist said

concerning Jerusalem, "Behold, her kings have
assembled."[59] It says that those who committed
fornication in her against the divine commandments will weep, since they see or hear of her
burning and her desolation, and they are thoroughly terrified at the sudden change that had
taken place in such a short time. COMMENTARY
ON THE APOCALYPSE 18.9-10.[60]

**ONLY PENITENCE WILL REMAIN FOR THE
IMPIOUS.** BEDE: This wailing of the kings, of the
merchants and of the seamen of Babylon may be
interpreted in a twofold sense. On the one hand,
it may mean that on the day of judgment when
all the glory of the world is passing away, only
penitence for their former life will remain for the
impious, who will then say, "What has pride
profited us? Or what has the vaunting of riches
brought us? All these things will pass away as a
cloud."[61] On the other hand, it may mean that
when in the present age an abundance of things
ceases and the downfall of various nations is
approaching, the opportunity for carnal pleasures, which was everywhere present for the sat-
ing of the desires of the wicked, will have been
taken away. "They see the smoke of her burning." That is, when they see the evidence of its
destruction, for smoke arises from fire. Indeed,
what else is the rioting of this world and its
crumbling other than the smoke of Gehenna,
which is close at hand? EXPLANATION OF THE
APOCALYPSE 18.9-10.[62]

## 18:11-14 *Merchants Will Weep*

**ALL THAT IS PLEASANT TO THE SENSES WILL
BE LOST.** BEDE: They bemoan the loss of all the
spectacles of the world and those things that are
pleasant to the senses of the body and that are
suitable for external use. For the various kinds of
metals pertain to sight, the odors to smell, the

---

[55]MTS 1 Sup 1:194-96. [56]See Ps 137:4, 6 (136:4, 6 LXX). [57]CCL
121A:477-79. [58]PL 35:2444-45. [59]Ps 48:4 (47:5 LXX). [60]MTS 1 Sup
1:196. [61]See Wis 5:8-9. [62]CCL 121A:479.

unguents to the touch, the wine, wheat and oils to the taste. In the mention of the beasts of burden and of the slaves, they lament the loss of other aids to humanity, and this in a double sense. For either they fail when this world passes away, or the miserable survivors of those who have left the joys of the world through death lament their ruin as though [it were] the ruin of their own city. EXPLANATION OF THE APOCALYPSE 18.11.[63]

## 18:15-19 *"Alas, Alas, for the Great City"*

**A FRUITFUL PENANCE IN FAITH.** PRIMASIUS: "They threw dust on their heads." This means that they reproached their leaders by whom they were led astray and so were lost.... "They wept and mourned."... To be sure, we know that many are often stricken by such contrition, and so it is not false to refer to the person these distances from which they are removed. That is, they will stand afar off and cry out when they see the smoke of its burning, since to stand afar off is not to fall with those who are lost but rather to acquire a stability from submitting to conversion. For "before one's own master does one stand or fall."[64] One ought not understand this standing in a bodily sense but as the conversion of a firm soul in faith, so that when they are said to weep over others who are perishing, they are themselves understood to be making a fruitful penance. For this reason the apostle says, "When you were dead through trespasses and sins in which you once walked, following the course of this world, following the prince of the power of the air, the spirit that is now at work in the sons of disobedience, among whom we all once lived in the passions of the flesh, following the desires of the flesh and mind, and so we were by nature children of wrath like the rest," or things like this.[65] According to these words of the apostle, I think that this passage can be rightly referred to the persons who convert. For no one can be found to be good who was not formerly evil. Therefore, the psalm says, "I have

reckoned all the sinners of the earth as transgressors."[66] COMMENTARY ON THE APOCALYPSE 18.17-19.[67]

**SINNERS WILL FEAR.** CAESARIUS OF ARLES: Whenever the Spirit says that they were made rich from her, he is indicating the abundance of their sins.... Can a city be dressed in fine linen and purple, rather than people? They lament for themselves, since they are despoiled of those riches mentioned here.... Can all those who are merchants and sailors and who work upon the sea be present to see the burning of a single city? Rather, it says that all who loved the world and were the workers of iniquity fear for themselves when they see the ruin of their own hope. EXPOSITION ON THE APOCALYPSE 18.15-17, HOMILY 16.[68]

**SINNERS WILL BE REPROACHED BY THEIR CONSCIENCE.** ANDREW OF CAESAREA: He leads before our eyes the sufferings of this Babylon, and through the laments made over her he depicts the greatness of her misfortune that she, who previously boasted of her royal majesty, will suffer.... He speaks figuratively of the present life as a "sea," since it is heaving with waves. Those who make commerce upon [the sea] swim in the turbulence of this life as though they were fishes. However, perhaps that city that suffers these things lies beside a physical sea and receives these misfortunes from those who sail upon it and receive from it an opportunity to loot it of its wealth. But it is necessary to add that the merchants of this universal Babylon, that is, Confusion, will suffer the same thing at the conclusion of the visible world and will sob inconsolably, since they are unwillingly deprived of the pleasures of this life and are reproached by their conscience because of their deeds.... But against this opinion is that of the ancient teachers of the church, which supposes

---

[63]CCL 121A:481. [64]Rom 14:4. [65]Eph 2:1-3. [66]Ps 119:119 (118:119 LXX). [67]CCL 92:257-58. [68]PL 35:2445.

that these things are prophesied against the Babylon of the Romans. They refer to the vision in which the ten horns are on the fourth beast, that is, upon the Roman rule, and from it another one comes that roots out three of the ten and subdues the others.[69] And when this king of the Romans comes in the pretense of assisting and helping their rule, he in fact comes to effect their complete ruin. Therefore, as we said, whoever interprets this kingdom as though it were one body that from the beginning until now exercised power and which truly has shed the blood of apostles, prophets and martyrs, such a one would not be mistaken concerning the present passage. For even as it is said that there is one chorus and one army and one city, although those who populate each of these might change, so also there is one kingdom, although it is divided into many times and places. COMMENTARY ON THE APOCALYPSE 18.15-19, 22.[70]

## 18:20 Rejoice, Heaven, Saints, Apostles and Prophets

**HEAVEN REJOICES AT THE VINDICATION OF THE MARTYRS.** APRINGIUS OF BEJA: That is, rejoice, because all of the blood of the martyrs which she poured out unto her damnation has been vindicated, and they see the avenging of the saints whom she persecuted. For, indeed, to show that the blood of the saints is to be requited, and to demonstrate the image of her ruin, there follows [the report of the mighty angel for] . . . the coming time of perdition is likened to a stone which is thrown with force. TRACTATE ON THE APOCALYPSE 18.20-21.[71]

**THE SOULS OF THE RIGHTEOUS REJOICE.** OECUMENIUS: While the merchants and the kings of the earth and all with whom the city did commerce while she yet stood and was prosperous will weep bitterly for her, the heavens will rejoice, that is, the angels in heaven and the souls of the righteous. The souls will rejoice because

their vindication from God has happened, while the angels will rejoice as those who are glad for the vindicated. Moreover, through the description of the behavior [of the kings and merchants] in the narrative, the suffering of the spiritual Babylon is highlighted. COMMENTARY ON THE APOCALYPSE 18.20-24.[72]

**THOSE WHO CONVERT ARE MADE GLAD.** PRIMASIUS: This refers to those who have converted, for they rejoice and are made glad because "God has given judgment for you against her." COMMENTARY ON THE APOCALYPSE 18.20.[73]

**BABYLON IS EVERYWHERE IN EVIL PEOPLE.** CAESARIUS OF ARLES: Is Babylon the only city in all the world that persecutes or has persecuted the saints of God, so that when she is destroyed all of them are avenged? Babylon is throughout the whole world in evil people, and throughout the world persecutes those who are good. EXPOSITION ON THE APOCALYPSE 18.20, HOMILY 17.[74]

**THE APOSTLES AND PROPHETS REJOICE.** ANDREW OF CAESAREA: By "heaven" he means either the angels or the saints who make their dwelling in heaven. The apostles and the prophets are urged to rejoice with these, and so to avenge those who were maltreated by [the city]. Their rejoicing would also avenge those who often were dishonored through transgressions of the divine laws while they vainly entreated the inhabitants of that city, or those who were forcibly scattered throughout the earth and were slaughtered for the sake of God and because they were servants of his words. In this way, the prophets were killed by the Jews, and the apostles by the Gentiles, to whom they especially preached the word. They rejoice for the coming of these chastisements, not because they rejoice in hardships but because they ardently desire a cessation to sin. And perhaps those who have been slaves to

---

[69]See Dan 7:8, 19-20. [70]MTS 1 Sup 1:199-200, 202. [71]CCL 107:70. [72]TEG 8:233. [73]CCL 92:258. [74]PL 35:2446.

sin might obtain a milder punishment in the age to come because they were tormented to some extent here. COMMENTARY ON THE APOCALYPSE 18.20.[75]

**THE DESTRUCTION OF THE WORLD.** BEDE: According to the Gospel, when the Lord was foretelling the destruction of the world, he added, "Now when you see these things taking place, look up and raise your heads,"[76] that is, make your hearts glad. . . . This is that judgment that the souls of the saints sought for with a loud cry, "How long, O Lord, holy and true, before you will judge and avenge our blood?"[77] EXPLANATION OF THE APOCALYPSE 18.20.[78]

## 18:21-24 A Mighty Angel Threw a Stone into the Sea

**CAIN ESTABLISHED BABYLON WITH THE BLOOD OF ABEL.** CAESARIUS OF ARLES: Babylon is likened to a great millstone which is thrown down, for the revolving of times, as though it were a millstone, grinds down those who love the world, and it sends them in circles. Of these the Scriptures say, "The wicked walk in a circle."[79] . . . "The sound of harpers and musicians and flute players and trumpeters is no longer heard in her." That is, the joy and happiness of the wicked passes away and is no longer to be found. And it adds the reason for this, "for your merchants were the great men of the earth," that is, they had received good things in their lives. "The blood of the prophets and the saints was found in her and of all who have been slain by [her] upon the earth." Did the same city kill the apostles that also killed the prophets and all of the rest of the martyrs? Rather, this is the city of all the proud and arrogant, which Cain established by the blood of his brother and which he named after the name of his son, Enoch, that is, after his posterity.[80] For all the wicked in whom Babylon resides succeed one another and persecute the church of God until the end of the world. In the city of Cain "all the righteous blood" is poured

out "from the blood of righteous Abel to the blood of Zechariah," that is, of the people and of the priests, "between the sanctuary and the altar," that is, between the people and the priests.[81] This was said because not only the people but also the priests conspired in the death of Zechariah. . . . This is the city which killed the prophets and stoned those who were sent to it. This is that city that is built upon blood, as the Scriptures say, "Woe to him who builds a city with blood and founds a city on iniquity."[82] EXPOSITION ON THE APOCALYPSE 18.21-24, HOMILY 17.[83]

**BABYLON WILL SUDDENLY DISAPPEAR.** ANDREW OF CAESAREA: Just as a millstone sinks with force into the sea, so also the destruction of this Babylon will be sudden, so that afterward no trace of her will be found. The absence of harpers, minstrels and the rest is an indication of this. And he gives the reason for this. [Babylon] deceived all nations with her sorcery and was the recipient of the blood of prophets and the other saints. It is possible that this passage depicts the impious Babylon among the Persians, for at various times until now she has received the blood of many saints and continually rejoices in sorceries and deceptions. And this gives us an occasion for prayer, that she receive the rewards prophesied for arrogance against Christ and his servants. COMMENTARY ON THE APOCALYPSE 18.21-24.[84]

**LIKE A STONE, BABYLON SINKS.** BEDE: The city of this age is compared with an unstable millstone because of the weight and error of sins. For "the wicked walk in a circle."[85] [Babylon] is rightly swallowed up by the waves of retribution, for its citizens oppressed Jerusalem with the waves of infidelity when, sitting by the rivers of Babylon, they bemoaned their absence from the heavenly Zion. For the Lord says that those who cause one to fall are to be punished with a similar

---

[75]MTS 1 Sup 1:200. [76]Lk 21:28. [77]Rev 6:10. [78]CCL 121A:483. [79]Ps 12:8 (11:9 LXX). [80]Gen 4:17. [81]Mt 23:35. [82]Hab 2:12. [83]PL 35:2446-47. [84]MTS 1 Sup 1:201-2. [85]Ps 12:8 (11:9 LXX).

punishment.[86] To be sure, the church is also likened to a stone, but one that is stable and firm and withstands the assaults of the tempestuous waves.[87] The millstone may also be understood to represent the crushing of punishments, for even the blessed Ignatius is reported to have said as he was about to suffer, "I am the wheat of God; I am being ground by the teeth of beasts, so that I might be made a pure loaf."[88] "And the sound of harpers and minstrels, of flute players and trumpeters shall be heard in it no more." Of the five senses, the text had until now neglected to mentioned the sense of hearing, which will be taken away along with the other senses.[89] It is as though it said, "What is beautiful to the eye, and melodious to the ear, and smooth to the touch, and sweet to the smell and delicious to the taste, all of that will pass away from the world." EXPLANATION OF THE APOCALYPSE 18.21-22.[90]

---

[86]See Mt 18:6-7. [87]Mt 7:24-25 [88]Ignatius of Antioch *To the Romans* 4.1. [89]See Bede's comments on Rev 18:11-14. [90]CCL 121A:485.

## 19:1-6 A HEAVENLY DOXOLOGY

[1]After this I heard what seemed to be the loud voice of a great multitude in heaven, crying,
"Hallelujah! Salvation and glory and power belong to our God,
[2]for his judgments are true and just;
he has judged the great harlot who corrupted the earth with her fornication,
and he has avenged on her the blood of his servants."
[3]Once more they cried,
"Hallelujah! The smoke from her goes up for ever and ever."
[4]And the twenty-four elders and the four living creatures fell down and worshiped God who is seated on the throne, saying, "Amen. Hallelujah!" [5]And from the throne came a voice crying,
"Praise our God, all you his servants,
you who fear him, small and great."
[6]Then I heard what seemed to be the voice of a great multitude, like the sound of many waters and like the sound of mighty thunderpeals, crying,
"Hallelujah! For the Lord our God the Almighty reigns.

---

**Overview**: The destruction of the traitorous city, the great harlot, evokes from the church songs of praise and of jubilation (TYCONIUS, APRINGIUS, CAESARIUS OF ARLES). The saints rejoice, for God has caused sin to cease (ANDREW OF CAESAREA) and has separated out for punishment all adulterous and arrogant persons (CAESARIUS OF ARLES) and has given retribution to the wicked and reward to the good (APRINGIUS). By her evil deeds and her persecution of the saints the harlot committed every type of sin (BEDE). For this reason the wicked city and all its inhabitants go into an eternal punishment (ANDREW OF CAESAREA). This punishment will reveal that burning up that is ongoing even now in the present age. The wicked die in their wickedness, even as Jerusalem is constantly moving into paradise as the saints die in faith (CAESARIUS OF ARLES).

The innumerable ranks of the holy angels join in the praise of the saints and sing a threefold "Hallelujah" to the Father, Son and Holy Spirit (OECUMENIUS, ANDREW OF CAESAREA). The twenty-four elders and the four creatures show their agreement with this angelic doxology (OECUMENIUS) by singing "Amen, Hallelujah." Thereby they concur also in the faithful praise that the church now sings on the Lord's day in the hope of the resurrection (BEDE). God receives this praise from his elect as pleasing to him (PRIMASIUS). Moreover, because this praise of the church is not only with her lips but out of affection and devotion (BEDE), God is pleased whether the praise be by faithful teachers or by those newly learning the faith (PRIMASIUS, OECUMENIUS), whether by those of great natural abilities or by those of lesser accomplishments (ANDREW OF CAESAREA).

From her beginning the church has preached the gospel and sung praises to the Trinity in unison with the angels (NICETAS OF REMESIANA, OECUMENIUS, PRIMASIUS). For the Trinity is the omnipotent God who created all things from nothing (PRIMASIUS, ANDREW OF CAESAREA). By his power he also mercifully made righteous his elect from those who were perishing from sin, and from these he made his church (PRIMASIUS). To this end, the only begotten Word of the Father became man. And although by nature the Word is King with the Father and the Holy Spirit, he in no manner ceased to be King after his incarnation (OECUMENIUS, ANDREW OF CAESAREA). We do not now see the glory of his reign, but when death is destroyed, we will see it, whether by way of subjection or by way of direct knowledge (OECUMENIUS).

## 19:1-3 Salvation and Glory Belong to God

**THE DESTRUCTION OF THE WICKED AND THE JOY OF THE CHURCH.** TYCONIUS: Concerning the harlot it says, "The smoke from her goes up forever and ever." That is to say, while the church remains in her joyful praise, the smoke of the destruction of the wicked also remains. Just as the beginning of fire is in smoke, so smoke is present as long as fire remains. I think that the Lord gave us an example of these good and evil persons in the figures of the pauper and the rich man.[1] COMMENTARY ON THE APOCALYPSE 19.3.[2]

**THE SAINTS EXULT.** APRINGIUS OF BEJA: The saints exult over the destruction of the traitorous city, and they praise God with the jubilation of praise. What does this describe other than the coming of the retribution of the evildoers and the rewarding of the good? This is that of which Daniel spoke, "Some will rise to everlasting life, and some to everlasting reproach,"[3] so that they might see [this] forever. For this reason it is said, "The smoke from her goes up forever and ever." TRACTATE ON THE APOCALYPSE 19.1-3.[4]

**THE HOLY ANGELS SING "HALLELUJAH" TO THE TRINITY.** OECUMENIUS: "I heard a voice from heaven as of a great multitude," it says. The ranks of the holy angels are without number. As one of the fathers has said, the ninety-nine sheep who were kept safe and did not go astray represent the angels, while the one sheep who went astray represents the entirety of humankind.[5] They said, "Hallelujah!" "Hallelujah" is a Hebrew expression that means "praise God" or "sing to God." Therefore, they are singing a hymn of thanksgiving for the righteous judgment of the spiritual Babylon. And they cried out the same hymn a "second time," and yet later they spoke it again. And so by this threefold offering of the Hallelujah they give glory to the holy and much to be praised Trinity, for this [Trinity] is God. "The smoke from her goes up forever and ever." The doxology of the Hallelujah interrupted the flow of the discourse, since clearly the sequence of the narrative is this: "And he has avenged on her the blood of his servants. And the smoke from her goes up forever and ever." He mentions "smoke" since the city of which he speaks is com-

---

[1]See Lk 16:19-30. [2]CCL 92:260. [3]Dan 12:2. [4]CCL 107:70-71. [5]For example, Epiphanius *Homilia in assumptionem Christi* (PG 43:481).

pletely in flames. For smoke is an indication of fire. COMMENTARY ON THE APOCALYPSE 19.1-5.[6]

### PUNISHMENT RISES UP AS DOES SMOKE.

CAESARIUS OF ARLES: This is the voice of the church when the separation has already occurred and when all wicked persons have gone out of her to be consumed with eternal fire. "And their[7] smoke goes up for ever and ever." Hear, O brothers, and fear and know that Babylon and the harlot whose smoke ascends forever and ever are not to be understood as anything other than lustful, adulterous and arrogant persons. And, therefore, if you wish to avoid these punishments, do not desire to commit such grievous sins. . . . Is it smoke of a burned-out city that is visible and goes up forever and ever, and not rather [the smoke] of people who remain in their arrogance? It says "it goes up," not "it will go up," for in the present age Babylon is always going into destruction and burning up in part, just as Jerusalem is moving into paradise in those saints who leave the world. The Lord showed this in the story of the poor man and the rich man.[8] EXPOSITION ON THE APOCALYPSE 19.1-3, HOMILY 18.[9]

### THROUGH PUNISHMENT GOD ACCOMPLISHES THE END OF SIN.

ANDREW OF CAESAREA: "Hallelujah" signifies divine praise, while "Amen" means "truly" or "let it be so." This praise is common both from the angelic powers as well as from humankind, which is similar to the angels, and this praise is sent up to God three times on account of the tri-hypostatic deity of the Father and of the Son and of the Holy Spirit, one God. God has "avenged the blood of his servants from the hand" of Babylon and has benefited her inhabitants by accomplishing the cessation of sin through its punishment. The words that the "smoke from the city goes up forever and ever" show either the unforgettable nature of the punishment that has come upon the city, or that although she meted out punishments in part and to some extent, she will, nonetheless, be punished eternally in the coming

age. COMMENTARY ON THE APOCALYPSE 19.1-4.[10]

### IN CORRUPTION AND PERSECUTION ALL SIN IS INCLUDED.

BEDE: It mentions two deeds of the harlot, namely, that she corrupted herself with evil deeds and that she persecuted those who are good. It seems to me that in these two acts every [type of] transgression is comprehended. EXPLANATION OF THE APOCALYPSE 19.2.[11]

## 19:4-5 "Praise Our God"

### THE ELDERS AND CREATURES JOIN IN THE PRAISE OF THE ANGELS.

OECUMENIUS: The elders and the living creatures say "Amen," signifying their agreement with the doxology that was proffered by the holy angels. For when rendered from the Hebrew into the Greek, "Amen" means γένοιτο [ "let it be"]. It says, "Praise our God, you small and you great." By "small" he refers to those who are greater in holiness; by "great" he refers to those who are outstanding in holiness. COMMENTARY ON THE APOCALYPSE 19.1-5.[12]

### GOD ACCEPTS THE PRAISE OF HIS ELECT.

PRIMASIUS: When [the voice] commands that this [praise] be done and then it is reported that [such praise] was given, it indicates that [God] has accepted the praise of his elect as pleasing, indeed, giving his approval to the praise that had been given and indicating that it is to be perpetual. The "great" in the church are those of whom the apostle said, "We speak wisdom among the perfect,"[13] and of whom the Lord said, "Whoever teaches men so shall be called great in the kingdom of heaven."[14] The "small" are those of whom it is said, "As babes in Christ, I have given you milk to drink, not solid food."[15] COMMENTARY ON THE APOCALYPSE 19.5.[16]

---

[6]TEG 8:234-35. [7]The text of Caesarius reads *eorum* ("their"), not *eius* ("her") (Bede) or *de illa* ("from her") (Primasius). [8]See Lk 16:19-30. [9]PL 35:2447-48. [10]MTS 1 Sup 1:203. [11]CCL 121A:487-89. [12]TEG 8:235. [13]1 Cor 2:6. [14]Mt 5:19. [15]1 Cor 3:1-2. [16]CCL 92:261.

**EVEN CHILDREN ARE GREAT WHEN THEY PRAISE GOD.** ANDREW OF CAESAREA: The throne of God is the seraphim and the cherubim. Whether these be great or small in their accomplishments, all are urged to praise God according to their abilities. However, I think that also those who are small in age and children who are not yet grown shall be great when they sing to God who has done such great things. COMMENTARY ON THE APOCALYPSE 19.5.[17]

**THE CHURCH SINGS "HALLELUJAH" ON THE LORD'S DAY.** BEDE: The church worships her Lord not only with her lips but also with the affection of the highest devotion. The words *Amen* and *Hallelujah* can be interpreted, for they refer to faith or to the truth and praise of the Lord. However, out of reverence for the holiness of the original language, the use and authority of these words is preserved. The church continues to sing Hallelujah on the days of the Lord and throughout the period of Quinquagesima[18] because of the hope of the resurrection, which in the praise of the Lord is future. . . . It says "the small and the great," because to be small in natural abilities does not matter if one's heart and tongue are full of the praise of the Lord. EXPLANATION OF THE APOCALYPSE 19.4-5.[19]

### 19:6 The Voice of a Great Multitude

**TO SING WITH TRUE FAITH.** NICETAS OF REMESIANA: We know that later on the apostles also [sang psalms and hymns], since not even in prison did they cease to sing. So, too, Paul speaks to the prophets of the church: "When you come together, each of you has a hymn, has an instruction, has a revelation, has a tongue, has an interpretation. Let all things be done for edification."[20] And again, in another place: "I will sing with the spirit, but I will sing with the understanding also."[21] So, too, James sets down in his epistle: "Is any one of you sad? Let him pray. Is any one in good spirits? Let him sing a hymn."[22] And John in the Apocalypse reports that when the Spirit revealed himself to him, he saw and heard "a voice of the heavenly army, as it were the voice of many waters and as the voice of mighty thunders, saying, Alleluia." From all this we may conclude that no one should doubt that this ministry, if only it is celebrated with true faith and devotion, is one with that of the angels, who, as we know, unhindered by sleep or other occupation, cease not to praise the Lord in heaven and to bless the Savior. LITURGICAL SINGING 10.[23]

**THE INCARNATE CHRIST WILL ACQUIRE A PERFECT SOVEREIGNTY.** OECUMENIUS: According to the holy prophet Isaiah,[24] the seraphim said "holy" three times and so composed a threefold hymn to one lordship. In this manner they showed that there are three individual existences or, which is to speak in a similar way, [three] persons of whom to sing, while there is one essence of the Godhead. Also in this passage the holy angels, having spoken the Hallelujah three times in the passages above and having rendered homage to each of the three holy hypostases, now sing the Hallelujah to the holy Trinity, showing that the holy and much-sung Trinity is in one unique essence and Godhead. "For the Lord our God reigns," it says. Our Lord, Jesus Christ, even before his saving incarnation, as the only begotten Son and Word of the Father and the Maker of all things, reigned over what is in heaven and on earth with the Father and the all-holy Spirit. But even after the incarnation he is similarly Lord and King of all things, for by his taking of flesh he was in no way made inferior in regards to his rule and dominion over all things. As the all-wise apostle says, we do not yet see all things subjected to him, but all things will rather be subjected to him in the coming age, including those who now until then behave insolently toward him. Even death itself is to be subjected—for "the last

---

[17]MTS 1 Sup 1:204. [18]The Sunday before Lent. [19]CCL 121A:489-91. [20]1 Cor 14:26. [21]1 Cor 14:15. [22]Jas 5:13. [23]FC 7:73. For a similar comment see Cassiodorus *Explanations of the Psalms* (ACW 53:162-63). [24]Is 6:3.

enemy to be destroyed is death"[25]—the holy angels properly say "the Lord our God reigns." [In this way they] lift up a doxology regarding the future age, since then by the subjection of all things, Christ will have acquired a perfect sovereignty over all things. Some will experience this subjection by way of torment, while others will experience it by way of a direct knowledge which is not "through a dim mirror or an enigma,"[26] as is the case now. COMMENTARY ON THE APOCALYPSE 19.6-9.[27]

**OUT OF HIS OMNIPOTENCE GOD CREATES, ELECTS AND PERFECTS.** PRIMASIUS: The trumpets[28] signify that preaching of which Isaiah spoke, saying, "Cry aloud, spare not, lift up your voice like a trumpet."[29] In this preaching the dread of the divine judgment is also indicated, which I think is also suggested by the mention of the thunder. . . . In the many waters those peoples are symbolized who praise God by saying "Hallelujah." And so, when the church preaches and fears and praises, she exults with trembling, as we read, "Serve the Lord with fear; praise him with trembling."[30] "For our Lord the Almighty reigns." The voice rightly mentions God's omnipotence. For he created from nothing that which did not exist, and he sought those who had perished from sin, and he found those who were deserving of punishment, and from these he mercifully made righteous those whom he willed. Then from these, as though from members, he made for himself the church, and when he had redeemed her for such a dignity, he made her to be his bride

since she did not merit to be his servant girl. COMMENTARY ON THE APOCALYPSE 19.6.[31]

**BY NATURE CHRIST RULES ALL THINGS AS CREATOR.** ANDREW OF CAESAREA: "The voice of a great multitude and of many waters and thunderpeals" signifies the piercing clarity of the hymn, for all the angelic and heavenly powers are without number, and some have interpreted these to be the waters above the heavens. With these [heavenly powers] the whole body of the righteous give glory to the Creator. Indeed, Christ rules as King. By nature he governs all those of whom he is the Creator, but he rules these also by virtue of his incarnation, either according to his free and purposeful fellowship [with them] or according to the authority which is proper to him as King and Judge. COMMENTARY ON THE APOCALYPSE 19.6-7.[32]

**THE HEART OF THE REDEEMED SINGS WITH GREAT DEVOTION.** BEDE: The great voice of those singing indicates the great devotion of the heart. By the manifold repetition of praise, [the voice] rejoices in the destruction of the wicked and in the eternal glory of the Lord and of those who are his. EXPLANATION OF THE APOCALYPSE 19.6.[33]

---

[25]1 Cor 15:26. [26]1 Cor 13:12. [27]TEG 8:235-36. [28]The text of Primasius reads *vocem tubarum* ("voice of trumpets"), not *vocem turbae* ("voice of a multitude"). [29]Is 58:1. [30]See Ps 2:11 LXX. [31]CCL 92:261-62. [32]MTS 1 Sup 1:204. [33]CCL 121A:491.

# 19:7-10 THE MARRIAGE SUPPER OF THE LAMB

[7]*Let us rejoice and exult and give him the glory,*
*for the marriage of the Lamb has come,*

*and his Bride has made herself ready;*

[8]*it was granted her to be clothed with fine linen, bright and pure"—*
*for the fine linen is the righteous deeds of the saints.*

[9]*And the angel said [1] to me, "Write this: Blessed are those who are invited to the marriage sup-*
*per of the Lamb." And he said to me, "These are true words of God." [10]Then I fell down at his feet*
*to worship him, but he said to me, "You must not do that! I am a fellow servant with you and your*
*brethren who hold the testimony of Jesus. Worship God." For the testimony of Jesus is the spirit of*
*prophecy.*

1 Greek *he said*

---

**OVERVIEW:** In the present age the church is in the stage comparable to courtship before a wedding. As a sign of courtship the church has received the Holy Spirit (OECUMENIUS) and so persists in her works of righteousness. However, at the end of the world, the church, having shown herself ready for the spiritual banquet (BEDE), will be united in the purity of faith with Christ (APRINGIUS, OECUMENIUS, BEDE). As now a husband becomes one flesh with his wife, then the church catholic will become one spirit with Christ and will receive ineffable gifts (OECUMENIUS) suitable to her manner of life and virtue (OECUMENIUS, BEDE).

The elect who will enjoy this marriage supper of the Lamb will partake of the wine of the Father's kingdom (APRINGIUS) and will recline at table with Abraham, Isaac and Jacob (APRINGIUS, PRIMASIUS). They will have new bodies, a new joy and a pure righteousness (APRINGIUS). This banquet will be sumptuous, not a light meal, for it will be nothing other than the refreshment of the heavenly vision (BEDE). Since this joy will surpass our present understanding, the Scriptures call it by various names, such as "paradise," "kingdom of heaven" or "marriage" (ANDREW OF CAESAREA).

The angels even now enjoy the happiness of eternal contemplation. However, the God of their contemplation, the changeless Wisdom of God, took upon himself our own nature to teach us that we must worship only what the angels worship (AUGUSTINE). Unlike the Greeks, therefore, who believe that multiple gods rule over the nations (OECUMENIUS), in the fullness of the catholic confession the church knows that all prophecy and the divine law testify to Christ and to his church (APRINGIUS, PRIMASIUS). With the angels, therefore, Christians worship the incarnate God alone (OECUMENIUS) and pray that they might have a humble mind as did the Savior and as do the holy angels, who out of their humility allow no worship to be directed to themselves (ANDREW OF CAESAREA).

## 19:7-8 The Marriage of the Lamb

**THE CATHOLIC CHURCH WILL BE JOINED TO CHRIST.** APRINGIUS OF BEJA: The fine linen is the righteous deeds of the saints. After thanksgiving has been given and after the voice of exhortation has been heard, the praise to God, as though the sound of claps of thunder, is loudly proclaimed by those who rejoice that the marriage feast of the Lamb has come. This will occur when, after the consummation of the world, "every rule and authority will have been destroyed and he will have delivered the kingdom to God the Father, so that God will be all in all."[1] This will occur, that is, when his wife, namely the catholic church, will be joined to him in the purity of faith. Concerning this the holy apostle said: "For I betrothed you to Christ to present you as a pure virgin to one husband."[2] And so, the fine linen which she [the church] wears does not

---

[1] 1 Cor 15:24.  [2] 2 Cor 11:2.

represent the beauty of a vestment, but the righteousness of the saints. TRACTATE ON THE APOCALYPSE 19.6-8.[3]

**THE CHURCH WILL BECOME ONE SPIRIT WITH CHRIST.** OECUMENIUS: In the present age the marriage of the Lord with the church is still in the stage of courtship and is not yet a consummated marriage. The holy apostle indicates this when he writes his second letter to the Corinthians and says, "For I betrothed you as a pure bride to one husband to present you to Christ."[4] Therefore, the time of courtship remains. For "I betrothed" refers to courtship, and we receive the pledge of the Spirit as a sign of courtship. However, when the church becomes one spirit with Christ, as a husband becomes one body with his wife, then will the marriage be perfected. For indeed the wise apostle has spoken wisely concerning bodily marriage when he wrote, "The two shall become one flesh."[5] But then he continues, "This is a great mystery, and I am saying that it refers to Christ and the church."[6] For this reason the holy angels say, "The marriage of the Lamb has come," signifying that the marriage, which now is in the stage of courtship, will then be consummated. And the Gospel also clearly gives this understanding to us. For on one occasion it introduces the wedding festivities of a son, prepared by his father who is a king. Although many have been invited to the banquet, some partake of the feasting while others excuse themselves from the supper, and one person is excluded because he is not dressed in a wedding garment.[7] On another occasion the Gospel speaks of ten virgins, five of whom are wise and they enter with the bridegroom into the blessed bridal chamber. The other [virgins] are locked outside since they did not fill up their lamps with sufficient oil.[8] It is not suitable to regard any of this as referring to the present time; it rather refers to that which is coming. Therefore, the marriage of the Lamb has come and his bride, the church, is presented as ready to receive those ineffable gifts that come by union with Christ. [The church] is

clothed, it says, with fine linen, that is, with a robe made of virtues. It is linen because it is bright and of fine texture, bright from her incomprehensible manner of life, and fine because of her teachings and convictions concerning God. COMMENTARY ON THE APOCALYPSE 19.6-9.[9]

**THE CHURCH WILL UNITE WITH CHRIST.** BEDE: The marriage supper of the Lamb occurs when the church will be united with her Lord in the wedding chamber of the heavenly kingdom. "And his bride has made herself ready." By always persisting in the works of righteousness, [the church] has shown herself worthy of the spiritual banquet and the eternal kingdom. One can also interpret this according to the parable of the Gospel, which speaks of the virgins who, when the bridegroom was coming, rose up to prepare their lamps,[10] that is, among themselves to consider their deeds for which they hope to receive eternal blessedness. . . . It was granted to [the church] to be clothed with her own deeds. But it is not so with the wicked who, according to Isaiah, "weave a spider's web and will not be covered by their works, for their works are without benefit."[11] EXPLANATION OF THE APOCALYPSE 19.7-8.[12]

### 19:9 Blessed Are Those Invited to the Marriage Supper

**PREPARATION FOR THE FEAST OF THE LAMB.** APRINGIUS OF BEJA: Who are those who have been invited to the feast of the Lamb, unless those to whom it is said: "I will not drink from this fruit of the vine until I will drink it new with you in the kingdom of my Father who is in heaven."[13] And again, "Many will come from east and west and will recline at table with Abraham, Isaac, and Jacob in the kingdom of heaven."[14] This is to drink the new cup, to prepare the new bodies of those being raised, to keep a new joy,

[3]CCL 107:71. [4]2 Cor 11:2. [5]Eph 5:31. [6]Eph 5:32. [7]Mt 22:2-14. [8]Mt 25:1-13. [9]TEG 8:236-37. [10]Mt 25:1-13. [11]See Is 59:5-6. [12]CCL 121A:491. [13]Mt 26:29. [14]Mt 8:11.

and to repay the sincere righteousness of a true faith. These are the blessed who are prepared for this feast and for this repast. Tractate on the Apocalypse 19.9-10.[15]

## At Table in the Kingdom of Heaven. Primasius:

The Lord spoke of this, saying, "They will recline at table with Abraham, Isaac and Jacob in the kingdom of heaven,"[16] and again, "He will come and serve them."[17] Certainly [the Lord] is indicating those "who are called according to his purpose"[18] and who enter the full number of the elect. "For many are called, but few are chosen."[19] Commentary on the Apocalypse 19.9.[20]

## The Many Blessings of the Coming Age.

Andrew of Caesarea: The marriage supper of Christ is the feast of those who are being saved and the joy that accompanies it. The blessed will come into these things when they enter into the eternal bridal chamber with the holy Bridegroom of their purified souls. For he who has promised this is faithful. Since there are many blessings in the coming age, which surpass every understanding, the participation in them is indicated through various terms. Sometimes they are called the "kingdom of heaven" on account of their glory and honor; sometimes they are called "paradise" on account of the everlasting banquet of good things; sometimes they are called the "bosom of Abraham" on account of the rest of those who repose there, or the "bridechamber" and "marriage" because of the endless joy and the perfect and inexpressible union of God with his servants. This union surpasses every carnal and bodily union as much as light is separated from darkness or a perfume from a foul odor. Commentary on the Apocalypse 19.7-9.[21]

## A Great Feast. Bede:

It says that they are invited to a supper, not to a mere lunch, for at the end of days the supper will certainly be a great feast. Therefore, when the time of the present life is ended, those who come to the refreshment of the heavenly contemplation are truly invited to the supper of the Lamb. Explanation of the Apocalypse 19.9.[22]

## 19:10 "Worship God"

## We Honor Angels with Love. Augustine:

The lowest person must worship the same God as is worshiped by the highest angel. In fact it is by refusing to worship him that human nature has been brought low. The source of wisdom and of truth is the same for angel and humankind, namely, the one unchangeable Wisdom and Truth. The very Virtue and changeless Wisdom of God who is consubstantial and coeternal with the Father, for our salvation deigned, in the temporal dispensation, to take upon himself our nature in order to teach us that humanity must worship what every rational intellectual creature must also worship. Let us believe that the highest angels and most excellent ministers of God want us to join them in the worship of the one God, in contemplation of whom they find their happiness. Even we are not made happy by seeing an angel but by seeing the Truth, by which we love the angels too and rejoice with them. We do not grudge that they should have readier access to the Truth and enjoy him without obstacle. Rather, we love them because we are bidden by our common Lord to hope for the same condition hereafter. So we honor them with love but not with divine worship. We do not build temples for them. They do not wish to be honored by us in that way, because they know that when we are good people we are ourselves the temples of the most high God. Of True Religion 110.[23]

## Truth, Judgment and Justice. Apringius of Beja:

When the royal commands of God were heard, he fell down to worship him who was speaking with him. However, to respect the nature of his own office and to show that God is

---

[15]CCL 107:72. [16]Mt 8:11. [17]Lk 12:37. [18]Rom 8:28. [19]Mt 22:14. [20]CCL 92:262. [21]MTS 1 Sup 1:205-6. [22]CCL 121A:491-93. [23]LCC 6:280-81.

above all things, he prohibited this, saying, "Do not do this, because I am a fellow servant with you and your brothers who hold the testimony of Jesus." The testimony of Jesus is the true profession of the catholic confession. "For the testimony of Jesus is the Spirit of prophecy." The Spirit of prophecy is truth and judgment and justice, which in their fullness are contained in the catholic faith. TRACTATE ON THE APOCALYPSE 19.9-10.[24]

**THE GREEKS REGARD AS DIVINE THOSE DEMONS THEY HAVE ASSIGNED TO THE NATIONS.** OECUMENIUS: The [pagan] Greeks, though accursed and hated by God, heard of the teaching given in our prophecies that by the good will of God the holy angels protect the nations and the churches and every individual. . . . Since [the Greeks] have heard that such things were being taught by us, they say to us, "Since you claim the same things as we do, O people, why do you find fault with the teaching that we advance concerning the gods that rule over the nations? For those whom you call angels we call gods, so that we differ only in the use of the names but not in the substance of the matter. But since you also call the order of angels gods, there is no difference with us even in regard to the use of names."

To such persons one must say the following: "O you accursed people. You worship the works of your own hands and until very recently have established for yourselves gods with whom you associated for every vile purpose. You have purloined most of our divine teachings and adding these to your own destructive teachings, you have made a grand mixture of them. But since you use your own mind as guide and not God, you have not been able to maintain the nobility of our teachings in every regard. Rather, although you followed him for a short while, somewhere at the beginning of things, you suffered shipwreck. There is, therefore, nothing in common between us and you, just as there is nothing in common between light and darkness or between Christ and Beliar, as it is written.[25] Assuming the gods,

or rather the unclean demons, to be the rulers of the nations, you bring yourselves into league with them, ascribing reverence to them and wishing to worship them as gods.

Moreover, [these demons] are regarded by you as divine, while no mention is made of that God who has ordered all things for the providential care of humankind, these rather governing the nations by their own counsel, as they themselves wish. Therefore, you have assigned to Ares[26] the most savage and bloodthirsty Scythians and Germans, who became such since they were ruled by that murderous plague of man, Ares. But you assigned the Greeks, because of their understanding, to Athena,[27] since from her they received understanding as their lot. And you assigned other peoples to other gods, each of the gods training the nations according to their own passions."

When the evangelist wished to worship the holy angel, . . . [the angel] says, "See that you do not do this! I am a fellow servant with you and your brothers who hold the testimony of Jesus." The exclamation "See!" is not simply the cry of someone who wishes temporarily to hinder something but of someone who wants to prevent something altogether. He calls himself a "fellow servant" with all of those who confess themselves to be servants of Christ and who testify that he is God incarnate. What, then, is to be done, O most holy angel, since you forbid yourself to be worshiped? "Worship God!" he says, "for the testimony of Jesus is the spirit of prophecy." This is as though he had said, "Do you seek to worship me, since I announced to you ahead of time what was to take place? Whoever witnesses to the lordship and deity of Christ is filled with the prophetic grace, not I alone. Why therefore, he says, do you worship that grace which I have in equal measure with my fellow servants? Are the things which the Greeks think about the rulers of the nations really the same as what the Christians say about

---

[24]CCL 107:72.  [25]See 2 Cor 6:14-15.  [26]The Greek god of war.  [27]The Greek goddess of wisdom, justice and war.

the holy angels?" COMMENTARY ON THE APOCA-
LYPSE 19.10.[28]

**EVERY WORK OF THE SPIRIT IS A TESTIMONY
TO JESUS CHRIST.** PRIMASIUS: Indeed, the
whole point of prophecy and of the sanctifying
work of the Spirit lies in the testimony of Jesus
Christ, whom the entire law and all prophecy
serve [as though slaves]. For this reason, when he
manifested himself on the mountain between
Moses and Elijah, his face and his clothing were
resplendent with his brightness, and he declared
that the law and the prophets had truly testified
of him. And so, whatever they had foretold, he
himself testifies that it serves Christ and the
church, for he said of Moses, "For he wrote of
me."[29] And when he had risen from the dead, he
said, "Everything written about me in the law of
Moses and the prophets and the psalms must be
fulfilled."[30] COMMENTARY ON THE APOCALYPSE
19.10.[31]

**THE HOLY ANGELS ARE OF HUMBLE DISPOSI-
TION.** ANDREW OF CAESAREA: "Do not worship
me as one who is foretelling the future," the holy
angel says. For the confession of Christ, that is,
the testimony is the gift of the prophetic Spirit.

And you should note also this. The prophecy [is
given] for this reason, so that the testimony of
Christ may be made strong and the faith be given
witness by the saints. Therefore, do not pay homage to me, as fellow servant, but to him who possesses power over all things. From this passage we
also learn of the humble disposition of the holy
angels, for they do not claim for themselves
divine glory as do the evil demons but ascribe this
glory to the Lord. May it be that we "outdo one
another" with a humble mind,[32] thus fulfilling the
saying of the Lord: "Learn from me, for I am gentle and lowly in heart, and you will find rest for
your souls."[33] And may we receive rest in the coming age, where "sorrow and pain and groaning
have fled,"[34] and where the dwelling is of all who
rejoice and gaze upon the light of the face of
Christ our God,[35] to whom every song of praise,
honor and worship be given, together with the
Father and the life-giving Spirit forever and ever.
Amen. COMMENTARY ON THE APOCALYPSE
19.10.[36]

---

[28]TEG 8:238-40. This is testimony to the continuing vigor of paganism at the time of Oecumenius. [29]Jn 5:46. [30]Lk 24:44. [31]CCL
92:263. [32]See Rom 12:10. [33]Mt 11:29. [34]See Is 35:10. [35]See Ps 87:7
(86:7 LXX); 2 Cor 4:6. [36]MTS 1 Sup 1:206-7.

---

## 19:11-16 A WHITE HORSE AND ITS RIDER

[11]*Then I saw heaven opened, and behold, a white horse! He who sat upon it is called Faithful
and True, and in righteousness he judges and makes war.* [12]*His eyes are like a flame of fire, and on
his head are many diadems; and he has a name inscribed which no one knows but himself.* [13]*He is
clad in a robe dipped in[m] blood, and the name by which he is called is The Word of God.* [14]*And the
armies of heaven, arrayed in fine linen, white and pure, followed him on white horses.* [15]*From his
mouth issues a sharp sword with which to smite the nations, and he will rule them with a rod of
iron; he will tread the wine press of the fury of the wrath of God the Almighty.* [16]*On his robe and
on his thigh he has a name inscribed, King of kings and Lord of lords.*

m Other ancient authorities read *sprinkled with*

**OVERVIEW:** The Word on earth is image and shadow; the Word in heaven is true. The words by which the divine Word opens heaven and makes known the higher things fight the irrational elements of the soul so that the Word in heaven might dwell in it with reason and justice. This Word is faithful and true and leads the soul higher than the words by which the divine Word speaks on earth, which are shadow, type and image. To be sure, we were introduced to the Word by his coming in our body. However, by his words he at the end destroys the material element of our thoughts and dispels all forms of falsehood by the illuminating clarity of God's wisdom (ORIGEN). When Christ assumed his pure, white body, he came to conquer the powers of the air (BEDE) and to free us from sin and to endure patiently the sinner (APRINGIUS). In this struggle Christ is our strength and also the prize to those who conquer in him (PRIMASIUS). At the end of time, Christ will come with his celestial army to establish his kingdom (VICTORINUS) and like a mighty general will make war against his enemies with the armies of his saints, who are without any spot of sin (OECUMENIUS). In Christ the saints obtain the beauty of their own crowns (TYCONIUS), while Christ offers the glory and honor of the saints to his Father (APRINGIUS).

Through the commandments and his Holy Spirit (BEDE) God has illumined and made bright the righteous, for his all-seeing power is like a flame of fire (ANDREW OF CAESAREA) that sees all things and scrutinizes all humankind (APRINGIUS). For the sinner, however, the all-seeing power of God does not make bright but rather burns (ANDREW OF CAESAREA). Indeed, sinners and heretics have no knowledge of the Word who gives to the church what it is worthy to know in him (PRIMASIUS). In his works Christ is known by many names, for he is Shepherd, Light, Holiness and Redemption (ANDREW OF CAESAREA). However, in the incomprehensibility of his divine essence, the Son is unapproachable, and his name known only to himself and to the Father and the Holy Spirit (OECUMENIUS, PRIMASIUS, ANDREW OF CAESAREA). Yet even though the nature of the Word is invisible and incorporeal and his peace is beyond every creaturely understanding (BEDE), the Word is for us the interpreter of the Father's wisdom. This Word, impassibly generated from the mind of the Father (ANDREW OF CAESAREA), appeared as man and instructed his church and gave to it knowledge and hope (PRIMASIUS, BEDE).

In the remission of their sins and with Christ suffering in them (PRIMASIUS), the saints, like a mighty army (BEDE), follow in the footsteps of Christ with bodies and minds made pure through the resurrection (APRINGIUS, PRIMASIUS). In this the saints are similar to the angels, who also are free from sin, pure by nature and bright in their union with God (OECUMENIUS, ANDREW OF CAESAREA). Indeed, in his incarnation the Word was in no way diminished as King and Lord (OECUMENIUS). Rather, united personally to the flesh taken from the Virgin (APRINGIUS, OECUMENIUS), the Word became Head of the church so that in Christ the church herself is a lord (CAESARIUS OF ARLES). Through faith Christ makes "sons" of God by adoption (APRINGIUS), and so by the posterity of spiritual offspring all the nations will be blessed (PRIMASIUS). These "sons" by faith are lords, for they have power over sin (CAESARIUS OF ARLES, ANDREW OF CAESAREA), they witness by a firm confession that Christ is King and Lord (APRINGIUS), and they will rule with Christ forever in the coming age (ANDREW OF CAESAREA).

In this age God instructed the humble by the Law and by persecution (PRIMASIUS, CAESARIUS OF ARLES). However, the proud are broken by the severity of God's justice and are not purified or made new. God will punish such unrepentant sinners with righteous anger and cast them into Gehenna (APRINGIUS, OECUMENIUS, PRIMASIUS, CAESARIUS OF ARLES).

### 19:11 He Is Called Faithful and True

**THE WORD IN HEAVEN IS TRUE.** ORIGEN: I think that heaven has been closed to those who are impious and who bear "the image of the earthly" but opened to those who are just and who have been adorned with "the image of the heavenly."[1] For the higher things have been closed to the impious, inasmuch as they are below and are still in the flesh. They cannot understand them or their beauty. They do not wish to perceive them, in that they are stooped over and do not devote themselves to lifting up their heads. But he opened the heavenly places with the key of David[2] to be contemplated by the just, inasmuch as they have citizenship in heaven. The divine Word opens them and explains them by riding a horse. The horse signifies the words that proclaim the meanings. He is white because the nature of the knowledge is remarkable and white and luminous. And he who is called "Faithful" sits on the white horse, seated more firmly and, if I may so speak, royally, on words that cannot be overturned, words that run faster and swifter than any horse and that surpass every opponent in their rush, that is, every supposed word that is a dissembler of the Word and every dissembler of truth that seems to be truth. But he who is on the white horse is called "Faithful," not so much because he trusts as because he is trustworthy, that is, he is worthy of being trusted, for according to Moses, the Lord is faithful and true.[3] For he is also true in contradistinction to a shadow, and a type, and an image, since the Word in the opened heaven is such. For the Word on earth is not like the Word in heaven, inasmuch as he has become flesh and is expressed by means of a shadow and types and images. . . . This Word of God, indeed, who is called faithful is also called true, and he judges and fights justly. He has received the ability from God to impart what each creature deserves and to judge with absolute justice and judgment. . . . Now just as it is said that the task of the Word is to judge with justice, so also his task is said to be to fight according to justice, that by thus fighting the soul's enemies with reason and justice, he may dwell in it and justify it when the irrational elements and injustice are destroyed. He casts out the hostile elements from that soul which, if I may speak in this way, has

been taken captive by Christ for salvation. COMMENTARY ON THE GOSPEL OF JOHN 2.47-54.[4]

**THE LORD COMES WITH HIS CELESTIAL ARMY.** VICTORINUS OF PETOVIUM: It shows "a white horse and him who sat upon it," namely, our Lord coming with his celestial army to establish his kingdom. At his coming all the nations will be gathered and will be slain with the sword. Those among them who are more noble will be preserved in order to serve the saints,[5] and it will be necessary that these at the end of time, when the kingdom of the saints is ended, before the judgment and when the devil is again released, be killed. The prophets prophesy about all these things in a similar manner. COMMENTARY ON THE APOCALYPSE 19.1.[6]

**THE INCARNATE CHRIST IS PATIENT.** APRINGIUS OF BEJA: The white horse is the body which [Christ] assumed. He who sits upon it is the Lord of Majesty; he is the Word of the most high Father; he is the only begotten of the unbegotten Father. Therefore, the true character of his person is expressed when he is called "Faithful" and "True." For of God it is said, "God is faithful, in whom there is no iniquity."[7] And "in righteousness he judges and makes war." For concerning him it is written, "God is a judge, just, strong and patient."[8] He makes war by freeing us from the adversity of sin; he is patient by enduring the sins we commit; he is called strong because he repels whatever opposes him. TRACTATE ON THE APOCALYPSE 19.11-13.[9]

**CHRIST CONQUERS HIS ENEMIES LIKE A MIGHTY GENERAL.** OECUMENIUS: The Evangelist now receives the revelation of the fall of the antichrist and of the arch-evil dragon. He sees moreover the punishment they will receive at the

---

[1]See 1 Cor 15:49. [2]See Rev 3:7. [3]See Deut 32:4. [4]FC 80:106-8. See also *Commentary on the Gospel of John* 1.277-78 (FC 80:90-91). [5]See Is 60:10; 61:5; Irenaeus *Against Heresies* 5.35.1 (ANF 1:565). [6]CSEL 49:136-38. [7]Cf. Deut 32:4. [8]Ps 7:12 LXX. [9]CCL 107:72-73.

time of the end and their recompense, as well as the fall of those kings who at that time will oppose the servants of Christ. And see what it says: "I saw heaven opened, and behold, a white horse," and the rider is faithful and true and just. He sees the Lord as he is about to join the battle and fight for the saints and make war against his adversaries. For this reason the vision depicts him in the form of a general, giving him a horse and a sword and the leadership of armies. "And, behold, a white horse" upon which the Lord was riding. By this the vision reveals that Christ depends upon no others than those who are pure and are not tainted by any stain of sin. For this reason, the Lord also said of that "chosen instrument," namely, Paul, that he would "carry my name before the Gentiles and kings and the sons of Israel."[10] You see, therefore, that Christ depends upon and rides on such persons as Paul. "He who sat upon it," that is, upon the horse, "is called Faithful and True, and in righteousness he judges and makes war." He who is true is also faithful, as the apostle said concerning him: "He remains faithful, for he cannot deny himself,"[11] and so he is the "Faithful" and "True." And about him two assertions are made which address the same matter. The prophet was witness that he judges righteously and that he makes war on behalf of his servants against their visible enemies: "O God, give your judgment to the king, and your righteousness to the king's son," that is, to Christ—for the son of Solomon was Christ according to the flesh, to whom the psalmist was referring—and then it continues, "that he might judge your people with righteousness and your poor with judgment."[12] That he also makes war [the psalmist] shows when he speaks of him arming himself as a soldier: "Gird your sword upon your thigh, O mighty one, in your comeliness and in your beauty, and bend [your bow] and prosper and reign." Then he adds, "Your weapons are sharpened, O mighty one, the nations shall fall under you."[13] COMMENTARY ON THE APOCALYPSE 19.11-16.[14]

**CHRIST IS HIMSELF THE PRIZE.** PRIMASIUS: He judges as the King of all ages. He makes war

as one who always suffers in his members. When he fights, he conquers; he crowns himself; he offers himself as strength to those who struggle; he promises himself as the prize for those who overcome. COMMENTARY ON THE APOCALYPSE 19.11.[15]

**THE LORD CONQUERS THE POWERS OF THE AIR.** BEDE: The Lord, who is "the Way, the Truth and the Life,"[16] and to whom it is said through the prophet, "For you have done wonderful things, plans ancient and faithful, Amen,"[17] mounts the throne of his white body, that is, his pure body, in order to conquer the powers of the air. EXPLANATION OF THE APOCALYPSE 19.11.[18]

### 19:12a On His Head Are Many Diadems

**THE WORD WEARS MANY CROWNS.** ORIGEN: As the flame is bright and at the same time illuminating, and further also has a nature that is fiery and consumes the more material elements, so the eyes of the Word, if I may speak in this way, with which he sees, and everyone who participates in him, destroy and obliterate the more material and gross elements of thoughts by grasping them by means of the spiritual powers inherent in him. Everything false, in any way whatsoever, has fled the subtlety and precision of the truth. . . . If the lie were one and simple against which the Word who is "faithful and true" prevailed, who received the crown when the lie was overcome, the Word who became master of God's opponents would also reasonably have been recorded to wear one diadem. But now, since the lies that profess the truth are many against which the Word has fought and is crowned, there are many diadems surrounding the head of him who has conquered them all. COMMENTARY ON THE GOSPEL OF JOHN 2.57-59.[19]

---

[10]Acts 9:15. [11]2 Tim 2:13. [12]Ps 72:2 (71:2 LXX). [13]Ps 44:3-5 LXX. [14]TEG 8:241-42. [15]CCL 92:264. [16]Jn 14:6. [17]Is 25:1. [18]CCL 121A:493-95. Caesarius of Arles interprets the white horse to be the church (PL 35:2447). [19]FC 80:109.

ALL SAINTS ARE CROWNED IN CHRIST. TYCO-
NIUS: In him "in whom we shall perform great
deeds,"[20] in him the multitude of the saints are
said to have the beauty of crowns. COMMENTARY
ON THE APOCALYPSE 19.12.[21]

THE EYES OF GOD PERVADE ALL THINGS.
APRINGIUS OF BEJA: As fire penetrates everything which contains it and leaves no portion
untouched by the force of its burning heat, so the
eyes of the Lord cannot be avoided, for they are
everywhere and pervade all things, and seeing all
things which people do, they investigate them
with a holy scrutiny. . . . There are many [dia-
dems] because he brings to God, who gathers all,
all the glory of the saints and all the honor of the
blessed. And these do not remain quiet, but bring
forth praise and thanksgiving. TRACTATE ON THE
APOCALYPSE 19.11-13.[22]

GOD'S POWER ILLUMINES THE RIGHTEOUS.
ANDREW OF CAESAREA: The flames of fire come
forth from his eyes, that is, from his all-seeing
power. For those who are righteous, this fire does
no harm but illumines and makes bright. However, for the sinners this fire burns but does not
make bright. The multiple diadems symbolize
either his kingdom, which is over all things in
heaven and on earth—as many as there are ranks
of angels and kingdoms upon the earth and
assemblies among holy people—or they signify
the victory against the sinners that was won for
us by all of his acts of mercy, as a certain holy person said, "And you will gain victory when you are
judged."[23] COMMENTARY ON THE APOCALYPSE
19.11-12.[24]

THE COMMANDMENTS AND THE SPIRIT. BEDE:
Sometimes he speaks of the commandments as
the "eyes of the Lord," sometimes he is speaking
of the Spirit. Of the commandments, he says,
"Your word, O Lord, is a lamp to my feet,"[25] and
of the Spirit, he says, "I came to cast fire upon the
earth."[26] EXPLANATION OF THE APOCALYPSE
19.12.[27]

## 19:12b A Name Which No One Knows

THE LIVING WORD ALONE UNDERSTANDS
ALL THINGS. ORIGEN: The living Word alone
understands some things because of the natural
inferiority in those who came into existence after
him. None of them can contemplate all the things
that he grasps. And perhaps also only those who
share in the Word, in contradistinction to those
who do not, know what the others are missing.
COMMENTARY ON THE GOSPEL OF JOHN 2.60.[28]

THE NAME OF THE ONLY BEGOTTEN REMAINS
UNKNOWN TO EVERYONE. OECUMENIUS: In
Exodus, God speaks to holy Moses: "I am the
Lord. I appeared to Abraham, to Isaac and to
Jacob, being their God, but I did not reveal to
them my name, the Lord,"[29] showing that it is to
be regarded as superior to any report of man. And
for this reason, the Lord also handed over to his
apostles how those who had turned to the knowledge of God ought to be baptized, saying, "baptizing them in the name."[30] And when he said
"name," he did not transmit the proper names—
for he had no power to give utterance to their
names. Rather, instead of the proper names, he
transmitted relational and personal names, for he
spoke names of relation when he said, "in the
name of the Father and of the Son," while he
added a personal name, "and in the Holy Spirit."
Therefore, most definitely, also in the Revelation
he allows the proper name of the Only Begotten
to remain unknown to everyone. COMMENTARY
ON THE APOCALYPSE 19.11-16.[31]

WHAT IS KNOWN BY THE SON IS KNOWN BY
THE FATHER AND THE SPIRIT. PRIMASIUS: Perfect knowledge of the Word of God is revealed to
those who are worthy to be the body of Christ
and members [of him], since the Head especially

---

[20]Ps 60:12 (59:14 LXX). [21]CCL 92:264. [22]CCL 107:73. [23]See Ps 51:4
(50:6 LXX). [24]MTS 1 Sup 1:208. According to Oecumenius, the fiery
eyes reveal Christ's wrath against his enemies (TEG 8:242). [25]Ps
119:105 (118:105 LXX). [26]Lk 12:49. [27]CCL 121A:495. [28]FC 80:109.
[29]Ex 6:2-3. [30]Mt 28:19. [31]TEG 8:242-43.

gives knowledge of himself to the body, and he knows what the church is worthy to know in him. The apostle says, "He who is united to the Lord is one spirit, for the two shall be one flesh."[32] Neither the Jews nor the foreigners nor the heretics will ever know this name, for "if they had [known], they would not have crucified the Lord of glory,"[33] and again, "The world has not known you."[34] And the Lord said again to his disciples, "You will see me; because I live, you will live also. In that day you will know that I am in my Father, and you in me, and I in you."[35] And the disciples answered, "Lord, how is it that you will manifest yourself to us and not to the world?"[36] Concerning the heretics, the Lord said, "To you it has been given to know the secret of the kingdom of God, but for those outside everything is in parables, so that they may indeed see but not perceive."[37] He has a great name inscribed that no one knows except himself. However, we must beware lest by a purely carnal wisdom we think that the name of the Son is unknown to the Father or to the Holy Spirit. . . . If the Son alone is said to know something, the whole Trinity is also regarded as knowing it. Similarly, if the Father alone is said to know something, he is without doubt thought to know it together with his Wisdom, who is Christ, and with his Spirit, who is believed to be the Spirit of the Father and of the Son. For when the Father alone was said to know the day of judgment,[38] certainly it was not denied that the Son and the Spirit also knew it. So also, when the Holy Spirit alone is said to know something, and the names of the Father and of the Son are unspoken, nevertheless it is declared that they know in the same manner. When the apostle says, "What person knows the thoughts of a man except the spirit of the man that is in him? So also no one comprehends the thoughts of God except the Spirit of God,"[39] it would be foolish to separate the Father and the Son from such knowledge. When he says elsewhere, "Do not grieve the Holy Spirit of God, in whom you were sealed for the day of redemption,"[40] he is not excluding the persons of the Father and of the Son from the work of our redemption, even though he does not mention their names. For through the undivided power of the one nature, we teach that the works of the Trinity are inseparable. COMMENTARY ON THE APOCALYPSE 19.12.[41]

**THE WORD IS WITHOUT NAME AND UNAPPROACHABLE.** ANDREW OF CAESAREA: That his name is unknown signifies the incomprehensibility of his essence. By virtue of his works he is known by many names, such as Good, Shepherd, Sun, Light, Life, Righteousness, Holiness, Redemption.[42] Similarly, he is called by terms of negation, such as Incorruptible, Invisible, Immortal, Unchangeable.[43] However, according to his essence he is without name and is unapproachable, being known by himself alone with the Father and the Spirit. COMMENTARY ON THE APOCALYPSE 19.12.[44]

## 19:13 He Is Called the Word of God

**WE WILL NOT FORGET HIS INCARNATION.** ORIGEN: John does not see the Word of God mounted on a horse naked. He is clothed with a garment sprinkled with blood, since the Word who became flesh, and died because he became flesh, is invested with traces of that passion, since his blood also was poured forth upon the earth when the soldier pierced his side. For perhaps, even if in some way we attain the most sublime and highest contemplation of the Word and of the truth, we shall not forget completely that we were introduced to him by his coming in our body. COMMENTARY ON THE GOSPEL OF JOHN 2.61.[45]

---

[32]1 Cor 6:16-17. [33]1 Cor 2:8. [34]Jn 17:25. [35]Jn 14:19-20. [36]Jn 14:22. [37]Mk 4:11-12. [38]See Mt 24:36. [39]1 Cor 2:11. [40]Eph 4:30. [41]CCL 92:264-65. [42]For these names, see Lk 18:19; Jn 10:11; Heb 13:20; Jn 1:9; 8:12; 14:6; 1 Cor 1:30. [43]For these names, see 1 Tim 1:17; Col 1:15; Mal 3:6; Heb 1:10-12. [44]MTS 1 Sup 1:208. See also Gregory of Nazianzus *Oration* 29.17 (NPNF 2 7:307); *Oration* 30.20, 21 (NPNF 2 7:316-17). [45]FC 80:110.

**PARTICIPATING IN HIS WORD DIPPED IN BLOOD.** PRIMASIUS: If no one is allowed to know his name, why is he now openly called the "Word of God"? When we read, "No one has ascended into heaven, but he who has descended from heaven, the Son of man who is in heaven,"[46] we are to understand that whoever of his members will ascend is allowed to ascend in the Head himself and through him. By promising this to his members, he has granted them hope, and by fulfilling this, he will give to them the possibility [to receive this]. So here, the Son alone is said to know what is allowed to his bride to know in him, through whom and in whom the church is instructed. In speaking of the robe sprinkled with blood, it is indicating the tokens of his passion, whether this be in the Head himself or in his body, which is the church. For this reason, the apostle teaches the Hebrews that from the beginning in the animal sacrifices demanded by the law there was no remission of sins with the shedding of blood.[47] Concerning the church he says, "that in my flesh I might complete what is lacking in Christ's sufferings,"[48] remembering the words which he heard, "Saul, Saul, why do you persecute me?"[49] For whatever the church suffers, Christ also truly suffers, and of him Paul says, "he suffered once to take away the sins of many,"[50] however, he suffers frequently in his members. Isaiah spoke of the appearance of this robe in this way, "Who is this that comes from Edom, in crimsoned garments from Bozrah? He is glorious in his apparel, marching in the greatness of his strength. It is I who speaks righteousness and who am a fighter for salvation. Why then is your garment red, and your apparel as though freshly trodden in a winepress? I alone have trodden the winepress, and from the peoples no one was with me."[51] COMMENTARY ON THE APOCALYPSE 19.13.[52]

**CHRIST INTERPRETS THE FATHER'S WISDOM.** ANDREW OF CAESAREA: How is it that he who is without name and is unknown to all is here named "Word"? This is either to demonstrate his filial personhood and his impassible generation from the Father, just as our speech comes from our minds [impassibly], or his name suggests that he bears within himself the causes of all things, or that he is the interpreter of the wisdom and power of the Father. COMMENTARY ON THE APOCALYPSE 19.13.[53]

**NOTHING IN HIS NATURE IS VISIBLE OR CORPOREAL.** BEDE: Apparently this passage refers to the passion, as his immaculate birth was indicated in the white horse and his innocent death is indicated in the bloodstained garment.[54] "His name is called Word of God" because the same who in time appeared as a man who was going to suffer in the beginning was God with God. He is called "Word," because nothing in the substance of his nature is visible or corporeal, or because through him the Father created all things. As it says above, perfect knowledge of his nature is known to himself alone, and to the Father. "For the peace of God passes all understanding,"[55] that is, that peace by which God himself is peace unto himself surpasses every creaturely understanding, all human understanding and even the understanding of the angels. "His wisdom is without end."[56] When it says, "And to whom the Son chooses to reveal [the Father],"[57] it means that one who knows the Son and the Father, knows them after the manner of the creature. EXPLANATION OF THE APOCALYPSE 19.13.[58]

## 19:14 The Armies of Heaven

**CLOTHED WITH THE REALITIES OF THE DIVINE WISDOM.** ORIGEN: All the hosts of heaven follow this Word of God. They follow the Word who leads them and imitate him in all things, especially in having mounted white horses like him, for all things are open to those who understand. And just as "pain and grief and

---

[46]Jn 3:13. [47]See Heb 9:22. [48]Col 1:24. [49]Acts 9:4. [50]Heb 9:28. [51]Is 63:1-3. [52]CCL 92:266-67. [53]MTS 1 Sup 1:209. [54]Caesarius of Arles interprets the bloody garment to be "the martyrs who are in the church" (PL 35:2447). [55]Phil 4:7. [56]See Ps 147:5 (146:5 LXX). [57]Mt 11:27. [58]CCL 121A:495-97.

groaning fled"[59] at the end of things, so, I think, obscurity and dismay fled when all the mysteries of God's wisdom burst forth with precision and clarity. And consider the white horses of those who follow the Word, clothed in "pure white linen."[60] [What does this mean] unless the linen garments, since linen comes from the earth, are types of the languages on earth in which the sounds have been clothed, which indicate the realities in a pure manner? COMMENTARY ON THE GOSPEL OF JOHN 2.62-63.[61]

**BODIES MADE NEW IN THE RESURRECTION.** APRINGIUS OF BEJA: We interpret the armies of heaven to be the bride herself, who above was said to be prepared for the marriage of the Lamb. When it says that they were "on white horses," it is speaking either of the purity of faith, or it is alluding to the members of our bodies made new through the resurrection. [The fine linen] is the righteous works of the saints. TRACTATE ON THE APOCALYPSE 19.14.[62]

**THE HOLY ANGELS ARE PURE BY NATURE.** OECUMENIUS: [Christ] is the commander-in-chief of the heavenly powers. The Lord in fact called himself that when bearing the name of Jesus, son of Nun, he said, "I, as commander of the army of the Lord have now come."[63] The horses that belong to the holy angels are also white, for the angels too rejoice over the pure deeds of humankind, since they are pure by nature and free from every stain. This is symbolized by their raiment of fine linen, which is pure and white. COMMENTARY ON THE APOCALYPSE 19.11-16.[64]

**THE CHURCH FOLLOWS THE FOOTSTEPS OF CHRIST.** PRIMASIUS: In heaven the churches, as though "with unveiled face beholding the glory of God,"[65] all being pure in heart and made whiter than snow by grace, are said to follow Christ. . . . They always go forward on white horses, that is, with pure bodies and minds, following the footsteps of Christ, who is going before and to whom

it is said in the Song of Songs, "We run after you for the aroma of your ointments."[66] COMMENTARY ON THE APOCALYPSE 19.14.[67]

**THE ANGELS ARE BRIGHT BY THEIR VIRTUE.** ANDREW OF CAESAREA: [The heavenly armies] signify the heavenly orders that are resplendent with the excellence of their nature, with the sublimity of their thoughts and with the brightness of their virtues and their intimate union with God. COMMENTARY ON THE APOCALYPSE 19.14.[68]

**THE CHURCH IS CALLED AN ARMY.** BEDE: With pure white bodies the church imitates [Christ], for because of the battle of her struggles, it receives by right the name of army. EXPLANATION OF THE APOCALYPSE 19.14.[69]

## 19:15 He Will Rule the Nations

**CHRIST WILL JUDGE THE NATIONS.** APRINGIUS OF BEJA: The sharp sword that issues from his mouth is the authority of the law and the severity of the judge. It remains sharp for justice, so that he might separate all things and reckon the deeds of every person. Then it says, "so that he might smite the nations with [the sword]." To smite means to strike, to determine, to free, to damn, to justify, to rescue, to save. . . . The rod of iron is the discipline of power by which he will make right all nations, equally changing them and judging them. . . . The wine press is hell, and the wine is the judgment by which those are restrained and subdued upon whom the righteous anger of God will have come. TRACTATE ON THE APOCALYPSE 19.15-16.[70]

**PUNISHMENT AWAITS THOSE WHOM THE WORD DOES NOT REFORM.** OECUMENIUS: The vision places [the sword] in the mouth. In this

---

[59]Is 35:10. [60]In the text of Origen, the white horses are clothed in white linen, not those who follow the Word. Codex Sinaiticus also has this reading. [61]FC 80:110. [62]CCL 107:73. [63]Josh 5:14. [64]TEG 8:243. [65]2 Cor 3:18. [66]Song 1:4 LXX. [67]CCL 92:267. [68]MTS 1 Sup 1:209. [69]CCL 121A:497. [70]CCL 107:73-74.

way it is indicated that all things have their existence by the Word of God and that whoever in any way disobeys him will not remain unpunished. "So that with it he might smite the nations." Which nations? Those that are arrayed with the antichrist for war against the servants of Christ and have been gathered under him. "And he will rule them," it says, "with a rod of iron." Since he is intrinsically good and merciful, the Lord desired to rule these nations ... with a staff of comfort, as would a shepherd and to lead them to "green pastures and to nourish them with the waters of rest."[71] But since they did not wish this, they will be governed with a "rod of iron," that is, with severity and death. For certainly punishment awaits those whom the Word does not reform. To indicate that the rod of iron is that of severity and punishment, the prophet suggests the rule of the Romans[72] about which Daniel spoke in saying, "Arise, devour much flesh,"[73] when he spoke to God, saying, "You will rule them with a rod of iron and dash them in pieces as a potter's vessel."[74] However, when there existed a favorable time, God ruled them with the former rod, but at the last time, he will rule them with this latter rod. "He will tread the winepress of the fury of the wrath of God the Almighty." In the Gospels, the Lord says of his own Father, "The Father judges no one but has given all judgment to the Son."[75] Most appropriately, therefore, it says in the Revelation that "he will tread the winepress of the fury of the wrath of God." For through the judgment and recompense of the wicked, he fulfills the will of his Father in that he fulfills the righteous anger of the Father. COMMENTARY ON THE APOCALYPSE 19.11-16.[76]

**PERSECUTION AND CALAMITY SERVE TO PURIFY THE CHURCH.** PRIMASIUS: The sharp sword symbolizes either the two Testaments or what we read concerning wisdom, "She carries law and kindness on her tongue,"[77] namely, judgment and mercy. On the other hand, the rod of iron symbolizes the unbending standard of justice.... As the action of threshing separates the

wheat from the chaff so that it is stored in the barn, so also the weight of the pressure of the winepress purifies the wine as it is separated from the grape skins or the oil from the dregs. The prophet referred to this when he said, "He dug out a wine vat in her."[78] This occurs in the church when persecution arises or some other kind of calamity happens. Then, some like dregs will run down by an irremediable fall, while others will shine more brightly by their faith which now is tested. COMMENTARY ON THE APOCALYPSE 19.15.[79]

**THE RIGHTEOUSNESS OF GOD.** CAESARIUS OF ARLES: The two-edged sharp sword is the power of Christ by which the righteous are defended and the unrighteous are punished. The rod of iron is the righteousness of God by which the humble are instructed but the proud are broken to pieces as though they were a clay pot.... He treads [the winepress of God's wrath] even now, when he permits the evil to persecute the good and leaves them to their own desires. However, later he will seek repayment, when he sends those into Gehenna who have not repented. EXPOSITION ON THE APOCALYPSE 19.15, HOMILY 17.[80]

### 19:16 King of Kings and Lord of Lords

**THROUGH FAITH THE SONS OF GOD CONFESS CHRIST.** APRINGIUS OF BEJA: Christ is the basis and the foundation on which Paul builds as an architect. Christ is the good Shepherd "who gives his life for the sheep."[81] Christ is the head of every dominion and power. He is himself the head of the church, wherefore it is said, "the head of man is Christ,"[82] because he is the head of the church. He is the father, because by him through baptism all the nations of the earth are born again. His thigh, on which his name is written,

---

[71]Ps 23:2 (22:2 LXX). [72]A traditional interpretation of the fourth beast spoken of in Dan 7:19. [73]Dan 7:5. [74]Ps 2:9. [75]Jn 5:22. [76]TEG 8:243-44. [77]See Prov 31:26. [78]Is 5:2. [79]CCL 92:267-68. [80]PL 35:2447. [81]Jn 10:15. [82]1 Cor 11:3.

are the believers whom the Son of God, that is, Christ, has willed to name "sons" through the adoption of faith. His robe is the assumed man, and because there is one person of two substances, we recognize his divinity in his robe, that is, in the sacrament of the Lord's body. Upon the vestment of his body it is said that his name was written, "King of kings and Lord of lords." Indeed, it is written on his thigh, because all who are called "sons" through faith witness with an unswerving confession that he is the King of kings and the Lord of lords. TRACTATE ON THE APOCALYPSE 19.15-16.[83]

### THE INCARNATION OF CHRIST DID NOT DIMINISH HIS RANK. OECUMENIUS: The robe symbolizes the flesh of the Lord, which was endowed with a rational soul. The holy angels spoke of his flesh through Isaiah, "Why are your garments red and your apparel as if from a trodden winepress, utterly stained by trodden [grapes]?"[84] Moreover, the thigh indicates his birth in the flesh, for it is written in Genesis, "All the souls that came with Jacob into Egypt, who came out of his thighs."[85] Therefore, when the vision shows that on the robe and on the thigh it is written that the Immanuel is king of all, it shows that the Word, united personally to the flesh and having undergone a fleshly birth from a virgin, was in no way established less a King and Lord of all things in heaven and upon earth; nor was he diminished in rank by virtue of his incarnation. For even as such he was God and is and shall be God. COMMENTARY ON THE APOCALYPSE 19.11-16.[86]

### THE SPIRITUAL OFFSPRING OF CHRIST. PRIMASIUS: [The name is inscribed] on his robe, that is, on the church with which Christ is clothed and which, according to the apostle, "he cleansed by the washing of water with the word, that he might present to himself a church glorious, without spot or wrinkle."[87] He cleansed the robe that

it might have no spot, and he stretched it that it might have no wrinkle. The thigh symbolizes the posterity of his offspring, by which all nations will be blessed, according to the apostle who teaches, "It does not say, 'and to offsprings,' referring to many, but referring to one, 'and to your offspring,' which is Christ."[88] As though to a dead brother, according to ancient custom, the same apostle raises offspring spiritually, saying, "Lest any one should say that you were baptized in my name,"[89] since he says that from Jerusalem as far as Illyricum he has done all things for the gospel, so that he might truthfully say to the Gentiles, "I became your father in Christ Jesus through the gospel."[90] Therefore, on this thigh, as though on children, the knowledge of Christ is written "not with ink but with the Spirit of the living God, not on tablets of stone but on tablets of human hearts,"[91] which confess him to be the King of kings and the Lord of all lords. COMMENTARY ON THE APOCALYPSE 19.16.[92]

### IN CHRIST THE CHURCH IS LORD. CAESARIUS OF ARLES: This is a name that the proud do not know. For by serving [Christ], the church reigns in Christ, and she is lord of lords, that is, she conquers vices and sins. EXPOSITION OF THE APOCALYPSE 19.16, HOMILY 17.[93]

### THOSE WHO RULE THEIR PASSIONS. ANDREW OF CAESAREA: This name reveals the unity of the divine incarnation. For in this unity he who is God suffered in the flesh, and although man, he is King of kings and Lord of lords. Those who have ruled the passions and in cooperation with Christ have possessed the authority and power over sin shall also rule with him in the coming age. COMMENTARY ON THE APOCALYPSE 19.16.[94]

---

[83]CCL 107:74. [84]Is 63:2. [85]Gen 46:26. [86]TEG 8:244-45. [87]Eph 5:26-27. [88]Gal 3:16. [89]1 Cor 1:15. [90]1 Cor 4:15. [91]2 Cor 3:3. [92]CCL 92:268-69. [93]PL 35:2446. [94]MTS 1 Sup 1:210.

## 19:17-21 THE SUPPER OF THE GREAT GOD

*<sup>17</sup>Then I saw an angel standing in the sun, and with a loud voice he called to all the birds that fly in midheaven, "Come, gather for the great supper of God, <sup>18</sup>to eat the flesh of kings, the flesh of captains, the flesh of mighty men, the flesh of horses and their riders, and the flesh of all men, both free and slave, both small and great." <sup>19</sup>And I saw the beast and the kings of the earth with their armies gathered to make war against him who sits upon the horse and against his army. <sup>20</sup>And the beast was captured, and with it the false prophet who in its presence had worked the signs by which he deceived those who had received the mark of the beast and those who worshiped its image. These two were thrown alive into the lake of fire that burns with sulphur. <sup>21</sup>And the rest were slain by the sword of him who sits upon the horse, the sword that issues from his mouth; and all the birds were gorged with their flesh.*

**OVERVIEW:** The angel in mid-heaven is the church's preaching (PRIMASIUS, CAESARIUS OF ARLES, BEDE). This preaching is without fear and is the more free the more it is oppressed (PRIMASIUS, BEDE). Those who hear the preaching of the one church and become faithful are sacrificially "eaten" and so are transformed into the body of the church (PRIMASIUS, CAESARIUS OF ARLES). The angels, too, are like birds because of their sublime and exalted natures (OECUMENIUS, ANDREW OF CAESAREA). The angel in mid-heaven, who may be Michael (APRINGIUS), invites all the angels to share in the joy of God's victory over his enemies (OECUMENIUS). These angels are in "mid-heaven" for they intervene and mediate for the saints of the catholic church (APRINGIUS, ANDREW OF CAESAREA), and they give commands in the light of the Spirit (OECUMENIUS).

Even as delight over the death of one's enemies may be called "food," so also the joy of believers is a "food" (OECUMENIUS). In a similar manner, Christ said that his food was the will of the Father. Those who do the will of the Father will eat the supper of the kingdom; those who are lustful and wicked will eat the supper of torment (ANDREW OF CAESAREA). Although the devil and the antichrist will gather their armies against the Lord and his angels (OECUMENIUS) and against

the saints who follow Jesus (APRINGIUS), the Lord will defeat them more quickly than it takes to speak a word (OECUMENIUS). By the unity of its mind and will the army of Christ will overcome the armies of sins and of heretical opinions, which the devil commands (ANDREW OF CAESAREA).

Finally, no one can resist Christ (APRINGIUS), and so the devil and his entire society will be destroyed (PRIMASIUS). The devil and the antichrist will be condemned to the lake of fire, where they will be immortal and live eternally (OECUMENIUS, ANDREW OF CAESAREA). By a great justice God does not condemn the devil and his followers with the same punishment (OECUMENIUS). The sword is swift, the second death eternal (OECUMENIUS, ANDREW OF CAESAREA). At that time the saints who hungered and thirsted after righteousness will be filled with the full knowledge of divine righteousness (PRIMASIUS).

### 19:17 One Angel Standing in the Sun

**THE ARCHANGEL MICHAEL INTERVENES.**
APRINGIUS OF BEJA: He saw an angel standing upon the sun. The sun upon which this angel is standing is the Faith of the catholic church. Concerning this angel also Daniel spoke as follows:

"At that time shall arise Michael, the great prince who stands before the sons of your people."[1] For just as then this holy archangel stood in the sight of God on behalf of the sons of the ancient people, so now he unceasingly intervenes for the people of the whole catholic church. "And there shall be a time, such as never has been since there was a nation till that time."[2] In the Revelation the holy John says that in that time the birds of the earth shall gather to consume the bodies of the impious. TRACTATE ON THE APOCALYPSE 19.17-18.[3]

### THE ANGELS DESTROY GOD'S ENEMIES.

OECUMENIUS: I think that this holy angel . . . is a certain military herald of the divine army and that he commands all the holy angels in heaven, here called "birds" because they are sublime and fly in the air, to partake of the slaughter of the enemies. To be sure, even one angel was sufficient to destroy an entire army of the enemy, as that one clearly demonstrated who destroyed 185,000 Assyrians in one night.[4] However, he orders all to partake so that all might share in the joy against [God's] enemies. For I think that also these say with the prophet, "Do I not hate them that hate you, O Lord? And have I not wasted away because of your enemies? I have hated them with a perfect hate, and they were counted among my enemies."[5] And since he commanded angels who were flying in mid-heaven, he too was standing in mid-heaven when he gave them orders. For the sun is established in the middle of the seven planets, with three above it and three below it. Either this [is the meaning], or he was giving his commands in the light, which is as it were, in the Spirit and was speaking of the coming slaughter. For the Spirit is the spiritual light, as the prophet teaches when he was discoursing with God the Father, and said, "In your Light, shall we see Light,"[6] that is, in the Spirit we shall see the Son. COMMENTARY ON THE APOCALYPSE 19.17-21.[7]

### BY PREACHING THE CHURCH TRANSFORMS UNBELIEVERS.

PRIMASIUS: The angel refers to the church in her preaching.[8] Rightly it adds "one," for "my dove is only one."[9] In this manner the mystery of unity is preserved. [The angel] is "in the sun," where it may be already brightly visible and not further hidden because of fear. "And with a loud voice it called out." In the loud voice we recognize the liberty of a great trust. . . . In some contexts birds are interpreted by the qualities of evil birds, in other contexts they are interpreted by the qualities of good birds.[10] As earlier the form of an eagle in flight was mentioned,[11] so in this passage those who are spiritual are invited to the feast. Peter, who bore the image of the present church, was told of this feast when it was said to him, "Kill and eat."[12] Since they kill what they had been so that they might become what he is, that is, faithful, they are transformed into the body of the church, and having been planted with the members of the Christ, they reign with them. For whatever we eat, we bring over into our body. COMMENTARY ON THE APOCALYPSE 19.L7.[13]

### AS THOUGH THEY WERE ONLY ONE CHURCH.

CAESARIUS OF ARLES: [The angel in the sun] is the preaching that takes place in the church. . . . Depending on the context, we interpret birds or beasts to represent the good or the wicked. For example, "The wild beast will bless me,"[14] or, "The Lion from the tribe of Judah."[15] In the present passage the birds flying in mid-heaven are the churches that, being considered as one body, it had said was an eagle flying in mid-heaven.[16] EXPOSITION ON THE APOCALYPSE 19.18, HOMILY 17.[17]

### THE ANGELS SHARE THEIR ASCENT AND JOY.

ANDREW OF CAESAREA: We think that this angel is one of the highest of the angels and exhorts the others to rejoice over the punishment of the

---

[1]Dan 12:1. [2]Dan 12:1. [3]CCL 107:75. [4]2 Kings 19:35. [5]Ps 138:21-22 LXX. [6]Ps 36:9 (35:10 LXX). [7]TEG 8:246. [8]This idea comes from Tyconius. [9]Song 6:9. [10]This point comes from Tyconius. [11]See Rev 8:13. [12]Acts 10:13; 11:7. Peter is to "kill and eat" the Gentiles, that is, to convert them. [13]CCL 92:269. [14]Is 43:20. [15]Rev 5:5. [16]See Rev 8:13. [17]PL 35:2446.

sinners and the cessation of sin. He has called the angels "birds" due to the exalted and sublime nature that they have in comparison with ours. In imitation of Christ, their food is the fulfilling of the divine will. They are "in mid-heaven" so that they might share their ascent and joy, just mentioned, with those people who are similar to the angels. For through their mediation there is a way up from the things below, and through them the saints "are caught up to meet the Lord."[18] COMMENTARY ON THE APOCALYPSE 19.17.[19]

**LIKE AN EAGLE IN FLIGHT.** BEDE: [The angel standing in the sun] represents preaching in the church, which shines the more brightly and thunders the more freely the more it is oppressed.... The birds refer to the saints who live a heavenly life, "for wherever the body is, there the eagles will be gathered together."[20] Considered as one body, he had referred to the saints as an eagle flying in mid-heaven.[21] EXPLANATION OF THE APOCALYPSE 19.17.[22]

### 19:17-18 Gather for the Supper of God

**TO THOSE WHO BELIEVE.** OECUMENIUS: "That you might," it says, "eat the flesh of kings." The delight over the death of one's enemies is called "food." Similarly, the Lord also speaks of joy [as food] when he says to his disciples and apostles, "I have food to eat which you do not know."[23] In this way he calls "food" that delight that will come to those who believe. COMMENTARY ON THE APOCALYPSE 19.17-21.[24]

**THE NATIONS BECOME THE BODY OF CHRIST.** CAESARIUS OF ARLES: We know that this in fact happens in the church. For when all nations are incorporated in the church, they are spiritually devoured. Indeed, those who have been devoured by the devil become the body of the devil, while those who have been received by the church are made to be members of Christ. EXPOSITION ON THE APOCALYPSE 19.17-18, HOMILY 17.[25]

**THROUGH OUR WORKS WE DESIRE THE KINGDOM OR TORMENT.** ANDREW OF CAESAREA: That will of God is to be regarded as foremost which is called both his "good pleasure" and the supper most desired by him, namely, that "people be saved and come to the knowledge of the truth" and that they turn and live.[26] But second, it is his will that those who have trusted in themselves suffer punishment. Therefore, Christ said that his food was the will of the Father.[27] In this passage he calls this the "supper of God," since each of those who are present desired through their works either the supper of the kingdom or the supper of torment. Through the eating of flesh it indicates the destruction of everything fleshly and the end of kings and rulers on the earth. It mentions horses, not because they will rise again, but through them it signifies either the excessive desire for women or those who have submitted to evil, or perhaps both. In the riders it symbolizes those who are especially wicked. A little further on it further clarifies, saying, "both free and slave, both great and small." By the free and great it refers to those who sinned freely and willingly, and by the slave and small it indicates those who transgressed in a lesser manner, either because of their intent or because of their age or because of weakness. COMMENTARY ON THE APOCALYPSE 19.17-18.[28]

**THE FAITHFUL WILL EAT THEIR FILL.** BEDE: "Come," it says, "you who hunger and thirst for righteousness,[29] to the supper of the kingdom that is to come, when the anger of the proud has been suppressed and you will eat your fill of the light of the divine righteousness." EXPLANATION OF THE APOCALYPSE 19.18.[30]

### 19:19 The Kings of the Earth Gathered Against Him

---

[18]1 Thess 4:17. [19]MTS 1 Sup 1:211. [20]Mt 24:28. [21]See Rev 8:13. [22]CCL 121A:499. [23]Jn 4:32. [24]TEG 8:246. [25]PL 35:2447. [26]See 1 Tim 2:4; 2 Tim 2:25. [27]Jn 4:34. [28]MTS 1 Sup 1:211-12. [29]See Mt 5:6. [30]CCL 121A:501.

**WAR AGAINST CHRIST AND THE SAINTS.**
APRINGIUS OF BEJA: If you compare the words of
the blessed Daniel, you will find one and the
same thing. "He will come with a great multitude
so that he might exterminate and destroy many."[31]
However, in the Revelation it is said that, when
the kings of the earth and their armies are gathered together, they will war against him who sits
on the horse, that is, against Jesus Christ, and
against his army, that is, against all saints who
follow him. TRACTATE ON THE APOCALYPSE
19.19.[32]

**THE LORD WILL DEFEAT HIS ENEMIES.**
OECUMENIUS: And they waged war against the
Lord and his holy angels, that is, the devil and the
antichrist—for it calls the latter the "false
prophet" of that brutal devil—and the kings who
are arrayed with them. However, they were
defeated more quickly than a word [is spoken].
For what do the divine Scriptures say about
them? Speaking of their sudden destruction, Isaiah says, "Let the ungodly be taken away, that he
not see the glory of the Lord."[33] And the apostle
says, "whom the Lord will slay with the breath of
his mouth."[34] For what is shorter than to breathe
or to blow upon one's enemies? COMMENTARY ON
THE APOCALYPSE 19.17-21.[35]

**CHRIST HAS ONE ARMY.** ANDREW OF CAE-
SAREA: It speaks of the armies allied with the
devil in the plural, because of the many forms of
their sin and their divisions and various opinions.
[By contrast], it speaks of the angelic powers and
of those persons like the angels who follow Christ
in the singular as an army, because of the unity of
their mind and their will which is well-pleasing to
the divine Word. COMMENTARY ON THE APOCA-
LYPSE 19.19.[36]

## 19:20 Thrown into the Lake of Fire

**AGAINST WHOM THE LORD FIGHTS.** APRING-
IUS OF BEJA: And Daniel says, "No one will help
him."[37] When the Lord fights against him, no one

is able to bring assistance to him.... [The two
thrown into the fire were] the devil, the leader of
every evil being, and that one who is most
wicked, who is called the antichrist. TRACTATE
ON THE APOCALYPSE 19.20.[38]

**FOREVER CONDEMNED.** ANDREW OF CAESAREA:
Although these, together with the kings and rulers who trusted them, arrayed themselves against
Christ the Savior, both the antichrist and the
false prophet, who by signs and wonders made
the rogue acceptable, are bested and overcome by
the divine wrath.... Perhaps these will not die
that death that is common to all, but in the twinkling of an eye will be made immortal by being
condemned to the second death of the lake of fire,
just as the apostle spoke of others who "will not
sleep but will be changed, in a moment, in the
twinkling of an eye."[39] These [mentioned by Paul]
will rightly go to judgment. But the two mentioned in this passage, being wicked and against
God, will not go to judgment but to condemnation. And although some do not hold this opinion, we base ourselves on the saying of the apostle
that the antichrist will be destroyed by the spirit
of the command of God[40] and on one of our
teachers who said that some will be found living
after the destruction of the antichrist.[41] We
affirm that those living are those blessed by
Daniel,[42] but that after the destruction of their
power these two will be handed over with their
incorruptible bodies to the fire of Gehenna. This
will be their death and destruction by the divine
command of Christ. COMMENTARY ON THE
APOCALYPSE 19.20.[43]

## 19:21a The Rest Were Slain by the Sword

**A GREAT JUSTICE.** OECUMENIUS: "These two
were thrown alive into the lake of fire. And the

---

[31]Dan 11:44. [32]CCL 107:75. [33]Is 26:10. [34]2 Thess 2:8. [35]TEG
8:246-47. [36]MTS 1 Sup 1:212. [37]Dan 11:45. [38]CCL 107:75.
[39]1 Cor 15:51-52. [40]See 2 Thess 2:8. [41]Reference unknown. [42]Dan
12:2-3. [43]MTS 1 Sup 1:213-14.

rest were slain by the sword." O, what a super-abundance of justice! He does not reckon those responsible for the war and those who were accomplices worthy of the same punishment. Rather, the two, namely, the devil and the anti-christ, were condemned to the fire, in which they will live for eternity—for this is the meaning of their being thrown alive into the fire. The rest are killed by the sword. It is, certainly, much different to give swift justice with the sword than to con-demn to fire. COMMENTARY ON THE APOCALYPSE 19.17-21.[44]

### THE DEVIL AND ALL HIS FOLLOWING WILL BE DESTROYED.

PRIMASIUS: "The beast was captured and with him the false prophet." This refers to the devil and the antichrist or the lead-ers and their entire following. . . . There are two, the head and the body, the devil and his society . . . which shall continue until the end of time. "The rest were slain by the sword . . . which issues from his mouth." It divides the one body into parts, wishing to show both those who have been dead a long time and those whom Christ will find living at his second coming, as we read, "whom the Lord Jesus will slay with the breath of his mouth and destroy him by the brightness of his coming."[45] COMMENTARY ON THE APOCA-LYPSE 19.20-21.[46]

## 19:21b The Birds Were Gorged with Their Flesh

### EATEN BY BIRDS.

APRINGIUS OF BEJA: All who have believed [the beast] will be killed by the judgment of our Lord Jesus Christ and by the breath of his mouth, and their flesh will be put out for the birds of the air and for the beasts of the earth. TRACTATE ON THE APOCALYPSE 19.21.[47]

### FILLED WITH THE KNOWLEDGE OF RIGHT-EOUSNESS.

PRIMASIUS: "And all the birds were gorged with their flesh." We ought not think of this in a carnal manner so that we believe that the saints, who seek higher things, are sated on the flesh of the impious. Rather, when the equity of the divine judgment has been revealed, through which [God] will determine the full number of the elect and so decree that the oth-ers are to be damned, [the saints] are said to be sated with the knowledge of that righteousness after which they hungered and thirsted in this life but were unable to comprehend perfectly. For even Isaiah said of the impious, "And they shall be a complete spectacle to all flesh."[48] I think it is the satiety of the birds that is men-tioned in this passage. Also the apostle admits that he has not yet understood perfectly when he says, "Not that I have already obtained this or am already perfect; but I press on so that I might understand because I have been known by Christ."[49] And so, they shall not rejoice at the damnation of the wicked, but sated by the light of the divine righteousness, they will at that time rejoice. One might interpret the birds in a negative way and regard them as the transgress-ing angels. Having led their followers into destruction, these angels are said to have ful-filled their evil desire and to be filled on the flesh of the lost. Thus, they acquire their satiety from the damnation of those to whom they had offered themselves as guides to error. COMMEN-TARY ON THE APOCALYPSE 19.21.[50]

### EVERY FLESHLY DEED IS LOATHSOME TO THE SAINTS.

ANDREW OF CAESAREA: There are two deaths, the first that of the separation of the soul and body, and the second that of being sent to Gehenna. Concerning those who ally themselves with the antichrist, there is reason to think that they will suffer the first death, that of the flesh, by the sword of God, that is, by his command, and that then the second death will follow. However, should this not be the case, then they will share with those who deceived them the second death, that of eternal torment. The birds are gorged on their flesh.

---

[44]TEG 8:247. [45]2 Thess 2:8. [46]CCL 92:270. [47]CCL 107:76. [48]See Is 66:24. [49]Phil 3:12. [50]CCL 92:270-71.

To this we might add, that just as God spoke to some through Isaiah, "You have become loathsome to me,"[51] so every fleshly deed is tiresome, grievous and loathsome to the saints. COMMEN-

TARY ON THE APOCALYPSE 19.21.[52]

[51]Is 1:14. [52]MTS 1 Sup 1:214.

# 20:1-3 THE DEVIL IS BOUND FOR A THOUSAND YEARS

[1]*Then I saw an angel coming down from heaven, holding in his hand the key of the bottomless pit and a great chain. *[2]*And he seized the dragon, that ancient serpent, who is the Devil and Satan, and bound him for a thousand years, *[3]*and threw him into the pit, and shut it and sealed it over him, that he should deceive the nations no more, till the thousand years were ended. After that he must be loosed for a little while.*

**OVERVIEW:** In Adam the devil had conquered man and held the human race in bondage, man's various sins subjecting man to death (IRENAEUS, AUGUSTINE). That humanity might regain life through the destruction of death (IRENAEUS), Christ came with the Father's power down into the flesh to wage war upon the devil (BEDE). By the sovereign power of his passion and cross (APRINGIUS, ANDREW OF CAESAREA), Christ bound the devil so that humanity might be set free (IRENAEUS) and the devil might be constrained in his power to seduce the elect (AUGUSTINE). In this way the Lord makes those who had been vessels of wrath into vessels of mercy (PRIMASIUS).

Those who serve in the office of ministry are called to bind the devil with the unbreakable bond of the divine judgment (APRINGIUS). During the "day of salvation," which is the time of the Lord's incarnation, the devil was unable to resist the Savior's deity, and the demons feared that the Lord had come to torment them (OECUMENIUS). The binding of Satan in the "day" of the Lord's incarnation continues in the "thousand" years of the church between the passion of Christ and his

coming again to raise the dead and to render judgment (AUGUSTINE). During this time the preaching of the gospel will go into all the world calling all to mature into the fullness of Christ, the "perfect man" (ANDREW OF CAESAREA).

Since the devil is bound and restrained, idol worship is disappearing and pagan temples are being destroyed (ANDREW OF CAESAREA). Yet during this time the devil will also take a deeper hold upon unbelievers causing them to hate the church from the abyss of their hearts. The elect, however, although known to God alone, will not be seduced by the devil to the point of damnation, for God has chosen from eternity to rescue them from the power of darkness (AUGUSTINE). Rather, as though bolted down by the cross, the devil is free only to tempt the saints to the extent the Lord allows (APRINGIUS), and such temptation is not beyond what the saints are able to withstand (CAESARIUS OF ARLES). To be sure, the final assault of the devil against the saints will be fierce. Yet this assault will reveal how great is the victory of the city of God and how immense is the glory of its Liberator and Redeemer. None of the haters of the church, however, will convert to the faith during this time of trial (AUGUSTINE). As the devil and the antichrist pour out their venom of wickedness, may God save us from the punishment prepared for them and grant to us the eternal blessings made ready for those who did not fall (ANDREW OF CAESAREA).

## 20:1 An Angel Came from Heaven

MINISTERS EXERCISE THE KEYS OF THE LORD. APRINGIUS OF BEJA: We must entreat the Lord more earnestly here, lest we consent in error concerning the number of the thousand years or through our own excess nurture error. Rather, [let us entreat the Lord] that he who is called "Faithful" and "True" might keep our faith safe. The Lord himself said at the beginning of this book, "I am the first and the last, and the living one although I was dead; and I have the keys of death and of hades."[1] By the key it speaks of him who bears the office of ministry, so that he might open the pit of the abyss. The great chain is the unbreakable bond of the divine commandment. It is in his hand, which means that he exercises it by work and deed. TRACTATE ON THE APOCALYPSE 20.1.[2]

VESSELS OF MERCY OUT OF VESSELS OF WRATH. PRIMASIUS: We understand the angel coming down from heaven to be our Lord, Jesus Christ, who is called the angel of great counsel. He visited the region of those who are mortal, for as one who is stronger he wished to bind the strong one, so that he might make vessels of mercy out of those who had earlier been vessels of wrath. And he accomplished this through that work that he had promised before when he said, "No one can enter a strong man's house and plunder his wares, unless he first binds the strong man,"[3] that is, the devil. The key of the bottomless pit is the depth of the divine judgments, for "the judgments of God are a great deep."[4] Indeed, to him alone is it known who from the mass of sinners are to be called out into the full number of the elect. COMMENTARY ON THE APOCALYPSE 20.1-2.[5]

CHRIST FREED THOSE BOUND BY THE DEVIL. ANDREW OF CAESAREA: This passage expresses the destruction of the devil that occurred through the passion of our Lord. For through his passion the one who is stronger than [the devil], namely, Christ our God, bound him who seemed to be strong and freed us, who were his spoils, from his hands and condemned him by throwing him into the pit. This is shown by those demons who pleaded that he not send them into the pit. The demonstration that the devil is bound is the disappearance of idol worship, the destruction of pagan temples, the abandonment of the defilement of altars and the knowledge of the will of God throughout the world. COMMENTARY ON THE APOCALYPSE 20.1-3.[6]

CHRIST CAME TO WAGE WAR ON THE DEVIL. BEDE: Summarizing again from the beginning, the author explains more fully what he had earlier spoken: "The beast that you saw was, and is not, and is to ascend from the bottomless pit and go to perdition."[7] Therefore, possessing the power of the Father, the Lord came down into the flesh, for he was going to wage war upon the leader of the world, and when he had been bound, he was going to free his captives. EXPLANATION OF THE APOCALYPSE 20.1.[8]

## 20:2 The Devil Bound for a Thousand Years

THE DESTRUCTION OF DEATH IS HUMANKIND'S SALVATION. IRENAEUS: This is the reason that he put enmity between the serpent and the woman and her seed, with both of them maintaining the enmity: he, the sole of whose foot should be bitten, has power also to tread upon the enemy's head; but the other bit, killed and impeded the steps of humanity until the seed came which was appointed to tread down his head. This was the seed who was born of Mary, of whom the prophet speaks, "You will tread

---

[1]Cf. Rev 1:17-18. [2]CCL 107:77. [3]Mt 12:29. [4]Ps 36:6 (35:7 LXX). [5]CCL 92:271-72. [6]MTS 1 Sup 1:215. [7]Rev 17:8. [8]CCL 121A:503.

upon the asp and the basilisk; you will trample down the lion and the dragon." This means that sin, which was set up and spread out against man, and which rendered him subject to death, would be deprived of its power, along with death, which rules [over people]. The lion, that is, antichrist, who will be rampant against humankind in the latter days, will be trampled down by him. He shall bind "the dragon, that old serpent," and subject him to the power of man, who had been conquered, so that all his might should be trodden down. Now Adam had been conquered, all life having been taken away from him. But the foe was conquered in his turn, and Adam received new life. The last enemy, death, is destroyed, which at the first had taken possession of humankind. Therefore, when man has been liberated, "what is written shall come to pass, Death is swallowed up in victory, O death, where is thy victory? O death, where is thy sting?"[9] This could not be said with justice, if that man, over whom death did first obtain dominion, were not set free. For his salvation is death's destruction. When therefore the Lord vivifies man, that is, Adam, death is at the same time destroyed. AGAINST HERESIES 3.23.7.[10]

**CHRIST RESTRAINS SATAN'S POWER TO SEDUCE THE ELECT.** AUGUSTINE: Our Lord Jesus Christ himself said, "No one can enter the strong man's house and plunder his goods, unless he first binds the strong man."[11] By "strong man" he means the devil, who was able to hold the human race in bondage. By his "goods" that Christ was to "plunder," he means God's future faithful ones whom the devil was keeping for himself because of their ungodliness and various sins. It was for the purpose of binding this strong man that John, in the Apocalypse, saw "an angel coming down from heaven . . . who bound [the ancient serpent] for a thousand years." The angel, that is, checked and repressed his power to seduce and possess those destined to be set free.

Now, the "thousand years" can, so far as I can see, be interpreted in one of two ways. One interpretation is that this event is to take place in the sixth and last millennium (the sixth "day"), the latter span of which is now passing, and that when John spoke of the last part of this millennium as a "thousand years" he was using, figuratively, the whole to indicate a part. (After this "sixth day" will come the "sabbath" that has no evening, namely, the endless repose of the blessed.)

The other interpretation makes the "thousand years" stand for all the years of the Christian era, a perfect number being used to indicate the "fullness of time." For the number one thousand is the cube of ten. Ten times ten equals one hundred, which is already a square, but still a plane figure. To give it depth and make it a cube, one hundred is further multiplied by ten to make a thousand. Now it is true that the number one hundred is sometimes made to stand for "all." Thus, the Lord promised to anyone leaving all things to follow him, "he shall receive a hundredfold."[12] . . . How much more properly, then, does the number one thousand stand for the whole, since it is the cube, whereas one hundred is only the square of ten? In the same way there is no better interpretation of the text, "he has remembered his covenant forever: the word that he commanded to a thousand generations,"[13] than to take "a thousand" as meaning "all" generations. CITY OF GOD 20.7.[14]

**THE CROSS IS THE DESTRUCTION OF THE ENEMY.** APRINGIUS OF BEJA: In Greek letters, one thousand is designated with an "alpha." In the alpha we have the beginning, which is Christ; in the name [of Christ] we have the cross,[15] which is our victory and the destruction of the evil enemy. Therefore, both by the cross of Christ and by the authority of the cross he bound the enemy of the world who deceived those who dwell upon the earth. For to that eternity no time is added, and the eternity of his time will be

---

[9]1 Cor 15:54-55. [10]ANF 1:457*. [11]Mt 12:29. [12]Mt 19:29. [13]Ps 105:8 (104:8 LXX). [14]FC 24:266-67*. Primasius follows Augustine's comments (CCL 92:272-73). [15]Apringius is thinking of the X in the name Χρίστος.

enclosed by no end, nor will there ever be an end to the number of years. And so by the sovereignty of the Lord through the power of the cross he bound him in the abyss. TRACTATE ON THE APOCALYPSE 20.2.[16]

**THE LIFE OF CHRIST IS THE DAY OF SALVATION.** OECUMENIUS: The Revelation does not present to us the millenialism of the atheistic Greeks and the transmigration of souls and the Lethian water and I do not know what other idle talk and nonsense when it says that the devil will be bound for a thousand years and will again be loosed to deceive the nations. Stay away from such destructive teachings, which are suitable to the silliness of the Greeks. What, however, does it say? The prophet says, "For a thousand years in your sight, O Lord, are as yesterday which is past, and as a watch in the night."[17] Therefore, a thousand years in the sight of God is regarded as one day. And in his second letter, the holy Peter says the same thing when he writes, "But do not ignore this one fact, beloved, that with the Lord one day is as a thousand years, and a thousand years as one day."[18] And this is so. Moreover, the holy Isaiah speaks of the entire incarnation of the Lord as a "day," saying, "In the time of favor I have answered you, in a day of salvation I have helped you."[19] And, not only this, the psalmist calls this same "day" also a "morning." For somewhere it says, "This is the day that the Lord has made; let us rejoice and be glad in it," speaking of the joy of our salvation.[20] And somewhere else the psalmist says, "In the morning you will hear my voice; in the morning I will wait upon you and you will see me."[21] For our prayers have become worthy in the sight of God the Father and become acceptable through the mediation and reconciliation of the Lord. And moreover, it says concerning Jerusalem, "God will help her right early."[22] And so, the incarnation of the Lord was a "day" and a "morning," since, as it were, the "sun of righteousness"—for Malachi speaks of him in this way—shone upon us, providing us with the "light of knowledge."[23] And Zechariah foretold of

this divine light when he said, "Whereby the dayspring will visit us from on high, to give light to those who sit in darkness and in the shadow of death."[24] And in agreement with this, the prophet said, "God is the Lord, and he has shined upon us; celebrate the feast with thick branches, even to the horns of the altar."[25] . . .

Since it says that the day is reckoned by God "as a thousand years," and moreover since the sojourn of the Lord on the earth is called a "day," it calls this day a "thousand years," as though with God there were no distinction between one day and a thousand years. At this time, the time of the incarnation of the Lord, the devil was bound, not being able to resist the marks of the Savior's deity. And, therefore, when they sensed that they were spiritually bound, the wicked demons cried out, "What have you to do with us, O Son of the living God? Have you come here to torment us before the time?"[26] And the Lord also made clear their bondage when he said, "Or how can one enter a strong man's house and plunder his goods, unless he first binds the strong man? Then indeed he may plunder his house."[27] Since, therefore, as it was indicated, we understand the incarnation of the Lord and his sojourn upon earth to be called "one day" and a "thousand years" without distinction in the holy Scriptures, such a number is used figuratively. Note, therefore, what the Revelation says. "I saw another angel coming down from heaven holding the key of the bottomless pit and a chain." And it says, when he seized the devil, "he bound him and threw him into the bottomless pit." That which is accomplished spiritually by the Lord is shown to the Evangelist as though on a painted tablet. For since John was a human being and could not see spiritual realities, that which occurred is depicted for him in material terms. . . . "That he should deceive the nations no more," it says, "till the

---

[16]CCL 107:77. [17]Ps 90:4 (89:4 LXX). [18]2 Pet 3:8. [19]Is 49:8. [20]Ps 118:24 (117:24 LXX). [21]See Ps 5:3 (5:4 LXX). [22]Ps 46:5 (45:6 LXX). [23]Hos 10:12. [24]Lk 1:78-79. [25]Ps 118:27 (117:27 LXX). [26]Mt 8:29. [27]Mt 12:29.

thousand years were ended." It was necessary that the sojourn of the Lord on the earth have a somewhat greater support and protection, to prohibit the unclean demons from attacking it in the same way as they did against humankind before the time of the incarnation. COMMENTARY ON THE APOCALYPSE 20.1-3.[28]

**DURING THE TIME OF PREACHING.** ANDREW OF CAESAREA: Also the great Justin says that at the coming of Christ the devil will first learn that he is condemned to the abyss, that is, to the Gehenna of fire.[29] It is, therefore, possible also to understand the sentence of Christ against the devil in the words just spoken. The seer says that the angel administers this sentence, thereby revealing that [the devil] is weaker in power than the ministering powers and showing the vanity of one who insolently opposes him who has rule over all things. For our understanding, he speaks of a "chain," meaning the work of restraining [the devil's] evil. It is in no way good to understand the "thousand years" as referring to a thousand years as such. For when David says "of the word that he commanded for a thousand generations,"[30] we ought not to understand this to mean a hundred years times ten. Rather, David means many [generations] taken as a whole. So also in this case, we regard the number "thousand" to signify either many or that which is complete. If we take it to mean "many," then it refers to the preaching of the gospel into all the world and the sowing of the seeds of piety in the world. [Or] should it mean "complete," then it signifies that during this time, having been released from the life learned from the law, we have been called to the "perfect man," to the measure of the maturity of the fullness of Christ. Therefore, the "thousand years" are the time from the incarnation of the Lord until the arrival of the antichrist. Whether the matter is as we have interpreted it, or the thousand years are one hundred times ten, as some believe, or the thousand years are less than this, this is known to God alone, who knows how long his patience is beneficial to us, and he

determines the continuance of the present life. COMMENTARY ON THE APOCALYPSE 20.1-3.[31]

**THE NAMES OF THE DEVIL INDICATE HIS WICKED WORKS.** BEDE: The devil is interpreted to mean "flowing downwards," although in the Greek it means "accuser," while Satan means "adversary" or "deceiver." Therefore, he is called "dragon" because of the wicked harm he inflicts; he is called "serpent" because of the cunning of his deception; he is called "devil" because of the fall from his previous status; and he is called "Satan" because of the stubbornness of his opposition to the Lord. EXPLANATION OF THE APOCALYPSE 20.2.[32]

## 20:3 Thrown into the Pit

**THE DEVIL SEDUCES NONE OF THE ELECT TO THE POINT OF DAMNATION.** AUGUSTINE: The devil was cast into the "abyss," taken in the sense of the countless number of godless people whose bitter hatred of God's church comes from the abysmal depths of their hearts. The devil was cast into those hearts, not in the sense that he was not there before, but because in proportion as he has been more and more shut out from believing hearts, he has taken still deeper hold upon unbelievers. It is bad enough to be a stranger to God, but gratuitously to hate God's servants is to have the devil's hold take even deeper root. . . . The words "closed it over him" mean that the angel rendered him powerless to escape, that is, forbade him to go beyond bounds. The further verb, "sealed," means, I think, that the angel wants no one to know the secret of who is on the devil's side and who is not. For to be sure, this secret division is absolutely unknowable in this world of time, inasmuch as we have no certainty whether the one who is now upright is going to fall, and the one who is now lying flat is going to rise to

---

[28]TEG 8:248-50. [29]The text of Justin is lost, but this view of Justin is quoted by Irenaeus *Against Heresies* 5.26.2 (ANF 1:555). [30]Ps 105:8 (104:8 LXX). [31]MTS 1 Sup 1:215-16. [32]CCL 121A:503.

righteousness. The nations or people freed from the devil's seductions, in virtue of this restraining and disabling chaining and imprisonment, are those whom he used to lead astray and hold captive but who now belong to Christ. For God chose, before the world was made, to rescue these from the power of darkness and to transfer them into the kingdom of his beloved Son, as Paul says.[33] With respect to others not predestined to eternal life, the devil continues to this very day to lead these people astray and to drag them down into eternal damnation, as every believer knows. And these assertions are not shaken by the fact that the devil often seduces those people, too, who have been reborn in Christ and walk in the ways of God. For "the Lord knows who are his."[34] Of these chosen ones the devil seduces no one to the point of eternal damnation. For the Lord's knowledge of his elect is a divine knowledge and perfect knowledge, wholly unlike the knowledge a person has of his fellow man. Even at the moment of looking, a man can hardly see another man, since he does not see his heart, and he has no foresight at all of how anyone, including himself, is going to turn out in the future. City of God 20.7.[35]

**The Devil Is Free Only by the Lord's Permission.** Apringius of Beja: "And sealed it over him," that is, placed upon it the bolt of the cross so that he might never regain his strength, nor any more seduce the nations, whom the resurrection will restore and make better. Nonetheless, to this explanation the following seems in opposition. "Until the thousand years shall be ended. After that he must be loosed for a little while." However, one can understand this to mean to the extent that the will of our Lord, Jesus Christ, and his command allow. "For a little while," that is, in a moment of time and by the power of the one who commands, [Satan] is dissolved into nothing and at the same time disappears. For if he is loosed so that he might be free, how then does he say, "I saw thrones?" This is similar to the most holy Daniel who speaks in the

same sense as follows: "In that day your people shall be saved, every one whose [name] shall be found written in the book. And many of those who sleep in the dust of the earth shall awake, some to eternal life, and some to disgrace, that they might eternally see."[36] For, how is he released from chains, if the resurrection is already celebrated and if the seats of judgment are seen? Tractate on the Apocalypse 20.3-4.[37]

**What They Are Able to Endure.** Caesarius of Arles: These thousand years are reckoned from the passion of Christ. During them it is not permitted to the devil to do whatever he wishes, for God does not permit his servants to be tempted beyond that which they are able to endure.[38] Exposition on the Apocalypse 20.3, Homily 17.[39]

### 20:3 Loosed for a Little While

**The Final Assault of the Devil.** Augustine: When he is let loose at last, there will be little time left, since, as we read, he and his [followers] will rage with the fullness of strength only for three years and six months. Moreover, the people upon whom he will make war are to be such people as will be beyond overpowering by his open attacks or hidden ambush. If he were never set free, the full measure of his malevolent power would never be known, nor would the full measure of the holy city's staunchness under fire be put to the test. Likewise, we would not have a full view of the good use to which almighty God puts the devil's great wickedness.[40] For example, [we would not see] how God allows him, even though driven from the saints' inmost hearts which cling to God in faith, to tempt the saints somewhat so that they may profit by these external assaults. We would not see how God, further,

---

[33]See Eph 1:4; Col 1:13. [34]2 Tim 2:19. [35]FC 24:267-68. Primasius follows Augustine's comments (CCL 92:273-74). [36]Dan 12:1-2. [37]CCL 107:77-78. [38]See 1 Cor 10:13. [39]PL 35:2447. [40]Bede quotes Augustine to this point in his commentary on Rev 20:3b (CCL 121A:507).

has bound him in those who belong to his camp, to make it impossible for him to spill out and set to work such quantities of his evil power as would topple down countless weak souls destined to increase and fill the church. These include already believing people whose constancy the devil would smash, and people destined to believe whom he would frighten from the faith. At last, God will loose him to the end that all people may see how mighty a foe God's city had overcome— all to the immense glory of its Liberator, Helper, Redeemer. . . . However, it may be asked whether, during the last three years and a half in which the unleashed devil will stage his all-out offensive, any one of these haters [of Christians] is to turn at last to the faith he formerly spurned? Think of the text: "How can anyone enter the strong man's house and plunder his goods, unless he first binds the strong man?"[41] How can these words remain true if the devil can be dispossessed just as well when he is loosed? The text seems to compel us to believe that the brief interval in question will witness no new conversions to Christianity, but that the devil will do battle only with those who are already Christians at the time of his unleashing—and, of course, any whom he may win over to his side will not have been numbered among the predestined sons of God. CITY OF GOD 20.8.[42]

### The Time Until the Consummation Is Short.
OECUMENIUS: "[The devil] must be loosed for a little while." What does he mean by "a little while"? He means the time between the incarnation of the Lord and the consummation of the present age. When measured and compared with that which is past and that which is future, this is "little," even though it should seem to be great. For if our Lord appears bodily at the "last" hour, indeed at the "eleventh" hour, as the faith of the holy writings claim, the time until the consummation is properly called "little." After [this] the devil will again be bound, this time with an eternal and neverending bond. However, although he has been loosed, bind yet again, O Lord, his works of cunning against us. For you are our King, and it is proper to give you glory forever. Amen. COMMENTARY ON THE APOCALYPSE 20.1-3.[43]

### The All-Merciful God Will Save Us.
ANDREW OF CAESAREA: After this, the antichrist will put the whole world into confusion, bearing in himself the activity of the evil one and pouring out upon humankind the wine of his venomous wickedness, since he knows that his torment is without end. Redeeming us from his works, the all-merciful God will save us from the punishment that has been "prepared for him and his angels,"[44] and he will manifest those who partake of the eternal blessings that are being made ready for those who opposed him [antichrist] even to the shedding of blood. For it is proper to ascribe to him mercy for those who trusted him, and he is worthy of thanksgiving and worship from every holy power, together with the Father and the life-giving Spirit forever and ever. Amen. COMMENTARY ON THE APOCALYPSE 20.1-3.[45]

---

[41]Mt 12:29. [42]FC 24:271-73. [43]TEG 8:250. [44]See Mt 25:41. [45]MTS 1 Sup 1:216-17.

# 20:4 THE RIGHTEOUS REIGN WITH CHRIST FOR A THOUSAND YEARS

*[4]Then I saw thrones, and seated on them were those to whom judgment was committed. Also I saw the souls of those who had been beheaded for their testimony to Jesus and for the word of God, and who had not worshiped the beast or its image and had not received its mark on their foreheads or their hands. They came to life, and reigned with Christ a thousand years.*

**OVERVIEW:** During the life of the incarnate Lord, the apostles in a partial way rendered judgment, for they condemned those responsible for the death of the Christ (OECUMENIUS). Moreover, teaching thrones were given to them for the enlightenment of the nations, even as in the age to come thrones will be given to them for the judgment of those who rejected their teaching (ANDREW OF CAESAREA). However, even now in the present age the church is the kingdom of Christ in which the saints reign with Christ. These saints are themselves the kingdom of Christ, while the "weeds," although in the church, do not even now reign with Christ. The temporal church in which the saints reign is of the living and of the departed saints, and this is indicated by the commemoration of the saints in the liturgy and by the necessity of baptism and of penance (AUGUSTINE).

Already at the time of Christ many who refused to conspire against Christ were martyred and their property confiscated (OECUMENIUS). The martyrs of the church do reign in death with a special splendor (AUGUSTINE), and the authority they have over the demons is evident in their miracles and their healings (ANDREW OF CAESAREA). However, the promises of God are not only for the martyrs and for the persecuted. Those who remain firm in their faith and do not succumb to idolatry will also be honored along with the martyrs of Christ (CYPRIAN). Similarly, those who live according to their faith by refusing the hypocrisy of deception and bad morals will reign with Christ (AUGUSTINE). Finally, even as those who followed Christ lived the reasonable life and defeated demons with works of power (OECUMENIUS), so at the resurrection of the dead the martyrs and all faithful will reign with Christ by the sign of Christ's most glorious passion (APRINGIUS).

### 20:4a Those to Whom Judgment Was Committed

**THOSE REIGN WITH CHRIST WHO ARE HIS KINGDOM. AUGUSTINE:** During the "thousand years" when the devil is bound, the saints also reign for a "thousand years" and, doubtless, the two periods are identical and mean the span between Christ's first and second coming. For not only in that future kingdom to which Christ referred in the words, "Come, blessed of my Father, take possession of the kingdom prepared for you,"[1] but even now those saints reign with him in some authentic though vastly inferior fashion. To them he said, "Behold, I am with you all days, even to the consummation of the world."[2] . . . This, to be sure, is the period in which the scribe instructed in the kingdom of heaven brings forth from his storeroom things new and old, as I mentioned above.[3] So, too, the reapers are to gather up out of the church the weeds, which he allows to grow intermixed with the wheat up to the time of harvest. . . . This

---

[1]Mt 25:34. [2]Mt 28:20. [3]See *City of God* 20.4 (FC 24:255-56).

certainly cannot be the kingdom that is to be utterly without scandals.[4] The kingdom from which scandals are gathered out, then, must be the church on earth. . . . The mixed kingdom must be the church, such as she exists in her temporal stage, while the unmixed kingdom is the church such as she will be when she is to contain no evildoer. Consequently the church, even in this world, here and now, is the kingdom of Christ and the kingdom of heaven. Here and now Christ's saints reign with him, although not in the way they are destined to reign hereafter; but the "weeds" do not reign with him, even now, though they grow along with the "wheat" in the church. . . . Those alone reign with Christ whose presence in his kingdom is such that they themselves are his kingdom. . . . Now it is of this militant stage of the kingdom, during which there is still war with our enemy, alternating victory over, and defeat before, our evil inclinations, that the Apocalypse speaks. The "thousand years" are to last until we come to that kingdom, free of the foe, where the saints reign in fullest peace. . . . After mentioning the devil's chaining for a thousand years and his brief interval of freedom to follow, John sums up the activity of and in the church during the "thousand years": "And I saw thrones, and men sat upon them and judgment was given to them." Now there is no question of the last judgment in this verse. The thrones and the enthroned people are the prelates who govern the church here and now. And the judgment is best interpreted as the one contained in the words, "Whatever you bind on earth shall be bound also in heaven, and whatever you loose on earth shall be loosed also in heaven."[5] City of God 20.9.[6]

**The Apostles Judged Those Who Did Not Believe.** Oecumenius: He explains yet more fully the life of the incarnate Lord, namely, that which now meets us in the vision. For it says, "Then I saw thrones, and seated on them were those to whom judgment was committed." He sees the holy apostles to whom the promise was made that they would "sit on twelve thrones, judging the twelve tribes of Israel."[7] Although this will be fulfilled more completely in the coming age, it did happen partially at the time of the incarnation. For when they believed in the Lord and shared in a multitude of blessings, they condemned those who did not wish to come to the faith and those who, although they had been taught by the grace given to the apostles, did not advance to the same piety but rather plotted his death on the cross. Commentary on the Apocalypse 20.4-8.[8]

**Condemnation for Those Who Reject the Gospel.** Andrew of Caesarea: Indeed, the teaching thrones had already been given to the holy apostles through whom the nations have been enlightened. However, thrones will also be given according to the purpose of God in the age to come for the condemnation of those who rejected the preaching of the gospel. As David said, "For there the tribes went up, the tribes of the Lord, as a testimony for Israel," and again, "For there are set thrones for judgment."[9] Commentary on the Apocalypse 20.4.[10]

### 20:4b *The Souls Who Had Been Beheaded*

**The Firm in Faith and Life Will Be Honored.** Cyprian: The rewards of divine promise do not await only the persecuted and the slain. If passion is lacking in the faithful, yet if the faith has remained sound and unconquered and, after forsaking all his possessions and so continuing in this way, shows that he follows Christ, he also is honored among the martyrs of Christ, as he himself says: "There is no one who leaves house, or land, or parents, or brothers or wife or children for the sake of the kingdom of God who shall not receive much more in the present

---

[4]Augustine has quoted Mt 13:39-41. [5]Mt 16:19; 18:18. [6]FC 24:274-77*. Primasius follows the argument of Augustine (CCL 92:275-76). [7]Mt 19:28. [8]TEG 8:251-52. [9]Ps 122:4-5 (121:4-5 LXX). [10]MTS 1 Sup 1:218.

time, and in the age to come life everlasting."[11] In the same way in the Apocalypse he says: "And I saw the souls of those who had been beheaded because of the name of Jesus and the Word of God." And when he had put those beheaded in the first place, he added saying, "And who did not worship the image of the beast, and did not accept his mark upon their foreheads or in their hands." And all these he joins together as seen by him in the same place and says, "And they came to life and reigned with Christ." He says that all live and reigned with Christ, not only those who have been slain. He is referring to those who stand in the firmness of their faith and who in the fear of God have not adored the image of a beast and have not consented to his deadly sacrilegious edicts. EXHORTATION TO MARTYRDOM 5.12.[12]

### THE CHURCH REIGNS WITH CHRIST. AUGUSTINE:
We are to understand as implied by the words that come further on that these souls of the martyrs "reigned with Christ a thousand years"—of course, not yet reunited with their bodies. For the souls of the faithful departed are not divorced from Christ's kingdom, which is the temporal church. If they were, we should not be mindful of them at God's altar in the communion of the body of Christ; nor would there be any point in hastening one's baptism in time of danger, lest one die unbaptized; nor in seeking reconciliation, when one has been cut off from Christ's body by a sinful conscience or by the church's penitential discipline. Why do we go to all this trouble if the faithful departed are not still Christ's members? We may be sure, then, that their souls reign with him, just as their bodies will in time to come, even while the thousand years are rolling on. . . . We conclude, therefore, that even now, in time, the church reigns with Christ both in its living and departed members. "For to this end Christ died," says Paul, "and rose again, that he might be Lord both of the dead and of the living."[13] If John mentions only the souls of the martyrs, that is because they who have bat-

tled for the truth unto death reign in death with a special splendor. But as the part is here used for the whole, we know that the words apply to the remaining faithful who belong to the same church, which is Christ's kingdom. CITY OF GOD 20.9.[14]

### BLESSED ARE THOSE WHO DID NOT CONSPIRE AGAINST CHRIST. OECUMENIUS:
And it says, "and the souls of those who had been beheaded for their testimony to Jesus and for the word of God." These, in common with the others, he saw sitting on thrones and judging the rest of humankind. It says that they were "beheaded," for they had been killed by the axe. He is speaking figuratively about the members of those who died for the sake of the faith in Christ and especially those who were martyred for the faith. For to be sure, [the Jews] caused them to be thrown outside the synagogues with much revilement and they confiscated for themselves their property, as the wise apostle testifies,[15] for they believed completely in Christ. The Lord also spoke about these persons: "Blessed are you when men revile you and persecute you and utter all kinds of evil against you falsely on my account."[16] And following the thought of the narrative and holding captive every idea in obedience to the holy Scriptures, you will consider those who did not worship the beast or receive his mark and his image to be those who did not conspire with the rest of the Jews in their plots against the Lord, nor [did they wish] to obey the suggestions of the devil, who is hated of God. For this would be to worship him and also his image. The imprint of his will upon the hearts of the Jews he calls an "image," which he also calls a "mark," which encompasses both their guiding and their active principles. For the head, of which the forehead is a member, is representative of the guiding

---

[11]Lk 18:29-30. [12]FC 36:342-43. [13]Rom 14:9. [14]FC 24:277-78. Primasius follows the argument of Augustine (CCL 92:276). [15]See Heb 10:34. [16]Mt 5:11.

principle, while the hand is representative of the active principle. COMMENTARY ON THE APOCALYPSE 20.4-8.[17]

**MARTYRS CONTINUE TO DEMONSTRATE THEIR POWER OVER THE DEMONS.** ANDREW OF CAESAREA: Judgment, that is, the authority to judge, was given to the rest of the saints, namely, to the martyrs who suffered for Christ and did not receive the mark of that spiritual beast, the devil, that is, the image of his apostasy. And as we can see, even to the present time they judge the demons by this authority, for they reign with Christ until the consummation of the present age and are honored by pious kings and faithful rulers and demonstrate their God-given power against every bodily weakness and demonic activity. It is clear that the devil, the antichrist and the false prophet share with one another both their deeds and their names, since each of them is called "beast," and the dragon, clearly Satan, is shown with seven heads and ten horns with as many diadems. Moreover, the beast that comes up out of the sea, clearly the antichrist, appears in a similar form and testifies to the same will and activity for the destruction of those who have been deceived. Those who have been freed from this will reign with Christ in the manner just mentioned until his second coming, and after that they will enjoy more abundantly the promises of God. COMMENTARY ON THE APOCALYPSE 20.4.[18]

**THEY REIGN WITH CHRIST WHO REFUSE FALSE FAITH AND BAD MORALS.** AUGUSTINE: This verse should be applied to both the living and the dead. . . . As to the identity of the beast in question, there is need of very careful study. Nevertheless, consistently with sound faith, one may take it to be the godless city as opposed to the city of God, men and women without faith as opposed to those who believe. The beast's "image," I think, is his deception as found, for example, in such people as profess the faith yet live like pagans. For they pretend to be what, in fact, they are not, and are called Christians, not because of full faith but of false face. The beast possesses, in addition to the openly avowed enemies of Christ's name and of his glorious city, the "weeds" that are marked for uprooting from his kingdom, the church, at the end of the world. Those who do not follow the beast or his image are surely those who follow Paul's admonition: "Do not bear the yoke with unbelievers."[19] Their not worshiping means their not agreeing with, their not becoming subjects to, unbelievers. Their not accepting his "mark" upon their "foreheads" and "hands" means that they refuse the stigma of false faith and bad morals. Such people, alive or dead, keep themselves aloof from such evils and so reign with Christ, even now, in a fashion befitting the passage of time, throughout this whole era indicated by the "thousand years." CITY OF GOD 20.9.[20]

### 20:4c They Came to Life

**ALL MARTYRS AND FAITHFUL REIGN BY THE SIGN OF THE CROSS.** APRINGIUS OF BEJA: The souls of all the martyrs and of all the Christian faithful who rise again and awaken from the dust of the earth shall reign, it says, with Christ for a thousand years. That is, they will reign by the sign of the cross and by the pre-eminence of the Lord's passion. TRACTATE ON THE APOCALYPSE 20.4.[21]

**THOSE WHO FOLLOWED CHRIST.** OECUMENIUS: "They came to life and reigned with Christ a thousand years." He again speaks of a "thousand years" to indicate, as we said above, the sojourn of the Lord on the earth. During this time they lived the spiritual life and reigned with Christ, confronting demons and giving honor to suffering and bringing about a great many mira-

---

[17]TEG 8:252-53. [18]MTS 1 Sup 1:218-19. [19]2 Cor 6:14. [20]FC 24:278-79. Primasius follows the argument of Augustine (CCL 92:276-77). [21]CCL 107:78.

cles. Not that one is only to be present with Christ, the King of glory, one should also reign with him. And so it is spoken by the prophet concerning them: "When the heavenly One scatters kings upon it, they will become white as snow on Zalmon."[22] COMMENTARY ON THE APOCALYPSE 20.4-8.[23]

---

[22]Ps 67:15 LXX. [23]TEG 8:253.

---

# 20:5-6 THE FIRST RESURRECTION

[5]*The rest of the dead did not come to life until the thousand years were ended. This is the first resurrection.* [6]*Blessed and holy is he who shares in the first resurrection! Over such the second death has no power, but they shall be priests of God and of Christ, and they shall reign with him a thousand years.*

---

**OVERVIEW:** The apostle Paul speaks of two trumpets, indicating two resurrections. The first resurrection is that of the saints and the believing Jews, who will reign with Christ a thousand years. The second is the final resurrection of the sinners and impious, who will suffer the second death of damnation in hell (VICTORINUS). One might, however, understand the first resurrection to be that of faith (OECUMENIUS) by which one passes from death unto life (AUGUSTINE). For although he was largely hidden in the Old Testament and even during the time of the incarnation, the divine Holy Spirit became manifest and perceptible when he led many to receive faith in Christ (OECUMENIUS). In Adam all are dead in sins and trespasses (CAESARIUS OF ARLES), but the holy person whom Christ baptizes with the Holy Spirit (ORIGEN) receives the first resurrection through the remission of sins in baptism (CAESARIUS OF ARLES, ANDREW OF CAESAREA). Those who participate in this first resurrection by rising from the death of sin and persevering in the new life (AUGUSTINE) will not suffer the second death of the eternal punishment for sin (AUGUSTINE, OECUMENIUS). Christ baptizes the holy man in the Spirit, the sinner in fire. Those who sin after the first resurrection of the Holy Spirit, however, must receive another resurrection through the purifying baptism of fire (ORIGEN). Those who rise to the second death of unending torment (ANDREW OF CAESAREA) will remain as though dead, for there is no true life where there is no joy and happiness (AUGUSTINE, APRINGIUS). Moreover, in the second death pain afflicts but never destroys, so that the corruption of death continues without itself dying (AUGUSTINE). Those who rise to be eternally with Christ will reign with him in the strength of the cross and in the sovereignty of his might (APRINGIUS). As now the saints reign with Christ by keeping themselves free of temptation (CAESARIUS OF ARLES) and reign as priests in him who is the true Priest (AUGUSTINE), so then when things eternal arrive and temporal reality passes away, the saints will possess the kingdom of Christ more certainly (ANDREW OF CAESAREA). And so, there is a first death which is physical and temporary, and a second death, which is spiritual and eternal (OECUMENIUS, ANDREW OF CAESAREA). And there is a first resurrection, which is that of faith, and a second resurrection, which is universal and for all, even for the unwilling (Oecumenius).

## 20:5-6 The First Resurrection

**Those Who Did Not Pass from Death to Life.** Augustine: Compare [John's] other words: "The hour is coming, and now is here, when the dead shall hear the voice of the Son of God, and those who hear shall live"[1]—implying that the rest of the dead (who do not hear) will "not come to life." The added clause, "until the thousand years were finished," means that during that time "the rest of the dead" did "not come to life" as they should by passing over from death to life. Therefore, in the day of the body's resurrection, they will go forth from their tombs, not to life but to "judgment," meaning that condemnation that is called the second death. Anyone at all who will have failed to "come to life" during this millennium, this whole era of the first resurrection, by not hearing "the voice of the Son of God" and by not passing from death to life will certainly, when the second and bodily resurrection comes, pass to the second death, body and soul together. City of God 20.9.[2]

**They Are as Though Dead.** Apringius of Beja: "Until the thousand years were ended," that is, until such time as the sacrament of the faith and the mystery of the cross is perfected in them and that those who are beginning to flourish might appear in their eternal blessedness. "The rest of the dead did not come to life." He did not say, "they did not arise again," but that they did not come to life, because without joy and happiness, and without the reward of eternity, in their torments they shall be regarded as though dead.[3] "This is the first resurrection." That is to say, the happiness of the saints and their reward; for it is said to be the "first" because of its splendor and its preeminence. Tractate on the Apocalypse 20.5.[4]

**Most Come to Faith by the Power of the Divine Spirit.** Oecumenius: "The rest of the dead did not come to life until the thousand years were ended." He calls those "dead" who remained in unbelief. The Lord also spoke of these when he said, "Let the dead bury their own dead."[5] To be sure, the unbelievers did not live the reasonable life until the time of the incarnation, which is the thousand years, was completed. But after this they lived. How so? By the visitation and presence of the Holy Spirit. For then most of the Jews believed in Christ, as many as did not believe in him when he was living among them in the flesh. This was accomplished in a most divine manner, not as the human mind might have expected. For while in the Old Testament the Son was proclaimed and was made known through his incarnation and his many signs and wonders, the Holy Spirit was not yet clearly revealed to humankind. In the Old Testament there was only talk concerning him, as there was of the Son, but there was no manifest and perceptible activity, which especially leads people to faith. He was, however, perceived by those who progressed into the depths of the divine purpose, For to be sure, everything which is done and accomplished is produced by the Holy Trinity. The Lord establishes this clearly when he says somewhere, "The Father has given me commandment what to say and what to speak"[6] and again, "I am able to do nothing from myself,"[7] referring to whatever happens in the Trinity; and again from John, "The Son of man can do nothing from himself, unless he sees his Father doing it,"[8] and somewhere he vigorously claims, "If I by the Spirit of God cast out demons."[9] Since, as we said, there was no perceptible activity of the Holy Spirit among humankind, it was determined by plan that virtually all people would receive faith in Christ by the presence and power of the Paraclete and of God

---

[1]Jn 5:25. [2]FC 24:279. Primasius follows the argument of Augustine (CCL 92:277). [3]The text of CCL 107 excludes the comment on "the rest of the dead" as not authentic to Apringius. We have chosen to follow SEHL. [4]SEHL 11:59. [5]Mt 8:22. [6]Jn 12:49. [7]Jn 5:30. [8]Jn 5:19. [9]Mt 12:28.

the Father, so that it might be clearly evident to all that he also is of the same substance and of equal power with the Father and the Son. To be sure, we are given no information that during the time of the incarnation any more than 120 had come to faith. The Acts [of the Apostles] numbers those who had gathered together in the upper room to have been so many.[10] But since the power of the Lord's teaching had reached many, certainly the conviction concerning this coming of the Spirit would have been preserved [among them]. Just as when seed is scattered upon the ground and the rains come and the sun shines upon it, all the seeds that had remained hidden and concealed in the ground until this time now start to spring up and become visible, for they had been simply kept in the earth, so also did it happen at the visitation of the Holy Spirit. All those to whom the teaching of the Lord had been thrown [as seed] began to spring up unto faith. Therefore, it is said with greater accuracy in the Revelation, "the rest of the dead did not come to life until the thousand years were ended." COMMENTARY ON THE APOCALYPSE 20.4-8.[11]

### CHRIST BAPTIZES THE HOLY PERSON IN THE SPIRIT, THE SINNER IN FIRE. ORIGEN: Jesus

baptizes "in the Holy Spirit and in fire,"[12] not the same person "in the Holy Spirit and in fire," but the holy person "in the Holy Spirit," while another person, after he has believed, after he has been deemed worthy of the Holy Spirit and after he has sinned again, Jesus washes in fire. So . . . it is not the same person who is baptized by Jesus in the Holy Spirit and in fire. Blessed, then, is the one who is baptized in the Holy Spirit and does not need the baptism by fire, but three times unhappy is that person who has need to be baptized in fire, though Jesus takes care of both of them. For "a shoot from the stump of Jesse will come forth, and a branch will grow out of the root,"[13] a shoot for those who are punished, a branch for the righteous. So God is a consuming fire and God is light, a consuming fire to sinners, a light to the just and holy ones. And blessed is he

"who shares in the first resurrection," he who has kept the baptism of the Holy Spirit. Who is he who is saved in another resurrection? He who needs the baptism from fire, when he comes before that fire and the fire tests him, and when that fire finds wood, hay and stubble to burn. HOMILIES ON JEREMIAH 2.3.1-3.[14]

### THE FIRST RESURRECTION AND THE FINAL RESURRECTION. VICTORINUS OF PETOVIUM:

Everyone should know that the "scarlet devil" and all of his rebellious angels are shut up in the Tartarus of Gehenna[15] at the Lord's coming, and that after one thousand years they are released because of the nations who will have served the antichrist so that they alone might perish and therefore have merited [such a punishment]. Thereupon the universal judgment will occur. Therefore it says, "The dead [who are written in the Book of Life] came to life, and they will reign with Christ a thousand years. This is the first resurrection. Blessed and holy is he who shares in the first resurrection.[16] Over such the second death has no power." Concerning this resurrection he says, "And I saw the Lamb standing and with him—that is, standing[17] with him—144,000."[18] Namely, these are those from among the Jews who will come to believe at the end of time through the preaching of Elijah and who, the Spirit testifies, are chaste not only in body but also in tongue.[19] And therefore, it is mentioned above that the twenty-four elders had said, "We give thanks to you, Lord God, that you have begun to reign, and the nations have become enraged."[20] At the time of this first resurrection will also be that future, beautiful city that this

---

[10]Acts 1:15. [11]TEG 8:253-55*. [12]Lk 3:16. [13]Is 11:1. [14]FC 97:26-27. Those who sin seriously after receiving the Holy Spirit in baptism must receive also a baptism of purifying fire, and then "another" resurrection. See also Homilies on Jeremiah 16.6 (FC 97:173-74); 20.3 (FC 97:227). [15]See 2 Pet 2:4-5. [16]Irenaeus also understands the first resurrection to be to an earthly interregnum of a thousand years (Against Heresies 5.34.2; ANF 1:564). He combines Rev 20:5-6 with Is 30:25-26; Is 58:14; Lk 12:37-38; Is 6:11; Dan 7:27; Dan 12:13. [17]Victorinus understands "standing" to refer to the resurrection of the saints from the dead. [18]Rev 14:1. [19]See Rev 14:4-5. [20]See Rev 11:17-18.

writing has described. Also Paul spoke in this manner to the church in Macedonia concerning this first resurrection: "For this we declare to you by the word of God, that at the trumpet of God the Lord himself will descend from heaven to arouse [the dead from sleep]. And the dead in Christ will rise first; then we who are alive shall be caught up together with them in the clouds to meet the Lord in the air, and so we shall always be with the Lord."[21] We have heard that he speaks of a trumpet. We observe that in another place the apostle mentions another trumpet. He says to the Corinthians, "At the last trumpet the dead will rise"—they become immortal— "and we shall be changed."[22] He says that the dead will rise immortal in order to suffer their punishments; however, it is clear that we will be changed and clothed in glory. When, therefore, we hear that there is a "last trumpet," we must understand that there has also been a first trumpet. Now these are the two resurrections. Therefore, however many shall not rise previously in the first resurrection and reign with Christ over the world—over all the nations—they will rise at the last trumpet after the thousand years, that is, at the final resurrection among the impious, the sinners and those guilty in various ways. Rightly, then, does the passage continue by saying, "Blessed and holy is he who shares in the first resurrection; over such the second death has no power." Now, the second death is damnation in hell. COMMENTARY ON THE APOCALYPSE 20.1-2.[23]

**THOSE WHO RISE FROM SIN AND PERSEVERE IN THEIR NEW LIFE.** AUGUSTINE: Anyone who thus participates [in the first resurrection] is one who not only rises from the death of sin but also perseveres in his newfound life. "Over these," says John, "the second death has no power." Therefore, it has power over all the others of whom he said above: "The rest of the dead did not come to life till the thousand years were finished." They may have lived long enough in their bodies, in the period John calls the "thousand years," but they did not rise from the binding

death of their ungodliness. If they had, they would have shared in the first resurrection and thus escaped the power of the second death. CITY OF GOD 20.9.[24]

**IN THE SECOND DEATH PAIN AFFLICTS BUT NEVER DESTROYS.** AUGUSTINE: Whoever are not liberated from that mass of perdition (brought to pass through the first man) by the one Mediator between God and humankind, they will also rise again, each in his own flesh, but only that they may be punished together with the devil and his angels. Whether these people will rise again with all their faults and deformities, with their diseased and deformed members—is there any reason for us to labor such a question? For obviously the uncertainty about their bodily form and beauty need not weary us, since their damnation is certain and eternal. And let us not be moved to inquire how their body can be incorruptible if it can suffer—or corruptible if it cannot die. For there is no true life unless it be lived in happiness; no true incorruptibility save where health is unscathed by pain. But where an unhappy being is not allowed to die, then death itself, so to say, dies not; and where pain perpetually afflicts but never destroys, corruption goes on endlessly. This state is called, in the Scripture, "the second death." ENCHIRIDION 92.[25]

**THE SAINTS SHALL REIGN IN THE STRENGTH OF THE CROSS.** APRINGIUS OF BEJA: He indicates that those over whom the second death has power did not come to life. To be sure, they have been resurrected unto the second death, that is, they have been damned to the lake of fire, even as it is stated in the psalms: "As though living he swallows them as in anger."[26] Indeed, concerning those over whom the second death has no power, it says, "they shall be priests of God and they shall reign with him a thousand years." All those

---

[21]1 Thess 4:15-17. [22]1 Cor 15:52. [23]CSEL 49:138-44. [24]FC 24:279. [25]LCC 7:393. See also *Sermon* 231 (*WSA* 3 7:19-20); 306 (*WSA* 3 9:19-20). [26]Ps 57:9 (57:10 LXX).

who shall have been in the congregation of the saints, shall be called saints, and they shall be priests of Christ our God, and they shall reign with him in the strength of the cross and in the sovereignty of his might. TRACTATE ON THE APOCALYPSE 20.6.[27]

**A FIRST AND SECOND DEATH, A FIRST AND SECOND RESURRECTION.** OECUMENIUS: "This is," it says, "the first resurrection," clearly that of faith. For the second resurrection will be the universal resurrection of the body. Therefore, "blessed is he who shares in the first resurrection!" For we will all take part in the second resurrection, even those who are unwilling. Upon those who share in the first resurrection, that is, upon the faithful, "the second death has no power." What sort of death is this second death? Clearly it is that of sin and of the subsequent punishment. For just as he spoke of a first and a second resurrection, so also is there a first and a second death. The first death is physical and results in the separation of the soul and the body. The second death . . . is spiritual and is caused by sin. Of this death also the Lord spoke: "Do not fear those who kill the body; rather fear him who can destroy both soul and body in hell."[28] COMMENTARY ON THE APOCALYPSE 20.4-8.[29]

**WE RISE IN THE FIRST RESURRECTION THROUGH BAPTISM.** CAESARIUS OF ARLES: [The first resurrection] is that by which we rise through baptism. As the apostle says, "If you have been raised with Christ, seek the things which are above."[30] And again he says, "living as [those who have been brought to life] from the dead."[31] For sin is death, as the apostle says, "when you were dead through trespasses and sins."[32] Therefore, just as the first death is in this life because of sin, so also the first resurrection is in this life through the remission of sins. EXPOSITION ON THE APOCALYPSE 20.5, HOMILY 18.[33]

**THE FIRST LIFE AND DEATH ARE TEMPORARY; THE SECOND LIFE AND DEATH ARE**

**ETERNAL.** ANDREW OF CAESAREA: From the holy Scriptures we are taught that there are two lives and two deaths. The first life, which is after the transgression of the commandment, is temporary and fleshly. The [second] life is eternal and is promised to the saints because of Christ's obedience to the divine commandments. Likewise, there are two deaths. The first is that of the flesh and is temporary. The other is eternal and is the reward for sins. It occurs in the age to come; this is the Gehenna of fire. We also know a distinction among the dead. There are the accused, of whom Isaiah wrote, "The dead shall not see life."[34] These are those persons who by their deeds bring upon themselves both stench and death. There are . . . the praiseworthy, who in Christ put to death the deeds of the body and crucified themselves with Christ and died to the world. The dead who are rejected, who were not buried with Christ and did not rise with him through baptism but who remained in that death which comes through sins, they shall not live with him until the completion of the thousand years, that is, that perfect number that extends from his first appearance until his second, glorious appearance. . . . Having been born only from the earth and not from the Spirit, these return to the earth. Their death becomes the beginning of the punishment coming to them. However, those who have a portion in the first resurrection, that is, in the rising from thoughts that bring death and from dead works, these are blessed, for the second death, that is, the unending torment, shall have no power over them. COMMENTARY ON THE APOCALYPSE 20.5-6.[35]

## 20:6 They Shall Be Priests of God

**AS MEMBERS OF THE ONE PRIEST, ALL CHRISTIANS ARE PRIESTS.** AUGUSTINE: Here he is speaking not just of bishops and of presbyters (who are now priests in the church) but of all Christians. For just as we call all of them Christs

---

[27]CCL 107:78-79. [28]Mt 10:28. [29]TEG 8:255. [30]Col 3:1. [31]See Rom 6:13. [32]Eph 2:1. [33]PL 35:2448. [34]Is 26:14. [35]MTS 1 Sup 1:219-20.

by reason of their mystical chrism, we call them all priests insomuch as they are members of the one Priest. Peter speaks of them as a "chosen race, a royal priesthood."[36] Surely, too, this text implies, however briefly and incidentally, that Christ is God. The words "priests of God and Christ" mean priests of the Father and Son, even though it was in his servant form that Christ was both made Son of man and also ordained a priest forever according to the order of Melchizedek. CITY OF GOD 20.10.[37]

**THOSE WHO KEEP THEMSELVES FROM TEMPTATION.** CAESARIUS OF ARLES: The Spirit repeats what he had written before, that the church is going to reign a thousand years in this age until the end of the world. It is clear that no one ought doubt about the eternal rule when the saints rule even in this present age. For those are rightly said to reign who with God's aid govern well both themselves and others in the temptations of the present world. EXPOSITION ON THE APOCALYPSE 20.6, HOMILY 18.[38]

**THOSE WHO NOW REIGN WITH CHRIST.** ANDREW OF CAESAREA: [Those who have a portion of the first resurrection] shall serve as

priests and shall reign with Christ, as we see, for the thousand years as they are interpreted by us, until Satan is loosed and deceives the nations. Not that these will then be deprived of the kingdom. Rather, they will possess it more certainly and more manifestly with the passing of temporal reality and the arrival of things eternal. For the time between the loosing of the devil and the verdict against him and his punishment in gehenna is short. So, that "they shall be priests of God and of Christ" ought to be regarded as the restoration of former things. . . . Therefore, since there are two deaths, it is necessary also to accept two resurrections. There is the first, physical death, given as a wage for human disobedience. The second death is eternal punishment. The first resurrection is the giving of life[39] from dead works. The second resurrection is the transformation from the corruption of our bodies into incorruptibility. COMMENTARY ON THE APOCALYPSE 20.5-6.[40]

---

[36]1 Pet 2:9. [37]FC 24:281. Primasius follows the argument of Augustine (CCL 92:278). [38]PG 35:2448. [39]The Greek word ζωοποίησις suggests the work of the Holy Spirit in baptism. [40]MTS 1 Sup 1:220-21.

---

## 20:7-10 GOG AND MAGOG

[7]And when the thousand years are ended, Satan will be loosed from his prison [8]and will come out to deceive the nations which are at the four corners of the earth, that is, Gog and Magog, to gather them for battle; their number is like the sand of the sea. [9]And they marched up over the broad earth and surrounded the camp of the saints and the beloved city; but fire came down from heaven[n] and consumed them, [10]and the devil who had deceived them was thrown into the lake of fire and sulphur where the beast and the false prophet were, and they will be tormented day and night for ever and ever.

n Other ancient authorities read *from God, out of heaven,* or *out of heaven from God*

**Overview:** During the time of the Lord's incarnation, the devil's power was restrained so that the mystery of the incarnation might not be ineffective and without benefit. However, when Christ had ascended into heaven, the devil was once more released to do his customary work of deceiving the nations. In this activity he serves as a sort of athletic trainer for humankind, granting opportunity to the apostles, martyrs, pastors, ascetics and every righteous person to display the strength of their faith (Oecumenius). During this period of time the preaching of the gospel will bring in the full and complete harvest of the faithful. After this, the antichrist will come so that unbelievers might be condemned (Andrew of Caesarea), while the saints receive the reality of eternity under the headship of Christ. At this time, too, the nether regions will be freed from the devil who will disappear into eternal perdition (Apringius).

While even now the wicked are hostile to good works (Apringius), at the end of time the devil will gather the nations, Gog and Magog, which are loyal to him to fight against the saints. Although some believe that this has already occurred during the time of the Old Testament or the time of the Maccabees (Andrew of Caesarea), it is clear that this climatic battle will occur at the time of the consummation (Oecumenius, Andrew of Caesarea). These nations do not yet exist, or they exist but are given different names in Scripture (Oecumenius). It may well be, however, that we should not think of specific tribes or nations. Rather, this last persecution will be against the city of Christ, which exists everywhere in the world. For the city of the devil also is worldwide (Augustine), and wherever the devil abides in his own people, there a hostile people will emerge out of his arrogance to fight the church (Augustine, Apringius).

Exalted in their own pride (Apringius, Caesarius of Arles), the devil and his followers will encompass the church, for they are intermixed and intermingled with it (Augustine, Apringius). However, the blazing zeal of the saints will torment the ungodly (Augustine) even as the ungodly are consumed by the fire of their sins. Some of the ungodly may convert to Christ through the fire of the Holy Spirit and be spiritually consumed by the holy church (Caesarius of Arles). In any case, Satan, that originator of evil, will be thrown into the lake of fire at the end (Oecumenius), and the church will remain safe, for not a single angel but many angels surround and protect those who fear God. When Christ comes, he will slay the devil and his followers with the breath of his mouth (Andrew of Caesarea) and hand them over to punishment, which, as the Lord teaches, will be eternal and neverending (Augustine).

## 20:7 *Satan Will Be Loosed*

**The Nether Regions Will Be Freed from Satan.** Apringius of Beja: [We have here a difficulty] for we must inquire how it is that when the thousand years have ended, the enemy is given his freedom and the nations [continue to] live upon the earth within that infinity [which occurs after the end]. For indeed, after the resurrection, when the judgment of the living and the dead has been rendered, all things everlasting are given and those who reign with Christ, namely, the saints, will come with God's aid to the eternal blessings, that is, to the very reality of eternality itself. Moreover, they will be rewarded with the contemplation of him who is the Beginning, and possessing the presence of a vision of such a majesty they will be established in its bliss. When the rewards of all the blessed have been consummated and perfected, and all things have been brought to the one headship of our Lord Jesus Christ and in him all things are held together,[1] "Satan will be loosed from his prison." Then the nether regions themselves will be freed from him, at the same time the author of darkness will be dissolved and disappear, "and go out," into eternal perdition. Tractate on the Apocalypse 20.7.[2]

---

[1]See Col 1:17.  [2]CCL 107:79.

**SATAN SERVES AS AN ATHLETIC TRAINER FOR HUMANKIND.** OECUMENIUS: When the Lord completed the economy according to the flesh and ascended into heaven, the devil was to be released from his spiritual chains again to deceive the nations. It was said in an earlier book that the Lord's manner of life among men destroyed the work of the devil.[3] But when the Lord had ascended into heaven, the devil once more effected that which is proper and customary to him, and the people upon the earth were again subject to his authority, as was their custom. For the devil attempts to lead all astray. Some are persuaded by him, while others are not persuaded and struggle against the evil one. However, perhaps someone might say, "Why is it that when he was restrained and his own assaults were repulsed by the coming of the Lord in the flesh, he was let loose again against us, to lead those on earth astray? Were it not better had he been bound and humankind left free of [further] deception?" To such a person it must be said, Why do you not rather inquire after the existence of the devil at the very beginning? Or, why do you not inquire why he was not utterly destroyed when he first existed and had become a transgressor, so that he would have no access to mankind?

But, O friend, how would athletes continue to receive vigorous exercise were there no one to wrestle against? And how would athletes demonstrate their strength were there no opponent? For those persons who are lazy and subject to pleasures are inherently perverse, whether or not the devil is present and prodding them on. But the people of God who are noble athletes would be wrongly treated were their courage against the passions not put on public display. So, as it happens, the lazy would receive no benefit and the zealous would be very greatly wronged, were there no Satan. In a way, Satan serves as an athletic trainer for humankind, providing for those who contend an opportunity for victories. For as we said, those enamored with sin are in no way harmed, since, even were the devil not present, they would use their own sluggishness in place of him. And so, although unwilling, the devil does good to those [strong athletes], while he harms these not at all, or very little. But for my sake and yours, lest we be further injured by the work of the devil in any manner small or great, you [O friend] were willing that the lovers of sin be left unconstrained [by any discipline] and in a state of defeat and that the patriarchs and the prophets be despoiled of the glory [of their victories], along with the apostles, the Evangelists and those who had remained steadfast even to the point of blood for the witness of Christ and had preserved their nobility for him. Furthermore, you would have the confessors and those pastors who govern the churches well to be deprived of their glory, together with the ascetics, who endure very great hardships, and every righteous person who is perfected by their faith in Christ. "Of none of these is this world worthy." As a result, those noble and virtuous combatants mitigate to some extent the penalty of sinners who are altogether responsible for their hurts. For one who is upright is honored more by God than are thousands of those who do evil.

Therefore, both of these actions were exceptionally good and inspired, that at the coming of the Lord the impious attacks of the devil were stopped and that after his ascension into heaven the devil was loosed to tempt humankind. For had Satan been allowed to display all of his spiritual power while the Lord sojourned upon the earth, he would not have allowed anyone to become a hearer of the divine teaching. Nor would anyone have learned who is the true God by nature and what is the pure worship of him and what is vice and what is virtue. Rather, [Satan] would have prepared the cross for Christ prematurely, even before the Lord had begun to teach. And had this happened, such a great and admirable mystery as the Lord's incarnation would have been ineffective and without any benefit. COMMENTARY ON THE APOCALYPSE 20.4-8.[4]

---

[3]1 Jn 3:8. [4]TEG 8:255-57.

**THE PERIOD OF THE PREACHING OF THE GOS-PEL.** ANDREW OF CAESAREA: Some interpret the period of a thousand years to be the three and a half years from the baptism of Christ to his ascension into heaven, and they believe that after this the devil is to be loosed.[5] Others say that after the completion of six thousand years the first resurrection of the dead will occur for the saints alone, so that on this very earth on which they endured suffering, they might enjoy temporal largess and glory for a thousand years, and that after this [period] the general resurrection will occur, which will be not only of the righteous but also of the sinners.[6] It is unnecessary to say that the church receives nothing of this.

Rather, we listen to the Lord when he says to the Sadducees that the righteous will be "as the angels in heaven."[7] We listen also to the apostle who says, "the kingdom of God is not food and drink."[8] And so we interpret the thousand-year period to be that of the preaching of the gospel. ... It is not necessary to think of these thousand years in terms of a number. When it is said in the Song of Songs "everyone was to bring for its fruit a thousand pieces of silver," and again, "Solomon shall have a thousand and they who keep its fruit two hundred,"[9] the precise number is not indicated, but the full and complete harvest. So also here, the harvest of faith in its entirety is meant, after which "the son of perdition, the man of lawlessness" will come "so that all may be condemned who did not believe the truth but had pleasure in unrighteousness," as the apostle says.[10] And the Lord said, "I have come in my Father's name, and you do not receive me; another will come in his own name, him you will receive."[11] COMMENTARY ON THE APOCALYPSE 20.7-8.[12]

## 20:8 Satan Will Deceive the Nations

**GOG AND MAGOG ARE THE DEVIL AND HIS PEO-PLE.** AUGUSTINE: At that time the devil will have a single objective in his deception, namely, to bring on this battle, rather than deceive by the multifarious means of his previous malice. The expression "will go forth" means that his secret hatred will blaze out into open persecution. For this is to be the very last of all persecutions immediately preceding the very last of all judgments—a persecution that Holy church, the worldwide city of Christ, is to suffer at the hands of the worldwide city of the devil, in every place where the two cities will then extend. The peoples John calls Gog and Magog are not to be thought of as some definite barbarians dwelling in a certain part of the earth, such as the Getae and Massagetae[13] (as some have imagined on account of the initial letters), or any other foreign tribes beyond the pale of the Roman Empire.[14] John clearly indicates that they are to be everywhere in the world, "nations that are in the four corners of the earth, Gog and Magog." Of these names I am told that, literally, Gog means "a roof" and Magog "from the roof."[15] Thus we may take the words to mean an "abode" and a "person issuing from this abode" and, therefore, "the peoples in whom the devil abides as in an abyss" and "the devil himself, lifting himself up and coming out of them." They are the "roof," and he is "from the roof." If ... we apply both names to the peoples (rather than the first to them, the second to the devil), then they are the "roof" because the ancient foe is now shut up and roofed over in them, and they will issue "from the roof" when their concealed hatred bursts forth and is revealed in the open. CITY OF GOD 20.11.[16]

---

[5]Andrew is referring to Oecumenius. [6]For example, Irenaeus *Against Heresies* 5.32.1; 35.1-2 (ANF 1:561, 565-66). [7]Mt 22:41. [8]Rom 14:17. [9]Song 8:11-12. [10]2 Thess 2:3, 12. [11]Jn 5:43. Irenaeus also referred this passage to the coming of the antichrist (*Against Heresies* 5.25.4; ANF 1:554). [12]MTS 1 Sup 1:221-23. [13]Scythian Goths who were spread from the Balkans to east of the Caspian Sea and whom some believe were the displaced tribes of Israel. See also Herodotus 1.212ff. [14]Ambrose identified Gog with the Goths (*On the Christian Faith* 2.138; NPNF 2 10:241). He wrote this as Emperor Gratian was preparing to confront the Goths in A.D. 378. [15]See Jerome *Commentary on Ezekiel* 11.38 (CCL 95:525-27). In the Hebrew *gōg* means "roof" or "top." However, *gāg is* not equivalent to *Gōg*. [16]FC 24:281-82. Primasius follows the argument of Augustine (CCL 92:278-79).

**THE WICKED WILL "COME OUT" FROM THE DEVIL'S ARROGANT PRIDE.** APRINGIUS OF BEJA: In this passage "to deceive" means to scatter or to spoil, that is, to drag the nations along with him into condemnation, namely, all the wicked whom he has deceived in every part of the earth. And he will cause those who have been gathered together with him in one single condemnation to be delivered over to eternal torments. For Gog means "roof" and Magog means "out of the covering" or "out from the roof." Everyone whom he has brought out and led to the collapse of his own arrogance, or those whom he supported by the roof of his pride, or those who will be recognized as coming from the same cover and height of his arrogance, all these persons will be taken at the same time in one condemnation and by an eternal fire. When it says, "he will gather them for battle," it describes as something future what is in the past, for in some manner this battle is the hostility that the wicked have toward good works. And since those who are wicked are many and numerous, he adds, "whose number is like the sand of the sea." TRACTATE ON THE APOCALYPSE 20.7.[17]

**LEADING THE NATIONS AGAINST THE SERVANTS OF CHRIST.** OECUMENIUS: The holy prophet Ezekiel also spoke concerning Gog and Magog, relating how evil persons perish in an evil way. These are certain nations that shall lead the nations at the time of the consummation. These nations do not at present exist, or they are certain nations which do at present exist but that are called different names by the divine Scripture. These, therefore, will fight with that God-hated Satan against the servants of Christ. COMMENTARY ON THE APOCALYPSE 20.8-10.[18]

**GOG AND MAGOG WILL ARISE AT THE END OF TIME.** ANDREW OF CAESAREA: Satan will be loosed from his prison and will deceive all nations and will entice Gog and Magog to war for the devastation of the world. Some believe that these two are the remote northern people of the Scythians,[19] whom we call the Huns,[20] and, as we see,

are the most populous and warlike of any kingdom on earth and are kept from seizing the whole earth until the loosing of the devil by the hand of God alone. . . . Some interpret on the basis of the Hebrew language and render Gog as "one who gathers" or "that which is gathered" and Magog as "one who is exalted." In this way, these names signify either the gathering of the nations or their exaltation. We should note that Ezekiel prophesied that these nations would come upon the earth with great power at the end of time, that Israel would fall and for a period of seven years would burn by their arms as though through a great fire. Some interpreters refer this to the fall of the Assyrians under Sennacherib at the time of Hezekiah, which happened a long time prior to the prophecy of Ezekiel.[21] Others refer this to the destruction of the nations that attacked those coming to rebuild Jerusalem after the conquest by the Babylonians, when first Cyrus the Persian and then Darius ordered the governors of Syria to do this. Yet others refer to the forces of Antiochus, which were defeated by the Maccabees. However, it is clear that the arrival of these nations best suits the final times. First of all, it is nowhere written that the nation of the Scythians waged war against the Jews at that time, but only those nations round about them that envied their prosperity. Second, concerning Gog it is written, "He will be prepared from the days of old and will come at the end of time."[22] Third, in the present Revelation, which foretells future events, it is written that Gog and Magog will come toward the end of this age. COMMENTARY ON THE APOCALYPSE 20.7-8.[23]

## 20:9-10 *Fire Consumed Them*

---

[17]CCL 107:79-80. [18]TEG 8:259. [19]Already Josephus, who writes that Magog founded the Magogites whom the Greeks call "Scythians" (*Jewish Antiquities* 1.6.1). [20]Theodoret identifies Gog and Magog (= Scythians) with the Huns under Rugila (*Ecclesiastical History* 5.37.4; GCS 19:340). Later Byzantine writers, such as Andrew, called "Huns" any barbarian people who, like the Huns, threaten Byzantium. [21]2 Chron 32:1-23. It is unknown to which interpreters Andrew is referring. [22]Ezek 38:8. [23]MTS 1 Sup 1:223-25.

**BY GOD'S GRACE THE SAINTS WILL PROVE
UNCONQUERABLE.** AUGUSTINE: [That they
encompassed the beloved city] obviously does not
mean that they gathered or will gather in some
one place where, we must suppose, the camp of
the saints and the beloved city is to be. For, of
course, this city is Christ's church, which is
spread over the whole world. Wherever his
church will be (and it will be among all nations,
"over the breadth of the earth"), there is to be the
camp of the saints and the beloved city of God.
There will she be, surrounded by all her enemies,
intermingled with her as they are and will be in
every people, girded with the appalling magnitude of that besetting, hemmed in, straitened and
encompassed by the pressures of that mighty
affliction; but never will [the church] give up her
fighting spirit, her "camp," as John says. [The fire
from heaven] must not be taken to indicate that
supreme punishment of the ungodly, which is to
begin only with the words "Depart from me,
accursed ones, into the everlasting fire."[24] For it is
then that the wicked are to be cast into fire rather
than to have fire fall on them. John's words, "fire
from heaven," can well be interpreted as symbolizing the staunchness of the saints, their refusal
to give in and do the bidding of their raging enemies. For the heavens are called a "firmament,"
and by its firmness the ungodly will be tormented
by blazing zeal, because [they are] powerless to
win over Christ's holy ones to the camp of antichrist. This is the devouring fire, and it is said to
come from God because it is by God's grace that
the saints are to be unconquerable, to the great
torment of their foes. CITY OF GOD 20.11-12.[25]

**THE IMPIOUS ARE LIFTED UP BY THEIR
ARROGANCE.** APRINGIUS OF BEJA: "And they
ascended upon the height[26] of the earth and surrounded the camp of the saints." Lifted up by their
arrogance, the impious ascended into the heights,
but their earthly arrogance holds them back. They
are wise in nothing heavenly, nor do they fear the
power of celestial greatness. "They surrounded the
camp of the saints." [This means that] they wished

to exist in common with the saints, but of them
the prophecy is fulfilled that says, "They shall
return at evening and be hungry as a dog and go
around about the city."[27] In the present passage he
calls the city "beloved," saying, "they shall surround the camp of the saints and the beloved city."
TRACTATE ON THE APOCALYPSE 20.8.[28]

**SATAN, THE ORIGINATOR OF EVIL, WILL BE
PUNISHED FOREVER.** OECUMENIUS: "And they
surrounded the beloved city," that is, the church.
However, "fire brought from heaven" will destroy
all of them, and moreover when the consummation has occurred, Satan, the originator of evil,
together with the devil and the antichrist, will be
thrown into the lake of fire, that is, Gehenna. Let
the one who reads take note that in earlier material the Revelation has transmitted information
about three figures: the first was the dragon, who
was shown in heaven and who is the originator of
evil; the second is the beast who rose from the sea
and whom we claimed was second to Satan but
prominent among the rest of the demons; and the
third was the antichrist, who is also called the
false prophet.[29] However, it was stated a little earlier that the second, the devil and the antichrist
were "thrown into the lake of fire that burns with
brimstone."[30] But now it speaks of Satan, or the
devil, who earlier it had called "dragon." Therefore, you who read this book know that we have
interpreted the phrase "the thousand years," in
which the devil was bound and thrown into the
bottomless pit and again loosed, to refer very precisely to the incarnation of the Lord and his life
upon the earth, during which the devil's activity
was for a short time impeded. But now it is
revealed that his punishment and that of those
deceived by him is not a thousand years and then
there is a loosing of the evil one. Rather, this pun-

---

[24]Mt 25:41. [25]FC 24:282-83. Primasius follows the argument of
Augustine (CCL 92:279-80). [26]The text of Apringius and of Caesarius of Arles reads *ascenderunt super altitudinem terrae*, not *super lati-
tudinem* as in the text of Primasius and Bede. [28]Ps 59:6 (58:7 LXX).
[28]CCL 107:80. [29]See Rev 12:3; 13:1, 11. [30]Rev 19:20.

ishment is "forever and ever." COMMENTARY ON THE APOCALYPSE 20.8-10.[31]

**THOSE WHO PERSECUTE THE CHURCH.** CAESARIUS OF ARLES: "And the devil and his people went up into the height of the earth," that is, in the presumption of their arrogance, and "they surrounded the camp of the saints and the city of the beloved," that is, the church. This refers to what was earlier said about those assembled at Armageddon.[32] They cannot be gathered into one city from the four corners of the earth. Rather, in every corner [of the earth] each people will be gathered together for opposition to the holy city, that is, for persecution of the church. "And fire shall descend out of heaven from God," that is, out of the church, "and consume them." In this passage the fire may be interpreted in two ways. Either they will believe in Christ through the fire of the Holy Spirit, and they will be spiritually consumed by the church, that is, incorporated into the church, or they will be consumed by the fire of their own sins and will perish. EXPOSITION ON THE APOCALYPSE 20.9, HOMILY 18.[33]

**MANY ANGELS WILL PROTECT THE CHURCH.** ANDREW OF CAESAREA: Just as fierce animals come out of their caves, so, it says, those led by the devil and the demons with him will come from their various locations and spread themselves out over the earth to ravage the camp of the saints, clearly meaning the church, which is established throughout the four corners of the world. But they do not know that it is not only a single angel but many angels who encamp round about them who fear God, as the psalm says.[34] They will come to subdue the new Jerusalem, the beloved city, from which the divine law has gone into all the world through the apostles. Then, they say, the antichrist will seat himself in the temple of God. This refers either to the ancient temple of God among the Jews that was destroyed because of their audacity against Christ and which those Jews who hate God still expect to be rebuilt by him, or it refers to the true temple

of God, namely, the catholic church. The antichrist will usurp for himself what does not belong to him and "proclaim himself to be God," as the apostle says.[35] Not long afterward, it says, fire comes down from heaven. This will be either a physical fire such as that which burned the two groups of fifty at the time of Elijah,[36] or the passage refers to the glorious coming of Christ, who will slay them "by the breath of his mouth"[37] and consume the aforementioned nations and their leader, the devil. Christ will hand them, along with the antichrist and the false prophet, over to the lake of fire, where they will be tormented forever and ever. Christ the Savior has taught us to pray that we enter not into temptation, and so, recognizing our weakness, let us do that earnestly, that we be saved from the trials of that which is prophesied. COMMENTARY ON THE APOCALYPSE 20.9-10.[38]

**THE DEVIL WILL BE PUNISHED FOREVER.** AUGUSTINE: John goes on to state succinctly the full punishment that is to be meted out in the last judgment to the hostile city and its prince, the devil. . . . Why has the church been so intolerant with those who defend the view that, however greatly and however long the devil is to be punished, he can be promised ultimately that all will be purged or pardoned?[39] Certainly it is not because so many of the church's saints and biblical scholars have begrudged the devil and his angels a final cleansing and the beatitude of the kingdom of heaven. Nor is it because of any lack of feeling for so many and such high angels that must suffer such great and enduring pain. This is not a matter of feeling but of fact. The fact is that there is no way of waiving or weakening the

---

[31]TEG 8:259-60. [32]Rev 16:16. [33]PL 35:2448-49. [34]See Ps 34:7 (33:8 LXX). At the time of Hezekiah, God saved Jerusalem with but a single angel (2 Chron 32:21); at the end there will many angels protecting the saints. How certain, then, the outcome! [35]2 Thess 2:4. [36]2 Kings 1:9-12. [37]2 Thess 2:8. [38]MTS 1 Sup 1:225-26. [39]Augustine has Origen and his followers in mind; they believed that ultimately all divine punishment was purgative, not retributive. This doctrine is sometimes called *apokatastasis* (the "restoration" of all things).

words that the Lord has told us that he will pronounce in the last judgment: "Depart from me,
accursed ones, into the everlasting fire which was
prepared for the devil and his angels."[40] In this
way he showed plainly that it is an eternal fire in
which the devil and his angels are to burn. Then
we have the words of the Apocalypse: "and they

will be tormented day and night forever and ever."
In the one text we have "everlasting," in the other,
"forever and ever." These are words that have a
single meaning in the divine Scripture, namely, of
unending duration. CITY OF GOD 20.14; 21.23.[41]

---

[40]Mt 25:41. [41]FC 24:286, 385.

---

## 20:11-15 THE FINAL JUDGMENT AND THE SECOND DEATH

[11]*Then I saw a great white throne and him who sat upon it; from his presence earth and sky fled away, and no place was found for them.* [12]*And I saw the dead, great and small, standing before the throne, and books were opened. Also another book was opened, which is the book of life. And the dead were judged by what was written in the books, by what they had done.* [13]*And the sea gave up the dead in it, Death and Hades gave up the dead in them, and all were judged by what they had done.* [14]*Then Death and Hades were thrown into the lake of fire. This is the second death, the lake of fire;* [15]*and if any one's name was not found written in the book of life, he was thrown into the lake of fire.*

---

**OVERVIEW**: With the appearance of Christ the rest that God will establish among the saints is revealed (ANDREW OF CAESAREA). God will be enthroned among them with a radiant rule reflected in the splendor of their virtue. At that time the corruption under which the heavens and the earth had been subjected will be cast off (OECUMENIUS, ANDREW OF CAESAREA), and they will be changed into something better by way of a transformation, not by destruction into nonexistence (AUGUSTINE, OECUMENIUS, ANDREW OF CAESAREA). This final transformation of the world proves that it was originally created by God from nothing (TERTULLIAN).

At that time also, all people will be judged according to the commandments of God written in the Old and New Testaments (AUGUSTINE, BEDE). All persons, whether old or young, righteous or sinner (OECUMENIUS, ANDREW OF CAE-

SAREA), will be judged when Christ, who is the Book of Life, renders to each according to his deeds (APRINGIUS). The book that shall be opened is not a physical book but a spiritual book (AUGUSTINE, APRINGIUS). Perhaps we should think of this book as the conscience of each person who by divine illumination "reads" the record of his or her deeds (AUGUSTINE). Perhaps the book is the Lord Jesus Christ, who is merciful in the giving of recompense (APRINGIUS). Certainly in the single Book of Life only a few will be inscribed, for only few walk on the narrow way that leads to life (OECUMENIUS).

Those whose bodies were drowned in the sea or otherwise dissolved into the elements will be raised bodily to face their judgment (APRINGIUS, OECUMENIUS). This will not be too difficult for God, for he is able to do as he wishes, and originally he brought all bodies into existence from nonexistence (Oecumenius). All the dead, therefore, will be given up for judgment, those who are dead because of the separation of body and soul (Bede) as well as those who are "dead" because their bodies are destined to eternal death in view of their death-bearing sins (Augustine, Andrew of Caesarea, Bede).

In the final judgment the devil and all the friends of death will be condemned to everlasting torment (Augustine, Andrew of Caesarea). With them all who are worthy of death and of hades will be cast into the second death (Oecumenius, Andrew of Caesarea). For such persons it would be better were they not to rise at all. For in the second death there is nothing but misery and groaning in outer darkness (Aphrahat). There the life of the soul, which comes from God, is gone while the soul, united with the body, enables the body to feel the torment it endures. That "life" apart from God that is given over to perpetual pain is more properly called death than life (Augustine). With an infallible foreknowledge God knows who will be condemned to this life of eternal death (Augustine, Bede). For already in the present time God begins his judgment by deserting evil persons and leaving them in their sins (Fulgentius of Ruspe). Such persons, neither believing in life nor confessing with their mouths, shall be destroyed in hell (Apringius). With their evil thoughts and deeds made known to all (Bede), the condemned will forever be punished in the sight of the angels and the just (Lactantius). Yet even in the lake of fire there will be a distinction of punishments (Oecumenius).

## 20:11 Earth and Sky Fled

**Heaven and Earth Will Come to Nothing.** Tertullian: It is enough for us, both that it is certain that all things were made by God and that there is no certainty whatever that they were made out of matter. . . . The belief that everything was made from nothing will be impressed upon us [also] by that ultimate dispensation of God

that will bring back all things to nothing. For "the very heaven shall be rolled together as a scroll";[1] no, it shall come to nothing along with the earth itself, with which it was made in the beginning. "Heaven and earth shall pass away," he says.[2] "The first heaven and the first earth passed away,"[3] "and there was found no place for them," because, of course, that which comes to an end loses locality. Against Hermogenes 33-34.[4]

**The Visible Appearance of the World Will Pass Away.** Augustine: John picks up again the theme of the last judgment (which is to accompany the second and bodily resurrection of the dead) and describes the manner of its revelation to him. . . . Note that he does not say, "One who sat upon it, *and* from his face earth and heaven fled away," because this "flight" had not yet taken place, that is, not before the judgment of the living and the dead. What he says is that he beheld One sitting on the throne "from *whose* face earth and heaven fled away"—not then but subsequently. The fact is that it will be after the judgment is completed that heaven and earth will end with the beginning of the new heaven and earth. For it will be by a transformation rather than by a wholesale destruction that this world of ours will pass away. This explains Paul's words: "This world as we see it is passing away. I would have you free from care."[5] It is, to be sure, the visible appearance of the world that is destined to pass away, not its nature. City of God 20.14.[6]

**The Corruption of the Heaven and Earth Will Be Cast Off.** Oecumenius: By the words *white throne* he speaks of a throne that is bright and radiant. By the figure of the flight of the heaven and the earth, the passage indicates their change and transformation. For if "the heavens will pass away with a loud noise," as the holy Peter says,[7] and as the prophet who says, "In the

---

[1]Is 34:4; Rev 6:14. [2]Mt 24:35. [3]Rev 21:1. [4]ANF 3:496-97. [5]1 Cor 7:31-32. [6]FC 24:286-87. Primasius follows the argument of Augustine (CCL 92:281-82). [7]2 Pet 3:10.

beginning, O Lord, you did lay the foundation of the earth, and the heavens are the works of your hands; they shall perish, but you remain, and they all shall grow old as a garment, and as a vesture you shall fold them, and they shall be changed,"[8] then certainly the Revelation speaks of their passing away and their destruction, which signify their change, as a "flight," since no place was found for them. For where would one find that corruption that had been cast off? Therefore, in the present passage he speaks of their change, while a little further on he says that they shall become new. COMMENTARY ON THE APOCALYPSE 20.11-12.[9]

**THE CREATION WILL RECEIVE A CHANGE FOR THE BETTER.** ANDREW OF CAESAREA: The image of the "white throne" signifies the divine rest that God will establish among the saints, who are resplendent with virtues and among whom God will be enthroned. The flight of the earth and sky signifies their transformation from what they were into something better. And there will be found no longer any place for change. For if the creation was subjected to corruption because of us, as the apostle says, it will also be transformed with us into the freedom of the glory of the children of God,[10] being made new into that which is more brilliant.[11] [The creation] will not be subjected to complete annihilation, as we learn from Irenaeus, Antipater[12] and other saints. For the blessed Irenaeus writes, "For neither is the substance nor the essence of the creation annihilated (for faithful and true is he who has established it), but the fashion of the world passes away, that is, those things among which transgression has occurred, since humankind has grown old in them. And therefore this fashion has been formed temporary, God foreknowing all things."[13] Similarly, the great Methodius comments as follows in On the Resurrection: "It is not satisfactory to say that the universe will be utterly destroyed, and sea and air and sky will be no longer. For the whole world will be deluged with fire from heaven and burned for the purpose of

purification and renewal; it will not, however, come to complete ruin and corruption." And a little later he says, "And Paul clearly testifies this, saying, 'For the creation waits with eager longing for the manifestation of the sons of God; for the creation was subjected to futility, not willingly but through him who subjected it in hope. Therefore, the creation itself will be set free from its bondage to decay' "[14] and so on. But before these saints the holy David sang to the Lord, saying, "You sent forth your Spirit, and they are created; and you renew the face of the ground."[15] And Isaiah says, "There will be a new heaven and a new earth, and the former things will not be remembered or come into mind; but they will find gladness and rejoicing in it."[16] Certainly in the superabundance of joy and in the greatness of their rewards they will forget the struggles and pains that they endured. In another place Isaiah says, "For as the new heavens and the new earth which I will make shall remain before me, so shall your descendants and your name remain."[17] It follows, therefore, that the creation, which was made for our sake, receives with us a change for the better, not going into nonexistence, just as we do not go into nonexistence after our death. COMMENTARY ON THE APOCALYPSE 20.11.[18]

## 20:12 The Book of Life

**EACH PERSON WILL MENTALLY REVIEW HIS OR HER DEEDS.** AUGUSTINE: He says he saw scrolls opened, and another scroll, but he makes

---

[8]Ps 102:25-26 (101:26-27 LXX). [9]TEG 8:260-61. [10]Rom 8:20-21. [11]Against Origen On First Principles 1.6.2; 2.1.1-2, who argues that "the end is like the beginning" so that rational creatures will return to a previous, primordial position. [12]Antipater of Bostra in John of Damascus Sacra Parallela (PG 96:497). Antipater argues, against Origen, that the saints will become more glorious in the resurrection and uses the story of Christ's transfiguration to illustrate his point. [13]Against Heresies 5.36.1. Irenaeus does not quote Rev 20:11 in connection with "the fashion of the world" passing away. Rather, he quotes Rev 21:1-4 (Against Heresies 5.35.2; ANF 1:566). [14]Rom 8:19-21. On the Resurrection 1.8 (ANF 6:365). Methodius does not quote Rev 20:11 in this context. Methodius also was arguing against Origen. [15]Ps 104:30 (103:30 LXX). [16]Is 65:17-18. [17]Is 66:22. [18]MTS 1 Sup 1:227-29.

clear the character of the latter, "which is the book of each person's life."[19] The first scrolls he mentions, then, must represent the holy Scriptures of the Old and New Testaments. These will be opened to show the commandments of God, and the other scroll [will] show how these commandments were kept or disobeyed by each and every person. As for this latter scroll, if one considers it materially, it surpasses all powers of thought for size and length. And if it contains the entire life record of all people, how much time would it take to read it? Are we to suppose that there will be an equal number of angels and people present in the judgment and that each person will hear his life record read out by an angel accredited to him for this task? In this supposition, there would not be one book for all but a book for each. Yet, the Apocalypse wants us to think of one book. . . . No, the book in question must symbolize some divine action in virtue of which each person will recall his deeds, good or bad, and review them mentally so that, without a moment's delay, each one's conscience will be either burdened or unburdened and thus, collectively and individually, all will be judged at the same moment. And because, in virtue of this divine illumination, each person will, so to speak, read the record of his deeds, God's action is called a "book." CITY OF GOD 20.14.[20]

**THE LORD JESUS WILL BE MADE MANIFEST.** APRINGIUS OF BEJA: Who is free before God if not those who are declared to be by the power of him who judges the works of each one? God is said to have a book, which is not a physical book but a spiritual book, that is, the eternal memory in which the names of the elect are kept. And so the psalm says, "The righteous shall be in everlasting remembrance."[21] "Also another book was opened, which is the Book of Life." The Book of Life, and Life itself, is the Lord Jesus Christ. Then he shall be opened, that is, made manifest to every creature, when he will render to each according to his work. "And the dead were judged by what was written in the books, by what they had done."

"God has spoken once, and I have heard these two things," it says.[22] And what these two things are he makes clearer when he says, "The kingdom is the Lord's, and he is the governor of the nations."[23] There he heard of the kingdom; here he has beheld the book. There he heard two things; here he has also seen another book. And what is contained in these two books he says there, "the power of God is also yours, O Lord, and mercy."[24] The power is in the judging and the mercy is in the giving of recompense. "And the dead were judged by what was written in the books, by what they had done." And so he says there, "for you will recompense everyone according to his works."[25] TRACTATE ON THE APOCALYPSE 20.12.[26]

**THOSE WHO HAVE WALKED IN VIRTUE ARE IN THE BOOK OF LIFE.** OECUMENIUS: By *great* he speaks of the just, not because they are great by any physical measurement but because of their glory and the brightness of their virtue. By *small* he means the sinners, since they have become as nothing through their baseness and worthlessness. "And books were opened, and another book was opened, which is the Book of Life." In the Gospels, the Lord says that the way that leads to destruction is broad and wide and that many walk on it, but that the way that leads to life is narrow and cramped and that not only are there few who are walking on it, but few who even find it.[27] For this reason he saw many books and one book. There are many books because all of humankind is inscribed in them, and there is a great number in them. There is but one Book of Life, because in it are inscribed those who are the elect, that is, those blameless in virtue, who have trodden every rugged and steep path of virtue. Everyone in the books, it says, were judged deservedly according to their works. [Earlier]

---

[19]The text of Augustine reads *qui est vitae uniuscuiusque.* This is also the text of Primasius and of Caesarius of Arles. Bede mentions this reading as an *alia editio.* [20]FC 24:287-88. Primasius follows the argument of Augustine (CCL 92:282). [21]Ps 112:6 (111:6 LXX). [22]Ps 62:11 (61:12 LXX). [23]Ps 22:28 (21:29 LXX). [24]Ps 62:11-12 (61:12-13 LXX). [25]Ps 62:12 (61:13 LXX). [26]CCL 107:83-84. [27]See Mt 7:13-14.

mention was also made of another book, which was called a "little scroll."[28] But now he speaks of a "book," even a "scroll of life," as if there were three different ones. He speaks of a "little scroll" in which are listed the most impious according to the thoughts there asserted. He also speaks of the "Book of Life" in which are listed the most pious and righteous. And finally he speaks of "books" in which all those are listed who are, as it were, in between evil and virtue. COMMENTARY ON THE APOCALYPSE 20.11-12.[29]

**THE RIGHTEOUS AND THE SINNERS WILL BE JUDGED.** ANDREW OF CAESAREA: By the *dead* he means either all persons, since they experience the death of the body, or those who have died because of [their] transgressions. The "great and small" are either those who are older or younger, or more likely those who have done the works of death and will appropriately be punished for these acts. Or the great are the righteous and the small those sinners who are worthless because of the baseness of their soul. The books that are opened are indicative of the deeds and of the conscience of each person. There is but one book of Life in which the names of the saints are written. COMMENTARY ON THE APOCALYPSE 20.12.[30]

**THE WICKED WILL READ OF THE GOOD THEY CHOSE NOT TO DO.** BEDE: "The dead were judged by what was written in the books, by what they had done." This means that they were judged from the [two] Testaments according to what they had done and what they had not done. It is possible also to understand these books to refer to the deeds of the righteous. For in comparison with these the wicked are damned, since in the opening of these books they read of that good that they did not choose to do. EXPLANATION OF THE APOCALYPSE 20.12.[31]

## 20:13 All Were Judged

**THOSE DESTINED TO DEATH ARE DEAD EVEN WHILE THEY ARE ALIVE.** AUGUSTINE: Who,

now, are these dead people who were in the sea and whom the sea will give up? Surely we are not to think that because a person drowns, his soul does not go to hell, or that his body is preserved in the sea, or—what is still more absurd—that the sea keeps the good dead people and hell the bad ones. No one could entertain such a notion. Surely those are right who take the sea in this text to stand for this world of ours.[32] To indicate, accordingly, that the living who Christ is to find on earth are to be judged along with the arisen dead, John termed the former dead, too. Such are the good "dead" to whom the words were addressed: "For you have died, and your life is hidden with Christ in God."[33] The bad "dead" . . . are addressed in the verse: "Leave the dead to bury their own dead."[34] There is another reason why living people can be called dead, namely, because they carry around bodies destined for death. This was Paul's thought when he wrote, "The body, it is true, is dead by reason of sin, but the spirit is life by reason of justification"[35]—a text in which he shows that both life and death exist in a person living in his body, death in his body, life in the spirit. . . . The sea is said to "deliver up" its dead, because they are presented for judgment living, just as they are; whereas death and hell are said to "give back their dead," because they are actually restored to life.[36] And do not imagine that it would perhaps have been sufficient for John to say death or hell. He said both—death alone for the good people who, although they suffered death, did not go to hell; and hell for the evil people who, after death, suffer the pains of hell. CITY OF GOD 20.15.[37]

**NO FURTHER DEATH OF THE BODY AFTER THE RESURRECTION.** APRINGIUS OF BEJA: Lest anyone say that those who have died at sea or have been drowned by water or have been eaten

[28]See Rev 10:2, 10. [29]TEG 8:261-62. [30]MTS 1 Sup 1:229-30. [31]CCL 121A:515. [32]Augustine probably has Tyconius in mind. [33]Col 3:3. [34]Mt 8:22. [35]Rom 8:10. [36]For "deliver up" Augustine uses *exhibuit*; for "give back" he uses *reddiderunt*. [37]FC 24:289-90. Primasius follows the argument of Augustine (CCL 92:282-83).

by beasts or have been destroyed by fire cannot be raised again, [it says therefore that] they gave up their dead. And since no one will escape the judgment of God, it adds, "and all were judged by what they had done." Lest anyone should think that after the resurrection there follows a death of the body, an opinion that is profane to believe and even to mention, he adds [that death was sent into the lake of fire]. TRACTATE ON THE APOCALYPSE 20.13.[38]

### GOD IS ABLE TO RESTORE TO US OUR BODIES. OECUMENIUS:

Those who do not believe in the resurrection of the body smile at us and at our teaching, which asserts that these very bodies are to rise again, as though this were not only difficult but altogether impossible. They say moreover that every earthly body consists of the four elements of fire, water, earth, air, and that upon death bodies return to those elements from which they were constituted in the first place. So that which is of fire in us returns to that which is naturally and wholly fire; that which is of water returns to water, and the other two return to what belongs to them. "Since these elements," [they may argue], "have been mixed and compounded with their own substances, how is it possible that that which has become one simple, indistinguishable substance by mixture be restored as bodies, as you [Christians] say, unless you would say that different bodies are arising instead of the other [previous] ones?" To such persons one might quote the holy Scripture, "You are wrong, O people, because you do not know the power of God,"[39] by whose will all things received their being, since for him only to will a work is for it to be accomplished. For what is easier, to bring substances out of nothing, or, having once brought them forth and mixing them either with themselves or with other things, again to dissemble them and assign to each what is its own? Furthermore, even we are often successful by a certain technique in separating wine that has been mixed with water. Moreover, even the sun draws up through the mists and vapors what is

fresh and sweet from the sea, while it leaves that which is heavy, earthy, salty and bitter. But the primary consideration is this, that God alone is able to do whatever he wishes. If, therefore, God has brought that which had no existence into existence, how is it not easier for him to separate again what had been mixed completely with the elements simply by willing to do so and to assign to each body what belongs to it, even though for humans this would be impossible? It is impossible for you and for me to divide the brilliance of fire from its heat, yet this is possible with God—for it says, "There is a voice of the Lord who divides flames of fire."[40] In the same way it is impossible for you and me to separate what has been mixed together, while for God it is easy and readily done. The present passage of the Revelation now offers to us this marvelous doctrine [of the resurrection of the body], saying, "The sea gave up the dead in it" from the sea. This concerns the element of water. Signifying every watery substance, it says that the watery substance gave up everything that had been mixed with it from what was of water in human bodies. "And death and hades," it says, "gave up the dead in them." By *death* it means the earth, since our bodies had decayed in it. And so the holy prophet also speaks periphrastically of death as the "dust of death," saying, "He has brought me down into the dust of death."[41] And so the earth gave up everything in it which had been earthy in our [bodies]. In addition, hades gave up the dead in it. By *hades* it speaks of air and fire, for they are formless and invisible. For to be sure, because it is so fine, air is invisible, unless it becomes dense, and fire that smolders in wood is invisible, unless it burst into flame. Moreover, that element of fire, the ether, is invisible to us because it is obscured by the interposition of much air. And too, by *hades* he speaks of fire because of the destruction and formlessness it reeks upon that which it touches. And so many sayings name it "Unknown." Therefore, when

---

[38]CCL 107:84. [39]See Mt 22:29. [40]Ps 29:7 (28:7 LXX). [41]Ps 22:15 (21:16 LXX).

each element has given back whatever was mixed with it of the human being, the resurrection is accomplished. COMMENTARY ON THE APOCALYPSE 20.13-21.2.[42]

### DEATH AND HADES GIVE UP OUR BODIES AND SOULS.

ANDREW OF CAESAREA: It says that each body is returned to those elements from which it was constituted and given up, whether it had been given over to the earth or to the sea. Death and hades are not ensouled living creatures, as some have written.[43] Rather, death is the separation of the soul and the body, and hades is that place that is to us formless and unseen and that receives the souls that travel there. Those souls are "dead" that carry death-bearing deeds. As a wise man said, "The souls of the righteous are in the hand of God, and no torment shall touch them."[44] COMMENTARY ON THE APOCALYPSE 20.13.[45]

### GOOD AND WICKED SOULS WILL BE UNITED WITH THEIR BODIES.

BEDE: He indicates that the bodies and the souls are to be brought together, the bodies from the earth and the souls from their own locations. By *death* he indicates those good souls who endured only the separation of the flesh but would not suffer punishment, while by *hades* he indicates the wicked souls. It is also possible to interpret this literally to mean that all bodies that the waves of the sea carried away or that the beasts had devoured would be resurrected. Tyconius interpreted the passage this way: "Those nations that he shall find here still living are the dead of the sea; while 'death and hades gave up their dead' refers to the nations that are dead and buried."[46] EXPLANATION OF THE APOCALYPSE 20.13.[47]

## 20:14 The Lake of Fire, the Second Death

### IT WOULD BE BETTER FOR THE WICKED WERE THEY NOT TO RISE.

APHRAHAT: It is right for us to be afraid of the second death, that which is full of weeping and gnashing of teeth and of groanings and miseries, that which is situated in outer darkness. But blessed shall be the faithful and the righteous in that resurrection, in which they expect to be awakened and to receive the good promises made them. But as for the wicked who are not faithful, in the resurrection woe to them, because of that which is laid up for them! It would be better for them, according to the faith that they possess, were they not to rise. For the servant for whom his Lord is preparing stripes and bonds, while he is sleeping desires not to awake, for he knows that when the dawn shall have come and he shall awake, his Lord will scourge and bind him. But the good servant, to whom his Lord has promised gifts, looks expectantly for the time when dawn shall come and he shall receive presents from his Lord. DEMONSTRATIONS 8.19.[48]

### THE DEVIL WILL BE SENT TO THE LAKE OF FIRE.

AUGUSTINE: In this verse, "hell and death" stand for the devil (together with the entirety of his followers) inasmuch as he is the author of death and of the torments of hell. CITY OF GOD 20.15.[49]

### TOTAL DEATH.

AUGUSTINE: There is also a total death for a person, a death of body and soul, namely, when a soul, abandoned by God, abandons the body. In this case, the soul has no life from God and the body no life from the soul. The consequence of such total death is the second death, so called on the authority of divine Revelation. This is the death that our Savior meant when he said, "Be afraid of him who is able to destroy both soul and body in hell."[50]

Since this second death does not occur until soul and body are reunited, never to be separated again, you might wonder how the body is said to die by a death in which it is not deserted by the

---

[42]TEG 8:262-64. [43]Reference is unknown. [44]Wis 3:1. [45]MTS 1 Sup 1:230. [46]"Sea" in this passage of Tyconius refers to this earthly life. Caesarius of Arles follows this interpretation of Tyconius (PL 35:2449). [47]CCL 121A:515-17. [48]NPNF 2 13:381. [49]FC 24:290. Primasius follows the argument of Augustine (CCL 92:283-84). [50]Mt 10:28.

soul but rather is given a life by the soul to feel the torment it endures. For in a person's last and everlasting punishment the soul is rightly said to be dead when its life from God is gone, but, since the body's life depends on the soul, how can the body be said to be dead? If the body were dead, it could not feel the bodily torments that are to be felt after the resurrection. It is because life of every kind is good, and pain is evil, that we decline to say that that body lives, in which the soul is the cause, not of life, but of pain?[51] The soul, then, lives by God when it lives well, for it cannot live well unless God is the cause of its good works.[52] The body, however, takes its life from the soul when the soul is alive in the body, whether the soul is receiving any life from God or not. . . . It is true that when a person is finally damned, he does not lose sensation; nevertheless, because his feelings are not gentle enough to give pleasure nor soothing enough to be restful but are purifying to the point of pain, they can more properly be called death rather than life. The reason why this death of damnation is called a second death is that it comes after that first death, which is a divorce of two natures meant to be in union, whether God and the soul or the soul and the body. It can be said of the first death, the death of the body, that it is good for saints and bad for sinners, but of the second that is certainly good for no one and nonexistent for the saints. CITY OF GOD 13.2.[53]

**NO ONE WHO DIES WILL DIE AGAIN.**
APRINGIUS OF BEJA: This is to show that since death has been overtaken no one will die again. Moreover, since the nether region has been condemned, hell will find no one further whom it might receive. TRACTATE ON THE APOCALYPSE 20.14.[54]

**THE SECOND DEATH HAS SIN AS ITS CAUSE.**
OECUMENIUS: Once the resurrection has happened and each soul has received its own body, death, namely, the formless, disembodied life of souls in death is destroyed. [The passage]

describes this in a figurative manner and speaks of their destruction symbolically when it says that death and hades were thrown into the lake of fire. The prophet Hosea also speaks similarly, saying, "Where is your penalty, O death? Where, O hades, is your sting?"[55] "This is," it says, "the second death, the lake of fire." In previous passages it spoke of physical death, that is, the separation of the soul and the body as the first death, while the second death was the spiritual death, punishment and torment, which has sin as its cause. COMMENTARY ON THE APOCALYPSE 20.13-21.2.[56]

**THE EVIL POWERS WILL BE CONDEMNED.**
ANDREW OF CAESAREA: Death and hades are thrown into the lake of fire. This shows either that "the last enemy to be destroyed is death"[57] or that the evil powers who are the friends of the death caused by sin and who have their abode in hades and escort their followers there will be condemned to this fire. For just as the inhabitants are encompassed in the term *city*, so also those worthy of death and hades are included in the terms *death* and *hades*. However, that fire has no destructive power over those who have been born of God and are exceptionally good. It is written, "God did not make death."[58] For this reason, this passage signifies that death and corruption shall be no more but that incorruptibility and immortality will reign. And it should not amaze if all who are not written in the Book of Life will be thrown into the lake of fire. For just as with the Father there are many mansions for those being saved, so also there are distinctions among the places and manners of punishment. Some punishments will be more harsh, some more endurable, which those not worthy to be in the Book of Life will suffer. COMMENTARY ON THE APOCALYPSE 20.14-15.[59]

---

[51]The Latin reads *ideo nec vivere corpus dicendum est, in quo anima non vivendi causa est, sed dolendi.* [52]The Latin reads *non enim potest bene vivere nisi Deo in se operante quod bonum est.* [53]FC 14:300-301*. [54]CCL 107:84. [55]Hos 13:14. [56]TEG 8:264-65. [57]1 Cor 15:26. [58]Wis 1:13. [59]MTS 1 Sup 1:231.

## 20:15 *Names Not Written in the Book of Life*

**THE IMPIOUS WILL BE BURNED.** LACTANTIUS: When, however, the thousand years shall be completed, the world will be renewed by God, heaven will be folded up and the earth changed. And God will transform people into the likeness of angels, and they will be white and shining as snow, and they will always be in the sight of the Omnipotent and will sacrifice to their God and serve him forever. At the same time, there will take place that second and public resurrection of all, during which the unjust will be raised to everlasting sufferings. These are they who worshiped idols made by hands, who did not know or who denied the Lord and Father of the universe. But their master will be seized with his ministers and will be condemned to punishment, and together with him the whole band of the impious will be burned in perpetual fire forever in the sight of the angels and the just. EPITOME OF THE DIVINE INSTITUTES 7.26.[60]

**GOD HAS AN INFALLIBLE FOREKNOWLEDGE OF THE ELECT.** AUGUSTINE: The "Book of Life" is not for jogging God's memory lest he forget. It is a figure of the predestination of those who are to receive eternal life. We are not to imagine that God does not know them and has to read in his books to find out who they are. On the contrary, the Book of Life is precisely his infallible prescience of those inscribed therein, whose very registration there means only that they are foreknown by him. CITY OF GOD 20.15.[61]

**CONCUPISCENCE GIVES BIRTH TO SIN; MATURE SIN BEGETS DEATH.** FULGENTIUS OF RUSPE: [In evil persons] God begins his judgment with desertion and ends with anguish. For in this present time as well in which God deserts the evil ones who go away from him, he does not work in them what displeases him but works through them what pleases him. Afterwards, he is going to give them what they deserve from

his justice. . . . Such people God has fitted for destruction as punishment that the just judge by his just predestination has decreed for the sinner. . . . Concupiscence, conceiving, has given birth to sin, but the mature sin has begotten death. The wicked, therefore, have not been predestined to the first death of the soul but have been predestined to the second, that is, to the pool of fire and sulphur.[62] . . . He calls the second death that which follows from the sentence of the just judge, not that which went before in the evil concupiscence of the sinner. . . . Therefore, the first death of the soul, which a person inflicted on himself, is the cause of the second death. And the second death, which God has rendered to the person, is the punishment for the first death. LETTER TO MONIMUS 1.27.1-6.[63]

**WHOEVER HAS NOT CONFESSED THE LORD.** APRINGIUS OF BEJA: Whoever did not believe during life and did not open his mouth in confession of our Lord Jesus Christ shall be destroyed along with death and hell because he failed to receive life. Nevertheless, we do not confess that everyone will die or come to punishment. Rather, that will be fulfilled which we read in Daniel, "Some shall rise to everlasting life, and some to everlasting contempt, so that they might always behold."[64] And what shall they always behold, if not that they are tormented while others are glorified? TRACTATE ON THE APOCALYPSE 20.15.[65]

**THERE IS A DISTINCTION OF PUNISHMENTS IN THE LAKE OF FIRE.** OECUMENIUS: All those who remained in sins and were not accounted worthy to be in the Book of Life suffered the same fate. Do not marvel that it says that even those who had sinned moderately were thrown into the lake of fire together with the devil and the antichrist. For even there, there is a distinction of punishments. Just as in a fire there is a

---

[60]FC 49:536.  [61]FC 24:290. Primasius follows the argument of Augustine (CCL 92:284).  [62]Fulgentius quotes Rev 20:10, 14-15; 21:8.  [63]FC 95:225-27.  [64]Dan 12:2.  [65]CCL 107:84.

part that is continuously very hot and a part that is not so hot and is somewhat temperate, yet every part is called fire, so you might, as I do, consider this also to be like that. COMMENTARY ON THE APOCALYPSE 20.13-21.2.[66]

**THE THOUGHTS AND DEEDS OF EACH PERSON ARE MADE KNOWN.** BEDE: [The passage] is speaking of those who are not judged by God to be living. For this reason, it seems to me that

those are correct who say that the open books above are the thoughts and deeds of each person that have been made known. However, the Book of Life is the foreknowledge of God, which cannot fail concerning those to whom eternal life will be given. They are written in this book, that is, they have been foreknown [by God]. EXPLANATION OF THE APOCALYPSE 20.15.[67]

---

[66]TEG 8:265. [67]CCL 121A:517.

---

## 21:1-4 THE NEW JERUSALEM

[1]*Then I saw a new heaven and a new earth; for the first heaven and the first earth had passed away, and the sea was no more.* [2]*And I saw the holy city, new Jerusalem, coming down out of heaven from God, prepared as a bride adorned for her husband;* [3]*and I heard a loud voice from the throne saying, "Behold, the dwelling of God is with men. He will dwell with them, and they shall be his people,*[o] *and God himself will be with them;*[p] [4]*he will wipe away every tear from their eyes, and death shall be no more, neither shall there be mourning nor crying nor pain any more, for the former things have passed away."*

o Other ancient authorities read *peoples*    p Other ancient authorities add *and be their God*

---

**OVERVIEW:** Through the transgression of humankind, creation suffers corruption and mortality (OECUMENIUS). However, God will establish heaven and earth (CASSIODORUS) when they lay aside their corruptible character like an old garment and become new (CASSIODORUS, OECUMENIUS, ANDREW OF CAESAREA). This renewal will not involve the annihilation of the world's substance and the replacing of it by another, different substance (OECUMENIUS, ANDREW OF CAESAREA). Rather, through fire that which is corruptible will burn away, leaving only a transformed substance suitable to bodies now made immortal (AUGUSTINE). In this new heaven and earth, transformed and made fit for people now remade, the soul is

restored to its integrity and the body is restored to its original strength (AUGUSTINE). Then there will be no evil, and the restless and stormy turbulence of human life will also be no more (AUGUSTINE, ANDREW OF CAESAREA).

Then, too, that city created by heavenly grace will appear. The new Jerusalem has been "coming down" since the beginning, for continuously on the earth saints have been made citizens of it through the Holy Spirit (AUGUSTINE). This heavenly Jerusalem was prefigured in the tabernacle at the time of Moses (IRENAEUS, ANDREW OF CAESAREA), and similarly the city of Jerusalem in the land of Israel was an image of it, for in it the righteous were disciplined for incorruption (IREnaeus). Yet at the last judgment God's gift of grace will shine with such splendor that all previous prefigurements of the new Jerusalem will vanish in the spiritual bliss of the saints (Augustine, Oecumenius). That new Jerusalem is the blessed destiny of the saints (Oecumenius) in which they are united with the Lord in holiness and righteousness (Apringius, Andrew of Caesarea). There the Trinity dwells and reigns (Andrew of Caesarea), for God will be the reward of eternal bliss for those who have become his temple (Apringius).

In the bliss that the church shall enjoy after the resurrection (Caesarius of Arles) all suffering and death will come to an end (Oecumenius, Andrew of Caesarea), and where there is no suffering there is no sorrow (Tertullian); where there is no death there is no more presence of the devil (Origen). Rather, when their bodies have become incorruptible (Bede), the saints will enjoy the vision of inexpressible gladness (Andrew of Caesarea) as the contemplation of the eternal King feeds their minds (Bede).

## 21:1a A New Heaven and a New Earth

**When the Soul Is Restored to Its Integrity.** Augustine: Every rational soul is made unhappy by its sins or happy by its well doing. Every irrational soul yields to one that is more powerful, or obeys one that is better, or is on terms of equality with its equals, exercising rivals or harming any it has overcome. Every body is obedient to its soul so far as permitted by the merits of the latter or the orderly arrangement of things. There is no evil in the universe, but in individuals there is evil due to their own fault. When the soul has been regenerated by the grace of God and restored to its integrity and made subject to him alone by whom it was created, its body too will be restored to its original strength, and it will receive power to possess the world, not to be possessed by the world. Then it will have no evil. For the lowly beauty of temporal changes will not involve it, for it will have been raised above change. There will be, as it is written, a new heaven and a new earth, and there souls will not have to do their part in toiling but will reign over the universe. "All things are yours," says the apostle, "and you are Christ's and Christ is God's."[1] And again: "The head of the woman is the man, the head of the man is Christ, and the head of Christ is God."[2] Accordingly, since the vice of the soul is not its nature but contrary to its nature and is nothing else than sin and sin's penalty, we understand that no nature, or, if you prefer it, no substance or essence, is evil. Of True Religion 23.44.[3]

**Terrestrial Fires.** Augustine: Having concluded his prophecy of the judgment awaiting bad people, John has to speak of what is to befall the good. . . . [The new heaven and earth] will happen in the order which he indicated, by anticipation, in the earlier verse where he said he saw sitting on a throne one from whose face heaven and earth fled away.[4] First, to be sure, will come the judgment of those uninscribed in the Book of Life and their consignment to eternal fire. . . . Afterwards, this world as we see it will pass away, burned away by terrestrial fires, just as the flood was caused by the overflowing of terrestrial waters. This conflagration will utterly burn away the corruptible characteristics proper to corruptible bodies, as such; whereupon our substance will possess only those qualities that are consistent with bodies immortalized in this marvelous transformation—to this end, that the world, remade into something better, will become fit for people now remade, even in their bodies, into something better. City of God 20.16.[5]

**Almighty God Establishes Heaven and Earth.** Cassiodorus: This passage announces the power and strength of the Lord with the words "He has established them forever, and for ages of ages: he has made a decree, and it shall not

---

[1]1 Cor 3:21-23. [2]1 Cor 11:3. [3]LCC 6:246. [4]Rev 20:11. [5]FC 24:291. Primasius follows the argument of Augustine (CCL 92:284-85).

pass away." This is to remove all doubt that God is almighty, for what he has established continues in being without change, since this conclusion is applied to the things of heaven. But we read of the world to come: "There will be a new heaven and a new earth," so how can one say of the present heaven "He has established them forever"? There is however no doubt that all things have been established by God. Though man himself dies, he is "established" in God's eyes when he rises again; similarly heaven and earth remain in God's sight when they are made new. Once they have laid aside their roughness or corruptible character, nature itself is made better and abides, since it has been bidden to exist in eternity. As Paul says about the transformation of our bodies: "When the corruptible has put on incorruption, and the mortal puts on immortality."[6] A "decree" means a law or condition, so that we may realize that all things are in his power. It cannot pass away because the Almighty established it, and Truth has promised it in return. EXPOSITION OF THE PSALMS 148.6.[7]

## HEAVEN AND EARTH WILL PUT OFF THEIR FILTH. OECUMENIUS: In his second letter Peter speaks in a similar way: "According to his promise we wait for new heavens and a new earth."[8] They do not say this as though heaven and earth and sea are destroyed and pass into nonexistence and that other things come into being in their place. Rather, they mean that the present realities have cast off their corruption and become new, putting off their filth as though it were an old and dirty garment. For that is called "new" which is not such as it was formerly but is as it has now become. The creation shall then be free of every corruption that it contracted through the transgression of humankind. The holy apostle is also a very trustworthy witness to these things when in his letter to the Romans he writes this about the [new] creation: "For the creation waits with eager longing for the revealing of the sons of God; for the creation was subjected to futility, not of its own will but by the will of him who subjected it

in hope, because the creation itself will be set free from its bondage to decay unto the glorious liberty of the children of God."[9] And not only he, but also the holy prophet sang of the heaven and the earth in the testimony just presented: "They will all wear out as a garment, and as a vesture you will fold them, and they will be changed."[10] COMMENTARY ON THE APOCALYPSE 20.13-21.2.[11]

## THE RENEWAL OF THE OLD. ANDREW OF CAESAREA: This passage does not speak of the obliteration of creation but of its renewal into something better. For as the apostle says, "this creation will be freed from the bondage of corruption into the freedom of the glory of the children of God."[12] Also the holy psalmist says, "You change them like a raiment, and they pass away."[13] The renewal of that which has grown old does not involve the annihilation of its substance but rather indicates the smoothing out of its agedness and its wrinkles. It is a custom among us to say concerning persons who have in some way become better or have become worse, "someone has become someone else." And so it is indicated concerning the heaven and the earth that they have "passed away" instead of have "changed." And this is also the same with us who have received death; we will change from a former condition to a better lot. COMMENTARY ON THE APOCALYPSE 21.1.[14]

## 21:1b The Sea Was No More

## THE RESTLESS AND STORMY LIFE OF PEOPLE WILL PASS AWAY. AUGUSTINE: It is hard to know whether [the sea] will be dried up by the terrible heat of those flames or will itself be transformed into something better. For though we read that there will be a new heaven and earth, I cannot recall having ever seen mentioned a new sea, save perhaps in that verse of the Apocalypse, "a sea of glass similar to crystal."[15] Yet in that pas-

---

[6]1 Cor 15:54. [7]ACW 53:452-53*. [8]2 Pet 3:13. [9]Rom 8:19-21. [10]Ps 101:27 LXX. [11]TEG 8:265-66. [12]See Rom 8:21. [13]Ps 102:26 (101:27 LXX). [14]MTS 1 Sup 1:232-33. [15]Rev 4:6; 15:2.

sage, John was not talking about the end of the world; moreover, he did not claim to have seen a sea proper, but something like a sea. Still, as prophecy is prone to intermingle the literal and metaphorical and so veil its meaning, it may be that in our present text, "and the sea is no more," John was speaking of the identical sea he spoke of earlier: "And the sea gave up the dead that were in it." For then, this world of ours, made restless and stormy by the lives of men (and, hence, figuratively, called the sea), will have passed away. City of God 20.16.[16]

**There Will Be No More Need of Commerce.** Andrew of Caesarea: Concerning the sea, it says that "the sea was no more." For what use is there of a sea when people no longer need to sail it or to acquire by means of it the goods grown in regions lying far away? Moreover the "sea" is symbolic of the turbulence and unsettledness of life, and so there will then be no need of it when there remains no trouble or fear among the saints. Commentary on the Apocalypse 21.1.[17]

### 21:2 The New Jerusalem Comes Down from Heaven

**In the New Jerusalem, Humanity Is Disciplined for Incorruption.** Irenaeus: Of this Jerusalem the former one is an image—that Jerusalem of the former earth in which the righteous are disciplined beforehand for incorruption and prepared for salvation. And of this tabernacle Moses received the pattern in the mount;[18] and nothing is capable of being allegorized, but all things are steadfast and true and substantial, having been made by God for righteous people's enjoyment. For as it is God truly who raises up humankind, so also does humankind truly rise from the dead, and not allegorically.... And as he rises actually, so also shall he be actually disciplined beforehand for incorruption and shall go forward and flourish in the times of the kingdom, in order that he may be capable of receiving the glory of the Father. Against Heresies 5.35.2.[19]

**In the New Jerusalem No Trace of Earthly Blemish Remains.** Augustine: This city is said to come down out of heaven in the sense that God created it by means of heavenly grace, as he told it through Isaiah: "I am the Lord creating thee."[20] Indeed, its descent from heaven began with the beginning of time, since it is by God's grace coming down from above through the "laver of regeneration" in the Holy Spirit sent from heaven that its citizenship has continuously grown up on earth. Yet only after God's last judgment, the one he has deputed to Jesus Christ his Son, will his tremendous gift of grace be revealed so brightly in [Jerusalem] that in this new brightness there will remain no traces of its earthly blemishes. For then its members' bodies will pass over from mortal corruptibility to the new immortality of incorruption. City of God 20.17.[21]

**The Saints Are United with Their Lord.** Apringius of Beja: The heavenly Jerusalem is the multitude of the saints who will come with the Lord, even as Zechariah said: "Behold, my Lord God will come, and all his saints with him."[22] These are being prepared for God as a fine dwelling, namely, those who will live with him. "As a bride adorned for her husband." Adorned with holiness and righteousness, they go to be united with their Lord and shall remain with him forever. Tractate on the Apocalypse 21.2.[23]

**Jerusalem Is the Blessed Destiny of the Saints.** Oecumenius: By Jerusalem he symbolizes the blessed destiny and dwelling of the saints, which he figuratively calls Jerusalem both here and in the following passages. He has described its adornment magnificently and becomingly, so that we might lead our minds from perceptible realities to the spiritual bliss of the life of the saints. Commentary on the Apocalypse 20.13-21.2.[24]

---

[16]FC 24:291-92. Primasius follows the argument of Augustine (CCL 92:285). [17]MTS 1 Sup 1:233. [18]Ex 25:40. [19]ANF 1:566. [20]See Is 45:8. [21]FC 24:292-93. Primasius follows the argument of Augustine (CCL 92:285-86). [22]Zech 14:5. [23]CCL 107:85. [24]TEG 8:266.

**THE KINGLY TRINITY DWELLS IN THE NEW JERUSALEM.** ANDREW OF CAESAREA: This passage shows the renewal and transformation to a more brilliant appearance that the Jerusalem above will acquire when it comes down from the incorporeal powers above to humankind, since Christ, our God, has become the common Head of both. This city is constructed of the saints concerning whom it is written, "Holy stones are rolled upon the land,"[25] and it has Christ as its cornerstone. It is called a "city," since it is the dwelling place of the kingly Trinity—for [the Trinity] dwells in it and walks in it, as he promised—and it is called "bride," since it is joined to the Lord and is united with him in the highest, inseparable conjunction. It is "adorned," since within, as the psalm says, it has glory and youth in its manifold virtues.[26] COMMENTARY ON THE APOCALYPSE 21.2.[27]

## 21:3 "The Dwelling of God Is with Men"

**THE LORD WILL REWARD HIS PEOPLE WITH GLADNESS.** APRINGIUS OF BEJA: The Lord gives witness to himself, for the multitude of the saints will become his temple, so that he might dwell with them forever and that he might be their Lord and they might be his people. He himself will take away all weeping and every tear from the eyes of those whom he rewards with eternal gladness and whom he makes bright with perpetual blessedness. TRACTATE ON THE APOCALYPSE 21.3-4.[28]

**WE WILL ALWAYS BE WITH THE LORD.** OECUMENIUS: He now unveils the symbolism [of Jerusalem as the spiritual destiny of the saints] and says, "Behold, the dwelling of God is with men, and he will dwell with them, and they shall be his people, and God himself will be with them and will be their God." The apostle indicated this even more clearly when he said, "Then we who are alive, who are left, shall be caught up in the clouds to meet the Lord in the air; and we shall always be with the Lord."[29] COMMENTARY ON THE APOCALYPSE 21.3-5.[30]

**THE CHURCH IS THE TYPE OF THE NEW JERUSALEM.** ANDREW OF CAESAREA: The saint is instructed from heaven that this is the true dwelling whose type was indicated by Moses, or rather the prefiguration of the type, since the type exists in the church of the present day. COMMENTARY ON THE APOCALYPSE 21.3-4.[31]

**GOD WILL BE THE REWARD OF ETERNAL BLISS.** BEDE: For the elect, God himself will be the reward of eternal bliss which, since they are possessed by him, they will possess into all eternity. EXPLANATION OF THE APOCALYPSE 21.3.[32]

## 21:4 Tears, Death and Pain Cease

**THERE WILL BE NO MORE SORROW.** TERTULLIAN: If sorrow, and mourning, and sighing and death itself assail us from the afflictions both of soul and body, how shall they be removed, except by the cessation of their causes, that is to say, the afflictions of flesh and soul? Where will you find adversities in the presence of God? Where incursions of an enemy in the bosom of Christ? Where attacks of the devil in the face of the Holy Spirit—now that the devil himself and his angels are "cast into the lake of fire"? Where now is necessity, and what [the pagans] call fortune or fate? What plague awaits the redeemed from death after their eternal pardon? What wrath is there for the reconciled after grace? What weakness after their renewed strength? What risk and danger after their salvation? ON THE RESURRECTION OF THE FLESH 58.[33]

**THE DEVIL WILL BE NO MORE WHEN DEATH IS NO MORE.** ORIGEN: It must be understood

---

[25]Zech 9:16. [26]Ps 45:13-14 (44:14 LXX). [27]MTS 1 Sup 1:233-34. Contrary to such spiritual interpretations of the new Jerusalem, Eusebius of Caesarea thinks of the new Christian monuments built by Constantine in Jerusalem: "On the very spot that witnessed the Savior's sufferings, a new Jerusalem was constructed" (*Life of Constantine* 33; NPNF 2 1:529). Eusebius is apparently referring to the Basilica of the Holy Sepulchre. [28]CCL 107:85. [29]1 Thess 4:17. [30]TEG 8:267. [31]MTS 1 Sup 1:234. [32]CCL 121A:519. [33]ANF 3:590-91.

concerning the devil that he has certainly been conquered and crucified, but for those who have been crucified with Christ, moreover for all believers and likewise for all people, the devil will also be crucified at the time when what the apostle says will be fulfilled: "As in Adam all die, so also in Christ will all be made alive."[34] Thus there is also in this a mystery of future resurrection. For then, too, the people will again be divided into two parts; then, too, there will also be certain ones in front and others behind, who when they unite into one for Jesus, then, at that time, the devil will certainly be no more "because death will be no more." . . . Concerning the devil, the apostle says, "Death, the last enemy, is destroyed"[35] because death is truly conquered when "this mortal is swallowed up by life."[36] HOMILIES ON JOSHUA 8.4.[37]

**THE SUFFERING OF THE SAINTS WILL COME TO AN END.** OECUMENIUS: "And he will wipe away every tear from their eyes," it says. The prophet Isaiah says something similar to this: "Death has prevailed and swallowed [people] up, but again God has taken every tear away from every face."[38] For if, as the holy apostle says, "pain and sorrow and sighing have fled away" in that blissful life of the saints,[39] how would any tears remain in the absence of those things? "The former things have passed away," it says. By this he means that the suffering of the saints has come to an end. Now the rewards for their toils have come. COMMENTARY ON THE APOCALYPSE 21.3-5.[40]

**IN THIS LIFE, HOLINESS RESULTS IN MORE ABUNDANT WEEPING.** PRIMASIUS: It is certain that all these benefits belong to the future life and not to this life. Indeed, in this life the more one is holy and the more full a person is of holy desires, the more abundant will be his weeping in prayer. For this reason we read, "My tears have been my

food day and night,"[41] and again, "Every night I flood my bed with tears."[42] COMMENTARY ON THE APOCALYPSE 21.4.[43]

**THE CHURCH WILL HAVE BLISS.** CAESARIUS OF ARLES: He has said all of this concerning the glory of the church such as it will possess after the resurrection. EXPOSITION ON THE APOCALYPSE 21.1-4, HOMILY 18.[44]

**THE VISION OF INEXPRESSIBLE GLADNESS.** ANDREW OF CAESAREA: In this tent made without hands there is no weeping nor any tears, for he who supplies the joy of the eternal temple will give to all the saints the vision of inexpressible gladness. That is, it is written, "pain and sorrow and sighing have passed away."[45] That "the first things have passed away" signifies that the suffering of the saints and the arrogance of the wicked have ceased, for an exchange of circumstances will occur for each of these groups. COMMENTARY ON THE APOCALYPSE 21.3-4.[46]

**INCORRUPTION TO THE BODY AND HEAVENLY CONTEMPLATION TO THE MIND.** BEDE: The glory of that city will be so great and so exalted from the goodness of God that no remnant of its [former] agedness will remain, namely, when the celestial incorruption will raise up all the bodies [of the saints] and the contemplation of the eternal King will feed their minds. . . . It was earlier said that death had been sent into the lake of fire. We can also now understand these statements in the same way, namely, that when the holy city has been glorified at the last judgment, mourning and crying and mortality will remain in Gehenna alone. EXPLANATION OF THE APOCALYPSE 21.4.[47]

---

[34]1 Cor 15:22. [35]1 Cor 15:26. [36]2 Cor 5:4. [37]FC 105:89. [38]Is 25:8. [39]Is 51:11. [40]TEG 8:267. [41]Ps 42:3 (41:4 LXX). [42]Ps 6:6 (6:7 LXX). [43]CCL 92:286. [44]PL 35:2449. [45]Is 51:11. [46]MTS 1 Sup 1:234-35. [47]CCL 121A:519-21.

## 21:5-8 "I MAKE ALL THINGS NEW"

*⁵And he who sat upon the throne said, "Behold, I make all things new." Also he said, "Write this, for these words are trustworthy and true." ⁶And he said to me, "It is done! I am the Alpha and the Omega, the beginning and the end. To the thirsty I will give from the fountain of the water of life without payment. ⁷He who conquers shall have this heritage, and I will be his God and he shall be my son. ⁸But as for the cowardly, the faithless, the polluted, as for murderers, fornicators, sorcerers, idolaters, and all liars, their lot shall be in the lake that burns with fire and sulphur, which is the second death."*

**OVERVIEW:** Truth himself speaks words that are true, and he here effects in reality (ANDREW OF CAESAREA) the renewal of the saints in all things, whereby they shine in splendor and are free from all sin and pain (APRINGIUS, OECUMENIUS). The words of him who is infinite God (OECUMENIUS) have nothing false in them and exclude all doubt about the future (PRIMASIUS). Moreover, the Truth who speaks "It is done!" is both the Creator of the world and he who consummates the world (BEDE). He is both God and man, and his providence extends from the first creature to the last (ANDREW OF CAESAREA). It is this One who shall bring all things to completion with a great suddenness (APRINGIUS).

To those who are still on the way to such completion, God freely gives the rain of the life-giving Spirit (PRIMASIUS, ANDREW OF CAESAREA). Those who here desired the remission of sins through baptism (CAESARIUS OF ARLES) will receive an inebriating abundance of spiritual rain in the fatherland of the new Jerusalem (PRIMASIUS). No suffering of this present world compares with that future life of the saints (OECUMENIUS, ANDREW OF CAESAREA). Those who remain steadfast in the labor of good works will become sons of God and enjoy the goodness of the Father (APRINGIUS, ANDREW OF CAESAREA). Those who remain in their sin and falsify virtue into evil counterfeits (OECUMENIUS) shall receive the painful wrath of the lake of fire (OECUMENIUS,

ANDREW OF CAESAREA). To keep us from such an inheritance, God urges us in every way, by harsh wrath and by kindness (ANDREW OF CAESAREA, BEDE), so that we might through the desire for bliss or through the fear of torment acquire the promised blessings (ANDREW OF CAESAREA). Let us pray God to keep us free from any weakness of our willpower (OECUMENIUS) but especially from the great detestable lie of religious hypocrisy (BEDE), so that we will not have received the grace of God in vain (ANDREW OF CAESAREA).

### 21:5 *"These Words Are True"*

**THE PROMISE OF THE MOST HIGH IS ACCOMPLISHED FOR THE SAINTS.** APRINGIUS OF BEJA: The promise of the Most High is accomplished for the saints, so that they might be renewed in all things and might shine with every splendor. Therefore, the apostle says, "and the dead will rise incorruptible,"[1] and they will change into glory. TRACTATE ON THE APOCALYPSE 21.5.[2]

**WHEN TEARS DO NOT INTERRUPT JOY, ALL THINGS ARE INDEED NEW.** OECUMENIUS: If the heaven, earth and the sea are new, and moreover if humankind and that which pertains to their joy and glory are new and in no way interrupted by tears or pains or sins, then indeed all things are

---

[1]1 Cor 15:52. [2]CCL 107:85.

new. "Do not think, O John," he says, "that because of their surpassing greatness what has been said and revealed to you is false or fantasy. All of these things are trustworthy and true. Therefore, write them down." COMMENTARY ON THE APOCALYPSE 21.3-5.[3]

**WORDS SPOKEN BY THE TRUTH.** ANDREW OF CAESAREA: These words are true, for they issue from the Truth himself and are [expressed] no longer by way of symbols. Rather, they are recognized by the realities themselves. COMMENTARY ON THE APOCALYPSE 21.5-6.[4]

## 21:6a "I Am the Alpha and Omega"

**THE PROMISES OF GOD ARE COMPLETED WITH QUICKNESS.** APRINGIUS OF BEJA: He declares that the matter is completed with such quickness so that it might be regarded as though it had already happened. Therefore, all these things are promised to those who conquer, so that the one who conquers might be called "son of God." TRACTATE ON THE APOCALYPSE 21.6-7.[5]

**GOD IS WITHOUT BEGINNING AND WITHOUT END.** OECUMENIUS: "They are done!" he says. What is done? These things, namely, that which is here spoken, and nothing in them is false. He has written "they are done," instead of "they shall be done." "I am the Alpha and the Omega, the beginning and the end," he says. Since he repeats what he had earlier said, also we, as it were following in his footsteps, repeat what we have said in previous passages. The phrase "Alpha and Omega, the beginning and the end" signifies that God is without any beginning and without any end. COMMENTARY ON THE APOCALYPSE 21.6-8.[6]

**NO ONE SHOULD DOUBT CONCERNING THE FUTURE.** PRIMASIUS: It is necessary that these [words] be believed not explained, especially since he said "It is done!" concerning the past so that no one might doubt concerning the future. COMMENTARY ON THE APOCALYPSE 21.5-6.[7]

**CHRIST IS DIVINE AND HUMAN.** ANDREW OF CAESAREA: Christ is "the first and the end," since he is "first" because of his divinity and "end" because of his humanity. Moreover, his providence extends from the first creation of the incorporeal creatures to the last human beings. COMMENTARY ON THE APOCALYPSE 21.5-6.[8]

**CHRIST CREATED THE WORLD AND CONSUMMATES IT.** BEDE: Just as he testified at the beginning of the book that he was [the Alpha and the Omega],[9] so now this is repeated for the third time,[10] so that no one might believe that there is any other god before him or any other god after him, as Isaiah says.[11] Indeed, since he is speaking of the end of the world, the one who consummates the world should be understood to be the same one as he who was its creator. EXPLANATION OF THE APOCALYPSE 21.6.[12]

## 21:6b To the Thirsty I Give Freely

**THE SUFFERINGS OF THE PRESENT NOT EQUAL TO THE FUTURE BLESSINGS.** OECUMENIUS: In the Gospels the Lord says, "Blessed are they who hunger and thirst after righteousness, for they shall be filled."[13] Therefore, to one who thirsts after such a thirst, I shall give life without payment. But how is it that he said "without payment," since the saints attain to the future life with very great hardships? Why, therefore, does he say that he gives it "without payment"? He says this to indicate that one never bears anything worthy of the blessings of that [future] time, no matter how much one might labor. And the apostle made the same point when he said, "For I consider that the sufferings of this present time are not worth comparing with the glory that is to be revealed to us."[14] COMMENTARY ON THE APOCALYPSE 21.6-8.[15]

---

[3]TEG 8:267. [4]MTS 1 Sup 1:235. [5]CCL 107:85. [6]TEG 8:268. [7]CCL 92:286. [8]MTS 1 Sup 1:235. [9]Rev 1:8. [10]Here and at Rev 22:13. [11]Is 43:10. [12]CCL 121A:521. [13]Mt 5:6. [14]Rom 8:18. [15]TEG 8:268.

**God Waters Those on the Way and Those in the Fatherland.** Primasius: From this fountain [God] refreshes believers who are now on the way. However, to those who conquer he will provide abundantly [from this fountain] and give them to drink in the fatherland. He causes rain to fall upon both, so that those who are still on the way are not deprived of drink in this desert and so that those who become citizens [of the new Jerusalem] might continually be inebriated from the stream of delights that come from God. Commentary on the Apocalypse 21.6.[16]

**The Remission of Sins Comes Through Baptism.** Caesarius of Arles: This is to say, [I will give from the fountain of life] to him who desires the remission of sins through the font of baptism. Exposition on the Apocalypse 21.6, Homily 18.[17]

**Christ Promises the Spirit to Those Who Believe.** Andrew of Caesarea: To the one who thirsts after righteousness he promises to grant the joy of the life-giving Spirit that he supplied in the Gospels to those who believed in him. It is "without payment" either because "the sufferings of this present time are not worth comparing with the glory that is to be revealed to the saints,"[18] or because it is not possessed except by the good works and the goodness of him who gives it. Commentary on the Apocalypse 21.6.[19]

## 21:7 "I Will Be His God"

**He Becomes a Son of God Who Conquers the Demons.** Andrew of Caesarea: He who conquers in the war against the invisible demons will receive these good things, becoming a son of God and reveling in the good gifts of the Father. Commentary on the Apocalypse 21.7.[20]

## 21:8 The Second Death

**Death Awaits Those Weak to Every**

**Good Work.** Oecumenius: But "for the vile and the unfaithful" and such as those, there will be an inheritance "in the lake of fire." He calls those "vile" who are weak to every good work, for the endurance of hardship is a matter of one's willpower. "And all liars," it says. He did not say "for all liars" but "for all deceivers," that is, those who behave contrary to nature and falsify the natural beauty of virtue into the base and counterfeit appearance of evil. Commentary on the Apocalypse 21.6-8.[21]

**God Exhorts Us Through Kindness and Anger.** Andrew of Caesarea: The God who thirsts after our salvation urges us in every way, both through kindness and through anger, toward the inheritance of his blessings. He brings now before our eyes the brightness of the heavenly Jerusalem and the dark, painful wrathfulness of the fiery Gehenna, so that whether through a desire for eternal bliss or through fear of unending torment, we might, as there is opportunity, acquire that which is good together with the rest of those in need. He indicates that those who were cowards and deserters in the battle against the devil will be condemned to the second death. May we propitiate him who desires mercy and does not will the death of sinners but their conversion, and so [let us] obtain his gifts by good deeds. To these [gifts] he exhorts us, not only through the enticement of words but also through the enticement of works and sufferings. For it suffices him to encourage toward the good and to discourage from evil, and afterward either to punish or to honor those worthy of glory or punishment. He did not disdain to suffer for us lest by his own power or by his appearance he might harm or disregard anything that pertains to our healing and restoration. Therefore, let us not receive the grace of God in vain, but let us render his beneficence effective by conversion and by the demonstra-

---

[16]CCL 92:286. [17]PL 35:2449. [18]Rom 8:18. [19]MTS 1 Sup 1:235-36. [20]MTS 1 Sup 1:236. [21]TEG 8:268-69.

tion of good works, so that we might attain to the promised blessings in Christ himself, our God, with whom be glory to the Father, together with the Holy Spirit forever and ever. Amen. Commentary on the Apocalypse 21.8.[22]

**God Encourages Watchfulness.** Bede: He always mixes harsh sayings in with the easy and appealing words, so that watchfulness is encouraged. Psalm 144 does the same when it mentions the grace of God's abundant mercies and suddenly mentions also his impending judgment: "The Lord watches over all who love him but will destroy all sinners."[23] He mentions the cowardly along with the unbelievers, since those who doubt the rewards for those who conquer will certainly be afraid to undergo trial. . . . He shows that there are many classes of liars. However, the greatest and most detestable liar is the one who sins in religion. The author spoke of such persons above: "They say that they are Jews but they are not, for they are lying; they are the synagogue of Satan."[24] Explanation of the Apocalypse 21.8.[25]

[22]MTS 1 Sup 1:236-37. [23]Ps 145:20 (144:20 LXX). [24]Rev 2:9. [25]CCL 121A:521-23.

## 21:9-27 THE BEAUTY AND GLORY OF THE HOLY CITY JERUSALEM

*9Then came one of the seven angels who had the seven bowls full of the seven last plagues, and*
*spoke to me, saying, "Come, I will show you the Bride, the wife of the Lamb." 10And in the Spirit he*
*carried me away to a great, high mountain, and showed me the holy city Jerusalem coming down out*
*of heaven from God, 11having the glory of God, its radiance like a most rare jewel, like a jasper, clear*
*as crystal. 12It had a great, high wall, with twelve gates, and at the gates twelve angels, and on the*
*gates the names of the twelve tribes of the sons of Israel were inscribed; 13on the east three gates, on*
*the north three gates, on the south three gates, and on the west three gates. 14And the wall of the city*
*had twelve foundations, and on them the twelve names of the twelve apostles of the Lamb.*

*15And he who talked to me had a measuring rod of gold to measure the city and its gates and*
*walls. 16The city lies foursquare, its length the same as its breadth; and he measured the city with*
*his rod, twelve thousand stadia;*[q] *its length and breadth and height are equal. 17He also measured*
*its wall, a hundred and forty-four cubits by a man's measure, that is, an angel's. 18The wall was*
*built of jasper, while the city was pure gold, clear as glass. 19The foundations of the wall of the city*
*were adorned with every jewel; the first was jasper, the second sapphire, the third agate, the fourth*
*emerald, 20the fifth onyx, the sixth carnelian, the seventh chrysolite, the eighth beryl, the ninth*
*topaz, the tenth chrysoprase, the eleventh jacinth, the twelfth amethyst. 21And the twelve gates*
*were twelve pearls, each of the gates made of a single pearl, and the street of the city was pure gold,*
*transparent as glass.*

*²²And I saw no temple in the city, for its temple is the Lord God the Almighty and the Lamb. ²³And the city has no need of sun or moon to shine upon it, for the glory of God is its light, and its lamp is the Lamb. ²⁴By its light shall the nations walk; and the kings of the earth shall bring their glory into it, ²⁵and its gates shall never be shut by day—and there shall be no night there; ²⁶they shall bring into it the glory and the honor of the nations. ²⁷But nothing unclean shall enter it, nor any one who practices abomination or falsehood, but only those who are written in the Lamb's book of life.*

q About fifteen hundred miles

---

**OVERVIEW:** John is granted a vision of the heavenly Jerusalem. Formed and betrothed in the blood of Christ (ANDREW OF CAESAREA), the church always gives birth to sons for God (BEDE) who live in spiritual splendor in God and with God (OECUMENIUS). The church is established upon the mountain of Christ (PRIMASIUS, CAESARIUS OF ARLES) and will appear at the first resurrection (VICTORINUS) but especially when she will be glorified by God (ANDREW OF CAESAREA). However, although the body of Christ is the light of the world (PRIMASIUS) and is pure in mind and faith (BEDE), yet her glory is not from herself. The city of Christ is illumined by Christ (APRINGIUS) who is the life-giving, pure and unfading radiance of the church (OECUMENIUS, ANDREW OF CAESAREA).

Christ also is the wall and the door of the glorious city. Through him the patriarchs and the apostles have entered into the city (APRINGIUS), and in Christ they have become themselves doors and walls of the city (OECUMENIUS, PRIMASIUS, CAESARIUS OF ARLES, ANDREW OF CAESAREA). Even as once angels assisted the apostles in the first proclamation of the gospel (OECUMENIUS, ANDREW OF CAESAREA), so now the teachers of the church proclaim that apostolic message (BEDE). That message is of the holy Trinity (OECUMENIUS), which has been preached throughout the world (APRINGIUS, CAESARIUS OF ARLES, BEDE) and is made firm in the spiritual sea of baptism that cleanses the world of its sins (ANDREW OF CAESAREA).

In the city of God all things are measured by the faith in the incarnation of the Lord (APRING-

IUS) who is the Wisdom of God (PRIMASIUS) and in whom all the saints are well founded, protected and made themselves wise (CAESARIUS OF ARLES, ANDREW OF CAESAREA, BEDE). Built upon the Rock, which is Christ (PRIMASIUS), the holy city is itself unchangeable and perfectly stable in faith, hope and love (APRINGIUS, OECUMENIUS, ANDREW OF CAESAREA, BEDE). In this perfection the saints will be like the angels (OECUMENIUS) enjoying an unfading life and wisdom in the flesh taken from the gentle Virgin (APRINGIUS, ANDREW OF CAESAREA). They will shine with every gift of the Holy Spirit (APRINGIUS, PRIMASIUS, CAESARIUS OF ARLES) and surpass the glory of the old covenant (ANDREW OF CAESAREA).

The city of God will possess the virtue of every precious jewel, for the twelve apostles possessed every spiritual virtue (ANDREW OF CAESAREA) as will every soul of the saints (BEDE). The splendor of that city is beyond our comprehension (ANDREW OF CAESAREA), for its glory is that of Christ, which he has given to it (ANDREW OF CAESAREA, BEDE). Of this splendor the Old Testament was but shadow (OECUMENIUS). Even though the glory of the saints will differ according to their merits (APRINGIUS, PRIMASIUS), all will be as pure as glass (OECUMENIUS) and none will be thought unworthy (PRIMASIUS). Possessing in perfection a blessed habitation in God (PRIMASIUS, CAESARIUS OF ARLES), the heavenly city will be also the temple of God (ANDREW OF CAESAREA) for one of the holy Trinity was incarnated (OECUMENIUS) so that the church might have all being, all knowledge and all love. In the ineffable light of Christ (PRIMASIUS) the darkness of our humanity will be made light in the humanity of Christ (APRINGIUS). There Christ will reward his saints for their suffering in the world (VICTORINUS). There Christ will be eternal Life (PRIMASIUS). There what was promised to Abraham (VICTORINUS) will be experienced in its fullness. There no sinner or heretic will intrude (APRINGIUS, OECUMENIUS, PRIMASIUS). For there, in the city above, all that is seen is loved, and what is loved is praised (PRIMASIUS).

## 21:9 *"I Will Show You the Bride"*

**THE BLISS OF THE SAINTS WILL BE IN GOD AND WITH GOD.** OECUMENIUS: The angel intends to show the church of the "firstborn who are enrolled in heaven," which he also calls the "heavenly Jerusalem." Paul spoke to the Hebrews of this church, writing, "For you have not come to a mountain that may be touched, to a blazing fire, darkness and gloom, and a tempest and the sound of a trumpet, and a voice whose words made the hearers entreat that no further message be spoken to them. For they could not endure the order that was given, 'If even a beast touches the mountain, it shall be stoned.' Indeed, so terrifying was the sight that he said, 'I tremble with fear.' But you have come to Mount Zion and to the city of the living God, the heavenly Jerusalem, and to innumerable angels in festal gathering, and to the assembly of the firstborn who are enrolled in heaven and to a judge who is God of all."[1] In the gathering or the assembly of all the saints into one, that is, by the image of the heavenly Jerusalem, the passage depicts the blessedness of the saints and the life that they will have in God and with God. As we indicated, he adorns it with physical and magnificent imagery in order to guide our mind to some extent from its depiction to its spiritual glory and splendor. COMMENTARY ON THE APOCALYPSE 21.9-14.[2]

**CHRIST BETROTHED THE CHURCH WITH HIS BLOOD.** ANDREW OF CAESAREA: Through this

passage it is shown that the angels not only induce the worst plagues but also act as physicians, at one time cutting and at another time applying healing medications. For he who once brought on a plague to those who deserved it, now shows to the saint the beatitude of the church. And fittingly does he call the bride the "wife" of the Lamb. For when Christ was slaughtered as a lamb, he at that time betrothed [the church] with his own blood. For just as when Adam was sleeping, the woman was formed through the taking of the rib, so also the church, formed through the shedding of blood from the side of Christ as he was sleeping voluntarily on the cross through death, was united with him who suffered for us. COMMENTARY ON THE APOCALYPSE 21.9.[3]

**THE CHURCH GIVES BIRTH TO SPIRITUAL SONS FOR GOD.** BEDE: He calls the church "bride" and "wife," for while remaining herself pure and immaculate, she is always giving birth to spiritual sons for God. Or, [she is called "bride" and "wife"] because although she is now betrothed to God, she will at that time be led to the neverending wedding feast. EXPLANATION OF THE APOCALYPSE 21.9.[4]

## 21:10 *He Showed Me the Holy City*

**AT THE TIME OF THE KINGDOM.** VICTORINUS OF PETOVIUM: At the time of the kingdom and of the first resurrection, the holy city will appear, which, it says, will come down from heaven. It will be foursquare and decorated with jewels of different value, color and kind, and it will be like pure gold, that is, clear and transparent. It says that its street will be paved with crystal and that the river of life will flow through the middle, as do fountains of the waters of life. The tree of life will produce different fruits each month. There will be there no light from the sun, since there

---

[1]Heb 12:18-23. [2]TEG 8:269-70. [3]MTS 1 Sup 1:238. [4]CCL 121A:523.

will be a more outstanding glory. For it says, the Lamb—that is, God—will be its light. COMMENTARY ON THE APOCALYPSE 21.1.[5]

**THROUGH THE SPIRIT THE CHURCH WILL BEAR THE HEAVENLY IMAGE.** PRIMASIUS: By the testimony of the Truth this is the "city set on a hill."[6] Also Isaiah says, "The mountain of the house of the Lord shall be established as the highest of the mountains and shall be raised above the hills."[7] [Isaiah says this] either because of the height of its righteousness, of which we read, "Your righteousness is like the mountains of God,"[8] or because both the apostles and the prophets are called mountains. However, being more excellent than all others, the Lord Christ towers as a mountain above the heights of mountains, and from his fullness, it says, we receive grace for grace.[9] Fittingly he says [that the city comes] down out of heaven from God, for [the church's] beauty will then be seen more fully, when through the Spirit, by whom her bridegroom is believed to have been conceived and born, she has merited to bear the heavenly image. Therefore, it is this very bride that is this city. COMMENTARY ON THE APOCALYPSE 21.9-10.[10]

**ESTABLISHED ON THE MOUNTAIN, WHICH IS CHRIST.** CAESARIUS OF ARLES: By the mountain he refers to Christ. . . . It is the church, the city established on the mountain, that is the bride of the Lamb. The city is then established on the mountain when on the shoulders of the Shepherd[11] it is called back like a sheep to its own sheepfold. For were the church one and the city coming down from heaven another, there would be two brides, which is simply not possible. He has called this city the "bride" of the Lamb, and therefore it is clear that it is the church itself that is going to be described. EXPOSITION ON THE APOCALYPSE 21.10, HOMILY 19.[12]

**THE SEER CONTEMPLATES THE SUBLIME LIFE OF THE SAINTS.** ANDREW OF CAESAREA: That

he was "carried away in the Spirit" indicates that through the Spirit he was elevated in his mind from earthly things to the contemplation of heavenly realities. The image of the "great mountain" indicates the sublime and transcendent life of the saints, in which the wife of the Lamb, the Jerusalem above, will be made beautiful and glorified by God. COMMENTARY ON THE APOCALYPSE 21.10-11.[13]

**THE HOLY CITY WILL FILL THE WHOLE WORLD.** BEDE: After the destruction of Babylon, the holy city, which is the bride of the Lamb, is seen located on a mountain. The stone which was cut out of the mountain without hands broke the image of the world's glory into small pieces, and it grew into a great mountain and filled the whole world.[14] EXPLANATION OF THE APOCALYPSE 21.10.[15]

### 21:11 Radiance Like Jasper, Clear as Crystal

**ILLUMINED BY THE LIGHT OF GOD ALONE.** APRINGIUS OF BEJA: We read of this very city in the prophets: "The sun shall be no more your light by day, nor shall the brightness of the moon give you light. But the Lord will be everlasting light, and your God will be your glory."[16] . . . As the brilliance of a stone shines neither in itself nor from the outside, but it is translucent by the clarity of its nature, so this city is described as illumined by no radiance of the stars but as invisibly illumined by the light of God alone. The shining clarity of the crystal signifies that in the city the grace of baptism shines with a reddish hue.[17] TRACTATE ON THE APOCALYPSE 21.10-11.[18]

**CHRIST IS LIFE-GIVING AND HOLY.** OECUMENIUS: "Its radiance," that is, Christ "the sun of

---

[5]CSEL 49:146. Victorinus gives a free rendering of Rev 21—22 to express his millenialist interpretation. [6]Mt 5:14. [7]Is 2:2. [8]See Is 48:18. [9]Jn 1:16. [10]CCL 92:287-88. [11]See Lk 15:5. [12]PL 35:2450. [13]MTS 1 Sup 1:239. [14]See Dan 2:34-35. [15]CCL 121A:525. [16]Is 60:19. [17]Baptism is into the death of Christ. [18]CCL 107:86. [19]Mal 4:2.

righteousness,"[19] was "like a jasper." Jasper has a certain green quality and so exhibits the life-bearing and life-giving nature of Christ, who "opens his hand and satisfies the desire of every living thing."[20] Indeed, green plants are the chief form of earthly food. The jasper was also like crystal and so symbolizes the purity and the holiness of Christ, for he "did no sin, and there was no deceit in his mouth," as the prophecy of Isaiah says.[21] COMMENTARY ON THE APOCALYPSE 21.9-14.[22]

## THE ENTIRE BODY OF CHRIST IS THE LIGHT OF THE WORLD. PRIMASIUS: [To which bride] the Lord says, "You are the light of the world."[23] This expression pertains to the entire body of Christ, although the apostles heard it from the mouth of the Truth, since they were first in both time and merit. . . . Although the jasper and the crystal are different kinds of stones with different colors, nonetheless here he aptly conjoins both of them for the sake of the metaphor. He compares them to a most precious stone, so that it would be understood to refer to Christ, of whom the blessed Peter spoke: "a cornerstone precious, laid firm in the foundation."[24] COMMENTARY ON THE APOCALYPSE 21.11.[25]

## THE GENEROSITY OF CHRIST. ANDREW OF CAESAREA: The radiance of the church is Christ, who here is depicted as a jasper and clear as crystal to indicate that he is unfading and life-giving and pure. He is also depicted by means of other images. For the manifold diversity of his generosity for us cannot be described merely through the illustration of one form. COMMENTARY ON THE APOCALYPSE 21.11.[26]

## PURE OF MIND AND SINCERE IN FAITH. BEDE: The precious stone is Christ, who said, "The glory that you have given to me, I have given to them."[27] . . . [The city's light is likened] to jasper because of the clarity of its virtues, and to crystal because of the inner purity of its mind and its sincere faith. EXPLANATION OF THE APOCALYPSE 21.11.[28]

## 21:12 Twelve Gates, Twelve Angels, the Names of Twelve Tribes

### THE PATRIARCHS AND APOSTLES KNOW THE OMNIPOTENT GOD. APRINGIUS OF BEJA: "And it had a great, high wall." Zechariah said, "For I will be," says the Lord, "a wall of fire round about."[29] What is so great and high as the Lord of majesty, who with the protection of his presence surrounds the holy city? "And it had twelve gates and at the gates twelve corners,[30] and the names of the twelve tribes of the sons of Israel were written [on the gates]." In the Gospel we read that the Lord spoke concerning himself: "I am the door; if any one enters by me, he will enter and will find pasture."[31] Therefore, Christ is the door. However, the ancient people of our faith are named together not as doors, but their names are written on the gates, that is, on the doors. Thus our Lord shows to all the saints that he is the door of truth and freedom. This shows that the whole band of the patriarchs belonged to the faith in our Lord Jesus Christ. The twelve corners of the gates, and the twelve gates and the twelve foundations on which the names of the apostles and of the Lamb are written yield the number of thirty-six. It is clear that this is the number of hours that our Lord Jesus Christ lay in the grave after his passion. This demonstrates that the host of leaders who came beforehand and the chorus of apostles who came afterwards had been redeemed by the one faith and passion of the Lord, and that they have come to the knowledge of the omnipotent God through the one entrance of faith in Christ, who is the door. For also the names of apostles themselves are said to be written upon the twelve foundations, because Christ is the foundation, as Paul says, "For no other foundation can anyone lay than that which is laid, which is Jesus Christ."[32] And he himself is in each, and each is in him. The Lord says, "You are

[20]Ps 145:16 (144:16 LXX). [21]Is 53:9. [22]TEG 8:270-71. [23]Mt 5:14. [24]1 Pet 2:6. [25]CCL 92:288. [26]MTS 1 Sup 1:239. [27]Jn 17:22. [28]CCL 121A:525. [29]Zech 2:5. [30]The text of Apringius reads *angylos* ("corners"), not *angelos* ("angels") as does the text of Caesarius and Bede. [31]Jn 10:9. [32]1 Cor 3:11.

Peter, and on this rock I will build my church."[33] And it is written in the words of the most blessed Paul that "the rock was Christ."[34] Therefore, it is Peter to whom the Lord spoke: "On this rock I will build my church."[35] That is, the church is built upon faith in the incarnation, passion and resurrection of the Lord. Tractate on the Apocalypse 21.12.[36]

**Holy Angels Assisted in the Proclamation of the Gospel.** Oecumenius: The wall of the saints, or of the church, is Christ himself, since he is our bulwark, our fence and our help. "It had," it says, "twelve gates." This symbolizes the holy apostles who proclaimed to us the way of faith in Christ. "And at the gates there were twelve angels." I am convinced that there were also holy angels who worked with the holy apostles for the faith of the world. For if the law that came from Moses was proclaimed by angels, as the apostle says: "For if the message declared by angels was valid,"[37] how much more would not the proclamation of the gospel possess the cooperation of angels? "And names inscribed," it says, "that are the names of the twelve tribes of Israel." In a material sense, Israel is those who were begotten from Jacob the patriarch. However, spiritually, Israel is those who walk by the faith of our father Abraham. Of this the apostle is witness, saying, "The father of the circumcision not only for those who are of the circumcision but also for those who follow the example of the faith of our father Abraham."[38] For Israel interpreted means "a mind that beholds God" or a mind that has spiritual discernment. And who, other than the faithful, have seen God with the mind or have acquired spiritual discernment by the abundant working of the Spirit? Therefore, their names are written upon the gates of the city. To be sure, the twelve tribes symbolize the complete number of the saints. For having once called the faithful Israel, he mentions also the number, which signifies their fullness, saying, "twelve tribes." Commentary on the Apocalypse 21.9-14.[39]

**Israel Came Directly from the Patriarchs.** Primasius: The wall of the church is Christ, and we read [that this wall] is both great and high: "Great is the Lord and greatly to be praised in the city of our God, on his holy mountain,"[40] and "The Lord is high above all the nations."[41] Of this wall the prophet Isaiah said, "In this day this song will be sung in the land of Judah, 'We have a strong city; a savior is placed in it as a wall and bulwark. Open the gates, so that a righteous nation that keeps truth may enter in and the ancient error stay away.'"[42] Singing together by one Spirit, they are seen to relate similar realities. He continues by speaking of the gates. There are twelve gates, and at the gates twelve angels and the names of the twelve tribes of the sons of Israel are inscribed [on the gates]. We know that our Lord originally offered entrance to the faith through the twelve apostles. However, the context of this passage prohibits that meaning when it now mentions the twelve tribes of the sons of Israel. The passage intends that we first consider the patriarchs from whose stock we know that the whole race of the Israelites was directly propagated. From these, according to the apostle, "there is a remnant saved by the election of grace,"[43] and he adds that "God has not rejected his people."[44] Therefore, in this passage we ought to interpret the [twelve] gates to signify the twelve patriarchs, especially since we hear that "you do not support the root, but the root supports you."[45] . . . I think that the angels signify those elders and princes whose administration and leadership marvelously ruled that nation [of Israel]. Commentary on the Apocalypse 21.12.[46]

**The Church Is Built on the Prophets and the Apostles.** Caesarius of Arles: The twelve gates and the twelve angels are the apostles

---

[33]Mt 16:18. [34]1 Cor 3:11. [35]Mt 16:18. [36]CCL 107:86-87. [37]Heb 2:2. [38]See Rom 4:12. [39]TEG 8:271-72. [40]Ps 48:1 (47:1 LXX). [41]Ps 113:4 (112:4 LXX). [42]Is 26:1-3. [43]Rom 11:5. [44]Rom 11:2. [45]Rom 11:18. [46]CCL 92:288-89.

and the prophets, for as it is written, we "are built upon the foundation of the apostles and the prophets."[47] The Lord also spoke in a similar way to Peter: "Upon this rock I shall build my church."[48] EXPOSITION ON THE APOCALYPSE 21.12, HOMILY 19.[49]

**PROMINENT ANGELS ASSIST THE SOWERS OF THE WORD.** ANDREW OF CAESAREA: Christ is the great and high wall of the church that protects those in the holy city. In the wall are twelve gates, which are his holy apostles through whom we have acquired access and entry to the Father. And these are assisted by twelve angels who are preeminent and especially close to God in their holiness. For if we believe that a protecting angel follows each one of the faithful, how much more does it follow that those ranked first among the angels [accompany] those who are the foundations of the church and are sowers of the evangelical word and serve as assistants in the preaching of the gospel? The names of the tribes of the spiritual Israel are written over the gates of the apostles, even as they were written on the shoulder strap of the physical high priest long ago. The writing of these names now testifies to the solicitude of the apostles for the faithful, just as Paul said that he had "anxiety for all the churches"[50] and that "his heart is wide"[51] and that he comes to all "those whom he begot through the gospel."[52] COMMENTARY ON THE APOCALYPSE 21.12.[53]

**THE TEACHERS OF THE CHURCH.** BEDE: [The wall represents] the unconquerable strength of [the church's] faith, hope and love. The Lord himself can be understood to be this great wall that protects the church on every side. Isaiah spoke of this: "A wall and a bulwark is set up in it."[54] [Isaiah is speaking] of the protection of the Lord and of the intercession of the saints who make a path to the city by addressing their teaching to the hearts of the faithful. The twelve gates are the apostles who by their writing and their work first made known to all the Gentiles the

entrance into the church. [The twelve angels] are the teachers who in the mystery of faith and word follow in the footsteps of the apostles. . . . [The names of the twelve sons of Israel] signify the remembrance of the ancient fathers that is implanted in the hearts of preachers. For this reason when the high priest entered the tabernacle, he was commanded to carry the remembrance of the fathers in his mind and understanding.[55] EXPLANATION OF THE APOCALYPSE 21.12.[56]

### 21:13 Three Gates Each Toward the Four Directions

**THE WHOLE WORLD HAS ACCEPTED THE TRINITY.** APRINGIUS OF BEJA: It says that the gates are divided into four groups: "on the east three gates, on the north three gates, on the south three gates, and on the west three gates." This signifies that the four parts of the world have accepted the mystery of the Trinity. That the names of the patriarchs are inscribed demonstrates that the ancient faith has been fulfilled. TRACTATE ON THE APOCALYPSE 21.13.[57]

**THE APOSTLES PROCLAIMED THE CONSUBSTANTIAL TRINITY.** OECUMENIUS: It says that there were three gates on each of the four corners of the world. For the holy apostles conceived all things [in threes], proclaiming the consubstantial Trinity to the nations and "baptizing them in the name of the Father and of the Son and of the Holy Spirit."[58] COMMENTARY ON THE APOCALYPSE 21.9-14.[59]

**THE TRINITY IS PREACHED IN THE CHURCH.** CAESARIUS OF ARLES: The city that is described is the church, which is extended throughout the whole world. There are groups of three gates on each of the four sides because throughout the four quarters of the world the mystery of the

---

[47]Eph 2:20. [48]Mt 16:18. [49]PL 35:2450. [50]2 Cor 11:28. [51]2 Cor 6:11. [52]1 Cor 4:15. [53]MTS 1 Sup 1:239-40. [54]Is 26:1. [55]Ex 28:12. [56]CCL 121A:525-27. [57]CCL 107:87. [58]Mt 28:19. [59]TEG 8:272.

Trinity is preached in the church. Exposition on the Apocalypse 21.13, Homily 19.[60]

**The Spiritual Sea of Baptism.** Andrew of Caesarea: The four-sided form of the gates and their threefold entries signifies the understanding of the one who worships the Trinity. This understanding is throughout the four-cornered universe, and we have received it through the life-giving cross. For the cruciform shape of the position of the gates is according to the form of the twelve oxen that bore the Sea erected by Solomon.[61] These oxen signify the threefold grouping of the apostles by fours, the herald of the Holy Trinity and the extension of the four Gospels into the four corners of the earth. Through this is symbolized the spiritual sea of baptism that cleanses the world from its sins and that was instituted by the spiritual Solomon. Commentary on the Apocalypse 21.13.[62]

**Faith in the Trinity Throughout the World.** Bede: In my opinion this skillful description of the gates intends to indicate the mystery of the number twelve. It can therefore suggest either the whole number of the apostles or the perfection of the church, for through her the faith in the holy Trinity is made known to the four corners of the earth. Explanation of the Apocalypse 21.13.[63]

## 21:14 Twelve Foundations, the Names of Twelve Apostles

**Christ Rests on the Preaching of the Apostles.** Oecumenius: "The wall of the city," it says, "had twelve foundations." Christ, whom we consider to be the wall, rests upon the preaching of the apostles, and he is placed upon them as "a precious cornerstone," as it is written.[64] On them, that is, upon the foundations, are the "twelve names of the twelve apostles of the Lamb." He has clearly revealed the symbol, saying explicitly that the apostles are the gates and the foundations of the holy city, the church. "Avoid-

ing the profane chatter of what is falsely called knowledge"[65] by the heretics, may we all remain in their teaching by the grace of Christ, our Guide and chief Shepherd, to whom be glory forever. Amen. Commentary on the Apocalypse 21.9-14.[66]

**In Christ, the One Foundation.** Primasius: Having mentioned the patriarchs, he now mentions the apostles. Although we know that the church has but a single foundation, that is, Christ, it is not surprising that here it is said to have twelve [foundations]. In Christ the apostles have merited to be foundations of the church, and of [Christ] the apostle said, "No other foundation can any one lay than that which is laid, which is Christ Jesus."[67] In Christ the apostles are also said to be "light," as he said to them, "You are the light of the world,"[68] although Christ alone is "the true light that enlightens every person coming into this world."[69] Therefore, Christ is the Light that enlightens, while the apostles are a light that is enlightened. The Holy Scripture often suggests many similar ideas. . . .[70] Therefore, in this passage we ought to recognize the twelve foundations to be the apostles, although as those called to be in the one Foundation, which is Jesus Christ. . . . Therefore, the apostles are foundations, but in the one foundation, Jesus. Moreover, Jesus alone, even without the apostles, is rightly called "foundation," while the apostles are without Christ in no way said to be foundations of the church. Commentary on the Apocalypse 21.14.[71]

**The Church Is Founded on the Apostles.** Andrew of Caesarea: The foundations of the wall are the blessed apostles, upon whom church of Christ has been established. Their names have been inscribed upon them, as upon a

---

[60]PL 35:2450. [61]See 1 Kings 7:23-25. [62]MTS 1 Sup 1:240-41. [63]CCL 121A:527. [64]Is 28:16. [65]1 Tim 6:20. [66]TEG 8:272. [67]1 Cor 3:11. [68]Mt 5:14. [69]Jn 1:9. [70]Primasius refers to Jas 1:18; 1 Cor 4:15; Mt 23:8-10; 1 Cor 1:13; Ps 120:1-2 (119:1-2 LXX). [71]CCL 92:290-91.

public placard, for the easy instruction of those who read them. COMMENTARY ON THE APOCALYPSE 21.14.[72]

**FOUNDED ON THE PATRIARCHS, APOSTLES, TEACHERS AND VIRTUES.** BEDE: By "foundations" the patriarchs can be designated, for in themselves, that is, by way of figure they entail the persons of the apostles. This city was founded through [the patriarchs], although it is through the apostles, as though through gates more wide, that the city is open to the nations that are going to believe. It should also be noted that when "foundation" is used in the plural, it means either the teachers of the church or its virtues. However, when "foundation" is used in the singular, it signifies the Lord himself, who is the foundation of foundations. EXPLANATION OF THE APOCALYPSE 21.14.[73]

### 21:15 A Golden Measuring Rod

**THE INCARNATE LORD IS THE MEASURE OF THE FAITH.** APRINGIUS OF BEJA: The wall of fire surrounding it is the Lord, as we have already said. The golden measuring rod is the faith concerning the Lord's incarnation, for on account of its purity and sinlessness his body is revealed to be clearer and more brilliant than any metal. He alone is the one through whom the measure of the faith and the integrity of the holy city is established, and he only is recognized as the measure of its gates and the height of its wall. TRACTATE ON THE APOCALYPSE 21.15.[74]

**CHRIST IS THE WISDOM OF GOD.** PRIMASIUS: Earlier John had said that a measuring rod was given to him, namely, the commission given to him to preach.[75] Now he says that the angel speaking with him has a golden measuring rod to measure the city and its gates and walls. It is necessary, therefore, to understand this angel as Christ, who is the Wisdom of God and by his power extends from one end [of the earth] to the other and "orders all things well."[76] Therefore, we

read, "Receive wisdom as gold."[77] Moreover, to Christ alone is it given to measure the city, for it is he who distributes to each one of the faithful the gifts of the spiritual graces, and who, as we read, "has ordered all things in number and measure and weight."[78] COMMENTARY ON THE APOCALYPSE 21.15-16.[79]

**FOUNDED ON THE FAITH.** CAESARIUS OF ARLES: In the golden rod he shows the members of the church, who, although weak in the flesh, are well founded in the golden faith. As the apostle says, "[We] have this treasure in earthen vessels."[80] EXPOSITION ON THE APOCALYPSE 21.15, HOMILY 19.[81]

**THE SAINTS WILL BE PROTECTED BY CHRIST.** ANDREW OF CAESAREA: The "golden measuring rod" indicates the excellence of the angel who measures, whom he saw in the form of a man. It indicates as well the excellence of the city that is being measured, whose wall we have interpreted to be Christ. The city is measured not by people but by an angel because of the purity and wisdom of its transcendent nature, to whom, as is probable, the greatness or the comely dignity of the city above is known. However, in this passage we think that the "wall" is suggestive of the divine covering and shelter by which the saints will be protected. COMMENTARY ON THE APOCALYPSE 21.15.[82]

**THE TEACHERS OF THE CHURCH EXAMINE THE MERITS OF EACH.** BEDE: One could also[83] think of the teachers of the church, who though weak in their bodies are heavenly in their mind and with wisdom examine the merits of each person. EXPLANATION OF THE APOCALYPSE 21.15.[84]

### 21:16 The City Is Foursquare

---

[72]MTS 1 Sup 1:241. [73]CCL 121A:527. [74]CCL 107:87. [75]See Rev 11:1. [76]Wis 8:1. [77]See Prov 16:16. [78]Wis 11:20. [79]CCL 92:292. [80]2 Cor 4:7. [81]PL 35:2451. [82]MTS 1 Sup 1:241. [83]Bede mentions first the interpretation of Primasius. [84]CCL 121A:529.

**PERFECT AND WHOLE IN FAITH AND HOLI-NESS.** APRINGIUS OF BEJA: [The city is four-square], that is, it persists in the faith of the four-fold gospel. It is said that its length is the same as its breadth, so that one might see that in its faith there is nothing disproportionate, nothing that has been added, and nothing that has been taken away. . . . He measured the city with his rod, which we understand to be the body of Christ, and it was twelve stadia. For the faith in Christ and the integrity of the holy people is recognized by means of these twelve stadia, that is, by means of the teaching of the apostles and the faith of the ancient fathers. "For the length and the breadth were the same." All things are equal, for nothing is found in the saints that is superfluous or that comes from the outside, nor is anything inferior found within them. TRACTATE ON THE APOCALYPSE 21.16.[85]

**THE BLISS OF THE SAINTS WILL BE UNCHANGEABLE.** OECUMENIUS: The four-square shape is called by the experts a cube. It is a flat surface of four corners, and when it is four-square and equal in all of its dimensions, they say that the cube exhibits great stability. For the blessings of the saints are permanent and un-changeable, since there is no change to corrupt their bliss. The grandeur of the city and the mag-nificence of the saints signify that although they are considerably less in number than are the sin-ners, they are not so small in number as not to fill such a city. COMMENTARY ON THE APOCALYPSE 21.15-22.[86]

**THE CHURCH IS BUILT ON THE UNSHAKEABLE ROCK.** PRIMASIUS: The apostle certainly recalls the dimension of the city when he says, "accord-ing to the measure of Christ's gift,"[87] and again, "To me, though I am the least of all the saints, this grace was given to me, to preach to the Gen-tiles."[88] Therefore, the city is said to be four-square and each side given an equal dimension, so that nothing might be marked by inequality. To be perfect, according to the apostle,[89] is to

have the same wisdom and to have peace, that is, truly to exist in the strength of a square. This is, then, that city that the Lord said in the Gospel was built on a hill, that is, was built on him-self.[90] And concerning this he also said to Peter, who is the image of the whole church, "You are Peter, and upon this rock I shall build my church."[91] It is as if he had said, "I will build you upon me." For Christ was the Rock, and there-fore from the Rock is the rock,[92] even as the Christian is from Christ. And Christ indeed teaches that every invention of human error is to be avoided and only the monuments of divine truth are to be followed. COMMENTARY ON THE APOCALYPSE 21.15-16.[93]

**PERFECTION OF LIFE AND OF REST FOR SOUL AND BODY.** ANDREW OF CAESAREA: The city is foursquare because of its stability and solidity. That which is of equal length in its depth and breadth and height is called by some a cube, and it suggests stability. The twelve thousand stadia that the city measures perhaps signify the size of the city, for, as David says, its inhabitants "shall be multiplied beyond the sand."[94] Or perhaps they are mentioned because of the number of the apostles through whom the city was estab-lished. The number seven, which is mystical, presents a solution through a certain line of rea-soning. The thousands of stadia, which are men-tioned, are equivalent to 1,714 miles, the thou-sand representing the perfection of eternal life, the seven hundred indicating the perfection of the rest, and the fourteen indicating the twofold sabbath of the soul and the body. For seven times two is fourteen. COMMENTARY ON THE APOCALYPSE 21.16.[95]

**THE CHURCH IS PERFECTLY STABLE IN FAITH, HOPE AND LOVE.** BEDE: [The twelve

---

[85]CCL 107:87-88. [86]TEG 8:274. [87]Eph 4:7. [88]Eph 3:8. [89]See 1 Cor 1:10; Phil 2:2. [90]See Mt 5:14. [91]Mt 16:18. [92]The Latin reads *Petra enim erat Christus; sic ergo a petra Petrus.* [93]CCL 92:292-93. [94]Ps 139:18 (138:18 LXX). [95]MTS 1 Sup 1:242.

thousand stadia] means that he looked upon the church in her faith and works and made her to be perfect. For the perfection of the four cardinal virtues is lifted up by the faith in the holy Trinity, and so by the number twelve the dignity of the church is indicated. . . . "Its length and breadth and height are equal." This signifies the stability of unconquered truth by which the church, supported by the length of faith, the breadth of love and the height of hope, is not allowed to be blown about by every wind of doctrine. Were she to lack any one of these, the perfect stability of the church would not exist. EXPLANATION OF THE APOCALYPSE 21.16.[96]

## 21:17 *The Measure of Its Wall*

### EVERY PERFECTION AND ALL THE SAINTS.

APRINGIUS OF BEJA: We ought to regard the measure to be in the wall itself, for the wall of this city is our Lord Jesus Christ. That it was measured by the measure of a man indicates that the assumed man serves for the protection of the saints and as a guarantee of all bliss. This measure of a man is said to be that of an angel because he is himself the angel of the covenant of whom it is said, "He will suddenly come to his temple, whom you seek, indeed the messenger of the covenant, whom you desire."[97] And again it is said, "His name will be called Wonderful Counselor, Mighty God, Everlasting Father, Prince of Peace."[98] Let us see what mystery is contained in the fact that its height is measured to be 144 cubits. One hundred, composed of ten tens, passes to the right side, and from this it is shown that the complete fullness of the saints and all righteousness that is perfected in the fulfillment of the Decalogue and the prophecy of the gospel is blessedly held at the right hand of our Lord Jesus Christ. However, the forty-four when divided into four tens and the remaining four ones indicates similarly that the fourfold truth of the gospel and the perfection of every heavenly doctrine remains by his power. Moreover, the number twenty-four

itself is the sum of two equal parts so that it might show that the fullness of the ancient law and the power of the gospel rest in him and come from him. We know that this is a figure of the apostles of the Lamb and of the patriarchs and is the very image of the twenty-four elders. This number [i.e. , twenty-four] multiplied six times teaches that in the six days of this present week in which the world exists, the entire congregation and multitude of the saints is included, even as in our Lord Jesus Christ there is every perfection and [in him] the full righteousness of all the saints is shown to be safeguarded. TRACTATE ON THE APOCALYPSE 21.17.[99]

### BY THE CONTEMPLATION OF GOD, MEN

BECOME ANGELS. OECUMENIUS: It is often the habit of holy Scripture to use the word *men* when speaking of angels. This is clear from those passages in which the archangel Gabriel is interpreted as "man of God."[100] Moreover, the prophet said, "You will preserve men and beasts, O Lord,"[101] by "men" referring to angels and by "beasts" referring to men. For compared with the thoughts of the angels, men are irrational and like animals. . . . In addition, according to Luke, the Lord also called angels "men" when he said, "Let your loins be girded and your lamps burning, and be like men who are waiting for their master to come home from the marriage feast."[102] Therefore, since angels are often called "men," as we have said above, their gaze is directed toward God. For this reason it says here "by a man's measure, that is, an angel's." By this language is signified that what is divine is wholly incomprehensible—above we have interpreted the wall of the city to be Christ—but rather by the contemplation of the greatness of God men become angels. And so, the wall of the city is measured by an angelic cubit, not a human one. That the wall measures 144 cubits indicates a certain mystical number determined by the wisdom and the discerning mea-

---

[96]CCL 121A:529. [97]See Mal 3:1. [98]Is 9:6. [99]CCL 107:89-90. [100]See Dan 9:21. [101]Ps 36:6 (35:7 LXX). [102]Lk 12:35-36.

surement of the angels. Commentary on the Apocalypse 21.15-22.[103]

**The Church Longs for the Companionship of the Angels.** Primasius: Clearly in many passages an angel symbolizes the church. Since the church is gathered together from people and is lifted high by the promises of Christ, she hopes for equality with the angels and her every intent longs for their company, and for this reason it says, "the measure of a man," that is, of an angel's. Or this verse indicates that that city that will reign more fully consists partly of angels who already live there in perpetual happiness and partly of those who are on the way, that is, of people. Commentary on the Apocalypse 21.17.[104]

### 21:18 The City Was Gold, Pure as Glass

**The Holy Chorus of the Saints.** Apringius of Beja: Jasper glimmers with a certain faint greenness and so shows the modest face of virginity. This is so that you might understand that our Lord Jesus Christ is joined to every building of the city and that that body taken from the flesh of the Virgin rises up for the protection of the whole wall. "The city itself was pure gold, pure as glass." In this most pure gold, which is purified by the heat of fire and so is proven, we perceive the chorus of the saints who have been tested in the furnace of suffering and by the heat of temptation and so have been made pure through the power of the Lord. They are compared with pure glass to indicate the transparent and pure brightness of the holiness that is in them. Tractate on the Apocalypse 21.18.[105]

**The Thoughts of the Saints Will Shine with Wisdom.** Primasius: "The city was from pure gold, similar to pure glass." He uses this strange analogy so that in all metaphors he might confer a unique dignity upon the one true stone, which is Christ, and so teach that all things serve him. For who does not know that gold is much different from glass and differs from it also in

color? And although it is common that the church is symbolized by gold since it is often depicted by golden lampstands and bowls on account of its worship of Wisdom,[106] nonetheless that pure gold is compared to pure glass is somewhat puzzling. I think the significance of this is given in what the apostle said, "Do not pronounce judgment before the time until the Lord comes, who will bring to light the things now hidden in darkness and will disclose the purposes of [our] hearts."[107] For with glass nothing is seen on the outside that does not exist on the inside. And so, this book in announcing that time when the thoughts of each one will be openly declared to each other, boldly compares gold with glass. Whatever at that time will be in the thoughts of the saints shall shine with the adornment of the virtue of Wisdom.... But now, however much one might excel in virtue, "no one knows the thoughts of man except the spirit of the man which is in him."[108] Commentary on the Apocalypse 21.18.[109]

**The Saints Will Enjoy Unfading Life.** Andrew of Caesarea: The structure of the wall was of jasper to show the ever green and unfading life of the saints. The city is of "pure gold as though of glass" because of the clarity and brightness of its inhabitants. Commentary on the Apocalypse 21.18.[110]

### 21:19-20 The Twelve Foundations Adorned with Jewels

**The Heavenly Jerusalem Is a Spiritual Edifice.** Clement of Alexandria: Tradition assures us that the heavenly Jerusalem that is above is built up of holy gems, and we know that the twelve gates of the heavenly city, which signify the wonderful beauty of the apostolic teaching, are compared with precious jewels. These priceless stones are described as possessing cer-

---

[103]TEG 8:274-75. [104]CCL 92:293. [105]CCL 107:91. [106]See Rev 1:20; 5:8. [107]1 Cor 4:5. [108]1 Cor 2:11. [109]CCL 92:294. [110]MTS 1 Sup 1:243.

tain colors that are themselves precious, while the rest is left of an earthly substance. To say that the city of the saints is built of such jewels, even though it is a spiritual edifice, is a cogent symbol indeed. By the incomparable brilliance of the gems is understood the spotless and holy brilliance of the substance of the spirit. CHRIST THE EDUCATOR 2.12.118.[111]

**THE HOLY SPIRIT SHINES WITHIN EACH OF THE APOSTLES.** APRINGIUS OF BEJA: These foundations of the city are understood to be the apostolic faith and the preaching of the apostles, upon which our Lord Jesus Christ constructs his city. For he who is the Foundation of foundations is himself the builder who upon the faith in his own most blessed name builds the holy church, which consists of those who were the very first and of those who follow after them until the end of the world, which is unknown to us. The various precious stones signify the apostles because in each of them shine the gifts and miracles that belong to the Holy Spirit. Moreover, that the brightness of the unified light is seen within them indicates that what shines outward from them never ceases to exist within. TRACTATE ON THE APOCALYPSE 21.19.[112]

**DECORATED WITH EVERY VIRTUE OF THE SPIRIT.** PRIMASIUS: In the song of Tobit we read, "All your walls will be precious stones,"[113] and also in Isaiah, "Behold, I will set your stones in order and lay your foundations with sapphires, and I will place jasper for your buttresses, and I will put your gates in formed stones, and all your borders will be in precious stones."[114] And as though explaining what he had said, lest you think materially of an earthly edifice, he added, "All your sons will be taught by the Lord, and there shall be great peace for your children."[115] The blessed Paul also concurs with these thoughts: "Built upon the foundation of the apostles and prophets, Christ Jesus himself being the cornerstone, in whom the whole structure is joined together and grows into a holy

temple in the Lord."[116] . . . Having said that the foundation was from every precious stone, he now names them in turn. . . . By the images of all these stones the beauty and support of the virtues are signified by which each one of the saints is spiritually decorated. Moreover, the entire city itself is described as adorned with these same stones, both in their strength and in the elegance of their variety. COMMENTARY ON THE APOCALYPSE 21.18-20.[117]

**THE APOSTLES POSSESSED THE VARIOUS GIFTS OF THE SPIRIT.** CAESARIUS OF ARLES: He mentions the names of the various gems in the foundations so that he might show the various gifts of grace that have been given to the apostles, as was spoken concerning the Holy Spirit, "who apportions to each one individually as he wills."[118] EXPOSITION ON THE APOCALYPSE 21.19, Homily 19.[119]

**THE NEW COVENANT AND THE OLD.** ANDREW OF CAESAREA: The twelve "foundations" were twelve precious stones, eight of which were worn in ancient times on the breastplate of the high priest, and four have been added to show the agreement of the new [covenant] with the old [covenant] and the superiority of the things brought to light in it. And so, the apostles are decorated with every virtue, which is made clear through the precious stones. COMMENTARY ON THE APOCALYPSE 21.19.[120]

### 21:19a The First Foundation Is Jasper

**PETER GUIDES US TO GREEN PASTURES.** ANDREW OF CAESAREA: It is likely that through the jasper, which has the color green like the emerald, the chief apostle Peter is indicated. For he bore the death of Christ in the body and in his

---

[111]FC 23:191. Clement is speaking of the "passion for jewels" of some wealthy Christian women. [112]CCL 107:91. [113]Tob 13:16. [114]Is 54:11-12. [115]Is 54:13. [116]Eph 2:20-21. [117]CCL 92:294-96. [118]1 Cor 12:11. [119]PL 35:2451. [120]MTS 1 Sup 1:243.

love for [Christ] made known that which is ever-lasting and always new, guiding us to green pastures through the warmth of his faith. COMMENTARY ON THE APOCALYPSE 21.19.[121]

**ADORNED BY THE VIGOR OF FAITH.** BEDE: There are many kinds of jasper. Some are green in color and have the appearance of being dipped in the color of living plants. Some have the appearance of the wetness of an emerald but of an uncultured type. These are said to have the power to chase away phantasms. Another has the appearance of the gray foam of great waves with a misty color over it. The jasper stone, then, symbolizes the unflagging vigor of faith. Such faith arises in the sacrament of the Lord's passion through the living water of baptism, and, with assisting aid, it grows into the blossoms of spiritual graces. For he who has this faith chases away all fear, as the blessed apostle Peter reminds us: "Your adversary, the devil, prowls around like a roaring lion seeking whom he might devour. Resist him, firm in your faith."[122] Such a person is able to say with the bride, "My beloved is radiant and blushing red."[123] Therefore, with good reason is both the structure of the wall built up with this stone and as Isaiah says,[124] the fortress of the city is also adorned by it. EXPLANATION OF THE APOCALYPSE 21.19.[125]

## 21:19b The Second Foundation Is Sapphire

**PAUL'S CITIZENSHIP IS IN HEAVEN.** ANDREW OF CAESAREA: The sapphire stone is like the heavenly body, from which also the color azure comes, and symbolizes the blessed Paul. For he was caught up into the third heaven and drew there those who were persuaded by him, and there in the heavens he has his citizenship.[126] COMMENTARY ON THE APOCALYPSE 21.19.[127]

**THE SAINTS ARE DAILY RENEWED BY RAYS OF DIVINE LIGHT.** BEDE: Moses explains both the color and the significance of this stone when he describes the dwelling of God: "Under his feet was a work of sapphire stone, clear as the sky."[128] Ezekiel also says that the place where the throne of God is has the appearance of sapphire and that the glory of the Lord, who bears the image of highest heaven, consists of that color.[129] Therefore, whoever is such a person is able to declare with the apostle: "Our commonwealth is in heaven."[130] As if struck by the rays of the sun, sapphire glows in itself with burning brightness. So also the thoughts of the saints are always occupied with heavenly things, and so they are daily renewed by the rays of divine light. Therefore, they continually and ardently, in whatever way, search after eternal things and urge others as well towards those things for which they ought to seek. For what happened in the Red Sea is said to occur again when through the passion of the Lord and through the laver of holy baptism, the minds of mortals are raised high to taste beforehand heavenly things. EXPLANATION OF THE APOCALYPSE 21.19.[131]

## 21:19c The Third Foundation Is Chalcedony

**ANDREW WAS IGNITED BY THE SPIRIT.** ANDREW OF CAESAREA: This stone [chalcedony] was not borne on the breastplate of the high priest, but rather anthracite, which does not appear here. We are then of the opinion that at that time the saint called anthracite by another name. But anthracite indicates the blessed apostle Andrew, who like coal was ignited by the Spirit. COMMENTARY ON THE APOCALYPSE 21.19.[132]

**THE HUMILITY OF SAINTS IS HIDDEN.** BEDE: Chalcedony shines like the pale fire of a lamp out of doors in the daylight. By this is shown those who, supported by heavenly desires, remain hidden [by their humility] to people as they practice

---

[121]MTS 1 Sup 1:243. [122]1 Pet 5:8-9. [123]Song 5:10. [124]See Is 54:12. [125]CCL 121A:533. [126]See 2 Cor 12:2; Phil 3:20. [127]MTS 1 Sup 1:244. [128]Ex 24:10. [129]See Ezek 1:26; 10:1. [130]Phil 3:20. [131]CCL 121A:533-35. [132]MTS 1 Sup 1:244.

in secret their fasting, almsgiving and prayers. But when they are commanded to demonstrate their teaching or other acts of saintly service in public they quickly do so in order that their inner glory might be shown forth. For that which remains after the sculptor has done his work draws dross to itself by the working of the sun's rays or by the handling of warm hands. This property of chalcedony rightly agrees with those who do not permit their own strength to be conquered by anything but rather by their own light and ardor draw to themselves the more fragile, joining them to their own strength. Concerning one of these it was said, "He was a burning and shining lamp."[133] Clearly he was burning with love, and he was shining in speech. For in order that their own virtues might never go dark, they are always refreshed by the oil of internal charity. The fact that among the Nasmoneans, which is a region of Ethiopia, this stone is produced indicates those who are under the ardent fervor of love. However, there is an obscure opinion that this stone is dirty as with a dark skin. Explanation of the Apocalypse 21.19.[134]

## 21:19d The Fourth Foundation Is Emerald

JOHN'S PREACHING. ANDREW OF CAESAREA: The emerald is green in color, and when rubbed with oil [it] receives a brilliant shine and beauty. We believe that this stone indicates the proclamation of the Evangelist John, which by divine oil makes bright the sorrow that has come to us through sins and by the most precious gift of theology grants to faith that which is everlasting. COMMENTARY ON THE APOCALYPSE 21.19.[135]

THE EMERALD IS TESTED BY ADVERSITY. BEDE: The emerald has the quality of very deep green to the point that it surpasses all green plants, branches and buds. It is colored all around with the green of reflective copper. It also fittingly produces a green oil, to the extent that its nature allows. There are many different types of this stone, but the more noble are the Scythian,

the second is Bactrian and the third Egyptian. This stone further signifies those souls who are always growing in faith and when tested more and more by the adversities of this world (indicated by the coldness of the Scythian climate) the more fully do they hold on to that unfading inheritance kept in heaven. These souls advance to a contempt of this world through the chalice of the Lord's passion and by the fullness of the inner charity given to them by the Holy Spirit. Also, the very beautiful ancestral homeland of these stones is fitting. It is a rich but uninhabitable land. The ground there abounds with gold and gems, but griffins hold all of them. These griffins are very ferocious birds or, rather, flying beasts, for they are four-legged and have the body of a lion while their heads are similar to birds.[136] When these griffins fight the Arimaspi, who carry the mark of one eye in the midst of their forehead, the griffins take these stones and with amazing ferocity and fierce snatching, take the Arimapsi captive. The psalmist refers to this land filled with an abundance of virtues when he says, "Behold, I have fled afar off, and I remain in solitude."[137] That is, I have withdrawn my soul from the enticements of the world. He then strikes out at the hostile beasts when he prays, "Let the lying lips be dumb that speak iniquity against the righteous in pride and contempt."[138] He shows himself to have found desirable riches when he says with remarkable affection, "How abundant is your goodness, O Lord, which you have laid up for those who fear you,"[139] and on to the end of the psalm. Against the desire of such birds to snatch away the seed of the divine word, some of the saints with a heavenly desire keep watch with undivided attention, as though wondering with one eye, in order that they might discover and unearth the precious jewel of faith and other virtues. Where the [need for] strength is greater,

[133]Jn 5:35. [134]CCL 121A:535-37. [135]MTS 1 Sup 1:244. [136]Paleontologists have recently found fossils of a similar creature in Scythian lands that have rare gems. [137]Ps 55:7 (54:8 LXX). [138]Ps 31:18 (30:19 LXX). [139]Ps 31:19 (30:20 LXX).

there are fewer laborers and fewer of those who bear the terrible persecution by unclean spirits. As the dreadful earthly griffins fight for riches by violence, these few struggle tirelessly for spiritual riches, not to possess the riches for themselves but to offer them to others. And since such an exalted faith is made known throughout the whole world through the gospel, it is fitting that as there are four books of the gospel, the emerald is placed in the fourth place. EXPLANATION OF THE APOCALYPSE 21.19.[140]

### 21:20a *The Fifth Foundation Is Sardonyx*

**JAMES WAS THE FIRST APOSTLE TO SUFFER MARTYRDOM.** ANDREW OF CAESAREA: This stone, which has the color of a shining human fingernail, symbolizes the person of James. For before the others he received the bodily death of martyrdom for the sake of Christ, which the nail characterizes, for when cut it experiences no feelings. COMMENTARY ON THE APOCALYPSE 21.20.[141]

**IN THE HUMILITY OF THEIR MINDS, SAINTS EXAMINE THEMSELVES.** BEDE: This stone has the luster of onyx yet shows the redness of carnelian, and therefore from both receives the name of sardonyx. There are many kinds of this stone. One has the likeness of red earth. Another has the appearance of two colors, as though it were blood shining through a human fingernail. Another consists of three colors, on the bottom is black, the middle is white, and the top is red. This stone represents those who are red in the passion of the body, white in the purity of the spirit, but in the humility of their mind examine themselves and say with the apostle, "Although our outer man is wasting away, our inner man is being renewed every day."[142] And again, "I am aware of nothing against myself, but in this I am not justified."[143] Similarly the psalmist says, "A man walks in the image of God," that is, by the virtue of the mind, "however, in vain will he be disquieted,"[144] that is, by the weakness of the flesh. . . . It is fitting that sardonyx is said to be

the fifth foundation, since our bodies possess five senses. EXPLANATION OF THE APOCALYPSE 21.20.[145]

### 21:20b *The Sixth Foundation Is Carnelian*

**PHILIP HEALED SPIRITUAL WOUNDS.** ANDREW OF CAESAREA: Sardion has a shiny red color and possesses therapeutic power for swellings and wounds from iron. For this reason I believe that this stone represents the beauty of the virtue of Philip. For by the fire of the divine Spirit this makes bright and heals the spiritual wounds of those who are deceived, which they received from the attacks of the devil. COMMENTARY ON THE APOCALYPSE 21.20.[146]

**THE BLOOD OF THE MARTYRS SHOWED THEIR GLORY.** BEDE: Sardion has the color of pure blood and signifies the glory of the martyrs, of whom it is said, "Precious in the sight of the Lord is the death of his saints."[147] Rightly is it placed in the sixth position, for our Lord was both incarnated in the sixth age of the world and was crucified on the sixth day for the salvation of the whole world. EXPLANATION OF THE APOCALYPSE 21.20.[148]

### 21:20c *The Seventh Foundation Is Chrysolite*

**BARTHOLOMEW WAS GLORIOUS IN HIS VIRTUE AND PREACHING.** ANDREW OF CAESAREA: Chrysolite glitters like gold and perhaps symbolizes Bartholomew, for he was made glorious by his precious virtues and by his divine preaching. COMMENTARY ON THE APOCALYPSE 21.20.[149]

**SAINTS HAVE THE SEVENFOLD GIFTS OF THE SPIRIT.** BEDE: Chrysolite shines as though it

---

[140]CCL 121A:537-41. [141]MTS 1 Sup 1:245. [142]2 Cor 4:16. [143]1 Cor 4:4. [144]Ps 39:6 (38:7 LXX). [145]CCL 121A:541-43. [146]MTS 1 Sup 1:245. [147]Ps 116:15 (115:6 LXX). [148]CCL 121A:543. [149]MTS 1 Sup 1:245.

were sparkling gold. Its appearance represents those who shine with the knowledge of the heavenly and true wisdom and who by the words of exhortation to their neighbors or even by signs of power sparkle as though sparks of fire. . . . Since this happens only by the gift of spiritual grace, it is most proper that chrysolite stands as the seventh foundation, for the grace of the Holy Spirit is often symbolized by the number seven, of whom it was said above, "and from the seven spirits who are before his throne."[150] It is in agreement with this meaning that a kind of this stone is found in the color of blue-green, for which reason the Hebrews call this stone "tharsis"[151] because it has the color of the sea. The color green indeed corresponds to the reality of faith, which is said to be the beginning of wisdom, and water is a figure of the Holy Spirit, as the Lord indicates, saying, "He who believes in me, as the Scripture says, 'out of his heart shall flow rivers of living water.' Now this he said about the Spirit, which those who believed in him were to receive."[152] EXPLANATION OF THE APOCALYPSE 21.20.[153]

## 21:20d *The Eighth Foundation Is Beryl*

**THOMAS WAS SENT BEYOND THE SEA TO INDIA.** ANDREW OF CAESAREA: This stone [beryl] has the color of the sea and of the air and is close to that of the hyacinth. Beryl very likely represents Thomas, for he was sent on journeys far beyond the sea, even to India, for their salvation. COMMENTARY ON THE APOCALYPSE 21.20.[154]

**WISDOM IS PERFECTED IN THE PERFORMANCE OF WORKS.** BEDE: Just as water reflecting the brightness of the sun, beryl gives off a beautiful reddish color. However, it does not shine unless it has been shaped and polished into a six-sided form, for its brightness is accentuated by the reflection of the angles. This stone represents those persons who indeed are wise by their natural disposition but who reflect even more the light of divine grace. Solomon indicates that

water might symbolize the depth of understanding when he says, "The words of a man's mouth are deep waters."[155] But neither human nor divine wisdom is perfect in its light unless the performance of works is joined to them. For often the completion of a work is represented by the number six, especially when in this number it is a finished work of this world. Without doubt it is clear why it is said that the hand of one holding [this stone] is burned, since one who is joined to a holy person is truly recreated by the fire of his good behavior. EXPLANATION OF THE APOCALYPSE 21.20.[156]

## 21:20e *The Ninth Foundation Is Topaz*

**MATTHEW HEALED THOSE BLIND OF HEART.** ANDREW OF CAESAREA: By means of the topaz, which is deep red and like charcoal, and which, as they say, sends forth a milk-like juice that relieves the pain of those suffering from eye disease, it is possible that the soul of Matthew is indicated. For he was inflamed by divine zeal and was adorned by the pouring out of his own blood for the sake of Christ. Through the Gospel he also healed those who were blind in their hearts and gave milk to drink to those newly born in the faith. COMMENTARY ON THE APOCALYPSE 21.20.[157]

**THE FIRE OF INNER LOVE AND THE BRIGHTNESS OF HEAVENLY LIGHT.** BEDE: Since topaz is rare, it is very valuable. It comes in two colors, one of purest gold and the other glittering with an ethereal clarity. In color it has a pure rosy and reddish hue and is similar to chrysophrase in the brilliance of its color. For it especially shines when it is struck by the splendor of the sun, surpassing the most costly brilliance of all other stones and in its appearance giving uniquely the greatest delight to the eyes. Should one polish this stone, however, it

---

[150]See Rev 1:4. [151]A likely reference to the place where the stone originated. [152]Jn 7:38-39. [153]CCL 121A:543-45. [154]MTS 1 Sup 1:245-46. [155]Prov 18:4. [156]CCL 121A:545-47. [157]MTS 1 Sup 1:246.

becomes dull; yet should one leave it alone, it shines by virtue of its own natural properties. Kings themselves regard this stone as marvelous and consider nothing else among their riches as its equivalent. This most beautiful quality of its nature is most fittingly compared to the contemplative life. For saintly kings, whose hearts are in the hand of God, display this nature by the riches of good works and by the gems of all of the virtues. Especially guiding in it the contemplation and keen vision of their pure minds, they shall be more frequently struck by the splendor of the heavenly grace, the more fervently they behold the sweetness of the heavenly life with their soul. Therefore, saintly people possess a golden color by the fire of their inner love, while they have also a heavenly color from the contemplation of a supernal sweetness. Sometimes these persons become worthless through the turmoil of the present world, as though they were rubbed by a file. For at one and the same time a soul cannot easily be agitated by the difficulty of earthly toils and by cares and sorrows and, having taken delight in the joy of the heavenly life, also contemplate this with a tranquil mind. Rather, in its groaning such a soul rather protests, "My eye is troubled because of anger; I have grown old on account of my enemies."[158] This stone is said to be found on the island of Thebaide, which is named Topazion, and from that it also receives its name. We can understand this in two ways. First, these regions, that is, of Egypt, are especially filled with crowds of monks, and whoever dwells near to the Son of righteousness is truly colored by the brightness of the heavenly light. And since the perfection of the active life is designated by the eighth place, this stone, which represents the delight of the contemplative life, is fittingly put in ninth place. [Topaz is in ninth position either] because there are nine angelic orders mentioned in the holy Scriptures,[159] whose life is imitated, or because [the contemplative life] is removed from the ten of perfect bliss, as I shall put it, by the single step of death. Longing for this highest joy, the prophet said, "Therefore, I have loved thy commandments more than

gold and topaz."[160] That is to say, above the glory for every approved work and above every height of contemplative joy that is possible in this life, I have delighted in your commandments with the sweetest love. And the first and greatest of these commandments is that "you will love the Lord your God with the whole heart, the whole mind and with all your strength."[161] It is most certainly true that this cannot be perfected in its completeness except in the height of the celestial kingdom. EXPLANATION OF THE APOCALYPSE 21.20.[162]

### 21:20f The Tenth Foundation Is Chrysophrase

**THADDEUS PREACHED CHRIST TO THE KING OF EDESSA.** ANDREW OF CAESAREA: Chrysoprase is deeper in color than gold itself, and through it I think that Thaddeus is indicated. For to Abgar, king of Edessa, he proclaimed the kingdom of Christ, which is signified by gold, and his death, which is indicated by ashes. COMMENTARY ON THE APOCALYPSE 21.20.[163]

**THE SAINTS AND MARTYRS REVEAL THE BRIGHTNESS OF PERFECT CHARITY.** BEDE: Chrysophrase has a mixed color of green and gold and even brings forth a certain purple gleam intermingled with spots of gold. It is found in India. This stone symbolizes those who by the brightness of perfect charity deserve the verdant [garden] of the eternal fatherland and reveal it even to others by the purple light of their own martyrdom. Since those who despise the present life and prefer the eternal glory follow the example of the Lord who appeared in the flesh, they already display the brightness of their merits as though in India, that is, near the rising of the sun. And because they expect to shine as the sun in the kingdom of the Father and desire then to

---

[158]Ps 6:7 (6:8 LXX). [159]See Gregory the Great *Homilies on the Gospels* 34. [160]See Ps 119:127 (118:127 LXX). [161]Deut 6:5. [162]CCL 121A:547-51. [163]MTS 1 Sup 1:246.

reign with their king for whom they are now suffering, rightly are they listed in the tenth place. For through the denarius by which the workers in the Lord's vineyard were paid,[164] the image of the eternal king is to be perceived. There—and this would not have been possible in the ninth position—the Decalogue will be in every way fulfilled by a perfected love of God and of the neighbor. EXPLANATION OF THE APOCALYPSE 21.20.[165]

## 21:20g The Eleventh Foundation Is Hyacinth

**SIMON POSSESSED A HEAVENLY WISDOM.** ANDREW OF CAESAREA: It seems likely that the hyacinth, which is deep blue, that is, like the sky, symbolizes Simon. For he was zealous for the gifts of Christ and possessed a heavenly wisdom. COMMENTARY ON THE APOCALYPSE 21.20.[166]

**THOSE WHO APPROACH THE ANGELIC LIFE MUST PRESERVE THEIR HEARTS.** BEDE: Hyacinth is found in Ethiopia and has a dark blue color. At its best it is neither of loose texture nor dull by density, but rather [it] shines moderately and gives a pleasant, pure gleam. But this stone does not gleam the same all the time. Rather, it changes with the appearance of the sky, for when the sky is fair and clear, it is transparent and pleasing, but when the sky is cloudy, it becomes faint and pale to the eyes. This stone suggests those souls that are always devoted to the purpose of heaven and who, to the extent possible for mortals, approach in some manner to the angelic life. These are admonished to preserve their hearts with every diligence, lest they grow callous by an excessive subtlety of their understanding and dare to seek after higher things and to examine that which is more powerful. "For the glory of God is to conceal a word,"[167] that is, one is to intellectually scrutinize God and the human Christ only with caution. They are also to preserve their hearts lest through an idle torpor they fall back again to the weak beginnings of faith and to the rudiments of the words of God. Those

rather who travel the royal highway advance protected on the left and on the right by the weapons of righteousness,[168] and by apt observation of the times [they] change their style and form with the sky and say to their overseers, "If we are beside ourselves, it is for God; if we are in our right mind, it is for you."[169] As a hyacinth underneath a cloud, such a person says, "You are not restricted by us, but you are restricted in your own affection";[170] and again, "For I decided to know nothing among you except Jesus Christ and him crucified."[171] And as a hyacinth seen in the bright sun, he says, "We speak wisdom among the mature."[172] EXPLANATION OF THE APOCALYPSE 21.20.[173]

## 21:20h The Twelfth Foundation Is Amethyst

**MATTHIAS WAS WORTHY OF THE DIVINE FIRE.** ANDREW OF CAESAREA: It seems to me that through the amethyst, which is somewhat like fire in appearance, Matthias is indicated. He was accounted worthy of the divine fire at the distribution of the tongues and he filled the place of him who had fallen away, for by a fiery desire he wished to please him who elected him.[174] COMMENTARY ON THE APOCALYPSE 21.20.[175]

**THE WINE OF SUFFERING AND THE WINE THAT GLADDENS THE HEART.** BEDE: Amethyst is purple, a mixture of violet and the luster as of a rose, and it gently gives off little sparks. But it has a certain glow that is not purple through and through, but rather it appears like the red of a wine. The beauty of purple suggests the deportment of the heavenly kingdom, while the rosy violet indicates the humble modesty and the precious death of the saints. For to be sure, their minds are chiefly concerned with things on high, and although externally they

---

[164]Mt 20:2. [165]CCL 121A:551-53. [166]MTS 1 Sup 1:246. [167]Prov 25:2. [168]Num 20:17; 2 Cor 6:7. [169]2 Cor 5:13. [170]2 Cor 6:12. [171]1 Cor 2:2. [172]1 Cor 2:6. [173]CCL 121A:553-55. [174]See Acts 1:23-24. [175]MTS 1 Sup 1:247.

must endure misery, they remember among these adversities the Lord's promise, "Fear not, little flock, for it is your Father's good pleasure to give you the kingdom."[176] These persons do not extend the fire of love only toward one another but also toward their very persecutors, imploring on bended knee, "Lord, do not hold this sin against them."[177] Moreover, along with the wine of suffering that they must drink, by a continuous recollection they drink even more of that wine that gladdens the heart . . . and that the Lord promised that he would drink new with his disciples in the kingdom of the Father.[178] EXPLANATION OF THE APOCALYPSE 21.20.[179]

### 21:21a The Twelve Gates, Each Gate of a Single Pearl

THE STONES VIEWED TOGETHER. BEDE: These precious stones individually were allotted to each of the foundations because, although all the [stones] by which the city of our God is adorned and established upon his holy mountain are perfect and shine by the light of spiritual grace, nevertheless "to one is given through the Spirit the utterance of wisdom, to another the utterance of knowledge, to another gifts of healing, to another various kinds of tongues, to another faith by the same Spirit"[180] and the like. "Its builder and maker is God,"[181] who is the Foundation of foundations and who for our sake was also found worthy to be High Priest so that by the sacrifice of his own blood he might both wash clean and dedicate the walls of this very city, and that whatever the Father has he might possess as his own. For this reason these same stones with the names of the patriarchs inscribed upon them were commanded to be placed on the breast of the high priest, so that by this most wonderful mystery it might be shown that every spiritual grace that each saint received individually and in part has been wholly and perfectly fulfilled by the mediator of God and man, the man Jesus Christ.[182] EXPLANATION OF THE APOCALYPSE 21.20.[183]

THE APOSTOLIC TEACHING. APRINGIUS OF BEJA: It is one thing to speak of each of the pearls; it is another thing to speak of the one pearl from which they come. For when it speaks of each pearl, it is shown that in each pearl one pearl is shining forth and that this one pearl is our Lord Jesus Christ. And when the pearls are related to a single pearl, we are taught that the apostolic teaching possesses already the light of righteousness that it has received from him. Just as Christ is the door, so also [the apostles] are the doors through which we are taught and enter into the faith. TRACTATE ON THE APOCALYPSE 21.21.[184]

IN THE LAW THERE WAS SHADOW. OECUMENIUS: The gates of the city, which we have interpreted to represent the apostles, "each were of a single pearl." And so the pearl is now placed here as something new, for it was not numbered with the stones of the oracle. It is possible, then, to see that the stones just now enumerated are more precious than those listed by the Old Testament as woven in the oracle. Through this it is signified that the apostles understood the Old Testament and were well-versed in the laws and customs in it—and for that reason the wise apostle said "as to righteousness under the law blameless."[185] However, it also signified that they had become well-versed in the commandments of the New Testament and were rich in the knowledge of it. For it was much clearer, and as it were more precious than the knowledge of the Old Testament, since in the law there was a kind of shadow, while in the New Testament reality had come. And this is symbolized by the mingling of the jewels of the Old Testament and those of the New Testament that are in the foundations of the city, which indicate the apostles. In the Gospels the Lord also said the same thing: "Therefore every scribe who has been trained for the kingdom of heaven is like a householder who brings out of his treasure

---

[176]Lk 12:32. [177]Acts 7:60. [178]Mt 26:29. [179]CCL 121A:555-57. [180]See 1 Cor 12:8-10. [181]See Heb 11:10. [182]See 1 Tim 2:5. [183]CCL 121A:557-59. [184]CCL 107:91. [185]Phil 3:6.

what is new and what is old."[186] And the gates of the city, which we have interpreted as the apostles, were from a single pearl, indicating their honor, purity and splendor. COMMENTARY ON THE APOCALYPSE 21.15-22.[187]

**THE DOOR OF ETERNAL LIFE.** CAESARIUS OF ARLES: These pearls symbolize the apostles, who are also called "gates" because through their teaching they make known the door of eternal life. EXPOSITION ON THE APOCALYPSE 21.21, HOMILY 19.[188]

**THE APOSTLES RECEIVED THEIR SPLENDOR FROM CHRIST.** ANDREW OF CAESAREA: The twelve gates are manifestly the twelve disciples of Christ, through whom we have come to know the door and the way. And they are also the twelve pearls that have received their splendor from the one, most precious pearl, namely, Christ. COMMENTARY ON THE APOCALYPSE 21.21.[189]

**THE GLORY OF THE HEAD IS REFERRED TO THE BODY.** BEDE: All the glory of the head is referred to the body. Just as "the true light that enlightens every person"[190] has granted to the saints to be the light of the world, so also he himself, since he is the single pearl that the wise merchant purchased after selling all that he had, in similar manner compares his disciples with the bright appearance of pearls. EXPLANATION OF THE APOCALYPSE 21.21.[191]

## 21:21b *The Street Was of Gold, Clear as Glass*

**TOGETHER THE SAINTS SHINE BRIGHTLY.** APRINGIUS OF BEJA: These words reveal the difference of merit that exists within the very beatitude of the saints. For above it was said that the entirety of the city was like pure gold, clear as glass.[192] [Now it says that] "the streets of the city are pure gold, transparent as glass." These are the saints of the city that are of lesser merit. Nonetheless, gathered together into one congregation,

it is indicated that they do not shine with a lesser light. TRACTATE ON THE APOCALYPSE 21.21.[193]

**LIKE CLEAR GLASS.** OECUMENIUS: We have said that the gold and the purity and transparency of the glass signify the honor and purity of the life of the saints. COMMENTARY ON THE APOCALYPSE 21.15-22.[194]

**NONE WILL BE THOUGHT UNWORTHY.** PRIMASIUS: He had already said that the city was of pure gold, transparent as glass,[195] and that its foundations were from every precious jewel.[196] I think that this refers to those who have authority in the church. But now he speaks in addition of the streets and says that also they are from pure gold that is as clear as glass. It is as though in the earlier passage the streets were not included in the description of the city. It is my opinion that in this passage the little children [of God] are symbolized, of whom in the present time it is said, "Your eyes beheld my unformed substance and in your book all of them were written."[197] And again, "His conversation is with the simple,"[198] for they by this reward will certainly not be deceived and by this mutual conversation they will come to behold their own understandings. For as the streets are placed in a lesser position, so [the simple] seem to be reserved for a humble position. Although in the streets the breadth of love is to be discerned, he signifies the perfect through a variety of words. However, at that time no one will there [be regarded] as unworthy, no one will be found to be small or weak, although some may stand out with a greater clarity than others because of the difference of rewards. "For as star differs from star in glory," the apostle says, "so is it with the resurrection of the dead."[199] COMMENTARY ON THE APOCALYPSE 21.21.[200]

---

[186]Mt 13:52. [187]TEG 8:276-77. [188]PL 35:2451. [189]MTS 1 Sup 1:248. [190]Jn 1:9. [191]CCL 121A:559-61. [192]See Rev 21:18. [193]CCL 107:91-92. [194]TEG 8:277. [195]Rev 21:18. [196]Rev 21:19. [197]Ps 139:16 (138:16 LXX). [198]See Prov 3:32. [199]1 Cor 15:41-42. [200]CCL 92:296-97.

**UNDERSTANDING SURPASSES OUR MIND.**
ANDREW OF CAESAREA: It is not possible to
present in one image an exact description of the
good things of the heavenly city. Therefore, he
perceived the street of the city as gold on account
of its costliness and its beautiful color, and as
crystal, that is, as transparent glass on account of
its purity. We are not able to bring both of these
things together in one symbol. But the saint perceived all of these things as he was able. However,
an unsullied understanding of the city above surpasses our hearing and sight and mind. COM-
MENTARY ON THE APOCALYPSE 21.21.[201]

### 21:22 Its Temple Is God and the Lamb

**NO TEMPLE IS NECESSARY.** APRINGIUS OF BEJA:
God established the temple so that the people
gathered within the walls of the temple might call
upon him whom neither the world nor the temple
can contain. In this way their minds might obtain
through the work of faith what cannot be seen of
God. However, where he openly manifests himself to the faithful there a temple is neither
desired nor existent, for he who sanctifies the
temple is known in the sight of all. TRACTATE ON
THE APOCALYPSE 21.22.[202]

**ONE OF THE HOLY TRINITY WAS INCAR-
NATED.** OECUMENIUS: What need is there of a
temple when God is present and in some manner
lives with the saints and when God's face is to
some extent made visible? For the holy apostle
has said that in the present age the knowledge of
God is "in a mirror" and "in darkness" but that in
the coming age such knowledge will be "face to
face."[203] Someone might reasonably ask, "Why
did he mention God the Almighty, that is, the
Father of the Lord and the Lamb, the Son of
God, but did not yet mention the Holy Spirit?"
To such a person one must respond, "When he
says the Lord and God, he is naming the Father
and the Son and the Holy Spirit, for these are
God. And further, when he says the Lord God
the Almighty he indicates the holy Trinity by the

three designations." But someone might inquire
further, "Why, then, having mentioned the venerable Trinity by the words 'the Lord God the
Almighty is its temple,' does he make special
mention of the Lamb, who is Christ, so that we
no longer are to consider the Trinity?" Let it not
seem to him to be so, for we are not taught to
think that! Rather, when it mentions the holy
Trinity and the Lamb, the passage indicates that
one of the holy Trinity has become incarnate and
that with his flesh the Son fills the holy Trinity
and even now in heaven is not without his flesh.
For figuratively he signified the Son who became
flesh through the name God, who is the Son,
while by "Lamb" he indicated the very same
Christ incarnated, consubstantial with us and
endowed with a rational soul, to which flesh the
Word was united hypostatically. COMMENTARY
ON THE APOCALYPSE 21.15-22.[204]

**THE CHURCH WILL BE WHOLE.** PRIMASIUS:
Just as the body consists of individual members,
so is the temple constructed from precious
stones. Although we are accustomed to material
things, he does not want us here to think of
something physical as is our habit. Therefore,
relieving us from this manner of thinking, he
says, "I saw in it no temple, for its temple is the
Lord God Almighty and the Lamb." For when the
tares have been removed, then shall the church
especially exult in the elect alone and remain consecrated in God as though she were resting completely in a temple. In this way the church may
obtain a blessed habitation in him from whom
she had received the origin of her existence and
had come to know the gentleness of redemption.
For the church's wholeness is completed in these
three things: in being, in knowing and in loving.
God created her that she might be fashioned
[according to his will]; having called her, he
enlightened her; having elected her, he has made
her blessed. God intends that when perfected

---

[201]MTS 1 Sup 1:248. [202]CCL 107:92. [203]See 1 Cor 13:12. [204]TEG
8:277-78.

[the church] will dwell in him by way of the promised glorification, when she no longer walks by way of faith but rejoices in his sight. COMMENTARY ON THE APOCALYPSE 21.22.[205]

**THE CHURCH IS IN GOD.** CAESARIUS OF ARLES: [He saw no temple in the city] because the church is in God and God is in the church. EXPOSITION ON THE APOCALYPSE 21.22, HOMILY 19.[206]

**GOD IS TEMPLE AND INDWELLER.** ANDREW OF CAESAREA: For what need of a physical temple is there for one who will have God as protection and shelter, in whom we live and move and have our being? For he himself is both temple and indweller of the saints, dwelling in them and walking among them, as he promised. The "Lamb" is the Lamb of God who was slain for us, to whom manifestly the co-essential and life-giving Spirit is conjoined, who is mentioned a little later through [the image] of the river.[207] COMMENTARY ON THE APOCALYPSE 21.22.[208]

**GOD WILL BE THE HOUSE AND REST OF THE SAINTS.** BEDE: It says, "Although I have said that the city was constructed of stones, nevertheless I have not indicated by this that the rest of the saints will be in a material building. For God himself will be their sole house and light and rest." EXPLANATION OF THE APOCALYPSE 21.22.[209]

## 21:23 Its Lamp Is the Lamb

**THE GLORY OF GOD IS THE PRESENCE OF HIS MAJESTY.** APRINGIUS OF BEJA: What an image there is in these words, that the city, which has no need of a temple, has no need of the brightness of the heavenly luminaries! And what is the reason for this? Because the glory of God gives it light. The glory of God, that is, the presence of his majesty, about which it is said, "We shall see him as he is."[210] Therefore, why would those who shall see God have need of sun or moon? TRACTATE ON THE APOCALYPSE 21.23.[211]

**CHRIST IS A SUPERIOR AND INEFFABLE LIGHT.** PRIMASIUS: Wishing to relieve us altogether from the changeability characteristic of the luminaries of the day and the night, and to call us to that immutable Light, it says, "[The city] had no need of the sun," nor is that city illumined by that [natural] order. Rather, it is illumined by a much superior and ineffable Light, namely, the Sun of righteousness. Speaking of him, the prophet says, "Healing is in its wings."[212] "For he is himself the true Son and eternal life and the true light who enlightens every one coming into this world."[213] COMMENTARY ON THE APOCALYPSE 21.23.[214]

**THE SAINTS WILL SEE SPIRITUAL REALITIES.** OECUMENIUS: There is no need of physical light for those who enjoy the spiritual light of God. For to behold spiritual realities is the lot of the saints at that time. COMMENTARY ON THE APOCALYPSE 21.23-25.[215]

**CHRIST IS GLORY AND LIGHT.** ANDREW OF CAESAREA: Where there is the intellectual Sun of righteousness, there is no need of perceptible illuminaries. For he is both the glory and the lamp of the city, and "the nations" of those who are being saved will walk in its light. COMMENTARY ON THE APOCALYPSE 21.23.[216]

**THE CHURCH IS LED BY THE ETERNAL SUN.** BEDE: [The city has no need of sun or moon] because the church is not governed by the light or the elements of the world. Rather, she is led through the darkness of the world by Christ, the eternal Sun. EXPLANATION OF THE APOCALYPSE 21.23.[217]

## 21:24 The Nations Will Walk by Its Light

---

[205]CCL 92:297. [206]PL 35:2451. [207]See Rev 22:1. [208]MTS 1 Sup 1:248. [209]CCL 121A:561. [210]1 Jn 3:2. [211]CCL 107:92. [212]Mal 4:2. [213]See 1 Jn 5:20; Jn 1:9. [214]CCL 92:297-98. [215]TEG 8:279. [216]MTS 1 Sup 1:249. [217]CCL 121A:561.

**CHRIST ENLIGHTENS THE WHOLE.** APRINGIUS OF BEJA: By the light, the Lamb is clearly shown to be the [city's] lamp, and the kings and the nations will walk in his light. The prophet knew this and said, "In your light we shall see light."[218] The apostle also spoke concerning this light: "The night is far gone, the day is at hand."[219] The Evangelist also writes in a similar way: "The life was the light of men, and the light shines in the darkness, and the darkness did not comprehend it."[220] This is to say, what the nature of our weakness had concealed and what the shadow of our humanity had rendered dark was made clear by the assumption of the Lord's body. And while God, who is light, inhabits the lot of our flesh, he enlightens the whole by the greatness of his glory. For this reason the honor and the glory of the kings and the nations are given to him, because all have been made glorious through him, and the darkness of night shall not overcome his faithful, whom the presence of the Lamb and the Word of the ineffable, unbegotten Father illuminate. TRACTATE ON THE APOCALYPSE 21.24-26.[221]

**THE SAINTS WILL BRING THEIR VIRTUE INTO THE CITY.** OECUMENIUS: [By the nations] it speaks not only of the Gentiles but also of the saints from Israel who came to faith. For since the saints from the Gentiles are more numerous by far, it indicates also those [from Israel] in speaking of those who are more numerous. . . . By "kings of the earth" he means all the saints, of whom it is written, "When the heavenly One scatters kings upon it, they shall be made white as snow in Selmon."[222] . . . Therefore, since these possess a certain glory and honor—he speaks of that honor that comes from virtue—they shall carry it into that holy city. This is as though he said, the blessings arising from virtue shall dwell with the saints. COMMENTARY ON THE APOCALYPSE 21.23-25.[223]

**THE STRENGTH OF SPIRITUAL KINGS.** PRIMASIUS: With these words it is to be understood that the Lamb himself who then will be the life of the citizens [of the heavenly city] is the way for those who are underway [toward the heavenly city]. For it is necessary that whatever dignity they will have received is attributed through praise to the honor of him who was the giver. Here [the passage] is speaking of spiritual kings of whom we read, "He is powerful and gives strength to our kings and has exalted the horn of his Christ."[224] COMMENTARY ON THE APOCALYPSE 21.24.[225]

## 21:25 There Will Be No Night

**RECOMPENSE FOR SUFFERING IN THIS WORLD.** VICTORINUS OF PETOVIUM: In this kingdom [Christ] promised to his servants: "Whoever shall have left father or mother or brother or sister for my name's sake, he will receive as a reward a hundredfold now, and in the future he will possess eternal life."[226] In this kingdom those who have been defrauded of their goods for the name of the Lord,[227] also the many who have been killed by every kind of crime and imprisonment—for before the coming of the Lord, the holy prophets were stoned, killed and cut in half[228]—will receive their consolation, that is, their crowns and celestial rewards. In this kingdom the Lord promised that he would compensate for the years in which the grasshopper and locust and corruption destroyed. In this kingdom the whole of creation will be preserved and reestablished and will, by the command of God, bring forth good things within it. Here the saints will receive "gold for bronze and silver for iron and precious stones."[229] In this place "he will give over to them the wealth of the sea and power of the nations."[230] In this kingdom "they will be called priests of the Lord and ministers of God," just as they were called impious.[231] In this king-

---

[218]Ps 36:9 (35:10 LXX). [219]Rom 13:12. [220]Jn 1:4-5. [221]CCL 107:92. [222]Ps 68:14 (67:15 LXX). [223]TEG 8:279. [224]1 Sam 2:10. [225]CCL 92:298. [226]See Mt 19:29. Victorinus refers these passages of the Revelation to the millennial kingdom. [227]A common millenarian view. See Irenaeus *Against Heresies* 5.32.1. [228]See Heb 11:36-37. [229]See Is 60:17. [230]See Is 60:5. [231]See Is 61:6.

dom "they will drink wine and be anointed with oil and be given over to joy."[232] Before his passion, the Lord made mention of this kingdom when he said to the apostles, "I shall not drink again of the fruit of this vine until I shall drink it new with you in the future kingdom."[233] This is the "hundredfold," which is ten thousand more or less. And when he says that there will be stones that are different in kind and color, he is speaking of people, but he is also indicating the very precious variety of faith that exists in each person. The gates made of pearl refer to the apostles. And they will not be closed, it says, for through them grace has been given that will never be closed. In this place they will see face to face, and "one has not inquired after another."[234] And the names of the fathers and of the apostles shall be on the walls and the gates; we have already discussed and interpreted the twenty-four elders. And of those who will have reigned in this kingdom [it is said], "They shall judge the world."[235] COMMENTARY ON THE APOCALYPSE 21.5-6.[236]

**EVEN IN THE ETERNAL CITY THE APOSTLES WILL BE TEACHERS.** OECUMENIUS: This has two possible meanings. It may mean that there will be peace and security so that there will be no need for the city to set a sentry for itself or to ever close its gates and make them secure with bars. Or the words may say that the apostolic teachings—for we have noted that the gates are the apostles—will never fall silent there but rather that even there the apostles will be teachers of new and more divine teachings for the saints. For being "sons of day and of light,"[237] the righteous shall revel in the divine illumination of the praises and the mysteries, since the day and the light of divine illumination are perpetually around them. "For there shall be no night," it says. For were the divine illumination ever to be interrupted, there would be also night. But since it is impious to say this, for the divine light shines without interruption, how shall there be night for the saints? COMMENTARY ON THE APOCALYPSE 21.23-25.[238]

**WHAT IS SEEN IS LOVED, WHAT IS LOVED IS PRAISED.** PRIMASIUS: The passage refers to the perpetual light of the Lamb. Indeed, the Lamb himself will be the eternal [light] in that city when the time of night has been removed. As Isaiah said, "It shall be for them from month to month and from sabbath to sabbath."[239] By *month* he signifies the light because of the full splendor of the moon; by *sabbath* he is signifying the eternal rest. It is as though it had said, "For them there continues light from light and eternal rest from rest." That the gates are not closed is indicative of the most complete security. For [in that city] it is not said, "Watch and pray that you may not enter into temptation,"[240] but rather "Be still and see that I am the Lord."[241] There what is seen is truly loved; what is loved is praised without ceasing. There no one becomes feeble from sloth; nor does anyone grow weary from the activity of perpetual praise. COMMENTARY ON THE APOCALYPSE 21.25.[242]

## 21:26 The Glory and Honor of the Nations

**LANDS PROMISED TO ABRAHAM.** VICTORINUS OF PETOVIUM: Each of the gates are from a single pearl. There are three gates on each side, and these gates are not closed but open. The Scripture shows extensively that the kings of [every] region and nation, who are its servants, will bring their wealth into [the city]. It is speaking of the subduing of the last [nations], of which we have already spoken. However, *city* is not to be understood in a manner such as we know. For without a guide we are unable to conceive of anything grander and larger than what we have heard and seen. But here *city* refers to every region of the eastern provinces that were promised to the patriarch Abraham. He says, "Look into the heaven from the place in which you are now

---

[232]See Is 25:6-7. [233]Mt 26:29. Irenaeus *Against Heresies* 5.33.1, also refers this passage to the millennium. [234]See Is 34:16 LXX. [235]1 Cor 6:2. [236]CSEL 49:152-54. [237]See 1 Thess 5:5. [238]TEG 8:279. [239]Is 66:23. [240]Mt 26:41. [241]Ps 46:10 (45:11 LXX). [242]CCL 92:298-99.

standing"—that is, "from the great river Euphrates to the river of Egypt"—"all the land which you see I will give to you and to your seed."[243] Then the Holy Spirit said, "He shall have dominion from sea to sea"—that is, from the Red Sea, which is in Arabia, to the Sea of the North, which is the Sea of Phoenicia—"and to the ends of the earth,"[244] that is, the regions of great Syria. Therefore, it is manifest that all of these regions will be made level and cleansed at the coming of the Lord, and . . .when the splendor comes down from heaven as a cloud, they will be covered all around with a light from above that surpasses the splendor of the sun. COMMENTARY ON THE APOCALYPSE 21.2.[245]

**THE WORTHY GENTILES WILL COME TO THE HEAVENLY JERUSALEM.** OECUMENIUS: When it mentions the "glory and honor of the nations" which are carried into the holy city, it is speaking periphrastically of those from the Gentiles who were reputable and who had performed works worthy of life. For these shall be brought into the heavenly Jerusalem and shall live together with the saints there. COMMENTARY ON THE APOCALYPSE 21.26-22.5.[246]

### 21:27 Only Those in the Lamb's Book of Life Will Enter

**NO SINNER OR HERETIC.** APRINGIUS OF BEJA: It is true that no one enters into that communion of the saints who either refuses to be cleansed of former sin and from the guilt of their parents, or having become filthy after purification refused to be cleansed by the washing of humility and the

shedding of tears. Indeed, Judas committed such an abomination, and so does a heretic who worships God deceitfully. However, those are said to enter who are written in the Lamb's Book of Life, namely, those whom the heart of a true faith and a firm hope embrace. TRACTATE ON THE APOCALYPSE 21.27.[247]

**THE RIGHTEOUSNESS OF GOD ALLOWS NO SINFULNESS.** OECUMENIUS: "But nothing unclean shall enter it, nor any one who practices abomination, but only those who are written in the Lamb's Book of Life." For "what fellowship has light with darkness"[248] or the sinner with the righteousness of God, whom the Lord instructs us in the Gospels are separated by a wide chasm?[249] COMMENTARY ON THE APOCALYPSE 21.26-22.5.[250]

**THE CHURCH OF THE FUTURE.** PRIMASIUS: He is here describing the church of the future when, unlike at the present time, the evil will not be mixed in along with the good and allowed to live with them. For the good alone will reign with Christ with whom and in whom they will live happily forever, namely, in that heavenly Jerusalem that is the mother of all. Indeed, it says that they are written in the book of the Lamb [to whom] he said, "Rejoice that your names are written in heaven."[251] COMMENTARY ON THE APOCALYPSE 21.27.[252]

---

[243]Gen 13:14-15; 15:18. [244]Ps 72:8 (71:8 LXX). [245]CSEL 49:148. [246]TEG 8:280. [247]CCL 107:93. [248]2 Cor 6:14. [249]See Lk 16:26. [250]TEG 8:280. [251]Lk 10:20. [252]CCL 92:299.

# 22:1-5 THE REIGN OF GOD IS LIFE AND LIGHT

*[1]Then he showed me the river of the water of life, bright as crystal, flowing from the throne of God and of the Lamb [2]through the middle of the street of the city; also, on either side of the river, the tree of life[r] with its twelve kinds of fruit, yielding its fruit each month; and the leaves of the tree were for the healing of the nations. [3]There shall no more be anything accursed, but the throne of God and of the Lamb shall be in it, and his servants shall worship him; [4]they shall see his face, and his name shall be on their foreheads. [5]And night shall be no more; they need no light of lamp or sun, for the Lord God will be their light, and they shall reign for ever and ever.*

r Or the Lamb. In the midst of the street of the city, and on either side of the river, was the tree of life, etc.

**OVERVIEW:** The river of God is the Holy Spirit, who flows among the angelic powers in heaven (ANDREW OF CAESAREA). This river now flows within the church, for in baptism the Spirit makes clean those who are washed (CAESARIUS OF ARLES, ANDREW OF CAESAREA). By this living stream of the font the single kingship of the holy Trinity is confessed (JEROME), and this kingship is revealed through the incarnation of the Savior from whom all holiness of baptism flows (JEROME, APRINGIUS). The grace of Christ floods everlastingly upon the saints like a river (OECUMENIUS) and brings them into eternal life (PRIMASIUS). This river of the Holy Spirit that flows from the Father through the Son (ANDREW OF CAESAREA) is given witness in the two Testaments (JEROME, APRINGIUS).

In both Testaments one tree is planted which is Christ (JEROME, APRINGIUS, OECUMENIUS, ANDREW OF CAESAREA). Through the teaching of the apostles those who read the Scriptures may gather the fruit of the tree. For the divine meaning of Scripture (JEROME) speaks of the fullness of our salvation (APRINGIUS) and leads us to eat of the tree of Christ's cross (CAESARIUS OF ARLES). With an inexhaustible generosity (OECUMENIUS, PRIMASIUS) Christ perpetually offers himself (PRIMASIUS) and the Holy Spirit (ANDREW OF CAESAREA), so that the saints themselves attain to a blissful immortality (PRIMASIUS) and, like leaves clinging to a tree (OECUMENIUS), participate in his deity through the flesh that he assumed (ANDREW OF CAESAREA).

In this way the saints also become trees of life (ANDREW OF CAESAREA), for they will be untainted by any sinful stain (OECUMENIUS) and they will rejoice in the vision of Christ's face (APRINGIUS). Where the glory of the one Godhead is acknowledged (PRIMASIUS), there nothing belonging to the devil will exist (ANDREW OF CAESAREA). Rather, abiding in the presence of God (OECUMENIUS), the saints will see Christ as the apostles saw him on the mountain (ANDREW OF CAESAREA). For the reward of faith is the vision of God (PRIMASIUS), and the vision of God is the highest good (BEDE), neverending illumination (OECUMENIUS, ANDREW OF CAESAREA), eternal rest and the perfect fulfillment of every promise (BEDE).

## 22:1 The River of the Water of Life

**THE KINGSHIP OF THE TRINITY IS ONE.**
JEROME: We believe in the Father and the Son and the Holy Spirit, that is true, and that they are a Trinity; nevertheless the kingship is one. "I saw a single throne set up, and I saw a single Lamb standing in the presence of the throne."[1] This

---

[1]See Rev 5:6.

refers to the incarnation of the Savior. Scripture says, "Behold the lamb of God, who takes away the sin of the world."[2] "And there was a fountain of water coming forth from beneath the middle of the throne." Notice that it is from the midst of the throne that there issues forth a river of graces. That river does not issue forth from the throne unless the Lamb is standing before it, for unless we believe in the incarnation of Christ, we do not receive those graces. HOMILIES ON THE PSALMS 1 (Ps 1).[3]

**CHRIST IS THE LIVING WATER RECEIVED IN BAPTISM.** APRINGIUS OF BEJA: The living water is the Lord Jesus Christ. Of this water he spoke to the Samaritan woman: "If you knew the gift of God and who it was who says to you, 'give me to drink,' you would rather ask from him, and he would give to you the living water."[4] [He was speaking of] the knowledge of his deity and the fullness of a holy faith. For concerning him it is said, "For with you is the fountain of life."[5] For they are buried [with him] through baptism, as the apostle says: "For we have been buried with him by baptism into death."[6] Therefore, the living water which is like crystal and is perfectly clear is the washing of the holy font and the resulting brightness of most blessed faith. It is said to flow from the throne of God and the Lamb because the cleansing is from him, life is from him, and all righteousness and holiness of baptism flows from and proceeds from him. TRACTATE ON THE APOCALYPSE 22.1.[7]

**THE GRACE OF CHRIST IS LIKE A RIVER.** OECUMENIUS: The "river of life" is the abundant and plenteous gifts of the grace of Christ that are everlastingly poured out upon the saints. These sweep and flow upon them much like a river. COMMENTARY ON THE APOCALYPSE 22.1-5.[8]

**ETERNAL LIFE IS THE FRUIT OF BAPTISM.** PRIMASIUS: The river of life that flows in the midst of the city no longer signifies the administration of baptism. Rather, the fruit of that sacra-

ment is here revealed. For we sow now in tears what we shall then reap in joy, and so now the church "sows to the Spirit so that it might reap eternal life."[9] COMMENTARY ON THE APOCALYPSE 22.1.[10]

**THE FOUNTAIN OF BAPTISM.** CAESARIUS OF ARLES: This passage shows the fountain of baptism flowing from God and from Christ in the midst of the church. For what kind of honor would there be for this city were the river to flow through the streets to the hindrance of the inhabitants? EXPOSITION ON THE APOCALYPSE 22.1, HOMILY 19.[11]

**THE SPIRIT CLEANSES IN BAPTISM.** ANDREW OF CAESAREA: The river that flows from the church in the present life indicates the baptism of regeneration that is made effective through the Spirit and makes those who are washed more clean than snow and crystal. But the river of God, filled up with waters, namely, the Holy Spirit, flows through the Jerusalem above, flowing from God the Father through the Son. And [this river flows] in the midst of the most excellent powers, which are named here the "throne of God," making full the streets of the holy city, that is, the multitude of its inhabitants who are, according to the psalmist, "more in number than the sand."[12] COMMENTARY ON THE APOCALYPSE 22.1-2.[13]

### 22:2 The Tree of Life

**THE HOLY SPIRIT PRESENTS CHRIST IN BOTH TESTAMENTS.** JEROME: This tree bears twofold: it produces fruit and it produces foliage. The fruit that it bears contains the meaning of Scripture; the leaves, only the words. The fruit is in the meaning; the leaves are in the words. For that reason, whoever reads sacred Scripture, if he reads merely as the Jews read, grasps only the

---

[2]Jn 1:29. [3]FC 48:8-9. [4]Jn 4:10. [5]Ps 36:9 (35:10 LXX). [6]Rom 6:4. [7]CCL 107:93. [8]TEG 8:280. [9]Gal 6:8. [10]CCL 92:299. [11]PL 35:2451. [12]Ps 139:18 (138:18 LXX). [13]MTS 1 Sup 1:250.

words. If he reads with true spiritual insight, he gathers the fruit. "And whose leaves never fade."[14] The leaves of this tree are by no means useless. Even if one understands holy Scripture only as history, he has something useful for his soul. . . . A tree, he says, one lofty tree had been set up. He did not say trees, but only one tree. If there is but one tree, how can it be on both sides of the river? If he had said, "I saw trees," it would have been possible for some trees to be on one side of the river and other trees on the other side. Actually, one tree is said to be on both sides of the river. One river comes forth from the throne of God—the grace of the Holy Spirit—and this grace of the Holy Spirit is found in the river of the sacred Scriptures. This river, moreover, has two banks, the Old Testament and the New Testament, and the tree planted on both sides is Christ. During the year, this tree yields twelve fruits, one for each month, but we are unable to receive the fruits except through the apostles. If one approaches the tree through the apostles, he must receive the fruit; he gathers the fruit from the sacred Scriptures; he grasps the divine meaning abiding within the words. If, therefore, one comes to this tree through the apostles, he gathers its fruit. HOMILIES ON THE PSALMS I (Ps I).[15]

**THE FRUIT OF WISDOM IS FOR THE HEALTH OF THE NATIONS.** APRINGIUS OF BEJA: Concerning wisdom it is said, "She proclaims outside; she raises her voice in the streets, and she cries out on the top of the walls."[16] And should anyone refuse to come to the marriage of the king, she commands her servants and says, "Go to the streets and byways and invite whomever you meet to the wedding, that my house might be filled."[17] This water of salvation and the cleansing of grace is described as flowing in the streets. . . . The two banks of the river are the two Testaments in which the fullness of our salvation is written down. There is the tree of life. There is told [the story] of our Lord Jesus Christ, who is the tree of life: "Through him we live, move, and have our being."[18] The leaves are his words; they

are of use for the health of all nations. The twelve months are the apostles of the Lord, because the Lord himself is the "favorable year of forgiveness."[19] These are the twelve months, each bringing to the many the fruit of unending preaching out of an abundance of knowledge. TRACTATE ON THE APOCALYPSE 22.2.[20]

**CHRIST HEAPS GENEROSITY ON GENEROSITY.** OECUMENIUS: The Lord is the "tree of life" according to what the author of the Proverbs writes concerning wisdom. He says, "She is a tree of life to those who lay hold of her."[21] And the wise Paul has taught us that "Christ is the power of God and the wisdom of God."[22] He says that the saints are not only rich in the gracious gifts of Christ but also that they have him as one who lives in them and among them,[23] and this is the pinnacle of the highest blessedness. Continuously and without cessation the "tree of life," namely, Christ, produces ripe fruit and gifts for the saints, as though he were heaping generosity on generosity, and so they never become bereft of God's benefits. COMMENTARY ON THE APOCALYPSE 21.26-22.5.[24]

**CHRIST IS THE FOUNTAIN AND THE RIVER.** PRIMASIUS: By the twelve months he signifies all of time, and to be sure all of eternity. Therefore, where there is an eternal paradise, no aridity will ever be permitted to intrude. Where there is a perfect and certain well-being, absolutely no infirmity enters in. This is what the prophet promised when he said, "They shall obtain joy and gladness, and sorrow and sighing shall flee away."[25] This is the tree, as we read, which is "planted by streams of water,"[26] and of which Jeremiah says that it "sends out its roots by the stream."[27] This is to say that it places its hope and trust in the Lord. We may also interpret this passage concerning the river of the water of life to

---

[14]Jerome is quoting Ps 1:3. [15]FC 48:8-9. [16]Prov 1:20-21. [17]Lk 14:23. [18]Acts 17:28. [19]Is 61:2. [20]CCL 107:93-94. [21]Prov 3:18. [22]1 Cor 1:24. [23]See 2 Cor 6:16. [24]TEG 8:281. [25]Is 35:10. [26]Ps 1:3. [27]Jer 17:8.

refer to the Lord Jesus Christ, who is himself the fountain of life. For we read of him, "With you is the fountain of life; in your light we shall see light."[28] He is himself, as we read, "the image of God's majesty, who is powerful in all things, and remaining in himself renews all things and in every generation rests in holy souls."[29] And so he is the Fountain who is also the River. He is the Fountain, for he remains in himself inexhaustible, and he is the River because he offers himself generously and perpetually so that the saints might receive of [his] abundance. Where he is called fountain, he is also called a rushing stream. When the psalm says, "You shall give them drink from the river of your delights," it then continues, "for with you is the fountain of life, and in your light shall we see light."[30] Moreover, [it says that it flows] through the middle of the street for it is a good that is common to all the saints and that is not denied to any who are worthy, nor is it granted to any who are unworthy.... Indeed, it is in their midst as an undivided patrimony to all who see God. For that reason we read, "Jerusalem, a city whose fellowship is complete within itself."[31] If the fruit is understood to be the reward of a blissful immortality, then we rightly understand the leaves to be the song of perpetual praise, because for those who sing they fall in the well-being of a happy fate. For there exists the true healing of the nations, there is full redemption, there is eternal happiness. COMMENTARY ON THE APOCALYPSE 22.2-3.[32]

**THE FAITHFUL EAT THE CROSS OF THE LORD.**
CAESARIUS OF ARLES: It is speaking of the cross of the Lord. There is no tree that bears fruit in every season except the cross that the faithful, who are made wet by the water of the church's river, eat.[33] And these [faithful] in turn produce eternal fruit in every season. EXPOSITION ON THE APOCALYPSE 22.2, HOMILY 19.[34]

**WE KNOW CHRIST BY THE SPIRIT AND THROUGH THE SPIRIT.** ANDREW OF CAESAREA: This river waters the saints who are planted

alongside it. They are here figuratively called the "tree of life" by virtue of their participation and imitation of him who is the Tree of Life. Moreover, they give forth "twelve fruits," that is, they unceasingly yield the production of fruit. For there will be there no winter of sin that causes the trees of life to shed their leaves, such as we see now. Rather, the time of the production of fruit by the saints will be complete and uninterrupted, and [this time] is here said to be twelve months. It speaks in these terms equally because of the customary year among us, as well as because of the proclamation of the twelve apostles. This present passage may also be interpreted in another way. "The river" might signify the gifts of the life-giving Spirit, which flow down from the throne of the Father and of the Son, that is, from the ranks of the cherubim, among whom God is enthroned. [This river flows] into the streets of the city, that is, to the full citizenry of the saints, as coming from the first ranks into the second that are made to share in the well-ordered arrangement of the heavenly hierarchy. The "tree of life" signifies Christ, whom we know by the Holy Spirit and through the Spirit. For in him is the Spirit, and he is worshiped in Spirit, and he is the supplier of the Spirit, and through him the twelve fruits of the apostolic chorus give to us the inexhaustible fruit of the knowledge of God, through whom "the acceptable year of the Lord and the day of recompense" foretold by the prophet[35] is proclaimed to us. COMMENTARY ON THE APOCALYPSE 22.2.[36]

**THE WORDS OF SCRIPTURE ARE MEDICINE FOR THE NATIONS.** JEROME: If one cannot pluck the fruit [of the tree of the sacred Scriptures], it is because he is still too weak; he is not yet a disciple but belongs to the throng; he is an outsider, a stranger from the nations. Because he cannot

---

[28]Ps 36:9 (35:10 LXX). [29]See Wis 7:26-27. [30]Ps 36:8-9 (35:9-10 LXX). [31]Ps 122:3 (121:3 LXX). [32]CCL 92:300-301. [33]Caesarius is referring to baptism and the Eucharist. [34]PL 35:2451. [35]Is 61:2. [36]MTS 1 Sup 1:251-52.

pluck the fruit, he plucks only words, the leaves for the healing of the nations. . . . One who belongs to the nations, who is not a disciple, who is as yet only one of the crowd, gathers only leaves from the tree; he receives from Scripture plain words for a healing remedy; . . . in other words, the leaves are medicine. HOMILIES ON THE PSALMS 1 (Ps 1).[37]

**ALL WHO CLING TO CHRIST ARE LEAVES OF LIFE.** OECUMENIUS: The leaves of life are those who hang from Christ and cling to him: patriarchs, prophets, apostles, evangelists, martyrs and also confessors, those who perform the rites of the gospel at the proper time, the shepherds of the church and every righteous person, those who even now heal souls and will be for the saints the source of additional blessings. COMMENTARY ON THE APOCALYPSE 21.26-22.5.[38]

**TO SHARE IN CHRIST'S DEITY.** ANDREW OF CAESAREA: The "leaves of the tree," namely, of Christ, are the more exalted understandings of the divine judgments, even as its "fruits" are the more perfect knowledge that is to be revealed in the age to come. The leaves will be for healing, that is, for the cleansing of the ignorance of those who have been deficient in the exercise of the virtues, for "there is one glory of the sun, and another glory of the moon, and another glory of the stars."[39] Moreover, "in my Father's house there are many rooms,"[40] so that one is accounted worthy of less and another of more brightness according to the measure of the works of each. This present passage may also be interpreted otherwise. The "tree of life" produces twelve fruits, namely, the apostolic chorus that shares in him who is truly the Tree of Life, who through his participation in the flesh has given us to share in his deity. Their fruits are those who yield fruit a hundredfold. The leaves are those who yield sixtyfold. These carry to those who come later the illumination of the divine light that they had received from those who had yielded a hundredfold, and they bring healing to those from the

nations who yield thirtyfold. For at that time there will be a difference between those who are saved as great as there is a difference between fruit and leaves. Some will be glorified to a lesser extent, some to a greater extent, as it is written. It writes of a "tree" in the singular rather than "trees" in the plural to indicate the unity and harmony of the life which the saints have together. COMMENTARY ON THE APOCALYPSE 22.2.[41]

## 22:3 The Throne of God and of the Lamb

**JOY IN THE VISION OF CHRIST'S FACE.** APRINGIUS OF BEJA: There will be [in that city] nothing accursed, that is, no temptation will approach, no profane sin shall be recorded through the rashness of the envious one. Rather, in its midst will be the rule of the divine power and of the Lamb. All will serve him with the exaltation of that city's happiness. They shall rejoice in the vision of his face and in the sweetness of his presence, and they shall bear his name engraved in the sign of his cross on their foreheads. TRACTATE ON THE APOCALYPSE 22.3-4.[42]

**THE SAINTS WILL WORSHIP WITH JOY AND SPIRITUAL GLADNESS.** OECUMENIUS: Even were now curses especially put to flight, we are nonetheless tossed about by them, with thousands of allegations brought up against us with our knowledge and even without our knowledge. But then the saints will be clean and untainted of any stain of the soul as well as of the body. And the rule of God will exist in the city, for this is the meaning of "the throne." The saints "shall worship him," it says, not with a worship that is laborious but that done with joy and spiritual gladness. [Such worship] comes from the vision of his face. COMMENTARY ON THE APOCALYPSE 21.26-22.5.[43]

**THE RULE OF THE ONE GODHEAD IS INDIVISIBLE.** PRIMASIUS: He does not speak here of

---

[37]FC 48:9-10*. [38]TEG 8:281. [39]1 Cor 15:41. [40]Jn 14:2. [41]MTS 1 Sup 1:252-53. [42]CCL 107:94. [43]TEG 8:281-82.

thrones. For where there is a natural and undifferentiated unity, there the glory of the Godhead may be especially esteemed. There is one throne of an indivisible rule that cannot be divided by the cunning of Arian depravity or confounded by the doubts of Sabellian vanity.[44] Rather, it is able to be contemplated only by the reception of catholic truth and is proven to be rightly held by the confession of her faith. COMMENTARY ON THE APOCALYPSE 22.3.[45]

**NOTHING DEDICATED TO THE DEVIL WILL BE IN THE CITY.** ANDREW OF CAESAREA: *Anathema* can be interpreted in a twofold manner. It either refers to that which is holy for many but is dedicated to God alone, or it refers to that which is sacred to the whole of creation and to the holy powers but is attributed to the devil because of his utter alienation and separation from that which is good. We think that here *katathema*[46] is used in an emphatic sense. For such a thing is not dedicated to anyone, but it is "put aside" for the devil, being subordinated to him and condemned along with him. Such a thing will not exist within that city. COMMENTARY ON THE APOCALYPSE 22.3.[47]

### 22:4 His Name on Their Foreheads

**AN ABIDING MEMORY OF THEIR UNION WITH GOD.** OECUMENIUS: They will behold [the face of God] to the extent possible by human nature. "And his name," it says, "shall be on their foreheads." These words symbolize the abiding memory they have of God and their union with him. For just as God rests upon them and is imprinted on them, so he is always present with the saints. This is evident also from what Paul said: "And we shall always be with the Lord."[48] COMMENTARY ON THE APOCALYPSE 21.26-22.5.[49]

**THE VISION OF GOD IS THE REWARD OF FAITH.** PRIMASIUS: This[50] implies that there is in store for us a reward for our faith, that vision that John had in mind when he said, "When he

appears, we shall be like him, for we shall see him just as he is."[51] For, of course, *face* is to be understood not as the kind of face we now have as part of our body but as a manifestation of what God is. . . . God will be made known to and be perceived by us, in many ways. He will be seen in the spirit (whereby each of us will see him within ourselves and in one another); he will be seen in himself; he will be seen in the new heavens and the new earth and in every creature then existing.[52] COMMENTARY ON THE APOCALYPSE 22.4.[53]

**THE SAINTS WILL SEE CHRIST.** ANDREW OF CAESAREA: Those who become the throne of God because of the rest of the Lord among them will be the inhabitants of that city. They will see him no longer in shadows but face to face, even as the holy apostles saw him on the holy mount, as the great Dionysius says.[54] And instead of the golden breastplate worn in ancient times by the high priest, they will have the divine name imprinted not only on their foreheads but also within their hearts, and this shows their firm, bold and immoveable love toward him. For the writing upon the forehead symbolizes the ornamentation of boldness. COMMENTARY ON THE APOCALYPSE 22.3-4.[55]

**THE VISION OF GOD IS THE HIGHEST GOOD.** BEDE: The vision of God is preserved for us as the reward of faith. This is the highest good as Philip understood when he said, "Lord, show us the Father, and we shall be satisfied."[56] EXPLANATION OF THE APOCALYPSE 22.4.[57]

---

[44]The Arians claimed that the Son was "of another essence" than the Father; therefore, he was not "true God" and his rule by adoption only. The Sabellians did not believe that there were distinct "persons" in the Godhead and therefore "confounded" the persons in the trinitarian rule of the one Godhead. [45]CCL 92:301. [46]The prefixing of *kata* intensifies the meaning. [47]MTS 1 Sup 1:253. [48]1 Thess 4:17. [49]TEG 8:282. [50]The reference is to 1 Cor 13:12, "then we shall see face to face." [51]1 Jn 3:2. [52]For his commentary on Rev 22:4a, Primasius quotes Augustine. We have given Primasius's quotation from Augustine *City of God* 22.29 (FC 24:498, 504-5). Primasius also quotes Augustine *Letter* 147.51 (FC 20:220-21). [53]CCL 92:303. [54]Pseudo-Dionysius *De Div. Nom.* 1.4 (PG 3:592). [55]MTS 1 Sup 1:253-54. [56]Jn 14:8. [57]CCL 121A:565.

## 22:5 *They Shall Reign Forever*

**UNDERSTANDING AND WISDOM.** APRINGIUS OF BEJA: Neither the night of sin nor the darkness of unrighteousness will ever appear again. Nor in that bliss will they [the saints] live by the words of any teacher; nor established in such a fullness will they require the light of another's understanding. The Lord himself will give them great understanding and wisdom, for all knowledge that is desired is revealed in the brightness of his countenance. And they shall reign in all wisdom and truth. TRACTATE ON THE APOCALYPSE 22.5.[58]

**GOD WILL GIVE ETERNAL ILLUMINATION.** OECUMENIUS: The saints shall never have need of the light of the sun or that from a lamp, since the light of God will provide never-ending illumination. "And they shall reign," clearly the saints, "forever." The all-wise Daniel testified of these things, saying, "And the saints of the Most High shall receive the kingdom and possess it for ever and ever."[59] COMMENTARY ON THE APOCALYPSE 21.26-22.5.[60]

**THE LORD OF GLORY WILL BE LIGHT AND KING.** ANDREW OF CAESAREA: If, as the Lord says, "the righteous will shine as the sun,"[61] how will there be any necessity for the light of a lamp or of the sun for those who have the Lord of glory as their illumination and king? And they will be ruled by him forever, or rather they will reign with him, as the holy apostle says.[62] COMMENTARY ON THE APOCALYPSE 22.5.[63]

**THE VISION OF GOD IS THE PERFECTION OF ALL PROMISES.** BEDE: [In the city above] the weakness of our bodies will require neither the quiet of night nor the light of a fire. For then God will be all in all, namely, he who is the true light and the eternal rest of the saints. One might also interpret these words figuratively. The exhortation of the prophets and the preaching of the divine Law will not be necessary there, for these are now said to be lights in a dark place. But then, when all things have been fulfilled, the promise will be perfected in the vision and contemplation of God. EXPLANATION OF THE APOCALYPSE 22.5.[64]

---

[58]CCL 107:94. [59]Dan 7:18. [60]TEG 8:282. [61]Mt 13:43. [62]2 Tim 2:12. [63]MTS 1 Sup 1:254. [64]CCL 121A:567.

---

# 22:6-7 THE END WILL COME QUICKLY!

[6]*And he said to me, "These words are trustworthy and true. And the Lord, the God of the spirits of the prophets, has sent his angel to show his servants what must soon take place. [7]And behold, I am coming soon."*

*Blessed is he who keeps the words of the prophecy of this book.*

---

**OVERVIEW:** The words and the vision given to John are trustworthy and true, because they came from Christ, "the God of the prophets," who is himself the Truth. He gave the revelation in a manner corresponding to the economy of his condescension (ANDREW OF CAESAREA) so that we might learn what John saw (OECUMENIUS). Since the promise of Christ is true (APRINGIUS), the

Revelation is commended to the church since also those who will come later will have to learn from it (PRIMASIUS). Christ makes known that his coming will not tarry. Therefore, what is foreseen in this book will happen quickly and suddenly (APRINGIUS). Keeping in mind that the present time is short in comparison with the everlasting ages that are coming (OECUMENIUS, ANDREW OF CAESAREA), we should be eager to maintain our resolve to live a God-pleasing and pure life (OECUMENIUS, PRIMASIUS). Since the death of each person comes swiftly, let us pray that we not be fettered by the cares of this world, but rather that we might be preserved by God's mercy from a life of lost opportunities and from a death for which we are unprepared (ANDREW OF CAESAREA).

## 22:6 Trustworthy and True

**NOTHING IS SO CERTAIN AS THE PROMISE OF CHRIST.** APRINGIUS OF BEJA: What is so faithful and true as the promise of Christ and the future hope of the saints? He who spoke through his servants, the prophets, did so that he might be recognized as the Lord of the living and be called "the Spirit of the Lord." For the Spirit is life, and all flesh is made alive by the Spirit. TRACTATE ON THE APOCALYPSE 22.6-7.[1]

**THROUGH THE REVELATION WE HAVE LEARNED WHAT JOHN SAW.** OECUMENIUS: By "spirits of the prophets" he means the prophetic gifts, as we learn from the all-wise Paul, who said, "and the spirits of the prophets are subject to prophets,"[2] and from the holy prophet Isaiah: "We have conceived, O Lord, because of fear of you, and we have been in birth pangs and have brought forth the breath of your salvation that you have wrought upon the earth."[3] "To show his servants what must soon take place," it says. By means of John and his writings, all have learned what he saw. And appropriately he says "soon," for as we have noted earlier, in comparison with the everlasting ages that are coming, all time is short, even if

someone might think it a very long while. COMMENTARY ON THE APOCALYPSE 22.6-9.[4]

**THE REVELATION IS COMMENDED.** PRIMASIUS: He is not expressing any doubts about the trustworthiness of John. Rather, he is commending this vision to the whole church as true, for he knew that in the future there would also be those who are to learn from it. [By speaking of his angel], he teaches that he has always looked after the welfare of all. He is the Spirit of the prophets who is also the Holy Spirit and indeed is the Lord. For this reason the prophet said, "I will hear what the Lord God speaks to me,"[5] and "The beginning of the speaking of God to Hosea."[6] Because of the essence of the one, divine Trinity, he also fittingly mentions here the Holy Spirit, since above he had mentioned the Father and the Son.[7] For when we read that "God is spirit,"[8] it refers to the entire Trinity. COMMENTARY ON THE APOCALYPSE 22.6.[9]

**CHRIST KNOWS THE TIME OF THE CONSUMMATION.** ANDREW OF CAESAREA: These words are "trustworthy and true" because they come from the Truth.... Since Christ is "the God of the prophets, who sent his angel" by means of the blessed John who saw this vision, "to show his servants what is to take place," it is clear that he gave the Revelation for the sake of the flesh according to the condescension of the economy of the Son, as it said at the beginning.[10] For he who is the God of the prophets and who sent his angels as ministering spirits for the revelation of coming things would not be ignorant of the hour or the day of the consummation, so that he who has all "the hidden treasures of wisdom and knowledge"[11] would learn [these things] only now from the Father. COMMENTARY ON THE APOCALYPSE 22.6.[12]

---

[1]CCL 107:94-95. [2]1 Cor 14:32. [3]Is 26:18. [4]TEG 8:282-83. [5]Ps 85:8 (84:9 LXX). [6]Hos 1:2. [7]Rev 22:1. [8]Jn 4:24. [9]CCL 92:304. [10]Rev 1:1. [11]See Col 2:3. [12]MTS 1 Sup 1:254-55.

## 22:7 "I Am Coming Soon"

**THE QUICKNESS OF THE END.** APRINGIUS OF BEJA: By the messenger of truth the Lord himself reveals directly "to his servants what must soon take place." And unless anyone be in doubt about the expectation of the end, he indicates that what is to happen will happen quickly and that he is blessed who keeps the words of the prophets. TRACTATE ON THE APOCALYPSE 22.6-7.[13]

**THOSE WHO LIVE A GOD-PLEASING LIFE.** OECUMENIUS: Those who keep these words are [blessed, because they are] eager by a God-pleasing life not to fall into the punishments mentioned in it. COMMENTARY ON THE APOCALYPSE 22.6-9.[14]

**RESOLVE TO LIVE A MORE PURE LIFE.** PRIMASIUS: "To keep" means to believe in a reverent manner and to maintain one's resolve and intention to live a more pure life. COMMENTARY ON THE APOCALYPSE 22.7.[15]

**PRAY GOD TO PRESERVE US FROM AN UNPREPARED DEATH.** ANDREW OF CAESAREA: It is often customary for the prophets to speak divine words as though it were from their own person. The words "I am coming soon" indicate either the shortness of the present time in comparison with the future age or the sudden swiftness of the death of each person. For the departure from here is the end of every person. Therefore, since "we do not know at what hour the thief will come,"[16] we are commanded "to watch and to gird ourselves and to keep our lamps burning,"[17] letting our godly behavior shine even for our neighbor.[18] Therefore, let us not cease to beseech God with a contrite heart to "save us from all our pursuers," lest our souls, having been defeated by them, be snatched away unprepared "with no one to rescue or to save."[19] [Let us also pray God] lest any soul, bound by the chains of earthly affairs and not able to free itself from them, should vainly turn again to them and then, when constrained to leave them by the authority of the angels and the command of God, will lament in vain for the lost opportunities of a life now passed. Rather, singing without ceasing the song of David, "I prepared myself and was not fearful to keep your commandments,"[20] let us receive as a reward for keeping [his commandments] the praise of God, who will say, "Well done, good and faithful servant; you have been faithful over a little, I will set you over much; enter into the joy of your master."[21] Together with him glory, honor and power are fittingly given to the Father and also to the Holy Spirit now and always and forever and ever. Amen. COMMENTARY ON THE APOCALYPSE 22.7.[22]

---

[13]CCL 107:95. [14]TEG 8:283. [15]CCL 92:304. [16]See Mt 24:43. [17]See Lk 12:39, 45. [18]See Mt 5:16. [19]Ps 7:1-2 (7:2-3 LXX). [20]Ps 119:60 (118:60 LXX). [21]Mt 25:21, 23. [22]MTS 1 Sup 1:255-57.

---

## 22:8-9 "WORSHIP GOD"

[8]*I John am he who heard and saw these things. And when I heard and saw them, I fell down to worship at the feet of the angel who showed them to me;* [9]*but he said to me, "You must not do that! I am a fellow servant with you and your brethren the prophets, and with those who keep the words of this book. Worship God."*

**OVERVIEW:** John testifies that he is an eyewitness and earwitness of the revelation (ANDREW OF CAESAREA). Overcome by fright and awe at the greatness of what he had seen and heard, John fell at the feet of the revealing angel (APRINGIUS). But the heavenly piety of the angel would not allow any worship of himself (ANDREW OF CAESAREA). For no creature properly worships another creature (ATHANASIUS). Rather, since nothing is equal to the Creator, all creatures are to offer worship to God alone (APRINGIUS, ATHANASIUS). True worship appertains also to the Son, for he is not above the angels in glory only. He is the Father's proper Son according to essence, and therefore as God worthy of worship (ATHANASIUS). Although worshiped by the angels above, Christ has not yet chosen to avenge himself on earth. Taking his example, we ought not with shameless haste insist on our own revenge. Rather, we ought with patience await his coming (CYPRIAN).

### 22:8 I Fell Down to Worship

**JOHN WAS OVERCOME.** APRINGIUS OF BEJA: John, the most blessed of the apostles, says that when he heard [these words] he was overcome with fright by the power of the words and the magnitude of the vision and fell to the ground because of this. And he says that he was prostrate that he might adore the angel of truth "who showed these things to me." TRACTATE ON THE APOCALYPSE 22.8.[1]

**JOHN WAS AN EYEWITNESS AND EARWITNESS OF THE VISION.** ANDREW OF CAESAREA: [To witness by eye and ear] is characteristic of one who is an apostle. Just as he said in the Gospel, "He who has seen bears witness, and his testimony is true,"[2] so also in this passage [John] confesses that he is an eyewitness and earwitness of what has been foretold and so makes himself to be a guarantee of what has been seen. COMMENTARY ON THE APOCALYPSE 22.8-9.[3]

### 22:9 "Worship God!"

**NOW IS THE TIME FOR PATIENCE AND OBEDIENCE.** CYPRIAN: This is the Judge and the Avenger, beloved brothers, that we are to await who, when he revenges himself, is destined to revenge us, the people of his church, and the number of all the just from the beginning of the world. Let him who hastens and hurries too much to his own revenge consider that he alone who avenges has not yet avenged himself. . . . In the Apocalypse, when John wishes to adore him, the angel resists him and says, "You must not do this because I am a fellow servant of you and of your brothers. Adore Jesus the Lord." How wonderful then is Jesus our Lord, and what great patience this is that he who is adored in heaven is not yet avenged on earth! Let us think of his patience, beloved brothers, in our persecutions and sufferings. Let us show the full obedience that is inspired by our expectation of his coming, and let us not hasten with the impious and shameless haste of a servant to defend ourselves before the Lord. Let us rather persevere and let us labor, and [let us] be watchful with all our heart and steadfast even to total resignation; let us guard the precepts of the Lord, so that when the day of wrath and vengeance comes, we may not be punished with the impious and sinners but may be honored with the just and those who fear God. THE GOOD OF PATIENCE 24.[4]

**WORSHIP IS OWED TO GOD ALONE.** ATHANASIUS: The Father shows [the Son] to be his own proper and only Son, saying, "You are my Son,"[5] and "This is my beloved Son, in whom I am well pleased."[6] Accordingly the angels ministered to him, as being one beyond themselves; and they worship him, not as being greater in glory but as being some one beyond all the creatures, and beyond themselves, and alone the Father's proper Son according to essence. For if he was worshiped as excelling them in glory, each of the things subservient ought to worship what excels itself. But

---

[1]CCL 107:95. [2]Jn 21:24. [3]MTS 1 Sup 1:257. [4]FC 36:286-87. [5]Ps 2:7. [6]Mt 3:17.

this is not the case; for creature does not worship creature, but servant [worships the] Lord, and creature God. Thus Peter the apostle hinders Cornelius, who would worship him, saying, "I myself also am a man."[7] And an angel, when John would worship him in the Apocalypse, hinders him, saying, "See that you do not do it; . . . worship God." Therefore, to God alone appertains worship, and this the very angels know, that though they excel other beings in glory, yet they are all creatures and not to be worshiped but worship the Lord. DISCOURSES AGAINST THE ARIANS 2.23.[8]

### NOTHING IS EQUAL TO THE CREATOR.

APRINGIUS OF BEJA: Since there is no pride in the servant nor any vanity in the saints, [the angel] immediately exhorts him [not to worship him].

. . . The angel proclaims that nothing is equal to the Creator, and he declares that nothing can be offered to another that is owed to the Lord God only. TRACTATE ON THE APOCALYPSE 22.9.[9]

### THE PIETY OF THE ANGEL IS REVEALED.

ANDREW OF CAESAREA: He shows the piety of the angel who has described and interpreted the vision, indicating that [the angel] would not allow himself to be worshiped by a fellow servant. Rather, with a good conscience we are to give homage to [our] common Lord. COMMENTARY ON THE APOCALYPSE 22.8-9.[10]

---

[7]Acts 10:26. [8]NPNF 2 4:360*. [9]CCL 107:95. [10]MTS 1 Sup 1:257. For his commentary on Rev 22:9, Oecumenius refers to his comments on Rev 19:10 (above).

## 22:10-15 THE TIME IS AT HAND

[10]And he said to me, "Do not seal up the words of the prophecy of this book, for the time is near. [11]Let the evildoer still do evil, and the filthy still be filthy, and the righteous still do right, and the holy still be holy."

[12]"Behold, I am coming soon, bringing my recompense, to repay every one for what he has done. [13]I am the Alpha and the Omega, the first and the last, the beginning and the end."

[14]Blessed are those who wash their robes,[s] that they may have the right to the tree of life and that they may enter the city by the gates. [15]Outside are the dogs and sorcerers and fornicators and murderers and idolaters, and every one who loves and practices falsehood.

s Other ancient authorities read do his commandments

**OVERVIEW:** The time of the Lord's coming is not far distant, but it is not yet present. For this reason, Christ did not wish the words of the Revelation to be kept in the mind of John alone (OECUMENIUS). Rather, it was necessary that the promises and future judgments be revealed (BEDE) for the admonition of all (APRINGIUS, OECUMENIUS). The Scriptures remain closed to the proud and worldly (CAESARIUS OF ARLES, BEDE), but the faithful, the humble and the obedient who read the Revelation will receive their reward of eternal life (ANDREW OF CAESAREA, BEDE).

In the meantime, therefore, every person has opportunity to use free will for good or for evil (Oecumenius). Since God does not desire the punishment of sinners (Apringius), sinners are threatened so that they might abstain from wickedness and devote themselves rather to holiness (Apringius). Yet some will follow the hidden judgment of God and choose to become yet more evil (Primasius), perhaps by engaging in ever greater cruelty against the martyrs (Eusebius) or by allow-ing lesser sins to be the occasion for greater sins (Bede). Although those who crucified Christ seemed most wicked, worse still are those who sin willfully after the crucifixion of Jesus (Augustine).

Keeping in mind, therefore, that Christ will recompense each person at his coming (Oecumenius), we ought not be as lazy and negligent laborers who are ashamed when their employer comes. We should rather be eager to do good (Clement of Rome). In the future no conversion or penance will be possible; at the coming of the Lord no further workers will be called to the vineyard (Fulgentius of Ruspe). Blessed are those who are cleansed of every sinful stain by baptism or by the tears of repentance (Apringius). Such who have lived righteously will rest upon the tree of life (Oecumenius, Primasius) and delight in the vision of Christ (Andrew of Caesarea, Bede). The faith that possesses such power is that faith that is in Christ, who is both true God and true man and in the deity of the Holy Spirit, who is one God together with the Father and the Son (Primasius).

Outside of the ark of the church (Apringius) there is only the madness of the impious (Bede) and every kind of vice and impurity that is against nature. Virtue is according to nature and reflects a healthy soul (Oecumenius). Those who sin after their baptism are no better than the shameless and the unfaithful (Andrew of Caesarea).

## 22:10 *"The Time Is Near"*

**Written for the Admonition of All.** Apringius of Beja: He says that the time of retribution and of the end is near. With heavenly words he indicates the dire reason why those things that were commanded and spoken ought not be left in silence. Rather, they were written for the admonition of all. Tractate on the Apocalypse 22.10.[1]

**The End Is Not Far Off.** Oecumenius: "Do not seal up these words," it says. That is, you ought not keep these words to yourself nor lock them up in the treasury of your mind. Rather, make them known to everyone. "For the time is near," it says. He is saying something like this: While the right time when they will have need to hear these words is not far distant, as it once was, that time is not yet present either. For it is not good that the exhortation of these words be, as it were, superfluous—for what need of exhortation do those have who are still acquainting themselves with evil and good?—for it is untimely to instruct by word those who are learning from experience. But why does he say "it is near"? It is neither a long time away, nor is it already present. Commentary on the Apocalypse 22.10-14.[2]

**The Scriptures Are Open to the Humble.** Caesarius of Arles: Just as the divine Scriptures are sealed for those who are proud and who love the world more than God, so are they opened for those who are humble and who fear God. Exposition on the Apocalypse 22.10, Homily 19.[3]

**The Revelation Guides Those Who Read It.** Andrew of Caesarea: Until now he has presented the words of the angel, but here he changes to the person of the Lord Christ, saying, "Do not seal up the words of the prophecy." Indeed, the book is worthy to be read by the faithful. In view of the punishment prepared for the sinners and of the rest promised to the saints,

---

[1]CCL 107:95. [2]TEG 8:284. [3]PL 35:2451.

it guides those who read it to the true life. COM-MENTARY ON THE APOCALYPSE 22.10.[4]

**JUDGMENTS AND PROMISES MADE KNOWN.**
BEDE: Since the future judgment is approaching, it is necessary that the divine commandments, judgments and promises be made known. For by obedience to them those who are humble shall acquire their reward, while the proud and obstinate will incur condemnation by their neglect. EXPLANATION OF THE APOCALYPSE 22.10.[5]

## 22:11 *"Let the Holy Still Be Holy"*

**THE WICKED ARE ONLY INFLAMED BY WORKS OF RIGHTEOUSNESS.** EUSEBIUS OF CAESAREA: The blessed Blandina . . . rejoiced in her death as though she had been invited to a bridal banquet instead of being a victim of the beasts. After the scourges, the animals and the hot griddle, she was at last tossed into a net and exposed to a bull. After being tossed a good deal by the animal, she no longer perceived what was happening because of the hope and possession of all she believed in and because of her intimacy with Christ. Thus she too was offered in sacrifice. . . .But not even this was enough to satisfy their madness and their viciousness toward the Christians. For these wild and barbarous people once stirred up by the wild beast were difficult to satisfy, and their wickedness found another special form in what they did to the bodies of the dead. The [pagans] were not humiliated by their defeat, because they lacked human comprehension; rather, it enflamed their bestial anger, so that both the governor and the populace showed toward us the same undeserved hatred, that the Scriptures might be fulfilled: "Let the wicked be wicked and the righteous perform righteousness." ECCLESIASTICAL HISTORY 5.1.55-58.[6]

**THE EVIL OF THOSE WHO WILLFULLY SIN AFTER CHRIST'S DEATH.** AUGUSTINE: "Let the wickedness of sinners be consummated."[7] In this context, "consummated" means "brought to com-pletion," in tune with what is said in the Apocalypse, "Let the righteous become more righteous yet, and the filthy still wallow in their filth." The wickedness of those who crucified the Son of God seems to be complete, but greater still is the wickedness of those who do not wish to live uprightly and hate the commandments of truth for which the Son of God was crucified. The psalmist said, therefore, "Let the wickedness of sinners be consummated," that is, let it come to the pinnacle of wickedness, so that the righteous judgment can come immediately.[8] EXPLANATION OF PSALM 7.9.[9]

**THE ANGEL THREATENS THE EVIL AND ENCOURAGES THE RIGHTEOUS.** APRINGIUS OF BEJA: The angel does not desire that sinners perish. He rather warns those who do iniquity so that hearing the sound of a celestial threat, they might wish to abstain from evil works. Moreover, that the righteous might be made even better, he says, "Let the righteous still do right, and the holy still be holy." [He says this] that they might realize the imminent coming of the Lord and that they might more easily keep themselves from sin and from that time forward always devote themselves to holiness and righteousness. TRACTATE ON THE APOCALYPSE 22.11.[10]

**OPPORTUNITY TO USE FREE WILL.** OECUME-NIUS: He is not urging or commanding anyone to do that which is wicked or to defile themselves. Rather, he is saying that the short time remaining gives humankind yet an opportunity. Therefore, let each person do that which is pleasing to them, and let them use their free will as they choose, whether for that which is evil or for that which is good. COMMENTARY ON THE APOCALYPSE 22.10-14.[11]

---

[4]MTS 1 Sup 1:258. [5]CCL 121A:569. [6]ACM 78-80. Eusebius is quoting the *Letter of the Lyons Martyrs*. [7]Ps 7:9 (7:10 LXX). [8]In his commentary of Rev 22:11, Bede uses this idea of Augustine (CCL 121A:571). [9]WSA 3 15:120-21. [10]CCL 107:95. [11]TEG 8:284.

### THE JUDGMENTS OF GOD ARE HIDDEN AND JUST. PRIMASIUS:

He shows that the judgments of God by which evil people are allowed to become even more evil are hidden yet just. Yet here we ought not think that evil persons harm only others; they harm especially themselves. And therefore it continues, "Let him who is filthy be filthy still." For to whom will that person be good who is harmful to himself? COMMENTARY ON THE APOCALYPSE 22.11.[12]

### A LESSER SIN CAN BECOME CAUSE OF A GREATER SIN. BEDE:

[Herod knew that John the Baptist was a just man and kept him safe].[13] But his love for the woman prevailed, and she forced him to lay his hands on a man whom he knew to be holy and just. Since he was unwilling to restrain his lust, he incurred the guilt of homicide. What was a lesser sin for him became the cause of a greater sin. By God's strict judgment it happened to him that, as a result of his craving for the adulteress whom he knew he ought to reject, he caused the shedding of the blood of the prophet, who he knew was pleasing to God. Now this is [an illustration of] the divine dispensation of judgment, of which it is said, "Let the evildoer still do evil, and the filthy still be filthy." But what follows, "Let the holy still be holy," is appropriate to the person of blessed John. Already holy, he became more holy still when, through his office of spreading the good news, he reached the palm of martyrdom. HOMILIES ON THE GOSPELS 2.23.[14]

## 22:12 "I Am Coming Soon"

### WE MUST BE EAGER TO DO GOOD AND NOT BE LAZY. CLEMENT OF ROME:

What, then, brothers, ought we to do? Should we grow slack in doing good and give up love? May the Lord never permit this to happen at any rate to us! Rather, should we be energetic in doing "every good deed"[15] with earnestness and eagerness.... The good laborer accepts the bread he has earned with his head held high; the lazy and negligent workman cannot look his employer in the face.

We must, then, be eager to do good; for everything comes from him. For he warns us, "See, the Lord is coming. He is bringing his reward with him, to pay each one according to his work." He bids us, therefore, to believe on him with all our heart and not to be slack or negligent in "every good deed." He should be the basis of our boasting and assurance. We should be subject to his will. We should note how the whole throng of his angels stand ready to serve his will. For the Scripture says, "Ten thousand times ten thousand stood by him, and thousands of thousands ministered to him and cried out: Holy, holy, holy is the Lord of Hosts: all creation is full of his glory."[16] We too, then, should gather together for worship in concord and mutual trust and earnestly beseech him as it were with one mouth, that we may share in his great and glorious promises. For he says, "Eye has not seen and ear has not heard and human heart has not conceived what he has prepared for those who patiently wait for him."[17] 1 CLEMENT 33-34.[18]

### PENANCE WILL BE USELESS. FULGENTIUS OF RUSPE:

It is recognized that there is no forgiveness of sins if penance is not done at this moment; nor is penance in this time of any avail for those who despair of the forgiveness of sins. But in the future time, there is to be no conversion for the wicked, and the penance of such people will be endless as well as useless. Just as forgiveness will never be given to them, so their penance will never be ended. For they neglect the time in which penance is fruitfully done by sinners and in which divine pity grants the forgiveness of sins. Because of this the Lord himself in the Apocalypse of John, consoling his faithful and directing the attention of the wicked to the penalty of future punishment, speaks thus....[19] In order that we may more fully recognize that only the time of this present world is allotted for conversion, let us pay attention to those workers

---

[12]CCL 92:305. [13]Mk 6:20. [14]CS 111:232. [15]Tit 3:1. [16]Is 6:3. [17]1 Cor 2:9. [18]LCC 1:58-59. [19]Fulgentius quotes Rev 22:11-15.

whom the Lord called to his vineyard. Although he called for them at various hours, still at the eleventh hour he ended the call, that is, just before the end of the day. In those hours at which the call went out for workers are recognized the ages of the world, in which God has called to a good work those whom he converted to himself by a free justification. . . . Then the eleventh hour came in the first coming of Christ, in which he came in humility in mortal flesh, in which he, the immortal one, deigned to be killed for the sin of the world. . . . After the end of this hour, the Lord does not call workers to the vineyard, but he will come to render to each one the reward for his work, as he himself says, "Behold, I am coming soon; I bring with me the recompense." ON THE FORGIVENESS OF SINS 17.3-18.3.[20]

**CHRIST WILL REWARD EACH PERSON.** OECU-MENIUS: "I am coming," says the Lord, referring to his second coming. And he is bringing with him whatever is necessary for the rewarding of each person, whether that be good or evil. COMMENTARY ON THE APOCALYPSE 22.10-14.[21]

## 22:13 The Alpha and the Omega

**CHRIST JOINED PETER AND PAUL TOGETHER IN MARTYRDOM.** AUGUSTINE: As you know, all of you who know the holy Scriptures, among the disciples whom the Lord chose while present in the flesh, Peter was the first to be chosen. Paul . . . was not chosen among them nor with them, but a long time afterward, though not for all that unequal to them. So Peter is the first of the apostles, Paul the last; while God, whose servants these two are, whose heralds, whose preachers these two are, is "the first and the last." Peter first among the apostles, Paul last among the apostles; God both first and last, before whom nothing and after whom nothing. So God who has presented himself as eternally the first and the last, himself joined together the first and the last apostles in martyrdom. SERMON 299.2.[22]

**THE TWO NATURES OF CHRIST AND THE DEITY OF THE SPIRIT.** PRIMASIUS: Whenever the faithful proclamation of the truth and the pure form of the virtues is confirmed by repetition, our spiritual mind is disposed toward a deeper worship. This is briefly yet meaningfully indicated at the end of this book when it signifies the deity of the Word by an A and the assumed humanity by an Ω [he who is] the beginning without an end. When I note that in the present book A and Ω is repeated several times, I recognize that this occurs for a reason. For [they are repeated] either to assert more often the divinity and the humanity of the one [person] of Christ, in which we claim the fullness of the whole Christian faith to consist, or [they are repeated] to suggest the whole Trinity, which is of one nature. The Trinity spoke through the prophet, saying, "Before me no god was formed, nor shall there be any after me. I am God and besides me there is no savior."[23] And it is he to whom it is said through the prophet, You are God, and in you there is God, and beside you there is no other God. And should there be some other better and deeper mystery hidden in this, I have no doubt that this has been repeated so that it might remain beneficial for the understanding of the faithful. To be sure, the Greek letters A and Ω yield a number that we know is contained in the word *dove*. The Greek word for "dove" is περι-στερά and this word has the value of 801: π=80, ε=5, ρ=100, ι=10, σ=200, τ=300, ε=5, ρ=100, α=1. The letters A and Ω also yield 801: A=1, Ω=800. In the form of the dove we rightly recognize the person of the Holy Spirit, for it was in this form that he chose to appear when he came down.[24] And in this way the madness of the Arians and other heretics is brought to naught, who claim that he is alien to the nature of the Father and the Son. And so by the agreement of this number this revelation from heaven makes

---

[20]FC 95:174-76. [21]TEG 8:284. [22]WSA 3 8:229. This sermon commemorates the birthday of Peter and Paul. [23]See Is 47:8. [24]See Mt 3:16.

known that the Holy Spirit is consubstantial and co-eternal with the Father and the Son. COMMENTARY ON THE APOCALYPSE 22.13.[25]

**NO END TO THE KINGDOM AND POWER OF GOD.** ANDREW OF CAESAREA: There is no God before me, nor is there any God after me. For there is nothing more ancient than the beginning, and there is no end to the kingdom and power of God. In previous passages Christ has often been called "first" because of his deity and "last" because of his humanity. COMMENTARY ON THE APOCALYPSE 22.13.[26]

## 22:14 Entering the City by the Gates

**BAPTIZED AND REPENTING WITH SORROW.** APRINGIUS OF BEJA: He calls those blessed who either wash their nuptial garment in the blood of the Lord's passion through the washing of regeneration which they receive or who through the sorrow of their heart and with tears accomplish the washing away of sins committed at the present time. He indicates that without doubt these will have the right to possess the tree of life.[27] This is that right, that they see the face of our Lord, Jesus Christ, who is true life, and rejoice, and that they desire to be admitted to his presence through the gates, that is, through the doctrine of the apostles and the prophets, which they worked to fulfill. TRACTATE ON THE APOCALYPSE 22.14.[28]

**CLEANSED FROM EVERY SIN.** OECUMENIUS: By "robes" he means our bodies. Therefore, blessed are those who live well and cleanse themselves from every stain of sin. For those who have lived in such a manner will have the right to lean upon the tree of life and to rest upon it. The "tree of life" is the Lord, as we have noted earlier. "That they may enter the city by the gates." Through the gates, that is, by the apostolic doctrines and teachings they become partakers of the life and blessedness of the saints. COMMENTARY ON THE APOCALYPSE 22.10-14.[29]

**THE STRENGTH OF FAITH.** PRIMASIUS: After speaking of the faith he mentions the uprightness of our character, and by the washed robes he teaches about the keeping of the divine commandments. At the beginning of his Gospel John uses a different manner of speech but with the same meaning when he says, "In the beginning was the Word."[30] A little later he writes, "The Word became flesh,"[31] where the fullness of our entire faith consists, so that in one and the same Christ both perfect deity and true humanity are confessed. When he speaks of the uprightness of our character and habits, he says, "As many as received him, he gave to them power to become sons of God, namely, to those who believe in his name,"[32] making explicit the reward for faith and love. So also in this present passage [John] is speaking in a similar and equal manner, making mention of Christ in the A and Ω, and signifying the pure and stainless life in the white robes. Thus, in a similar manner he promises the same reward, saying, "That they might have power over the tree of life."[33] However, the tree of life is Christ, for we read, "Wisdom is a tree of life to those who lay hold of her."[34] We must not think, however, that they [who have this power] are over [i.e., more powerful than] Christ.[35] For "a disciple is not above his teacher, nor a servant above his master."[36] Therefore, when he says here "over the tree of life," he means that their strength consists in the tree of life, that is, in the Lord Christ, of whom the prophet also says, "They are made strong in the holy One of Israel."[37] From whatever source one receives strength, one is said to be "over this." In the same sense it is said to blessed Peter, "On this rock I will build my church,"[38] that is, "upon me."

---

[25]CCL 92:306-7. [26]MTS 1 Sup 1:259. [27]Apringius's text reads *super lignum vitae potestatem*. I have translated *potestas super* to suggest the idea of "a right granted in relation to." [28]CCL 107:96. [29]TEG 8:284-85. [30]Jn 1:1. [31]Jn 1:14. [32]Jn 1:12. [33]In the text of Primasius the term *potestas* occurs in Jn 1:12 and Rev 22:14. [34]Prov 3:18. [35]The text of Primasius reads *ut sit potestas eorum super lignum vitae*. Primasius clearly wishes to exclude any possible false conclusions drawn from *super* ("over," "above"). [36]Mt 10:24. [37]Reference unknown. [38]Mt 16:18. *Super hanc petram* ("upon this rock").

Also the prophet speaks the same meaning although with a different wording when he says, "I will keep my strength, [watching] for you."[39] [Concerning the gates] it is written, "Open to me the gates of righteousness, that I might enter through them and confess the Lord. This is the gate of the Lord; the righteous shall enter through it."[40] In addition we must also say that no one can enter into this city except through Christ who says, "I am the door,"[41] and "No one comes to the Father except through me."[42] COMMENTARY ON THE APOCALYPSE 22.14.[43]

**REST AND DELIGHT IN CHRIST.** ANDREW OF CAESAREA: Those [who keep the commandments] are truly worthy of blessedness. For in life eternal they shall possess authority to find rest in the tree of life, namely, Christ our God, and to delight in the vision of him without any evil power becoming a hindrance [to that bliss]. And they shall enter into that city above by the apostolic gates, that is, by the apostles' teachings, through the true door. Nor shall they, as though shepherds for hire, sneak in by some other way, but they will be guided in by the gatekeeper of life. COMMENTARY ON THE APOCALYPSE 22.14.[44]

**THROUGH GATES OF RIGHTEOUSNESS.** BEDE: In the image of the white robes he is promising a worthy and suitable reward, namely, that of a pure and stainless life. Clearly [he promises this] in order that one might receive the vision of the Lord, who is eternal life. "Blessed are the pure in heart, for they shall see God."[45] "That they might enter the city by the gates." Those who keep the commandments of the Lord, who said, "I am the door; if any one enters by me, he will be saved, and will go in and out and find pasture"[46]—these are the pastures that are also here promised, that is, the tree of life—these without doubt enter through the gates into the church, to be sure, through the gates of righteousness which the psalmist says are opened to him.[47] "However, he who climbs in by another way, that man is a thief and a robber."[48] EXPLA-

NATION OF THE APOCALYPSE 22.14.[49]

## 22:15 Those Who Are Outside

**THOSE OUTSIDE THE CHURCH.** APRINGIUS OF BEJA: Those who are outside the congregation of the saints will be manifestly thrown out of the ark of blessedness. He moreover declares by whose authority these things have been shown or said to saint John when he continues, "I, Jesus . . ." TRACTATE ON THE APOCALYPSE 22.15.[50]

**VIRTUE IS ACCORDING TO NATURE.** OECUMENIUS: "Outside are the dogs," it says. It is customary in the holy Scriptures to call homosexuals "dogs" because they are shameless and impure. In Deuteronomy the law of the holy teacher Moses says, "You shall not bring the hire of a harlot or the wages of a dog into the house of the Lord your God in payment for any vow,"[51] since indeed such persons are similar to dogs because of their shamelessness. Even a wise man outside [the church] gives witness to the same view, saying, "Flee every murder and adulterous couch of a woman, and also the oaths of the rich and shameless beds of boys."[52] Therefore, such dogs are outside the holy city and apart from the life with the righteous. For what do they have in common with the righteous of God? "And everyone who loves and practices falsehood" will be outside, it says. Everything against nature is false. Virtue is according to nature, since from the beginning the Creator has implanted in our makeup the seed of virtue, and so vice is against nature. For just as health is natural to our bodies and sickness is unnatural, and just as seeing and hearing are natural while blindness and deafness are unnatural, so also virtue in our souls is natural and evil is unnatural. Health is, then, analogous to virtue, and vice analogous to sickness. In a correspond-

---

[39]Ps 59:9 (58:10 LXX).   [40]Ps 118:19-20 (117:19-20 LXX).   [41]Jn 10:9.   [42]Jn 14:6.   [43]CCL 92:308-9.   [44]MTS 1 Sup 1:259.   [45]Mt 5:8.   [46]Jn 10:9.   [47]Ps 118:19 (117:19 LXX).   [48]Jn 10:1.   [49]CCL 121A:571-73.   [50]CCL 107:96.   [51]Deut 23:18.   [52]Oecumenius quotes an anonymous source.

ing way, falsehood is evil, for it often falsely presents itself as virtue. Temerity masquerades as courage, dishonorable conduct as prudence, sloth as wisdom, and false modesty as righteousness. All of these things are evils, cloaking themselves with a mask of virtue, to those who fall in with them, and therefore he casts outside the divine walls those who pursue such lying deceit. COMMENTARY ON THE APOCALYPSE 22.15-19.[53]

**THOSE WHO SIN AFTER BAPTISM.** ANDREW OF CAESAREA: The dogs are not only the shameless and the unfaithful and those evildoers in the circumcision, for whom the apostle wept,[54] but also those who, after their baptism, "returned to their own vomit."[55] Therefore, with the fornicators and

the murderers and the idolaters, they are foreigners to the heavenly city. COMMENTARY ON THE APOCALYPSE 22.15.[56]

**ALL KINDS OF MADNESS.** BEDE: Every kind of madness that characterizes the impious now tempts the church from without. But when the Father of the household enters in and the saints enter in with him to the wedding banquet, he shall close the door, and then [the impious] will stand outside and begin to knock upon the door.[57] EXPLANATION OF THE APOCALYPSE 22.15.[58]

---

[53]TEG 8:285-86. [54]See Phil 3:2. [55]2 Pet 2:22. [56]MTS 1 Sup 1:259-60. [57]See Lk 13:25. [58]CCL 121A:573.

---

## 22:16-21 "COME, LORD JESUS!"

[16]"I Jesus have sent my angel to you with this testimony for the churches. I am the root and the offspring of David, the bright morning star."
[17]The Spirit and the Bride say, "Come." And let him who hears say, "Come." And let him who is thirsty come, let him who desires take the water of life without price.
[18]I warn every one who hears the words of the prophecy of this book: if any one adds to them, God will add to him the plagues described in this book, [19]and if any one takes away from the words of the book of this prophecy, God will take away his share in the tree of life and in the holy city, which are described in this book.
[20]He who testifies to these things says, "Surely I am coming soon." Amen. Come, Lord Jesus!
[21]The grace of the Lord Jesus be with all the saints.[t] Amen.

t Other ancient authorities omit all; others omit the saints

---

**OVERVIEW:** Jesus gives witness to himself as the Lord who sent the angel of testimony so that churches everywhere might hear what the Revelation says (OECUMENIUS, ANDREW OF CAESAREA). Jesus refers to his majesty as the one who is true God and true man (OECUMENIUS, BEDE), and he

calls himself the "bright morning star." Although he was the star of truth who guided the magi (APRINGIUS), yet the chief priests did not see in Christ the "sun of righteousness" (OECUMENIUS). Nonetheless, it was he who after the night of suffering rose from the dead and revealed to the world the light of life (PRIMASIUS, BEDE). In like fashion, after the night of this present life he will reveal the unending day at the resurrection of all (ANDREW OF CAESAREA). In the light of his resurrection the Spirit and the church summon all to salvation (APRINGIUS) and pray to the Father for the second coming of the Son (OECUMENIUS, ANDREW OF CAESAREA).

Every grace of God is without cost and freely given, whether the gift be the rebirth of baptism, the healing of repentance (APRINGIUS) or the acquisition of virtue (OECUMENIUS). Indeed, even the desire and the will to receive grace are themselves gifts of grace. God wills to give his grace to all and so desires to move the idle and to restrain the reckless (PRIMASIUS). Therefore, his words are more trustworthy than any human words no matter how exalted (ANDREW OF CAESAREA), and God will not tolerate any falsification of them (APRINGIUS, BEDE). Since the coming of Christ is much desired (ANDREW OF CAESAREA), we ought to pray with the church, "Your kingdom come!" (PRIMASIUS). In the meantime, let us pray that the Lord Jesus will free us from the prison of this world (CAESARIUS OF ARLES) so that at his coming he finds nothing in us worthy of punishment (APRINGIUS). Rather, mindful of the singular gift of God's grace that is intended for all (BEDE), let us also pray, "Make us, O Christ, to be partakers of this grace through your goodness alone" (OECUMENIUS).

## 22:16 An Angel Sent for Testimony to the Churches

**SO THAT NO ONE WILL BE IGNORANT.** OECUMENIUS: "To testify" means to bear witness, not in private or in secret but so that the churches everywhere will hear and no one, feigning ignorance, will with evil intent do evil. COMMENTARY ON THE APOCALYPSE 22.15-19.[1]

**THE LORD SENT THE ANGEL.** ANDREW OF CAESAREA: Also here the lordship and dignity of him who sent the angel is demonstrated. COMMEN-

TARY ON THE APOCALYPSE 22.16.[2]

## 22:16a The Root of David

**ROOT AND OFFSPRING OF DAVID.** OECUMENIUS: We might think that it would have been more consistent had he said, "I am the branch that has sprung from the root of David." However, on the contrary, he has here called himself the root of David, and not only "root" but also the "offspring." He is "root" and cause of all things, including David, insofar as he is and is known to be God, while he is "offspring" of David and has sprung from him according to the flesh, insofar as he is and is known to be man. And so he is—as the holy apostle somewhere says of his own words, "it is not irksome to me to say the same things" often, and for those who read them it is safe[3]—and so he is the Immanuel, of divinity and of humanity, possessing both [natures] perfectly, according to the traditional language, unconfusedly, unchangeably, immutably, really.[4] We are convinced that after the inexpressible union there is one person, one hypostasis and one energy, "even if the difference of the natures, from which we state the ineffable union has been made is not perceived," nor the characteristic of each according to their natural quality, as our holy father, Cyril, says.[5] COMMENTARY ON THE APOCALYPSE 22.15-19.[6]

**THE CREATOR OF DAVID IS ALSO DESCENDED FROM DAVID.** BEDE: In this passage he is referring to the two natures of his person, for he who is the creator of David according to his divinity is

---

[1]TEG 8:286. [2]MTS 1 Sup 1:260. [3]Phil 3:1. [4]Oecumenius is referring to the Definition of Faith of the Council of Chalcedon (A.D. 451). Chalcedon confessed that the two natures of Christ were united "uncon-fusedly" (ἀσυγχύτως), "immutably" (ἀτρέπτως), "indivisibly" (ἀδιαιρέτως),"inseparably" (ἀχωρίστως). Oecumenius mentions the first two adverbs, but then uses the adverbs "unchangeably" (ἀναλλοιώτως) and "really" (ἀφαντασιάστως), that is, not merely in appearance only. [5]Cyril of Alexandria Letter 39.6 (FC 76:151). [6]TEG 8:286-87. Andrew of Caesarea follows Oecumenius who is interpreting "root" to refer to Christ's deity, "offspring" to his humanity.

he "who was descended from David according to the flesh."[7] In the Gospel the Lord put this question to the Jews, how it was that the Christ could be the son of David, when David, inspired by the Spirit, calls him his Lord.[8] EXPLANATION OF THE APOCALYPSE 22.16.[9]

### 22:16b *The Bright Morning Star*

THE STAR OF TRUTH. APRINGIUS OF BEJA: This is that star of truth by which the magi themselves were led to his salutary presence. For our exposition can bring forward nothing more clearly than do the very words of this book. TRACTATE ON THE APOCALYPSE 22.16.[10]

CHRIST IS THE SUN. OECUMENIUS: By *morning star* he means either the sun, since he is called the "sun of righteousness" in Malachi,[11] and further the prophet sings, "fire has fallen upon them," that is, upon the chief priests of the Jews, "and they did not see the sun," that is, him who is the "sun of righteousness," namely, Christ.[12] Or he means the morning star. For he is also called this by Peter in his second letter: "until the day dawns and the morning star rises in your hearts."[13] COMMENTARY ON THE APOCALYPSE 22.15-19.[14]

THE MORNING STAR. PRIMASIUS: Brightly reflecting the grace of the New Testament, he refers to the time of the first resurrection when Christ rose from the dead. For this reason we read, "From the morning watch until night, from the morning watch let Israel hope in the Lord."[15] COMMENTARY ON THE APOCALYPSE 22.16.[16]

CHRIST WILL SHINE. ANDREW OF CAESAREA: He is the "morning star," since he rose for us early in the morning after the three days. Moreover, after the night of the present life he will manifest himself to the saints in the early morning of the common resurrection and bring to pass the unending day. COMMENTARY ON THE APOCALYPSE 22.16.[17]

CHRIST REVEALED THE LIGHT OF RESURRECTION. BEDE: [The morning star] is he who after the night of his suffering appeared living and so revealed to the world the light of resurrection and life by both words and example. Of him Job speaks to the blessed One, "Have you ever brought forth the morning star at its own time?"[18] EXPLANATION OF THE APOCALYPSE 22.16.[19]

### 22:17a *The Spirit and the Bride Say, "Come"*

ALL ARE CALLED TO SALVATION. APRINGIUS OF BEJA: The Holy Spirit and the church call all to come to salvation. . . . And whoever keeps the words of this prophecy and hears him whom the Lord himself has commanded [to speak], he is worthy to be taught. TRACTATE ON THE APOCALYPSE 22.17.[20]

WE ARE TO PRAY FOR THE SECOND COMING. OECUMENIUS: "And the Spirit," that is, the prophetic Spirit, "and the bride," the church that is universal and in every place, say, "Come!" We are instructed to seek the second coming of the Lord, and indeed to pray for it. For to be sure, whoever prays "thy kingdom come" to God seeks the kingdom of Christ, which is also the kingdom of the Father and of the Spirit. "And let him who hears say, 'Come,'" it says. Everyone who hears these words, even you, John, ought to pray for the kingdom of the coming of Christ. He says this to exhort everyone to the works and practices of righteousness. For no one who is not fully aware of righteousness in himself would pray for the coming of Christ, at which he will demand an accounting of the life of all. COMMENTARY ON THE APOCALYPSE 22.15-19.[21]

THE CHURCH PRAYS FOR THE COMING OF THE SON. ANDREW OF CAESAREA: The church and

---

[7]Rom 1:3. [8]Mt 22:42-43. [9]CCL 121A:573. [10]CCL 107:96. [11]Mal 4:2. [12]See Ps 58:8 (57:9 LXX). [13]2 Pet 1:19. [14]TEG 8:287. [15]See Ps 130:6-7 (129:6 LXX). [16]CCL 92:309. [17]MTS 1 Sup 1:260-61. [18]See Job 38:32. [19]CCL 121A:573. [20]CCL 107:96. [21]TEG 8:287-88.

the Spirit in her crying out in our hearts "Abba, Father" call for the coming of the only begotten Son of God. Indeed, every faithful person who hears prays to God the Father as he has been taught, "Your kingdom come!" COMMENTARY ON THE APOCALYPSE 22.17.[22]

**WE ARE CALLED TO FAITH AND LOVE.** BEDE: The Head and body of the Church exhort each member to faith. . . . Whoever has received and possesses in their mind the interior light of faith and love, calls also others to share in this. EXPLANATION OF THE APOCALYPSE 22.17.[23]

## 22:17b *Who Is Thirsty*

**BAPTISM AND ABSOLUTION ARE FREELY GIVEN.** APRINGIUS OF BEJA: Salvation is given without any price and without any barter. Rather, he who desires to be saved, he will enter and will either receive free of charge the regeneration of baptism, or he will receive the remedy of repentance without cost or charge. The prophet spoke in a similar manner: "All who thirst, come to the waters; and you who have no money, hasten, come, buy and eat."[24] TRACTATE ON THE APOCALYPSE 22.17.[25]

**WE SHOULD DRINK IN THE PRACTICE OF VIRTUE.** OECUMENIUS: Since the time of my coming will come, says the Lord, place your mouth on the fountain of life, that is, on the practice of virtue. Already before the Lord came, Isaiah had said the same thing when he urged, "All who have no money, go and buy, and drink without money and without price."[26] . . . The acquisition of virtue through struggles and labors is received as a free gift, since "the sufferings of this present time are not worth comparing with the glory that is to be revealed to us," as the all-wise Paul says.[27] COMMENTARY ON THE APOCALYPSE 22.15-19.[28]

**EVEN THE WILL TO DRINK IS A GIFT OF GRACE.** PRIMASIUS: How is it that he who

wishes may take [of the tree of life] when he had said, "No one can come to me unless the Father who sent me draws him,"[29] unless because we know that one who was previously unwilling becomes willing through divine inspiration? So also here free will is fittingly included when he says, "Let him who desires take," since immediately grace is proclaimed when he says, "the water of life without price." To be sure, [this means] let him take the water of life without price, even though no good [works] have gone before. As the apostle says, "What have you that you did not receive?"[30] Therefore, we receive by grace from God even the will to come, and to this we have brought nothing beforehand so that we might be [willing]. How much more, therefore, [do we bring nothing] so that from being sinners we might be made righteous. COMMENTARY ON THE APOCALYPSE 22.17.[31]

## 22:18-19 *No Changes to This Book*

**JOHN FORBIDS HERETICAL FALSIFICATION OF HIS WORDS.** APRINGIUS OF BEJA: It is not that he denies that the words that he had spoken were not to be explained. Rather, around that very time in which the saint had his vision, the error of various teachers and heretics began to emerge and to take their rise. Therefore, in order that no one promoting error might through the usual deceit of their error intend either to add or to subtract from his words and in that way seek to confirm their views by the witness of this most holy man, he determined to conclude his book with this warning. And that no one might think that what he said was merely a human opinion, he now mentions [the Lord Jesus Christ] who is the author of these things. TRACTATE ON THE APOCALYPSE 22.18-19.[32]

---

[22]MTS 1 Sup 1:261. [23]CCL 121A:573-75. Primasius (CCL 92:309) and Caesarius of Arles (PL 35:2452) also believe that "the Spirit and the bride" refers to Christ and the church. [24]Is 55:1. [25]CCL 107:96-97. [26]See Is 55:1. [27]Rom 8:18. [28]TEG 8:288. [29]Jn 6:44; cf. Jn 14:6. [30]1 Cor 4:7. [31]CCL 92:309-10. [32]CCL 107:97.

**God Desires to Move the Idle and Restrain the Reckless.** Primasius: Solomon said, "Do not add to his words, lest you be rebuked and be found a liar."[33] In this passage he also adds the terror of the plagues so that he might urge and warn not only by the weight of his authority but also that he might either move the idle with threats or restrain the reckless. Commentary on the Apocalypse 22.19.[34]

**The Scriptures Are Trustworthy.** Andrew of Caesarea: The curse against those who falsify the divine Scriptures is terrible, since the daring insolence of such self-willed persons can deprive them of the blessings of the coming age. In order that we might not suffer that lot, he testifies to us who listen neither to add nor to subtract anything. Rather, we should regard the characteristics of the Scriptures as more trustworthy and venerable than Attic compositions and dialectical arguments. For even among those should anyone find anything that is contrary to the rules, he is referred to the trustworthiness of their poets and authors. How great the difference is between those who have a great reputation among them and those who are of repute among us is impossible to conceive. I would judge that it is greater than the difference between light and darkness. Commentary on the Apocalypse 22.18-19.[35]

**No One May Falsify Scripture.** Bede: He said this because of those who would falsify [the Scriptures], not because of those who speak their opinions in a simple manner, yet in no way wrongly change the prophecy. Explanation of the Apocalypse 22.18.[36]

## 22:20 "I Am Coming Soon"

**May We Keep Ourselves Pure.** Apringius of Beja: "He who testifies to these things says," that is, the very same Lord Jesus Christ who commanded me to write these things, "Surely, I am coming soon." He makes known the certainty and the quickness of his coming. And already certain of his own blessedness, this saint fervently declares, "Come, Lord Jesus!" May the almighty Jesus Christ grant to us that as we earnestly await his coming we might, with his protection, keep ourselves from every grave sin, and that when our desire is fulfilled, he find nothing in us worthy of punishment. But should there be anything to pardon, may he nevertheless have mercy upon the accused and not condemn the sinner. May he with whom the blessed One lives and reigns forever grant this. Amen. Tractate on the Apocalypse 22.20.[37]

**John Declares That He Will Soon Die.** Oecumenius: [John] says here what Paul also said, "For I am already on the point of being sacrificed, and the time of my departure has come."[38] I am he who teaches these things, he says, and I who am finally at the end of this life bears witness to them so that no one will forsake the word through doubt. . . . I write these things all but speaking to Christ who is calling me to a change of place, "I am coming soon!" Commentary on the Apocalypse 22.20.[39]

**The Church Devoutly Responds to Christ.** Primasius: The selfsame Christ who gave his testimony announces to the church that he is coming. And to him the church devoutly responds in the manner of the Song of Songs, "Amen, Come, Lord Jesus Christ."[40] And when the church prays, it says, "Your kingdom come!"[41] and "in the way that is blameless, when you will come to me."[42] Commentary on the Apocalypse 22.20.[43]

**May Christ Free Us.** Caesarius of Arles: Let us pray that the Lord Jesus Christ deign to come to us according to his promise and through

---

[33]Prov 30:6. [34]CCL 92:310-11. [35]MTS 1 Sup 1:262. [36]CCL 121A:575. [37]CCL 107:97. [38]2 Tim 4:6. [39]TEG 8:288-89. [40]See Song 2:8, 10, 13; 4:8; 7:11. [41]Mt 6:10. [42]Ps 101:2 (100:2 LXX). [43]CCL 92:311.

his mercy free us from the prison of this world and for the sake of his compassion lead us to his blessedness. With the Father and the Holy Spirit he lives and reigns into all eternity. Amen. EXPOSITION ON THE APOCALYPSE 22.20, HOMILY 19.[44]

**DESIRED BY THE SAINTS.** ANDREW OF CAESAREA: Also I who am speaking these things say to you, who are Life, "I am coming." And you yourself also come, O Lord. Or perhaps he is saying this in the person of Christ, "I who witness to these things," clearly the one who is testifying, "I am coming." Then what follows is said in the person of the apostle, "Come, Lord Jesus Christ." For the coming of Christ is much desired by the saints, since he will recompense those who have labored with a manifold reward. Therefore, this present book is holy and inspired by God and leads those who read it to their blessed end and inheritance. COMMENTARY ON THE APOCALYPSE 22.20-21.[45]

## 22:21 *The Grace of the Lord Jesus Christ*

**THE WORLDLY HAVE NO ENTRY.** OECUMENIUS: The worldly have already been banished from the life of the saints and from any entry into the spiritual Jerusalem. For how would the grace of Christ, our God, come upon those who had been declared excluded? Make us, O Christ, to be partakers of this grace through your goodness alone. For it is proper to give you glory now and always and forever. Amen. COMMENTARY ON THE APOCALYPSE 22.21.[46]

**THE GRACE OF GOD IS FOR ALL.** BEDE: Let the Pelagians be confident in their own power and deprive themselves of the grace of the Lord. However, when the apostle Paul was seeking for help, he said, "Who will deliver me from this body of death?"[47] Mindful of his own condition, let John respond and say, "The grace of God through Jesus Christ, our Lord." And lest the Donatists deceive themselves concerning the singular gift of God, let them hear that when John commends the grace of God, as if it were a final farewell, he adds, "and with you all, Amen."[48] EXPLANATION OF THE APOCALYPSE 22.21.[49]

---

[44]PL 35:2452. [45]MTS 1 Sup 1:262-63. [46]TEG 8:289. [47]Rom 7:24. [48]The Pelagians believed that grace was primarily the gift of free will; our holiness, therefore, lay in the correct use of the free will, not by virtue of the remedial, creative grace of God. The Donatists believed that they alone were the holy church; the church in its universality was then called into question. [49]CCL 121A:577.

# Early Christian Writers and the Documents Cited

The following table lists all the early Christian documents cited in this volume by author, if known, or by the title of the work. The English title used in this commentary is followed in parentheses with the Latin designation and, where available, the Thesaurus Linguae Graecae (=TLG) digital references or Cetedoc Clavis numbers. Printed sources of original language version may be found in the bibliography of work in original languages.

**Andrew of Caesarea**
Commentary on the Apocalypse (*Commentarii in Apocalypsin*)

**Aphrahat**
Demonstrations (*Demonstrationes*)

**Apringius of Beja**
Tractates on the Apocalypse (*Tractatus in Apocalypsin*)

**Athanasius**

| | |
|---|---|
| Discourses Against the Arians (*Orationes tres contra Arianos*) | TLG 2035.042 |
| On Luke (*In illud: Omnia mihi tradita sunt*) | TLG 2035.039 |

**Augustine**

| | |
|---|---|
| Admonition and Grace (*De corruptione et gratia*) | Cetedoc 0353 |
| City of God (*De civitate Dei*) | Cetedoc 0313 |
| Enchiridion (*Enchiridion de fide, spe et caritate*) | Cetedoc 0295 |
| Explanations of the Psalms (*Enarrationes in Psalmos*) | Cetedoc 0283 |
| Holy Virginity (*De sancta virginitate*) | Cetedoc 0300 |
| Of True Religion (*De vera religione*) | Cetedoc 0264 |
| Sermons (*Sermones*) | Cetedoc 0284 |
| Tractates on the Gospel of John (*In Johannis evangelium tractatus*) | Cetedoc 0278 |

**Bede**

| | |
|---|---|
| Explanation of the Apocalypse (*Explanatio Apocalypsis*) | Cetedoc 1363 |
| Homilies on the Gospels (*Homiliarum evangelii libri ii*) | Cetedoc 1367 |
| On the Tabernacle (*De tabernaculo et vasis eius ac vestibus sacerdotum libri iii*) | Cetedoc 1345 |

**Caesarius of Arles**

| | |
|---|---|
| Exposition on the Apocalypse (*Expositio in Apocalypsin*) | Cetedoc 1016 |

Sermons *(Sermones)*                                                                        Cetedoc 1008

**Cassiodorus**
Exposition of the Psalms *(Expositio psalmorum)*                                            Cetedoc 0900

**Clement of Alexandria**
Christ the Educator *(Paedagogus)*                                                         TLG 0555.002
Stromateis *(Stromata)*                                                                     TLG 0555.004

**Clement of Rome**
1 Clement *(Epistula i ad Corinthios)*                                                      TLG 1271.001

**Cyprian**
Exhortation to Martyrdom *(Ad Fortunatum [De exhortatione martyrii])*                       Cetedoc 0045
Letters *(Epistulae)*                                                                       Cetedoc 0050
The Dress of Virgins *(De habitu virginum)*                                                 Cetedoc 0040
The Good of Patience *(De bono patientiae)*                                                 Cetedoc 0048
The Lapsed *(De lapsis)*                                                                     Cetedoc 0042
The Unity of the Church *(De ecclesiae catholicae unitate)*                                 Cetedoc 0041
Works and Almsgiving *(De opere et eleemosynis)*                                            Cetedoc 0047

**Epiphanius of Salamis**
Panarion *(Panarion [Adversus haereses])*                                                   TLG 2021.002

**Eusebius of Caesarea**
Ecclesiastical History *(Historia ecclesiastica)*                                           TLG 2018.002

**Fulgentius of Ruspe**
Letters *(Epistulae)*                                                                       Cetedoc 0817
On the Forgiveness of Sins *(Ad Euthymium de remissione peccatorum libri II)*              Cetedoc 0821

**Gregory Thaumaturgus**
Oration and Panegyric Addressed to Origen *(In Originem oratio panegyrica)*                 TLG 2063.001

**Gregory the Great**
Dialogues *(Dialogorum libri iv libri duo)*                                                 Cetedoc 1713

**Hippolytus**
Commentary on Daniel *(Commentarium in Danielem)*                                           TLG 2115.030
On the Antichrist *(De antichristo)*                                                        TLG 2115.003

**Irenaeus**
Against Heresies *(Adversus haereses)*                                                      Cetedoc 1154
Proof of the Apostolic Preaching *(Demonstratio apostolicae praedicationis)*

## Jerome

| | |
|---|---|
| Against Jovinianus (*Adversus Jovinianum*) | Cetedoc 0610 |
| Dialogue Against the Luciferians (*Altercatio Luciferiani et Orthodoxi*) | Cetedoc 0608 |
| Homilies on the Psalms (*Tractatus lix in psalmos*) | Cetedoc 0592 |
| Homilies on Mark (*Tractatus in Marci evangelium*) | Cetedoc 0594 |
| Letters (*Epistulae*) | Cetedoc 0620 |

## Lactantius

| | |
|---|---|
| Epitome of the Divine Institutes (*Epitome divinarum institutionum*) | Cetedoc 0086 |

## Maximus of Turin

| | |
|---|---|
| Sermons (*Collectio sermonum antiqua*) | Cetedoc 0219a |

## Methodius

| | |
|---|---|
| Symposium or Banquet of the Ten Virgins (*Symposium sive Convivium decem virginum*) | TLG 2959.001 |

## Nicetas of Remesiana

Liturgical Singing (*De utilitate hymnorum*)

## Oecumenius

| | |
|---|---|
| Commentary on the Apocalpyse (*Commentarius in Apocalypsin*) | TLG 2866.001 |

## Origen

| | |
|---|---|
| Against Celsus (*Contra Celsum*) | TLG 2042.001 |
| Commentary on the Gospel of John (*Commentarii in evangelium Joannis [lib. 1, 2, 4, 5, 6, 10, 13]*) | TLG 2042.005 |
| Homilies on Jeremiah (*In Jeremiam [homiliae 1-11]*) | TLG 2042.009 |
| Homilies on Joshua (*In Jesu nave homiliae xxvi*) | TLG 2042.025 |
| Homilies on the Gospel of Luke (*Homiliae in Lucam*) | TLG 2042.016 |
| On First Principles (*De principiis*) | TLG 2042.002 |

## Primasius

| | |
|---|---|
| Commentary on the Apocalypse (*Commentarius in Apocalypsin*) | Cetedoc 0873 |

## Pseudo-Hippolytus

| | |
|---|---|
| On the End of the World, the Antichrist, and the Second Coming (*De consummatione mundi*) | TLG 2115.029 |

## Quodvultdeus

| | |
|---|---|
| On the Symbol (*De symbolo III*) | Cetedoc 0403 |

## Rufinus of Aquileia

| | |
|---|---|
| Commentary on the Apostles' Creed (*Expositio symboli*) | Cetedoc 0196 |

**Salvian the Presbyter**

The Governance of God (*De gubernatione Dei*)      Cetedoc 0485

**Tertullian**

Against Hermogenes (*Adversus Hermogenem*)      Cetedoc 0013

On Flight in Time of Persecution (*De fuga in persecutione*)      Cetedoc 0025

On Monogamy (*De monogamia*)      Cetedoc 0028

On Patience (*De patientia*)      Cetedoc 0009

On Penitence (*De paenitentia*)      Cetedoc 0010

On Prayer (*De oratione*)      Cetedoc 0007

On the Resurrection of the Flesh (*De resurrectione mortuorum*)      Cetedoc 0019

On the Soul (*De anima*)      Cetedoc 0017

Scorpiace (*Scorpiace*)      Cetedoc 0022

**Tyconius**

Commentary on the Apocalypse (*Tyconii Afri in Apocalypsin*)

**Victorinus of Petovium**

Commentary on the Apocalypse (*Scholia in Apocalypsin beati Joannis*)

# Biographical Sketches & Short Descriptions of Select Anonymous Works

This listing is cumulative, including all the authors and works cited in this series to date.

**Acacius of Beroea** (c. 340-c. 436). Syrian monk known for his ascetic life. He became bishop of Beroea in 378, participated in the council of Constantinople in 381, and played an important role in mediating between Cyril of Alexandria and John of Antioch; however, he did not take part in the clash between Cyril and Nestorius.

**Acacius of Caesarea** (d. c. 365). Pro-Arian bishop of Caesarea in Palestine, disciple and biographer of Eusebius of Caesarea, the historian. He was a man of great learning and authored a treatise on Ecclesiastes.

**Adamnan** (c. 624-704). Abbot of Iona, Ireland, and author of the life of St. Columba. He was influential in the process of assimilating the Celtic church into Roman liturgy and church order. He also wrote *On the Holy Sites*, which influenced Bede.

**Alexander of Alexandria** (fl. 312-328). Bishop of Alexandria and predecessor of Athanasius, on whom he exerted considerable theological influence during the rise of Arianism. Alexander excommunicated Arius, whom he had appointed to the parish of Baucalis, in 319. His teaching regarding the eternal generation and divine substantial union of the Son with the Father was eventually confirmed at the Council of Nicaea (325).

**Ambrose of Milan** (c. 333-397; fl. 374-397). Bishop of Milan and teacher of Augustine who defended the divinity of the Holy Spirit and the perpetual virginity of Mary.

**Ambrosiaster** (fl. c. 366-384). Name given by Erasmus to the author of a work once thought to have been composed by Ambrose.

**Ammonius** (c. fifth century). An Aristotelian commentator and teacher in Alexandria, where he was born and of whose school he became head. Also an exegete of Plato, he enjoyed fame among his contemporaries and successors, although modern critics accuse him of pedantry and banality.

**Amphilochius of Iconium** (b. c. 340-345, d.c. 398-404). An orator at Constantinople before becoming bishop of Iconium in 373. He was a cousin of Gregory of Nazianzus and active in debates against the Macedonians and Messalians.

**Andreas** (c. seventh century). Monk who collected commentary from earlier writers to form a catena on various biblical books.

**Andrew of Caesarea** (early sixth century). Bishop of Caesarea in Cappadocia. He produced one of the earliest Greek commentaries on Revelation and defended the divine inspiration of its author.

**Antony (or Anthony) the Great** (c. 251-c. 356).

An anchorite of the Egyptian desert and founder of Egyptian monasticism. Athanasius regarded him as the ideal of monastic life, and he has become a model for Christian hagiography.

**Aphrahat** (c. 270-350; fl. 337-345). "The Persian Sage" and first major Syriac writer whose work survives. He is also known by his Greek name Aphraates.

**Apollinaris of Laodicea** (310-c. 392). Bishop of Laodicea who was attacked by Gregory of Nazianzus, Gregory of Nyssa and Theodore for denying that Christ had a human mind.

**Aponius/Apponius** (fourth–fifth century). Author of a remarkable commentary on Song of Solomon (c. 405-415), an important work in the history of exegesis. The work, which was influenced by the commentaries of Origen and Pseudo-Hippolytus, is of theological significance, especially in the area of Christology.

*Apostolic Constitutions* (c. 381-394). Also known as *Constitutions of the Holy Apostles* and thought to be redacted by Julian of Neapolis. The work is divided into eight books, and is primarily a collection of and expansion on previous works such as the *Didache* (c. 140) and the *Apostolic Traditions.* Book 8 ends with eighty-five canons from various sources and is elsewhere known as the *Apostolic Canons.*

**Apringius of Beja** (middle sixth century). Iberian bishop and exegete. Heavily influenced by Tyconius, he wrote a commentary on Revelation in Latin, of which two large fragments survive.

**Arethas of Caesarea** (c. 860-940) Byzantine scholar and disciple of Photius. He was a deacon in Constantinople, then archbishop of Caesarea from 901.

**Arius** (fl. c. 320). Heretic condemned at the Council of Nicaea (325) for refusing to accept that the Son was not a creature but was God by nature like the Father.

**Arnobius the Younger** (fifth century). A participant in christological controversies of the fifth century. He composed *Conflictus cum Serapione,* an account of a debate with a monophysite monk in which he attempts to demonstrate harmony between Roman and Alexandrian theology. Some scholars attribute to him a few more works, such as *Commentaries on Psalms.*

**Athanasius of Alexandria** (c. 295-373; fl. 325-373). Bishop of Alexandria from 328, though often in exile. He wrote his classic polemics against the Arians while most of the eastern bishops were against him.

**Athenagoras** (fl. 176-180). Early Christian philosopher and apologist from Athens, whose only authenticated writing, *A Plea Regarding Christians,* is addressed to the emperors Marcus Aurelius and Commodius, and defends Christians from the common accusations of atheism, incest and cannibalism.

**Augustine of Hippo** (354-430). Bishop of Hippo and a voluminous writer on philosophical, exegetical, theological and ecclesiological topics. He formulated the Western doctrines of predestination and original sin in his writings against the Pelagians.

**Babai** (c. early sixth century). Author of the Letter to Cyriacus. He should not be confused with either Babai of Nisibis (d. 484), or Babai the Great (d. 628).

**Babai the Great** (d. 628). Syriac monk who founded a monastery and school in his region of Beth Zabday and later served as third superior at the Great Convent of Mount Izla during a period of crisis in the Nestorian church.

**Basil of Seleucia** (fl. 444-468). Bishop of Seleucia in Isauria and ecclesiastical writer. He took part in the Synod of Constantinople in 448 for the condemnation of the Eutychian errors and the deposition of their great champion, Dioscurus of Alexandria.

**Basil the Great** (b. c. 330; fl. 357-379). One of the Cappadocian fathers, bishop of Caesarea and champion of the teaching on the Trinity propounded at Nicaea in 325. He was a great administrator and founded a monastic rule.

**Basilides** (fl. second century). Alexandrian heretic of the early second century who is said to have believed that souls migrate from body to body and that we do not sin if we lie to protect the body from martyrdom.

**Bede the Venerable** (c. 672/673-735). Born in Northumbria, at the age of seven, he was put under the care of the Benedictine monks of Saints Peter and Paul at Jarrow and given a broad classical education in the monastic tradition. Considered one of the most learned men of his age, he is the author of *An Ecclesiastical History of the English People.*

**Benedict of Nursia** (c. 480-547). Considered the most important figure in the history of Western monasticism. Benedict founded many monasteries, the most notable found at Montecassino, but his lasting influence lay in his famous Rule. The Rule outlines the theological and inspirational foundation of the monastic ideal while also legislating the shape and organization of the cenobitic life.

**Besa the Copt** (5th century). Coptic monk, disciple of Shenoute, whom he succeeded as head of the monastery. He wrote numerous letters, monastic catecheses and a biography of Shenoute.

***Book of Steps*** (c. 400). Written by an anonymous Syriac author, this work consists of thirty homilies or discourses which specifically deal with the more advanced stages of growth in the spiritual life.

**Braulio of Saragossa** (c. 585-651). Bishop of Saragossa (631-651) and noted writer of the Visigothic renaissance. His *Life* of St. Aemilianus is his crowning literary achievement.

**Caesarius of Arles** (c. 470-543). Bishop of Arles renowned for his attention to his pastoral duties. Among his surviving works the most important is a collection of some 238 sermons that display an ability to preach Christian doctrine to a variety of audiences.

**Callistus of Rome** (d. 222). Pope (217-222) who excommunicated Sabellius for heresy. It is very probable that he suffered martyrdom.

**Cassia** (b. c. 805, d. between 848 and 867). Nun, poet and hymnographer who founded a convent in Constantinople.

**Cassian, John** (360-432). Author of the *Institutes* and the *Conferences,* works purporting to relay the teachings of the Egyptian monastic fathers on the nature of the spiritual life which were highly in-

fluential in the development of Western monasticism.

**Cassiodorus** (c. 485-c. 580). Founder of the monastery of Vivarium, Calabria, where monks transcribed classic sacred and profane texts, Greek and Latin, preserving them for the Western tradition.

**Chromatius** (fl. 400). Bishop of Aquileia, friend of Rufinus and Jerome and author of tracts and sermons.

**Clement of Alexandria** (c. 150-215). A highly educated Christian convert from paganism, head of the catechetical school in Alexandria and pioneer of Christian scholarship. His major works, *Protrepticus, Paedagogus* and the *Stromata,* bring Christian doctrine face to face with the ideas and achievements of his time.

**Clement of Rome** (fl. c. 92-101). Pope whose *Epistle to the Corinthians* is one of the most important documents of subapostolic times.

**Commodian** (probably third or possibly fifth century). Latin poet of unknown origin (possibly Syrian?) whose two surviving works suggest chiliast and patripassionist tendencies.

***Constitutions of the Holy Apostles.*** *See Apostolic Constitutions.*

**Cyprian of Carthage** (fl. 248-258). Martyred bishop of Carthage who maintained that those baptized by schismatics and heretics had no share in the blessings of the church.

**Cyril of Alexandria** (375-444; fl. 412-444). Patriarch of Alexandria whose extensive exegesis, characterized especially by a strong espousal of the unity of Christ, led to the condemnation of Nestorius in 431.

**Cyril of Jerusalem** (c. 315-386; fl. c. 348). Bishop of Jerusalem after 350 and author of *Catechetical Homilies.*

**Cyril of Scythopolis** (b. c. 525; d. after 557). Palestinian monk and author of biographies of famous Palestinian monks. Because of him we have precise knowledge of monastic life in the fifth and sixth centuries and a description of the Origenist crisis and its suppression in the mid-sixth century.

**Diadochus of Photice** (c. 400-474). Antimonophysite bishop of Epirus Vetus whose work *Discourse on the Ascension of Our Lord Jesus Christ* exerted influence in both the East and West through its Chalcedonian Christology. He is also the subject of the mystical *Vision of St. Diadochus Bishop of Photice in Epirus*.

**Didache** (c. 140). Of unknown authorship, this text intertwines Jewish ethics with Christian liturgical practice to form a whole discourse on the "way of life." It exerted an enormous amount of influence in the patristic period and was especially used in the training of catechumen.

**Didymus the Blind** (c. 313-398). Alexandrian exegete who was much influenced by Origen and admired by Jerome.

**Diodore of Tarsus** (d. c. 394). Bishop of Tarsus and Antiochene theologian. He authored a great scope of exegetical, doctrinal and apologetic works, which come to us mostly in fragments because of his condemnation as the predecessor of Nestorianism. Diodore was a teacher of John Chrysostom and Theodore of Mopsuestia.

**Dionysius of Alexandria** (d. c. 264). Bishop of Alexandria and student of Origen. Dionysius actively engaged in the theological disputes of his day, opposed Sabellianism, defended himself against accusations of tritheism and wrote the earliest extant Christian refutation of Epicureanism. His writings have survived mainly in extracts preserved by other early Christian authors.

**Dorotheus of Gaza** (fl. c. 525-540). Member of Abbot Seridos's monastery and later leader of a monastery where he wrote *Spiritual Instructions*. He also wrote a work on traditions of Palestinian monasticism.

**Ennodius** (474-521). Bishop of Pavia, a prolific writer of various genre, including letters, poems and biographies. He sought reconciliation in the schism between Rome and Acacius of Constantinople, and also upheld papal autonomy in the face of challenges from secular authorities.

**Ephrem the Syrian** (b. c. 306; fl. 363-373). Syrian writer of commentaries and devotional hymns which are sometimes regarded as the greatest specimens of Christian poetry prior to Dante.

**Epiphanius of Salamis** (c. 315-403). Bishop of Salamis in Cyprus, author of a refutation of eighty heresies (the *Panarion*) and instrumental in the condemnation of Origen.

**Epiphanius the Latin.** Author of the late fifth-century or early sixth century Latin text *Interpretation of the Gospels*, with constant references to early patristic commentators. He was possibly a bishop of Benevento or Seville.

**Epistle of Barnabas.** *See Letter of Barnabas.*

**Eucherius of Lyons** (fl. 420-449). Bishop of Lyons c. 435-449. Born into an aristocratic family, he, along with his wife and sons, joined the monastery at Lérins soon after its founding. He explained difficult Scripture passages by means of a threefold reading of the text: literal, moral and spiritual.

**Eugippius** (b. 460). Disciple of Severinus and third abbot of the monastic community at Castrum Lucullanum, which was made up of those fleeing from Noricum during the barbarian invasions.

**Eunomius** (d. 393). Bishop of Cyzicyus who was attacked by Basil and Gregory of Nyssa for maintaining that the Father and the Son were of different natures, one ingenerate, one generate.

**Eusebius of Caesarea** (c. 260/263-340). Bishop of Caesarea, partisan of the Emperor Constantine and first historian of the Christian church. He argued that the truth of the gospel had been foreshadowed in pagan writings but had to defend his own doctrine against suspicion of Arian sympathies.

**Eusebius of Emesa** (c. 300-c. 359). Bishop of Emesa from c. 339. A biblical exegete and writer on doctrinal subjects, he displays some semi-Arian tendencies of his mentor Eusebius of Caesarea.

**Eusebius of Gaul, or Eusebius Gallicanus** (c. fifth century). A conventional name for a collection of seventy-six sermons produced in Gaul and revised in the seventh century. It contains material from different patristic authors and focuses on ethical teaching in the context of the liturgical cycle (days of saints and other feasts).

**Eusebius of Vercelli** (fl. c. 360). Bishop of Vercelli who supported the trinitarian teaching of Nicaea (325) when it was being undermined by compromise in the West.

**Eustathius of Antioch** (fl. 325). First bishop of Beroea, then of Antioch, one of the leaders of the anti-Arians at the council of Nicaea. Later, he was banished from his seat and exiled to Thrace for his support of Nicene theology.

**Euthymius** (377-473). A native of Melitene and influential monk. He was educated by Bishop Otreius of Melitene, who ordained him priest and placed him in charge of all the monasteries in his diocese. When the Council of Chalcedon (451) condemned the errors of Eutyches, it was greatly due to the authority of Euthymius that most of the Eastern recluses accepted its decrees. The empress Eudoxia returned to Chalcedonian orthodoxy through his efforts.

**Evagrius of Pontus** (c. 345-399). Disciple and teacher of ascetic life who astutely absorbed and creatively transmitted the spirituality of Egyptian and Palestinian monasticism of the late fourth century. Although Origenist elements of his writings were formally condemned by the Fifth Ecumenical Council (Constantinople II, A.D. 553), his literary corpus continued to influence the tradition of the church.

**Eznik of Kolb** (early fifth century). A disciple of Mesrob who translated Greek Scriptures into Armenian, so as to become the model of the classical Armenian language. As bishop, he participated in the synod of Astisat (449).

**Facundus of Hermiane** (fl. 546-568). African bishop who opposed Emperor Justinian's *post mortem* condemnation of Theodore of Mopsuestia, Theodoret of Cyr and Ibas of Ebessa at the fifth ecumenical council. His written defense, known as "To Justinian" or "In Defense of the Three Chapters," avers that ancient theologians should not be blamed for errors that became obvious only upon later theological reflection. He continued in the tradition of Chalcedon, although his Christology was supplemented, according to Justinian's decisions, by the theopaschite formula *Unus ex Trinitate passus est*

("Only one of the three suffered").

**Fastidius** (c. fourth-fifth centuries). British author of *On the Christian Life*. He is believed to have written some works attributed to Pelagius.

**Faustinus** (fl. 380). A priest in Rome and supporter of Lucifer and author of a treatise on the Trinity.

**Faustus of Riez** (c. 400-490). A prestigious British monk at Lérins; abbot, then bishop of Riez from 457 to his death. His works include *On the Holy Spirit*, in which he argued against the Macedonians for the divinity of the Holy Spirit, and *On Grace*, in which he argued for a position on salvation that lay between more categorical views of free-will and predestination. Various letters and (pseudonymous) sermons are extant.

**The Festal Menaion.** Orthodox liturgical text containing the variable parts of the service, including hymns, for fixed days of celebration of the life of Jesus and Mary.

**Filastrius** (fl. 380). Bishop of Brescia and author of a compilation against all heresies.

**Firmicus Maternus** (fourth century). An anti-Pagan apologist. Before his conversion to Christianity he wrote a work on astrology (334-337). After his conversion, however, he criticized paganism in *On the Errors of the Profane Religion*.

**Fructuosus of Braga** (d. c. 665). Son of a Gothic general and member of a noble military family. He became a monk at an early age, then abbot-bishop of Dumium before 650 and metropolitan of Braga in 656. He was influential in setting up monastic communities in Lusitania, Asturia, Galicia and the island of Gades.

**Fulgentius of Ruspe** (c. 467-532). Bishop of Ruspe and author of many orthodox sermons and tracts under the influence of Augustine.

**Gaudentius of Brescia** (fl. 395). Successor of Filastrius as bishop of Brescia and author of twenty-one Eucharistic sermons.

**Gennadius of Constantinople** (d. 471). Patriarch of Constantinople, author of numerous commentaries and an opponent of the Christology of Cyril of Alexandria.

**Gerontius** (c. 395-c.480). Palestinian monk, later

archimandrite of the cenobites of Palestine. He led the resistance to the council of Chalcedon.

**Gnostics.** Name now given generally to followers of Basilides, Marcion, Valentinus, Mani and others. The characteristic belief is that matter is a prison made for the spirit by an evil or ignorant creator, and that redemption depends on fate, not on free will.

**Gregory of Elvira** (fl. 359-385). Bishop of Elvira who wrote allegorical treatises in the style of Origen and defended the Nicene faith against the Arians.

**Gregory of Nazianzus** (b. 329/330; fl. 372-389). Cappadocian father, bishop of Constantinople, friend of Basil the Great and Gregory of Nyssa, and author of theological orations, sermons and poetry.

**Gregory of Nyssa** (c. 335-394). Bishop of Nyssa and brother of Basil the Great. A Cappadocian father and author of catechetical orations, he was a philosophical theologian of great originality.

**Gregory Thaumaturgus** (fl. c. 248-264). Bishop of Neocaesarea and a disciple of Origen. There are at least five legendary *Lives* that recount the events and miracles which led to his being called "the wonder worker." His most important work was the *Address of Thanks to Origen*, which is a rhetorically structured panegyric to Origen and an outline of his teaching.

**Gregory the Great** (c. 540-604). Pope from 590, the fourth and last of the Latin "Doctors of the Church." He was a prolific author and a powerful unifying force within the Latin Church, initiating the liturgical reform that brought about the Gregorian Sacramentary and Gregorian chant.

**Hesychius of Jerusalem** (fl. 412-450). Presbyter and exegete, thought to have commented on the whole of Scripture.

**Hilary of Arles** (c. 401-449). Archbishop of Arles and leader of the Semi-Pelagian party. Hilary incurred the wrath of Pope Leo I when he removed a bishop from his see and appointed a new bishop. Leo demoted Arles from a metropolitan see to a bishopric to assert papal power over the church in Gaul.

**Hilary of Poitiers** (c. 315-367). Bishop of Poitiers and called the "Athanasius of the West" because of his defense (against the Arians) of the common nature of Father and Son.

**Hippolytus** (fl. 222-245). Recent scholarship places Hippolytus in a Palestinian context, personally familiar with Origen. Though he is known chiefly for *The Refutation of All Heresies*, he was primarily a commentator on Scripture (especially the Old Testament) employing typological exegesis.

**Horsiesi** (c. 305-c. 390). Pachomius's second successor, after Petronius, as a leader of cenobitic monasticism in Southern Egypt.

**Ignatius of Antioch** (c. 35-107/112). Bishop of Antioch who wrote several letters to local churches while being taken from Antioch to Rome to be martyred. In the letters, which warn against heresy, he stresses orthodox Christology, the centrality of the Eucharist and unique role of the bishop in preserving the unity of the church.

**Irenaeus of Lyons** (c. 135-c. 202). Bishop of Lyons who published the most famous and influential refutation of Gnostic thought.

**Isaac of Nineveh** (d. c. 700). Also known as Isaac the Syrian or Isaac Syrus, this monastic writer served for a short while as bishop of Nineveh before retiring to live a secluded monastic life. His writings on ascetic subjects survive in the form of numerous homilies.

**Isho'dad of Merv** (fl. c. 850). Nestorian bishop of Hedatta. He wrote commentaries on parts of the Old Testament and all of the New Testament, frequently quoting Syriac fathers.

**Isidore of Seville** (c. 560-636). Youngest of a family of monks and clerics, including sister Florentina and brothers Leander and Fulgentius. He was an erudite author of comprehensive scale in matters both religious and sacred, including his encyclopedic *Etymologies*.

**Jacob of Nisibis** (d. 338). Bishop of Nisibis. He was present at the council of Nicaea in 325 and took an active part in the opposition to Arius.

**Jacob of Sarug** (c. 450-c. 520). Syriac ecclesiastical writer. Jacob received his education at Edessa. At the end of his life he was ordained bishop of

Sarug. His principal writing was a long series of metrical homilies, earning him the title "The Flute of the Holy Spirit."

**Jerome** (c. 347-420). Gifted exegete and exponent of a classical Latin style, now best known as the translator of the Latin Vulgate. He defended the perpetual virginity of Mary, attacked Origen and Pelagius and supported extreme ascetic practices.

**John Chrysostom** (344/354-407; fl. 386-407). Bishop of Constantinople who was noted for his orthodoxy, his eloquence and his attacks on Christian laxity in high places.

**John of Antioch** (d. 441/42). Bishop of Antioch, commencing in 428. He received his education together with Nestorius and Theodore of Mopsuestia in a monastery near Antioch. A supporter of Nestorius, he condemned Cyril of Alexandria, but later reached a compromise with him.

**John of Apamea** (fifth century). Syriac author of the early church who wrote on various aspects of the spiritual life, also known as John the Solitary. Some of his writings are in the form of dialogues. Other writings include letters, a treatise on baptism, and shorter works on prayer and silence.

**John of Damascus** (c. 650-750). Arab monastic and theologian whose writings enjoyed great influence in both the Eastern and Western Churches. His most influential writing was the *Orthodox Faith*.

**John the Elder** (c. eighth century). A Syriac author who belonged to monastic circles of the Church of the East and lived in the region of Mount Qardu (northern Iraq). His most important writings are twenty-two homilies and a collection of fifty-one short letters in which he describes the mystical life as an anticipatory experience of the resurrection life, the fruit of the sacraments of baptism and the Eucharist.

**John the Monk.** Traditional name found in *The Festal Menaion*, believed to refer to John of Damascus. *See* John of Damascus.

**Josephus, Flavius** (c. 37-c. 101). Jewish historian from a distinguished priestly family. Acquainted with the Essenes and Sadducees, he himself became a Pharisee. He joined the great Jewish re-volt that broke out in 66 and was chosen by the Sanhedrin at Jerusalem to be commander-in-chief in Galilee. Showing great shrewdness to ingratiate himself with Vespasian by foretelling his elevation and that of his son Titus to the imperial dignity, Josephus was restored his liberty after 69 when Vespasian became emperor.

**Julian of Eclanum** (c. 385-450). Bishop of Eclanum in 416/417 who was removed from office and exiled in 419 for not officially opposing Pelagianism. In exile, he was accepted by Theodore of Mopsuestia, whose Antiochene exegetical style he followed. Although he was never able to regain his ecclesiastical position, Julian taught in Sicily until his death. His works include commentaries on Job and parts of the Minor Prophets, a translation of Theodore of Mopsuestia's commentary on the Psalms, and various letters. Sympathetic to Pelagius, Julian applied his intellectual acumen and rhetorical training to argue against Augustine on matters such as free will, desire and the locus of evil.

**Justin Martyr** (c. 100/110-165; fl. c. 148-161). Palestinian philosopher who was converted to Christianity, "the only sure and worthy philosophy." He traveled to Rome where he wrote several apologies against both pagans and Jews, combining Greek philosophy and Christian theology; he was eventually martyred.

**Lactantius** (c. 260-c. 330). Christian apologist removed from his post as teacher of rhetoric at Nicomedia upon his conversion to Christianity. He was tutor to the son of Constantine and author of *The Divine Institutes*.

**Leander** (c. 545-c. 600). Latin ecclesiastical writer, of whose works only two survive. He was instrumental in spreading Christianity among the Visigoths, gaining significant historical influence in Spain in his time.

**Leo the Great** (regn. 440-461). Bishop of Rome whose *Tome to Flavian* helped to strike a balance between Nestorian and Cyrilline positions at the Council of Chalcedon in 451.

***Letter of Barnabas*** (c. 130). An allegorical and typological interpretation of the Old Testament with a decidedly anti-Jewish tone. It was included with other New Testament works as a "Catholic epistle" at least until Eusebius of Caesarea (c. 260/263-340) questioned its authenticity.

**Letter to Diognetus** (c. third century). A refutation of paganism and an exposition of the Christian life and faith. The author of this letter is unknown, and the exact identity of its recipient, Diognetus, continues to elude patristic scholars.

**Lucifer** (d. 370/371). Bishop of Cagliari and vigorous supporter of Athanasius and the Nicene Creed. In conflict with the emperor Constantius, he was banished to Palestine and later to Thebaid (Egypt).

**Luculentius** (fifth century). Unknown author of a group of short commentaries on the New Testament, especially Pauline passages. His exegesis is mainly literal and relies mostly on earlier authors such as Jerome and Augustine. The content of his writing may place it in the fifth century.

**Macarius of Egypt** (c. 300-c. 390). One of the Desert Fathers. Accused of supporting Athanasius, Macarius was exiled c. 374 to an island in the Nile by Lucius, the Arian successor of Athanasius. Macarius continued his teaching of monastic theology at Wadi Natrun.

**Macrina the Younger** (c. 327-379). The elder sister of Basil the Great and Gregory of Nyssa, she is known as "the Younger" to distinguish her from her paternal grandmother. She had a powerful influence on her younger brothers, especially on Gregory, who called her his teacher and relates her teaching in *On the Soul and the Resurrection*.

**Manichaeans**. A religious movement that originated circa 241 in Persia under the leadership of Mani but was apparently of complex Christian origin. It is said to have denied free will and the universal sovereignty of God, teaching that kingdoms of light and darkness are coeternal and that the redeemed are particles of a spiritual man of light held captive in the darkness of matter (*see* Gnostics).

**Marcellus of Ancyra** (d. c. 375). Wrote a refutation of Arianism. Later, he was accused of Sabellianism, especially by Eusebius of Caesarea. While the Western church declared him orthodox, the

Eastern church excommunicated him. Some scholars have attributed to him certain works of Athanasius.

**Marcion** (fl. 144). Heretic of the mid-second century who rejected the Old Testament and much of the New Testament, claiming that the Father of Jesus Christ was other than the Old Testament God (*see* Gnostics).

**Marius Victorinus** (b. c. 280/285; fl. c. 355-363). Grammarian of African origin who taught rhetoric at Rome and translated works of Platonists. After his conversion (c. 355), he wrote against the Arians and commentaries on Paul's letters.

**Mark the Hermit** (c. sixth century). Monk who lived near Tarsus and produced works on ascetic practices as well as christological issues.

**Martin of Braga** (fl. c. 568-579). Anti-Arian metropolitan of Braga on the Iberian peninsula. He was highly educated and presided over the provincial council of Braga in 572.

**Martyrius.** *See* Sahdona.

**Maximus of Turin** (d. 408/423). Bishop of Turin. Over one hundred of his sermons survive on Christian festivals, saints and martyrs.

**Maximus the Confessor** (c. 580-662). Palestinian-born theologian and ascetic writer. Fleeing the Arab invasion of Jerusalem in 614, he took refuge in Constantinople and later Africa. He died near the Black Sea after imprisonment and severe suffering, having his tongue cut off and his right hand mutilated. He taught total preference for God and detachment from all things.

**Methodius of Olympus** (d. 311). Bishop of Olympus who celebrated virginity in a *Symposium* partly modeled on Plato's dialogue of that name.

**Minucius Felix** (second or third century). Christian apologist who was an advocate in Rome. His *Octavius* agrees at numerous points with the *Apologeticum* of Tertullian. His birthplace is believed to be in Africa.

**Montanist Oracles.** Montanism was an apocalyptic and strictly ascetic movement begun in the latter half of the second century by a certain Montanus in Phrygia, who, along with certain of his followers, uttered oracles they claimed were inspired by the Holy Spirit. Little of the authentic oracles remains and most of what is known of Montanism comes from the authors who wrote against the movement. Montanism was formally condemned as a heresy before by Asiatic synods.

**Nemesius of Emesa** (fl. late fourth century). Bishop of Emesa in Syria whose most important work, *Of the Nature of Man,* draws on several theological and philosophical sources and is the first exposition of a Christian anthropology.

**Nestorius** (c. 381-c. 451). Patriarch of Constantinople (428-431) who founded the heresy which says that there are two persons, divine and human, rather than one person truly united in the incarnate Christ. He resisted the teaching of *theotokos,* causing Nestorian churches to separate from Constantinople.

**Nicetas of Remesiana** (fl. second half of fourth century). Bishop of Remesiana in Serbia, whose works affirm the consubstantiality of the Son and the deity of the Holy Spirit.

**Nilus of Ancyra** (d. c. 430). Prolific ascetic writer and disciple of John Chrysostom. Sometimes erroneously known as Nilus of Sinai, he was a native of Ancyra and studied at Constantinople.

**Novatian of Rome** (fl. 235-258). Roman theologian, otherwise orthodox, who formed a schismatic church after failing to become pope. His treatise on the Trinity states the classic western doctrine.

**Oecumenius** (sixth century). Called the Rhetor or the Philosopher, Oecumenius wrote the earliest extant Greek commentary on Revelation. Scholia by Oecumenius on some of John Chrysostom's commentaries on the Pauline Epistles are still extant.

**Olympiodorus** (early sixth century). Exegete and deacon of Alexandria, known for his commentaries that come to us mostly in catenae.

**Origen of Alexandria** (b. 185; fl. c. 200-254). Influential exegete and systematic theologian. He was condemned (perhaps unfairly) for maintaining the preexistence of souls while purportedly

denying the resurrection of the body. His extensive works of exegesis focus on the spiritual meaning of the text.

**Pachomius** (c. 292-347). Founder of cenobitic monasticism. A gifted group leader and author of a set of rules, he was defended after his death by Athanasius of Alexandria.

**Pacian of Barcelona** (c. fourth century). Bishop of Barcelona whose writings polemicize against popular pagan festivals as well as Novatian schismatics.

**Palladius of Helenopolis** (c. 363/364-c. 431). Bishop of Helenopolis in Bithynia (400-417) and then Aspuna in Galatia. A disciple of Evagrius of Pontus and admirer of Origen, Palladius became a zealous adherent of John Chrysostom and shared his troubles in 403. His *Lausaic History* is the leading source for the history of early monasticism, stressing the spiritual value of the life of the desert.

**Paschasius of Dumium** (c. 515-c. 580). Translator of sentences of the Desert Fathers from Greek into Latin while a monk in Dumium.

**Paterius** (c. sixth-seventh century). Disciple of Gregory the Great who is primarily responsible for the transmission of Gregory's works to many later medieval authors.

**Paulinus of Milan** (late 4th-early 5th century). Personal secretary and biographer of Ambrose of Milan. He took part in the Pelagian controversy.

**Paulinus of Nola** (355-431). Roman senator and distinguished Latin poet whose frequent encounters with Ambrose of Milan (c. 333-397) led to his eventual conversion and baptism in 389. He eventually renounced his wealth and influential position and took up his pen to write poetry in service of Christ. He also wrote many letters to, among others, Augustine, Jerome and Rufinus.

**Paulus Orosius** (b. c. 380). An outspoken critic of Pelagius, mentored by Augustine. His *Seven Books of History Against the Pagans* was perhaps the first history of Christianity.

**Pelagius** (c. 354-c. 420). Contemporary of Augustine whose followers were condemned in 418 and 431 for maintaining that even before Christ there were people who lived wholly without sin and that salvation depended on free will.

**Peter Chrysologus** (c. 380-450). Latin archbishop of Ravenna whose teachings included arguments for adherence in matters of faith to the Roman see, and the relationship between grace and Christian living.

**Peter of Alexandria** (d. c. 311). Bishop of Alexandria. He marked (and very probably initiated) the reaction at Alexandria against extreme doctrines of Origen. During the persecution of Christians in Alexandria, Peter was arrested and beheaded by Roman officials. Eusebius of Caesarea described him as "a model bishop, remarkable for his virtuous life and his ardent study of the Scriptures."

**Philo of Alexandria** (c. 20 B.C.-c. A.D. 50). Jewish-born exegete who greatly influenced Christian patristic interpretation of the Old Testament. Born to a rich family in Alexandria, Philo was a contemporary of Jesus and lived an ascetic and contemplative life that makes some believe he was a rabbi. His interpretation of Scripture based the spiritual sense on the literal. Although influenced by Hellenism, Philo's theology remains thoroughly Jewish.

**Philoxenus of Mabbug** (c. 440-523). Bishop of Mabbug (Hierapolis) and a leading thinker in the early Syrian Orthodox Church. His extensive writings in Syriac include a set of thirteen *Discourses on the Christian Life*, several works on the incarnation and a number of exegetical works.

**Photius** (c. 820-891). An important Byzantine churchman and university professor of philosophy, mathematics and theology. He was twice the patriarch of Constantinople. First he succeeded Ignatius in 858, but was deposed in 863 when Ignatius was reinstated. Again he followed Ignatius in 878 and remained the patriarch until 886, at which time he was removed by Leo VI. His most important theological work is Address on the Mystagogy of the Holy Spirit, in which he articulates his opposition to the Western filioque, i.e., the procession of the Holy Spirit from the Father and the Son. He is also known for his Amphilochia and Library (Bibliotheca).

**Poemen** (c. fifth century). One-seventh of the sayings in the *Sayings of the Desert Fathers* are attributed to Poemen, which is Greek for shepherd. Poemen was a common title among early Egyptian desert ascetics, and it is unknown whether all of the sayings come from one person.

**Polycarp of Smyrna** (c. 69-155). Bishop of Smyrna who vigorously fought heretics such as the Marcionites and Valentinians. He was the leading Christian figure in Roman Asia in the middle of the second century.

**Potamius of Lisbon** (fl. c. 350-360). Bishop of Lisbon who joined the Arian party in 357, but later returned to the Catholic faith (c. 359?). His works from both periods are concerned with the larger Trinitarian debates of his time.

**Primasius** (fl. 550-560). Bishop of Hadrumetum in North Africa (modern Tunisia) and one of the few Africans to support the condemnation of the Three Chapters. Drawing on Augustine and Tyconius, he wrote a commentary on the Apocalypse, which in allegorizing fashion views the work as referring to the history of the church.

**Procopius of Gaza** (c. 465-c. 530). A Christian exegete educated in Alexandria. He wrote numerous theological works and commentaries on Scripture (particularly the Hebrew Bible), the latter marked by the allegorical exegesis for which the Alexandrian school was known.

**Prosper of Aquitaine** (c. 390-c. 463). Probably a lay monk and supporter of the theology of Augustine on grace and predestination. He collaborated closely with Pope Leo I in his doctrinal statements.

**Prudentius** (c. 348-c. 410). Latin poet and hymn-writer who devoted his later life to Christian writing. He wrote didactic poems on the theology of the incarnation, against the heretic Marcion and against the resurgence of paganism.

**Pseudo-Clementines** (third-fourth century). A series of apocryphal writings pertaining to a conjured life of Clement of Rome. Written in a form of popular legend, the stories from Clement's life, including his opposition to Simon Magus, illustrate and promote articles of Christian teaching. It is likely that the corpus is a derivative of a number of Gnostic and Judeo-Christian writings. Dating the corpus is a complicated issue.

**Pseudo-Dionysius the Areopagite** (fl. c. 500). Author who assumed the name of Dionysius the Areopagite mentioned in Acts 17:34, and who composed the works known as the *Corpus Areopagiticum* (or *Dionysiacum*). These writings were the foundation of the apophatic school of mysticism in their denial that anything can be truly predicated of God.

**Pseudo-Macarius** (fl. c. 390). An anonymous writer and ascetic (from Mesopotamia?) active in Antioch whose badly edited works were attributed to Macarius of Egypt. He had keen insight into human nature, prayer and the inner life. His work includes some one hundred discourses and homilies.

**Quodvultdeus** (fl. 430). Carthaginian bishop and friend of Augustine who endeavored to show at length how the New Testament fulfilled the Old Testament.

**Rufinus of Aquileia** (c. 345-411). Orthodox Christian thinker and historian who nonetheless translated and preserved the works of Origen, and defended him against the strictures of Jerome and Epiphanius. He lived the ascetic life in Rome, Egypt and Jerusalem (the Mount of Olives).

**Sabellius** (fl. 200). Allegedly the author of the heresy which maintains that the Father and Son are a single person. The patripassian variant of this heresy states that the Father suffered on the cross.

**Sahdona** (fl. 635-640). Known in Greek as Martyrius, this Syriac author was bishop of Beth Garmai. He studied in Nisibis and was exiled for his christological ideas. His most important work is the deeply scriptural *Book of Perfection* which ranks as one of the masterpieces of Syriac monastic literature.

**Salvian the Presbyter of Marseilles** (c. 400-c. 480). An important author for the history of his own time. He saw the fall of Roman civilization to the barbarians as a consequence of the reprehensible conduct of Roman Christians. In *The Governance of God* he developed the theme of divine providence.

*Second Letter of Clement* (c. 150). The so-called *Second Letter of Clement* is an early Christian sermon probably written by a Corinthian author, though some scholars have assigned it to a Roman or Alexandrian author.

**Severian of Gabala** (fl. c. 400). A contemporary of John Chrysostom, he was a highly regarded preacher in Constantinople, particularly at the imperial court, and ultimately sided with Chrysostom's accusers. He wrote homilies on Genesis.

**Severus of Antioch** (fl. 488-538). A monophysite theologian, consecrated bishop of Antioch in 522. Born in Pisidia, he studied in Alexandria and Beirut, taught in Constantinople and was exiled to Egypt.

**Shenoute** (c. 350-466). Abbot of Athribis in Egypt. His large monastic community was known for very strict rules. He accompanied Cyril of Alexandria to the Council of Ephesus in 431, where he played an important role in deposing Nestorius. He knew Greek but wrote in Coptic, and his literary activity includes homilies, catecheses on monastic subjects, letters, and a couple of theological treatises.

*Shepherd* of **Hermas** (second century). Divided into five *Visions*, twelve *Mandates* and ten *Similitudes*, this Christian apocalypse was written by a former slave and named for the form of the second angel said to have granted him his visions. This work was highly esteemed for its moral value and was used as a textbook for catechumens in the early church.

**Sulpicius Severus** (c. 360-c. 420). An ecclesiastical writer from Bordeaux born of noble parents. Devoting himself to monastic retirement, he became a personal friend and enthusiastic disciple of St. Martin of Tours.

**Symeon the New Theologian** (c. 949-1022). Compassionate spiritual leader known for his strict rule. He believed that the divine light could be perceived and received through the practice of mental prayer.

**Tertullian of Carthage** (c. 155/160-225/250; fl. c. 197-222). Brilliant Carthaginian apologist and polemicist who laid the foundations of Christology and trinitarian orthodoxy in the West, though he himself was later estranged from the catholic tradition due to its laxity.

**Theodore of Heraclea** (d. c. 355). An anti-Nicene bishop of Thrace. He was part of a team seeking reconciliation between Eastern and Western Christianity. In 343 he was excommunicated at the council of Sardica. His writings focus on a literal interpretation of Scripture.

**Theodore of Mopsuestia** (c. 350-428). Bishop of Mopsuestia, founder of the Antiochene, or literalistic, school of exegesis. A great man in his day, he was later condemned as a precursor of Nestorius.

**Theodore of Tabennesi** (d. 368) Vice general of the Pachomian monasteries (c. 350-368) under Horsiesi. Several of his letters are known.

**Theodoret of Cyr** (c. 393-466). Bishop of Cyr (Cyrrhus), he was an opponent of Cyril who commented extensively on Old Testament texts as a lucid exponent of Antiochene exegesis.

**Theodotus the Valentinian** (second century). Likely a Montanist who may have been related to the Alexandrian school. Extracts of his work are known through writings of Clement of Alexandria.

**Theophanes** (775-845). Hymnographer and bishop of Nicaea (842-845). He was persecuted during the second iconoclastic period for his support of the Seventh Council (Second Council of Nicaea, 787). He wrote many hymns in the tradition of the monastery of Mar Sabbas that were used in the *Paraklitiki*.

**Theophilus of Antioch** (late second century). Bishop of Antioch. His only surviving work is *Ad Autholycum*, where we find the first Christian commentary on Genesis and the first use of the term *Trinity*. Theophilus's apologetic literary heritage had influence on Irenaeus and possibly Tertullian.

**Theophylact of Ohrid** (c. 1050-c. 1108). Byzantine archbishop of Ohrid (or Achrida) in what is now Bulgaria. Drawing on earlier works, he wrote commentaries on several Old Testament books and all of the New Testament except for Revelation.

**Tyconius** (c. 330-390). A lay theologian and exegete of the Donatist church in North Africa who influenced Augustine. His *Book of Rules* is the first manual of scriptural interpretation in the Latin West. In 380 he was excommunicated by the Donatist council at Carthage.

**Valentinus** (fl. c. 140). Alexandrian heretic of the mid-second century who taught that the material world was created by the transgression of God's Wisdom, or Sophia (*see* Gnostics).

**Valerian of Cimiez** (fl. c. 422-439). Bishop of Cimiez. He participated in the councils of Riez (439) and Vaison (422) with a view to strengthening church discipline. He supported Hilary of Arles in quarrels with Pope Leo I.

**Verecundus** (d. 552). An African Christian writer, who took an active part in the christological controversies of the sixth century, especially in the debate on Three Chapters. He also wrote allegorical commentaries on the nine liturgical church canticles.

**Victorinus of Petovium** (d. c. 304). Latin biblical exegete. With multiple works attributed to him, his sole surviving work is the *Commentary on the Apocalypse* and perhaps some fragments from *Commentary on Matthew*. Victorinus expressed strong millenarianism in his writing, though his was less materialistic than the millenarianism of Papias or Irenaeus. In his allegorical approach he could be called a spiritual disciple of Origen. Victorinus died during the first year of Diocletian's persecution, probably in 304.

**Vincent of Lérins** (d. before 450). Monk who has exerted considerable influence through his writings on orthodox dogmatic theological method, as contrasted with the theological methodologies of the heresies.

# Timeline of Writers of the Patristic Period

| Location<br>Period | British Isles | Gaul | Spain, Portugal | Rome* and Italy | Carthage and Northern Africa |
|---|---|---|---|---|---|
| **2nd century** | | | | Clement of Rome, fl. c. 92-101 (Greek) | |
| | | | | Shepherd of Hermas, c. 140 (Greek) | |
| | | | | Justin Martyr (Ephesus, Rome), c. 100/110-165 (Greek) | |
| | | Irenaeus of Lyons, c. 135-c. 202 (Greek) | | Valentinus the Gnostic (Rome), fl. c. 140 (Greek) | |
| **3rd century** | | | | Marcion (Rome), fl. 144 (Greek) | |
| | | | | Callistus of Rome, regn. 217-222 (Latin) | Tertullian of Carthage, c. 155/160-c. 225 (Latin) |
| | | | | Minucius Felix of Rome, fl. 218-235 (Latin) | |
| | | | | Hippolytus (Rome, Palestine?), fl. 222-235/245 (Greek) | Cyprian of Carthage, fl. 248-258 (Latin) |
| | | | | Novatian of Rome, fl. 235-258 (Latin) | |
| | | | | Victorinus of Petovium, 230-304 (Latin) | |

*One of the five ancient patriarchates

| Alexandria* and Egypt | Constantinople* and Asia Minor, Greece | Antioch* and Syria | Mesopotamia, Persia | Jerusalem* and Palestine | Location Unknown |
|---|---|---|---|---|---|
| Philo of Alexandria, c. 20 B.C. – c. A.D. 50 (Greek) | | | | Flavius Josephus (Rome), c. 37-c. 101 (Greek) | |
| Basilides (Alexandria), 2nd cent. (Greek) | Polycarp of Smyrna, c. 69-155 (Greek) | *Didache* (Egypt?), c. 100 (Greek) | | | |
| *Letter of Barnabas* (Syria?), c. 130 (Greek) | | Ignatius of Antioch, c. 35– 107/112 (Greek) | | | |
| Theodotus the Valentinian, 2nd cent. (Greek) | Athenagoras (Greece), fl. 176-180 (Greek) | Theophilus of Antioch, c. late 2nd cent. (Greek) | | | *Second Letter of Clement* (spurious; Corinth, Rome, Alexandria?) (Greek), c. 150 |
| Clement of Alexandria, c. 150-215 (Greek) | *Montanist Oracles*, late 2nd cent. (Greek) | | | | |
| Sabellius (Egypt), 2nd–3rd cent. (Greek) | | | | | Pseudo-Clementines 3rd cent. (Greek) |
| | | | Mani (Manichaeans), c. 216-276 | | |
| *Letter to Diognetus*, 3rd cent. (Greek) | Gregory Thaumaturgus (Neocaesarea), fl. c. 248-264 (Greek) | | | | |
| Origen (Alexandria, Caesarea of Palestine), 185-254 (Greek) | | | | | |
| Dionysius of Alexandria, d. 264/5 (Greek) | | | | | |
| | Methodius of Olympus (Lycia), d. c. 311 (Greek) | | | | |

## Timeline of Writers of the Patristic Period

| Location / Period | British Isles | Gaul | Spain, Portugal | Rome* and Italy | Carthage and Northern Africa |
|---|---|---|---|---|---|
| **4th century** | | | | Firmicus Maternus (Sicily), fl. c. 335 (Latin) | |
| | | Lactantius, c. 260-330 (Latin) | | Marius Victorinus (Rome), fl. 355-363 (Latin) | |
| | | | | Eusebius of Vercelli, fl. c. 360 (Latin) | |
| | | | Hosius of Cordova, d. 357 (Latin) | Lucifer of Cagliari (Sardinia), d. 370/371 (Latin) | |
| | | Hilary of Poitiers, c. 315-367 (Latin) | Potamius of Lisbon, fl. c. 350-360 (Latin) | Faustinus (Rome), fl. 380 (Latin) | |
| | | | | Filastrius of Brescia, fl. 380 (Latin) | |
| | | | Gregory of Elvira, fl. 359-385 (Latin) | Ambrosiaster (Italy?), fl. c. 366-384 (Latin) | |
| | | | Prudentius, c. 348-c. 410 (Latin) | Faustus of Riez, fl. c. 380 (Latin) | |
| | | | Pacian of Barcelona, 4th cent. (Latin) | Gaudentius of Brescia, fl. 395 (Latin) | Paulus Orosius, b. c. 380 (Latin) |
| | | | | Ambrose of Milan, c. 333-397; fl. 374-397 (Latin) | |
| | | | | Paulinus of Milan, late 4th early 5th cent. (Latin) | |
| | | | | Rufinus (Aquileia, Rome), c. 345-411 (Latin) | |
| **5th century** | Fastidius (Britain), c. 4th-5th cent. (Latin) | Sulpicius Severus (Bordeaux), c. 360-c. 420/425 (Latin) | | Aponius, fl. 405-415 (Latin) | Quodvultdeus (Carthage), fl. 430 (Latin) |
| | | | | Chromatius (Aquileia), fl. 400 (Latin) | |
| | | John Cassian (Palestine, Egypt, Constantinople, Rome, Marseilles), 360-432 (Latin) | | Pelagius (Britain, Rome), c. 354-c. 420 (Greek) | Augustine of Hippo, 354-430 (Latin) |
| | | | | Maximus of Turin, d. 408/423 (Latin) | Luculentius, 5th cent. (Latin) |
| | | Vincent of Lérins, d. 435 (Latin) | | Paulinus of Nola, 355-431 (Latin) | |
| | | Valerian of Cimiez, fl. c. 422-449 (Latin) | | Peter Chrysologus (Ravenna), c. 380-450 (Latin) | |
| | | Eucherius of Lyons, fl. 420-449 (Latin) | | Julian of Eclanum, 386-454 (Latin) | |

*One of the five ancient patriarchates

| Alexandria* and Egypt | Constantinople* and Asia Minor, Greece | Antioch* and Syria | Mesopotamia, Persia | Jerusalem* and Palestine | Location Unknown |
|---|---|---|---|---|---|
| Antony, c. 251-355 (Coptic /Greek) | Theodore of Heraclea (Thrace), fl. c. 330-355 (Greek) | Eustathius of Antioch, fl. 325 (Greek) | Aphrahat (Persia) c. 270-350; fl. 337-345 (Syriac) | Eusebius of Caesarea (Palestine), c. 260/263-340 (Greek) | Commodius, c. 3rd or 5th cent. (Latin) |
| Peter of Alexandria, d. c. 311 (Greek) | Marcellus of Ancyra, d.c. 375 (Greek) | Eusebius of Emesa, c. 300-c. 359 (Greek) | Jacob of Nisibis, fl. 308-325 (Syriac) | | |
| Arius (Alexandria), fl. c. 320 (Greek) | Epiphanius of Salamis (Cyprus), c. 315-403 (Greek) | Ephrem the Syrian, c. 306-373 (Syriac) | | | |
| Alexander of Alexandria, fl. 312-328 (Greek) | Basil (the Great) of Caesarea, b. c. 330; fl. 357-379 (Greek) | | | | |
| Pachomius, c. 292-347 (Coptic/Greek?) | Macrina the Younger, c. 327-379 (Greek) | | | | |
| Theodore of Tabennesi, d. 368 (Coptic/Greek) | Apollinaris of Laodicea, 310-c. 392 (Greek) | | | | |
| Horsiesi, c. 305-390 (Coptic/Greek) | Gregory of Nazianzus, b. 329/330; fl. 372-389 (Greek) | Nemesius of Emesa (Syria), fl. late 4th cent. (Greek) | | Acacius of Caesarea (Palestine), d. c. 365 (Greek) | |
| Athanasius of Alexandria, c. 295-373; fl. 325-373 (Greek) | Gregory of Nyssa, c. 335-394 (Greek) | Diodore of Tarsus, d. c. 394 (Greek) | | Cyril of Jerusalem, c. 315-386 (Greek) | |
| Macarius of Egypt, c. 300-c. 390 (Greek) | Amphilochius of Iconium, c. 340/345- c. 398/404 (Greek) | John Chrysostom (Constantinople), 344/354-407 (Greek) | | | |
| Didymus (the Blind) of Alexandria, 313-398 (Greek) | Evagrius of Pontus, 345-399 (Greek) | Apostolic Constitutions, c. 375-400 (Greek) | | | |
| Tyconius, c. 330-390 (Latin) | Eunomius of Cyzicus, fl. 360-394 (Greek) | Didascalia, 4th cent. (Syriac) | | | |
| | | Theodore of Mopsuestia, c. 350-428 (Greek) | | Diodore of Tarsus, d. c. 394 (Greek) | |
| | Pseudo-Macarius (Mesopotamia?), late 4th cent. (Greek) | Acacius of Beroea, c. 340-c. 436 (Greek) | | Jerome (Rome, Antioch, Bethlehem), c. 347-420 (Latin) | |
| | Nicetas of Remesiana, d. c. 414 (Latin) | | | | |
| Palladius of Helenopolis (Egypt), c. 365-425 (Greek) | Nestorius (Constantinople), c. 381-c. 451 (Greek) | Book of Steps, c. 400 (Syriac) | Eznik of Kolb, fl. 430-450 (Armenian) | Jerome (Rome, Antioch, Bethlehem), c. 347-419 (Latin) | |
| | | Severian of Gabala, fl. c. 400 (Greek) | | | |
| Cyril of Alexandria, 375-444 (Greek) | Basil of Seleucia, fl. 440-468 (Greek) | Nilus of Ancyra, d.c. 430 (Greek) | | Hesychius of Jerusalem, fl. 412-450 (Greek) | |
| | Diadochus of Photice (Macedonia), 400-474 (Greek) | | | | |
| | | | | Euthymius (Palestine), 377-473 (Greek) | |

## Timeline of Writers of the Patristic Period

| Location / Period | British Isles | Gaul | Spain, Portugal | Rome* and Italy | Carthage and Northern Africa |
|---|---|---|---|---|---|
| 5th century (cont.) | | Hilary of Arles, c. 401-449 (Latin) | | | |
| | | Eusebius of Gaul, 5th cent. (Latin) | | Leo the Great (Rome), regn. 440-461 (Latin) | |
| | | Prosper of Aquitaine, c. 390-c. 463 (Latin) | | Arnobius the Younger (Rome), fl. c. 450 (Latin) | |
| | | Salvian the Presbyter of Marseilles, c. 400-c. 480 (Latin) | | Ennodius (Arles, Milan, Pavia) c. 473-521 (Latin) | |
| | | Gennadius of Marseilles, d. after 496 (Latin) | | | |
| 6th century | | Caesarius of Arles, c. 470-543 (Latin) | Paschasius of Dumium (Portugal), c. 515-c. 580 (Latin) | Epiphanius the Latin, late 5th–early 6th cent. (Latin) | Fulgentius of Ruspe, c. 467-532 (Latin) |
| | | | Apringius of Beja, mid-6th cent. (Latin) | | Verecundus, d. 552 (Latin) |
| | | | Leander of Seville, c. 545-c. 600 (Latin) | Eugippius, c. 460- c. 533 (Latin) | |
| | | | | Benedict of Nursia, c. 480-547 (Latin) | Primasius, fl. 550-560 (Latin) |
| | | | Martin of Braga, fl. 568-579 (Latin) | | Facundus of Hermiane, fl. 546-568 (Latin) |
| | | | | Cassiodorus (Calabria), c. 485-c. 540 (Latin) | |
| 7th century | | | | Gregory the Great (Rome), c. 540-604 (Latin) | |
| | | | | Gregory of Agrigentium, d. 592 (Greek) | |
| | | | Isidore of Seville, c. 560-636 (Latin) | Paterius, 6th/7th cent. (Latin) | |
| | | | Braulio of Saragossa, c. 585-651 (Latin) | | |
| | Adamnan, c. 624-704 (Latin) | | Fructuosus of Braga, d.c. 665 (Latin) | | |
| 8th-12th century | Bede the Venerable, c. 672/673-735 (Latin) | | | | |

*One of the five ancient patriarchates

| Alexandria* and Egypt | Constantinople* and Asia Minor, Greece | Antioch* and Syria | Mesopotamia, Persia | Jerusalem* and Palestine | Location Unknown |
|---|---|---|---|---|---|
| Ammonius of Alexandria, c. 460 (Greek) | Gennadius of Constantinople, d. 471 (Greek) | John of Antioch, d. 441/2 (Greek) | | Gerontius of Petra c. 395-c.480 (Syriac) | |
| Poemen, 5th cent. (Greek) | | Theodoret of Cyr, c. 393-466 (Greek) | | | |
| Besa the Copt, 5th cent. | | Pseudo-Victor of Antioch, 5th cent. (Greek) | | | |
| Shenoute, c. 350-466 (Coptic) | | John of Apamea, 5th cent. (Syriac) | | | |
| | Andrew of Caesarea (Cappadocia), early-6th cent. (Greek) | | | | |
| Olympiodorus, early 6th cent. | Oecumenius (Isauria), 6th cent. (Greek) | Philoxenus of Mabbug (Syria), c. 440-523 (Syriac) | Jacob of Sarug, c. 450-520 (Syriac) | Procopius of Gaza (Palestine), c. 465-530 (Greek) | Pseudo-Dionysius the Areopagite, fl. c. 500 (Greek) |
| | | Severus of Antioch, c. 465-538 (Greek) | Babai the Great, c. 550-628 (Syriac) | Dorotheus of Gaza, fl. 525-540 (Greek) | |
| | | Mark the Hermit (Tarsus), c. 6th cent. (4th cent.?) (Greek) | Babai, early 6th cent. (Syriac) | Cyril of Scythopolis, b. c. 525; d. after 557 (Greek) | |
| | Maximus the Confessor (Constantinople), c. 580-662 (Greek) | Sahdona/Martyrius, fl. 635-640 (Syriac) | Isaac of Nineveh, d. c. 700 (Syriac) | | (Pseudo-) Constantius, before 7th cent.? (Greek) |
| | | | | | Andreas, c. 7th cent. (Greek) |
| | | John of Damascus (John the Monk), c. 650-750 (Greek) | | | |
| | Theophanes (Nicaea), 775-845 (Greek) | | John the Elder of Qardu (north Iraq), 8th cent. (Syriac) | | |
| | Cassia (Constantinople), c. 805-c. 848/867 (Greek) | | Isho'dad of Merv, d. after 852 (Syriac) | | |
| | Arethas of Caesarea (Constantinople/Caesarea), c. 860-940 (Greek) | | | | |
| | Photius (Constantinople), c. 820-891 (Greek) | | | | |
| | Symeon the New Theologian (Constantinople), 949-1022 (Greek) | | | | |
| | Theophylact of Ohrid (Bulgaria), 1050-1126 (Greek) | | | | |

This bibliography refers readers to original language sources and supplies Thesaurus Linguae Graecae (=TLG) or Cetedoc Clavis (=Cl.) numbers where available. The edition listed in this bibliography may in some cases differ from the edition found in TLG or Cetedoc databases.

Andrew of Caesarea. *Commentary on the Apocalypse.* In Josef Schmid, *Studien zur Geschichte des griechischen Apokalypse-Testes, part 1.* MTS 1 Sup 1. Munich, Germany: K. Zink, 1955-56.

Aphrahat. "Demonstrationes (IV)" In *Opera omnia.* Edited by R. Graffin. Patrologia Syriaca 1, cols. 137-82. Paris: Firmin-Didor, 1910.

[Apringius of Beja]. *Apringii Pacensis episcopi Tractatus in Apocalypsin.* Edited by A. C. Vega. SEHL 10, 11. Madrid: Typis Augustianis Monasterii Escurialensis, 1940.

———. "Apringi Pacensis episcopi Tractatus in Apocalypsin Fragmenta quae supersunt." In *Commentaria minora in Apocalypsin Johannis,* pp. 11-97. Edited by Roger Gryson. CCL 107. Turnhout: Brepols, 2003.

Athanasius. "In Illud: Omnia mihi tradita sunt." In *Opera omnia.* PG 25, cols. 208-20. Edited by J.-P. Migne. Paris: Migne, 1857. TLG 2035.039.

———. "Orationes tres contra Arianos." In *Opera omnia.* PG 26, cols. 813-920. Edited by J.-P. Migne. Paris: Migne, 1887. TLG 2035.042.

Augustine. *De civitate Dei.* In *Aurelii Augustini opera.* Edited by Bernhard Dombart and Alphons Kalb. CCL 47, 48. Turnhout, Belgium: Brepols, 1955. Cl. 0313.

———. "De corruptione et gratia." In *Opera omnia.* PL 44, cols. 915-46. Edited by J.-P. Migne Paris: Migne, 1845. Cl. 0353.

———. "De sancta virginitate." In *De bono coniugali; De sancta virginitate,* pp. 66-147. Translated and edited by P. G. Walsh. Oxford Early Christian Texts. Oxford: Clarendon Press, 2001. Cl. 0300.

———. "De vera religione." In *Aurelii Augustini opera.* Edited by K. D. Daur. CCL 32, pp. 169-260. Turnhout, Belgium: Brepols, 1962. Cl. 0264.

———. "Enarrationes in Psalmos." In *Aurelii Augustini opera.* Edited by D. E. Dekkers and John Fraipont. CCL 38, 39, 40. Turnhout, Belgium: Brepols, 1956. Cl. 0283.

———. "Enchiridion de fide, spe et caritate." In *Aurelii Augustini opera.* Edited by E. Evans. CCL 46, pp. 49-114. Turnhout, Belgium: Brepols, 1969. Cl. 0295.

———. "In Johannis evangelium tractatus." Edited by R. Willems. CCL 36. Turnhout, Belgium: Brepols, 1954. Cl. 0278.

———. "Sermones." In *Augustini opera omnia.* PL 38 and 39. Edited by J.-P. Migne. Paris: Migne, 1844-1865. Cl. 0284.

Bede. "De tabernaculo et vasis eius ac vestibus sacerdotum libri iii." In *Bedae opera.* Edited by D. Hurst. CCL 119A, pp. 5-139. Cl. 1345.

———. "Homiliarum evangelii." In *Bedae opera.* Edited by D. Hurst. CCL 122, pp. 1-378. Turnhout, Belgium: Brepols, 1956. Cl. 1367.

[Bede]. *Bedae Presbyteri. Expositio Apocalypseos.* Edited by Roger Gryson. CCL 121A. Turnhout: Brepols, 2001. Cl. 1363.

Caesarius of Arles. "Expositio in Apocalypsin." In *Aurelii Augustini opera omnia.* Edited by J.-P. Migne. PL 35, cols. 2417-52. Paris: Migne, 1845. Cl. 1016.

[Caesarius of Arles]. *Sermones Caesarii Arelatensis.* Edited by Germain Morin. CCL 103, 104. Turnhout, Belgium: Brepols, 1953. Cl. 1008.

Cassiodorus. *Expositio Psalmorum.* Edited by Marcus Adriaen. CCL 97, 98. Turnhout: Brepols, 1958. Cl. 0900.

Clement of Alexandria. "Paedagogus." In *Le pédagogue [par] Clement d'Alexandrie.* Translated by Mauguerite Harl, Chantel Matray and Claude Mondésert. Introduction and notes by Henri-Irénée Marrou. SC 70, 108, 158. Paris: Éditions du Cerf, 1960-1970. TLG 0555.002.

———. "Stromata." In *Clemens Alexandrinus.* Vol. 2, 3rd ed., and vol. 3, 2nd ed. Edited by Otto Stählin, Ludwig Früchtel and Ursula Treu. GCS 15, pp. 3-518 and GCS 17, pp. 1-102. Berlin: Akademie-Verlag, 1960-1970. TLG 0555.004.

Clement of Rome. "Epistula i ad Corinthios." In *Clément de Rome: Épître aux Corinthiens.* Edited by Annie Jaubert. SC 167. Paris: Éditions du Cerf, 1971. TLG 1271.001.

Cyprian. "Ad Fortunatum (De exhortatione martyrii)." In *Sancti Cyprian episcopi opera.* Edited by R. Weber. CCL 3, pp. 183-216. Turnhout, Belgium: Typographi Brepolis Editores Pontificii, 1972. Cl. 0045.

———. "De bono patientiae." In *Sancti Cypriani episcopi Epistularum.* Edited by C. Moreschini. CCL 3A, pp. 118-33. Turnhout, Belgium: Typographi Brepolis Editores Pontificii, 1976. Cl. 0048.

———. "De ecclesiae catholicae unitate." In *Sancti Cypriani episcopi opera.* Edited by Maurice Bévenot. CCL 3, pp. 249-68. Turnhout, Belgium: Brepols, 1972. Cl. 0041.

———. "De habitu virginum." In *S. Thasci Caecili Cypriani opera omnia.* Edited by William Hartel. CSEL 3.1, pp. 185-205. Vienna, Austria: Gerold, 1868. Cl. 0040.

———. "De lapsis." In *Sancti Cyprian episcopi opera.* Edited by R. Weber. CCL 3, pp. 221-42. Turnhout, Belgium: Typographi Brepolis Editores Pontificii, 1972. Cl. 0042.

———. "De opera et eleemosynis." In *Sancti Cypriani episcopi opera.* Edited by Manlio Simonetti. CCL 3A, pp. 53-72. Turnhout, Belgium: Brepols, 1976. Cl. 0047.

———. *Epistulae.* Edited by G. F. Diercks. CCL 3B, 3C. Turnhout, Belgium: Brepols, 1994-1996. Cl. 0050.

Epiphanius of Salamis. "Panarion." In *Epiphanius.* Edited by Karl Holl. GCS 25, 31. Leipzig: Hinrichs, 1915-1922. TLG 2021.002.

Eusebius of Caesarea. "Historia ecclesiastica." See "The Martyrs of Lyons," in *The Acts of the Christian Martyrs,* pp. 62-85. Edited and translated by Herbert Musurillo. Oxford Early Christian Texts. Oxford: Clarendon Press, 1972.

[Eusebius of Caesarea]. *Eusèbe de Césarée. Histoire ecclésiastique.* Edited by G. Bardy. SC 31, pp. 3-215; SC 41, pp. 4-231; SC 55, pp. 3-120. Paris: Éditions du Cerf, 1952-1958. TLG 2018.002.

Fulgentius of Ruspe. "Ad Euthymium de remissione peccatorum libri II." In *Opera.* Edited by John Fraipont. CCL 91A, pp. 649-707. Turnhout, Belgium: Brepols, 1968. Cl. 0821.

———. *Epistulae XVIII.* In *Sancti Fulgentii episcopi Ruspensis Opera.* Edited by John Fraipont. CCL 91, pp. 189-280, 311-12, 359-444; and CCL 91A, 447-57, 551-629. Turnhout, Belgium: Brepols, 1968. Cl. 0817.

Gregory Thaumaturgus. "In Originem oratio panegyrica." In *Remerciement à Origène/Grégoire le Thaumaturge. Suivi de la lettre d'Origène à Grégoire.* Edited by H. Crouzel. SC 148, pp. 94-183. Paris: Éditions du Cerf, 1969. TLG 2063.001.

Gregory the Great. "Dialogorum libri iv." In *Dialogues*. Translation, introduction and notes by Paul Antin and Adalbert de Vogüé. SC 251, 260, 265. Paris: Éditions du Cerf, 1978-1980. Cl. 1713.

Hippolytus. "Commentarium in Danielem." In *Hippolyte. Commentaire sur Daniel*. Edited by Maurice Lefèvre. SC 14, pp. 70-386. Paris: Éditions du Cerf, 1947. TLG 2115.030.

——. "De antichristo." In *Hippolyt's kleinere exegetische und homiletische Schriften*. Edited by Hans Achelis. GCS 1.2, pp. 1-47. Leipzig: Hinrichs, 1897. TLG 2115.003.

Irenaeus. "Adversus haereses [liber 3]." In *Irénée de Lyon. Contre les heresies, livre 3*, vol. 2. Edited by Adelin Rousseau and Louis Doutreleau. SC 211. Paris: Éditions du Cerf, 1974. Cl. 1154.

——. *Démonstration de la Prédication Apostolique*. Edited by Adelin Rousseau. SC 406. Paris: Éditions du Cerf, 1995.

Jerome. "Adversus Jovinianum." In *Opera omnia*. PL 23, cols. 221-352. Edited by J.-P. Migne. Paris: Migne, 1845. Cl. 0610.

——. "Altercatio Luciferiani et Orthodoxi." In *Opera omnia*. PL 23, cols. 155-182. Edited by J.-P. Migne. Paris: Migne, 1845. Cl. 0608.

——. *Epistulae*. Edited by I. Hilberg. CSEL 54, 55, 56. Vienna, Austria: F. Tempsky; Leipzig, Germany: G. F. Freytag, 1910-1918. Cl. 0620.

——. "Tractatus lix in psalmos." In *S. Hieronymi presbyteri opera*. Edited by Germain Morin. CCL 78, pp. 3-352. Turnhout, Belgium: Brepols, 1958. Cl. 0592.

——. "Tractatus in Marci evangelium." In *Opera, Part 2*. Edited by G. Morin. CCL 78, pp. 449-500. Turnhout, Belgium: Typographi Brepols Editores Pontificii, 1958. Cl. 0594.

Lactantius. "Epitome divinarum institutionum." In *L. Caeli Firmiani Lactanti Opera omnia*. Edited by Samuel Brandt. CSEL 19, pp. 673-761. Vienna, Austria: F. Tempsky; Leipzig, Germany: G. Freytag, 1890. Cl. 0086.

Maximus of Turin. "Collectio sermonum antiqua." In *Maximi episcopi Taurinensis Sermones*. Edited by Almut Mutzenbecher. CCL 23, pp. 1-364. Turnhout, Belgium: Brepols, 1962. Cl. 0219a.

Methodius. "Symposium *sive* Convivium decem virginum." In *Opera omnia*. PG 18, cols. 27-220. Edited by J.-P. Migne. Paris: Migne, 1857. TLG 2959.001.

Nicetas of Remesiana. "De utilitate hymnorum." In "Niceta of Remesiana II. Introduction and Text of *De psalmodiae bono*." Edited by C. Turner. *Journal of Theological Studies* 24 (1923): 233-41.

[Oecumenius]. *Oecumenii Commentarius in Apocalypsin*. Edited by Marc de Groote. TEG 8. Louvain: Peters, 1999. TLG 2866.001.

Origen. "Commentarii in evangelium Joannis (lib. 1, 2, 4, 5, 6, 10, 13)." In *Origène. Commentaire sur saint Jean*, 3 vols. Edited by Cécil Blanc. SC 120, 157, 222. Paris: Éditions du Cerf, 1966-1975. TLG 2042.005.

——. "Commentarii in evangelium Joannis (lib. 19, 20, 28, 32)." In *Origenes Werke*. Vol. 4. Edited by Erwin Preuschen. GCS 10, 298-480. Leipzig: Hinrichs, 1903. TLG 2042.079.

——. "Contra Celsum." In *Origène Contre Celse*. Edited by M. Borret. SC 132, 136, 147 and 150. Paris: Éditions du Cerf, 1967-1969. TLG 2042.001.

——. "De principiis." In *Origenes vier Bücher von den Prinzipien*, pp. 462-560, 668-764. Edited by Herwig Görgemanns and Heinrich Karpp. Darmstadt, Germany: Wissenschaftliche Buchgesellschaft, 1976. TLG 2042.002.

——. "Homiliae in Lucam." In *Opera omnia*. PG 13, cols. 1799-1902. Edited by J.-P. Migne. Paris: Migne, 1862. TLG 2042.016.

——. "In Jeremiam (homiliae 1-11)." In "Homiliae 2-3." *Origenes Werke*. Vol. 8. Edited by W. A. Baehrens. GCS 33, pp. 290-317. Leipzig: Teubner, 1925. TLG 2042.009.

———."In Jeremiam [homiliae 12-20]." In *Origenes Werke*. Vol. 3. Edited by Erich Klostermann. GCS 6, pp. 85-194. Berlin: Akademie-Verlag, 1901. TLG 2042.021.

———."In Jesu nave." In *Homélies sur Josué*. Edited by Annie Jaubert. SC 71. Paris: Éditions du Cerf, 1960. TLG 2042.025.

Primasius. *Commentarius in Apocalypsin*. Edited by A. W. Adams. CCL 92. Turnholt, Brepols, 1985. Cl. 0873.

[Pseudo-Hippolytus]. "De consummatione mundi." In *Hippolyt's kleinere exegetische und homiletische Schriften*. Edited by H. Achelis. Die griechischen christlichen Schriftsteller 1.2, pp. 289-309. Leipzig: Hinrichs, 1897. TLG 2115.029.

Quodvultdeus. "De symbolo III." Edited by R. Braun. CCL 60, pp. 349-363. Turnhout, Belgium: Brepols, 1976. Cl. 0403.

Rufinus of Aquileia. "Expositio symboli." In *Opera*. Edited by Manlio Simonetti. CCL 20, pp. 125-82. Turnhout, Belgium: Brepols, 1961. Cl. 0196.

Salvian the Presbyter. "De gubernatione Dei." In *Ouvres*. Edited by Georges LaGarrigue. SC 220. Paris: Éditions du Cerf, 1975. Cl. 0485.

Tertullian. "Adversus Hermogenem." In *Tertulliani opera*. Edited by E. Kroymann. CCL 1, pp. 397-435. Turnhout, Belgium: Brepols, 1954. Cl. 0013.

———."De anima." In *Tertulliani opera*. Edited by J. H. Waszink. CCL 2, pp. 781-869. Turnholt, Belgium: Brepols, 1954. Cl. 0017.

———."De fuga in persecutione." In *Tertulliani opera*. Edited by J. J. Thierry. CCL 2, pp. 1135-55. Turnhout, Belgium: Brepols, 1954. Cl. 0025.

———. "De monogamia." In *Tertulliani opera*. Edited by E. Dekkers. CCL 2, pp. 1229-53. Turnholt, Belgium: Brepols, 1954. Cl. 0028.

———."De oratione." In *Tertulliani opera*. Edited by G. F. Diercks. CCL 1, pp. 255-74. Turnhout, Belgium: Brepols, 1954. Cl. 0007.

———."De paenitentia." In *Tertulliani opera*. Edited by J. W. P. Borleffs. CSEL 76, pp. 140-70. Vienna: Hoelder-Pichler-Tempsky, 1957. Cl. 0010.

———."De patientia." In *Tertulliani opera*. Edited by J. G. Ph. Borleffs. CCL 1, pp. 299-317. Turnhout, Belgium: Brepols, 1954. Cl. 0009.

———."De resurrectione mortuorum." In *Tertulliani opera*. Edited by J. G. Ph. Borleffs. CCL 2, pp. 919-1012. Turnhout, Belgium: Brepols, 1954. Cl. 0019.

———."Scorpiace." In *Tertulliani opera*. Edited by A. Reifferscheid and G. Wissowa. CCL 2, pp.1067-97. Turnhout, Belgium: Brepols, 1954. Cl. 0022.

[Tyconius]. *The Turin Fragments of Tyconius' Commentary on Revelation*. Edited by Francesco Lo Bue and Geoffrey Grimshaw Willis. TSNS 7. Cambridge: Cambridge University Press, 1963.

———. *See* Primasius. *Commentarius in Apocalypsin*. Edited by A. W. Adams. CCL 92. Turnholt, Brepols, 1985. Cl. 0873.

Victorinus of Petovium. *Commentarii in Apocalypsim Joannis*. Edited by Johannes Haussleiter. CSEL 49, pp. 14-154. Vienna: F. Tempsky; Leipzig: G. Freytag, 1916.

# Bibliography of Works
## in English Translation

[Aphrahat]. "Select Demonstrations." In *Gregory the Great, Ephraim Syrus, Aphrahat*, pp. 345-412. Translated by James Barmby. NPNF 13. Series 2. Edited by Philip Schaff and Henry Wace. 14 vols. 1886-1900. Reprint, Peabody, Mass.: Hendrickson, 1994.

[Athanasius]. *Selected Works and Letters*. Translated by Archibald Robertson. NPNF 4. Series 2. Edited by Philip Schaff and Henry Wace. 14 vols. 1886-1900. Reprint, Peabody, Mass.: Hendrickson, 1994.

Augustine. "Admonition and Grace." In *Saint Augustine*, pp. 239-305. Translated by John Courtney Murray. FC 2. Washington, D.C.: The Catholic University of America Press, 1947.

———. *The City of God Books VIII-XVI*. Translated by Gerald Walsh and Grace Monahan. FC 14. Washington, D.C.: The Catholic University of America Press, 1952.

———. *The City of God Books XVII-XXII*. Translated by Gerald G. Walsh and Daniel J. Honan. FC 24. Washington, D.C.: The Catholic University of America Press, 1954.

———. *Confessions and Enchiridion*, pp. 337-412. Translated and edited by Albert C. Outler. LCC 7. London, SCM, 1955.

———. *Expositions on the Book of Psalms*. Edited from the Oxford translation by A. Cleveland Coxe. NPNF 8. Series 1. Edited by Philip Schaff. 14 vols. 1886-1889. Reprint, Peabody, Mass.: Hendrickson, 1994.

———. *Expositions of the Psalms, vol. 1-2*. Translated by Maria Boulding. WSA 15 and 16. Part 3. Edited by John E. Rotelle. New York: New City Press, 2000.

———. "On Holy Virginity." In *De bono coniugali; De sancta virginitate*, pp. 66-147. Translated and edited by P. G. Walsh. Oxford Early Christian Texts. Oxford: Clarendon Press, 2001.

———. "Of True Religion." In *Earlier Works*, pp. 218-83. Translated by John H. S. Burleigh. LCC 6. London: SCM Press, 1953.

———. *Sermons*. Translated by Edmund Hill. WSA 7, 8, 9 and 10. Part 3. Edited by John E. Rotelle. New York: New City Press, 1990-1995.

———. *Tractates on the Gospel of John, 28-54*. Translated by John W. Rettig. FC 88. Washington, D.C.: The Catholic University of America Press, 1993.

Bede, the Venerable. *Homilies on the Gospels*. Translated by Lawrence T. Martin and David Hurst. 2 vols. CS 110 and 111. Kalamazoo, Mich.: Cistercian Publications, 1991.

———. *On the Tabernacle*. Translated with notes and introduction by Arthur G. Holder. TTH 18. Liverpool: Liverpool University Press, 1994.

Caesarius of Arles. *Sermons*. Translated by Mary Magdeleine Mueller. 3 vol.s FC 31, 47 and 66. Washington, D.C.: The Catholic University of America Press, 1956-1973.

Cassiodorus. *Explanation of the Psalms*. Translated by P. G. Walsh. ACW 52 and 53. New York: Paulist Press, 1990-1991.

Clement of Alexandria. *Christ the Educator*. Translated by Simon P. Wood. FC 23. Washington, D.C.: The Catholic University of America Press, 1954.

———. *Stromateis: Books 1-3*. Translated by John Ferguson. FC 85. Washington, D.C.: The Catholic University of America Press, 1991.

[Clement of Rome]. "The Letter of the Church of Rome to the Church of Corinth, Commonly Called Clement's First Letter." In *Early Christian Fathers*, pp. 33-73. Translated by Cyril C. Richardson. LCC 1. Philadelphia: Westminster Press, 1953.

Cyprian. *Treatises*. Translated and edited by Roy J. Deferrari. FC 36. Washington, D.C.: The Catholic University of America Press, 1958.

———. *Letters 1-81*. Translated by Rose Bernard Donna. FC 51. Washington, D.C.: The Catholic University of America Press, 1964.

———. "Works and Almsgiving." In *Hippolytus, Cyprian, Caius, Novatian*, pp. 476-84. Arranged by A. Cleveland Coxe. ANF 5. Edited by Alexander Roberts and James Donaldson. 10 vols. 1885-1887. Reprint, Peabody, Mass.: Hendrickson, 1994.

Epiphanius of Salamis. *The Panarion: Books II and III*. Translated by F. Williams. NHMS 36. Leiden: E. J. Brill, 1994.

Eusebius of Caesarea. "Ecclesiastical History." See "The Martyrs of Lyons," in *The Acts of the Christian Martyrs*, pp. 62-85. Edited and translated by Herbert Musurillo. Oxford Early Christian Texts. Oxford: Clarendon Press, 1972.

———. "The Church History of Eusebius." In *Church History, Life of Constantine the Great, Oration in Praise of Constantine*, pp. 73-387. Translated by Arthur Cushman McGiffert. NPNF 1. Series 2. Edited by Philip Schaff and Henry Wace. 14 vols. 1886-1900. Reprint, Peabody, Mass.: Hendrickson, 1994.

[Fulgentius of Ruspe]. *Selected Works*. Translated by Robert B. Eno. FC 95. Washington, D.C.: The Catholic University of America Press, 1997.

Gregory Thaumaturgus. "The Oration and Panegyric Addressed to Origen." In *Gregory Thaumaturgus, Dionysius the Great, Julius Africanus, Anatolius and Minor Writers, Methodius, Arnobius*, pp. 21-39. Arranged by A. Cleveland Coxe. ANF 6. Edited by Alexander Roberts and James Donaldson. 10 vols. 1885-1887. Reprint, Peabody, Mass.: Hendrickson, 1994.

Gregory the Great. *Dialogues*. Translated by Odo John Zimmerman. FC 39. Washington, D.C.: The Catholic University of America Press, 1959.

[Hippolytus]. *Hippolytus, Cyprian, Caius, Novatian, Appendix*. Arranged by A. Cleveland Coxe. ANF 5. Edited by Alexander Roberts and James Donaldson. 10 vols. 1885-1887. Reprint, Peabody, Mass.: Hendrickson, 1994.

Irenaeus. "Against Heresies." In *The Apostolic Fathers with Justin Martyr and Irenaeus*, pp. 315-567. Arranged by A. Cleveland Coxe. ANF 1. Edited by Alexander Roberts and James Donaldson. 10 vols. 1885-1887. Reprint, Peabody, Mass.: Hendrickson, 1994.

———. *Proof of the Apostolic Preaching*. Translated by Joseph P. Smith. ACW 16. Mahwah, NJ: Paulist Press, 1952.

Jerome. *Letters and Select Works*. Translated by W. H. Fremantle, G. Lewis, and W. G. Martley. NPNF 6. Series 2. Edited by Philip Schaff and Henry Wace. 14 vols. 1886-1900. Reprint, Peabody, Mass.: Hendrickson, 1994.

———. *Homilies on the Psalms: 1-59*. Translated by Sister Marie Liguori Ewald. FC 48. Washington, D.C.: The Catholic University of America Press, 1964.

———. "Homilies on Mark." In *Homilies 60-96*, pp. 121-92. Translated by Sister Marie Liguori Ewald. FC 57. Washington, D.C.: The Catholic University of America Press, 1966.

Lactantius. *The Divine Institutes: Books I-VII*. Translated by Sister Mary Francis McDonald. LC 49. Washington, D.C.: The Catholic University of America Press, 1964.

[Maximus of Turin]. *The Sermons of St. Maximus of Turin*. Translated and annotated by Boniface Ramsey. ACW 50. Mahwah, N.J.: Paulist Press, 1989.

Methodius. "Banquet of the Ten Virgins." In *The Writings of Methodius, Alexander of Lycopolis, Peter of Alexandria, and Several Fragments*, pp. 1-119. ANCL 14. Edited by Alexander Roberts and James Donaldson. Edinburgh: T & T Clark, 1869.

———. *The Symposium: A Treatise on Chastity*. Translated by Herbert Musurillo. ACW 27. Mahwah, NJ: Paulist Press, 1958.

Nicetas of Remesiana. "Liturgical Singing." In *Niceta of Remesiana, Sulpicius Severus, Vincent of Lerins, Prosper of Aquitaine*, pp. 65-76. Translated by Gerald G. Walsh. FC 7. New York: Fathers of the Church, Inc., 1949.

Origen. "Against Celsus." In *Tertullian (IV); Minucius Felix; Commodian; Origen (I and III)*, pp. 395-669. Translated by Frederick Combie. ANF 4. Edited by Alexander Roberts and James Donaldson. 10 vols. 1885-1887. Reprint, Peabody, Mass.: Hendrickson, 1994.

———. *Commentary on the Gospel According to John, Books 1-10*. Translated by Ronald E. Heine. FC 80. Washington, D.C.: The Catholic University of America Press, 1989.

———. *Homilies on Jeremiah, Homily on 1 Kings 28*. Translated by John Clark Smith. FC 97. Washington, D.C.: The Catholic University of America Press, 1998.

———. *Homilies on Joshua*. Translated by Cynthia White. FC 105. Washington, D.C.: The Catholic University of America Press, 2002.

———. *Homilies on Luke*. In *Homilies on Luke, Fragments on Luke*, pp. 1-162. Translated by Joseph T. Lienhard. FC 94. Washington D.C.: The Catholic University of America Press, 1996.

———. *On First Principles*. Translated by G. W. Butterworth. London: SPCK, 1936. Reprint, Gloucester, Mass.: Peter Smith, 1973.

[Pseudo-Hippolytus]. "On the End of the World, the Antichrist, and the Second Coming." In *Hippolytus, Cyprian, Caius, Novatian, Appendix*, pp. 242-55. Arranged by A. Cleveland Coxe. ANF 5. Edited by Alexander Roberts and James Donaldson. 10 vols. 1885-1887. Reprint, Peabody, Mass.: Hendrickson, 1994.

Rufinus of Aquileia. *A Commentary on the Apostles' Creed*. Translated by J. N. D. Kelly. ACW 20. Mahwah, N.J.: Paulist Press, 1954.

Salvian the Presbyter. "The Governance of God." In *The Writings of Salvian the Presbyter*, pp. 21-232. Translated by Jermiah F. O'Sullivan. FC 3. Washington, D.C.: The Catholic University of America Press, 1962.

Tertullian. *Disciplinary, Moral and Ascetical Works*. Translated by Emily Joseph Daly. FC 40. Washington, D.C.: The Catholic University of America Press, 1959.

———. *Latin Christianity: Its Founder, Tertullian*. Arranged by A. Cleveland Coxe. ANF 3. Edited by Alexander Roberts and James Donaldson. 10 vols. 1885-1887. Reprint, Peabody, Mass.: Hendrickson, 1994.

———. "On Monogamy." In *Treatises on Marriage and Remarriage: To His Wife, an Exhortation to Chastity, Monogamy*, pp. 70-108. Translated by William P. Le Saint. ACW 13. Mahwah, N.J.: Paulist Press, 1951.

———. "On Penitence." In *Treatises on Penance: On Penitence and On Purity*, pp. 14-37. Translated by William P. Le Saint. ACW 28. Mahwah, N.J.: Paulist Press, 1959.

———. "On the Soul." In *Tertullian: Apologetical Works, and Minucius Felix: Octavius*, pp. 179-309. Translated by Rudolph Arbesmann, Sister Emily Joseph Daly, and Edwin A. Quain. FC 10. Washington, D.C.: The Catholic University of America Press, 1950.